Parallel and Distributed Programming Using C++

Parallel and Distributed Programming Using C++

CAMERON HUGHES • TRACEY HUGHES

✦ Addison-Wesley

Boston • San Fransisco • New York • Toronto • Montreal
London • Munich • Paris • Madrid
Cape Town • Sydney • Tokyo • Singapore • Mexico City

Many of the designations used by manufacturers and sellers to distinguish their products are claimed as trademarks. Where those designations appear in this book, and Addison-Wesley was aware of a trademark claim, the designations have been printed with initial capital letters or in all capitals.

The authors and publisher have taken care in the preparation of this book, but make no expressed or implied warranty of any kind and assume no responsibility for errors or omissions. No liability is assumed for incidental or consequential damages in connection with or arising out of the use of the information or programs contained herein.

The publisher offers discounts on this book when ordered in quantity for bulk purchases and special sales. For more information, please contact:

U.S. Corporate and Government Sales
(800) 382-3419
corpsales@pearsontechgroup.com

For sales outside of the U.S., please contact:

International Sales
(317) 581-3793
international@pearsontechgroup.com

Visit Addison-Wesley on the Web: www.awprofessional.com

A CIP catalog record for this book can be obtained from the Library of Congress.

Pearson Education, Inc.
Rights and Contracts Department
75 Arlington Street, Suite 300
Boston, MA 02116
Fax: (617) 848-7047

ISBN: 0-13-101376-9
Text printed on recycled paper
1 2 3 4 5 6 7 8 9 10
First printing, June 2003

This book is dedicated to all the code warriors, white hat hackers, midnight engineers, and countless volunteers who have tirelessly given their skill, talent, experience, and time to make the open-source movement a reality and the Linux revolution possible. Without their tremendous contributions, the software needed to explore cluster programming, MPP programming, SMP programming, and distributed programming would simply not be as widely accessible and available to everyone in the world as it now is.

Contents

5   SYNCHRONIZING CONCURRENCY BETWEEN TASKS. 184

Preface

Wfe present an architectural approach to distributed and parallel programming using the C++ language. Particular attention is paid to how the C++ standard library, algorithms, and container classes behave in distributed and parallel environments. Methods for extending the C++ language through class libraries and function libraries to accomplish distributed and parallel programming tasks are explained. Emphasis is placed on how C++ works with the new POSIX and Single UNIX standards for multithreading. Combining C++ executables with other language executables to achieve multilingual solutions to distributed or parallel programming problems is also discussed. Several methods of organizing software that support parallel and distributed programming are introduced.

We demonstrate how to remove the fundamental obstacles to concurrency. The notion of emergent parallelization is explored. Our focus is not on optimization techniques, hardware specifics, performance comparisons, or on trying to apply parallel programming techniques to complex scientific or mathematical algorithms; rather, on how to structure computer programs and software systems to take advantage of opportunities for parallelization. Furthermore, we acquaint the reader with a multiparadigm approach to solving some of the problems that are inherent with distributed and parallel programming. Effective solutions to these problems often require a mix of several software design and engineering approaches. For instance, we deploy object-oriented programming techniques to tackle data race and synchronization problems. We use agent-oriented architectures to deal with multiprocess and multithread management. Blackboards are used to minimize communication issues. In addition to object-oriented, agent-oriented, and AI-oriented programming, we use parameterized programming to implement generalized algorithms that are suitable where concurrency is required. Our experience with the development of software of all sizes and shapes has led us to believe that successful software design and implementation demands versatility. The suggestions, ideas, and solutions we present in this book reflect that experience.

The Challenges

There are three basic challenges to writing parallel or distributed programs:

1. Identifying the natural parallelism that occurs within the context of a problem domain.
2. Dividing the software appropriately into two or more tasks that can be performed at the same time to accomplish the required parallelism.
3. Coordinating those tasks so that the software correctly and efficiently does what it is supposed to do.

These three challenges are accompanied by the following obstacles to concurrency:

Data race	Deadlock detection
Partial failure	Latency
Deadlock	Communication failures
Termination detection	Lack of global state
Multiple clock problem	Protocol mismatch
Localized errors	Lack of centralized resource allocation

This book explains what these obstacles are, why they occur, and how they can be managed.

Finally, several of the mechanisms we use for concurrency use TCP/IP as a protocol. Specifically the MPI (Message Passing Interface) library, PVM (Parallel Virtual Machine) library, and the MICO (CORBA) library. This allows our approaches to be used in an Internet/Intranet environment, which means that programs cooperating in parallel may be executing at different sites on the Internet or a corporate intranet and communicating through message passing. Many of the ideas serve as foundations for infrastructure of Web services. In addition to the MPI and PVM routines, the CORBA objects we use can communicate from different servers accross the Internet. These components can be used to provide a variety of Internet/intranet services.

The Approach

We advocate a component approach to the challenges and obstacles found in distributed and parallel programming. Our primary objective is to use framework classes as building blocks for concurrency. The framework classes are supported by object-oriented mutexes, semaphores, pipes, and sockets. The complexity of task synchronization and communication is significantly reduced through the use of interface classes. We deploy agent-driven threads and processes to facilitate thread and process management. Our primary approach to a global state and its related problems involve the use of blackboards. We combine agent-oriented and object-oriented architectures to accomplish multiparadigm solutions. Our multiparadigm approach is made possible using the support C++ has for object-oriented programming, parameterized programming, and structured programming.

Why C++?

There are C++ compilers available for virtually every platform and operating environment. The ANSI (American National Standards Institute) and ISO (International Standard Organization) have defined standards for the C++ language and its library. There are robust open-source implementations as well as commercial implementations of the language. The language has been widely adopted by researchers, designers, and professional developers around the world. The C++ language has been used to solve problems of all sizes and shapes from device drivers to large-scale industrial applications. The language supports a multiparadigm approach to software development and libraries that add parallel and distributed programming capabilities are readily available.

Libraries for Parallel and Distributed Programming

The MPICH, an implementation of MPI, the PVM library, and the Pthreads (POSIX Threads) library, are used to implement parallel programming using C++. MICO, a C++ implementation of the CORBA standard, is used to achieve distrbuted programming. The C++ Standard Library, in combination with CORBA and the Pthreads library, provides the support for agent-oriented and blackboard programming concepts that are discussed in this book.

The New Single UNIX Specification Standard

The new Single UNIX Specification Standard, Version 3, a joint effort between IEEE and the Open Group, was finalized and released in December 2001. The new Single UNIX Specification encompasses the POSIX standards and promotes portability for application programmers. It was designed to give software developers a single set of APIs to be supported by every UNIX system. It provides a reliable road map of standards for programmers who need to write multitasking and multithreading applications. In this book we rely on the Single UNIX Specification Standard for our discussions on process creations, process management, the Pthreads library, the new `posix_spawn()` routines, the POSIX semaphores, and FIFOs. Appendix B in this book contains excerpts from the standard that can be used as a reference to the material that we present.

Who is This Book For?

This book is written for software designers, software developers, application programmers, researchers, educators, and students who need an introduction to parallel and distributed programming using the C++ language. A modest knowledge of the C++ language and standard C++ class libraries is required. This book is not intended as a tutorial on programming in C++ or object-oriented programming. It is assumed that the reader will have a basic understanding of object-oriented programming techniques such as encapsulation, inheritance, and polymorphism. This book introduces the basics of parallel and distributed programming in the context of C++.

Development Environments Supported

The examples and programs presented in this book were developed and tested in the Linux and UNIX environments, specifically with Solaris 8, Aix, and Linux (SuSE, Red Hat). The PVM and MPI code was developed and tested on a 32-node Linux-based cluster. Many of the programs were tested on Sun Enterprise 450s. We used Sun's C++ Workshop, The Portland Group's C++ compiler, and GNU C++. Most examples will run in both the UNIX and Linux environments. In the cases where an example will not run in both environments, this fact is noted in the Program Profiles that are provided for all the complete program examples in the book.

Ancillaries

UML Diagrams

Many of the diagrams in this book use the UML (Unified Modeling Language) standard. In particular, activity diagrams, deployment diagrams, class diagrams, the state diagrams are used to describe important concurrency architectures and class relationships. Although a knowledge of the UML is not necessary, familarity is helpful. Appendix A contains an explanation and description of the UML symbols and language that we use in this book.

Program Profiles

Each complete program in the book is accompanied by a program profile. The profile will contain implementation specifics such as headers required, libraries required, compile instructions, and link instructions. The profile also includes a Notes section that will contain any special considerations that need to be taken when executing the program. Code that is not accompanied by a profile is meant for exposition purposes only.

Sidebars

We made every attempt to stay away from notation that is too theoretical for a introductory book such as this one. However, in some cases the theoretical or mathematical notation was unavoidable. In those cases we use the notation but we provide a detailed explanation of the notation in a sidebar.

Testing and Code Reliability

Although all examples and applications in this book were tested to ensure correctness, we make no warranties that the programs contained in this book are free of defects or error, are consistent with any particular standard or merchantability, or will meet your requirement for any particular application. They should not be relied upon for solving problems whose incorrect solution could result in injury to person or loss of property. The authors and publishers disclaim all liability for direct or consequential damages resulting from your use of the examples, programs, or applications present in this book.

Acknowledgments

We could not have successfully pulled this project off without the help, suggestions, constructive criticisms, and resources of many of our friends and colleagues. In particular, we would like to thank Terry Lewis and Doug Johnson from OSC (Ohio Super-Computing) for providing us with complete access to a 32-node Linux-based cluster. To Mark Welton from YSU for his expertise and help with configuring the cluster to support our PVM and MPI programs. To Sal Sanders from YSU for providing us with access to Power-PCs running Mac OSX and Adobe Illustrator. To Brian Nelson from YSU for allowing us to test many of our multithreaded and distributed programs on multiprocessor Sun E-250s and E-450s. We are also indebted to Mary Ann Johnson and Jeffrey Trimble from YSU MAAG for helping us locate and hold on to the technical references we required. Claudio M. Stanziola, Paulette Goldweber, and Jacqueline Hansson from the IEEE Standards and Licensing and Contracts Office for obtaining permission to reprint parts of the new Single-UNIX/POSIX standard; Andrew Josey and Gene Pierce from The Open Group was also helpful in this regard. Thanks to Trevor Watkins of the Z-Group for all his help with the testing of the program examples; his multi-Linux distribution environment was especially important in the testing process. A special thanks to Steve Tarasweki for agreeing to provide a technical review for this book while it was in its roughest form. To Dr. Eugene Santos for pointing us in the right direction as we explored how categorical data structures could be used with PVMs. To Dr. Mike Crescimanno from the Advanced Computing Work Group at YSU for allowing us to present some of the materials from this book at one of the ACWG meetings. Finally, to Paul Petralia and the production team (especially Gail Cocker-Bogusz) from Prentice Hall who had to put up with all of our missed deadlines and strange UNIX/Linux file formats—we are extremely indebted to their patience, encouragement, enthusiasm, and professionalism.

1 The Joys of Concurrent Programming

"I suspect that concurrency is best supported by a library and that such a library can be implemented without major language extensions."

—*Bjarne Stroustrup, inventor of C++*

In this Chapter

What is Concurrency? • The Benefits of Parallel Programming • The Benefits of Distributed Programming • The Minimal Effort Required • The Basic Layers of Software Concurrency • No Keyword Support for Parallelism in C++ • Programming Environments for Parallel and Distributed Programming • Summary—Toward Concurrency

The software development process now requires a working knowledge of parallel and distributed programming. The requirement for a piece of software to work properly over the Internet, on an intranet, or over some network is almost universal. Once the piece of software is deployed in one or more of these environments it is subjected to the most rigorous of performance demands. The user wants instantaneous and reliable results. In many situations the user wants the software to satisfy many requests at the same time. The capability to perform multiple simultaneous downloads of software and data from the Internet is a typical expectation of the user. Software designed to broadcast video must also be able to render graphics and digitally process sound seamlessly and without interruption. Web server software is often subjected to hundreds of thousands of hits per day. It is not uncommon for frequently used e-mail servers to be forced to survive the stress of a million sent and received messages during business hours. And it's not just the quantity of the messages that can require tremendous work, it's also the content. For instance, data transmissions containing digitized music, movies, or graphics devour network bandwidth and can inflict a serious penalty on server software that has not been properly designed. The typical computing environment is networked and the computers involved have multiple processors. The more the software does, the more it is required to do. To meet the minimal user's requirements, today's software must work harder and smarter. Software must be designed to take advantage of computers that have multiple processors. Since networked computers are more the rule than the exception, software must be designed to correctly and effectively run, with some of its pieces executing simultaneously on different computers. In some cases, the different computers have totally different operating systems with different network protocols! To accommodate these realities, a software development repertoire must include techniques for implementing concurrency through parallel and distributed programming.

1.1   What is Concurrency?

Two events are said to be concurrent if they occur within the same time interval. Two or more tasks executing over the same time interval are said to execute concurrently. For our purposes, concurrent doesn't necessarily mean at the same exact instant. For example, two tasks may occur concurrently within the same second but with each task executing within different fractions of the second. The first task may execute for the first tenth of the second and pause, the second task may execute for the next tenth of the second and pause, the first task may start again executing in the third tenth of a second, and so on. Each task may alternate executing. However, the length of a second is so short that it appears that both tasks are executing simultaneously. We may extend this notion to longer time intervals. Two programs performing some task within the same hour continuously make progress of the task during that hour, although they may or may not be executing at the same exact instant. We say that the two programs are executing concurrently for that hour. Tasks that exist at the same time and perform in the same time period are concurrent. Concurrent tasks can execute in a single or multiprocessing environment. In a single processing environment, concurrent tasks exist at the same time and execute within the same time period by context switching. In a multiprocessor environment, if enough processors are free, concurrent tasks may execute at the same instant over the same time period. The determining factor for what makes an acceptable time period for concurrency is relative to the application.

Concurrency techniques are used to allow a computer program to do more work over the same time period or time interval. Rather than designing the program to do one task at a time, the program is broken down in such a way that some of the tasks can be executed concurrently. In some situations, doing more work over the same time period is not the goal. Rather, simplifying the programming solution is the goal. Sometimes it makes more sense to think of the solution to the problem as a set of concurrently executed tasks. For instance, the solution to the problem of losing weight is best thought of as concurrently executed tasks: diet and exercise. That is, the improved diet and exercise regimen are supposed to occur over the same time interval (*not necessarily at the same instant*). It is typically not very beneficial to do one during one time period and the other within a totally different time period. The concurrency of both processes is the natural form of the solution. Sometimes concurrency is used to make software faster or get done with its work sooner. Sometimes concurrency is used to make software do more work over the same interval where speed is secondary to capacity. For instance, some web sites want customers to stay logged on as long as possible. So it's not how fast they can get the customers on and off of the site that is the concern—it's how many customers the site can support concurrently. So the goal of the software design is to handle as many connections as possible for as long a time period as possible. Finally, concurrency can be used to make the software simpler. Often, one long, complicated sequence of operations can be implemented easier as a series of small, concurrently executing operations. Whether concurrency is used to make the software faster, handle larger loads, or simplify the programming solution, the main object is software improvement using concurrency to make the software better.

1.1.1 The Two Basic Approaches to Achieving Concurrency

Parallel programming and distributed programming are two basic approaches for achieving concurrency with a piece of software. They are two different programming paradigms that sometimes intersect. *Parallel programming techniques* assign the work a program has to do to two or more processors within a single physical or a single virtual computer. *Distributed programming techniques* assign the work a program has to do to two or more processes—where the processes may or may not exist on the same computer. That is, the parts of a distributed program often run on different computers connected by a network or at least in different processes. A program that contains parallelism executes on the same physical or virtual computer. The parallelism within a program may be divided into *processes* or *threads*. We discuss processes in Chapter 3 and threads in Chapter 4. For our purposes, distributed programs can only be divided into processes. Multithreading is restricted to parallelism. Technically, parallel programs are sometimes distributed, as is the case with PVM (Parallel Virtual Machine) programming. Distributed programming is sometimes used to implement parallelism, as is

Figure 1-1 Typical architecture for a parallel and distributed program.

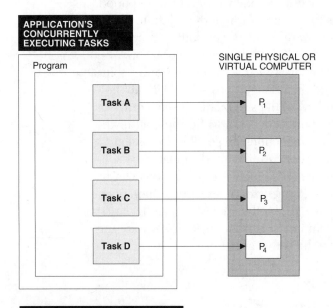

the case with MPI (Message Passing Interface) programming. However, not all distributed programs involve parallelism. The parts of a distributed program may execute at different instances and over different time periods. For instance, a software calendar program might be divided into two parts: One part provides the user with a calendar and a method for recording important appointments and the other part provides the user with a set of alarms for each different type of appointment. The user schedules the appointments using part of the software, and the other part of the software executes separately at a different time. The alarms and the scheduling component together make a single application, but they are divided into two separately executing parts. In pure parallelism, the concurrently executing parts are all components of the same program. In distributed programs, the parts are usually implemented as separate programs. Figure 1–1 shows the typical architecture for a parallel and distributed program.

The parallel application in Figure 1–1 consists of one program divided into four tasks. Each task executes on a separate processor, therefore, each task may execute simultaneously. The tasks can be implemented by either a process or a thread. On the other hand, the distributed application in Figure 1–1 consists of three separate programs with each program executing on a separate computer. Program 3 consists of two separate parts that execute on the same computer. Although Task A and D of Program 3 are on the same computer, they are distributed because they are implemented by two separate processes. Tasks within a parallel program are more tightly coupled than tasks within a distributed program. In general, processors associated with distributed programs are on different computers, whereas processors associated with programs that involve parallelism are on the same computer. Of course, there are hybrid programs that are both parallel and distributed. These hybrid combinations are becoming the norm.

1.2 The Benefits of Parallel Programming

Programs that are properly designed to take advantage of parallelism can execute faster than their sequential counterparts, which is a market advantage. In other cases the speed is used to save lives. In these cases *faster* equates to *better*. The solutions to certain problems are represented more naturally as a collection of simultaneously executing tasks. This is especially the case in many areas of scientific, mathematical, and artificial intelligence programming. This means that parallel programming techniques can save the software developer work in some situations by allowing the developer to directly implement data structures, algorithms, and heuristics developed by researchers. Specialized hardware can be exploited. For instance, in high-end multimedia programs the logic can be distributed to specialized processors for increased performance, such as specialized graphics chips, digital sound processors, and specialized math processors. These processors can usually be accessed simultaneously. Computers with MPP (Massively Parallel Processors) have hundreds, sometimes thousands of processors and can be used to solve problems that simply cannot realistically be solved using sequential methods. With MPP computers, it's the combination of fast with pure *brute force* that makes the impossible possible. In this category would fall environmental modeling, space exploration, and several areas in biological research such as the Human Genome Project. Further parallel programming techniques open the door to certain software architectures that are specifically designed for parallel environments. For example, there are certain multiagent and blackboard architectures designed specifically for a parallel processor environment.

1.2.1   The Simplest Parallel Model (PRAM)

The easiest method for approaching the basic concepts in parallel programming is through the use of the PRAM (Parallel Random Access Machine). The PRAM is a simplified theoretical model where there are n processors labeled as P_1, P_2, P_3, ... P_n and each processor shares one global memory. Figure 1–2 shows a simple PRAM.

All the processors have read and write access to a shared global memory. In the PRAM the access can be simultaneous. The assumption is that each processor can perform various arithmetic and logical operations in parallel. Also, each of the theoretical processors in Figure 1–2 can access the global shared memory in one *uninterruptible* unit of time. The PRAM model has

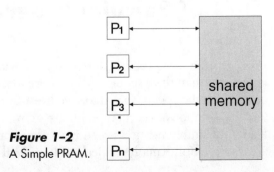

Figure 1–2
A Simple PRAM.

both concurrent and exclusive read algorithms. Concurrent read algorithms are allowed to read the same piece of memory simultaneously with no data corruption. Exclusive read algorithms are used to ensure that no two processors ever read the same memory location at the same time. The PRAM model also has both concurrent and exclusive write algorithms. Concurrent write algorithms allow multiple processors to write to memory, while exclusive write algorithms ensure that no two processors write to the same memory at the same time. Table 1–1 shows the four basic types of algorithms that can be derived from the read and write possibilities.

Table 1–1 Four Basic Read-Write Algorithms	
Read-Write Algorithm Types	*Meaning*
EREW	Exclusive read exclusive write
CREW	Concurrent read exclusive write
ERCW	Exclusive read concurrent write
CRCW	Concurrent read concurrent write

We will refer to these algorithm types often in this book as we discuss methods for implementing concurrent architectures. The blackboard architecture is one of the important architectures that we implement using the PRAM model and it is discussed in Chapter 13. It is important to note that although PRAM is a simplified theoretical model, it is used to develop practical programs, and these programs can compete on performance with programs that were developed using more sophisticated models of parallelism.

1.2.2   The Simplest Parallel Classification

The PRAM gives us a simple model for thinking about how a computer can be divided into processors and memory and gives us some ideas for how those processors may access memory. A simplified scheme for classifying the parallel computers was introduced by M.J. Flynn.[1] These schemes were SIMD (Single Instruction Multiple Data) and MIMD (Multiple Instruction Multiple Data). These were later extended to SPMD (Single Program Multiple Data) and MPMD (Multiple Program Multiple Data). The SPMD (SIMD) scheme

---

[1]M.J. Flynn. Very high-speed computers. In Proceedings of the IEEE, 54, 1901–1909 (December 1966).

allows multiple processors to execute the same instruction or program with each processor accessing different data. The MPMD (MIMD) scheme allows for multiple processors with each executing different programs or instructions and each with its own data. So in one scheme all the processors execute the same program or instructions and in the other scheme each processor executes different instructions. Of course, there are hybrids of these models where the processors are divided up and some are SPMD and some are MPMD. Using SPMD, all of the processors are simply doing the same thing only with different data. For example, we can divide a single puzzle up into groups and assign each group to a separate processor. Each processor will apply the same rules for trying to put together the puzzle, but each processor has different pieces to work with. When all of the processors are done putting their pieces together, we can see the whole. Using MPMD, each processor executes something different. Even though they are all trying to solve the same problem, they have been assigned a different aspect of the problem. For example, we might divide the work of securing a Web server as a MPMD scheme. Each processor is assigned a different task. For instance, one processor monitors the ports, another processor monitors login attempts, another processor analyzes packet contents, and so on. Each processor works with its own data relative to its area of concern. Although the processors are each doing different work using different data, they are working toward a single solution: security. The parallel programming concepts that we discuss in this book are easily described using PRAM, SPMD (SIMD), and MPMD (MIMD). In fact, these schemes and models are used to implement practical small- to medium-scale applications and should be sufficient until you are ready to do advanced parallel programming.

1.3   The Benefits
of Distributed Programming

Distributed programming techniques allow software to take advantage of resources located on the Internet, on corporate and organization intranets, and on networks. Distributed programming usually involves network programming in one form or another. That is, a program on one computer on a network needs some hardware or software resource that belongs to another computer either on the same network or on some remote network. Distributed programming is all about one program talking to another program over some kind of network connection, which may involve everything from modems to satellites. The distinguishing feature of distributed programs is they are broken into parts. Those parts are usually implemented as separate programs. Those programs typically execute on separate computers and the program's parts communicate with each other over a network. Distributed programming techniques provide access to resources that may be geographically distant. For example, a distributed program divided into a Web server component and a Web client component can execute on two separate computers. The Web server component can be located in Africa and the Web client component can be located in Japan. The Web client part is able to use software and hardware resources of the Web server component, although they are separated by a great distance and almost certainly located on different networks running different operating environments. Distributed programming techniques provide shared access to expensive hardware and software resources. For instance, an expensive, high-end holographic printer may have print server software that provides print services to client software. The print client software resides on one computer and the print server software resides on another computer. Only one print server is needed to serve many print clients. Distributed computing can be used for redundancy and fail over. If we divide the program up into a number of parts with each running on different computers, then we may assign some of the parts the same task. If one of the computers fails for some reason then another part of the same program executing on a different computer picks up the work. Databases can be used to hold billions, trillions, even quadrillions of pieces of information. It is simply not practical for every user to have a copy of the database. The problem is some users are located in different buildings than where the computer with the database is located. Some users are located in different cities, states, and in some instances, countries. Distributed programming techniques are used to allow users to share the massive database regardless of where they are located.

1.3.1 The Simplest Distributed Programming Models

The client-server model of distributed computing is perhaps the easiest to understand and the most commonly used. In this model, a program is divided up into two parts: One part is called the server and the other the client. The server has direct access to some hardware or software resource that the client wants to use. In most cases, the server is located on a different machine than the client. Typically, there is a many-to-one relationship between the server and the client, that is, there is usually one server fulfilling the requests of many clients. The server usually mediates access to a large database, an expensive hardware resource, or an important collection of applications. The client makes requests for data, calculations, and other types of processing. A search engine is a good example of a client-server application. Search engines are used to locate information on the Internet or on corporate and organization intranets. The client is used to obtain a keyword or phrase that the user is interested in. The client software part then passes the request to the server software part. The server has the muscle to perform the massive search for the user's keyword or phrase. The server has either direct access to the information or to other servers that have access to the information. Ideally, the server finds the keyword or phrase the user requested and returns that information to the client component. Although the client and the server are separate programs on separate computers, they make up a single application. This division of a piece of software into a client and a server is the primary method of distributed programming. The client-server model also has other forms depending on the environment. For instance, the term *producer-consumer* is a close cousin of client-server. Typically, client-server applications refer to larger programs and producer-consumer refers to smaller programs. Usually when the programs are at the operating system level or lower they are called producer-consumer, and when they are above the operating system level they are usually called client-server (however, there are always exceptions).

1.3.2   The Multiagent (Peer-to-Peer) Distributed Model

Although the client-server model is the most prevalent distributed programming model in use, it is not the only model. Agents are rational software components that are self directed, often autonomous, and can continuously execute. Agents can both make requests of other software components and fulfill requests of other software components. Agents can cooperate within groups to perform certain tasks collectively. In this model there is no specific client or server. The agents form a kind of peer-to-peer model where each of the components are on somewhat equal footing and each component has something to offer to the other. For example, an agent that is providing a price quote for the refurbishing of a vintage sports car might work together with other agents. Where one agent specializes in engine work, another specializes in body work, another specializes in interior design and so on. These agents may cooperatively and collectively come up with the most competitive quote for refurbishing the car. The agents are distributed because each agent is located on a different server on the Internet. The agents use an agreed-upon Internet protocol to communicate. The client-server model is a natural fit for certain types of distributed programming and the peer-to-peer agent model is a natural fit for certain types of distributed programming. We explore both types in this book. The client-server and peer-to-peer models can be used to satisfy most distributed programming demands.

1.4   The Minimal Effort Required

Parallel and distributed programming come with a cost. Although there are many benefits to writing parallel and distributed programming, there are also some challenges and prerequisites. We discuss some challenges in Chapter 2. We mention the prerequisites here. Before a program is written or a piece of software is developed, it must first go through a design process. For parallel and distributed programs, the design process will include three issues: decomposition, communication, and synchronization.

1.4.1   Decomposition

Decomposition is the process of dividing up the problem and the solution into parts. Sometimes the parts are grouped into logical areas (i.e., searching, sorting, calculating, input, output, etc.). In other situations the parts are grouped by logical resource (i.e., file, communication, printer, database, etc.). The decomposition of the software solution amounts to the WBS (work breakdown structure). The WBS determines which piece of software does what. One of the primary issues of concurrent programming is identifying a natural WBS for the software solution at hand. There is no simple or cookbook approach to identifying the WBS. Software development is the process of translating concepts, ideas, patterns of work, rules, algorithms, or formulas into sets of instructions and data that can be executed or manipulated by a computer. This is largely a process of modeling. Software models are reproductions in software of some real-world task, process, or ideal. The purpose of the model is to imitate or duplicate the behavior and characteristics of some real-world entity in a particular domain. This process of modeling uncovers the natural WBS of a software solution. The better the model is understood and developed the more natural the WBS will be. Our approach is to uncover the parallelism or distribution within a solution through modeling. If parallelism doesn't naturally fit, don't force it. The question of how to break up an application into concurrently executing parts should be answered during the design phase and should be obvious in the model of the solution. If the model of the problem and the solution don't imply or suggest parallelism and distribution then try a sequential solution. If the sequential solution fails, that failure may give clues to how to approach the parallelism.

1.4.2 Communication

Once the software solution is decomposed into a number of concurrently executing parts, those parts will usually do some amount of communicating. How will this communication be performed if the parts are in different processes or different computers? Do the different parts need to share any memory? How will one part of the software know when the other part is done? Which part starts first? How will one component know if another component has failed? These issues have to be considered when designing parallel or distributed systems. If no communication is required between the parts, then the parts don't really constitute a single application.

1.4.3 Synchronization

The WBS designates who does what. When multiple components of software are working on the same problem, they must be coordinated. Some component has to determine when a solution has been reached. The components' order of execution must be coordinated. Do all of the parts start at the same time or does some work while others wait? What two or more components need access to the same resource? Who gets it first? If some of the parts finish their work long before the other parts, should they be assigned new work? Who assigns the new work in such cases? DCS (decomposition, communication, and synchronization) is the minimum that must be considered when approaching parallel or distributed programming. In addition to considering DCS, the location of DCS is also important. There are several layers

of concurrency in application development. DCS is applied a little differently in each layer.

1.5   The Basic Layers
of Software Concurrency

In this book we are concerned with concurrency within the application as opposed to concurrency at the operating system level, or concurrency within
hardware. Although the concurrency within hardware and the concurrency
at the operating system level support application concurrency, our focus is on
the application. For our purposes, concurrency occurs at:

- Instruction level
- Routine (function/procedure) level
- Object level
- Application level

1.5.1   Concurrency at the Instruction Level

Concurrency at the instruction level occurs when multiple parts of a single
instruction can be executed simultaneously. Figure 1–3 shows how a single
instruction can be decomposed for simultaneous execution.

In Figure 1-3, the component (A + B) can be executed at the same time as
(C − D). This is an example of concurrency at the instruction level. This kind
of parallelism is normally supported by compiler directives and is not under
the direct control of a C++ programmer.

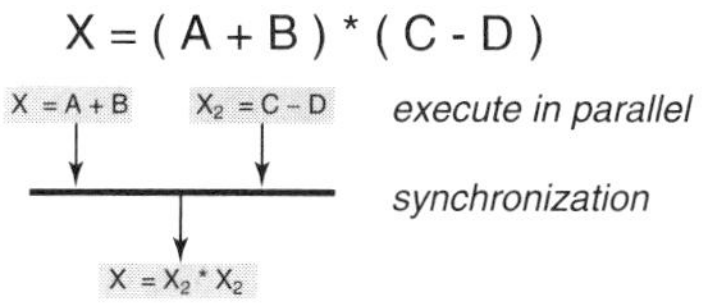

$X = (A + B) * (C - D)$

$X = A + B$ $X_2 = C - D$ *execute in parallel*

synchronization

$X = X_2 * X_2$

Figure 1–3
Decomposition of a single instruction.

1.5.2   Concurrency at the Routine Level

The WBS structure of a program may be along function lines, that is, the total work involved in a software solution is divided between a number of functions. If these functions are assigned to threads, then each function can execute on a different processor and if enough processors are available, each function can execute simultaneously. We discuss threads in more detail in Chapter 4.

1.5.3   Concurrency at the Object Level

The WBS of a software solution may be distributed between objects. Each object can be assigned to a different thread, or process. Using the CORBA (Common Object Request Broker Architecture) standard, each object may be assigned to a different computer on the network or different computer on a different network. We discuss CORBA in more detail in Chapter 8. Objects residing in different threads or processes may execute their methods concurrently.

1.5.4   Concurrency of Applications

Two or more applications can cooperatively work together to solve some problem. Although the application may have originally been designed separately and for different purposes, the principles of code reuse often allow applications to cooperate. In these circumstances two separate applications work together as a single distributed application. For example, the Clipboard was not designed to work with any one application but can be used by a variety of applications on the desktop. Some uses of the Clipboard had not been dreamed of during its original design.

The second and the third layers are the primary layers of concurrency that we will focus on in this book. We show techniques for implementing concurrency in these layers. Operating system and hardware issues are presented only where they are necessary in the context of application design. Once we have an appropriate WBS for a parallel programming or distributed programming design, the question is how do we implement it in C++.

1.6   No Keyword Support for Parallelism in C++

The C++ language does not include any keyword primitives for parallelism. The C++ ISO standard is for the most part silent on the topic of multithreading. There is no way within the language to specify that two or more statements should be executed in parallel. Other languages use built-in parallelism as a selling feature. Bjarne Stroustrup, the inventor of the C++ language, had something else in mind. In Stroustrup's opinion:

> It is possible to design concurrency support libraries that approach built-in concurrency support both in convenience and efficiency. By relying on libraries, you can support a variety of concurrency models, though, and thus serve the users that need those different models better than can be done by a single built-in concurrency model. I expect this will be the direction taken by most people and that the portability problems that arise when several concurrency-support libraries are used within the community can be dealt with by a thin layer of interface classes.

Furthermore, Stroustrup says, "I recommend parallelism be represented by libraries within C++ rather than as a general language feature." The authors have found Stroustrup's position and recommendation on parallelism as a library the most practical option. This book is only made possible because of the availability of high-quality libraries that can be used for parallel and distributed programming. The libraries that we use to enhance C++ implement national and international standards for parallelism and distributed programming and are used by thousands of C++ programmers worldwide.

1.6.1   The Options for Implementing Parallelism Using C++

Although there are special versions of C++ that implement parallelism, we present methods on how parallelism can be implemented using the ISO (International Standard Organization) standard for C++. The library approach to parallelism is the most flexible. System libraries and user-level libraries can be used to support parallelism in C++. System libraries are those libraries provided by the operating system environment. For example, the POSIX threads library is a set of system calls that can be used in conjunction with C++ to support parallelism. The POSIX (Portable Operating System Interface) threads are part of the new Single UNIX Specification. The POSIX threads are included in the IEEE Std. 1003.1-2001. The Single UNIX Specification is sponsored by the Open Group and developed by the Austin Common Standards Revision Group. According to the Open Group, the Single UNIX Specification is:

- Designed to give software developers a single set of APIs to be supported by every UNIX system.
- Shifts the focus from incompatible UNIX system product implementations to compliance to a single set of APIs.
- It is the codification and dejure standardization of the common core of UNIX system practice.
- The basic objective is portability of both programmers and application source code.

The Single UNIX Specification Version 3 includes the IEEE Std 1003.1-2001 and the Open Group Base Specifications Issue 6. The IEEE POSIX standards are now a formal part of the Single UNIX Specification and vice versa. There is now a single international standard for a portable operating system interface. C++ developers benefit because this standard contains APIs for creating threads and processes. Excluding instruction-level parallelism, dividing a program up into either threads or processes is the only way to achieve parallelism with C++. The new standard provides the tools to do this. The developer can use:

- POSIX threads (also referred to as pthreads)
- POSIX spawn function
- the exec() family of functions

These are all supported by system API calls and system libraries. If an operation system complies with the Single UNIX Specification Version 3, then these APIs will be available to the C++ developer. These APIs are discussed in Chapters 3 and 4. They are used in many of the examples in this book. In addition to system-level libraries, user-level libraries that implement other international standards such as the MPI (Message Passing Interface), PVM (Parallel Virtual Machine), and CORBA (Common Object Request Broker Architecture) can be used to support parallelism with C++.

1.6.2 MPI Standard

The MPI is the standard specification for message passing. The MPI was designed for high performance on both massively parallel machines and on workstation clusters. This book uses the MPICH implementation of the MPI standard. MPICH is a freely available, portable implementation of MPI. The MPICH provides the C++ programmer with a set of APIs and libraries that support parallel programming. The MPI is especially useful for SPMD and MPMD programming. The authors use the MPICH implementation of MPI on a 32-node cluster running Linux and an 8-node cluster running Solaris and Linux. Although C++ doesn't have parallel primitives built in, it can take advantage of power libraries such as MPICH that does support parallelism. This is one of the benefits of C++. It is designed for flexibility.

1.6.3 PVM: A Standard for Cluster Programming

The PVM is a software package that permits a heterogeneous collection of computers hooked together by a network to be used as a single large parallel computer. The overall objective of the PVM system is to enable a collection of computers to be used cooperatively for concurrent or parallel computation. A PVM library implementation supports:

- Heterogeneity in terms of machines, networks, and applications
- Explicit message-passing model
- Process-based computation
- Multiprocessor support (MPP, SMP)
- Translucent access to hardware (applications can either ignore or take advantage of hardware differences)
- Dynamically configurable host pool (processors can be added and deleted at runtime and can include processor mixes)

The PVM is the easiest to use and most flexible environment available for basic parallel programming tasks that require the involvement of different types of computers running different operating systems. The PVM library is especially useful for several single processor systems that can be networked together to form a virtual parallel processor machine. We discuss techniques for using PVM with C++ in Chapter 6. The PVM is the de facto standard for implementing heterogeneous clusters and is freely available and widely used. The PVM has excellent support for MPMD (MIMD) and SPMD (SIMD) models of parallel programming. The authors use PVM for small- to medium-size parallel programming tasks and the MPI for larger, more complex MPI tasks. PVM and MPI are both libraries that can be used with C++ to do cluster programming.

1.6.4   The CORBA Standard

CORBA is the standard for distributed cross-platform object-oriented programming. We mention CORBA here under parallelism because implementations of the CORBA standard can be used to develop multiagent systems. Multiagent systems offer important models of peer-to-peer distributed programming. Multiagent systems can work concurrently. This is one of the areas where parallel programming and distributed programming overlap. Although the agents are executing on different computers, they are executing during the same time period, working cooperatively on a common problem. The CORBA standard provides an open, vendor-independent architecture and infrastructure that computer applications use to work together over networks. Using the standard protocol IIOP, a CORBA-based program from any vendor, on almost any computer, operating system, programming language, and network, can interoperate with a CORBA-based program from the same or another vendor on almost any other computer operating system, programming language, and network. In this book we use the MICO implementation. MICO is a freely available and fully compliant implementation of the CORBA standard. MICO supports C++.

1.6.5   Library Implementations
Based on Standards

MPICH, PVM, MICO, and POSIX threads are each library implementations based on standards. This means that software developers can rely on these implementations to be widely available and portable across multiple platforms. These libraries are freely available and used by software developers worldwide. The POSIX threads library can be used with C++ to do multithreaded programming. If the program is running on a computer that has multiple processors, then each thread can possibly run on a separate processor and thereby execute concurrently. If only a single processor is available, then the illusion of parallelism is provided and concurrency is achieved through the process of context switching. POSIX threads are perhaps the easiest way to introduce parallelism within a C++ program. Whereas the MPICH, PVM, and MICO libraries will have to be downloaded or obtained (they are readily available), any operating system environment that is client with the POSIX standard or the new UNIX Specification Version 3 will have a POSIX threads implementation. Each library offers a slightly different model of parallelism. Table 1–2 shows how each library can be used with C++.

Table 1–2 MPICH, PVM, MICO, and POSIX Threads Used with C++	
Libraries	*C++ Usage*
MPICH	Supports large-scale, complex cluster programming. Strong support for SPMD model. Also supports SMP, MPP, and multiuser configurations.
PVM	Supports cluster programming of heterogeneous environments. Easy to use for single-user, small to medium cluster applications. Also supports MPP.
MICO	Supports either distributed or object-oriented parallel programming. Contains nice support for agent and multiagent programming.
POSIX	Supports parallel processing within a single application at the function or object level. Can be used to take advantage of SMP or MPP.

Whereas languages that depend on built-in support for parallelism are restricted to the models supplied, the C++ developer is free to mix and match parallel programming models. As the nature of the applications change, a C++ developer can select different libraries to match the scenario.

1.7 Programming Environments for Parallel and Distributed Programming

The most common environments for parallel and distributed programming are clusters, MPPs, and SMP computers.

Clusters are collections of two or more computers that are networked together to provide a single, logical system. The group of computers appear to the application as a single virtual computer. MPP (Massively Parallel Processors) is a single computer that has hundreds of processors. SMP (Symmetric Multiprocessing) is a single system that has processors that are tightly coupled where the processors share memory and the data path. SMP processors share the resources and are all controlled by a single operating system. This book provides a gentle introduction to parallel and distributed programming, therefore we focus our attention on small clusters of 8 to 32 processors and on multiprocessor machines with 2 to 4 processors. Although many of the techniques we discuss can be used in MPP environments or in large SMP environments, our primary attention is on moderate systems.

Summary—Toward Concurrency

Throughout this book we present an architectural approach to parallel and distributed programming. The emphasis is placed on uncovering the natural parallelism within a problem and its solution. This parallelism is captured within the software model for the solution. We suggest object-oriented methods to help manage the complexity of parallel and distributed programming. Our mantra is *function follows form*. We use the library approach to provide parallelism support for the C++ language. The libraries we recommend are based on national and international standards. Each library is freely available and widely used. Techniques and concepts presented in the book are vendor independent, nonproprietary, and rely on open standards and open architectures. The C++ programmer and software developer can use different parallel models to serve different needs because each parallelism model is captured within a library. The library approach to parallel and distributed programming gives the C++ programmer the greatest possible flexibility. While parallel and distributed programming can be fun and rewarding, it presents several challenges. In the next chapter we will provide an overview of the most common challenges to parallel and distributed programming.

2 The Challenges of Parallel and Distributed Programming

"The idea that you should really indicate the exact values of any physical quantity — temperature, density, potential field strength or whatever . . . is a bold extrapolation."

—*Erwin Shrodinger,* Causality and Wave Mechanics

In this Chapter

The Big Paradigm Shift • Coordination Challenges • Sometimes Hardware Fails and Software Quits • Too Much Parallelization or Distribution Can Have Negative Consequences • Selecting a Good Architecture Requires Research • Different Techniques for Testing and Debugging are Required • The Parallel or Distributed Design Must Be Communicated • Summary

In the basic sequential model of programming, a computer program's instructions are executed one at a time. The program is viewed as a recipe and each step is to be performed by the computer in the order and amount specified. The designer of the program breaks up the software into a collection of tasks. Each task is performed in order, and each task must wait its turn. Every program is perceived as having a beginning, middle, and end. The designer or developer envisions each program as a linear progression of tasks. Not only must the tasks march in single file, but the tasks are related so that if the first task cannot complete its work for some reason then the second task may never start. In other words, each task is made to wait on the result of the previous task's work before it can execute. In the sequential model tasks are often serially interdependent. This means that A needs something from B, B needs something from C, C needs something from D, and so on. If B fails for some reason, then C and D will never execute. In a sequential world the developer is accustomed to designing the software to perform step 1 first, then step 2, then step 3. This sequential model is so entrenched in the software design and development process that many programmers find it hard to see things any other way. The solution to every problem, the design of every algorithm, and the layout of every data structure all rely on the computer accessing each instruction or piece of data one at a time.

2.1   The Big Paradigm Shift

All of this changes in the world of parallel programming. In this world, multiple instructions can execute at the same instant. A single instruction might be broken down into smaller pieces with each piece being executed simultaneously. A program can be broken into multiple tasks that can each execute at the same time. Instead of one task, a program might consist of hundreds or thousands of routines executing concurrently. In the world of parallel programming, the sequence and location of things is not always predictable. Multiple tasks can start at the same time on any processor with no guarantee what task will finish first, in what order they'll finish, or on what processor they will execute. In addition to tasks executing in parallel, a single task may have concurrently executing parts or subtasks. In some configurations, it is possible for the subtasks to run on separate processors, possibly separate computers. Figure 2–1 shows three levels of parallelism that are possible within a single computer program.

The programmer and developer's model of a program undergoes a big paradigm shift because of the three levels of parallelism shown in Figure 2–1 and how these levels of parallelism can be distributed to multiple processors. Figure 2–2 illustrates how the three levels of parallelism are combined with the basic parallel processor configurations.

Notice in Figure 2–2 that multiple tasks can run on a single processor even when the computer has more than one processor. This situation can be created by operating system scheduling policies. Scheduling policies, process priorities, thread priorities, and input/output device performance all impact where and for how long a task, subtask, or partial instruction will execute. Figure 2–2 emphasizes the different architectures that a programmer must face when moving from the sequential programming model to a parallel programming model. The model changes from a strictly ordered sequence of tasks to only a partially ordered (possibly unordered) collection of tasks. Parallelism turns order of execution, time of execution, and location of execution into wildcards. Any combination of these wildcards is subject to change values in often unpredictable ways.

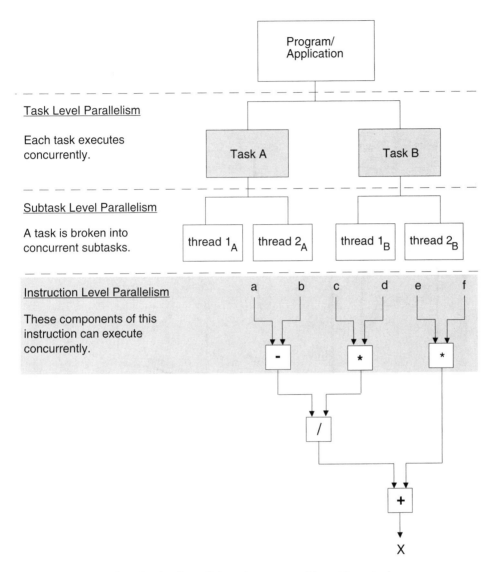

Figure 2-1 The three levels of parallelism that are possible within a single computer program.

2.2 Coordination Challenges

If a program has routines that can execute in parallel, and these routines share any files, devices, or memory locations, then several coordination issues are introduced. For example, lets say we have an electronic bank with-

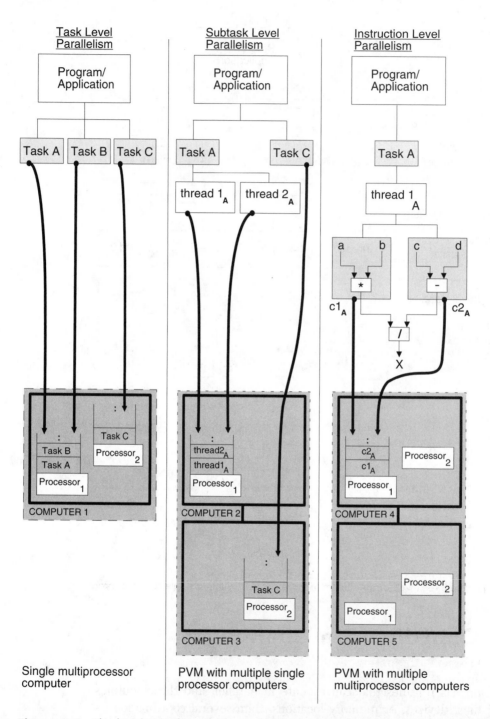

Figure 2–2   The three levels of parallelism combined with the basic parallel processor configurations.

drawal and deposit program that is divided into three tasks that can execute in parallel. We label the tasks A, B, C.

Task A receives requests from Task B to make withdrawals from an account. Task A also receives requests from Task C to make deposits to an account. Task A accepts and processes requests on a first-come, first-serve basis. What if we have an account that has a balance of $1,000 and Task C wants to make a $100 deposit to the account and Task B wants to make a $1,100 withdrawal from the account? What happens if Task B and Task C both try to update the same account at the same time? What would the balance be? Obviously an account balance can only hold one value at a time. Task A can only apply one transaction at a time to the account, so there's a problem. If Task B's request executes a fraction of a second faster than Task C, then the account will have a negative balance. On the other hand, if Task C gets to the account first, then the account will not have a negative balance. So the balance of the account depends on which task happens to get its request to Task A first. Furthermore, we can execute Tasks B and C several times, each time starting with the same amounts, and sometimes Task B would execute a fraction of a second faster and sometimes Task C would execute faster. Clearly some form of coordination is in order.

To coordinate tasks that are executing in parallel requires communication between the tasks and synchronization of their work. Four common types of problems occur when the communication or the synchronization is incorrect.

Problem #1 Data Race

If two or more tasks attempt to change a shared piece of data at the same time and the final value of the data depends simply on which tasks get there first, then a *race condition* has occurred. When two or more tasks are attempting to update the same data resource at the same time, the race condition is called *data race*. In our electronic banking program, which task gets to the account balance first turns out to be a matter of operating system scheduling, processor states, latency, and chance. This situation creates a race condition. Under these circumstances, what should the bank report as the account's real balance?

So while we would like our electronic banking program to be able to simultaneously handle many banking deposits and withdrawals, we need to coordinate the tasks in the program if the deposits and withdrawals happen to be applied to the same account. Whenever tasks concurrently share a modifiable resource, rules and policies will have to be applied to the task's access. For instance, in our banking program we might apply any deposits to the account before we apply any withdrawals. We might set a rule that only one transaction has access to an account at a time. If more than one transaction for the same account arrives at the same time, then the transactions must be held and organized according to some rule and then granted access one at a time. These organization rules help to accomplish proper synchronization.

Problem #2 Indefinite Postponement

Scheduling one or more tasks to wait until some event or condition occurs can be tricky. First, the event or condition must take place in a timely fashion. Second, it requires carefully placed communications between tasks. If one or more tasks are waiting for a piece of communication before they execute and that communication either never comes, comes too late, or is incomplete, then the tasks may never execute. Likewise, if the event or condition that we assumed would eventually happen actually never occurs, then the tasks that we have suspended will wait forever. If we suspend one or more tasks waiting on some condition or event that never occurs, this is known as *indefinite postponement*. In our electronic banking example, if we set up rules that cause the withdrawal tasks to wait until all deposit tasks are completed, then the withdrawal tasks could be headed for indefinite postponement.

The assumption is that there are deposit tasks. If no deposit requests are made, what will cause the withdrawal tasks to execute? What if the reverse happens, that is, what if deposit requests are continuously made to the same account? As long as a deposit is in progress, no withdrawal can be made. This situation can indefinitely postpone withdrawals.

Indefinite postponement might take place if no deposit tasks appear or if deposit tasks constantly appear. What if deposit requests appear correctly but we fail to properly communicate the event? So as we try to coordinate our parallel task's access to some shared data resource, we have to be mindful of situations that can create indefinite postponement. We discuss techniques for avoiding indefinite postponement in Chapter 5.

Problem #3 Deadlock

Deadlock is another *waiting-type* pitfall. To illustrate an example of deadlock, lets assume that the three tasks in our electronic banking program example are working with two accounts instead of one. Recall that Task A receives withdrawal requests from Task B and deposit requests from Task C. Tasks A, B, and C can execute concurrently. However, Tasks B and C may only update one account at a time. Task A grants access on a first-come, first-serve basis. Lets say that Task B has exclusive access to Account 1, and Task C has exclusive access to Account 2. But Task B needs access to Account 2 to complete its processing and Task C needs access to Account 1 to complete its processing. Task B holds on to Account 1 waiting for Task C to release Account 2 and Task C holds on to Account 2 waiting for Task B to release Account 1. Tasks B and C are engaged in a *deadly embrace,* also known as a *deadlock.* Figure 2–3 shows the deadlock situation between Tasks B and C.

The form of deadlock shown in Figure 2–3 requires concurrently executing tasks that have access to some shared writeable data to wait on each other for access to that shared data. In Figure 2–3 the shared data are Accounts 1 and 2. Both tasks have access to these accounts. It happens that instead of one task getting access to both accounts at the same time, each task got access to one of the accounts. Since Task B can't release Account 1 until it gets Account 2, and Task C can't release Account 2 until it gets Account 1, the electronic banking program is locked. Notice that Tasks B and C can drive another task(s) into indefinite postponement. If other tasks are waiting on access to Accounts 1 or 2 and Tasks B and C are engaged in a deadlock, then those tasks are waiting for a condition that will never happen. In attempting to coordinate concurrently executing tasks, deadlock and indefinite postponement are two of the ugliest obstacles that must be overcome.

Figure 2–3   The deadlock situation between Tasks B and C.

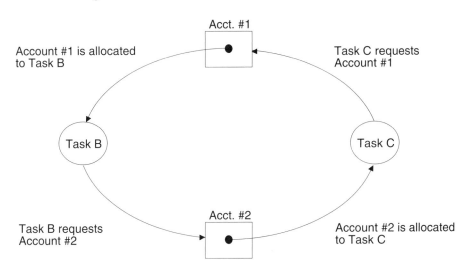

Problem #4 Communication Difficulties

Many commonly found parallel environments (e.g., clusters) often consist of *heterogeneous computer networks*. Heterogeneous computer networks are systems that consist of different types of computers often running different operating systems with different network protocols. The processors involved may have different architectures, different word sizes, and different machine languages. Besides different operating systems, different scheduling and priority schemes might be in effect. To make matters worse, each system might have different qualities of data transmission. This makes error and exception handling particularly challenging. The heterogeneous nature of the system might include other differences. For instance, we might need to share data and logic between programs written in different languages or developed using different software models. The solution might be partially implemented in Fortran, C++, and Java. This introduces interlanguage communication issues. Even when the distributed or parallel environment is not heterogeneous, there is the problem of communicating between two or more processes or between two or more threads. Because each process has its own address space, sharing variables, parameters, and return values between processes requires the use of IPC (inter-process communication) techniques. While IPC is not necessarily difficult, it adds another level of design, testing, and debugging to the system.

The POSIX specification supports five basic mechanisms used to accomplish communication between processes:

- Files with lock and unlock facilities
- Pipes (unnamed and named, also called fifos)
- Shared memory and messaging
- Sockets
- Semaphores

Each of these IPC mechanisms have strengths, weaknesses, traps, and pitfalls that the software designer and developer must manage in order to facilitate reliable and efficient communication between two or more processes. Communication between two or more threads (sometimes called lightweight processes) is easier because threads share a common address space. This means that each thread in the program can easily pass parameters, get return values from functions, and access global data. However, if the communication is not appropriately designed, then deadlock, indefinite postponement, and other data race conditions can easily occur. Both parallel and distributed programming have these four types of coordination problems in common.

Although purely parallel processing systems are different from purely distributed processing systems, we have purposely blurred the lines between the coordination problems in a distributed system versus the coordination problems in a parallel system. This is partly because there is an overlap between the kinds of problems encountered in parallel programming and those encountered in distributed programming. It's also partly because the solutions to the problems in one area are often applicable to problems in the other. However, the primary reason we lose the distinction is that hybrid systems that are part parallel and part distributed are quickly becoming the norm. The state of the art in parallel computing involves clusters, beowolfs, and grids. Exotic cluster configurations is comprised of commodity, off-the-shelf parts that are readily available. These architectures involve multiple computers with multiple processors. Furthermore, single processor systems are on the decline. So, in the future purely distributed systems will be built with computers that have multiple processors (forcing the hybrid issue). This means that as a practical matter the software designer and developer will most likely be faced with problems of distribution and parallelization. Therefore, we discuss the problems in the same space. Table 2–1 presents a matrix of the combinations of parallel and distributed programming with hardware configurations.

Table 2–1   A Matrix of the Combinations of Parallel and Distributed Programming with Hardware Configurations

	Single Computer	*Multiple Computers*
Parallel programming	Accomplished with multiple processors and breaking up the logic into multiple threads or processes. Threads or processes can run on different processors. IPC required to coordinate tasks.	Accomplished with libraries such as PVM. This requires the type of message passing normally associated with distributed programming.
Distrubuted programming	Multiple processors are not necessary. The logic may be broken up into multiple processors or threads. IPC required to coordinate tasks.	Accomplished with sockets and components such as CORBA ORB (Object Request Broker). Can use communication that is normally associated with parallel programming.

Notice in Table 2–1 that there are configurations where parallelism is accomplished by using multiple computers. This can be the case using the PVM library. Likewise, there are configurations where distribution can be accomplished on a single computer using multiple processes, or threads. The fact that multiple processes or threads are involved means that the work of the program is "distributed." The combinations in Table 2–1 imply that coordination problems that are normally associated with distributed programming can pop up in parallel programming situations and problems that are normally associated with parallel programming can appear in distributed programming situations.

Regardless of the hardware configuration, there are two basic mechanisms for communicating between two or more tasks: shared memory, and message passing. To effectively use the shared memory mechanism, the programmer must constantly be aware of data race, indefinite postponement, and deadlock pitfalls. The message passing scheme offers other showstoppers such as interrupted transmissions (partial execution), garbled messages, lost messages, wrong messages, too long messages, late messages, early messages, and so on. Much of this book is about the effective use of both mechanisms.

2.3 Sometimes Hardware Fails and Software Quits

When multiple processors are cooperating to provide the solution to some problem, what happens if one or more of the processors fail? Should the program halt or should the work be redistributed somehow? When multiple computers are involved in the solution to some problem, what happens if the communications link between two or more of the computers is temporarily interrupted? What if instead of the communications link being interrupted, the traffic is so slow that processes on each end of the communications time out? How should the software respond in these situations? If we have 50 computers cooperatively solving a problem and only two of the computers fail, should the other 48 pick up the work? If in our electronic banking programming we have a $1,000 withdrawal and deposit tasks executing simultaneously and two of the tasks are deadlocked, should we shut down the server task? What do we do about the two tasks that are locked? What if the withdrawal and deposit tasks are working properly and for some reason the server task locks up? Should we terminate all the pending withdrawal and deposit tasks?

What do we do about partial failures or partial executions? These kinds of considerations are not necessary in single computer sequential programs. Sometimes the failure is a result of some administration or security policy. For instance, if we have 1,000 routines working on some problem and several of the routines need write access to a file but don't have the write access, this could cause indefinite postponement, deadlock, or partial failure. What if some of the routines are blocked because they don't have security access to the resources they need? Should the entire system be shut down in such cases? How can the information or processing performed be useful if there are hardware interruptions, communications failures, and partial executions? Yet these situations represent normal processing within distributed and parallel environments. In this book, we present several software architectures and programming techniques that can be used to manage these situations.

2.4   Too Much Parallelization or Distribution Can Have Negative Consequences

There is a point where the overhead in managing multiple processors outweighs the speedup and other advantages gained from parallelization. The old adage "you can never have enough processors" is simply not true. Communication between computers or synchronization between processors comes at a cost. The complexity of the synchronization or the amount of communication between processors can require so much computation that the performance of the tasks that are doing the work can be negatively impacted. How many processes, tasks, or threads should a program be divided into? Is there an optimal number of processors for any given parallel program? At what point does adding more processors or computers to the computation pool slow things down instead of speeding them up? It turns out that the numbers change depending on the program. Some scientific simulations may max out at several thousand processors, while for some business applications several hundred might be sufficient. For some client-server configurations, eight processors are optimal and nine processors would cause the server to perform poorly.

There is the work and resources involved in managing parallel hardware and the work involved in managing concurrently executing processes and threads in software. The limit of software processes might be reached before we've reached the optimum number of processors or computers. Likewise, we might see diminishing returns in the hardware before we've reached the optimum number of concurrently executing tasks.

2.5   Selecting a Good Architecture Requires Research

There are many software architectures that support concurrency. The correct architecture needs to be matched with the WBS (Work Breakdown Structure) of a piece of software. Not all parallel and distributed architectures are created equal. While some distributed architectures would work fine in a Web environment, they would fail immediately in a real-time environment. For instance, distributed architectures that support long latency times that would be acceptable in a Web environment are unacceptable for many real-time environments. Compare the distributed processing in a Web-based e-mail system to the distributed processing that takes place with banking ATMs (automated teller machines). Latency that is present in many e-mail systems would simply be unacceptable in real-time systems such as ATMs. Certain distributed architectures (some asynchronous models) manage latency times better than others. Care must also be taken to select the proper parallel processing architectures. For instance, vector processing techniques may work well for certain mathematical and simulation problems, but are ineffective when applied to multiagent planning algorithms. Table 2–2 shows commonly found software architectures that support parallel and distributed programming.

The four basic models listed in Table 2–2 and their variations provide the basic foundations for all the concurrency architectures (i.e., agent, blackboard, object-oriented) that we discuss in this book. It is necessary to become familiar with each of these models and their applications to parallel and distributed programming. We provide an introduction to these models and the bibliography contains material that covers more advanced treatment of each of these models. It is best to find the natural or inherent parallelism in the work being done or in the solution to a problem. The architecture chosen should match this natural or inherent parallelism as closely as possible. For instance, the parallelism in a solution may be better described using a peer-to-peer model, where all workers are considered equal, as opposed to a

Model	Architecture	Distributed Programming	Parallel Programming
Table 2–2 Commonly Found Software Architectures that Support Parallel and Distributed Programming			
Host node also called • master/slave • boss/worker • loosely (client server)	Master control tasks that monitors and delegates work to subordinate tasks.	✔	✔
Peer or node only	All tasks are basically equal and work is distributed evenly.		✔
Vector processing loosely pipeline or array processing	One worker for each element of the array or stage in the pipeline.	✔	✔
Tree (parent–child)	Dynamically generated workers in a parent–child relationship. Useful in these types of algorithms: • recursion • divide and conquer • AND/OR • tree processing	✔	✔

boss worker model, where there is a master process managing all the other processes as subordinates.

2.6   Different Techniques for Testing and Debugging are Required

When testing a sequential program the developer can trace the logic of a program in a step-by-step manner. If the developer starts with the same data and makes sure the system is in the same state, then the outcome or flow of the logic is predictable. The programmer can find bugs in the software by starting the program in the necessary state, using the appropriate input and then tracing through the logic step-by-step. Testing and debugging in the sequential model depends on the predictability of the program's initial state, and current state given the specified input.

This changes with parallel and distributed environments. It is difficult to reproduce the exact context of parallel or distributed tasks because of operating system scheduling policies, dynamic workloads on the computer, processor time slices, process and thread priorities, communication latency, execution latency, and the random chance involved in parallel and distributed contexts. To reproduce the exact state the environment was in during testing and debugging requires that every task the operating system was working on be recreated. The processor scheduling state must be known. The status of virtual memory and context switching all must be reproduced exactly. Interrupt and signal conditions must be recreated. In some cases, networking traffic would have to be recreated! Even the testing and debugging tools impact the exact environment. This means that recreating the same sequence of events in order to test or debug a program is often out of the question. The reason these things would have to be recreated is because they can all help to determine which process or thread can execute and on what processor they can execute. Moreover, it is the particular mix of executing processes and threads that could be the reason for a deadlock, indefinite postponement, data race, or another kind of problem. Although some of these issues also affect sequential programming, they don't disrupt the assumptions of the sequential model. The kind of predictability that is present in the sequential model is simply not available in concurrency programming. This forces the developer to acquire new tactics for testing and debugging programs. It also requires that the developer find new ways to prove program correctness.

2.7   The Parallel or Distributed Design Must Be Communicated

There is also the challenge of how to accurately capture a parallel or distributed design in documentation. We must be able to describe the work breakdown structure as well as the synchronization and communication between tasks, objects, processes, and threads. Designers must be able to effectively communicate to developers. Developers must be able to communicate with those that must maintain and administer the system. Ideally, this should be done using a standard notation and representation that is readily available to all concerned. However, finding a single documentation language that is

Table 2–3	Seven UML Diagrams Helpful for Documenting Multithreaded, Parallel, and Distributed Programs

UML Diagrams	*Descriptions*
Activity diagram	A type of state diagram in which most (if not all) of the states represent activity and most of the transitions (if not all) are activated by completion of an activity in the source states.
Interaction	A type of diagram that shows the interaction among a set of objects; the interaction is described as a message exchanged among them. These diagrams include: • collaboration diagrams • sequence diagrams • activity diagrams
State/concurrent state diagram	A diagram that shows the sequence of an object's transformation as it responds to events. In the case of concurrent state diagram, these transformations can occur during the same time interval.
Sequence diagram	An interaction diagram that shows the organization of the structure of objects that receive and send messages.
Collaboration diagram	An interaction diagram that shows the organization of the structure of objects that receive and send messages.
Deployment diagram	A diagram that shows the runtime configuration of processing nodes, hardware, and software components in a system.
Component diagram	An interaction diagram that shows the dependencies and organization among a set of physical modules of code (packages) in a system.

broadly understood and can clearly represent the multiparadigm nature of some of these systems is elusive. We have chosen the UML (Unified Modeling Language) for this purpose. Table 2–3 lists the seven UML diagrams that are helpful for multithreaded, parallel, or distributed programs.

The seven diagram types in Table 2–3 are only a subset of the diagram types available in the UML, but these types of diagrams are immediately applicable to what we want to capture in our concurrency designs. In particular, the UML's activity, deployment, and state diagrams are very useful in communicating parallel and distributed processing behavior. Since the UML is the de facto standard for communicating object-oriented and agent-oriented designs, we rely upon its use in this book. The Appendix contains a description and explanation for the notation and symbols used in these diagrams.

Summary

Parallel and distributed programming present challenges in several areas. New approaches to software design and architectures must be adopted. Many of the fundamental assumptions that are held in the sequential model of programming don't apply in the realm of parallel and distributed programming. The four primary coordination problems, data race, indefinite postponement, deadlock, and communication synchronization, are among the major obstacles to programs that require concurrency. Every aspect of the software development life cycle is impacted when the requirements include parallelism or distribution from the initial design down to the testing and documentation. In this book, we present architectural approaches to many of these problems. In addition to the architectural approach, we take advantage of the multiparadigm capabilities of C++ to provide techniques for managing the complexity of parallel and distributed programs.

3   Dividing C++ Programs into Multiple Tasks

"Hence, whatever parallel processes may be going on at a lower (neural) level, at the symbolic level the human mind is fundamentally a serial machine, accomplishing its work through temporal sequences of processes, each typically requiring hundreds of milliseconds for execution."

—*Herbert A Simon*, The Machine As Mind

In this Chapter

Process: A Definition • Anatomy of a Process • Process States • Process Scheduling • Context Switching • Creating a Process • Terminating a Process • Process Resources • What are Asynchronous and Synchronous Processes? • Dividing the Program into Tasks • Summary

Concurrency in a C++ program is accomplished by factoring your program into either multiple processes or multiple threads. While there are variations on how the logic for a C++ program can be organized (e.g, within objects, functions, generic templates), the options for (with the exception of instruction level) parallelization is accounted for through the use of multiple processes and threads. This chapter focuses on the notion of a process and how C++ programs can be divided into multiple processes.

3.1   Process: A Definition

A *process* is a unit of work created by the operating system. It is important to note that processes and programs are not necessarily equivalent. A program may consist of multiple processes. In some situations, a process might not be associated with any particular program. Processes are artifacts of the operating system and programs are artifacts of the developer. Current operating systems such as UNIX/Linux are capable of managing hundreds or even thousands of concurrently loaded processes.

In order for a unit of work to be called a process it must have an address space assigned to it by the operating system. It must have a process id. It must have a state and an entry in the process table. According to the POSIX standard, it must have one or more flows of controls executing within that address space and the required system resources for those flows of control. A process has a set of executing instructions that reside in the address space of that process. Space is allocated for the instructions, any data that belongs to the process, and stacks for function calls and local variables.

3.1.1   Two Kinds of Processes

When a process executes, the operating system assigns the process to a processor. The process executes its instructions for a period a time. The process is preempted so another process can be assigned the processor. The operating system scheduler switches between the code of one process, user, or system to the code of another process, giving each process a chance to execute their instructions. There are *user* and *system* processes. Processes that execute system code are called system processes. System processes administer to the whole system. They perform housekeeping tasks such as allocating memory, swapping pages of memory between internal and secondary storage, checking devices, and so on. They also perform tasks on behalf of the user processes such as fulfill I/O requests, allocate memory, and so on. User processes execute its own code and sometimes they make system function calls. When a user process executes its own code, it is in *user mode*. In *user mode*, the process cannot execute certain privileged machine instructions. When a user process makes a system function call, for example `read()`, `write()`, `open()`, it is executing operating system instructions. What occurs is the user process is put on hold until the system call has completed. The processor is given to the kernel to complete the system call. At that time the user process is said to be in *kernel mode* and cannot be preempted by any user processes.

3.1.2   Process Control Block

Processes have characteristics used for identification and determining their behavior during execution. The kernel maintains data structures and provides system functions that allow the user to have access to this information. Some information is stored in the PCB (process control block). The information stored in the PCB describes the process to the operating system. This information is needed in order for the operating system to manage each process. When the operating system switches between a process utilizing the CPU to another process, it saves the current state of the executing process and its context to the PCB save area in order to restart the process the next time it is assigned to the CPU. The PCB is read and changed by various modules of the operating system. Modules concerned with the monitoring the operating system's performance, scheduling, allocating resources, and interrupt processing access and/or modify the PCB. PCB information includes:

- current state and priority of the process
- process, parent, and child identifiers
- pointers to allocated resources
- pointers to location of the process's memory
- pointer to the process's parent and child processes
- processor utilized by process
- control and status registers
- stack pointers

The information stored in the PCB can be organized as information concerned with *process control* such as the current state and priority of the process, pointers to parent/child PCBs, allocated resources, and memory. This also includes any scheduling-related information, process privileges, flags, messages, and signals that have to do with communication between processes (IPC, or interprocess communication). The process control information is required by the operating system in order to coordinate the concurrently active processes. Stack pointers and the content of user, control, and status registers describe information concerned with the *state of the processor.* When a process is running, information is placed in the registers of the CPU. Once the operating system decides to switch to another process, all the information in those registers has to be saved. When the process gains the use of the CPU again, this information can be restored. Other information has to do with *process identification.* This is the process id (PID), and the parent id (PPID). These identification numbers are unique for each process. They are positive, nonzero integers.

3.2   Anatomy of a Process

The address space of a process is divided into three logical segments: *text* (program code), *data* and *stack* segments. Figure 3–1 shows the logical layout of a process. The text segment is at the bottom of the address space. The text segment contains the instructions to be executed, called the *program code*. The data segment above it contains the initialized global, external, and static variables for the process. The stack segment contains locally allocated variables and parameters passed to functions. Because a process can make system function calls as well as user-defined function calls, two stacks are maintained in the stack segment, the *user-stack* and the *kernel-stack*. When a function call is made, a stack-frame is constructed and pushed onto either the user or kernel stack depending on whether the process is in user or kernel mode. The stack segment grows downward toward the data segment. The stack frame is popped from the stack when the function returns. The text, data, stack segments, and process control block are part of what forms the *process image*.

Figure 3–1   The address space of a process divided into the text, data, and stack segments. This is the logical layout of a process.

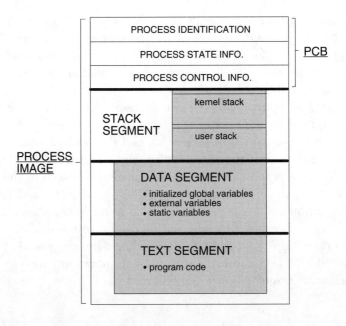

The address space of a process is *virtual*. Virtual storage dissociates the addresses referenced in an executing process from the addresses actually available in internal memory. This allows the addressing of storage space much larger than what is available. The segments of the process's virtual address space are contiguous blocks of memory. Each segment and physical address space are broken up into chunks called *pages*. Each page has a unique *page frame number*. The virtual page frame number is used as an index into

Figure 3–2 The contiguous virtual page frames mapped to pages in physical memory.

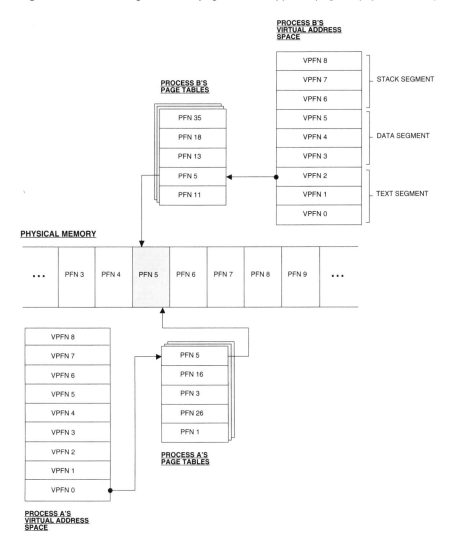

the process's page tables. The *page table* entries contain a physical page frame number, thus mapping the virtual page frames to physical page frames. This is depicted in Figure 3–2. As illustrated, virtual address space is contiguous but it is mapped to physical pages in any order.

Although the virtual address space of each process is protected to prevent another process from accessing it, the text segment of a process can be shared among several processes. Figure 3–2 also shows how two processes can share the same program code. The same physical page frame number is stored in the page table entries of both processes' page tables. As illustrated in Figure 3–2, process A virtual page frame 0 is mapped to physical page frame 5 as well as process B's virtual page frame 2.

In order for the operating system to manage all the processes stored in internal memory, it creates and maintains *process tables*. Actually, the operating system has a table for all of the entities that it manages. Keep in mind that the operating system manages not only processes but all the resources of the computer including devices, memory, and files. Some of the memory, devices, and files are managed on behalf of the user processes. This informa-

Figure 3–3   The operating system control tables. Each entry in the process table stores represents a process in the system.

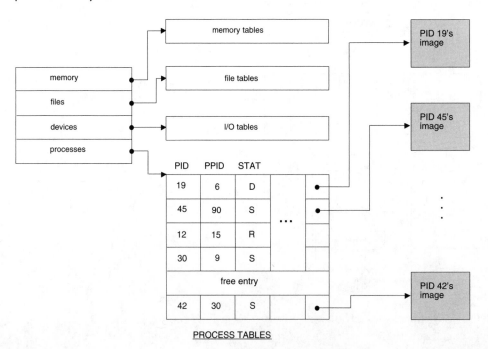

PROCESS TABLES

tion is referenced in the PCB as resources allocated to the process. The process table will have an entry for each process image in memory. Each entry contains the process and parent process id, real and effective user id and group id, list of pending signals, the location of the text, data, and stack segments, and the current state of the process. When the operating system needs to access a process, the process is looked up in the process table and then the process image is located in memory. This is depicted in Figure 3–3.

3.3 Process States

During a process' execution, the process's *state* changes. The state of the process is the current condition or status of the process. In the UNIX environment, a process can be in the following states:

- running
- runnable (ready)
- zombied
- waiting (blocked)
- stopped

The process changes its state when certain circumstances created by the process or the operating system exist. The *state transition* is the circumstance that causes the process to change its state. Figure 3–4 is the state diagram for the UNIX environment. The state diagram has nodes and directed edges between the nodes. Each node represents the state of the process. The directed edges between the nodes are *state transitions*. Table 3–1 lists the state transitions with a brief description. As Figure 3–4 and Table 3–1 show, only certain transitions are allowed between states. For example, there is a transition, an edge, between ready and running but there is no transition between sleeping and running, meaning there are circumstances that cause a process to move from the ready state to the running state but there are no circumstances that cause a process to move from the sleeping state to a running state.

When a process is created, it is ready to execute its instructions but must first wait until the processor is available. Each process is only allowed to use a processor for a discrete interval called a *time slice*. Processes waiting to use

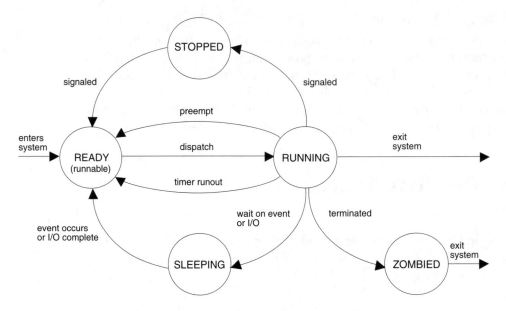

Figure 3–4   The process states and transitions in the UNIX/Linux environments.

a processor are placed in a ready queues. Only processes in the ready queues are selected (by the scheduler) to use the processor. Processes in the ready queues are *runnable*. When the processor is available, a runnable process is assigned a processor by the dispatcher. When the time slice has expired, the process is removed from the processor, whether it has finished executing all its instructions or not. The process is placed back in the ready queue to wait for its next turn to use the processor. A new process is selected from a ready queue and is given its time slice to execute. System processes are not preempted. When they are given the processor, they run until completion. If the time slice has not expired, a process may voluntarily give up the processor if it cannot continue to execute. The process may have made a request to access an I/O device by making a system call or it may need to wait on a synchronization variable to be released. Processes that cannot continue to execute because they are waiting for an event to occur are in a *sleeping state*. They are placed in a queue with other sleeping processes. They are removed from that queue and placed back in the ready queue when the event occurrs. The processor may be taken away from a process before its time slice has run out if a process with a higher priority, like a system

Table 3–1	Process Transitions

State transitions	*Descriptions*
READY→RUNNING (dispatch)	The process is assigned to the processor.
RUNNING→READY (timer runout)	The time slice the process is assigned to the processor has run out. The process is placed back in the ready queue.
RUNNING→READY (preempt)	The process has been preempted before the time slice ran out. This can occur if a process with a higher priority is runnable. The process is placed back in the ready queue.
RUNNING→SLEEPING (block)	The process gives up the processor before the time slice has run out. The process may need to wait for an event or has made a system call, for example, a request for I/O. The process is placed in a queue with other sleeping processes.
SLEEPING→READY (unblock)	The event the process was waiting for has occured or the system call has completed, for example, I/O request is filled. The process is placed back in the ready queue.
RUNNING→STOPPED	The process gives up the processor because it has received a signal to stop.
STOPPED→READY	The process has received the signal to continue and is placed back in the ready queue.
RUNNING→ZOMBIED	The process has been terminated and awaits the parent to retrieve its exit status from the process table.
ZOMBIED→EXIT	The parent process has retrieved the exit status and the process exits the system.
RUNNING→EXIT	The process has terminated, the parent has retrieved the exit status, and the process exits the system.

process, is runnable. The preempted process is still runnable and therfore placed back in the ready queue.

A running process can receive a signal to stop executing. The *stopped state* is different from a sleeping state because the time slice has not expired nor has the process made any requests of the system. The process may receive a signal to stop because it is being debugged or some situation in the system has occured. The process makes a transition from running state to *stopped state*. Later, the process may be awakened or destroyed.

When a process has executed all its instructions, it exits the system. The process is removed from the process table, the PCB is destroyed, and all of its resources are deallocated and returned to the system pool of available resources. A process that is unable to continue executing and cannot exit the system is *zombied*. A zombied process does not use any system resources but it still maintains an entry in the process table. When the process tables contain too many zombied processes, the performance of the system is affected, which can possibly cause the system to reboot.

3.4   Process Scheduling

When a ready queue contains several processes, the scheduler must determine which process should be assigned to a processor first. The scheduler maintains data structures that allow it to schedule the processes in an efficient manner. Each process is given a priority class and placed in a priority queue with other runnable processes with the same priority class. There are multiple priority queues, each representing a different priority class used by the system. These priority queues are stratified and placed in a dispatch array called the *multilevel priority queue,* illustrated in Figure 3–5. Each element in the array points to a priority queue. The scheduler assigns the process at the head of the nonempty highest priority queue to the processor.

Priorities can be *dynamic* or *static*. Once a static priority of a process is set, it cannot be changed. Dynamic priorities can be changed. Processes of the highest priority can monopolize the use of the processor. If the priority of a process is dynamic, the initial priority can be adjusted to a more appropriate value. The process is placed in a priority queue that has a higher priority. A process monopolizing the processor can also be given a lower priority or other processes can be given a higher priority than that process. In the UNIX/Linux environments, the range of priority levels is from -20 to 19. The higher the value, the lower the priority.

When assigning priority to a user process, what the process spends most of its time doing should be considered. Some processes are CPU intensive. CPU-intensive processes use the processor for the whole time slice. Some processes spend most of their time waiting for I/O or some other event to

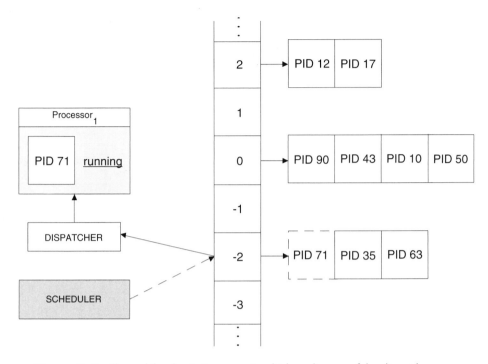

Figure 3–5 The multilevel priority queue in which each entry of the dispatch array points to a ready queue of processes with the same priority level.

occur. When such a process is ready to use a processor, it should be given the processor immediately so it can make its next request for I/O. Processes that are interactive may require a high priority to ensure good response time. System processes have a higher priority than user processes.

3.4.1 Scheduling Policy

The processes are placed in a priority queue according to a scheduling policy. Two of the scheduling policies used by the UNIX/Linux systems are FIFO (First-In-First-Out) and round-robin (RR) policies. Figure 3–6(a) shows the FIFO scheduling policy. With a FIFO scheduling policy, processes are assigned a processor according to the arrival time in the queue. When a running process time slice has expired, it is placed at the head of its priority queue. When a sleeping process becomes runnable, the process is placed at the end of its priority queue. A process can make a system call and give up a

(a) FIFO SCHEDULING

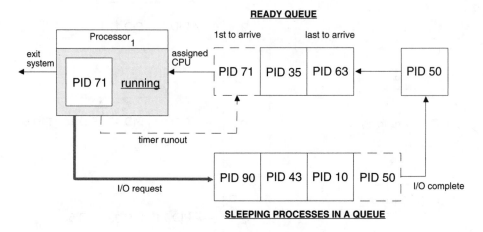

(b) RR SCHEDULING

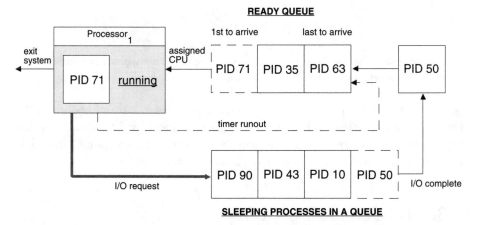

Figure 3–6   The behavior of the First-In-First-Out (FIFO) and round-robin (RR) scheduling policies. The FIFO scheduling policy assigns processes to the processor according to its arrival time in the queue. The process runs until completion. The RR scheduling policy assigns processes using FIFO scheduling but when the time slice runs out the process is placed at the back of the ready queue.

processor to another process with the same priority level. The process will be placed at the end of its priority queue.

In a round-robin scheduling policy, all processes are considered equal. Figure 3–6(b) depicts the RR scheduling policy. RR scheduling is the same as FIFO scheduling with an exception: when the time slice expires, the process is placed at the back of the queue and the next process in the queue is assigned the processor.

3.4.2 Using the `ps` Utility

The `ps` utility generates a report that summarizes execution statistics for the current processes. This information can be used to monitor the status of current processes. Table 3–2 lists the common headers and the meaning of the output for the `ps` utility for the Solaris/Linux environments. In a multi-processor environment, the `ps` utility is quite useful to monitor the state, CPU and memory usage, processor utilized, priority, and start time of the current processes executing. Command options control which processes are listed and what information is displayed about each process. In the Solaris environment, by default (no command options used), information about processes with the same effective user id and controlling terminal of the calling invoker is displayed. In the Linux environment, by default, the processes with the same user id as the invoker are displayed. In both environments, the only information that will be displayed is PID, TTY, TIME and COMMAND. These are some of the options that control which processes are displayed:

-t term	List the processes associated with the terminal specified by `term`
-e	All current processes
-a	(Linux) All processes with `tty` terminal except the session leaders
	(Solaris) Most frequently requested processes except group leaders and processes not associated with a terminal
-d	All current processes except session leaders
T	(Linux) All processes in this terminal
a	(Linux) All processes including those of other users
r	(Linux) Only running processes

Table 3–2	Common Headers Used for **ps** Utility in the Solaris/Linux Environments		
Headers	*Description*	*Headers*	*Description*
USER, UID	Username of process owner	TT, TTY	Process's controlling terminal
PID PPID	Process ID Parent process ID	S, STAT	Current state of the process
PGID	ID of process group leader	TIME	Total CPU time used by the process (HH:MM:SS)
SID	ID of session leader		
%CPU	Percentage of CPU time used by the process in the last minute	STIME, START	Time or date the process started
RSS	Amount of real RAM currently used by the process in k	NI	Nice value of the process
%MEM	Percentage of real RAM used by the process in the last minute	PRI	Priority of the process
SZ	Size of virtual memory of the process's data and stack in k or pages	C, CP	Short-term CPU-use factor used by the scheduler to compute PRI
WCHAN	Address of an event for which a process is sleeping	ADDR	Memory address of a process
COMMAND CMD	Command name and arguments	LWP	ID of the lwp (thread)
		NLWP	The number of lwps

Synopsis

```
(Linux)
ps -[Unix98 options]
    [BSD-style options]
    --[GNU-style long options

(Solaris)
ps [-aAdeflcjLPy][-o format][-t termlist][-u userlist]
    [-G grouplist][-p proclist][-g pgrplist][-s sidlist]
```

The following list contains some of the command options used to control the information displayed about the processes:

-f full listings

-l long format

-j jobs format

Below is an example of using the ps utility in Solaris/Linux environments:

ps -f

This will display information about the default processes in each environment. Figure 3–7 shows the output in the Solaris environment. The command options can also be used in tandem. Figure 3–7 also shows the output of using -l and -f together in the Solaris environment:

ps -lf

The l command option shows the additional headers: F, S, C, PRI, NI, ADDR, and WCHAN. The P command option will display the PSR header. Under this header is the number of the processor to which the process is assigned or bound.

Figure 3–8 shows the output of the ps utility using the Tux command options in the Linux environment. The %CPU, %MEM, and STAT information is displayed for the processes. In a multiprocessor environment, this information can be used to monitor which processes are dominating CPU and memory usage. The STAT header shows the state or status of the process. Table 3–3 lists how the status is encoded and their meanings. The STAT header can reveal additional information about the status of the process:

D (BSD) Disk wait

P (BSD) Page wait

X (System V) Growing: waiting for memory

W (BSD) Swapped out

K (AIX) Available kernel process

N (BSD) Niced: execution priority lowered

> (BSD) Niced: execution priority artificially raised

< (Linux) High priority process

L (Linux) Pages are locked in memory

```
//SOLARIS

$ ps -f
      UID  PID  PPID C   STIME    TTY    TIME CMD
  cameron 2214 2212 0 21:03:35 pts/12   0:00 -ksh
  cameron 2396 2214 2 11:55:49 pts/12   0:01 nedit

$ ps -lf
F S   UID  PID  PPID C PRI NI   ADDR SZ    WCHAN   STIME    TTY TIME  CMD
8 S cameron 2214 2212 0  51 20 70e80f00 230 70e80f6c 21:03:35 pts/12 0:00  -ksh
8 S cameron 2396 2214 1  53 24 70d747b8 843 70152aba 11:55:49 pts/12 0:01 nedit
```

Figure 3-7   Output of ps -f and ps -lf in the Solaris environment.

These codes will precede the status codes. If an N precedes the status, this means that the process is running at a lower priority level. If a process has a status SW< , this means the process is sleep, swapped out, and has a high priority level.

3.4.3   Setting and Returning the Process Priority

The priority level of a process can be changed by using the nice() function. Each process has a nice value that is used to calculate the priority level of the calling process. A process inherits the priority of the process that created it. The priority of a process can lowered by raising its nice value. Only superuser and kernel processes can raise their priority levels.

Figure 3-8   Output of ps Tux in the Linux environment.

```
//Linux

[tdhughes@colony]$ ps Tux
USER       PID %CPU %MEM   VSZ   RSS   TTY  STAT   START    TIME COMMAND
tdhughes 19259  0.0  0.1  2448  1356  pts/4   S   20:29    0:00 -bash
tdhughes 19334  0.0  0.0  1732   860  pts/4   S   20:33    0:00 /home/tdhughes/pv
tdhughes 19336  0.0  0.0  1928   780  pts/4   S   20:33    0:00 /home/tdhughes/pv
tdhughes 19337 18.0  2.4 26872 24856  pts/4   R   20:33    0:47 /home/tdhughes/pv
tdhughes 19338 18.0  2.3 26872 24696  pts/4   R   20:33    0:47 /home/tdhughes/pv
tdhughes 19341 17.9  2.3 26872 24556  pts/4   R   20:33    0:47 /home/tdhughes/pv
tdhughes 19400  0.0  0.0  2544   692  pts/4   R   20:38    0:00 ps Tux
tdhughes 19401  0.0  0.1  2448  1356  pts/4   R   20:38    0:00 -bash
```

Synopsis

```
#include <unistd.h>
int nice(int incr);
```

A low nice value raises the priority level of the process. The `incr` parameter is the value added to the current nice value of the calling process. The `incr` can be negative or positive. The nice value is a non-negative number. A positive `incr` value will raise the nice value, therefore lowering the priority level. A negative `incr` value will lower the nice value, therefore raising the priority level. If the `incr` value raises the nice value above or below its limits, the nice value of the process will be set to the highest or lowest limit accordingly. If successful, the `nice()` function will return the new nice value of the process. If unsuccessful, the function will return `-1` and the nice value is not changed.

Synopsis

```
#include <sys/resource.h>

int getpriority(int which, id_t who);
int setpriority(int which, id_t who, int value);
```

The `setpriority()` function sets the nice value for a process, process group, or user. The `getpriority()` returns the priority of a process, process group, or user. Example 3.1 shows the syntax to the functions `setpriority()` and `getpriority()` to set and return the nice value of the current process.

```
//Example 3.1 Using setpriority() and getpriority().

#include <sys/resource.h>

//...
id_t pid = 0;
int which  = PRIO_PROCESS;
int value = 10;
int nice_value;
int ret;
nice_value = getpriority(which,pid);
if(nice_value < value){
```

```
    ret = setpriority(which,pid,value);
}
//...
```

In Example 3.1, the priority of the calling process is being returned and set. If the calling process's nice value is < 10, the nice value of the process is set to 10. The target process is determined by the values stored in the which and who parameters. The which parameter can specify a process, process group, or user. It can have the following values:

PRIO_PROCESS	Indicates a process
PRIO_PGRP	Indicates a process group
PRIO_USER	Indicates a user

Depending on the value of which, the who parameter is the id number of a process, process group, or effective user. In Example 3.1, which is assigned PRIO_PROCESS. A 0 value for who indicates the current process, process group, or user. In Example 3.1, the who is set to 0, indicating the current process. The value parameter for setpriority() shall be the new nice value for the specified process, process group, or user. The range of nice value in the Linux environment is -20 to 19. In Example 3.1, the value of nice is set to 10 if the current nice value is less than 10. Unlike the function nice(), the value passed to setpriority() is the actual value of nice and not an offset to be added to the current nice value.

In a process with multiple threads, the modification of the priority will affect the priority of all the threads in that process. If successful, getpriority() will return the nice value of the specified process. If successful, setpriority() will return 0. If unsuccessful, both functions will return -1. The return value -1 is a legitimate nice value for a process. To determine if an error has occurred, check the external variable errno.

3.5   Context Switching

A context switch occurs when the use of the processor is switched from one process to another process. When a context switch occurs, the system saves the context of the current running process and restores the context of the next process selected to use the processor. The PCB of the preempted process is updated. The process state field is changed from the running to the appropriate state (runnable, blocked, zombied, etc.). The contents of the processor's registers, state of the stack, user and process identification and privileges, and scheduling and accounting information are saved and updated.

The system must keep track of the status of the process's I/O and other resources, and any memory management data structures. The preempted process is placed in the appropriate queue.

A context switch occurs when:

- a process is preempted
- a process voluntarily gives up the processor
- a process makes an I/O request or needs to wait for an event
- a process switches from user mode to kernel mode

When the preempted process is selected again to use the processor, its context is restored and execution continues where it left off.

3.6   Creating a Process

To run any program the operating system must first create a process. When a new process is created, a new entry is placed in the main process table. A new PCB is created and initialized and the process identification portion of the PCB contains a unique process id number and the parent process id. The program counter is set to point to the program entry point and the system stack pointers are set to define the stack boundaries for the process. The process is initialized with any of the attributes requested. If the process is not given a priority value, it is given the lowest priority value by default. The process initially does not own any resources unless there is an explicit request for resources or they have been inherited from the creator process. The state of the process is runnable and placed in the runnable or ready queue. Address space is allocated for the process. How much space to be set aside can be determined by default based on the type of process. The size can also be set as a request by the creator of the process. The creator process can pass the size of the address space to the system at the time the process is created.

3.6.1   Parent–Child Process Relationship

A process that creates or *spawns* another process is a *parent* process to the spawned *child* process. The init process is the parent of all user processes. The init process is the very first process visible to the UNIX system when booted up. The init process brings the system up, runs other programs when necessary, and starts daemons. It has a PID of 1. The child process has its own unique PID, PCB, and a separate entry in the process table. The child process can also spawn a process. An executing application can create a tree of processes. For example, a parent process searches a hard drive for a specified HTML document. The HTML document name is written to a global data structure like a list, which contains all the request for documents. Once the document is located, it is removed from the request list and the path is written to another global data structure, which contains the paths of located documents. To ensure a good response to the user requests, the process has a limit of five requests pending in the list. Once the limit has been reached, two new processes are spawned to handle to work load. For each process that reaches its limits, two new processes are spawned. Figure 3–9 shows a tree of processes created in this manner. A process has only one parent process, but a parent process can have many children.

A child process can be created with its own executable image or as a duplication of the parent process. As a duplicate of the parent, the child inherits many of the attributes of the parent, including its environment, priority and scheduling policy, resource limits, open files, and shared memory segments. If the child process advances a file's position pointer, or closes the file, this will also be seen by the parent process. If the parent allocates any additional resources after the child has been created, they are not accessible to the child. In turn, if the child process allocates any resources, they are not accessible by the parent.

Some attributes of the parent are not inherited by the child. As mentioned earlier, the child does not inherit the parent's PID or PCB. Of course, each process will have different parents. The child does not inherit any file locks created by the parent or any pending signals. Timing information such as processor usage and creation time are reset for the child process. Although these processes have this relationship, they function as separate processes. The program and stack counters operate separately. Because the data segments are copied, not shared, the child can change the values of its variables without affecting the parent's copy. The child and parent share the code segment and execute the instructions immediately following the system call that

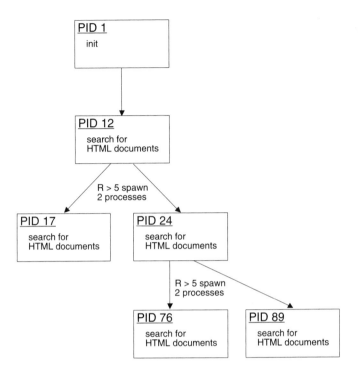

Figure 3-9   A tree of processes. A process spawns two new processes if a certain condition is met.

creates the child process. They do not execute those instructions in lock step because they compete for the processor with all the other processes loaded in the memory.

Once created, the child process image can be replaced with another executable image. The code, data, and stack segments as well as its heap is overwritten with the new process image. The new process preserves its PID and PPID. Table 3–3 lists the attributes preserved by the new process after its executable image has been replaced. It also lists the system calls that return these attributes. The environment variables are also preserved unless new environment variables were specified at time of the executable was replaced. Files that were open before the executable was replaced will still be open afterward. The new process will create files with the same file permissions. The CPU time will not be reset.

Table 3–3   Attributes Preserved by the New Process After Its Process Image Has Been Replaced with a New Process Image

Attributes preserved	*Description*
Process ID	`getpid()`
Parent Process ID	`getppid()`
Process Group ID	`getpgid()`
Session membership	`getsid()`
Real User ID	`getuid()`
Real Group ID	`getgid()`
Supplementary Group IDs	`getgroups()`
Time left on an alarm signal	`alarm()`
Nice value	`nice()`
Time used so far	`times()`
Process signal mask	`sigprocmask()`
Pending signals	`sigpending()`
File size limit	`ulimit()`
Resource limit	`getrlimit()`
File mode creation mask	`umask()`
Current working directory	`getcwd()`
Root directory	

3.6.1.1   The `pstree` Utility

The `pstree` utility in the Linux environment displays a tree of processes. It shows the running processes in a tree structure. The root of the tree is the `init` process.

Synopsis

```
pstree [-a] [-c] [-h | -Hpid] [-l] [-n] [-p] [-u] [-G] | -U]
[pid | user]
pstree -V
```

These are some of the options that can be used with this utility:

-a   Show command-line arguments

-h   Highlight the current process and its ancestors

-H   Like -h but highlight the specified process instead

-n   Sort processes with the same ancestor by PID instead of by name

-p   Show PIDs

Figure 3–10 shows the output of pstree -h in the Linux environment.

Figure 3-10   Output of pstree -h in the Linux environment.

```
ka:~ # pstree -h
init-+-applix
     |-atd
     |-axmain
     |-axnet
     |-cron
     |-gpm
     |-inetd
     |-9*[kdeinit]
     |-kdeinit   -+-kdeinit
     |             |-kdeinit---bash---gimp---script-fu
     |             '-kdeinit---bash       -+-man---sh---sh---less
     |                              '-pstree
     |-kdeinit---cat
     |-kdm-+-X
     |     '-kdm---kde---ksmserver
     |-kflushd
     |-khubd
     |-klogd
     |-knotify
     |-kswapd
     |-kupdate
     |-login---bash
     |-lpd
     |-mdrecoveryd
     |-5*[mingetty]
     |-nscd---nscd---5*[nscd]
     |-sshd
     |-syslogd
     |-usbmgr
     '-xconsole
```

3.6.2   Using the `fork()` Function Call

The `fork()` call creates a new process that is a duplication of the calling process, the parent. The `fork()` returns two values if it succeeds, one to the parent and one to the child process. It will return 0 to the child process and return the PID of the child to the parent process. The parent and child processes continue to execute from the instruction immediately following the `fork()` call. If not successful, meaning no child process was created, -1 is returned to the parent process.

Synopsis

```
#include <unistd.h>

pid_t fork(void);
```

The `fork()` will fail if the system does not have the resources to create another process. If there is a limit to the number of child processes the parent can spawn or the number of system-wide executing processes and that limit has been exceeded, the `fork()` will fail. In that case, `errno` will be set to indicate the error.

3.6.3   Using the `exec` Family of System Calls

The `exec` family of functions replaces the calling process image with a new process image. The `fork()` call creates a new process that is a duplication of the parent process where the `exec` function replaces the duplicate process image with a new one. The new process image is a regular executable file and is immediately executed. The executable can be specified as a path or a filename. These functions can pass command-line arguments to the new process. Environment variables can also be specified. There is no return value if the function is not successful because the process image that contained the call to the exec is overwritten. If unsuccessful, -1 is returned to the calling process.

All of the `exec()` functions can fail under these conditions:

- *Permissions are denied*
  Search permission is denied for the executable's file directory
  Execution permission is denied for the executable file

- *Files do not exist*
  Executable file does not exist
  Directory does not exist

- *File is not executable*
  File is not executable because it is open for writing by another process
  File is not an executable file

- *Problems with symbolic links*
  Loop exists when symbolic links are encountered while resolving the pathname to the executable
  Symbolic links cause the pathname to the executable to be too long

The `exec` functions are used with the `fork()`. The `fork()` creates and initializes the child process with the duplicate of the parent. The child process then replaces its process image by calling an `exec()`. Example 3.2 shows an example of the `fork-exec` usage.

```
// Example 3.2 Using the fork-exec system calls.

//...
RtValue = fork();
if(RtValue == 0){
   execl("/path/direct","direct",".");
}
```

In Example 3.2, the `fork()` function is called and the return value is stored in `RtValue`. If `RtValue` is 0, then it is the child process. The `execl()` function is called. The first parameter is the path to the executable module, the second parameter is the execution statement, and the third parameter is the argument. `direct` is utility that lists all the directories and subdirectories from a given directory. There are six versions of the exec functions, each having a different calling convention and use.

3.6.3.1 `execl()` Functions

The `execl()`, `execle()`, `execlp()` functions pass the command-line arguments as a list. The number of command-line arguments should be known at compile time in order for these functions to be useful.

- `int execl(const char *path,const char *arg0,.../*, (char *)0 */);`
  `path` is the pathname to the program executable. It can be specified as an absolute pathname or a relative pathname from the cur-

rent directory. The next arguments are the list the command-line arguments, from `arg0` to `argn`. There can be n number of arguments. The list is to be followed by a NULL pointer.

- `int execle(const char *path,const char *arg0,.../*,`
  `(char *)0 *, char *const envp[]*/);`
  This function is identical to `execl()` except it has an additional parameter, `envp[]`. This parameter contains the new environment for the new process. `envp[]` is a pointer to a null-terminated array of null-terminated strings. Each string has the form:

  `name=value`
  where `name` is the name of the environment variable and `value` is the string to be stored. `envp[]` can be assigned in this manner:

  `char *const envp[] = {"PATH=/opt/kde2:/sbin",`
  `"HOME=/home",NULL};`
  `PATH` and `HOME` are the environment variables in this case.

- `int execlp(const char *file,const char *arg0,.../*,`
  `(char *)0 */);`
  `file` is the name of the program executable. It uses the `PATH` environment variable to locate the executables. The remaining arguments list the command-line arguments as explained for `execl()` function.

These are examples of the syntax of the `execl()` functions using these arguments:

```
char *const args[] = {"direct",".",NULL};
char *const envp[] = {"files=50",NULL};
execl("/path/direct","direct",".",NULL);
execle("/path/direct","direct",".",NULL,envp);
execlp("direct","direct",".",NULL);
```

Each shows the syntax of how each `execl()` function creates a process that executes the `direct` program.

Synopsis

```
#include <unistd.h>

int execl(const char *path,const char *arg0,.../*,(char *)0 */);
int execle(const char *path,const char *arg0,.../*,
        (char *)0 *,char *const envp[]*/);
```

```
int execlp(const char *file,const char *arg0,.../*,(char *)0 */);
int execv(const char *path,char *const arg[]);
int execve(const char *path,char *const arg[],
          char *const envp[]);
int execvp(const char *file,char *const arg[]);
```

3.6.3.2 **execv()** Functions

The execv(), execve(), and execvp() functions pass the command-line arguments in a vector of pointers to null-terminated strings. The number of command-line arguments should be known at compile time in order for these functions to be useful. argv[0] is usually the execution statement.

- int execv(const char *path,char *const arg[]);
  path is the pathname to the program executable. It can be specified as an absolute pathname or relative pathname to the current directory. The next argument is the null-terminated vector that contains the command-line arguments as null-terminated strings. There can be n number of arguments. The vector is to be followed by a NULL pointer. arg[] can be assigned in this manner:

  ```
  char *const arg[] = {"traverse",".", ">","1000",NULL};
  ```

  This is an example of a function call:

  ```
  execv("traverse",arg);
  ```

  In this case, the traverse utility will list all files in the current directory larger than 1000 bytes.

- int execve(const char *path,char *const arg[],char *const envp[]);
  This function is identical to execv() except it has the additional parameter envp[], described earlier.

- int execvp(const char *file,char *const arg[]);
  file is the name of the program executable. The next argument is the null-terminated vector that contains the command-line arguments as null-terminated strings. There can be n number of arguments. The vector is to be followed by a NULL pointer.

These are examples of syntax of the execv() functions using these arguments:

```
char *const arg[] = {"traverse",".", ">","1000",NULL};
char *const envp[] = {"files=50",NULL};
```

```
execv("/path/traverse",arg);
execve("/path/traverse",arg,envp);
execvp("traverse",arg);
```

Each shows the syntax of how each `execv()` function creates a process that executes the `traverse` program.

3.6.3.3   Determining Restrictions on **exec()** Functions

There is a limit on the size `argv[]` and `envp[]` can be when passed to the `exec()` functions. The `sysconf()` can be used to determine the maximum size of command-line arguments plus the size of environment variables for the `exec()` functions that accept the `envp[]` parameter. To return the size, `name` should have the value `_SC_ARG_MAX`.

Synopsis

```
#include <unistd.h>

long sysconf(int name);
```

Another restriction when using `exec()` and the other functions used to create processes is the maximum number of simultaneous processes allowed per user id. To return this number, `name` has the value `_SC_CHILD_MAX`.

3.6.3.4   Reading and Setting Environment Variables

Environment variables are null-terminated strings that store system-dependent information such as paths to directories that contain commands, libraries, functions, and procedures used by a process. They can also be used to transmit any useful user-defined information between the parent and the child processes. They provide a mechanism for providing specific information to a process without having it hardcoded in the program code. System environment variables are predefined and common to all shells and processes in that system. The variables are initialized by startup files. Below are the common system variables:

$HOME   The absolute pathname of your home directory

$PATH   A list of directories to search for commands

$MAIL	The absolute pathname of your mailbox
$USER	Your user id
$SHELL	The absolute pathname of your login shell
$TERM	Your terminal type

They can be stored in a file or in an environment list. The environment list will contain pointers to null-terminated strings. The variable:

```
extern char **environ
```

points to the environment list when the process begins to execute. These strings will have the form:

```
name=value
```

as explained earlier. Processes initialized with the functions execl(), exe-clp(), execv(), and execvp() will inherit the environment of the parent process. Processes initialized with the functions execve() and execle() set the environment for the new process.

There are functions and utilities that can be called to examine, add, or modify environment variables. The getenv() is used to determine whether a specific variable has been set. The parameter name is the environment variable in question. The function will return NULL if the specified variable has not been set. If the variable has been set, the function will return a pointer to a string containing the value.

Synopsis

```
#include <stdlib.h>

char *getenv(const char *name);
int setenv(const char *name, const char *value,
          int overwrite);
void unsetenv(const char *name);
```

For example:

```
string Path;

Path = getenv("PATH");
```

the string Path is assigned the value contained in the predefined environment PATH.

The `setenv()` is used to change or add a variable to the environment of the calling process. The parameter `name` contains the name of the environment variable to be changed or added. It is assigned the value stored in `value`. If the `name` variable already exists, then the value is changed to `value` if the `overwrite` parameter is nonzero. If `overwrite` is 0, the content of the specified environment variable is not modified. `setenv()` return 0 if it is successful and -1 if unsuccessful. The `unsetenv()` removes the environment variable specified by `name`.

3.6.4   Using `system()` to Spawn Processes

The `system()` is used to execute a command or executable program. The `system()` causes the execution of `fork-exec`, and a shell. The `system()` function executes a `fork()` and the child process calls an `exec()` with a shell that executes the given command or program.

Synopsis

```
#include <stdlib.h>


int system(const char *string);
```

The `string` parameter can be a system command or the name of an executable file. If successful, the function returns the termination status of the command or return value (if any) of the program. Errors can happen at several levels, the `fork()` or `exec()` functions may fail or the shell may not be able to execute the command or program.

The function returns a value to the parent process. The function returns 127 if the `exec()` fails and -1 if some other error occurs. The return code of the command is returned if the function succeeds. This function does not affect the wait status of any of the children processes.

3.6.5   The POSIX Functions for Spawning Processes

Similar to the `system()` and `fork-exec` method of process creation, the `posix_spawn()` functions create new child processes from specified process images. But the `posix_spawn()` functions create child processes can be created with more fine-grained control. These functions control the attributes the child process inherits from the parent process including:

- file descriptors
- scheduling policy
- process group id
- user and group id
- signal mask

They also control whether signals ignored by the parent will be ignored by the child or reset to a default action. Controlling file descriptors allow the child process independent access to the data stream independent opened by the parent. Being able to set the child's process group id affects how the child's job control will relate to that of the parent. The child's scheduling policy can be set to be different from the scheduling policy of the parent.

Synopsis

```
#include <spawn.h>

int posix_spawn(pid_t *restrict pid, const char *restrict path,
                const posix_spawn_file_actions_t *file_actions,
                const posix_spawnattr_t *restrict attrp,
                char *const argv[restrict],
                char *const envp[restrict]);

int posix_spawnp(pid_t *restrict pid, const char *restrict file,
                 const posix_spawn_file_actions_t *file_actions,
                 const posix_spawnattr_t *restrict attrp,
                 char *const argv[restrict],
                 char *const envp[restrict]);
```

The difference between these two functions is `posix_spawn()` has a `path` parameter and `posix_spawnp()` has a `file` parameter. The `path` parameter in the `posix_spawn()` function is the absolute or relative pathname to the executable program file. The `file` parameter in the `posix_spawnp()` function is the name of the executable program. If the parameter contains a slash, then `file` will be used as a pathname. If not, then the path to the executable is determined by the PATH environment variable.

The `file_action` parameter is a pointer to a `posix_spawn_file_actions_t` structure:

```
struct posix_spawn_file_actions_t{
{
    int __allocated;
    int __used;
    struct __spawn_action *actions;
    int __pad[16];
};
```

The `posix_spawn_file_actions_t` is a data structure that contains information about the actions to be performed in the new process with respect to file descriptors. The `file_action` parameter is used to modify the parent's set of open file descriptors to a set of file descriptors for the spawned child process. This structure can contain several file action operations to be performed in the sequence in which they were added to the spawn file action object. These file action operations are performed on the open file descriptors of the parent process. These operations can duplicate, reset, add, delete or close a specified file descriptors on behalf of the child process even before it's spawned. If the `file_action` parameter is a null pointer, then the file descriptors opened by the parent process will remain open for the child process without any modifications. Table 3–4 lists the functions used to add file actions to the `posix_spawn_file_actions` object.

The `attrp` parameter points to a `posix_spawnattr_t` structure:

```
struct posix_spawnattr_t
{
    short int __flags;
    pid_t __pgrp;
    sigset_t __sd;
    sigset_t __ss;
    struct sched_param __sp;
    int __policy;
    int __pad[16];
};
```

This structure contains information about the scheduling policy, process group, signals and flags for the new process. The descriptions of individual attributes are as follows:

__flags   Used to indicate which process attributes are to be modified in the spawned process.

Table 3–4	Functions Used to Add File Actions to the `posix_spawn_file_actions` Object

File Action Attributes Functions	*Descriptions*

`int`
`posix_spawn_file_actions_addclose`
`  (posix_spawn_file_actions_t`
`   *file_actions, int fildes);`
	Adds a `close()` action to a spawn file action object specified by `file_actions`. This causes the file descriptor `fildes` to be closed when the new process is spawned using this file action object.

`int`
`posix_spawn_file_actions_addopen`
`  (posix_spawn_file_actions_t`
`   *file_actions, int fildes,`
`   const char *restrict path,`
`   int oflag, mode_t mode);`
	Adds an `open()` action to a spawn file action object specified by `file_actions`. This causes the file named `path` with the returned file descriptor `fildes` to be opened when the new process is spawned using this file action object.

`int`
`posix_spawn_file_actions_adddup2`
`  (posix_spawn_file_actions_t`
`   *file_actions, int fildes,`
`   int new fildes);`
	Adds a `dup2()` action to spawn a file action object specified by `file_actions`. This causes the file descriptor `fildes` to be duplicated with the file descriptor `newfildes` when the new process is spawned using this file action object.

`int`
`posix_spawn_file_actions_destroy`
`  (posix_spawn_file_actions_t`
`   *file_actions);`
	Destroys the specified `file_actions` object. This causes the object to be uninitialized. The object can then become reinitialized using `posix_spawn_file_actions_init()`.

`int`
`posix_spawn_file_actions_destroy`
`(posix_spawn_file_actions_t`
`*file_actions);`
	Initializes the specified `file_actions` object. Once initialized, it will contain no file actions to be performed.

They are bitwise-inclusive OR of 0 or more of the following:

        `POSIX_SPAWN_RESETIDS`

        `POSIX_SPAWN_SETPGROUP`

        `POSIX_SPAWN_SETSIGDEF`

        `POSIX_SPAWN_SETSIGMASK`

        `POSIX_SPAWN_SETSCHEDPARAM`

        `POSIX_SPAWN_SETSCHEDULER`

__pgrp   The id of the process group to be joined by the new process.

__sd   Represents the set of signals to be forced to use default signal handling by the new process.

__ss   Represents the signal mask to be used by the new process.

__sp   Represents the scheduling parameter to be assigned to the new process.

__policy   Represents the scheduling policy to be used by the new process.

Table 3–5 lists the functions used to set and retrieve the individual attributes contained in the posix_spawnattr_t structure.

Table 3–5   Functions Used to Set and Retrieve the Individual Attributes Contained in the `posix_spawnattr_t` **Structure**

Spawn Process Attributes functions	*Descriptions*
int posix_spawnattr_getflags (const posix_spawnattr_t *restrict attr, short *restrict flags);	Returns the value of the __flags attribute stored in the specified attr object.
int posix_spawnattr_setflags (posix_spawnattr_t *attr, short flags);	Sets the value of the __flags attribute stored in the specified attr object to flags.
int posix_spawnattr_getpgroup (const posix_spawnattr_t *restrict attr, pid_t *restrict pgroup);	Returns the value of the __pgroup attribute stored in the specified attr object and stores it in the pgroup parameter.
int posix_spawnattr_setpgroup (posix_spawnattr_t *attr, pid_t pgroup);	Sets the value of the __pgroup attribute stored in the specified attr object to the pgroup parameter if POSIX_SPAWN_SETPGROUP is set in the __flags attribute.
int posix_spawnattr_getschedparam (const posix_spawnattr_t *restrict attr, struct sched_param *restrict schedparam);	Returns the value of the __sp attribute stored in the specified attr object and stores it in the schedparam parameter.
int posix_spawnattr_setschedparam (posix_spawnattr_t *attr const struct sched_param *restrict schedparam);	Sets the value of the __sp attribute stored in the specifed attr object to the schedparam parameter if POSIX_SPAWN_SETSCHEDPARAM is set in the __flags attribute.

Table 3–5 (cont.)

Spawn Process Attributes functions	Descriptions
`int posix_spawnattr_getschedpolicy (const posix_spawnattr_t *restrict attr, int *restrict schedpolicy);`	Returns the value of the __policy attribute stored in the specifed `attr` object and stores it in the `schedpolicy` parameter.
`int posix_spawnattr_setschedpolicy (posix_spawnattr_t *attr, int schedpolicy);`	Sets the value of the __policy attribute stored in the specified `attr` object to the `schedpolicy` parameter if `POSIX_SPAWN_SETSCHEDULER` is set in the __flags attribute.
`int posix_spawnattr_getsigdefault (const posix_spawnattr_t *restrict attr, sigset_t *restrict sigdefault);`	Returns the value of the __sd attribute stored in the specified `attr` object and stores it in the `sigdefault` parameter.
`int posix_spawnattr_setsigdefault (posix_spawnattr_t *attr, const sigset_t *restrict sigdefault);`	Sets the value of the __sd attribute stored in the specified `attr` object to the `sigdefault` parameter if `POSIX_SPAWN_SETSIGDEF` is set in the __flags attribute.
`int posix_spawnattr_getsigmask (const posix_spawnattr_t *restrict attr, sigset_t *restrict sigmask);`	Returns the value of the __ss attribute stored in the specified `attr` object and stores it in the `sigmask` parameter.
`int posix_spawnattr_setsigmask (posix_spawnattr_t *restrict attr, const sigset_t *restrict sigmask);`	Sets the value of the __ss attribute stored in the specified `attr` object to the `sigmask` parameter if `POSIX_SPAWN_SETSIGMASK` is set in the __flags attribute.
`int posix_spawnattr_destroy (posix_spawnattr_t *attr);`	Destroys the specified `attr` object. The object can then become reinitialized using `posix_spawnattr_init()`.
`int posix_spawnattr_init (posix_spawnattr_t *attr);`	Initializes the specified `attr` object with default values for all of the attributes contained in the structure. The object can then become reinitialized using `posix_spawnattr_init()`.

Example 3.3 shows how the `posix_spawn()` function can be used to create a process.

```
// Example 3.3 Spawning a process, using the posix_spawn()
// function, that calls the ps utility .

#include <spawn.h>
#include <stdio.h>
#include <errno.h>
#include <iostream>
{
   //...
   posix_spawnattr_t X;
   posix_spawn_file_actions_t Y;
   pid_t Pid;
   char *const argv[] = {"/bin/ps","-lf",NULL};
   char *const envp[] = {"PROCESSES=2"};
   posix_spawnattr_init(&X);
   posix_spawn_file_actions_init(&Y);
   posix_spawn(&Pid,"/bin/ps",&Y,&X,argv,envp);
   perror("posix_spawn");
   cout << "spawned PID: " << Pid << endl;
   //...
   return(0);

}
```

In Example 3.3, the `posix_spawnattr_t` and `posix_spawn_file_actions_t` objects are initialized. The `posix_spawn()` function is called with the arguments: `PID`, the path, `Y`, `X`, and `argv`, which contains the command as the first element and the argument as the second, and the `envp`, the environment list. If the `posix_spawn()` function is successful, then the value stored in `Pid` will be the `PID` of the spawned process. `perror` will display:

```
posix_spawn: Success
```

and the `Pid` is sent to output. The spawned process, in this case, executes:

```
/bin/ps -lf
```

These functions return the process id of the child process to the parent process in the `pid` parameter and returns 0 as the return value. If the function is unsuccessful, no child process is created, thus no `pid` is returned and an error value is returned as the return value of the function.

Errors can occur on three levels when using the spawn functions. An error can occur if the `file_actions` or `attr` objects are invalid. If this occurs after the function has successfully returned (the child process was spawned), then the child process may have an exit status of `127`. If the spawn attribute functions cause an error, then the error produced for that particular function (listed in Tables 3–4 and 3–5) is returned. If the spawn function has already successfully returned, then the child process may have an exit status of `127`.

Errors can also occur when attempting to spawn the child process. These errors would be the same errors produced by `fork()` or `exec()` functions. If they occur, they will be the return values for the spawn functions. If the child process produces an error, it is not returned to the parent process. In order for the parent process to be aware that the child has produced an error, other mechanisms would have to be used since it will not be stored in the child's exit status. Interprocess communication can be used or the child could set some flag visible to the parent.

3.6.6 *Identifying the Parent and Child with Process Management Functions*

There are two functions that return the calling process's PID and the parent process's PID .`getpid()` returns the process id of the calling process. `getppid()` returns the parent id of the calling process. These functions are always successful, therefore no errors are defined.

```
Synopsis

#include <unistd.h>

pid_t getpid(void);
pid_t getppid(void);
```

3.7 Terminating a Process

When a process is terminated, the PCB is erased and the address space and resources used by the terminated process are deallocated. An exit code is placed in its entry in the main process table. The entry is removed once the parent has accepted the exit code. The termination of the process can occur under several conditions:

- All instructions have executed.
- The process makes an explicit return or makes a system call that terminates the process.
- Child processes may automatically terminate when the parent has terminated.
- The parent sends a signal to terminate its child processes.

Abnormal termination of a process can occur when the process itself does something that it shouldn't:

- The process requires more memory than the system can provide.
- The process attempts to access resources it is not allowed to access.
- The process attempts to perform an invalid instruction or a prohibited computation.

The termination of a process can also be initiated by a user when the process is interactive.

The parent process is responsible for the termination/deallocation of its children. The parent process should wait until all its child processes have terminated. When a parent process retrieves a child process's exit code, the child process exits the system normally. The process is in a zombied state until the parent accepts the signal. If the parent never accepts the signal because it has already terminated and exited the system or because it is not waiting for the child process, the child remains in the zombied state until the init process (the original system process) accepts its exit code. Many zombied processes can negatively affect the performance of the system.

3.7.1 The exit(), kill() and abort() Calls

There are two functions a process can call for self termination, exit() and abort(). The exit() function causes a normal termination of the calling process. All open file descriptors associated with the process will be closed.

The function will flush all open streams that contain unwritten buffered data, then the open streams are closed. The `status` parameter is the process's exit status. It is returned to the waiting parent process, which is then restarted. The value of `status` may be `0`, `EXIT_FAILURE`, or `EXIT_SUCCESS`. The `0` value means the process has terminated successfully. The waiting parent process only has access to the lower 8 bits of `status`. If the parent process is not waiting for the process to terminate, the zombied process is adopted by the `init` process.

The `abort()` function causes an abnormal termination of the calling process. An abnormal termination of the process causes the same effect as `fclose()` on all open streams. A waiting parent process will receive a signal that the child process aborted. A process should only abort when it encounters an error that it cannot deal with programmatically.

Synopsis

```
#include <stdlib.h>

void exit(int status);
void abort(void);
```

The `kill()` function can be used to cause the termination of another process. The `kill()` function sends a signal to the processes specified or indicated by the parameter `pid`. The parameter `sig` is the signal to be sent to the specified process. The signals are listed in the header `<signal.h>`. To kill a process, `sig` has the value `SIGKILL`. The calling process must have the appropriate privileges to send a signal to the process, or it has a real or effective user id that matches the real or saved set user-ID of the process that receives the signal. The calling process may have permission to send only certain signals to processes and not others. If the function successfully sends the signal, `0` is returned to the calling process. If it fails, `-1` is returned.

The calling process can send the signal to one or several processes under these conditions:

`pid > 0`   The signal will be sent to the process whose PID is equal to the `pid`.

`pid = 0`	The signal will be sent to all the processes whose process group id is the same as the calling process.
`pid = -1`	The signal will be sent to all processes for which the calling process has permission to send that signal.
`pid < -1`	The signal will be sent to all processes whose process id group is equal to the absolute value of `pid` and for which the calling process has permission to send that signal.

Synopsis

```
#include <signal.h>

int kill(pid_t pid, int sig);
```

3.8   Process Resources

In order for a process to perform whatever task it is instructed to perform, it may need to write data to a file, send data to a printer, or display data to a screen. A process may need input from the user via the keyboard or input from a file. Processes can also use other processes, such as a subroutine, as a resource. Subroutines, files, semaphores, mutexes, keyboards, and display screens are all examples of resources that can be utilized by a process. A *resource* is anything used by a process at any given time as a source of data, a means to process, compute, or display data or information.

In order for a process to access a resource, it must first make a request to the operating system. If the resource is available, the operating system allows the process to use the resource. The process uses the resource, then releases it so it will be available to other processes. If the resource is not available, the request is denied and the process must wait. When the resource becomes available, the process is awakened. This is the basic approach to resource allocation. Figure 3–11 shows a resource allocation graph, which shows which processes hold resources and which processes are requesting resources. In

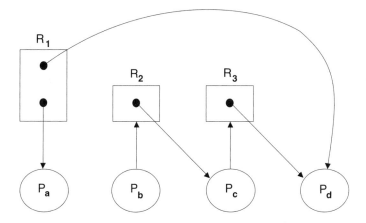

Figure 3–11 A resource-allocation graph that shows which processes hold resources and which processes are requesting resources.

Figure 3–11, process B makes a request for resource 2, which is held by process C. Process C makes a request for resource 3, which is held by process D.

When more than one request to access a resource is granted, the resource is *sharable,* which is shown in Figure 3–11 as well. Process A shares resource 1 with process D. A resource may allow many processes concurrent access or may only allow one process limited time before allowing another process access. An example of this type of shared resource is the processor. A process is assigned a processor for a short interval and then another process is assigned the processor. When only one request to access a resource is granted at a time and that occurs after the resource has been released by another process, the resource is *unshared* and the process has *exclusive access* to the resource. In a multiprocessor environment, it is important to know whether a shared resource can be accessed simultaneously or by only one process at a time in order to avoid some of the pitfalls inherent in concurrency.

Some resources can be changed or modified by a process. Other resources will not allow a process to change it. The behavior of shared modifiable or unmodifiable resources is determined by the resource type.

Resource Allocation Graph

Resource allocation graphs are directed graphs that show how the re-sources in a system are allocated. The graph consists of a set of vertices V and a set of edges E. The set of vertices is partitioned into two types:

$P = \{P_1, P_2, \ldots, P_n)$
$R = \{R_1, R_2, \ldots, R_m\}$

Set P is the set of all the processes in the system and set R is the set of all resources in the system. A directed edge from a process to a resource is called a request edge *and a directed edge from a resource to a process is called an* assignment edge. *These directed edges are denoted:*

$P_i \rightarrow R_j$ Request edge : Process P_i requests an instance of resource type R_j

$R_j \rightarrow P_i$ Assignment egde : Instance of resource type R_j has been al-located to Process P_i

Each process in the resource-allocation graph is depicted as a circle and each resource is depicted as a square. Since there may be many instances of a resource type, each instance of the resource type is represented as a dot within the square. A request edge points to the perimeter of the re-source square but an assignment edge originates from the dot to the perimeter of the process circle.

The resource-allocation graph in Figure 3–11. depicts the following:

Sets P, R, and E
$P = \{P_a, P_b, P_c, P_d\}$
$R = \{R_1, R_2, R_3\}$
$E = \{R_1 \rightarrow P_a, R_1 \rightarrow P_d, P_b \rightarrow R_2, R_2 \rightarrow P_c, P_c \rightarrow R_3, R_3 \rightarrow P_d\}$

3.8.1   Types of Resources

There are three basic types of resources: hardware, data, and software. *Hardware resources* are physical devices connected to the computer. Exam-ples of hardware resources are processors, main memory, and all other I/O devices including printers, hard disk, tape, and zip drives, monitors, keyboards, sound, network, graphic cards, and modems. All these devices can be shared by several processes.

Some hardware resources are preempted to allow different processes access. For example, a processor is preempted to allow different processes time to run. RAM is another example of a shared, preemptible resource. When a process is not executing, some of the physical page frames it occupies may be swapped out to secondary storage in order for another process to be swapped in to occupy those now-available page frames. A range of memory can only be occupied by the page frames of one process at any given time. An example of a shared, nonpreemptible resource is a printer. When a printer is shared, the jobs sent to the printer by each process is stored in a queue. Each job is printed to completion before another job starts. The printer is not preempted by any waiting printer jobs unless the current job is canceled.

Data resources such as objects; system data such as environment variables, files, and handles, and globally defined variables such as semaphores and mutexes are all resources shared and modified by processes. Regular files and files associated with physical devices such as the printer can be opened in such a manner, restricting the type of access processes have to that file. Processes may be granted only read or write access, or read/write access. A child process inherits the parent process's resources and access rights to those resources existing at the time the child's process was created. The child process can advance the file pointer, close, modify, or overwrite the contents of a file opened by the parent. Shared memory and files with write permission require their access to be synchronized. Shared data such as semaphores or mutexes can be used to synchronize access to other shared data resources.

Shared libraries are examples of *software resources*. Shared libraries provide a common set of services or functions to processes. Processes can also share applications, programs, and utilities. In such a case, only one copy of the program(s) code is brought into memory. There will be separate copies of the data, one for each user (process). Program code that is not changed (also called *reentrant*) can be accessed by several processes simultaneously.

3.8.2   POSIX Functions to Set Resource Limits

POSIX defines functions that restrict a process's ability to use certain resources. The operating system sets limitations on a process's ability to utilize system resources. These resource limits affect the following:

- size of the process's stack
- size of file and core file creation
- amount of CPU usage (size of time slice)
- amount of memory usage
- number of open file descriptors

The operating system sets a hard limit on resource usage by a process. The process can set or change the soft limit of its resources but its value should not exceed the hard limit set by the operating system. A process can lower its hard limit but this value should be greater than or equal to the soft limit. When a process lowers its hard limit, it is irreversible. Only processes with special privileges can raise their hard limit.

Synopsis

```
#include <sys/resource.h>

int setrlimit(int resource, const struct rlimit *rlp);
int getrlimit(int resource, struct rlimit *rlp);
int getrusage(int who, struct rusage *r_usage);
```

The setrlimit() function is used to set limits on the consumption of specified resources. This function can set both hard and soft limits. The parameter resource represents the resource type. Table 3–6 lists the values for resource with a brief description. The soft and hard limits of the specified resource are represented by the rlp paramater. The rlp parameter points to a struct rlimit that contains two objects of type rlim_t:

```
struct rlimit
{
      rlim_t rlim_cur;
      rlim_t rlim_max;
};
```

rlim_t is an unsigned integer type. rlim_cur contains the current or soft limit. rlim_max contains the maximum or hard limit. rlim_cur and rlim_max can be assigned any value. They can also be assigned these symbolic constants defined in the header <sys/resource.h>:

RLIM_INFINITY   Indicates no limit
RLIM_SAVED_MAX   Indicates an unrepresentable saved hard limit
RLIM_SAVED_CUR   Indicates an unrepresentable saved soft limit

The soft or hard limit can be set to RLIM_INFINITY, which means the resource is unlimited.

Table 3–6   Values for resource

Resource definitions	Descriptions
RLIMIT_CORE	Maximum size of a core file in bytes that may be created by a process.
RLIMIT_CPU	Maximum amount of CPU time in seconds that may be used by a process.
RLIMIT_DATA	Maximum size of a process data segment in bytes.
RLIMIT_FSIZE	Maximum size of a file in bytes that may be created by a process.
RLIMIT_NOFILE	A number 1 greater than the maximum value that the system may assign to a newly created file descriptor.
RLIMIT_STACK	Maximum size of a process stack in bytes
RLIMIT_AS	Maximum size of a process total available memory in bytes.

The getrlimit() returns the soft and hard limit of the specified resource in the rlp object. Both functions return 0 if successful and -1 if unsuccessful. Example 3.4 contains an example of a process setting the soft limit for file size in bytes.

```
//Example 3.4 Using setrlimit() to set the soft limit for
file size.

#include <sys/resource.h>

//...
struct rlimit R_limit;
struct rlimit R_limit_values;

//...
```

```
R_limit.rlim_cur = 2000;
R_limit.rlim_max = RLIM_SAVED_MAX;
setrlimit(RLIMIT_FSIZE,&R_limit);
getrlimit(RLIMIT_FSIZE,&R_limit_values);
cout << "file size soft limit: " << R_limit_values.rlim_cur
     << endl;
```

```
//...
```

In Example 3.4, the file size soft limit is set to 2000 bytes and the hard limit is set to the hard limit maximum. R_limit and the RLIMIT_FSIZE are passed to the setrlimit() function. getrlimit() are passed RLIMIT_FSIZE and R_limit_value. The soft value is sent to cout.

The getrusage() function returns information about the measures of resources used by the calling process. It also returns information about the terminated child process the calling process is waiting for. The parameter who can have these values:

```
RUSAGE_SELF
RUSAGE_CHILDREN
```

If the value for who is RUSAGE_SELF, then the information returned will pertain to the calling process. If the value for who is RUSAGE_CHILDREN, then the information returned is pertaining to the calling process's children. If the calling process did not wait for its children, then the information pertaining to the child process is discarded. The information is returned in the r_usage. r_usage points to a struct rusage that contains information listed and described in Table 3–7. If the function is successful, it returns 0, if unsuccessful, it returns -1.

3.9   What are Asynchronous and Synchronous Processes?

Asynchronous processes execute independent of each other. Process A runs until completion without any regard to process B. Asynchronous processes may or may not have a parent–child relationship. If process A creates process B, they can both execute independently but at some point the parent retrieves the exit status of the child. If they do not have a parent–child relationship, they may share the same parent.

Table 3–7 Information Contained in `struct rusage`	
`struct rusage` Attributes	**Description**
`struct timeval ru_utime`	User time used
`struct timeval ru_sutime`	System time used
`long ru_maxrss`	Maximum resident set size
`long ru_maxixrss`	Shared memory size
`long ru_maxidrss`	Unshared data size
`long ru_maxisrss`	Unshared stack size
`long ru_minflt`	Number of page claims
`long ru_majflt`	Number of page faults
`long ru_nswap`	Number of page swaps
`long ru_inblock`	Block input operations
`long ru_oublock`	Block output operations
`long ru_msgsnd`	Number of messages sent
`long ru_msgrcv`	Number of messages received
`long ru_nsignals`	Number of signals received
`long ru_nvcsw`	Number of voluntary context switches
`long ru_nivcsw`	Number of involuntary context switches

Asynchronous processes may execute serially, simultaneously, or overlap. These scenarios are depicted in Figure 3–12. In case 1, process A runs until completion, process B runs until completion, then process C runs until completion. This is serial execution of these processes. Case 2 depicts simultaneous execution of processes. Processes A and B are active processes. While process A is running, process B is sleeping. At some point both processes are sleeping. Process B awakens before process A, process A awakens, and now both processes are running at the same time. This shows that asynchronous processes may execute simultaneously only during certain intervals of their execution. In case 3, the execution of processes A and B overlaps.

Asynchronous processes may share resources like a file or memory. This may or may not require synchronization or cooperation of the use of the resource. If the processes are executing serially (case 1), then they will not require any synchronization. For example, all three processes, A, B, and C,

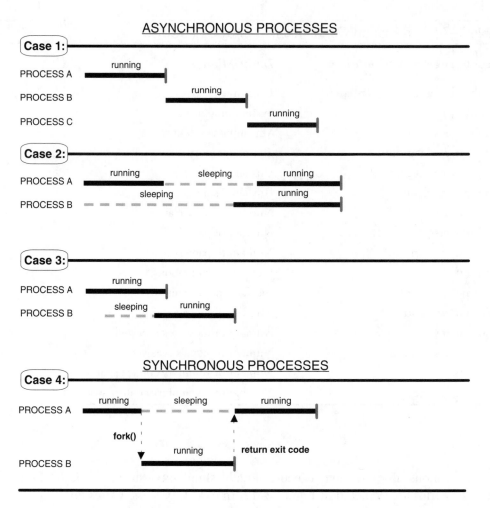

Figure 3-12   Possible scenarios of asynchronous and synchronous processes.

may share a global variable. Process A writes to the variable before it terminates, then when process B runs, it reads the data stored in the variable and
before it terminates it writes to the variable. When it runs, process C reads
data from the variable. But in cases 2 and 3, the processes may attempt to
modify the variable at the same time, thus requiring synchronization of its
use.

For our purposes, we define *synchronous* processes as processes with interleaved execution, one process suspends its execution until another process fin-

ishes. For example, process A, the parent process, executes and creates process B, the child process. Process A suspends its execution until process B runs until completion. When process B terminates, its exit code is placed in the process table. Process A is informed that process B has terminated. Process A can resume additional processing, then terminate or it can immediately terminate. Process A and process B are synchronous processes. Figure 3–12 contrasts synchronous and asynchronous execution of processes A and B.

3.9.1 Synchronous and Asynchronous Processes Created with `fork()`, `exec()`, `system()`, and `posix_spawn()` Functions

Processes created by `fork()`, fork-exec, and `posix_spawn()` functions will create asynchronous processes. When using the `fork()` function, the parent process image is duplicated. Once the child process has been created, the function returns to parent the child's PID and a return value of `0`, indicating process creation was successful. The parent does not suspend execution; both processes continue to execute independently from the statement immediately preceding the `fork()`. Child processes created using the fork-exec combination initializes the child's process image with a new process image. The `exec()` functions do not return to the parent process unless the initialization was not successful. The `posix_spawn()` functions create the child process images and initialize it within one function call. The PID is returned to the `posix_spawn()` as well as a return value indicating if the process was spawned successfully. After `posix_spawn()` returns, both processes are executing at the same time. Processes created by the `system()` function will create synchronous processes. A shell is created that executes the system command or executable file. The parent process is suspended until the child process terminates and the `system()` call returns.

3.9.2 The `wait()` Function Call

Asynchronous processes can suspend execution until a child process terminates by executing the `wait()` system call. After the child process terminates, a waiting parent process collects the child's exit status, which prevents zombied processes. The `wait()` function obtains the exit status from the process table. The `status` parameter points to a location that contains the exit status of the child process. If the parent process has more than one child process and several of them have terminated, the `wait()` function only retrieves the exit status for one child process from the process table. If the status information is available before the execution of the `wait()` function, the function will return immediately. If the parent process does not have any children, the function returns with an error code. The `wait()` function can also be called when the calling process is to wait until a signal is delivered then perform some signal handling action.

Synopsis

```
#include <sys/wait.h>

pid_t wait(int *status);
pid_t waitpid(pid_t pid, int *status, int options);
```

The `waitpid()` function is the same as `wait()` except it takes an additional parameter, `pid`. The `pid` parameter specifies a set of child processes for which the exit status is retrieved. Which processes are in the set is determined by the value of `pid`:

`pid > 0`	A single child process.
`pid = 0`	Any child process whose group id is the same as the calling process.
`pid < -1`	Any child processes whose group id is equal to the absolute value of pid.
`pid = -1`	Any child processes.

The `options` parameter determines how the wait should behave and can have the value of the following constants defined in the header `<sys/wait.h>`:

WCONTINUED	Reports the exit status of any continued child process (specified by pid) whose status has not been reported since it continued.
WUNTRACED	Reports the exit status of any child process (specified by pid) that has stopped whose status has not been reported since they stopped.

WNOHANG   The calling process is not suspended if the exit status for the specified child process is not available.

These constants can be logically OR'ed and passed as the `options` parameter (e.g., `WCONTINUED || WUNTRACED`).

Both functions return the PID of the child process whose exit status was obtained. If the value stored in `status` is 0, then the child process has terminated under these conditions:

- Process returned 0 from the function `main()`
- Process called some version of `exit()` with a 0 argument
- Process was terminated because the last thread of the process terminated

Table 3–8 lists the macros in which the value of the exit status can be evaluated.

Table 3–8 Macros in Which the Value of the Exit Status Can be Evaluated

Macros for evaulating `status`	Description
WIFEXITED	Evaluates to nonzero if status was returned by a normally terminated child process.
WEXITSTATUS	if `WIFEXITED` is nonzero, this evaluates to the low-order 8 bits of the `status` argument the terminated child process passed to `_exit()`, `exit()`, or value returned from `main()`.
WIFSIGNALED	Evaluates to nonzero if `status` was returned from a child process that terminated because it was sent a signal that was not caught.
WTERMSIG	If `WIFSIGNALED` is nonzero, this evaluates to the number of the signal that caused the child to terminate.
WIFSTOPPED	Evaluates to nonzero if `status` was returned from a child process that currently stopped.
WSTOPSIG	If `WIFSTOPPED` is nonzero, this evaluates to the number of the signal that caused the child process to stop.
WIFCONTINUED	Evaluates to nonzero if `status` was returned from a child process that has continued from a job control stop.

3.10   Dividing the Program into Tasks

When considering dividing your program into multiple tasks, you are introducing concurrency into your program. In a single processor environment,
concurrency is implemented with *multitasking*. This accomplished by
process switching. Each process executes for a short interval, then the
processor is given to another process. This occurs so quickly that it gives the
illusion that the processes are executing simultaneously. In a multiprocessor
environment, processes belonging to a single program can all be assigned to
the same processor or different processors. If the processes are assigned to
different processors, then the processes will execute in parallel.

Two levels for concurrent processing within an application or system are
the process level and the thread level. Concurrent processing on the thread
level is called *multithreading*, which will be discussed in the next chapter.
The key to dividing your program into concurrent tasks is identifying where
concurrency occurs, and where you can take advantage of it. Sometimes concurrency is not absolutely necessary. Your program may have a concurrency
interpretation yet serially execute just fine. The concurrency might benefit
your program with increased speed and less complexity. Some programs have
natural parallelism, while others are naturally sequential by nature. Some
programs have dual interpretations.

When decomposing your program into functions or objects, the top-down
approach is used to break down the program into functions and the bottom-
up approach is used to break down the program into objects. Once this is
done, it is necessary to determine which functions or objects are best served
as separate programs or subprograms while others will be executed by
threads. These subprograms will be executed by the operating system as
processes. The separate or processes perform the tasks you have designated
them to do.

A program separated into tasks can execute simultaneously in three ways:

1. Divide the program into a main task that creates a number of
    subtasks.
2. Divide the program into a set of separate binaries.
3. Divide the program into several types of tasks in which each task
    type is responsible for creating only certain tasks as needed.

PROGRAM

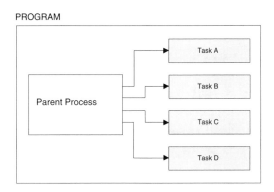

APPROACH 1:

Divide the program into a parent process
that creates a number of child processes

PROGRAM

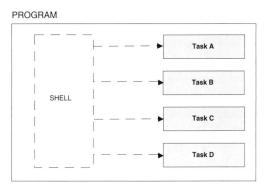

APPROACH 2:

Divide the program into a set of separate
binaries.

PROGRAM

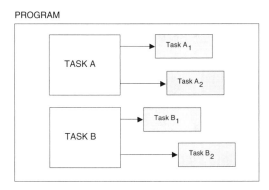

APPROACH 3:

Divide the program into several types of
processes in which each process is
responsible for creating certain processes
as needed.

Figure 3–13   Approaches that can be used to divide a program up into separate tasks.

These approaches are depicted in Figure 3–13.

For example, a rendering program can use these approaches. Rendering describes the process of going from a database representation of a 3D object to a shaded 2D projection on a view surface (computer screen). The image is represented as shaded polygons that exact the form of the object. The stages of the render process are shown in Figure 3–14. It can be broken down into separate tasks:

1. Set up the data structure for polygon mesh models.
2. Apply linear transformations.
3. Cull back-facing polygons.
4. Perform rasterization.
5. Apply hidden surface removal algorithm.
6. Shade the individual pixels.

The first task is representing the object as an array of polygons in which each vertex in the polygon uses 3D world coordinates. The second task is applying linear transformations to the polygon mesh model. These transformations are used to position objects into a scene and to create the view point or view surface (what is seen by the observer from the view point they are observing the scene or object). The third task is culling back-facing surfaces of the objects in the scene. This means lines generated from the back portion of

Figure 3-14   The stages of the render process.

STAGES OF RENDERING PROCESS

vertex #	x	y	z
1	1.40000	0.00000	2.30000
2	1.40000	-0.78400	2.30000
3	0.78400	-1.40000	2.30000
4	0.00000	-1.40000	2.30000
5	1.33750	0.00000	2.53125
6	1.33750	-0.75000	2.53125
7	0.74900	-1.33700	2.53125
8	0.00000	-1.33700	2.53125
9	1.43750	0.00000	2.53125
10	1.43750	-0.90500	2.53125
.			
.			
.			
306	1.42500	-0.79800	0.00000

1. Database representation
   of 3D object.

2. Polygon mesh model
   of 3D object.

3. Shaded 3D object.

objects not visible from the view point are removed. This is also called back-face elimination. The fourth task is converting the vertex-based model to a set of pixel coordinates. The fifth task is removing any hidden surfaces. If there are objects interacting in the seen, objects behind others, for example, these surfaces are removed. The sixth task is shading the surfaces.

Each task is saved separately and compiled into standalone executable files. Task1, Task2, and Task3 are executed sequentially and Task4, Task5, and Task6 are executed simultaneously. In Example 3.5, approach 1 is used to execute our rendering program.

```
// Example 3.5 Using approach 1 to create processes.

#include <spawn.h>
#include <stdlib.h>
#include <stdio.h>
#include <sys/wait.h>
#include <errno.h>
#include <unistd.h>

int main(void)
{
   posix_spawnattr_t Attr;
   posix_spawn_file_actions_t FileActions;
   char *const argv4[] = {"Task4",...,NULL};
   char *const argv5[] = {"Task5",...,NULL};
   char *const argv6[] = {"Task6",...,NULL};
   pid_t Pid;
   int stat;
   //...

   // execute first 3 tasks synchronously
   system("Task1 ...");
   system("Task2 ...");
   system("Task3 ...");

   // initialize structures
   posix_spawnattr_init(&Attr);
   posix_spawn_file_actions_init(&FileActions);

   // execute last 3 tasks asynchronously
   posix_spawn(&Pid,"Task4",&FileActions,&Attr,argv4,NULL);
   posix_spawn(&Pid,"Task5",&FileActions,&Attr,argv5,NULL);
   posix_spawn(&Pid,"Task6",&FileActions,&Attr,argv6,NULL);
```

```
// like a good parent, wait for all your children
wait (&stat);
wait (&stat);
wait (&stat);
return(0);
}
```

In Example 3.5, from `main()` Task1, Task2, and Task3 are executed using the `system()` function. Each of these tasks is performed synchronously to the parent process. Task4, Task5, and Task6 are performed asynchronously to the parent process using `posix_spawn()` functions. The ellipse (...) is used to indicate whatever files the tasks require. Parent process calls three `wait()` functions. Each waits for one of the Task4, Task5, and Task6 to terminate.

Using approach 2, the rendering program can be launched from a shell script. The advantage of using a shell script is all of the shell commands and operators can be used. For our render program, the & and && metacharacters are used to manage the execution of the task:

```
Task1 ... && Task2 ... && Task3
Task4 ... & Task5 ... & Task6
```

Here, Task1, Task2, and Task3 are executing sequentially under the condition the previous task executed successfully by using the && metacharacter. Task4, Task5, and Task6 executed simultaneously using the & metacharacter. The UNIX/Linux environments use metacharacters to control the way commands are executed. These are some of the metacharacters that can be used to control execution of several commands:

&&   Commands separated by && tokens causes the next command to be executed only if the previous command executes successfully.

|| Commands separated by || tokens causes the next command to be executed only if the previous command fails to execute successfully.

;   Commands separated by ; tokens causes the next command to be executed next in the sequence.

&   Commands separated by & tokens causes all the commands to be executed simultaneously.

Using approach 3, the tasks are categorized. When decomposing a program, it is a good technique to see if there are categories of tasks present. For example, some tasks are concerned with the user interface, creating it, extracting input from it, sending it to output, and so on. Other tasks perform computations, manage data, and so on. This is a useful technique when designing a progam. It can also be used in implementing a program. In our render-program, we can group tasks into several categories:

- *Tasks that perform linear transformations*
    Viewing transformations
    Scene transformations
- *Tasks that perform rasterization*
    Line drawing
    Solid area filling
    Rasterizing polygons
- *Tasks that perform surface removal*
    Hidden surface
    Back-surface elimination
- *Tasks that perform shading*
    Pixel
    Scheme

Categorizing our tasks will allow our program to be more general. Processes only create other processes of a certain category of work as needed. For example, if our program is to render a single object and not a scene, then it would not be necessary to spawn a process that performs hidden surface removal; back-surface elimination may be sufficient. If the object is not to be shaded, then it would not be necessary to spawn a task that performs shading; only line drawing rasterization would be nesssary. A parent process or a shell script can be used to launch our program using approach 3. The parent can determine what type of rendering is necessary and pass that information to each of the dedicated processes so that they will know which processes to spawn. The information can also be redirected to each of the dedicated processes from the shell script. In Example 3.6, approach 3 is used.

```
// Example 3.6 Using approach 3 to create processes.
// The tasks are launched from a parent process.

#include <spawn.h>
#include <stdlib.h>
#include <stdio.h>
#include <sys/wait.h>
#include <errno.h>
#include <unistd.h>
```

```cpp
int main(void)
{
   posix_spawnattr_t Attr;
   posix_spawn_file_actions_t FileActions;
   pid_t Pid;
   int stat;

   //...

   system("Task1 ...");    //performed regardless of the type
                             rendering used

   // determine what type of rendering is needed, this can be
   // obtained from the user or by performing some other type
   // of analysis, communicate this to other tasks through
   // arguments

   char *const argv4[] = {"TaskType4",...,NULL};
   char *const argv5[] = {"TaskType5",...,NULL};
   char *const argv6[] = {"TaskType6",...,NULL};

   system("TaskType2 ...");
   system("TaskType3 ...");

   // initialize structures
   posix_spawnattr_init(&Attr);
   posix_spawn_file_actions_init(&FileActions);

   posix_spawn(&Pid,"TaskType4",&FileActions,&Attr,argv4,
            NULL);
    posix_spawn(&Pid,"TaskType5",&FileActions,&Attr,argv5,
            NULL);
   if(Y){
         posix_spawn(&Pid,"TaskType6",&FileActions,&Attr,
                  argv6,NULL);
   }
   // like a good parent, wait for all your children
   wait(&stat);
   wait(&stat);
   wait(&stat);
   return(0);

}


// Each TaskType will be similar
```

```
//...

int main(int argc, char *argv[])
{
    int Rt;

    //...

    if(argv[1] == X){

        // initialize structures
        //...
        posix_spawn(&Pid,"TaskTypeX",&FileActions,&Attr,...,
                    NULL);
    }
    else{
            // initialize structures
            //...
            posix_spawn(&Pid,"TaskTypeY",&FileActions,&Attr,
                        ...,NULL);
    }
    wait(&stat);
    exit(0);
}
```

In Example 3.6, each task type will determine what processes need to be spawned based on the information passed to it from the parent or shell script.

3.10.1 Processes Along Function and Object Lines

Processes can be spawned from functions called from `main()`, as in Example 3.7.

```
// Example 3.7 The mainline which calls the function.

int main(int argc, char *argv[])
{
    //...

    Rt = func1(X, Y, Z);
```

```
   //...
}

// This is the function definition

int func1(char *M, char *N, char *V)
{
   //...

   char *const args[] = {"TaskX",M,N,V,NULL};

   Pid = fork();
   if(Pid == 0)
   {
       exec("TaskX",args);

   }
   if(Pid > 0)
   {
       //...
   }
   wait(&stat);
}
```

In Example 3.7 `func1()` is called with three arguments. These arguments are passed to the spawned process.

Processes can also be spawned from methods that belong to objects. The objects can be declared in any process, as in Example 3.8.

```
// Example 3.8   A process declaring an object.

//...

my_object MyObject;

//...

// Class declaration and definition

class my_object
{
public:
     //...
     int spawnProcess(int X);
     //...
};
```

```
int my_object::spawnProcess(int X)
{
    //...

    // posix_spawn() or system()

    //...
}
```

In Example 3.8, the object can create any number of processes from whatever method necessary.

Summary

Concurrency in a C++ program is accomplished by factoring your program into either multiple processes or multiple threads. A *process* is a unit of work created by the operating system. It is an artifact of the operating system where programs are artifacts of the developer. A program may consist of multiple processes that might not be associated with any particular program. Operating systems are capable of managing hundreds even thousands of concurrently loaded processes.

Some information and attributes of a process are stored in the *process control block* (PCB) used by the operating system to identify the process. This information is needed by the operating system to manage each process. The operating system multitasks between processes by performing a context switch. It saves the current state of the executing process and its context to the PCB save area in order to restart the process the next time it is assigned to the CPU. When the process is utilizing a processor, it is in a running state. When it is waiting to use the CPU, it is in a ready state. The ps utility can be used to monitor the executing processes on the system.

Processes that create other processes have a parent–child relationship with the created process. The creator of the process is the parent and the created process is the child process. Child processes inherit many attributes from the parent. The parent's key responsibility is to wait for the child process so it can exit the system. There are several system calls that can be used to create processes: fork(), fork-exec, system(), and posit_spawn(). fork(), fork-exec(), and posix_spawn() creates processes that are asynchronous to the parent process where system() creates a child process that is synchronous to the parent process. Asynchronous parents can call the `wait()` function and at that point synchronously wait for child processes to terminate or retrieve exit codes for already terminated child processes.

A program can be divided into several processes. These processes can be spawned from a parent process, or launched from a shell script as separate binaries. Dedicated processes can spawn other processes as needed that only perform certain types of work. Processes can be spawned from functions or from methods.

4

Dividing C++ Programs into Multiple Threads

"As our computer systems become more complicated, this kind of abstraction gives us hope of being able to continue to manage them."

—*Andrew Koening and Barbara Moo,* Ruminations on C++

In this Chapter

Threads: A Definition • The Anatomy of a Thread • Thread Scheduling • Thread Resources • Thread Models • Introduction to the Pthread Library • The Anatomy of a Simple Threaded Program • Creating Threads • Managing Threads • Thread Safety and Libraries • Dividing Your Program into Multiple Threads • Summary

The work of a sequential program can be divided between routines within a program. Each routine is assigned a specific task, and the tasks are executed one after another. The second task cannot start until the first task finishes, the third task cannot start until the second task finishes, and so on. This scheme works fine until performance and complexity boundaries are encountered. In some cases, the only solution to a performance problem is to allow the program to do more than one task simultaneously. In other situations the work that routines within a program have to do is so involved that it makes sense to think of the routines as mini-programs within the main program. Each mini-program executes concurrently within the main program. Chapter 3 presented methods for breaking a single process up into multiple processes, where each process executes a separate program. This method allows an application to do more than one thing at a time. However, each process has its own address space and resources. Because each program is in a separate address space, communication between routines becomes an issue. Interprocess communication techniques such as pipes, fifos, and environment variables are needed to communicate between the separately executing parts. Sometimes it is desirable to have a single program do more than one task at a time without dividing the program into multiple programs. Threads can be used in these circumstances. Threads allow a single program to have concurrently executing parts, where each part has access to the same variables, constants, and address space. Threads can be thought of as mini-programs within a program. When a program is divided into separate processes, as we did in Chapter 3, there is a certain amount of overhead associated with executing each of the separate programs. Threads require less overhead to execute. Threads can be thought of as *lightweight processes*, offering many of the advantages of processes without the communication requirements that separate processes require. Threads provide a means to divide the main flow of control into multiple, concurrently executing flows of control.

4.1   Threads: A Definition

A thread is a stream of executable code within a UNIX or Linux process that has the ability to be scheduled. A thread is a lighter burden on the operating system to create, maintain, and manage because very little information is associated with a thread. This lighter burden suggests that a thread has less overhead compared to a process. All processes have a *main* or *primary thread*. The main thread is a process's flow of control or thread of execution. A process can have multiple threads and therefore have as many flows of control as there are threads. Each thread will execute independently and concurrently with its own sequence of instructions. A process with multiple threads is called *multithreaded*. Figure 4–1 shows the multiple flows of control of a process with multiple threads.

4.1.1   Thread Context Requirements

All threads within the same process exist in the same address space. All of the resources belonging to the process are shared among the threads. Threads do not own any resources. Any resources owned by the process are sharable among all of the threads of that process. Threads share file descriptors and file pointers but each thread has its own program pointer, register set, state, and stack. The threads' stacks are all within the stack segment of its process. The data segment of the process is shared with its thread. A thread can read and write to the memory locations of its process and the main thread has access to the data. When the main thread writes to memory, any of the child

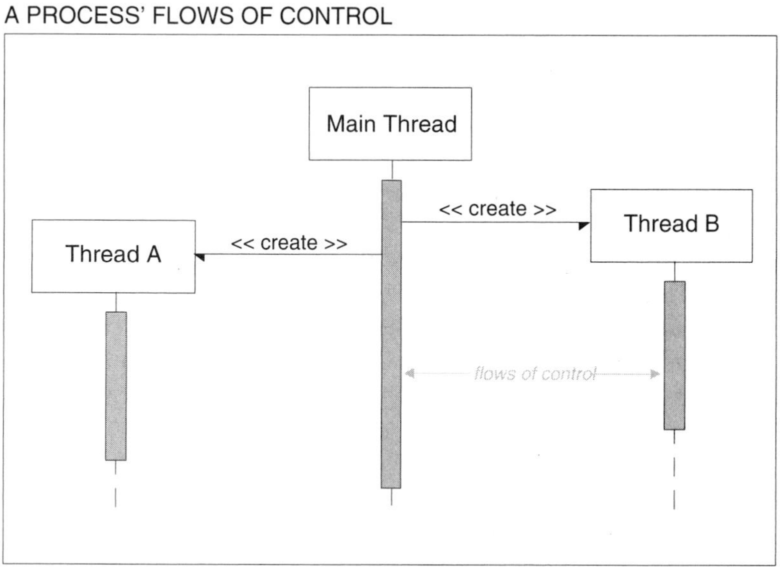

A PROCESS' FLOWS OF CONTROL

Figure 4–1   The flows of control of a multithreaded process.

threads can have access to the data. Threads can create other threads within the same process. All the threads in a single process are called *peers*. Threads can also suspend, resume, and terminate other threads within its process.

Threads are executing entities that compete independently for processor usage with threads of the same or different processes. In a multiprocessor system, threads within the same process can execute simultaneously on different processors. The threads can only execute on processors assigned to that particular process. If processors 1, 2, and 3 are assigned to process A, and process A has three threads, then a thread will be assigned to each processor. In a single processor environment, threads compete for processor usage. Concurrency is achieved through *context switching*. Context switches take place when the operating system is multitasking between tasks on a single processor. *Multitasking* allows more than one task to execute at the same time on a single processor. Each task executes for a designated time interval. When the time interval has expired or some event occurs, the task is removed from the processor and another task is assigned to it. When threads are executing concurrently within a single process, then the process is *multithreaded*. Each thread executes a subtask allowing these subtasks of the process to execute independently without regard to the process's main flow of control. With multithreading, the threads can compete for a single processor or be assigned to different processors. In any case, a context switch occurring between threads of the same process requires fewer resources than a context switch occurring between threads of different processes. A process uses many system resources to keep track of its information and a process context switch takes time to manage that information. Most of the information contained in the process context describes the address space of the process and resources owned by the process. When a switch occurs between threads in different address spaces, a process context switch must take place. Since threads within the same process do not have their own address space or resources, less information tracking is needed. The context of a thread only consists of an id, a stack, a register set, and a priority. The register set contains the program or instruction pointer and the stack pointer. The text of a thread is contained in the text segment of its process. A thread context switch will take less time and use fewer system resources.

4.1.2   Threads and Processes: A Comparison

There are many aspects of a thread that are similar to a process. Threads and processes have an id, a set of registers, a state, a priority, and adhere to a scheduling policy. Like a process, threads have attributes that describe it to the operating system. This information is contained in a thread information block similar to a process information block. Threads and child processes share the resources of its parent process. The resources opened by the process (main thread) are immediately accessible to the threads and child processes of the parent process. No additional initialization or preparation is needed. Threads and child processes are independent entities from its parent or creator and compete for processor usage. The creator of the process or thread exercises some control over the child process or thread. The creator can cancel, suspend, resume, or change the priority of the child process or thread. A thread or process can alter its attributes and create new resources but cannot access the resources belonging to other processes. However, threads and processes differ in several ways.

4.1.2.1   Differences between Threads and Processes

The major difference between threads and processes is each process has its own address space and threads don't. If a process creates multiple threads, all the threads will be contained in its address space. This is why they share resources so easily and interthread communication is so simple. Child processes have their own address space and a copy of the data segment. Therefore, when a child changes its variables or data, it does not affect the data of its parent process. A shared memory area has to be created in order for parent and child processes to share data. Interprocess communication mechanisms, such as pipes and fifos, are used to communicate or pass data between them. Threads of the same process can pass data and communicate by reading and writing directly to any data that is accessible to the parent process.

4.1.2.2   Threads Controlling Other Threads

Whereas processes can only exercise control over other processes in which it has a parent–child relationship, threads within a process are considered peers and are on an equal level regardless of who created whom. Any thread that has access to the thread id of another thread in the same process can cancel, suspend, resume, or change the priority of that thread. In fact, any thread within a process can kill the process by canceling the main or primary thread. Canceling the main thread would result in terminating all the threads of the process—killing the process. Any changes to the main thread may affect all the threads of the process. When changing the priority of the process, all the threads within the process that inherited that priority and have not changed its priorities would also be altered. Table 4–1 summarizes the similarities and differences between threads and processes.

4.1.3   Advantages of Threads

There are several advantages of using multiple threads to manage the subtasks of an application as compared to using multiple processes. These advantages include:

- Less system resources needed for context switching
- Increased throughput of an application
- No special mechanism required for communication between tasks
- Simplify program structure

Table 4–1 Similarities and Differences between Threads and Processes	
Similarities Between Threads and Processes	*Differences Between Threads and Processes*
• Both have an id, set of registers, state, priority, and scheduling policy. • Both have attributes that describe the entity to the OS. • Both have an information block. • Both share resources with the parent process. • Both function as independent entities from the parent process. • The creator can exercise some control over the thread or process. • Both can change their attributes. • Both can create new resources. • Neither can access the resources of another process.	• Threads share the address space of the process that created it; processes have their own address. • Threads have direct access to the data segment of its process; processes have their own copy of the data segment of the parent process. • Threads can directly communicate with other threads of its process; processes must use interprocess communication to communicate with sibling processes. • Threads have almost no overhead; processes have considerable overhead. • New threads are easily created; new processes require duplication of the parent process. • Threads can exercise considerable control over threads of the same process; processes can only exercise control over child processes. • Changes to the main thread (cancellation, priority change, etc.) may affect the behavior of the other threads of the process; changes to the parent process does not affect child processes.

4.1.3.1 Context Switches during Low Processor Availability

When creating a process, the main thread may be the only thread needed to carry out the function of the process. If the process has many concurrent subtasks, multiple threads can provide asynchronous execution of the subtasks with less overhead for context switching. When processor availability is low or there is only a single processor, concurrently executing processes involve heavy overhead because of the context switching required. Under the same condition using threads, a process context switch would only occur when a thread from a different process is the next thread to be assigned the processor. Less overhead means less system resources used and less time taken for context switching. Of course, if there are enough processors to go around then context switching is not an issue.

4.1.3.2 Better Throughput

Multiple threads can increase the throughput of an application. With one thread, an I/O request would halt the entire process. With multiple threads, as one thread waits for an I/O request, the application can continue executing. As one thread is blocked, another can execute. The entire application does not wait for each I/O request to be filled. Other tasks can be performed that does not depend on the blocked thread.

4.1.3.3 Simpler Communication between Concurrently Executing Parts

Threads do not require special mechanisms for communication between subtasks. Threads can directly pass and receive data from other threads. This also saves system resources that would have to be used in the setup and maintenance of special communication mechanisms if multiple processes were used. Threads communicate by using the memory shared within the address space of the process. Processes can also communicate by shared memory but processes have separate address spaces and therefore the shared memory exists outside the address space of both processes. This increases the time and space used to maintain and access the shared memory. Figure 4–2 illustrates the communication between processes and threads.

4.1.3.4 Simplify Program Structure

Threads can be used to simplify the program structure of an application. Each thread is assigned a subtask or subroutine for which it is responsible. The thread will independently manage the execution of the subtask. Each thread can be assigned a priority reflecting the importance of the subtask it is executing to the application. This will result in more easily maintained code.

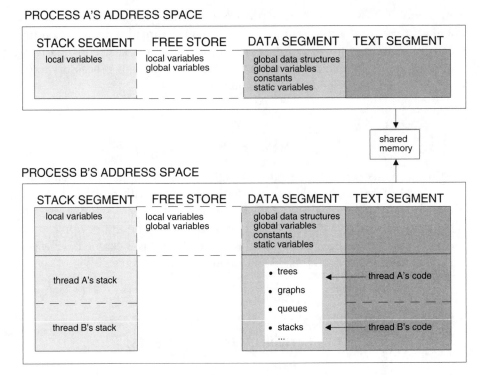

Figure 4-2   Communication between threads of a single process and communication between multiple processes.

4.1.4   Disadvantages of Threads

The easy accessibility threads have to the memory of a process has its disadvantages. For example:

- Threads can easily pollute address space of a process.
- Threads will require synchronization for concurrent read/write access to memory.
- One thread can kill the entire process or program.
- Threads only exist within a single process and are therefore not reusable.

4.1.4.1 Threads Can Corrupt Process Data Easier

It's easier for threads to corrupt the data of a process through data race because multiple threads have write access to the same piece of data. This is not so with processes. Each process has its own data and other processes don't have access unless special programming is done. The separate address spaces of processes protect the data. The fact that threads share the same address space exposes the data to corruption. For example, a process has three threads, A, B, and C. Threads A and B write to a memory location and Thread C reads the value and uses it in a calculation. Threads A and B may both attempt to write to the memory location at the same time. Thread B overwrites the data written by Thread A before Thread C gets a chance to read it. The threads need to be synchronized so that Thread C can read the data deposited in the memory location by Thread A before Thread B overwrites it. Synchronization is needed to prevent either thread from overwriting the values before the data is used. The issues of synchronization between threads will be discussed in Chapter 5.

4.1.4.2 One Bad Thread Can Kill the Entire Program

Since threads don't have their own address space, they are not isolated. If a thread causes a fatal access violation, this may result in the termination of the entire process. Processes are isolated. If one process corrupts its address space, the problems are restricted to that process. A process can have an access violation that causes the process to terminate and all of the other processes will continue executing if the violation isn't too bad. Data errors can be restricted to a single process. Errors caused by a thread are more costly than errors caused by processes. Threads can create data errors that affect the entire memory space of all the threads. Processes can protect its resources from indiscriminate access by other processes. Threads share resources with all the other threads in the process. A thread that damages a resource affects the whole process or program.

4.1.4.3 Threads are Not as Reusable by Other Programs

Threads are dependent and cannot be separated from the process in which they reside. Processes are more independent than threads. An application can divide tasks among many processes and those processes can be packaged as modules that can be used in other applications. Threads cannot exist outside the process that created it and therefore are not reusable. Table 4–2 lists the advantages and disadvantages of threads.

Table 4–2   Advantages and Disadvantages of Threads

Advantages of Threads	Disadvantages of Threads
• Less system resources needed for context switching	• Require synchronization for concurrent read/write access to memory
• Increased throughput of an application	• Can easily pollute address space of its process
• No special mechanism required for communication between tasks	• Only exist within a single process and therefore not reusable
• Simplification of program structure	

4.2   The Anatomy of a Thread

The layout of a thread is embedded in the layout of a process. As discussed in Chapter 3, a process has a code, data, and stack segment. The thread shares the code and data segment with the other threads of the process. Each thread has its own stack allocated in the stack segment of the process's address space. The thread's stack size is set when the thread is created. If the creator of the thread does not specify the size of the thread's stack, a default size is assigned by the system. The default size of the stack is system dependent and will depend on the maximum number of threads a process can have, the allotted size of a process's address space, and the space used by system resources. The thread's stack size must be large enough for any functions called by the thread, any code that is external to the process like library code, and local variable storage. A process with multiple threads should have a stack segment large enough for all of its thread's stacks. The address space allocated to the process limits the stack size, thus limiting the size possible for each thread's stack. Figure 4–3 shows the layout of a process that contains multiple threads.

In Figure 4–3, the process contains two threads and the thread's stacks are located in the stack segment of the process. Each thread executes different functions: thread A executes function 1 and thread B executes function 2.

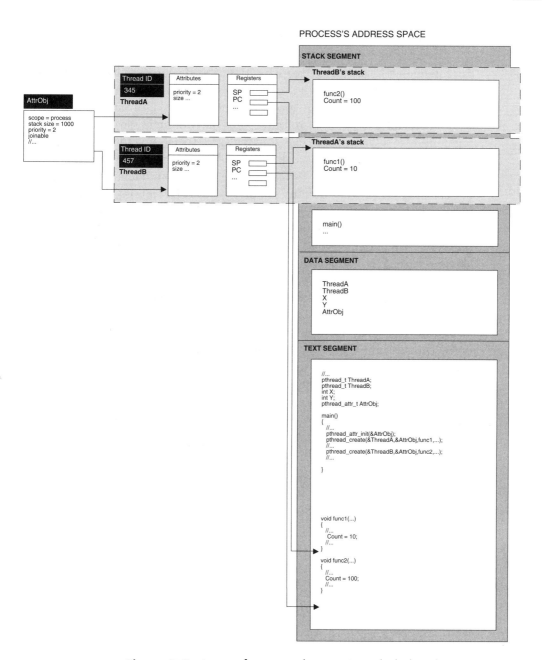

Figure 4-3 Layout of a process that contains multiple threads.

4.2.1   Thread Attributes

The attributes of a process are what describe the process to the operating system. The operating system uses this information to manage processes and distinguish one process from another. The process shares almost everything with its thread including its resources and environment variables. The data segment, text segment, and all resources are associated with the process and not the threads. Everything a thread needs to operate is supplied and defined by the process. What distinguishes threads from one another is the id, the set of registers that defines the state of the thread, its priority, and its stack. These attributes are what give each thread their identity. Like the process, the information about a thread is stored in data structures and returned by functions supplied by the operating system. Some information about a thread is contained in a structure called the *thread information block,* created at the time the thread is created.

The thread id is a unique value that identifies each thread during its lifetime in a process. The priority of a thread determines which threads are given preferential access to an available processor at a given time. The state of the thread is the condition a thread is in at any given time. The set of registers for a thread includes the program counter and the stack pointer. The program counter contains the address of the instruction the thread is to execute and the stack pointer points to the top of the thread's stack.

The POSIX thread library defines a thread *attribute object* that encapsulates the properties of the thread accessible and modifiable to the creator of the thread. The thread attribute defines the following attributes:

- scope
- stack size
- stack address
- priority
- detached state
- scheduling policy and parameters

A thread attribute object can be associated with one thread or multiple threads. When an attribute object is used, it is a profile that defines the behavior of a thread or group of threads. All the threads that use the attribute object take on all the properties defined by the attribute object. Figure 4–3 also shows the attributes associated with each thread. As you can see, both threads A and B share an attribute object but they maintain their separate thread ids and set of registers. Once the attribute object is created and initialized, it can be referenced in any calls to the thread creation function. Therefore, a group of threads can be created that has a "small stack, low priority" or "large stack, high priority and detached." Detached threads are threads that are not synchronized with other threads in the process. In other words, there are no threads waiting for the detached thread to exit. Therefore, once the thread exits, its resources, namely thread id, can be instantly reused. Several methods can be invoked to set and retrieve the values of these attributes. Once a thread is created, its attributes cannot be changed while the thread is in use.

The scope attribute describes which threads a particular thread will compete with for resources. Threads contend for resources within two contention scopes: *process scope* (threads of the same process) and *system scope* (all threads in the system). Threads compete with threads within the same process for file descriptors while threads with system-wide contention scope compete for resources that are allocated across the system (e.g., real memory). Threads compete with threads that have process scope and threads from other processes for processor usage depending on the contention scope and the allocation domains (the set of processors to which it is assigned). A thread that has system scope will be prioritized and scheduled with respect to all of the system-wide threads. Table 4–3 lists the settable properties for the POSIX thread attribute object with a brief description.

4.3   Thread Scheduling

When a process is scheduled to be executed, it is the thread that utilizes the processor. If the process has only one thread, it is the primary thread assigned to a processor. If a process has multiple threads and there are multiple processors, all of the threads are assigned to a processor. Threads compete for processor usage either with all the threads from active processes in the system or just the threads from a single process. The threads are placed in the ready queues sorted by their priority value. The threads in the queue with the same priority are scheduled to processors according to a scheduling policy. When there are not enough processors to go around, then a thread with a higher pri-

Table 4–3	Settable Properties for the Thread Attribute Object	

Settable Thread Attributes	*Functions*	*Description*
detachstate	int pthread_attr_ setdetachstate (pthread_attr_t *attr, int detachstate);	The detachstate attribute controls whether the newly created thread is detachable. If detached, the thread's flow of control cannot be joined to any thread.
guardsize	int pthread_attr_ setguardsize (pthread_attr_t *attr, size_t guardsize);	The guardsize attribute controls the size of the guard area for the newly created thread's stack. It creates a buffer zone the size of guardsize at the overflow end of the stack.
inheritsched	int pthread_attr_ setinheritsched (pthread_attr_t *attr, int inheritsched);	The inheritsched attribute determines how the scheduling attributes of the newly created thread will be set. It determines whether the new thread's scheduling attributes are inherited from the creating thread or set by an attribute object.
param	int pthread_attr_ setschedparam (pthread_attr_t *restrict attr, const struct sched_param *restrict param);	The param attribute is a structure that can be used to set the priority of the newly created thread.
schedpolicy	int pthread_attr_ setschedpolicy (pthread_attr_t *attr, int policy);	The schedpolicy determines the scheduling policy of the newly created thread.
contentionscope	int pthread_attr_ setscope (pthread_attr_t *attr, int contentionscope);	The contentionscope attribute determines which set of threads the newly created thread will compete with for processor usage. A process scope means the thread will compete with the set of threads of the same process; system scope means the thread will compete with system-wide threads (this includes threads from other processes).

Settable Thread Attributes	Functions	Description
stackaddr stacksize	```int pthread_attr_ setstack (pthread_attr_t *attr, void *stackaddr, size_t stacksize);```	The stackaddr and stacksize attributes determine the base address and minimum size in bytes of the stack for the newly created thread.
stackaddr	```int pthread_attr_ setstackaddr (pthread_attr_t *attr, void *stackaddr);```	The stackaddr attribute determines the base address of the stack for the newly created thread.
stacksize	```int pthread_attr_ setstacksize (pthread_attr_t *attr, size_t stacksize);```	The stacksize attribute determines the minimum size in bytes of the stack for the newly created thread.

ority can preempt an executing thread. If the newly active thread is of the same process as the preempted thread, then the context switch is between threads. If the newly active thread is of another process, a process context switch occurs and then the thread context switch is performed.

4.3.1 Thread States

Threads have the same states and transitions mentioned in Chapter 3 that processes have. Figure 4–4 is a duplication of the state diagram 3.4 from Chapter 3. To review, there are four commonly implemented states: runnable, running (active), stopped, and sleeping (blocked). A thread state is the mode or condition a thread is in at any given time. A thread is in a runnable state when it is ready for execution. All runnable threads are placed in a ready queue with other threads with the same priority that are ready to be executed. When a thread is selected and assigned to a processor, the thread is in the running state. A thread is preempted once it has

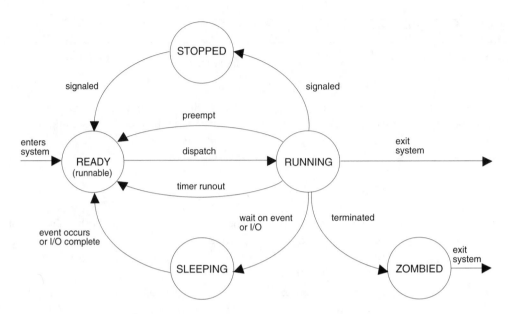

Figure 4–4 Thread states and transitions.

executed for its time slice or when a thread of higher priority becomes runnable. The thread is then placed back into the ready queue. A thread is in the sleeping state if it is waiting for an event to occur or I/O request to complete. A thread is stopped when it receives a signal to stop executing. It remains in that state until it receives a signal to continue. Once the signal is received, the thread moves from the stopped to a runnable state. As the thread moves from one state to another, it undergoes a state transition that signals some event has occurred. When a thread changes from the runnable to the running state it is because the system has selected that thread to run—the thread has been *dispatched*. A thread is *preempted* if its makes an I/O request or some other request of the kernel or for some external reason.

One thread can determine the state of an entire process. The state of a process with one thread is synonymous with the state of its primary thread. If the primary thread is sleeping, the process is sleeping. If the primary thread is running, the process is running. For a process that has multiple threads, all threads of the process would have to be in a sleeping or stopped state in order to consider the whole process sleeping or stopped. On the other hand, if one thread is active (runnable or running) then the process is considered active.

4.3.2 Scheduling and Thread Contention Scope

The contention scope of the thread determines which set of threads a thread will compete with for processor usage. If a thread has process scope, it will only compete with the threads of the same process for processor usage. If the thread has system scope, it will compete with its peers and with threads of other processes for processor usage. For example, in Figure 4–5, there are two processes in a multiprocessor environment of three processors. Process A has four threads and Process B has three threads. Process A has three threads that have process scope and one thread with system scope. Process B has two threads with process scope and one thread with system scope. Process A's threads with process scope competes for processor A and Process B's threads with process scope compete for processor C. Process A and B's threads with system scope compete for processor B.

Figure 4–5 Scheduling with process and system scope threads in a multiprocessor environment.

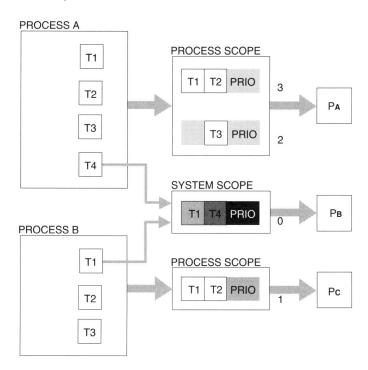

NOTE: Threads should have system scope when modeling true real-time behavior in your application.

4.3.3   Scheduling Policy and Priority

The scheduling policy and priority of the process belong to the primary thread. Each thread can have its own scheduling policy and priority separate from the primary thread. Threads have an integer priority value that has a maximum and minimum value. A priority scheme is used to determine which thread is assigned the processor. Each thread has a priority and the thread with the highest priority is executed before the threads of lower priority. When threads are prioritized, tasks that require immediate execution or response from the system are allotted the processor time it requires. In a preemptive operating system, executing threads are preempted if a thread of higher priority and the same contention scope is available. For example, in Figure 4–5, threads with process scope compete for the processor with threads of the same process that also have process scope. Process A has two threads with priority 3 in which one is assigned the processor. Once the thread with priority 2 becomes runnable, the active thread is preempted and the processor is given to the thread with higher priority. Yet, in Process B, it has two process scope threads that have priority 1, a higher priority than 2. One thread is assigned the processor. Although the other thread with priority 1 is runnable, it does not preempt Process A's thread with priority 2. The thread with system scope and a lower priority is not preempted by any of the threads of Process A or B. They only compete for processor usage with other threads that have system scope.

As discussed in Chapter 3, the ready queues are organized as a sorted list in which each element is a priority level. Each priority level in the list is a queue of threads with the same priority level. All threads of the same priority level are assigned to the processor using a scheduling policy: FIFO, round-robin, or other. With the FIFO (First-In, First-Out) scheduling policy, when the time slice expires the thread is placed at the head of the queue of its priority level. Therefore, the thread will run until it completes execution, it sleeps, or it receives a signal to stop. When a sleeping thread is awakened, it is placed at the end of the queue of its priority level. Round-robin scheduling is similar to FIFO scheduling except the thread is placed at the end of the queue when the time slice expires and the processor is given to the next thread in the queue.

The round-robin scheduling policy considers all threads to be of equal priority and each thread is given the processor for only a time slice. Task executions are interweaved. For example, a program that searches files for specified keywords is divided into two threads. One thread, thread 1, searches for all files with a specified file extension and places the path of the file into a container. Another thread, thread 2, extracts the name of the files from the container, searches each file for the specified keywords, then writes the name of the files that contains all the keywords to a file. If the threads used a round-robin scheduling policy with a single processor, thread 1 would use its time slice to find files and insert the paths into the container. Thread 2 would use its time slice to extract file names and then perform the keyword search. In a perfect world, this interweaves the execution of threads 1 and 2. But thread 2 may execute first when there are no files in the container or thread 1 may only get as far as finding a file, the time slice expiring before it had a chance to insert the file name into the container. This situation requires synchronization, which will be discussed briefly later in this chapter and in Chapter 5. The FIFO scheduling policy allows each thread to run until execution is complete. Using the same example, thread 1 would have time to locate all the files and insert the paths into the container. Thread 2 would then extract the filenames and perform its keyword search on each file. In a perfect world, this would be the end of the program. But thread 2 may be assigned to a processor before thread 1 and there would be no files in the container to search. Thread 1 would then execute, locate, and insert file names into the container but no keyword search would be performed. The program would fail. With FIFO scheduling, there is no interweaving of the execution of these tasks. A thread assigned to a processor dominates the processor until it completes execution. This scheduling policy can be used for applications where a set of threads need to complete as soon as possible. The "other" scheduling policy can be user-defined customization of a scheduling policy. For example, the FIFO scheduling policy can be customized to allow random unblocking of threads.

4.3.3.1   Changing Thread Priority

The priorities of threads should be changed in order to speed up the execution of threads on which other threads depend. They should not be changed in order for a specific thread to get more processor time. This will affect the overall performance of the system. High-priority class threads receive more processor time than threads of a lower class because they are executed more frequently. Threads of higher priority will dominate the processor, preventing other threads of lower priority valuable processor time. This is called *starvation*. Systems that use dynamic priority mechanisms respond to this situation by assigning priorities that last for short periods of time. The system adjusts the priority of threads in order for threads of lower priority execution time. This will improve the overall performance of the system.

The temptation to ensure that a process or specific thread runs to completion is to give it the highest priority but this will affect the overall performance of the system. Such threads may preempt communications over networks, causing the loss of data. Threads that control the user interface may be drastically affected, causing the keyboard, mouse, and screen response to be sluggish. Some systems prevent user processes and threads from having a higher priority than system processes. Otherwise, system processes or threads would be prevented from responding to critical system changes. Generally speaking, most user processes and threads fall in the category of normal or regular priority.

4.4   Thread Resources

Threads share most of its resources with other threads of the same process. Threads do own resources that define the thread's context. This includes the thread id, set of registers including the stack pointer and program counter, and stack. Threads must share other resources such as the processor, memory, and file descriptors required in order for it to perform its task. File descriptors are allocated to each process separately and threads of the same process compete for access to these descriptors. In memory, the processor, and other globally allocated resources, threads contend with other threads of its process as well as the threads of other processes for access to these resources.

A thread can allocate additional resources such as files or mutexes, but they are accessible to all the threads of the process. There are limits on the resources that can be consumed by a single process. Therefore, all the threads in combination must not exceed the resource limit of the process. If a thread attempts to consume more resources than the soft resource limit defines, it is sent a signal that the process's resource limit has been reached. Threads that allocate resources must be careful not to leave resources in an unstable state when they are canceled. A thread that has opened a file or created a mutex may be terminated, leaving the file open or the mutex locked. If the file has not been properly closed and the application is terminated, this may result in damage to the file or loss of data. A thread terminating after locking a mutex prevents access to whatever critical section that mutex is protecting. Before it terminates, a thread should perform some cleanup, preventing these unwanted situations from occurring.

4.5 Thread Models

The purpose of a thread is to perform work on behalf of the process. If a process has multiple threads, each thread performs some subtask as part of the overall task to be performed by the process. Threads are delegated work according to a specific strategy or approach that structures how delegation is implemented. If the application models some procedure or entity, then the approach selected should reflect that model. Some common models are:

- delegation (boss–worker)
- peer-to-peer
- pipeline
- producer-consumer

Each model has its own WBS (Work Breakdown Structure) that determines who is responsible for thread creation and under what conditions threads are created. For example, there is a centralized approach where a single thread creates other threads and delegates work to each thread. There is an assembly-line approach where threads perform different work at different stages. Once the threads are created, they can perform the same task on different data sets, different tasks on the same data set, or different tasks on different data sets. Threads can be categorized to only perform certain types of tasks. For example, there can be a group of threads that only perform computations, process input, or produce output.

It may be true that what is to be modeled is not homogeneous throughout the process and it may be necessary to mix models. In Chapter 3, we discussed a rendering process. Tasks 1, 2, and 3 were performed sequentially and tasks 4, 5, and 6 can be performed simultaneously. Each task can be executed by a different thread. If multiple images were to be rendered, threads 1, 2, and 3 can form the pipeline of the process. As thread 1 finishes, the image is passed to thread 2 while thread 1 performs its work on the next image. As these images are buffered, threads 4, 5, and 6 can use a workpile approach. The thread model is a part of the structuring of parallelism in your application where each thread can be executing on a different processor. Table 4–4 lists the thread models with a brief description.

Table 4–4 Thread Models	
Thread Models	*Description*
Delegation model	A central thread (boss) creates the threads (workers), assigning each worker a task. Each worker is assigned a task by the boss thread. The boss thread may wait until each thread completes that task.
Peer-to-peer model	All the threads have an equal working status. Threads are called peer threads. A peer thread creates all the threads needed to perform the tasks but performs no delegation responsibilities. The peer threads can process requests from a single input stream shared by all the threads or each thread may have its own input stream.
Pipeline	An assembly-line approach to processing a stream of input in stages. Each stage is a thread that performs work on a unit of input. When the unit of input has been through all the stages, then the processing of the input has been completed.
Producer–consumer model	A producer thread *produces* data to be *consumed* by the consumer thread. The data is stored in a block of memory shared by the producer and consumer threads.

4.5.1   Delegation Model

In the *delegation* model, a single thread (boss) creates the threads (workers) and assigns each a task. It may be necessary for the boss thread to wait until each worker thread completes its task. The boss thread delegates the task each worker thread is to perform by specifying a function. As each worker is assigned its task, it is the responsibility of each worker thread to perform that task and produce output or synchronize with the boss or other thread to produce output.

The boss thread can create threads as a result of requests made to the system. The processing of each type of request can be delegated to a thread worker. In this case, the boss thread executes an event loop. As events occur, thread workers are created and assigned their duties. A new thread is created for every new request that enters the system. Using this approach may cause the process to exceed its resource or thread limits. Alternatively, a boss thread can create a pool of threads that are reassigned new requests. The boss thread creates a number of threads during initialization and then each thread is suspended until a request is added to their queue. As requests are placed in the queue, the boss thread signals a worker thread to process the request. When the thread completes, it dequeues the next request. If none are available, the thread suspends itself until the boss signals the thread that more work is available in the queue. If all the worker threads are to share a single queue, then the threads can be programmed to only process certain types of requests. If the request in the queue is not of the type a particular thread is to process, the thread can again suspend itself. The primary purpose of the boss thread is to create all the threads, place work in the queue, and awaken worker threads when work is available. The worker threads check the request in the queue,

Figure 4-6 The two approaches to the delegation model.

DELEGATION APPROACH 1:

Boss thread creates a new thread for each new request.

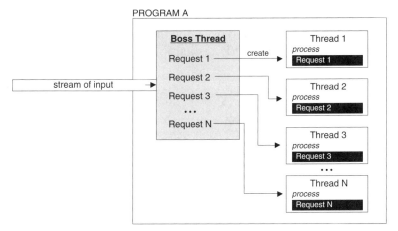

DELEGATION APPROACH 2:

Boss thread creates a pool of threads that processes all requests.

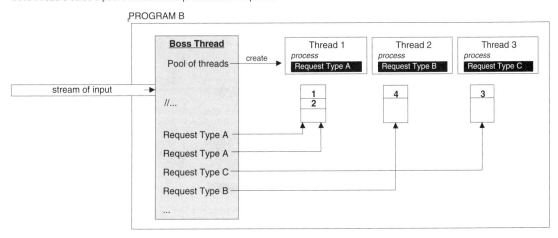

perform the assigned task, and suspend itself if no work is available. All the worker threads and the boss thread execute concurrently. Figure 4–6 contrasts these two approaches for the delegation model.

4.5.2   Peer-to-Peer Model

Where the delegation model has a boss thread that delegates tasks to worker threads, in the *peer-to-peer* model all the threads have an equal working status. Although there is a single thread that initially creates all the threads needed to perform all the tasks, that thread is considered a worker thread and does no delegation. In this model, there is no centralized thread. The worker (peer) threads have more responsibility. The peer threads can process requests from a single input stream shared by all the threads or each thread may have its own input stream for which it is responsible. The input can also be

Figure 4–7   Peer-to-peer thread model.

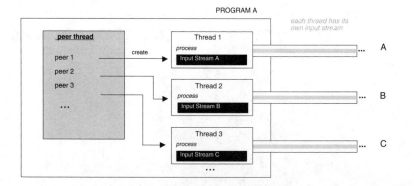

stored in a file or database. The peer threads may have to communicate and share resources. Figure 4–7 shows the peer-to-peer thread model.

4.5.3 Pipeline Model

The *pipeline* model is characterized as an assembly line in which a stream of items are processed in stages. At each stage, work is performed on a unit of input by a thread. When the unit of input has been through all the stages, then the processing of the input has been completed. This approach allows multiple inputs to be processed simultaneously. Each thread is responsible for producing its interim results or output, making them available to the next stage or next thread in the pipeline. The last stage or thread produces the result of the pipeline.

As the input moves down the pipeline, it may be necessary to buffer units of input at certain stages as threads process previous input. This may cause a slowdown in the pipeline if a particular stage's processing is slower than other stages, causing a backlog. To prevent backlog, it may be necessary for that stage to create additional threads to process incoming input. The stages of work in a pipeline should be balanced where one stage does not take more time than the other stages. Work should be evenly distributed throughout the pipeline. More stages and therefore more threads may also be added to the pipeline. This will also prevent backlog. Figure 4–8 shows the pipeline model.

4.5.4 Producer-Consumer Model

In the *producer-consumer* model, there is a producer thread that *produces* data to be *consumed* by the consumer thread. The data is stored in a block of memory shared between the producer and consumer threads. The producer thread

Figure 4–8 The pipeline model.

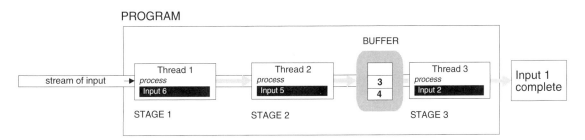

Figure 4–9   The producer–consumer model.

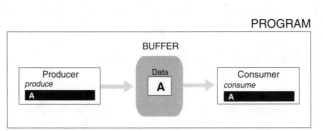

must first produce data, then the consumer threads retrieve it. This process will require synchronization. If the producer thread deposits data at a much faster rate than the consumer thread consumes it, then the producer thread may at several times overwrite previous results before the consumer thread retrieves it. On the other hand, if the consumer thread retrieves data at a much faster rate than the producer deposits data, then the consumer thread may retrieve identical data or attempt to retrieve data not yet deposited. Figure 4–9 shows the producer-consumer model. The producer-consumer model is also called the client-server model for larger-scaled programs and applications.

4.5.5   SPMD and MPMD for Threads

In each of the previous thread models, the threads are performing the same task over and over again on different data sets or are assigned different tasks performed on different data sets. These thread models utilize SIMD (Single Instruction Multiple Data) or MPMD (Multiple Programs Multiple Data). These are two models of parallelism that classify programs by instruction and data streams. They can be used to describe the type of work the thread models are implementing in parallel. For our purposes, MPMD is better stated as MTMD (Multiple Threads Multiple Data). These models describe a system that executes different threads processing different sets of data or data streams. SPMD means Single Program Multiple Data or, for our purposes, STMD (Single Thread Multiple Data). This model describes a system that executes a single thread that processes different sets of data or data streams. This means several identical threads executing the same routine are given different sets of data to process.

The delegation and peer-to-peer models can both use STMD or MTMD models of parallelism. As described, the pool of threads can execute different

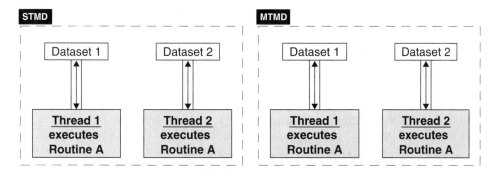

Figure 4–10 The STMD and MTMD models of parallelism.

routines processing different sets of data. This utilizes the MTMD model. The pool of threads can also be given the same routine to execute. The requests or jobs submitted to the system could be different sets of data instead of different tasks. In this case, a set of threads implementing the same instructions but on different sets of data thus utilizes STMD. The peer-to-peer model can be threads executing the same or different tasks. Each thread can have its own data stream or several files of data that each thread is to process. The pipeline model uses the MTMD model of parallelism. At each stage different processing is performed so multiple input units are at different stages of completion. The pipeline metaphor would be useless if at each stage the same processing was performed. Figure 4–10 contrasts the STMD and MTMD models of parallelism.

4.6 Introduction to the Pthread Library

The Pthread library supplies the API to create and manage the threads in your application. The Pthread library is based on a standardized programming interface for the creation and maintenance of threads. The thread interface has been specified by the IEEE standards committee in the POSIX 1003.1c standard. Third-party vendors supply an implementation that adheres to the POSIX standard. Their implementation is referred to as Pthreads or POSIX thread library.

The Pthread library contains over 60 functions that can be classified into the following categories:

I. Thread Management Functions
   1. Thread configuration
   2. Thread cancellation
   3. Thread scheduling
   4. Thread specific data
   5. Signals
   6. Thread attribute functions
      a. Thread attribute configuration
      b. Thread attribute stack configuration
      c. Thread attribute scheduling configuration
II. Mutex Functions
   1. Mutex configuration
   2. Priority management
   3. Mutex attribute functions
      a. Mutex attribute configuration
      b. Mutex attribute protocol
      c. Mutex attribute priority management
III. Condition Variable Functions
   1. Condition variable configuration
   2. Condition variable attribute functions
      a. Condition variable attribute configuration
      b. Condition variable sharing functions

The Pthread library can be implemented in any language but in order to be compliant with the POSIX standard, they must comply to the standardized interface and behave in the manner specified. The Pthread library is not the only thread API implementation. Hardware and third-party vendors have implemented their own proprietary thread APIs. For example, the Sun environment supports the Pthread library and their own Solaris thread library. In this chapter, we discuss some Pthread functions that implement thread management.

4.7   The Anatomy of a Simple Threaded Program

Any simple multithreaded program will consist of a main or creator thread and the functions that the threads will execute. The thread models determine the manner in which the threads are created and managed. They can

be created all at once or under certain conditions. In Example 4.1 the delegation model is used to show a simple multithreaded program.

```
// Example 4.1. Using the delegation model in a simple threaded program.

#include <iostream>
#include <pthread.h>

void *task1(void *X) //define task to be executed by ThreadA
{
   //...
   cout << "Thread A complete" << endl;

}

void *task2(void *X) //define task to be executed by ThreadB

{
   //...
   cout << "Thread B complete" << endl;

}

int main(int argc, char *argv[])
{
   pthread_t ThreadA,ThreadB; // declare threads

   pthread_create(&ThreadA,NULL,task1,NULL); // create threads
   pthread_create(&ThreadB,NULL,task2,NULL);
   // additional processing
   pthread_join(ThreadA,NULL); // wait for threads
   pthread_join(ThreadB,NULL);
   return (0);
}
```

In Example 4.1, the main line of the example defines the set of instructions for the primary thread. The primary thread, in this case, is also the
boss thread. The boss thread declares two threads, ThreadA and ThreadB.
By using the pthread_create() function, these two threads are associated
with the tasks they are to execute. The two tasks, task1 and task2, are defined. They simply send a message to the standard out but could be programmed to do anything. The pthread_create() function causes the
threads to immediately execute their assigned tasks. The pthread_join()
function works the same way as wait() for processes. The primary thread
waits until both threads return. Figure 4–11 shows the layout of Exam-

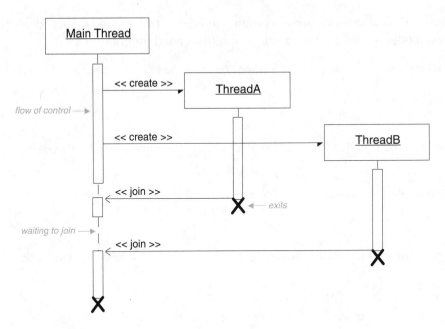

Figure 4-11   The layout, output, and flow of control for Example 4.1.

ple 4.1. It also shows what happens to the flow of controls as the `pthread_create()` and `pthread_join()` functions are called.

In Figure 4–11, the `pthread_create()` function causes a fork in the flow of control in the main line or primary thread. Two additional flows of control, one for each thread, are executing concurrently. The `pthread_create()` function returns immediately after the threads are created. It is an asynchronous function. As each thread executes its set of instructions, the primary thread executes its instructions. The `pthread_join()` causes the primary thread to wait until each thread terminates and rejoins the main flow of control.

4.7.1   *Compiling and Linking Multithreaded Programs*

All multithreaded programs using the POSIX thread library must include the header:

```
<pthread.h>
```

In order to compile and link multithreaded applications in the UNIX or Linux environments using the `g++` or `gcc` command-line compilers, be sure to link the Pthreads library to your application. Use the `-l` option that specifies a library.

```
-lpthread
```

will cause your application to link to the library that is compliant with the multithreading interface defined by POSIX 1003.1c standard. The Pthread library, `libpthread.so`, should be located in the directory where the system stores its standard library, usually `/usr/lib`. If it is not located in a standard location, use the `-L` option to make the compiler look in a particular directory first before searching the standard locations.

```
g++ -o blackboard -L /src/local/lib blackboard.cpp -lpthread
```

tells the compiler to look in the `/src/local/lib` directory for the Pthread library before searching in the standard locations.

The complete programs in this book are accompanied by a *program profile*. The program profile contains implementation specifics such as headers and libraries required and compile and link instructions. The profile also includes a note section that will contain any special considerations that need to be taken when executing the program.

4.8   Creating Threads

The Pthreads library can be used to create, maintain, and manage the threads of multithreaded programs and applications. When creating a multithreaded program, threads can be created any time during the execution of a process because they are dynamic. The `pthread_create()` function creates a new thread in the address space of a process. The `thread` parameter points to a thread handle or thread id of the thread that will be created. The new thread will have the attributes specified by the attribute object `attr`. The `thread` parameter will immediately execute the instructions in `start_routine` with the arguments specified by `arg`. If the function successfully creates the thread, it will return the thread id and store the value in the `thread` parameter.

If `attr` is `NULL`, the default thread attributes will be used by the new thread. The new thread takes on the attributes of `attr` when it is created. If `attr` is changed after the thread has been created, it will not affect any of the thread's attributes. If `start_routine` returns, the thread returns as if

---

Synopsis

```
#include <pthread.h>

int pthread_create(pthread_t *restrict thread,
                   const pthread_attr_t *restrict attr,
                   void *(*start_routine)(void*),
                   void *restrict arg);
```

---

pthread_exit() had been called using the return value of start_routine as its exit status.

If successful, the function will return 0. If the function is not successful, no new thread is created and the function will return an error number. If the system does not have the resources to create the thread or the thread limit for the process has been reached, the function will fail. The function will also fail if the thread attribute is invalid or the caller thread does not have permission to set the necessary thread attributes.

These are examples of creating two threads with default attributes:

```
pthread_create(&threadA,NULL,task1,NULL);
pthread_create(&threadB,NULL,task2,NULL);
```

These are the two pthread_create() function calls from Example 4.1. Both threads are created with default attributes.

Program 4.1 shows a primary thread passing an argument from the command line to the functions executed by the threads.

```cpp
// Program 4.1

#include <iostream>
#include <pthread.h>
#include <stdlib.h>

int main(int argc, char *argv[])
{
   pthread_t ThreadA,ThreadB;
   int N;

   if(argc != 2){
      cout << "error" << endl;
      exit (1);
   }
```

```
    N = atoi(argv[1]);
    pthread_create(&ThreadA,NULL,task1,&N);
    pthread_create(&ThreadB,NULL,task2,&N);
    cout << "waiting for threads to join" << endl;
    pthread_join(ThreadA,NULL);
    pthread_join(ThreadB,NULL);
    return (0);
}
```

Program 4.1 shows how the primary thread can pass arguments from the command line to each of the thread functions. A number is typed in at the command line. The primary thread converts the argument to an integer and passes it to each function as a pointer to an integer as the last argument to the `pthread_create()` functions. Program 4.2 shows each of the thread functions.

```
// Program 4.2

void *task1(void *X)
{
    int *Temp;
    Temp = static_cast<int *>(X);

    for(int Count = 1;Count < *Temp;Count++){
        cout << "work from thread A: " << Count << " * 2 = "
            << Count * 2 << endl;
    }
    cout << "Thread A complete" << endl;

}

void *task2(void *X)
{
    int *Temp;
    Temp = static_cast<int *>(X);

    for(int Count = 1;Count < *Temp;Count++){
        cout << "work from thread B: " << Count << " + 2 = "
            << Count + 2 << endl;
    }
    cout << "Thread B complete" << endl;

}
```

In Program 4.2, `task1` and `task2` executes a loop that is iterated the number of times as the value passed to the function. The function either adds or multiplies the loop invariant by 2 and sends the results to standard `out`. Once complete, each function outputs a message that the thread is complete. The instructions for compiling and executing Programs 4.1 and 4.2 are contained in Program Profile 4.1.

Program Profile 4.1

Program Name
`program4-12.cc`

Description
Accepts an integer from the command line and passes the value to the thread functions. Each function executes a loop that either adds or multiples the loop invariant by 2 and sends the result to standard `out`. The main line or primary thread is listed in Program 4.1 and the functions are listed in Program 4.2.

Libraries Required
`libpthread`

Headers Required
`<pthread.h> <iostream> <stdlib.h>`

Compile and Link Instructions
`c++ -o program4-12 program4-12.cc -lpthread`

Test Environment
SuSE Linux 7.1, gcc 2.95.2,

Execution Instructions
`./program4-12 34`

Notes
This program requires a command-line argument.

This is an example of passing a single argument to the thread function. If it is necessary to pass multiple arguments to the thread function, create a `struct` or container containing all the required arguments and pass a pointer to that structure to the thread function.

4.8.1   Getting the Thread Id

As mentioned earlier, the process shares all its resources with the threads in its address space. Threads have very few resources of their own. The thread id is one of the resources unique to each thread. The `pthread_self()` function returns the thread id of the calling thread.

Synopsis

```
#include <pthread.h>

pthread_t pthread_self(void);
```

This function is similar to `getpid()` for processes. When a thread is created, the thread id is returned to the creator or calling thread. The thread id will not know the created thread. Once the thread has its own id, it can be passed to other threads in the process. This function returns the thread id with no errors defined.

Here is an example of calling this function:

```
//...
pthread_t  ThreadId;
ThreadId = pthread_self();
```

A thread calls this function and the function returns the thread id stored in the variable `ThreadId` of type `pthread_t`.

4.8.2   Joining Threads

The `pthread_join()` function is used to join or rejoin flows of control in a process. The `pthread_join()` causes the calling thread to suspend its execution until the target thread has terminated. It is similar to the `wait()` function used by processes. This function can be called by the creator of a thread. The creator thread waits for the new thread to terminate and return, thus *rejoining* flows of control. The `pthread_join()` can also be called by peer threads if the thread handle is global. This will allow any thread to join flows of control with any other thread in the process. If the calling thread is canceled before the target thread returns, the target thread will not become a detached thread (discussed in the next section). If different peer threads simultaneously call the `pthread_join()` function on the same thread, this behavior is undefined.

Synopsis

```
#include <pthread.h>


int pthread_join(pthread_t thread, void **value_ptr);
```

The `thread` parameter is the thread (target thread) the calling thread is waiting on. If the function returns successfully, the exit status is stored in `value_ptr`. The exit status is the argument passed to the `pthread_exit()` function called by the terminated thread. The function will return an error number if it fails. The function will fail if the target thread is not a joinable thread or, in other words, created as a detached thread. The function will also fail if the specified thread `thread` does not exist.

There should be a `pthread_join()` function called for all joinable threads. Once the thread is joined, this will allow the operating system to reclaim storage used by the thread. If a joinable thread is not joined to any thread or the thread that calls the join function is canceled, then the target thread will continue to utilize storage. This is a state similar to a zombied process when the parent process has not accepted the exit status of a child process, the child process continues to occupy an entry in the process table.

4.8.3   Creating Detached Threads

A detached thread is a terminated thread that is not joined or waited upon by any other threads. When the thread terminates, the limited resources used by the thread, including the thread id, are reclaimed and returned to the system pool. There is no exit status for any thread to obtain. Any thread that attempts to call `pthread_join()` for a detached thread will fail. The `pthread_detach()` function detaches the thread specified by `thread`. By default, all threads are created as joinable unless otherwise specified by the thread attribute object. This function detaches already existing joinable threads. If the thread has not terminated, a call to this function does not cause it to terminate.

Synopsis

```
#include <pthread.h>


int pthread_detach(pthread_t thread thread);
```

If successful, the function will return 0. If not successful, it will return an error number. The `pthread_detach()` function will fail if thread is already detached or the thread specified by thread could not be found.

This is an example of detaching an already existing joinable thread:

```
//...
pthread_create(&threadA,NULL,task1,NULL);
pthread_detach(threadA);
//...
```

This causes `threadA` to be a detached thread. To create a detached thread, as opposed to dynamically detaching a thread, requires setting the `detachstate` of a thread attribute object and using that attribute object when the thread is created.

4.8.4   Using the Pthread Attribute Object

The thread attribute object encapsulates the attributes of a thread or group of threads. It is used to set the attributes of threads during their creation. The thread attribute object is of type `pthread_attr_t`. This structure can be used to set these thread attributes:

- size of the thread's stack
- location of the thread's stack
- scheduling inheritance, policy, and parameters
- whether the thread is detached or joinable
- the scope of the thread

The `pthread_attr_t` has several methods that can be invoked to set and retrieve each of these attributes. Table 4–3 lists the methods used to set the attributes of the attribute object.

The `pthread_attr_init()` and `pthread_attr_destroy()` functions are used to initialize and destroy a thread attribute object.

```
Synopsis

#include <pthread.h>


int pthread_attr_init(pthread_attr_t *attr);
int pthread_attr_destroy(pthread_attr_t *attr);
```

The `pthread_attr_init()` function initializes a thread attribute object with the default values for all the attributes. The `attr` parameter is a pointer to a `pthread_attr_t` object. Once `attr` has been initialized, its attribute values can be changed by using the `pthread_attr_set` functions listed in Table 4–3. Once the attributes have been appropriately modified, `attr` can be used as a parameter in any call to the `pthread_create()` function. If successful, the function will return 0. If not successful, the function will return an error number. The `pthread_attr_init()` function will fail if there is not enough memory to create the object.

The `pthread_attr_destroy()` function can be used to destroy a `pthread_attr_t` object specified by `attr`. A call to this function deletes any hidden storage associated with the thread attribute object. If successful, the function will return 0. If not successful, the function will return an error number.

4.8.4.1 Creating Detached Threads Using the Pthread Attribute Object

Once the thread object has been initialized, its attributes can be modified. The `pthread_attr_setdetachstate()` function can be used to set the `detachstate` attribute of the attribute object. The `detachstate` parameter describes the thread as detached or joinable.

```
Synopsis

#include <pthread.h>


int pthread_attr_setdetachstate(pthread_attr_t *attr,
                           int *detachstate);
int pthread_attr_getdetachstate(const pthread_attr_t *attr,
                           int *detachstate);
```

The `detachstate` can have one of these values:

```
PTHREAD_CREATE_DETACHED
PTHREAD_CREATE_JOINABLE
```

The `PTHREAD_CREATE_DETACHED` value will cause all the threads that use this attribute object to be detached. The `PTHREAD_CREATE_JOINABLE` value will cause all the threads that use this attribute object to be joinable. This is the default value of `detachstate`. If successful, the function will return 0. If not successful, the function will return an error number. The `pthread_attr_setdetachstate()` function will fail if the value of `detachstate` is not valid.

The `pthread_attr_getdetachstate()` function will return the `detachstate` of the attribute object. If successful, the function will return the value of `detachstate` to the `detachstate` parameter and 0 as the return value. If not successful, the function will return an error number. In Example 4.2, the threads created in Program 4.1 are detached. This example uses an attribute object when creating one of the threads.

```
// Example 4.2. Using an attribute object to create a detached thread.

//...

int main(int argc, char *argv[])
{

   pthread_t ThreadA, ThreadB;
   pthread_attr_t DetachedAttr;
   int N;

   if(argc != 2){
      cout << "error" << endl;
      exit (1);
   }
   N = atoi(argv[1]);
   pthread_attr_init(&DetachedAttr);
   pthread_attr_setdetachstate(&DetachedAttr,PTHREAD_CREATE_DETACHED);
   pthread_create(&ThreadA,NULL,task1,&N);
   pthread_create(&ThreadB,&DetachedAttr,task2,&N);
   cout << "waiting for thread A to join" << endl;
   pthread_join(ThreadA,NULL);
   return (0);
}
```

Example 4.2 declares an attribute object `DetachedAttr`. The `pthread_attr_init()` function is used to allocate the attribute object. Once initialized, the `pthread_attr_detachstate()` function is used to change the `detachstate` from joinable to detached using the `PTHREAD_CREATE_DETACHED` value. When creating `ThreadB`, the `Detached-Attr` is the second argument in the call to the `pthread_create()` function. The `pthread_join()` call is removed for `ThreadB` because detached threads cannot be joined.

4.9   Managing Threads

When creating applications with multiple threads, there are several ways to control how threads perform and how threads use and compete for resources. Part of managing threads is setting the scheduling policy and priority of the threads. This contributes to the performance of the thread. Thread performance is also determined by how the threads compete for resources, either on a process or system scope. The scheduling, priority, and scope of the thread can be set by using a thread attribute object. Because threads share resources, access to resources will have to be synchronized. This will briefly be discussed in this chapter and fully discussed in Chapter 5. Thread synchronization also includes when and how threads are terminated and canceled.

4.9.1   Terminating Threads

A thread's execution can be discontinued by several means:

- By returning from the execution of its assigned task with or without an exit status or return value
- By explicitly terminating itself and supplying an exit status
- By being canceled by another thread in the same address space

When a joinable thread function has completed executing, it returns to the thread calling `pthread_join()`, for which it is the target thread. The `pthread_join()` returns the exit status passed to the `pthread_exit()` function called by the terminating thread. If the terminating thread did not make a call to `pthread_exit()`, then the exit status will be the return value of the function, if it has one; otherwise, the exit status is NULL.

It may be necessary for one thread to terminate another thread in the same process. For example, an application may have a thread that monitors the work of other threads. If a thread performs poorly or is no longer needed, to save system resources it may be necessary to terminate that thread. The terminating thread may terminate immediately or defer termination until a logical point in its execution. The terminating thread may also have to perform some cleanup tasks before it terminates. The thread also has the option to refuse termination.

The `pthread_exit()` function is used to terminate the calling thread. The `value_ptr` is passed to the thread that calls `pthread_join()` for this thread. Cancellation cleanup handler tasks that have not executed will execute along with the destructors for any thread-specific data. No resources used by the thread are released.

Synopsis

```
#include <pthread.h>


int pthread_exit(void *value_ptr);
```

When the last thread of a process exits, then the process has terminated with an exit status of `0`. This function cannot return to the calling thread and there are no errors defined.

The `pthread_cancel()` function is used to cancel the execution of another thread in the same address space. The `thread` parameter is the thread to be canceled.

Synopsis

```
#include <pthread.h>


int pthread_cancel(pthread_t thread thread);
```

A call to the `pthread_cancel()` function is a request to cancel a thread. The request can be granted immediately, at a later time, or ignored. The cancel type and cancel state of the target thread determines when or if thread cancellation actually takes place. When the request is granted, there is a cancellation process that occurs asynchronously to the returning of the pthread_cancel() function to the calling thread. If the thread has cancellation cleanup handler tasks, they are performed. When the last handler returns, the destructors for thread-specific data, if any, are called and the thread is terminated. This is the cancellation process. The function returns 0 if successful and an error if not successful. The pthread_cancel() function will fail if the thread parameter does not correspond to an existing thread.

Some threads may require safeguards against untimely cancellation. Installing safeguards in a thread's function may prevent undesirable situations. Threads share data and depending on the thread model used, one thread may be processing data that is to be passed to another thread for processing. While the thread is processing data, it has sole possession by locking a mutex associated with the data. If a thread has locked a mutex and is canceled before the mutex is released, this could cause deadlock. The data may be required to be in some state before it can be used again. If a thread is canceled before this is done, an undesirable condition may occur. To put it simply, depending on the type of processing a thread is performing, thread cancellation should be performed when it is safe. A vital thread may prevent cancellation entirely. Therefore, thread cancellation should be restricted to threads that are not vital or points of execution that do not have locks on resources. Cancellations can also be postponed until all vital cleanups have taken place.

The *cancelability state* describes the cancel condition of a thread as being cancelable or uncancelable. A thread's *cancelabilty type* determines the thread's ability to continue after a cancel request. A thread can act upon a cancel request immediately or defer the cancellation to a later point in its execution. The cancelability state and type are dynamically set by the thread itself.

The pthread_setcancelstate() and pthread_setcanceltype() functions are used to set the cancelability state and type of the calling thread. The pthread_setcancelstate() function sets the calling thread to the cancelability state specified by state and returns the previous state in oldstate.

Synopsis

```
#include <pthread.h>

int pthread_setcancelstate(int state, int *oldstate);
int pthread_setcanceltype(int type, int *oldtype);
```

The values for `state` and `oldstate` are:

```
PTHREAD_CANCEL_DISABLE
PTHREAD_CANCEL_ENABLE
```

`PTHREAD_CANCEL_DISABLE` is a state in which a thread will ignore a cancel request. `PTHREAD_CANCEL_ENABLE` is a state in which a thread will concede to a cancel request. This is the default state of any newly created thread. If successful, the function will return 0. If not successful, the function will return an error number. The `pthread_setcancelstate()` may fail if not passed a valid `state` value.

The `pthread_setcanceltype()` function sets the calling thread to the cancelability type specified by `type` and returns the previous state in `oldtype`. The values for `type` and `oldtype` are:

```
PTHREAD_CANCEL_DEFFERED
PTHREAD_CANCEL_ASYNCHRONOUS
```

`PTHREAD_CANCEL_DEFFERED` is a cancelability type in which a thread puts off termination until it reaches its cancellation point. This is the default cancelability type for any newly created threads. `PTHREAD_CANCEL_ASYNCHRONOUS` is a cancelability type in which a thread terminates immediately. If successful, the function will return 0. If not successful, the function will return an error number. The `pthread_setcanceltype()` may fail if not passed a valid `type` value.

The `pthread_setcancelstate()` and `pthread_setcanceltype()` functions are used together to establish the cancelability of a thread. Table 4–5 list combinations of state and type and a description of what will occur for each combination.

Table 4–5   Combinations of Cancelabililty State and Type

Cancelability State	Cancelability Type	Description
PTHREAD_CANCEL_ ENABLE	PTHREAD_CANCEL_ DEFERRED	*Deferred cancellation.* The default cancellation state and type of a thread. Thread cancellation takes places when it enters a cancellation point or when the programmer defines a cancellation point with a call to `pthread_testcancel()`.
PTHREAD_CANCEL_ ENABLE	PTHREAD_CANCEL_ ASYNCHRONOUS	*Asynchronous cancellation.* Thread cancellation takes place immediately.
PTHREAD_CANCEL_ DISABLE	Ignored	*Disabled cancellation.* Thread cancellation does not take place.

4.9.1.1   Cancellation Points

When a cancel request is deferred, the termination of the thread takes place later in the execution of the thread's function. Whenever it occurs, it should be "safe" to cancel the thread because it is not in the middle of executing critical code, locking a mutex, or leaving the data in some usable state. These safe locations in the code's execution are good locations for *cancellation points*. A cancellation point is a check point where a thread checks if there are any cancellation requests pending and, if so, concede to termination.

Cancellation points can be marked by a call to `pthread_testcancel()`. This function checks for any pending cancellation request. If a request is pending, then it causes the cancellation process to occur at the location this function is called. If there are no cancellations pending, then the function continues to execute with no repercussions. This function call can be placed at any location in the code where it is considered safe to terminate the thread.

Synopsis

```
#include <pthread.h>

void pthread_testcancel(void);
```

Program 4.3 contains functions that use the `pthread_setcancel-state()`, `pthread_setcanceltype()`, and `pthread_testcancel()` functions. Program 4.3 shows three functions setting their cancelability types and states.

```
// Program 4.3

#include <iostream>
#include <pthread.h>


void *task1(void *X)
{
    int OldState;

    // disable cancelability
    pthread_setcancelstate(PTHREAD_CANCEL_DISABLE,&OldState);
```

```
   for(int Count = 1;Count < 100;Count++)
   {
      cout << "thread A is working: " << Count << endl;

   }

}

void *task2(void *X)
{
   int OldState,OldType;

   // enable cancelability, asynchronous
   pthread_setcancelstate(PTHREAD_CANCEL_ENABLE,&OldState);
   pthread_setcanceltype(PTHREAD_CANCEL_ASYNCHRONOUS,&OldType);

   for(int Count = 1;Count < 100;Count++)
   {
      cout << "thread B is working: " << Count << endl;

   }

}


void *task3(void *X)
{
   int OldState,OldType;

   // enable cancelability, deferred
   pthread_setcancelstate(PTHREAD_CANCEL_ENABLE,&OldState);
   pthread_setcanceltype(PTHREAD_CANCEL_DEFERRED,&OldType);

   for(int Count = 1;Count < 1000;Count++)
   {
     cout << "thread C is working: " << Count << endl;
     if((Count%100) == 0){
        pthread_testcancel();
     }

   }

}
```

In Program 4.3, each task has set its cancelability condition. In `task1`, the cancelability of the thread has been disabled. What follows is critical code that must be executed. In `task2`, the cancelability of the thread is enabled. A call to the `pthread_setcancelstate()` is unnecessary because all new threads have an enabled cancelability state. The cancelability type is set to `PTHREAD_CANCEL_ASYNCHRONOUS`. This means whenever a cancel request is issued, the thread will start its cancellation process immediately, regardless of where it is in its execution. Therefore, it should not be executing any vital code once this type is activated. If it is making any system calls, they should be cancellation-safe functions (discussed later). In `task2`, the loop iterates until the cancel request is issued. In `task3`, the cancelability of the thread is also enabled and the cancellation type is `PTHREAD_CANCEL_DEFFERED`. This is the default state and type of a newly created thread, therefore, calls to the `pthread_setcancelstate()` and `pthread_setcanceltype()` are unnecessary. Critical code can be executed after the state and type are set because the termination will not take place until the `pthread_testcancel()` function is called. If there is no request pending, then the thread will continue executing until, if any, calls to `pthread_testcancel()` are made. In `task3`, the `pthread_cancel()` function is called whenever `Count` is evenly divisible by `100`. Code between cancellation points should not be critical because it may not execute.

Program 4.4 shows the boss thread that issues the cancellation request for each thread.

```
// Program 4.4

int main(int argc, char *argv[])
{
    pthread_t Threads[3];
    void *Status;

    pthread_create(&(Threads[0]),NULL,task1,NULL);
    pthread_create(&(Threads[1]),NULL,task2,NULL);
    pthread_create(&(Threads[2]),NULL,task3,NULL);

    pthread_cancel(Threads[0]);
    pthread_cancel(Threads[1]);
    pthread_cancel(Threads[2]);

    for(int Count = 0;Count < 3;Count++)
    {
        pthread_join(Threads[Count],&Status);
```

```
    if(Status == PTHREAD_CANCELED){
        cout << "thread" << Count << " has been canceled" << endl;
    }
    else{
            cout << "thread" << Count << " has survived" << endl;
    }
  }
  return (0);
}
```

The boss thread in Program 4.4 creates three threads, then it issues a cancellation request for each thread. The boss thread calls the `pthread_join()` function for each thread. The `pthread_join()` function does not fail if it attempts to join with a thread that has already been terminated. The join function just retrieves the exit status of the terminated thread. This is good because the thread that issues the cancellation request may be a different thread than the thread that calls `pthread_join()`. Monitoring the work of all the worker threads may be the sole task of a single thread that also cancels threads. Another thread may examine the exit status of threads by calling the `pthread_join()` function. This type of information may be used to statistically evaluate which threads have the best performance. In this program, the boss thread joins and examines each exit thread's exit status in a loop. `Thread[0]` was not canceled because its cancelability was disabled. The other two threads were canceled. A canceled thread may return an exit status, for example, PTHREAD_CANCELED. Program Profile 4.2 contains the profile for Programs 4.3 and 4.4.

Program Profile 4.2

Program Name
program4-34.cc

Description
Demonstrates the use of thread cancellation. Three threads have different cancellation types and states. Each thread executes a loop. The cancellation state and type determines the number of loop iterations or whether the loop is executed at all. The primary thread examines the exit status of each thread.

Libraries Required
libpthread

Headers Required
`<pthread.h> <iostream>`

Compile and Link Instructions
`c++ -o program4-34 program4-34.cc -lpthread`

Test Environment
SuSE Linux 7.1, gcc 2.95.2,

Execution Instructions
`./program4-34`

Cancellation points marked by a call to the `pthread_testcancel()` function are used in user-defined functions. The Pthread library defines the execution of other functions as cancellation points. These functions block the calling thread and while blocked the thread is safe to be canceled. These are the Pthread library functions that act as cancellation points:

```
pthread_testcancel()
pthread_cond_wait()
pthread_timedwait
pthread_join()
```

If a thread with a deferred cancelability state has a cancellation request pending when making a call to one of these Pthread library functions, the cancellation process will be initiated. As far as system calls, Table 4–6 lists some of the system calls required to be cancellation points.

While these functions are safe for deferred cancellation, they may not be safe for asynchronous cancellation. An asynchronous cancellation during a library call that is not an asynchronously safe function may cause library data to be left in an incompatible state. The library may have allocated memory on behalf of the thread and when the thread is canceled, may still have a hold on that memory. For other library and systems functions that are not cancellation safe (asynchronously or deferred), it may be necessary to write code preventing a thread from terminating by disabling cancellation or deferring cancellation until after the function call has returned.

4.9.1.2   Cleaning Up Before Termination

Once the thread concedes to cancellation, it may need to perform some final processing before it is terminated. The thread may have to close files, reset shared resources to some consistent state, release locks, or deallocate re-

Table 4–6   POSIX System Calls Required to be Cancellation Points

POSIX System Calls (Cancellation Points)

accept()	nanosleep()	sem_wait()
aio_suspend()	open()	send()
clock_nanosleep()	pause()	sendmsg()
close()	poll()	sendto()
connect()	pread()	sigpause()
creat()	pthread_cond_timedwait()	sigsuspend()
fcntl()	pthread_cond_wait()	sigtimedwait()
fsync()	pthread_join()	sigwait()
getmsg()	putmsg()	sigwaitinfo()
lockf()	putpmsg()	sleep()
mq_receive()	pwrite()	system()
mq_send()	read()	usleep()
mq_timedreceive()	readv()	wait()
mq_timedsend()	recvfrom()	waitpid()
msgrcv()	recvmsg()	write()
msgsnd()	select()	writev()
msync()	sem_timedwait()	

sources. The Pthread library defines a mechanism for each thread to perform last-minute tasks before terminating. A cleanup stack is associated with every thread. The stack contains pointers to routines that are to be executed during the cancellation process. The pthread_cleanup_push() function pushes a pointer to the routine onto the cleanup stack.

Synopsis

```
#include <pthread.h>

void pthread_cleanup_push(void (*routine)(void *), void *arg);
void pthread_cleanup_pop(int execute);
```

The `routine` parameter is a pointer to the function to be pushed onto the stack. The `arg` parameter is passed to the function. The function `routine` is called with the `arg` parameter when the thread exits by calling `pthread_exit()`, when the thread concedes to a termination request, or when the thread explicitly calls the `pthread_cleanup_pop()` function with a nonzero value for `execute`. The function does not return.

The `pthread_cleanup_pop()` function removes `routine`'s pointer from the top of the calling thread's cleanup stack. The `execute` parameter can have a value of `1` or `0`. If the value is `1`, the thread executes `routine` even if it is not being terminated. The thread continues execution from the point after the call to this function. If the value is `0`, the pointer is removed from the top of the stack without executing.

It is required for each push there be a pop within the same lexical scope. For example, `funcA()` requires a cleanup handler to be executed when the function exits or cancels:

```
void *funcA(void *X)
{
    int *Tid;
    Tid = new int;
    // do some work
    //...
    pthread_cleanup_push(cleanup_funcA,Tid);
    // do some more work
    //...
    pthread_cleanup_pop(0);
}
```

Here, `funcA()` pushes cleanup handler `cleanup_funcA()` onto the cleanup stack by calling the `pthread_cleanup_push()` function. The `pthread_cleanup_pop()` function is required for each call to the `pthread_cleanup_push()` function. The pop function is passed `0`, which means the handler is removed from the cleanup stack but is not executed at this point. The handler *will* be executed if the thread that executes `funcA()` is canceled.

The `funcB()` also requires a cleanup handler:

```
void *funcB(void *X)
{
    int *Tid;
    Tid = new int;
    // do some work
    //...
    pthread_cleanup_push(cleanup_funcB,Tid);
```

```
   // do some more work
   //...
   pthread_cleanup_pop(1);
}
```

Here, `funcB()` pushes cleanup handler `cleanup_funcB()` onto the cleanup stack. The difference in this case is the `pthread_cleanup_pop()` function is passed 1, which means the handler is removed from the cleanup stack but will execute at this point. The handler *will* be executed regardless of whether the thread that executes `funcA()` is canceled or not. The cleanup handlers, `cleanup_funcA()` and `cleanup_funcB()`, are regular functions that can be used to close files, release resources, unlock mutexes, and so on.

4.9.2   *Managing the Thread's Stack*

The address space of a process is divided into the text and static data segments, free store, and the stack segment. The location and size of the thread's stacks are cut out of the stack segment of the process. A thread's stack will store a stack frame for each routine it has called but has not exited. The stack frame contains temporary variables, local variables, return addresses, and any other additional information the thread needs to find its way back to previously executing routines. Once the routine is exited, the stack frame for that routine is removed from the stack. Figure 4–12 shows how stack frames are placed onto a stack.

In Figure 4–12, Thread A executes Task 1. Task 1 creates some local variables, does some processing, then calls Task X. A stack frame is created for Task 1 and placed on the stack. Task X does some processing, creates local variables, then calls Task C. A stack frame for Task X is placed on the stack. Task C calls Task Y, and so on. Each stack must be large enough to accommodate the execution of each thread's function along with the chain of routines that will be called. The size and location of a thread's stack are managed by the operating system but they can be set or examined by several methods defined by the attribute object.

The `pthread_attr_getstacksize()` function returns the default stack size minimum. The `attr` parameter is the thread attribute object from which the default stack size is extracted. When the function returns, the default stack size, expressed in bytes, is stored in the `stacksize` parameter and the return value is 0. If not successful, the function returns an error number.

The `pthread_attr_setstacksize()` function sets the stack size minimum. The `attr` parameter is the thread attribute object for which the stack

PROCESS'S ADDRESS SPACE

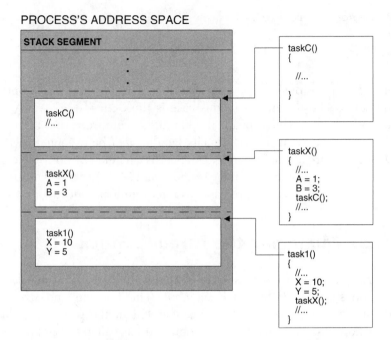

Figure 4-12   Stack frames generated from a thread.

size is set. The stacksize parameter is the minimum size of the stack expressed in bytes. If the function is successful, the return value is 0. If not successful, the function returns an error number. The function will fail if stacksize is less than PTHREAD_MIN_STACK or exceeds the system minimum. The PTHREAD_STACK_MIN will probably be a lower minimum than the default stack minimum returned by pthread_attr_getstacksize(). Consider the value returned by the pthread_attr_getstacksize() before raising the minimum size of a thread's stack. A stack's size is fixed so the stack's growth during runtime will only be within the fixed space of the stack set at compile time.

Synopsis

```
#include <pthread.h>

void pthread_attr_getstacksize(const pthread_attr_t *restrict attr,
                               void **restrict stacksize);
void pthread_attr_setstacksize(pthread_attr_t *attr, void *stacksize);
```

The location of the thread's stack can be set and retrieved by the `pthread_attr_setstackaddr()` and `pthread_attr_getstackaddr()` functions. The `pthread_attr_setstackaddr()` function sets the base location of the stack to the address specified by the parameter `stackattr` for the thread created with the thread attribute object `attr`. This address `addr` should be within the virtual address space of the process. The size of the stack will be at least equal to the minimum stack size specified by `PTHREAD_STACK_MIN`. If successful, the function will return 0. If not successful, the function will return an error number.

The `pthread_attr_getstackaddr()` function retrieves the base location of the stack address for the thread created with the thread attribute object specified by the parameter `attr`. The address is returned and stored in the parameter `stackaddr`. If successful, the function will return 0. If not successful, the function will return an error number.

Synopsis

```
#include <pthread.h>

void pthread_attr_setstackaddr(pthread_attr_t *attr, void *stackaddr);
void pthread_attr_getstackaddr(const pthread_attr_t *restrict attr,
                               void **restrict stackaddr);
```

The stack attributes (size and location) can be set by a single function. The `pthread_attr_setstack()` function sets both the stack size and stack location of a thread created using the specified attribute object `attr`. The base location of the stack will be set to the `stackaddr` parameter and the size of the stack will be set to the `stacksize` parameter. The `pthread_attr_getstack()` function retrieves the stack size and stack location of a thread created using the specified attribute object `attr`. If successful, the stack location will be stored in the `stackaddr` parameter and the stack size will be stored in the `stacksize` parameter. If successful, these functions will return 0. If not successful, an error number is returned. The `pthread_setstack()` function will fail if the `stacksize` is less than `PTHREAD_STACK_MIN` or exceeds some implementation-defined limit.

Synopsis

```
#include <pthread.h>

void pthread_attr_setstack(pthread_attr_t *attr, void *stackaddr,
                           size_t stacksize);
void pthread_attr_getstack(const pthread_attr_t *restrict attr,
                           void **restrict stackaddr, size_t stacksize);
```

Example 4.3 sets the stack size of a thread using a thread attribute object.

```
// Example 4.3. Changing the stack size of a thread
//              using an offset.

//...

pthread_attr_getstacksize(&SchedAttr,&DefaultSize);
if(DefaultSize < Min_Stack_Req){
   SizeOffset = Min_Stack_Req - DefaultSize;
   NewSize = DefaultSize + SizeOffset;
   pthread_attr_setstacksize(&Attr1,(size_t)NewSize);
}
```

In Example 4.3, the thread attribute object retrieves the default size from the attribute object then determines whether the default size is less than the minimum stack size desired. If so, the offset is calculated then added to the default stack size. This becomes the new minimun stack size for this thread.

NOTE: Setting the stack size and stack location may cause your program to be nonportable. The stack size and location you set for your program on one platform may not match the stack size and location of another platform.

4.9.3   *Setting Thread Scheduling and Priorities*

Like processes, threads execute independently. Each thread is assigned to a processor in order to execute the task it has been given. Each thread is assigned a scheduling policy and priority that dictates how and when it is assigned to a processor. The scheduling policy and priority of a thread or group of threads can be set by an attribute object using these functions:

```
pthread_attr_setinheritsched()
pthread_attr_setschedpolicy()
pthread_attr_setschedparam()
```

These functions can be used to return scheduling information about the thread:

```
pthread_attr_getinheritsched()
pthread_attr_getschedpolicy()
pthread_attr_getschedparam()
```

Synopsis

```
#include <pthread.h>
#include <sched.h>

void pthread_attr_setinheritsched(pthread_attr_t *attr,
                            int inheritsched);
void pthread_attr_setschedpolicy(pthread_attr_t *attr, int policy);
void pthread_attr_setschedparam(pthread_attr_t *restrict
                        attr, const struct sched_param
                        *restrict param);
```

The `pthread_attr_setinheritsched()`, `pthread_attr_setsched-policy()`, and `pthread_attr_setschedparam()` are used together to set the scheduling policy and priority of a thread. The `pthread_attr_set-inheritsched()` function is used to determine how the thread's scheduling attributes will be set, either by inheriting the scheduling attributes from the creator thread or from an attribute object. The `inheritsched` parameter can have one of these values:

PTHREAD_INHERIT_SCHED   Thread scheduling attributes shall be inherited from the creator thread and any scheduling attributes of the `attr` parameter will be ignored.

PTHREAD_EXPLICIT_SCHED Thread scheduling attributes shall be set to the scheduling attributes of the attribute object `attr`.

If the `inheritsched` parameter value is `PTHREAD_EXPLICIT_SCHED`, then the `pthread_attr_setschedpolicy()` function is used to set the scheduling policy and the `pthread_attr_setschedparam()` function is used to set the priority.

The `pthread_attr_setschedpolicy()` function sets the scheduling policy of the thread attribute object `attr`. The policy parameter values can be one of the following defined in the `<sched.h>` header:

`SCHED_FIFO`	First-In-First-Out scheduling policy where the executing thread runs to completion.
`SCHED_RR`	Round-robin scheduling policy where each thread is assigned to a processor only for a time slice.
`SCHED_OTHER`	Other scheduling policy (implementation-defined). By default, this is the scheduling policy of any newly created thread.

The `pthread_attr_setschedparam()` function is used to set the scheduling parameters of the attribute object `attr` used by the scheduling policy. The `param` parameter is a structure that contains the parameters. The `sched_param` structure has at least this data member defined:

```
struct sched_param {
   int sched_priority;
   //...
};
```

It may also have additional data members along with several functions that return and set the priority minimum, maximum, scheduler, paramaters, and so on. If the scheduling policy is either `SCHED_FIFO` or `SCHED_RR`, then the only member required to have a value is `sched_priority`.

To obtain the maximum and minimum priority values, use the `sched_get_priority_min()` and `sched_get_priority_max()` functions.

Synopsis

```
#include <sched.h>

int sched_get_priority_max(int policy);
int sched_get_priority_min(int policy);
```

Both functions are passed the scheduling policy `policy` for which the priority values are requested and both will return either the maximum or minimum priority values for the scheduling policy.

Example 4.4 shows how to set the scheduling policy and priority of a thread by using the thread attribute object.

```
// Example 4.4 Using the thread attribute object to set the
//              scheduling policy and priority of a thread.

//...
#define Min_Stack_Req 3000000

pthread_t ThreadA;
pthread_attr_t SchedAttr;
size_t DefaultSize,SizeOffset,NewSize;
int MinPriority,MaxPriority,MidPriority;
sched_param SchedParam;

int main(int argc, char *argv[])
{
   //...
   // initialize attribute object
   pthread_attr_init(&SchedAttr);

   // retrieve min and max priority values for scheduling policy
   MinPriority = sched_get_priority_max(SCHED_RR);
   MaxPriority = sched_get_priority_min(SCHED_RR);

   // calculate priority value
   MidPriority = (MaxPriority + MinPriority)/2;

   // assign priority value to sched_param structure
   SchedParam.sched_priority = MidPriority;

   // set attribute object with scheduling parameter
   pthread_attr_setschedparam(&Attr1,&SchedParam);

   // set scheduling attributes to be determined by attribute object
   pthread_attr_setinheritsched(&Attr1,PTHREAD_EXPLICIT_SCHED);

   // set scheduling policy
   pthread_attr_setschedpolicy(&Attr1,SCHED_RR);

   // create thread with scheduling attribute object
   pthread_create(&ThreadA,&Attr1,task2,Value);
}
```

In Example 4.4, the scheduling policy and priority of ThreadA is set using the thread attribute object SchedAttr. This is done in eight steps:

1. Initialize attribute object.
2. Retrieve min and max priority values for scheduling policy.
3. Calculate priority value.
4. Assign priority value to sched_param structure.
5. Set attribute object with sceduling parameter.
6. Set scheduling attributes to be determined by attribute object.
7. Set scheduling policy.
8. Create thread with scheduling attribute object.

With this method, the scheduling policy and priority is set before the thread is running. In order to dynamically change the scheduling policy and priority, use the pthread_setschedparam() and pthread_setsched-prio() functions.

Synopsis

```
#include <pthread.h>

int pthread_setschedparam(pthread_t thread, int policy,
                          const struct sched_param *param);
int pthread_getschedparam(pthread_t thread, int *restrict policy,
                          struct sched_param *restrict param);
int pthread_setschedprio(pthread_t thread, int prio);
```

The pthread_setschedparam() function sets both the scheduling policy and priority of a thread directly without the use of an attribute object. The thread parameter is the id of the thread, policy is the new scheduling policy, and param contains the scheduling priority. The pthread_getschedparam() function shall return the scheduling policy and scheduling parameters and store their values in policy and param parameters, respectively, if successful. If successful, both functions will return 0. If not successful, both functions will return an error number. Table 4–7 lists the conditions in which these functions may fail.

The pthread_setschedprio() function is used to set the scheduling priority of an executing thread whose thread id is specified by the thread para-

Table 4–7 Conditions in Which the Scheduling Policy and Priority Functions May Fail	
Pthread Scheduling and Priority Functions	*Failure Conditions*

`int pthread_getschedparam`
`(pthread_t thread,`
` int *restrict policy,`
` struct sched_param`
` *restrict param);`
	• The `thread` parameter does not refer to an existing thread.

`int pthread_setschedparam`
`(pthread_t thread,`
` int *policy,`
` const struct sched_param`
` *param);`
	• The `policy` parameter or one of the scheduling parameters associated with the `policy` parameter is invalid.
	• The `policy` parameter or one of the scheduling paramaters has a value that is not supported.
	• The calling thread does not have the appropriate permission to set the scheduling parameters or policy of the specified thread.
	• The `thread` parameter does not refer to an existing thread.
	• The implementation does not allow the application to change one of the parameters to the specified value.

`int pthread_setschedprio`
`(pthread_t thread,`
` int prio);`
	• The `prio` parameter is invalid for the scheduling policy of the specified thread.
	• The priority parameter has a value that is not supported.
	• The calling thread does not have the appropriate permission to set the scheduling priority of the specified thread.
	• The `thread` parameter does not refer to an existing thread.
	• The implementation does not allow the application to change the priority to the specified value.

meter. The scheduling priority of the thread will be changed to the value specified by `prio`. If the function fails, the priority of the thread will not be changed. If successful, the function will return `0`. If not successful, an error number is returned. The conditions in which this function fails are also listed in Table 4–7.

NOTE: Remember to carefully consider why it is necessary to change the scheduling policy or priority of a running thread. This may diversely affect the overall performance of your application. Threads with higher priority preempt running threads with lower priority. This may lead to starvation, or a thread constantly being preempted and therefore not able to complete execution.

4.9.3.1   Setting Contention Scope of a Thread

The contention scope of the thread determines which set of threads with the same scheduling policy and priority, the thread will compete for processor usage. The contention scope of a thread is set by the thread attribute object.

Synopsis

```
#include <pthread.h>

int pthread_attr_setscope(pthread_attr_t *attr, int contentionscope);
int pthread_attr_getscope(const pthread_attr_t *restrict attr,
                   int *restrict contentionscope);
```

The pthread_attr_setscope() function sets the contention scope attribute of the thread attribute object specified by the parameter attr. The contention scope of the thread attribute object will be set to the value stored in the contentionscope parameter. The contentionscope parameter can have the values:

PTHREAD_SCOPE_SYSTEM   System scheduling contention scope

PTHREAD_SCOPE_PROCESS   Process scheduling contention scope

The pthread_attr_getscope() function returns the contention scope attribute from the thread attribute object specified by the parameter attr. If successful, the contention scope of the thread attribute object will be returned and stored in the contentionscope parameter. Both functions return 0 if successful and an error number otherwise.

4.9.4 *Using* `sysconf()`

It is important to know the thread resource limits of your system in order for your application to appropriately manage its resources. For example, the maximum number of threads per process places an upper bound on the number of worker threads that can be created for a process. The `sysconf()` function is used to return the current value of configurable system limits or options.

Synopsis

```
#include <unistd.h>
#include <limits.h>


int sysconf(int name);
```

The `name` parameter is the system variable to be queried. What is returned is the POSIX IEEE Std. 1003.1-2001 values for the system variable queried. These values can be compared to the constants defined by your implementation of the standard to see how compliant they are. There are several variables and constant counterparts concerned with threads, processes, and semaphores, some of which are listed in Table 4–8.

The `sysconf()` function will return -1 and set `errno` to indicate an error has occurred if the parameter name is not valid. The variable may have no limit defined and may return -1 as a valid return value. In that case, `errno` will not be set. No defined limit does not mean there is an infinite limit. It simply indicates that no maximum limit is defined and higher limits are supported depending upon the system resources available.

Here is an example of a call to the `sysconf()` function:

```
if(PTHREAD_STACK_MIN == (sysconf(_SC_THREAD_STACK_MIN))){
    //...
}
```

The constant value of `PTHREAD_STACK_MIN` is compared to the `_SC_THREAD_STACK_MIN` value returned by the `sysconf()` function.

Table 4–8   Systems Variables and Their Corresponding Symbolic Constants

Variable	Name Value	Description
_SC_THREADS	_POSIX_THREADS	Supports threads.
_SC_THREAD_ATTR_STACKADDR	_POSIX_THREAD_ATTR_STACKADDR	Supports thread stack address attribute.
_SC_THREAD_ATTR_STACKSIZE	_POSIX_THREAD_ATTR_STACKSIZE	Supports thread stack size attribute.
_SC_THREAD_STACK_MIN	PTHREAD_STACK_MIN	Minimum size of thread stack storage in bytes.
_SC_THREAD_THREADS_MAX	PTHREAD_THREADS_MAX	Maximum number of threads per process.
_SC_THREAD_KEYS_MAX	PTHREAD_KEYS_MAX	Maximum number of keys per process.
_SC_THREAD_PRIO_INHERIT	_POSIX_THREAD_PRIO_INHERIT	Supports priority inheritance option.
_SC_THREAD_PRIO	_POSIX_THREAD_PRIO_	Supports thread priority option.
_SC_THREAD_PRIORITY_SCHEDULING	_POSIX_THREAD_PRIORITY_SCHEDULING	Supports thread priority scheduling option.
_SC_THREAD_PROCESS_SHARED	_POSIX_THREAD_PROCESS_SHARED	Supports process-shared synchronization.
_SC_THREAD_SAFE_FUNCTIONS	_POSIX_THREAD_SAFE_FUNCTIONS	Supports thread-safe functions.
_SC_THREAD_DESTRUCTOR_ITERATIONS	_PTHREAD_THREAD_DESTRUCTOR_ITERATIONS	Determines the number of attempts made to destroy thread-specific data on thread exit.
_SC_CHILD_MAX	CHILD_MAX	Maximum number of processes allowed to a UID.
_SC_PRIORITY_SCHEDULING	_POSIX_PRIORITY_SCHEDULING	Supports process scheduling.
_SC_REALTIME_SIGNALS	_POSIX_REALTIME_SIGNALS	Supports real-time signals.
_SC_XOPEN_REALTIME_THREADS	_XOPEN_REALTIME_THREADS	Supports X/Open POSIX real-time threads feature group.
_SC_STREAM_MAX	STREAM_MAX	Determines the number of streams one process can have open at a time.
_SC_SEMAPHORES	_POSIX_SEMAPHORES	Supports semaphores.

Variable	Name Value	Description
_SC_SEM_NSEMS_MAX	SEM_NSEMS_MAX	Determines the maximum number of semaphores a process may have.
_SC_SEM_VALUE_MAX	SEM_VALUE_MAX	Determines the maximum value a semaphore may have.
_SC_SHARED_MEMORY _OBJECTS	_POSIX_SHARED_MEMORY _OBJECTS	Supports shared memory objects.

Table 4–8   (Continued)

4.9.5   Managing a Critical Section

Concurrently executing processes, or threads within the same process, can share data structures, variables, or data. Sharing global memory allows the processes or threads to communicate or share access to data. With multiple processes, the shared global memory is external to the processes that the processes in question have access. This data structure can be used to transfer data or commands among the processes. When threads need to communicate, they can access data structures or variables that are part of the same process to which they belong.

Whether there are processes or threads accessing shared modifiable data, the data structures, variables, or data is in a critical region or section of the processes' or threads' code. A critical section in the code is where the thread or process is accessing and processing the shared block of modifiable memory. Classifying a section of code as a critical section can be used to control race conditions. For example, in a program two threads, thread A and thread B, are used to perform a multiple keyword search through all the files located on a system. Thread A searches each directory for text files and writes the paths to a list data structure TextFiles then increments a FileCount variable. Thread B extracts the filenames from the list TextFiles, decrements the FileCount, then searches the file for the multiple keywords. The file that contains the keywords is written to a file and another variable, FoundCount, is incremented. FoundCount is not shared with thread A. Threads A and B can be executed simultaneously on separate processors. Thread A executes until all directories have been searched while thread B searches each file extracted from TextFiles. The list is maintained in sorted order and can be requested to display its contents any time.

A number of problems can crop up. For example, thread B may attempt to extract a filename from `TextFiles` before thread A has added a filename to `TextFiles`. Thread B may attempt to decrement `SearchCount` before thread A has incremented `SearchCount` or both may attempt to modify the variable simultaneously. Also `TextFiles` may be sorting its elements while thread A is simultaneously attempting to write a filename to it or thread B is simultaneously attempting to extract a filename from it. These problems are examples of race conditions in which two or more threads or processes are attempting to modify the same block of shared memory simultaneously.

When threads or processes are simply simultaneously reading the same block of memory, race conditions do not occur. Race conditions occur when multiple processes or threads are simultaneously accessing the same block of memory with at least one of the threads or processes attempting to modify the block of memory. The section of code becomes critical when there are simultaneous attempts to change the same block of memory. One way to protect the critical section is to only allow exclusive access to the block of memory. Exclusive access means one process or thread will have access to the shared block of memory for a short period while all other processes or threads are prevented (blocked) from entering their critical section where they are accessing the same block of memory.

A locking mechanism, like a mutex semaphore, can be used to control race condition. A mutex, short for "mutual exclusion," is used to block off a critical section. The mutex is locked before entering the critical section then unlocked when exiting the critical section:

```
lock mutex
   // enter critical section
   // access shared modifiable memory
   // exit critical section
unlock mutex
```

The `pthread_mutex_t` models a mutex object. Before the `pthread_mutex_t` object can be used, it must first be initialized. The `pthread_mutex_init()` initializes the mutex. Once initialized the mutex can be locked, unlocked, and destroyed with the `pthread_mutex_lock()`, `pthread_mutex_unlock()`, and `pthread_mutex_destroy()` functions. Program 4.5 contains the function that searches a system for text files. Program 4.6 contains the function that searches each text file for specified keywords. Each function is executed by a thread. Program 4.7 contains the primary thread. These programs implement the producer-consumer model for thread delegation. Program 4.5 contains the producer thread and Program 4.6 contains the consumer thread. The critical sections are bolded.

```
// Program 4.5

 1  int isDirectory(string FileName)
 2  {
 3    struct stat StatBuffer;
 4
 5    lstat(FileName.c_str(),&StatBuffer);
 6    if((StatBuffer.st_mode & S_IFDIR) == -1)
 7    {
 8       cout << "could not get stats on file" << endl;
 9       return (0);
10    }
11    else{
12          if(StatBuffer.st_mode & S_IFDIR){
13              return (1);
14          }
15    }
16    return (0);
17  }
18
19
20  int isRegular(string FileName)
21  {
22    struct stat StatBuffer;
23
24    lstat(FileName.c_str(),&StatBuffer);
25    if((StatBuffer.st_mode & S_IFDIR) == -1)
26    {
27       cout << "could not get stats on file" << endl;
28       return (0);
29    }
30    else{
31          if(StatBuffer.st_mode & S_IFREG){
32              return (1);
33          }
34    }
35    return (0);
36  }
37
38
39  void depthFirstTraversal(const char *CurrentDir)
40  {
```

```
41   DIR *DirP;
42   string Temp;
43   string FileName;
44   struct dirent *EntryP;
45   chdir(CurrentDir);
46   cout << "Searching Directory: " << CurrentDir << endl;
47   DirP = opendir(CurrentDir);
48
49   if(DirP == NULL){
50      cout << "could not open file" << endl;
51      return;
52   }
53   EntryP = readdir(DirP);
54   while(EntryP != NULL)
55   {
56      Temp.erase();
57      FileName.erase();
58      Temp = EntryP->d_name;
59      if((Temp != ".") && (Temp != "..")){
60         FileName.assign(CurrentDir);
61         FileName.append(1,'/');
62         FileName.append(EntryP->d_name);
63         if(isDirectory(FileName)){
64            string NewDirectory;
65            NewDirectory = FileName;
66            depthFirstTraversal(NewDirectory.c_str());
67         }
68         else{
69                if(isRegular(FileName)){
70                   int Flag;
71                   Flag = FileName.find(".cpp");
72                   if(Flag > 0){
73                      pthread_mutex_lock(&CountMutex);
74                      FileCount++;
75                      pthread_mutex_unlock(&CountMutex);
76                      pthread_mutex_lock(&QueueMutex);
77                      TextFiles.push(FileName);
78                      pthread_mutex_unlock(&QueueMutex);
79                   }
80                }
81         }
82
83      }
84      EntryP = readdir(DirP);
85   }
```

```
86    closedir(DirP);
87  }
88
89
90
91  void *task(void *X)
92  {
93    char *Directory;
94    Directory = static_cast<char *>(X);
95    depthFirstTraversal(Directory);
96    return(NULL);
97
98  }
```

Program 4.6 contains the consumer thread that performs the search.

```
// Program 4.6

 1  void *keySearch(void *X)
 2  {
 3    string Temp, Filename;
 4    less<string> Comp;
 5
 6    while(!Keyfile.eof() && Keyfile.good())
 7    {
 8       Keyfile >> Temp;
 9       if(!Keyfile.eof()){
10          KeyWords.insert(Temp);
11       }
12    }
13    Keyfile.close();
14
15    while(TextFiles.empty())
16    { }
17
18    while(!TextFiles.empty())
19    {
20       pthread_mutex_lock(&QueueMutex);
21       Filename = TextFiles.front();
22       TextFiles.pop();
23       pthread_mutex_unlock(&QueueMutex);
24       Infile.open(Filename.c_str());
25       SearchWords.erase(SearchWords.begin(),SearchWords.end());
```

```
26
27      while(!Infile.eof() && Infile.good())
28      {
29          Infile >> Temp;
30          SearchWords.insert(Temp);
31      }
32
33      Infile.close();
34      if(includes(SearchWords.begin(),SearchWords.end(),
            KeyWords.begin(),KeyWords.end(),Comp)){
35          Outfile << Filename << endl;
36          pthread_mutex_lock(&CountMutex);
37          FileCount--;
38          pthread_mutex_unlock(&CountMutex);
39          FoundCount++;
40      }
41  }
42  return(NULL);
43
44 }
```

Program 4.7 contains the primary thread for producer–consumer threads
in Programs 4.5 and 4.6.

```
// Program 4.7

 1 #include <sys/stat.h>
 2 #include <fstream>
 3 #include <queue>
 4 #include <algorithm>
 5 #include <pthread.h>
 6 #include <iostream>
 7 #include <set>
 8
 9 pthread_mutex_t QueueMutex = PTHREAD_MUTEX_INITIALIZER;
10 pthread_mutex_t CountMutex = PTHREAD_MUTEX_INITIALIZER;
11
12 int FileCount = 0;
13 int FoundCount = 0;
14
15 int keySearch(void);
16 queue<string> TextFiles;
```

```
17  set <string,less<string> >KeyWords;
18  set <string,less<string> >SearchWords;
19  ifstream Infile;
20  ofstream Outfile;
21  ifstream Keyfile;
22  string KeywordFile;
23  string OutFilename;
24  pthread_t Thread1;
25  pthread_t Thread2;
26
27  void depthFirstTraversal(const char *CurrentDir);
28  int isDirectory(string FileName);
29  int isRegular(string FileName);
30
31  int main(int argc, char *argv[])
32  {
33    if(argc != 4){
34      cerr << "need more info" << endl;
35      exit (1);
36    }
37
38    Outfile.open(argv[3],ios::app||ios::ate);
39    Keyfile.open(argv[2]);
40    pthread_create(&Thread1,NULL,task,argv[1]);
41    pthread_create(&Thread2,NULL,keySearch,argv[1]);
42    pthread_join(Thread1,NULL);
43    pthread_join(Thread2,NULL);
44    pthread_mutex_destroy(&CountMutex);
45    pthread_mutex_destroy(&QueueMutex);
46
47    cout << argv[1]  << " contains " << FoundCount
            << " files that contains all keywords." << endl;
48    return(0);
49  }
```

With mutexes, one thread at a time is permitted to read from or write to the shared memory. There are other mechanisms and techniques that can be used to ensure thread safety for user-defined functions implementing one of the PRAM models:

EREW (exclusive read and exclusive write)

CREW (concurrent read and exclusive write)

ERCW (exclusive read and concurrent write)

CRCW (concurrent read and concurrent write)

Mutexes are used to implement EREW algorithms, which will be discussed in Chapter 5.

4.10   Thread Safety and Libraries

According to Klieman, Shah, and Smaalders (1996): *"A function or set of functions is said to be thread safe or reentrant when the functions may be called by more than one thread at a time without requiring any other action on the caller's part."* When designing a multithread application, the programmer must be careful to ensure that concurrently executing functions are thread safe. We have already discussed making user-defined functions thread safe but an application often calls functions defined by the system- or a third-party-supplied library. Some of these functions and/or libraries are thread safe where others are not. If the functions are not thread safe, then this means the functions contain one or more of the following: static variables, accesses global data, and/or is not reentrant.

If the function contains static variables, then those variables maintain their values between invocations of the function. The function requires the value of the static variable in order to operate correctly. When concurrent multiple threads invoke this function, then a race condition occurs. If the function modifies a global variable, then multiple threads invoking that function may each attempt to modify that global variable. If multiple concurrent accesses to the global variable are not synchronized, then a race condition can occur here as well. For example, multiple concurrent threads can execute functions that set `errno`. With some of the threads, the function fails and `errno` is set to an error message while other threads execute successfully. Depending on the compiler implementation, `errno` is thread safe. If not, when a thread checks the state of `errno`, which message will it report?

A block of code is considered *reentrant* if the code cannot be changed while in use. Reentrant code avoids race conditions by removing references to global variables and modifiable static data. Therefore, the code can be shared by multiple concurrent threads or processes without a race condition occurring. The POSIX standard defines several functions as reentrant. They are easily identified by a _r attached to the function name of the nonreen-trant counterpart. Some are listed below:

```
getgrgid_r()
getgrnam_r()
getpwuid_r()
sterror_r()
strtok_r()
readdir_r()
rand_r()
ttyname_r()
```

If the function accesses unprotected global variables; contains static, modifiable variables; or is not reentrant, then the function is considered thread unsafe.

System- or third-party-supplied libraries may have different versions of their standard libraries. One version is for single-threaded applications and the other version for multithreaded applications. Whenever a multithreaded environment is anticipated, the programmer should link to these multi-threaded versions of the library. Other environments do not require multi-threaded applications to be linked to the multithreaded version of the library but only require macros to be defined in order for reentrant versions of func-tions to be declared. The application will then be compiled as thread safe.

It is not possible in all cases to use multithreaded versions of functions. In some instances, multithreaded versions of particular functions are not avail-able for a given compiler or environment. Some function's interface cannot be simply made thread safe. In addition, the programmer may be faced with adding threads to an environment that uses functions that were only meant to be used in a single-threaded environment. Under these conditions, in gen-eral use mutexes to wrap all such functions within the program. For example, a program has three concurrently executing threads. Two of the threads, thread1 and thread2, both concurrently execute funcA(), which is not thread safe. The third thread, thread3, executes funcB(). To solve the problem of funcA(), the solution may be to simply wrap access to funcA() by thread1 and thread2 with a mutex:

```
thread1              thread2              thread3
{                    {                    {
    lock()               lock()               funcB()
    funcA()              funcA()          }
    unlock()             unlock()
}                    }
```

If this is done then only one thread accesses `funcA()` at a time. But there is still a problem. If `funcA()` and `funcB()` are both thread-unsafe functions, they may both modify a global or static variable. Although `thread1` and `thread2` are using mutexes with `funcA()`, `thread3` will be executing `funcB()` concurrently with either of these threads. In this situation, a race condition occurs because `funcA()` and `funcB()` may both modify the same global or static variable.

To illustrate another type of race condition when dealing with the `iostream` library, let's say we have two threads, thread A and thread B, sending output to the standard output stream, `cout`. `cout` is an object of type `ostream`. Using inserters, (`>>`), and extractors, (`<<`), invokes the methods of the `cout` object. Are these methods thread safe? If thread A is sending the message "We are intelligent beings" to `stdout` and thread B is sending the message "Humans are illogical beings," will the output be interleaved and produce a message "We are Humans are illogical beings intelligent beings"? In some cases, thread-safe functions are implemented as *atomic* functions. Atomic functions are functions that once they begin to execute cannot be interrupted. In the case of `cout`, if the inserter operation is implemented as atomic, then this interweaving cannot take place. When there are multiple calls to the inserter operation, they will be executed as if they were in serial order. Thread A's message will be displayed, then thread B's, or vice versa, although they invoked the function simultaneously. This is an example of serializing a function or operation in order to make it thread safe. This may not be the only way to make a function thread safe. A function may interweave operations if it has no adverse effect. For example, if a method adds or removes elements to or from a structure that is not sorted and two different threads invoke that method, interweaving their operations will not have an adverse effect.

If it is not known which functions from a library are thread safe and which are not, the programmer has three choices:

- Restrict use of all thread-unsafe functions to a single thread.
- Do not use any of the thread-unsafe functions.
- Wrap all potential thread-unsafe functions within a single set of synchronization mechanisms.

An additional approach is to create interface classes for all thread-unsafe functions that will be used in a multithreaded application. The unsafe functions are encapsulated within an interface class. The interface class can be combined with the appropriate synchronization objects through inheritance or composition. The interface class can be used by the host class through inheritance or composition. The approach eliminates the possibility of race conditions.

4.11   Dividing Your Program into Multiple Threads

Earlier in this chapter we discussed the delegation of work according to a specific strategy or approach called a thread model. Those thread models were:

- delegation (boss–worker)
- peer-to-peer
- pipeline
- producer–consumer

Each model has its own WBS (Work Breakdown Structure) that determines who is responsible for thread creation and under what conditions threads are created. In this section we will show an example of a program for each model using Pthread library functions.

4.11.1   Using the Delegation Model

We discussed two approaches that can be used to implement the delegation approach to dividing a program into threads. To recall, in the *delegation* model, a single thread (boss) creates the threads (workers) and assigns each a task. The boss thread delegates the task each worker thread is to perform by specifying a function. With one approach, the boss thread creates threads as a result of requests made to the system. The boss thread processes each type of request in an event loop. As events occur, thread workers are created and assigned their duties. Example 4.5 shows the event loop in the boss thread and the worker threads in pseudocode.

```
// Example 4.5. Approach 1: Skeleton program of boss and worker
             thread model.

//...
pthread_mutex_t Mutex = PTHREAD_MUTEX_INITIALIZER
int AvailableThreads
pthread_t Thread[Max_Threads]
void decrementThreadAvailability(void)
void incrementThreadAvailability(void)
int threadAvailability(void);


// boss thread
{
   //...
   if(sysconf(_SC_THREAD_THREADS_MAX) > 0){
      AvailableThreads = sysconf(_SC_THREAD_THREADS_MAX)
   }
   else{
         AvailableThreads = Default
   }

   int Count = 1;

   loop while(Request Queue is not empty)
      if(threadAvailability()){
         Count++
         decrementThreadAvailability()
         classify request
         switch(request type)
         {
            case X : pthread_create(&(Thread[Count])...taskX...)
            case Y : pthread_create(&(Thread[Count])...taskY...)
            case Z : pthread_create(&(Thread[Count])...taskZ...)
            //...
         }
      }
      else{
            //free up thread resources
      }
   end loop
}
```

```
void *taskX(void *X)
{
   // process X type request
   incrementThreadAvailability()
   return(NULL)
}

void *taskY(void *Y)
{
   // process Y type request
   incrementThreadAvailability()
   return(NULL)
}

void *taskZ(void *Z)
{
   // process Z type request
   decrementThreadAvailability()
   return(NULL)
}

//...
```

In Example 4.5, the boss thread dynamically creates a thread to process each new request that enters the system, but there are a maximum number of threads that will be created. There are n number of tasks to process n request types. To be sure the maximum number of threads per process will not be exceeded, these additional functions can be defined:

```
threadAvailability()
incrementThreadAvailability()
decrementThreadAvailability()
```

Example 4.6 shows pseudocode for these functions.

```
// Example 4.6  Functions that manage thread availability count.

void incrementThreadAvailability(void)
{
   //...
   pthread_mutex_lock(&Mutex)
   AvailableThreads++
   pthread_mutex_unlock(&Mutex)
}
```

```
void decrementThreadAvailability(void)
{
   //...
   pthread_mutex_lock(&Mutex)
   AvailableThreads—
   pthread_mutex_unlock(&Mutex)
}

int threadAvailability(void)
{
   //...
   pthread_mutex_lock(&Mutex)
   if(AvailableThreads > 1)
      return 1
   else
      return 0
   pthread_mutex_unlock(&Mutex)
}
```

The threadAvailability() function will return 1 if the maximum number of threads allowed per process has not been reached. This function accesses a global variable ThreadAvailability that stores the number of threads still available for the process. The boss thread calls the decrementThreadAvailability() function, which decrements the global variable before the boss thread creates a thread. The worker threads call incrementThreadAvailability(), which increments the global variable before a worker thread exits. Both functions contain a call to pthread_mutex_lock() before accessing the variable and a call to pthread_mutex_unlock() after accessing the global variable. If the maximum number of threads are exceeded, then the boss thread can cancel threads if possible or spawn another process, if necessary. taskX(), taskY(), and taskZ() execute code that processes their type of request.

The other approach to the delegation model is to have the boss thread create a pool of threads that are reassigned new requests instead of creating a new thread per request. The boss thread creates a number of threads during initialization and then each thread is suspended until a request is added to the queue. The boss thread will still contain an event loop to extract requests from the queue. But instead of creating a new thread per request, the boss thread signals the appropriate thread to process the request. Example 4.7 shows the boss thread and the worker threads in pseudocode for this approach to the delegation model.

```
// Example 4.7 Approach 2: Skeleton program of boss and worker thread
             model.

//...

pthread_t Thread[N]

// boss thread
{

    pthread_create(&(Thread[1]...taskX...);
    pthread_create(&(Thread[2]...taskY...);
    pthread_create(&(Thread[3]...taskZ...);
    //...

    loop while(Request Queue is not empty
       get request
       classify request
       switch(request type)
       {
           case X :
                   enqueue request to XQueue
                   signal Thread[1]

           case Y :
                   enqueue request to YQueue
                   signal Thread[2]

           case Z :
                   enqueue request to ZQueue
                   signal Thread[3]
               //...
       }

    end loop
}

void *taskX(void *X)
{
   loop
       suspend until awaken by boss
       loop while XQueue is not empty
          dequeue request
          process request
```

```
          end loop
     until done
}

void *taskY(void *Y)
{
   loop
       suspend until awaken by boss
       loop while YQueue is not empty
          dequeue request
          process request
       end loop
    until done
}

void *taskZ(void *Z)
{
   loop
       suspend until awaken by boss
       loop while (ZQueue is not empty)
          dequeue request
          process request
       end loop
    until done
}

//...
```

In Example 4.7, the boss thread creates N number of threads, one thread for each task to be executed. Each task is associated with processing a request type. In the event loop, the boss thread dequeues a request from the request queue, determines the request type, enqueues the request to the appropriate request queue, then signals the thread that processes the request in that queue. The functions also contain an event loop. The thread is suspended until it receives a signal from the boss that there is a request in its queue. Once awakened, in the inner loop, the thread processes all the requests in the queue until it is empty.

4.11.2   Using the Peer-to-Peer Model

In the *peer-to-peer* model, a single thread initially creates all the threads needed to perform all the tasks called peers. The peer threads process requests from their own input stream. Example 4.8. shows a skeleton program of the peer-to-peer approach of dividing a program into threads.

```
// Example 4.8  Skeleton program using the peer-to-peer model

//...

pthread_t Thread[N]

// initial thread
{

    pthread_create(&(Thread[1]...taskX...);
    pthread_create(&(Thread[2]...taskY...);
    pthread_create(&(Thread[3]...taskZ...);
    //...

  }

void *taskX(void *X)
{
    loop while (Type XRequests are available)
        extract Request
        process request
    end loop
    return(NULL)
}

//...
```

In the peer-to-peer model, each thread is responsible for its own stream of input. The input can be extracted from a database, file, and so on.

4.11.3   Using the Pipeline Model

In the pipeline model, there is a stream of input processed in stages. At each stage, work is performed on a unit of input by a thread. The input continues to move to each stage until the input has completed processing. This approach allows multiple inputs to be processed simultaneously. Each thread is responsible for producing its interim results or output, making them available to the next stage or next thread in the pipeline. Example 4.9 shows the skeleton program for the pipeline model.

```
// Example 4.9 Skeleton program using the pipeline model.

//...
```

```
pthread_t Thread[N]
Queues[N]

// initial thread
{
    place all input into stage1's queue
    pthread_create(&(Thread[1]...stage1...);
    pthread_create(&(Thread[2]...stage2...);
    pthread_create(&(Thread[3]...stage3...);
    //...
  }

void *stageX(void *X)
{
    loop
      suspend until input unit is in queue
      loop while XQueue is not empty
          dequeue input unit
          process input unit
          enqueue input unit into next stage's queue
        end loop
    until done
    return(NULL)
}

//...
```

In Example 4.9, N queues are declared for N stages. The initial thread enqueues all the input into stage 1's queue. The initial thread then creates all the threads needed to execute each stage. Each stage has an event loop. The thread sleeps until an input unit has been enqueued. The inner loop continues to iterate until its queue is empty. The input unit is dequeued, processed, then that unit is then enqueued into the queue of the next stage.

4.11.4   Using the Producer–Consumer Model

In the producer-consumer model, the producer thread *produces* data *consumed* by the consumer thread or threads. The data is stored in a block memory shared between the producer and consumer threads. This model was used in Programs 4.5, 4.6, and 4.7. Example 4.10 shows the skeleton program for the producer-consumer model.

```
// Example 4.10 Skeleton program using the producer-consumer model.

pthread_mutex_t Mutex = PTHREAD_MUTEX_INITIALIZER
pthread_t Thread[2]
Queue

// initial thread
{
    pthread_create(&(Thread[1]...producer...));
    pthread_create(&(Thread[2]...consumer...));
    //...
  }


void *producer(void *X)
{
   loop
      perform work
        pthread_mutex_lock(&Mutex)
          enqueue data
      pthread_mutex_unlock(&Mutex)
          signal consumer
      //...
   until done
}

void *consumer(void *X)
{
   loop
      suspend until signaled
      loop while(Data Queue not empty)
          pthread_mutex_lock(&Mutex)
            dequeue data
        pthread_mutex_unlock(&Mutex)
            perform work
      end loop
   until done
}
```

In Example 4.9, an initial thread creates the producer and consumer threads. The producer thread executes a loop in which it performs work then locks a mutex on the shared queue in order to enqueue the data it has produced. The producer unlocks the mutex then signals the consumer thread that there is data in the queue. The producer iterates through the loop until all work is done. The consumer thread also executes a loop in which it suspends itself until it is signaled. In the inner loop, the consumer thread processes all the data until the queue is empty. It locks the mutex on the shared queue before it dequeues any data and unlocks the mutex after the data has been dequeued. It then performs work on that data. In Program 4.6, the consumer thread enqueues its results to a file. The results could have been inserted into another data structure. This is often done by consumer threads in which it plays both the role of consumer and producer. It plays the role of consumer of the unprocessed data produced by the producer thread, then it plays the role of producer when it processes data stored in another shared queue consumed by another thread.

4.11.5 Creating Multithreaded Objects

The delegation, peer-to-peer, pipeline. and producer–consumer models demonstrate approaches to dividing a program into multiple threads along function lines. When using objects, member functions can create threads to perform multiple tasks. Threads can be used to execute code on behalf of the object: free-floating functions and other member functions.

In either case, the threads are declared within the object and created by one of the member functions (e.g., the constructor). The threads can then execute some free-floating functions (function defined outside the object), which invokes member functions of the object that are global. This is one approach to making an object multithreaded. Example 4.10 contains an example of a multithreaded object.

```
// Example 4.10. Declaration and definition of
//               multithreading an object.

#include <pthread.h>
#include <iostream>
#include <unistd.h>

void *task1(void *);
void *task2(void *);

class multithreaded_object
{
    pthread_t Thread1,Thread2;
public:
```

```cpp
    multithreaded_object(void);
    int c1(void);
    int c2(void);
    //...
};

multithreaded_object::multithreaded_object(void)
{
    //...
    pthread_create(&Thread1,NULL,task1,NULL);
    pthread_create(&Thread2,NULL,task2,NULL);
    pthread_join(Thread1,NULL);
    pthread_join(Thread2,NULL);
    //...

}

int multithreaded_object::c1(void)
{
    // do work
    return(1);
}

int multithreaded_object::c2(void)
{
    // do work
    return(1);
}

multithreaded_object MObj;

void *task1(void *)
{
    //...
    MObj.c1();
    return(NULL);
}

void *task2(void *)
{
    //...
    MObj.c2();
    return(NULL);
}
```

In Example 4.10, the class `multithread_object` declares two threads. From the constructor of the class, the threads are created and joined. `Thread1` executes `task1` and `Thread2` executes `task2`. `task1` and `task2`, then invokes member functions of the global object `MObj`.

Summary

In a sequential program, work can be divided between routines within a program where one task finishes then another task can perform work. With other programs, work is executed as mini-programs within the main program where the mini-programs execute concurrently with the main program. These mini-programs can be executed as processes or threads. With processes, each process has its own address space and requires interprocess communication if the processes are to communicate. Threads sharing the address space of the process do not require special communication techniques between threads of the same process. Synchronization mechanisms such as mutexes are needed to protect share memory in order to control race conditions.

There are several models that can be used to delegate work among threads and manage when threads are created and canceled. In the *delegation* model, a single thread (boss) creates the threads (workers) and assigns each a task. The boss thread waits until each worker thread completes its task. With the *peer-to-peer* model, there is a single thread that initially creates all the threads needed to perform all the tasks; that thread is considered a worker thread and does no delegation. All threads have equal status. The *pipeline* model is characterized as an assembly line in which a stream of items are processed in stages. At each stage, a thread executes work performed on the unit of input. The input moves from one thread to the next, processing it until completion. The last stage or thread produces the result of the pipeline. In the producer–consumer model, there is a producer thread that *produces* data to be *consumed* by the consumer thread. The data is stored in a block of memory shared between the producer and consumer threads. Objects can be made to be multithreaded. The threads are declared within the object. A member function can create a thread that executes a free-floating function that in turn invokes one of the member functions of the object.

The Pthread library can be used to create and manage the threads of a multithreaded application. The Pthread library is based on a standardized programming interface for the creation and maintenance of threads. The thread interface has been specified by the IEEE standards committee in the POSIX 1003.1c standard. Third-party vendors supply an implementation that adheres to the POSIX standard.

Synchronizing Concurrency between Tasks

> "The relation of these mechanisms to time demands careful study.... We are scarcely ever interested in the performance of a communication-engineering machine for a single input. To function adequately, it must give a satisfactory performance for a whole class of inputs, and this means a statistically satisfactory performance for the class of input which it is statistically expected to receive . . ."
>
> —*Norbert Wiener,* Cybernetics

In this Chapter

Coordinating Order of Execution • Synchronizing Access to Data • What are Semaphores? • Synchronization: An Object-Oriented Approach • Summary

With any computer system, resources are limited. There is only so much memory, I/O devices and ports, hardware interrupts, and processors. In an environment of limited hardware resources, an application consisting of multiple processes and threads must compete for memory locations, peripheral devices, and processor time. It is the job of the operating system to determine when the process or thread utilizes system resources and for how long. With preemptive scheduling, the operating system can interrupt the process or thread in order to accommodate all the processes and threads competing for the system resources. Processes and threads must also compete for software and data resources. An example of software resources is shared libraries that provide a common set of services or functions to processes and threads. Other shareable software resources are applications, programs, and utilities. When sharing software resources, only one copy of the program(s) code is brought into memory. Data resources are objects, system data (e.g., environment variables) files, globally defined variables, and data structures. With data resources, it is possible for processes and threads to have their own copy. In other cases, it is desirable and maybe necessary that data is shared. Some processes and threads work together to use the system's limited resources while other processes and threads work independently and asynchronously, competing for the use of the shareable resource. There are several techniques and mechanisms that can be used by the programmer to manage competing processes and threads to share data resources.

Synchronization is also needed to coordinate the order of execution of concurrent tasks. The producer-consumer model discussed in Chapter 4 is a prime example. It is necessary for the producer to execute before the consumer, not necessarily finish before the consumer. Synchronization is required to coordinate these tasks in order for work to progress. Data (*access synchronization*) and task synchronization (*sequence synchronization*) are two types of synchronization required when executing multiple concurrent tasks.

5.1   Coordinating Order of Execution

Let's say we have three threads executing concurrently labeled thread A, thread B, and thread C. All three threads are involved in list processing. The list is to be sorted and searched and the results displayed. Each thread is assigned a task; thread A is to display the results of the search, thread B is to sort the list, and thread C is to search the list. First, the list has to be sorted then multiple concurrent searches can occur on the list. The results of the searches are then displayed. If these threads' tasks are not synchronized properly, thread A may attempt to display results not yet generated that violates the postcondition of the process. The precondition in the list must be sorted prior to searching. If searches start before the list is sorted, the search may generate the wrong results. The three threads require *task synchronization*. Task synchronization enforces preconditions and postconditions of logical processes. Figure 5–1 shows a UML activity diagram for this process.

The thread B's sort must occur first, then forking to the multiple searches spawned by thread C takes place. The threads are then joined and thread A displays the results.

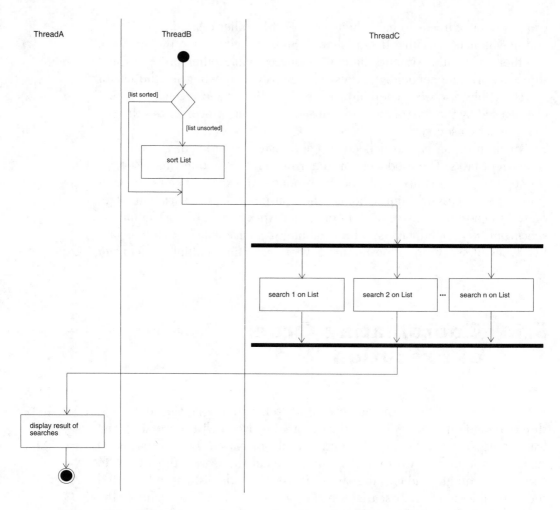

Figure 5–1   Activity diagram for sorting, searching, and displaying the contents of a list.

5.1.1   Relationships between Synchronized Tasks

There are four basic synchronization relationships between any two threads in a single process or between any two processes within a single application: start-to-start (SS), finish-to-start (FS), start-to-finish (SF), and finish-to-finish (FF). These four basic relationships characterize the coordination of

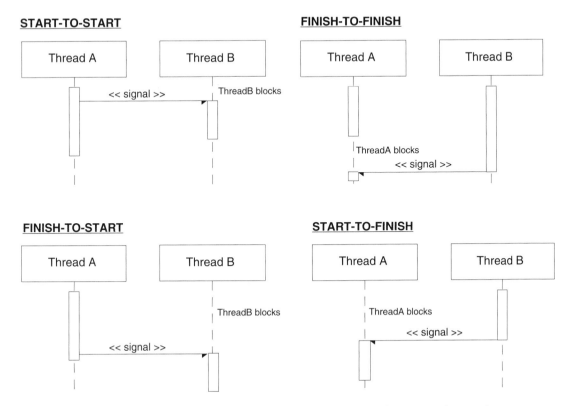

Figure 5–2   The synchronization relationships that can exist between tasks A and B.

work between threads and processes. Figure 5–2 shows activity diagrams for each synchronization relationship.

5.1.2   Start-to-Start (SS) Relationship

In a *start-to-start* synchronization relationship, one task cannot start until another task starts. One task may start before the other but never after. For example, let's say we have a program that implements an avatar. The avatar is a computer-generated talking head. The avatar provides a kind of personality for the software. The program that implements the avatar has several threads. Here, we will focus on thread A, which controls the animation of the mouth and thread B, which controls the sound or voice. We want to give the illusion that the sound and mouth animation are synchronized. Ideally, they should execute at the same precise moment. If multiple processors are involved, both threads may start simultaneously. The threads have a start-to-start relationship. Because of timing conditions, it is allowed that thread A start slightly before thread B (not much before for illusion's sake) but thread B cannot start before thread A. The voice has to wait for the animation. It is not desirable to hear a voice before the mouth animates (unless it is simulating voice dubbing).

5.1.3   Finish-to-Start (FS) Relationship

In a *finish-to-start* synchronization relationship, task A cannot finish until task B starts. This type of relationship is common with parent–child processes. The parent process cannot complete execution of some operation until it spawns a child process or it receives a communication from the child process that it has started its operation. The child process continues to execute once it has signaled the parent or supplied the needed information. The parent process is then free to complete its operation.

5.1.4   Start-to-Finish Relationship

A *start-to-finish* synchronization relationship is the reverse of the finish-to-start relationship. In a *start-to-finish* synchronization relationship, one task cannot start until another task finishes. Task A cannot start execution until task B finishes executing or completes a certain operation. If process A is reading from a pipe connected to process B, process B must first write to the pipe before process A reads from it. Process B must at least complete one operation, writing a single element to the pipe before process A starts. The producer-consumer threads in Chapter 4 are another example of a finish-to-start relationship. The sort-search threads in Figure 5–1 also demonstrate this relationship. The sort thread had to complete its work before the search threads were to search the list. In all these cases, one thread or process has to complete an operation before another thread or process attempts to execute its operation. Unless this work is coordinated, the goal of the process, thread, or application would fail or give inaccurate results.

The finish-to-start relationship usually suggests there is an information dependency between the tasks. With information dependency, interthread or interprocess communication is required from one or more tasks in order for a thread or process to operate correctly. The search would produce incorrect results unless the sort was performed. The consumer thread would have no files to process unless the producer thread produced the files to be searched.

5.1.5   Finish-to-Finish Relationship

In a *finish-to-finish* synchronization relationship, one task cannot finish until another task finishes. Task A cannot finish until task B finishes. This again can describe the relationship between parent and child processes discussed in Chapter 3. The parent process must wait until all its child processes have terminated before it is allowed to terminate. If the parent process terminates before its child processes, those terminated child processes become zombied. Parent processes should not finish (exit the system in this case) until all its child processes have finished executing. The parent process achieves this by either calling a `wait()` function for each of its child processes, or waiting for a mutex or condition variable that can be broadcast by child threads. Another example of a finish-to-finish relationship is the boss–worker model. The boss thread's job is to delegate work to the worker threads. It would be undesirable for the boss thread to terminate before the worker threads. New requests to the system would not be processed, existing threads would have no work to perform, and no new threads would be created. If the boss thread is the primary thread and it terminates, the process would terminate along with all the worker threads. In a peer-to-peer model, if thread A dynamically allocates an object passed to thread B and thread A terminates, the object is destroyed along with thread A. If this is done before thread B has had a chance to use, a segmentation fault or data access violation will occur. In order to prevent these kinds of errors with threads, termination of threads is synchronized by using the `pthread_join()` function. A call to this function causes the calling thread to wait on the target thread until it finishes. This creates finish-to-finish synchronization.

5.2   Synchronizing Access to Data

There is a difference between data shared between processes and data shared between threads. Threads share the same address space. Processes have separate address spaces. If there are two processes, A and B, then data declared in process A is not available to process B and vice versa.

Therefore, one method used by processes to share data is to create a block of memory that is then mapped to the address space of the processes that are to share the memory. Another approach is to create a block of memory that exists outside the address space of both processes. These are types of IPC (interprocess communication) that include: pipes, files, and message passing.

It is the block of memory shared between threads within the same address space and the block of memory shared between processes outside both address spaces that requires data synchronization. Figure 5–3 contrasts memory shared between threads and processes.

Data synchronization is needed in order to control race conditions and allow concurrent threads or processes to safely access a block of memory. Data synchronization controls when a block of memory can be read or modified. Concurrent access to shared memory, global variables, and files must be synchronized in a multithreaded environment. Data synchronization is

Figure 5–3   The memory shared between threads and processes.

PROCESS A'S ADDRESS SPACE

STACK SEGMENT	FREE STORE	DATA SEGMENT	TEXT SEGMENT
local variables	local variables global variables	global data structures global variables constants static variables	

messages   shared memory   files   fifos/pipes   — IPC MECHANISMS

PROCESS B'S ADDRESS SPACE

STACK SEGMENT	FREE STORE	DATA SEGMENT	TEXT SEGMENT
local variables	local variables global variables	global data structures global variables constants static variables	
thread A's stack		trees • graphs • queues • stacks ...	thread A's code
thread B's stack			thread B's code

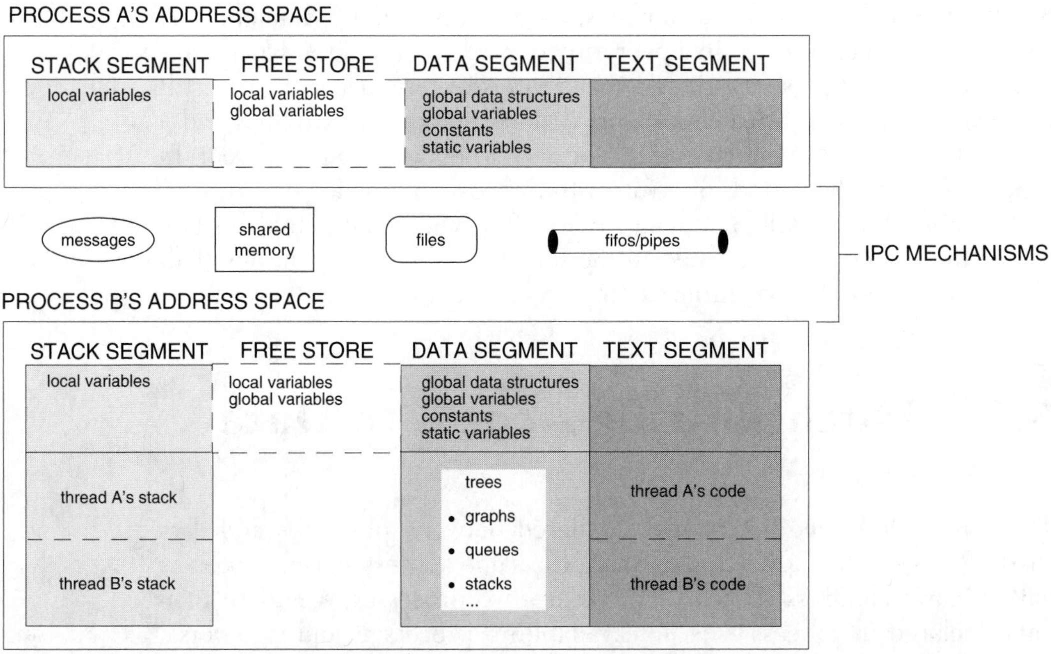

needed at the location in a task's code when it attempts to access the block of memory, global variable, or file shared with other concurrently executing processes or threads. This block of code is called the *critical section*. The critical section can be any block of code that changes the file pointer's position, writes to the file, closes the file, and reads or writes global variables or data structures. Classifying the tasks as read or write tasks is one step in managing concurrent access to the shared memory.

5.2.1 PRAM Model

The PRAM (Parallel Random-Access Machine) is a simplified theoretical model where there are N processors, labeled as P_1, P_2, P_3, . . . P_n, share one global memory. All the processors have simultaneous read and write access to shared global memory. Each of these theoretical processors can access the global shared memory in one *uninterruptible* unit of time. The PRAM model has concurrent read and write algorithms and exclusive read and write algorithms. Concurrent read algorithms are allowed to read the same piece of memory simultaneously with no data corruption. Concurrent write algorithms allow multiple processors to write to the shared memory. Exclusive read algorithms are used to ensure that no two processors ever read the same memory location at the same time. Exclusive write ensures that no two processors write to the same memory at the same time. The PRAM model can be used to characterize concurrent access to shared memory by multiple tasks.

5.2.1.1 Concurrent and Exclusive Memory Access

The concurrent and exclusive read-write algorithms can be combined into the following types of algorithm combinations that are possible for read-write access:

EREW (exclusive read and exclusive write)

CREW (concurrent read and exclusive write)

ERCW (exclusive read and concurrent write)

CRCW (concurrent read and concurrent write)

These algorithms can be viewed as the access policy implemented by the tasks sharing the data. Figure 5–4 illustrates these access policies. EREW

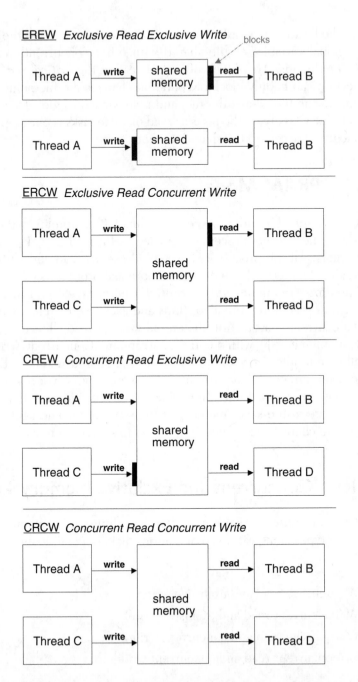

Figure 5-4   EREW, CREW, ERCW, and CRCW access policies.

means access to the shared memory is serialized. Only one task at a time is given access to the shared memory. An example of EREW access policy is the producer-consumer example discussed in Chapter 4. Access to the queue that contained the filenames was restricted to exclusive write by the producer and exclusive read by the consumer. Only one task was allowed access to the queue at any given time. CREW access policy allows multiple reads of the shared memory and exclusive writes. This means there are no restrictions on how many tasks can read the shared memory concurrently but only one task can write to the shared memory. Concurrent reads can occur while an exclusive write is taking place. With this type of access policy, each reading task may read a different value. As a task reads the shared memory, another task modifies it. The next task that reads the shared memory will see different data. The ERCW access policy is the direct reverse of CREW. With ERCW, concurrent writes are allowed but only one task at a time is allowed to read the shared memory. CRCW access policy allows concurrent reads and concurrent writes.

Each of these four algorithm types requires different levels and types of synchronization. They can be analyzed on a continuum with the access policy that requires the least amount of synchronization to implement on one end and the access policy that requires the most amount of synchronization at the other end. The goal is to implement these policies and maintain data integrity and satisfactory system performance. EREW is the policy that is the simplest to implement. This is because EREW essentially forces sequential processing. At first blush, you may consider CRCW is the simplest but it presents the most challenges. It may appear as if it has no policy. The memory can be accessed without restriction. But this is the furthest from the truth. This is the most difficult to implement and requires the most synchronization in order to meet our goal.

5.3 What are Semaphores?

A semaphore is a synchronization mechanism that can be used to manage synchronization relationships and implement the access policies. A *semaphore* is a special kind of variable that can only be accessed by very specific operations. The semaphore is used to help threads and processes synchronize access to shared modifiable memory or manage access to a device or other resource. The semaphore is used as a key to access the resource. This key can only be owned by one process or thread at a time. Whichever task owns the key or semaphore locks the resource for its exclusive use. Locking the resource causes any other task that wishes to use the resource to wait until the resource has been unlocked, making it available again. Once unlocked, the next task waiting for the semaphore is given the semaphore, thus accessing the resource. The *next task* is determined by the scheduling policy in effect for that thread or process.

5.3.1   Semaphore Operations

As mentioned earlier, a semaphore can only be accessed by specific operations like an object. There are two operations that can be performed on a semaphore. The P() operation is a decrement operation and the V() operation is an increment operation. If Mutex is the semaphore, then here are the logical implementations of the P(Mutex) and V(Mutex) operations:

```
P(Mutex)

if(Mutex > 0){
  Mutex--;
}
else {
    Block on Mutex;
}

V(Mutex)
if(Blocked on Mutex N processes){
  pass on Mutex;
}
else{
    Mutex++;
}
```

The actual implementation will be system dependent. These operations are indivisible, meaning once the operation is in progress, it cannot be preempted. If several tasks attempt to make a call to the P() operation, only one task will be allowed to proceed. If the Mutex has already been decremented, then the task will block and be placed in a queue. The V() operation is called by the task that has the Mutex. If other tasks are waiting on the Mutex, it is given to the next task in the queue. If no tasks are waiting, then the Mutex is incremented.

Semaphore operations can go by other names:

```
P() operation:    V() operation:
lock()            unlock()
```

The value of the semaphore will depend on the type of semaphore it is. There are several types of semaphores. A *binary semaphore* will have the value 0 or 1. A *counting semaphore* will have some non-negative integer value.

The POSIX standard defines several types of semaphores. These semaphores are used by processes or threads. Table 5–1 lists the types of semaphores. The table also lists some of their basic operations.

Table 5–1	Semaphore Types Defined by the POSIX Standard and Their Use by Threads and/or Processes	
Types of Semaphores	*Processes/Threads*	*Description*
Mutex semaphores	Processes or threads	Mechanism used to implement mutual exclusion in a critical section of code.
Read–write locks	Processes or threads	Mechanism used to implement read-write access policy between threads.
Condition variables	Processes or threads	Mechanism used to broadcast a signal between threads that an event has taken place. When a thread locks an event mutex, it blocks until it receives the broadcast.
Multiple condition variables	Processes or threads	Same as an event mutex but includes multiple events or conditions.

Any operating system that is compliant with the Single UNIX Specification or POSIX Standard will supply an implementation of these semaphores. They are a part of the `libpthread` library and the functions are declared in the `pthread.h` header.

5.3.2 Mutex Semaphores

The POSIX standard defines a mutex semaphore used by threads and processes of type `pthread_mutex_t`. This mutex provides the basic operations necessary to make it a practical synchronization mechanism:

- initialization
- request ownership
- release ownership
- try ownership
- destruction

Table 5–2 lists the `pthread_mutex_t` functions that are used to perform these basic operations. The *initialization* process allocates memory required to hold the mutex semaphore and give the memory some initial values. For a binary semaphore, its initial value will be 0 or 1. If it's a counting semaphore, its initial value is a non-negative number that represents the number of resources available. It can be used to represent the request limit a program is capable of processing in a single session. Unlike regular variables, there is no guarantee that the initialization operation of a mutex will occur. After calling the initialization operation, take precautions to ensure that the mutex was initialized (i.e., checking the return value or checking the `errno` value). The system shall fail to create the mutex if the space set aside for mutexes has been used, the number of allowable semaphores will be exceeded, the named semaphore already exists, or there is some other memory allocation problem.

Similar to a thread, the Pthread mutex has an attribute object that encapsulates all the attributes of the mutex. This mutex attribute will be discussed

Table 5–2 `pthread_mutex_t` Functions

Mutex Operations	Function Prototypes/Macros `#include <pthread.h>`
Initialization	`int pthread_mutex_init(pthread_mutex_t *restrict mutex, const pthread_mutexattr_t *restrict attr);`
	`pthread_mutex_t mutex = PTHREAD_MUTEX_INITIALIZER;`
Request ownership	`<time.h>`
	`int pthread_mutex_lock(pthread_mutex_t *mutex);`
	`int pthread_mutex_timedlock(pthread_mutex_t *restrict mutex, const struct tiemspec *restrict abs_timeout);`
Release ownership	`int pthread_mutex_unlock(pthread_mutex_t *mutex);`
Try ownership	`int pthread_mutex_trylock(pthread_mutex_t *mutex);`
Destruction	`int pthread_mutex_destroy(pthread_mutex_t *mutex);`

later. It can be passed to the initialization function, creating a mutex with attributes of those set in the mutex object. If no attribute object is used, the
mutex will be intialized with default values. The `pthread_mutex_t` is initialized as unlocked and private. A *private* mutex is shared between threads of
the same process. A *shared* mutex is shared between threads of multiple
processes. If default attributes are to be used, the mutex can be initialized
statically for statically allocated mutex objects by using the macro:

```
pthread_mutext Mutex = PTHREAD_MUTEX_INITIALIZER;
```

This method uses less overhead but performs no error checking.

A mutex can be owned or unowned. The *request ownership* operation
grants ownership of the mutex to the calling process or thread. Once the
mutex is owned, the thread or process has exclusive access to the resource.
If there is any attempt to own the mutex (by calling this operation) by any
other processes or threads, they are blocked until the mutex is made available. Releasing the mutex causes the next process or thread that has
blocked on this mutex to unblock and obtain ownership of the mutex.
With `pthread_mutex_lock()`, the thread granted ownership of a given
mutex is the only thread that can release the mutex. A timed version of
this function is also available. In that case, if the mutex is owned the
process or thread will wait for some specified period of time. If the mutex
is not released in that time interval, the process or thread will continue executing.

The *try ownership* operation tests the mutex to see if it is already owned.
If owned, the function returns some value indicating that. The advantage of
this operation is the thread or process is not blocked if the mutex is owned. It
will be able to continue executing. If the mutex is not owned, then ownership
is granted.

The *destruction* operation frees the memory associated with the mutex.
The memory cannot be destroyed or closed if it is owned or a thread or
process is waiting for the mutex.

5.3.2.1   Using the Mutex Attribute Object

The `pthread_mutex_t` has an attribute object used in a similar way as the
thread attribute. The attribute object encapsulates all the attributes of a
mutex object. Once initialized, it can be used by multiple mutex objects
when passed to the `pthread_mutex_init()` function. The mutex attribute
defines several functions used to set these attributes: priority ceiling, protocol, and type. These functions and other attribute functions are listed in
Table 5–3 with a brief description.

Table 5–3   `pthread_mutex_t` Attribute Object Functions

`pthread_mutex_t` Attribute Object Function Prototypes **`#include <pthread.h>`**	**Description**
`int pthread_mutexattr_init` `(pthread_mutexattr_t * attr);`	Initializes a mutex attribute object specified by the parameter `attr` with default values for all of the attributes defined by the implementation.
`int pthread_mutexattr_destroy` `(pthread_mutexattr_t * attr);`	Destroys a mutex attribute object specified by the parameter `attr`, which causes the mutex attribute object to become uninitialized. Can be reinitialized by calling the `pthread_mutexattr_init()` function.

`int pthread_mutexattr_`
`setprioceiling`
`(pthread_mutexattr_t * attr,`
` int prioceiling);`
 	
`int pthread_mutexattr_`
`getprioceiling`
`(const pthread_mutexattr_t *`
` restrict attr, int *restrict`
`prioceiling);`
	Sets and returns the priority ceiling attribute of the mutex specified by the parameter `attr`. The parameter `prioceiling` contains the priority ceiling of the mutex. The `prioceiling` attribute defines the minimum priority level at which the critical section guarded by the mutex is executed. The values are within the maximum range of priorities defined by SCHED_FIFO.

`int pthread_mutexattr_`
`setprotocol`
`(pthread_mutexattr_t * attr,`
` int protocol);`
 	
`int pthread_mutexattr_`
`getprotocol`
`(const pthread_mutexattr_t *`
` restrict attr,`
` int *restrict protocol);`
	Sets and returns the protocol of the mutex attribute specified by the parameter `attr`. The `protocol` parameter contains the value of the `protocol` attribute:
	
	PTHREAD_PRIO_NONE
	The priority and scheduling of the thread is not affected by the ownership of the mutex.
	
	PTHREAD_PRIO_INHERIT
	Thread blocking other threads of higher priority due to ownership of such a mutex, shall execute at the highest priority of any of the threads waiting on any of the mutexes owned by this thread with such a protocol.

Table 5–3 (cont.)	
pthread_mutex_t *Attribute Object* *Function Prototypes* `#include <pthread.h>`	*Description*
	PTHREAD_PRIO_PROTECT Threads owning such a mutex shall execute at the highest priority ceilings of all mutexes owned by this thread with such a protocol, regardless of whether other threads are blocked on any of these mutexes.

`int pthread_mutexattr_`
`setpshared`
`(pthread_mutexattr_t * attr,`
` int pshared);`
	Sets or returns the `process-shared` attribute of the mutex attribute object specified by the parameter `attr`. The `pshared` parameter contains a value:

`int pthread_mutexattr_`
`getpshared`
`(const pthread_mutexattr_t *`
` restrict attr, int *restrict`
`pshared);`
	PTHREAD_PROCESS_SHARED
	Permits a mutex to be shared by any threads that have access to the allocated memory of the mutex even if the threads are in different processes.

	PTHREAD_PROCESS_PRIVATE Mutex is shared between threads of the same process as the initialized mutex.

`int pthread_mutexattr_`
`settype`
`(pthread_mutexattr_t * attr,`
` int type);`
	Sets and returns the `type` mutex attribute of the mutex attribute specified by the parameter `attr`. The mutex `type` attribute is used to describe the behavior of the mutex, which includes whether the mutex will determine deadlock, perform error checking, etc. The `type` parameter contains a value:

`int pthread_mutexattr_`
`gettype`
`(const pthread_mutexattr_t *`
` restrict attr,`
` int *restrict type);`
	PTHREAD_MUTEX_DEFAULT
	PTHREAD_MUTEX_RECURSIVE
	PTHREAD_MUTEX_ERRORCHECK
	PTHREAD_MUTEX_NORMAL

The most interesting of the attributes is setting whether the mutex will be private or shared. *Private* mutexes are only shared among threads of the same process. It can be declared as global or a handle can be passed between threads. *Shared* mutexes are used by any threads that have access to the memory in which the mutex is located. This includes threads of different processes. Figure 5–5 contrasts the idea of private and shared mutexes between different processes. If threads of different processes are to share a mutex, it must be allocated in memory shared between processes. POSIX defines several functions used to allocate shared memory between objects using memory-mapped files and shared memory objects. Mutexes between processes can be used to protect critical sections that access files, pipes, shared memory, and devices.

5.3.2.2   Using Mutex Semaphores to Manage Critical Sections

Mutexes can be used to manage critical sections of processes and threads in order to control race conditions. Mutexes avoid race conditions by serializing access to the critical section. Example 5.1 shows two threads. Mutexes are used to protect their critical sections.

```
//Example 5.1 Using mutexes to protect critical sections
//               of threads.

// ...
pthread_t ThreadA,ThreadB;
pthread_mutex_t Mutex;
pthread_mutexattr_t MutexAttr;

void *task1(void *X)
{
   pthread_mutex_lock(&Mutex);
   // critical section of code
   pthread_mutex_unlock(&Mutex);
   return(0);
}

void *task2(void *X)
{
   pthread_mutex_lock(&Mutex);
   // critical section of code
   pthread_mutex_unlock(&Mutex);
   return(0);
}
```

PROCESS A'S ADDRESS SPACE

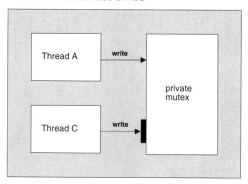

PROCESS B'S ADDRESS SPACE

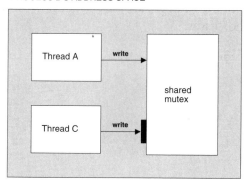

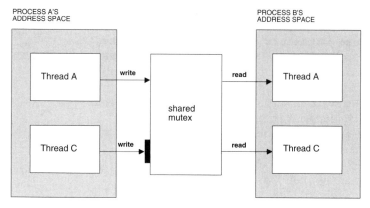

Figure 5–5   Private and shared mutexes.

```
int main(void)
{
    //...
    pthread_mutexattr_init(&MutexAttr);
    pthread_mutex_init(&Mutex,&MutexAttr);
    //set mutex attributes
    pthread_create(&ThreadA,NULL,task1,NULL);
    pthread_create(&ThreadB,NULL,task2,NULL);
    //...
    return(0);
}
```

In Example 5.1, ThreadA and ThreadB have critical sections protected by their use of Mutex.

Example 5.2 shows how mutexes can be used to protect the critical sections of currently executing processes.

```
// Example 5.2 Mutexes used to protect critical sections.
//...
int Rt;
pthread_mutex_t Mutex1;
pthread_mutexattr_t MutexAttr;


int main(void)
{
    //...
    pthread_mutexattr_init(&MutexAttr);
    pthread_mutexattr_setpshared(&MutexAttr,
                             PTHREAD_PROCESS_SHARED);
    pthread_mutex_init(&Mutex1,&MutexAttr);

    if((Rt = fork()) == 0){ // child process
        pthread_mutex_lock(&Mutex1);
        //critical section
        pthread_mutex_unlock(&Mutex1);
    }
    else{ // parent process
        pthread_mutex_lock(&Mutex1);
        //critical section
        pthread_mutex_unlock(&Mutex1);
    }
    //...
    return(0);
}
```

In Example 5.2, it is important to note that the mutex has been initialized as shared by calling:

```
pthread_mutexattr_setpshared(&MutexAttr,PTHREAD_PROCESS_SHARED);
```

This allows `Mutex` to be shared by threads of different processes. Once `fork()` is called, the child process and parent process can protect their critical section with `Mutex`. Their critical sections will contain some resource shared by both processes.

5.3.3 Read–Write Locks

Mutex semaphores are used to manage a critical section by serializing entry to that section. Only one thread or process is permitted to enter the critical section at a time. With *read-write locks*, multiple threads are allowed to enter the critical section if they are to read the shared memory only. Therefore, any number of threads can own a read-write lock for reading. But if multiple threads are to write or modify the shared memory, only one thread is given access. No other threads are allowed to enter the critical section if one thread is given exclusive access to write to the shared memory. This can be used when applications more often read data than write data. If the application has multiple threads, mutex exclusion can be extreme. The performance of the application can benefit by allowing multiple reads. The POSIX standard defines a read-write lock of type `pthread_rwlock_t`.

Similar to mutex semaphores, the read-write locks have the same operations. Table 5–4 lists the read-write lock operations.

The difference between regular mutexes and read-write mutexes is their locking request operations. Instead of one locking operation there are two:

```
pthread_rwlock_rdlock()
pthread_rwlock_wrlock()
```

`pthread_rwlock_rdlock()` obtains a read-lock and `pthread_rwlock_wrlock()` obtains a write lock. If a thread requests a read lock, it is granted the lock as long as there are no threads that hold a write lock. If so, the calling thread is blocked. If a thread request a write lock, it is granted as long as there are no threads that hold a read lock or a write lock. If so, the calling thread is blocked.

The read-write lock is of type `pthread_rwlock_t`. This type also has an attribute object that encapsulates its attributes. The attribute functions are listed in Table 5–5.

Table 5–4 Read–Write Lock Operations	
Read–write Lock Operations	**Function Prototypes** **#include <pthread.h>**
Initialization	int pthread_rwlock_init(pthread_rwlock_t *restrict rwlock, const pthread_rwlockattr_t *restrict attr);

Request ownership	#include <time.h>
	
	int pthread_rwlock_rdlock(pthread_rwlock_t *rwlock);
	
	int pthread_rwlock_wrlock(pthread_rwlock_t *rwlock);
	
	int pthread_rwlock_timedrdlock(pthread_rwlock_t *restrict rwlock, const struct timespec *restrict abs_timeout);
	
	int pthread_rwlock_timedwrlock(pthread_rwlock_t | *restrict rwlock, const struct timespec *restrict abs_timeout);

Release ownership	int pthread_rwlock_unlock(pthread_rwlock_t *rwlock);

Try ownership	int pthread_rwlock_tryrdlock(pthread_rwlock_t *rwlock);
	
	int pthread_rwlock_trywrlock(pthread_rwlock_t *rwlock);

Destruction	int pthread_rwlock_destroy(pthread_rwlock_t *rwlock);

The `pthread_rwlock_t` can be private between threads or shared between threads or different processes.

5.3.3.1 Using Read-Write Locks to Implement Access Policy

Read-write locks can be used to implement an access policy, namely CREW. Several tasks can be granted concurrent reads but only one task is granted write access. Using read-write locks will not permit concurrent reads to occur with the exclusive write. Example 5.3 contains tasks using read-write locks to protect critical sections.

Table 5–5   Attribute Object Functions for **pthread_rwlock_t**

pthread_rwlock_t *Attribute Object Function Prototypes* `#include <pthread.h>`	*Description*
`int pthread_rwlockattr_init` `(pthread_rwlockattr_t * attr);`	Initializes a read-write lock attribute object specified by the parameter `attr` with default values for all of the attributes defined by the implementation.
`int pthread_rwlockattr_destroy` `(pthread_rwlockattr_t * attr);`	Destroys a read-write lock attribute object specified by the parameter `attr`. Can be reinitialized by calling the `pthread_rwlockattr_init()` function.

`int pthread_rwlockattr_`
`setpshared`
`(pthread_rwlockattr_t * attr,`
` int pshared);`
	Sets or returns the `process-shared` attribute of the read-write lock attribute object specified by the parameter `attr`. The `pshared` parameter contains a value:

`int pthread_rwlockattr_`
`getpshared`
`(const pthread_rwlockattr_t *`
` restrict attr,`
` int *restrict pshared);`
	PTHREAD_PROCESS_SHARED
	Permits a read-write lock to be shared by any threads that have access to the allocated memory of the read-write lock even if the threads are in different processes.

	PTHREAD_PROCESS_PRIVATE The read-write lock is shared between threads of the same process as the initialized rwlock.

```
// Example 5.3 Threads using read-write locks.

//...
pthread_t ThreadA,ThreadB,ThreadC,ThreadD;
pthread_rwlock_t RWLock;


void *producer1(void *X)
{
   pthread_rwlock_wrlock(&RWLock);
   //critical section
   pthread_rwlock_unlock(&RWLock);
   return(0);
}
```

```c
void *producer2(void *X)
{
   pthread_rwlock_wrlock(&RWLock);
   //critical section
   pthread_rwlock_unlock(&RWLock);
}

void *consumer1(void *X)
{
   pthread_rwlock_rdlock(&RWLock);
   //critical section
   pthread_rwlock_unlock(&RWLock);
   return(0);
}

void *consumer2(void *X)
{
   pthread_rwlock_rdlock(&RWLock);
   //critical section
   pthread_rwlock_unlock(&RWLock);
   return(0);
}

int main(void)
{

   pthread_rwlock_init(&RWLock,NULL);
   //set mutex attributes
   pthread_create(&ThreadA,NULL,producer1,NULL);
   pthread_create(&ThreadB,NULL,consumer1,NULL);
   pthread_create(&ThreadC,NULL,producer2,NULL);
   pthread_create(&ThreadD,NULL,consumer2,NULL);
   //...
   return(0);
}
```

In Example 5.3, four threads are created. Two threads are producers, ThreadA and ThreadC, and two threads are consumers, ThreadB and ThreadD. All the threads have a critical section and each section is protected with the read–write lock RWLock. As mentioned, ThreadB and ThreadD can enter their critical sections concurrently or serially but neither thread can enter their critical sections if either ThreadA or ThreadC is in theirs. ThreadA and ThreadC cannot enter their critical sections concurrently. Table 5–6 shows part of the decision table for Example 5.3.

	Part of the Decision Table for Example 5.3		
Table 5–6			
Thread A *(writer)*	*Thread B* *(reader)*	*Thread C* *(writer)*	*Thread D* *(reader)*
N	N	N	Y
N	N	Y	N
N	Y	N	N
N	Y	N	Y
Y	N	N	N

5.3.4 Condition Variables

A *condition variable* is a semaphore used to signal an event has occurred. One or more processes or threads can wait for the signal sent by other processes or threads once the event has taken place. Some make a distinction between condition variables and the mutex semaphores discussed. The purpose of the mutex semaphore and read–write locks is to synchronize data access whereas condition variables are typically used to synchronize the sequence of operations. W. Richard Stevens, in his book *UNIX Network Programming,* states it best: "Mutexes are for *locking* and cannot be used for *waiting*."

In Program 4.6, our consumer thread contained a busy loop:

```
15   while(TextFiles.empty())
16   {}
```

The consumer thread looped until there were items in the TextFiles queue. This can be replaced by a condition variable. The producer can signal the consumer that items have been inserted into the queue. The consumer can wait until it receives the signal then continue to process the queue.

The condition variable is of type pthread_cond_t. These are the types of operations it can perform:

- initialize
- destroy
- wait
- timed wait

- signal
- broadcast

The initialize and destroy operations work in a similar manner as the other mutexes. Table 5–7 lists the functions for the pthread_cond_t that implement these operations.

Table 5–7	Functions for the **pthread_cond_t** that Implement Condition Variables Operations
Condition Variables Operations	*Function Prototypes/Macros* **#include <pthread.h>**
Initialization	int pthread_cond_init(pthread_cond_t *restrict cond, const pthread_condattr_t *restrict attr); pthread_cond_t cond = PTHREAD_COND_INITIALIZER;
Waiting	int pthread_cond_wait(pthread_cond_t * restrict cond, pthread_mutex_t *restrict mutex); int pthread_cond_timedwait(pthread_cond_t * restrict cond, pthread_mutex_t *restrict mutex, const struct timespec *restrict abstime);
Signaling	int pthread_cond_signal(pthread_cond_t *cond); int pthread_cond_broadcast(pthread_cond_t *cond);
Destruction	int pthread_cond_destroy(pthread_cond_t *cond);

Condition variables are used in conjunction with mutexes. If a thread or process attempts to lock a mutex, we know that it will block until the mutex is released. Once unblocked, it obtains the mutex then continues. If a condition variable is used, it must be associated with a mutex.

```
//...
pthread_mutex_lock(&Mutex);
pthread_cond_wait(&EventMutex,&Mutex);
//...
pthread_mutex_unlock(&Mutex);
```

A task attempts to lock a mutex. If the mutex is already locked then the task will block. Once unblocked, the task will release the mutex, `Mutex`, while it waits on the signal for the condition variable, `EventMutex`. If the mutex is not locked, it will release the mutex and wait indefinitely. With a timed wait, the task will only wait for a specified period of time. If the time expires before the task is signaled, the function will return an error. It will then reacquire the mutex.

The signal operation causes a task to signal to another thread or process that an event has occurred. If a task is waiting for that condition variable, it will be unblocked and given the mutex. If there are several tasks waiting for the condition variable, only one will be unblocked. The tasks will be waiting in a queue and unblocked according to the scheduling policy. The broadcast operation signals all the task waiting for the condition variable. If multiple tasks are unblocked, the tasks shall compete for the ownership of the mutex according to a scheduling policy. In contrast to the wait operation, the signaling task is not required to own the mutex, although it is recommended.

The condition variable also has an attribute object. Table 5–8 lists the functions of the attribute object with a brief description.

5.3.4.1 Using Condition Variables to Manage Synchronization Relationships

The condition variable can be used to implement the synchronization relationships mentioned earlier: start-to-start (SS), finish-to-start (FS), start-to-finish (SF), and finish-to-finish (FF). These relationships can exist between threads of the same processes or different processes. Examples 5.4 and 5.5 contain examples of how to implement an FS and FF synchronization relationship. There are two mutexes used in each example. One mutex is used to synchronize access to the shared data and the other mutex is used to synchronize execution of code.

```
//Example 5.4 FS synchronization relationship between two threads.

//...
float Number;
pthread_t ThreadA,ThreadB;
pthread_mutex_t Mutex,EventMutex;
pthread_cond_t Event;

void *worker1(void *X)
{
```

Table 5–8   Functions of the Attribute Object for the Condition Variable of Type `pthread_cond_t`

`pthread_cond_t` *Attribute Object Function Prototypes* `#include <pthread.h>`	*Description*
`int pthread_condattr_init (pthread_condattr_t * attr);`	Initializes a condition variable attribute object specified by the parameter `attr` with default values for all of the attributes defined by the implementation.
`int pthread_condattr_destroy (pthread_condattr_t * attr);`	Destroys a condition variable attribute object specified by the parameter `attr`. Can be reinitialized by calling the `pthread_condattr_init()` function.
`int pthread_condattr_ setpshared (pthread_condattr_t * attr, int pshared);`	Sets or returns the `process-shared` attribute of the condition variable attribute object specified by the parameter `attr`. The `pshared` parameter contains a value:
`int pthread_condattr_ getpshared (const pthread_condattr_t * restrict attr, int *restrict pshared);`	`PTHREAD_PROCESS_SHARED` Permits a read–write lock to be shared by any threads that have access to the allocated memory of the condition variable even if the threads are in different processes. `PTHREAD_PROCESS_PRIVATE` The condition variable is shared between threads of the same process as the initialized condition.
`int pthread_condattr_ setclock (pthread_condattr_t * attr, clockid_t clock_id);` `int pthread_condattr_ getclock (const pthread_condattr_t * restrict attr, clockid_t * restrict clock_id);`	Sets and returns the `clock` attribute for the condition variable attribute object specified by the parameter `attr`. The `clock` attribute is the clock id of the clock used to measure the timeout service of the `pthread_cond_timedwait()` function. The default value of the `clock` attribute is the system clock.

```
    for(int Count = 1;Count < 100;Count++){
        pthread_mutex_lock(&Mutex);
        Number++;
        pthread_mutex_unlock(&Mutex);
        cout << "worker1: number is " << Number << endl;
        if(Number == 50){
            pthread_cond_signal(&Event);
        }
    }
    cout << "worker 1 done" << endl;
    return(0);
}

void *worker2(void *X)
{
    pthread_mutex_lock(&EventMutex);
    pthread_cond_wait(&Event,&EventMutex);
    pthread_mutex_unlock(&EventMutex);
    for(int Count = 1;Count < 50;Count++){
        pthread_mutex_lock(&Mutex);
        Number = Number + 20;
        pthread_mutex_unlock(&Mutex);
        cout << "worker2: number is " << Number << endl;
    }
    cout << "worker 2 done" << endl;
    return(0);
}


int main(int argc, char *argv[])
{
    pthread_mutex_init(&Mutex,NULL);
    pthread_mutex_init(&EventMutex,NULL);
    pthread_cond_init(&Event,NULL);
    pthread_create(&ThreadA,NULL,worker1,NULL);
    pthread_create(&ThreadB,NULL,worker2,NULL);
    //...
    return (0);
}
```

In Example 5.4, the FS synchronization relationship is implemented. ThreadA cannot finish until ThreadB starts. ThreadA signals to ThreadB once Number has a value of 50. It can now continue execution until finished. ThreadB cannot start its computation until it gets a signal from ThreadA.

ThreadB uses the EventMutex with the condition variable Event. Mutex is used to synchronize write access to the shared data Number. A task can use several mutexes to synchronize different critical sections and synchronize different events.

Example 5.5 contains an implementation of a FF synchronization relationship.

```
//Example 5.5 FF synchronization relationship between
//            two threads.

//...
float Number;
pthread_t ThreadA,ThreadB;
pthread_mutex_t Mutex,EventMutex;
pthread_cond_t Event;

void *worker1(void *X)
{
   for(int Count = 1;Count < 10;Count++){
      pthread_mutex_lock(&Mutex);
      Number++;
      pthread_mutex_unlock(&Mutex);
      cout << "worker1: number is " << Number << endl;
   }
   pthread_mutex_lock(&EventMutex);
   cout << "worker1 done now waiting " << endl;
   pthread_cond_wait(&Event,&EventMutex);
   pthread_mutex_unlock(&EventMutex);
   return(0);
}

void *worker2(void *X)
{
   for(int Count = 1;Count < 100;Count++){
      pthread_mutex_lock(&Mutex);
      Number = Number * 2;
      pthread_mutex_unlock(&Mutex);
      cout << "worker2: number is " << Number << endl;
   }
   pthread_cond_signal(&Event);
   cout << "worker2 done now signalling " << endl;
   return(0);
}
```

```
int main(int argc, char *argv[])
{
   pthread_mutex_init(&Mutex,NULL);
   pthread_mutex_init(&EventMutex,NULL);
   pthread_cond_init(&Event,NULL);
   pthread_create(&ThreadA,NULL,worker1,NULL);
   pthread_create(&ThreadB,NULL,worker2,NULL);
   //...
   return (0);
}
```

In Example 5.5, `ThreadA` cannot finish until `ThreadB` finishes. `ThreadA` must iterate through the loop 10 times, where `ThreadB` must iterate through the loop only 100 times. `ThreadA` will complete its iterations before `ThreadB` but will wait until `ThreadB` signals that it is done.

SS and SF can be implemented in a similar manner. These techniques can easily be used to synchronize order of execution between processes.

5.4 Synchronization: An Object-Oriented Approach

One of the advantages of object-oriented programming is the protection encapsulation provides for the data component of an object. Encapsulation can provide "object-access policies and usage guidelines" (Hughes & Hughes, 1997) for the user of the object. In the examples presented in this chapter, access policies were the responsibility of the user of the data. With objects and encapsulation, the responsibility has switched from the user of the data to the data itself. This approach creates data, not unlike functions, which are thread safe.

In order to accomplish this, the data (wherever possible) of the multi-threaded application should be encapsulated using the C++ `class` or `struct` constructs. Then encapsulate the synchronization mechanism such as semaphores, read-write locks, and event mutexes. If the data or synchronization mechanisms are already objects, create an interface class for them. Lastly, combine the data object with the synchronization objects through inheritance or composition, to create data objects that are thread safe. This approach is discussed in detail in Chapter 11.

Summary

Synchronization can be used to coordinate the order of execution of processes and threads called *task synchronization* as well as access the shared data called *data synchronization*. There are four basic task synchronization relationships. A start-to-start relationship means task A cannot start until task B starts. A finish-to-start relationship means task A cannot finish until task B starts. A start-to-finish relationship means task A cannot start until task B finishes. A finish-to-finish (FF) relationship means task A cannot finish until task B finishes. The POSIX standard defines a condition variable of type `pthread_cond_t` that can be used to implement these task synchronization relationships.

The algorithm types of the PRAM model can be used to describe data synchronization. EREW (exclusive read exclusive write) access policy can be implemented with a mutex semaphore. The mutex semaphore protects the critical section by serializing entry into the critical section. Either read access or write access is allowed. The POSIX standard defines a mutex semaphore of type `pthread_mutex_t` that can be used to implement an EREW access policy. Read–write locks can be used to implement the CREW access policy. CREW access policy describes multiple concurrent reads of data but an exclusive write to that data. The POSIX standard defines a read–write lock of type `pthread_rwlock_t`. An object-oriented approach to data synchronization embeds synchronization inside the data object.

6

Adding Parallel Programming Capabilities to C++ Through the PVM

"We have thus divided our problem into two parts. The child-programme and the education process. These two remain very closely connected. We cannot expect to find a good child-machine at the first attempt. One must experiment with teaching one such machine, and see how well it learns . . ."

—*Alan Turing*, Can A Machine Think?

In this Chapter

The Classic Parallelism Models Supported by PVM • The PVM Library for C++ • The Basic Mechanics of the PVM • Accessing Standard Input (`stdin`) and Standard Output (`stdout`) within PVM Tasks • Summary

The PVM (Parallel Virtual Machine) is a software system that provides the software developer with the facilities to write and run programs that exploit parallelism. The PVM presents a collection of networked computers to the developer as a single logical machine with parallel capabilities. The collection of computers can all have the same architecture or the collection can consist of computers with different architectures. The PVM can even be connected to computers that fall into the MPP (Massively Parallel Processor) class. Although PVM programs can be developed for a single computer, the real advantages come when there are two or more computers connected.

The PVM supports the message passing model as a means of communication between concurrently executing tasks. An application interacts with the PVM through a library that consists of APIs for process control, sending messages, receiving messages, signaling processes, and so on. A C++ program interfaces with the PVM library in the same way that it interacts with any other function library. While a program that accesses PVM library calls does require certain functions to be called to initialize the environment, there is nothing that forces any particular form or architecture on a C++ program. This means that the C++ programmer can combine PVM capabilities with other styles of C++ programming (e.g., object-oriented, parameterized programming, agent-oriented programming, and structured programming). The use of libraries to provide additional functionality to C++ is considered one of its advantages. Through the use of libraries such as PVM, MPI, or Linda, a C++ developer can use different models of parallelism, whereas other languages are restricted to whatever parallel primitives are built into the language. The PVM library is perhaps the easiest way to add parallel programming capabilities to the C++ language.

6.1   The Classic Parallelism Models Supported by PVM

The PVM system supports the MIMD (Multiple Instruction Multiple Data) and SPMD (Single Program Multiple Data) models of parallelism. Actually, SPMD is a variation on the SIMD (Single Instruction Multiple Data) model. The models classify programs by instruction streams and data streams. In the MIMD model, a program consists of two or more concurrently executing instruction streams, each with its own local data stream. Essentially, each processor has its own memory. In the PVM environment the MIMD is considered a distributed memory model, which is in contrast to a shared memory model. In shared memory models each processor can see the same memory locations. In the distributed model memory values must be communicated through message passing. On the other hand, the SPMD model consists of a single program (the same set of instructions) concurrently executing on two or more machines with the program on each machine processing a different data stream. In other words, the same program on each machine is working with different pieces of data. The PVM environment supports both the MIMD and SIMD or a combination of these two models. Figure 6–1 shows the four classic models and where PVM programs are classified.

Notice in Figure 6–1 that the SISD and MISD models are not applicable to the PVM. The SISD model describes a uniprocessor machine and the MISD model has not yet been practically applied. The two models in Figure 6–1 that can be used with PVMs determine how a C++ program interacts with computers. The software developer sees one logical virtual computer as allowing either two or more different concurrently executing tasks, each with access to its own data, or the same task executing as a set of concurrent clones, with each clone accessing some different piece of data. For our pur-

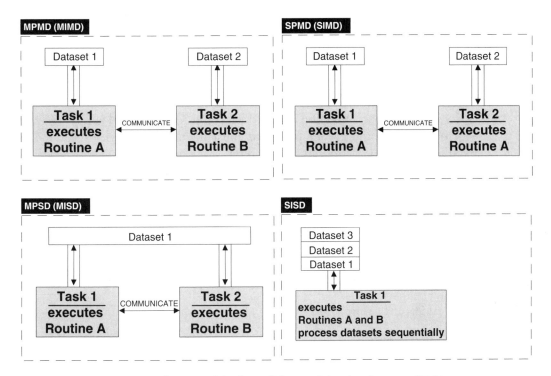

Figure 6-1 Four classic models of parallelism and the classification of PVM programs.

poses the Multiple Instructions and Single Program in Figure 6–1 refer to PVM tasks.

6.2   The PVM Library for C++

The PVM functionality is accessed by C++ through a collection of library routines provided by the PVM environment. The routines are typically divided into seven categories:

- Process Management and Control
- Messaging Packing and Sending
- Message Unpacking and Receiving
- Task Signaling

- Message Buffer Management
- Information and Utility Functions
- Group Operations

The library routines are easy to integrate into the C++ environment. The pvm_ prefix to each function helps to keep the namespace clear. To use the PVM library routines, your programs must include the pvm3.h header file and link to libpvm. Programs 6.1 and 6.2 show how a simple PVM program works. The instructions for compiling and executing Program 6.1 are contained in Program Profile 6.1.

```
//Program 6.1

#include "pvm3.h"
#include <iostream>
#include <string.h>

int main(int argc,char *argv[])
{
   int RetCode,MessageId;
   int PTid, Tid;
   char Message[100];
   float Result[1];
   PTid = pvm_mytid();
   RetCode = pvm_spawn("program6-2",NULL,0,"",1,&Tid);
   if(RetCode == 1){
      MessageId = 1;
      strcpy(Message,"22");
      pvm_initsend(PvmDataDefault);
      pvm_pkstr(Message);
      pvm_send(Tid,MessageId);
      pvm_recv(Tid,MessageId);
      pvm_upkfloat(Result,1,1);
      cout << Result[0] << endl;
      pvm_exit();
      return(0);
   }
   else{
         cerr << "Could not spawn task " << endl;
         pvm_exit();
         return(1);
   }
}
```

Program Profile 6.1

Program Name
program6-1.cc

Description
Uses pvm_send to send a number to another PVM task that is executing
(Program 6.2) and pvm_recv to receive a number from that task.

Libraries Required
libpvm3

Headers Required
<pvm3.h> <iostream> <string.h>

Compile and Link Instructions
c++ -o program6-1 -I $PVM_ROOT/include -L $PVM_ROOT/lib/
$PVM_ARCH -l pvm3

Test Environment
Solaris 8, PVM 3.4.3, SuSE Linux 7.1, gcc 2.95.2,

Execution Instructions
./program6-1

Notes
pvmd must be running.

Program 6.1 calls eight commonly used PVM routines: pvm_mytid(),
pvm_spawn(), pvm_initsend(), pvm_pkstr(), pvm_send(), pvm_recv(),
pvm_upkfloat(), and pvm_exit(). The pvm_mytid() routine returns the
task identifier of the calling process. The PVM system associates a task identifier with each process that it creates. The task identifier is used to send
messages between tasks, to receive messages from other tasks, to signal tasks,
to interrupt tasks, and so on. Any PVM task may communicate with any other
PVM task as long as it has access to the task identifier of the task it wants to
communicate with. The pvm_spawn() routine is used to start new PVM
processes. Program 6.1 uses the pvm_spawn() process to start a new process
to execute Program 6.2. The task identifier for the new task is returned in
the &Tid parameter of the pvm_spawn() call. The PVM environment uses
message buffers to pass data between tasks. Each task can have one or more
message buffers. However, only one buffer is considered the *active* message
buffer. Prior to sending each message the pvm_initsend() routine is called

to prepare or initialize the *active* message buffer. The `pvm_pkstr()` routine is used to pack the string contained in the `message` variable. This packing encodes the string for transport to another task in another process possibly on another machine with a different machine architecture. The PVM environment handles the details of the architecture-to-architecture conversions. The PVM environment requires the use of a packing routine prior to sending and an unpacking routine during receiving to make the message readable by the receiver. However, there is an exception to this, which we will discuss later. The `pvm_send()` and `pvm_recv()` are used to send and receive messages. The `MessageId` simply identifies which message the caller or sender is working with. Notice in Program 6.1 that the `pvm_send()` and `pvm_receive()` routines contain the task identifier of the task receiving the data and the task identifier of the task sending the data. The `pvm_upkfloat()` routine takes the message it retrieves from the active message buffer and unpacks it into an array of type `float`. Program 6.1 spawns a PVM task to execute Program 6.2.

Notice that Programs 6.1 and 6.2 both contain a call to the routine `pvm_exit()`. It's important that this function is called when the PVM processing for a task is finished. Although this routine does not kill the process or stop the process, it does PVM cleanup for the task and disconnects the task from the PVM. Notice that Programs 6.1 and 6.2 are self-contained, standalone programs that contain the `main()` function. Program Profile 6.2 has the implementation details for Program 6.2.

```
// Program 6.2

#include "pvm3.h"
#include "stdlib.h"

int main(int argc, char *argv[])
{
    int MessageId, Ptid;
    char Message[100];
    float Num,Result;
    Ptid = pvm_parent();
    MessageId = 1;
    pvm_recv(Ptid,MessageId);
    pvm_upkstr(Message);
    Num = atof(Message);
    Result = Num / 7.0001;
    pvm_initsend(PvmDataDefault);
    pvm_pkfloat(&Result,1,1);
```

```
     pvm_send(Ptid,MessageId);
     pvm_exit();
     return(0);
}
```

Program Profile 6.2

Program Name
program6-2.cc

Description
This program receives a number from its parent process and divides that
number by 7. It sends the result to its parent process.

Libraries Required
libpvm3

Headers Required
<pvm3.h> <stdlib.h>

Compile and Link Instructions
c++ -o program6-2 -I $PVM_ROOT/include program6-2.cc -L
$PVM_ROOT/lib/PVM_ARCH -lpvm3

Test Environment
SuSE Linux 7.1 gnu C++ 2.95.2 , Solaris 8 Workshop 6 , PVM 3.4.3

Execution Instructions
This program is spawned by Program 6.1.

Notes
pvmd must be running.

6.2.1   Compiling and Linking
a C++/PVM Program

Version 3.4.x of the PVM environment packages the routines in a single library, libpvm3.a . To compile a PVM program include the pvm3.h header
file and link with libpvm3.a:

```
$ c++ -o mypvm_program -I $PVM_ROOT/include mypvm_program.cc
-I$PVM_ROOT/lib -lpvm3
```

The $PVM_ROOT environment variable points to the PVM installed directory. This command will produce a binary called mypvm_program.

To execute Programs 6.1 and 6.2, you must have the PVM environment properly installed. Three basic methods can be used to execute a PVM program: as a standalone binary, using the PVM console, or using XPVM.

6.2.2   Executing a PVM Program as a Standalone

The pvmd program must be started and each host involved in the PVM must have the correctly compiled programs in the appropriate directory. The default directory for the compiled programs (binaries) is:

```
$HOME/pvm3/bin/$PVM_ARCH
```

where the PVM_ARCH contains the name of the machine's architecture. See Table 6–2 and items 1 and 2 from Section 6.1.5. The binaries should have the proper file permissions set to allow them to be accessed and executed. The pvmd program can be started as:

```
pvmd &
```

or:

```
pvmd hostfile &
```

where hostfile is a configuration file that has special options to be passed to the pvmd program. See item 5 from section 6.1.5. After the pvmd program has been started on one of the computers involved in the PVM, a PVM program can then be started simply by:

```
$MyPvmProgram
```

If this program spawns any other tasks they will be started automatically.

6.2.2.1   Starting PVM Programs Using the PVM Console

To execute the programs using the PVM console, type the following at the PVM console. Start the PVM console by typing:

```
$pvm
```

and at the pvm> prompt, type the name of the program to be executed:

```
pvm> spawn -> MyPvmProgram
```

6.2.2.2   Start PVM Programs Using XPVM

Besides starting the programs using the terminal-based PVM console, XPVM graphical interface for X Windows can be used. Figure 6–2 shows what to type in the tasks dialog of a XPVM session.

The PVM library does not force any particular structure on a C++ program. The first PVM routine called by a program enrolls that program into the PVM. It is good practice to always call pvm_exit() for every program that is part of the PVM. If this routine is not called for every PVM task, the system will hang. It is a good rule of thumb to call pvm_mytid() and pvm_parent() early in the processing of the task. Table 6–1 contains the library routines broken down into the seven commonly used categories.

Figure 6–2   The XPVM task dialog.

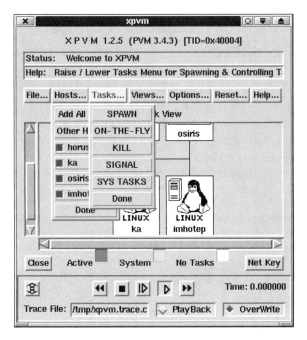

Table 6–1 Seven Categories of PVM Library Routines	
Categories of PVM Library Routines	*Description*
Process Management and Control	Routines used to manage and control PVM processes.
Message Packing and Sending	Routines used to pack messages into a send buffer and send messages from one PVM process to another.
Message Unpacking and Receiving	Routines used to receive messages and unpack the data from the active buffer.
Task Signaling	Routines used to signal and notify PVM processes about the occurrence of an event.
Message Buffer Management	Routines used to initialize, empty, dispose, and otherwise manage buffers used to receive and send messages between PVM processes.
Information and Utility Functions	Routines used to return information about a PVM process and perform other important tasks.
Group Operations	Routines used joining, leaving, and otherwise managing processes in a group.

6.2.3 A PVM Preliminary Requirements Checklist

In addition to obtaining and properly installing a PVM distribution, there are a few other minor considerations. When the PVM environment is implemented as a network of computers, the following items must be handled before your C++ program can interact with the PVM environment.

Item 1

The environment variable PVM_ROOT and PVM_ARCH should be set. The environment variable PVM_ROOT should be set to the directory where PVM is installed.

Using the Bourne Shell (bash)	*Using the C Shell*
`$ PVM_ROOT=/usr/lib/pvm3`	`setenv PVM_ROOT /usr/lib/pvm3`
`$ export PVM_ROOT`	

The PVM_ARCH environment variable identifies the architecture of the machine. Each machine involved in the PVM must be identified by architecture. For example, our Ultrasparcs have the designation SUN4SOL2 and our Linux machines have the designation LINUX. Table 6–2 shows the most commonly used architectures for the PVM environment. Check with your distribution of PVM if an appropriate architecture for your machines is not contained in Table 6–2.

Table 6–2 shows the name and machine type associated with the name. Set your PVM_ARCH environment variable to one of the names in Table 6–2. For instance:

Table 6–2   Most Commonly Used Architectures for the PVM Environment

PVM_ARCH	*Computer*	*PVM_ARCH*	*Computer*
AFX8	Alliance	LINUX	80386/486 PC Running UNIX
ALPHA	DEC Alpha	MASPAR	Maspar
BAL	Sequent Balance	MIPS	MIPS 4680
BFLY	BBN Butterfly TC2000	NEXT	NeXT
BSD386	80386/486 PC Running UNIX	PGON	Intel Paragon
CM2	Thinking Machine CM2	PMAX	DECstation 3100,5100
CM5	Thinking Machine CM5	RS6K	IBM/RS6000
CNVX	Convex C-series	RT	IBM RT
CNVXN	Convex C-series	SGI	Silicon Graphics IRIS
CRAY	C-90, YMP,T3D port available	SGI5	Silicon Graphics IRIS
CRAY2	Cray-2	SGIMP	SGI Multiprocessor
CRAYSIMP	Cray S-MP	SUN3	Sun 3
DGAV	Data General Aviion	SUN4	Sun 4, SPARCstation
E88K	Encore 88000	SUN2SOL2	Sun 4, SPARCstation
HP300	HP-9000 Model 300	SUNMP	SPARC Multiprocessor
HPPA	HP-9000 PA-RISC	SYMM	Sequent Symmetry
I860	Intel iPSC/860	TITN	Stardent Titan
IPSC2	Intel iPSC/2 386 Host	U370	IBM 370
KSRI	Kendall Square KSR-1	UVAX	DEC Licro VAX

Using the Bourne Shell (bash)	*Using the C Shell*
`$PVM_ARCH=LINUX`	`setenv PVM_ARCH LINUX`
`$export PVM_ARCH`	

Item 2

The binaries (executables) for any programs participating in the PVM have to be either located on all machines involved or accessible by all machines involved in the PVM. In addition to availability, each program must be compiled to work for the architecture it will run on. This means if we have UltraSparcs, PowerPCs, and Intel processors involved in the PVM, then we must have a version of the program compiled for each architecture. That version must be located in a place that the PVM is aware of. The location is often `$HOME/pvm3/bin`. However, the location can be specified in a PVM configuration file usually referred to as the `hostfile` or `.xpvm_hosts` if the XPVM environment is used. The `hostfile` would contain an entry such as:

```
ep=/usr/local/pvm3/bin
```

This specifies any user binaries needed by the PVM can be found in the `/usr/local/pvm3/bin` directory.

Item 3

The user initiating the PVM program must have network access to each machine involved in the PVM. This access is typically `rsh` or `ssh` access. See the main pages for more details on the `rsh` and `ssh` programs. By default, the PVM accesses each machine using the login name of the user initiating the PVM program or the account name of the machine starting the PVM program. If another account besides the initiating login account is required, an entry must be added to the host file or `.xpvm_hosts`. For example:

```
lo=flashgordon
```

Item 4

Create a `.rhosts` file on each host listing all the hosts you wish to use. These are the computers that have the potential to be involved in the PVM. Depending on the setting in the `.xpvm_hosts` file or the `pvm_hosts` file, these computers will automatically be added to the PVM when the `pvmd` is started. Computers listed in these files can also be dynamically added to the PVM at run-time.

Item 5

Create a `$HOME/.xpvm_hosts` and/or a `$HOME/pvm_hosts` file listing all the hosts you wish to use prepended by an `&`. The `&` means don't automatically ad the host. Not using `&` will cause the host to be automatically added. The `pvm_hostfile` is a user-created file. The name is arbitrary. However, `.xpvm_hosts` is the required name when using the XPVM environment. Figure 6–3 shows an example of a PVM hostfile. The same format would be used for the PVM console hostfile or for `.xpvm_hosts`.

The primary thing to keep in mind is network access of the user running the PVM program. The owner of the PVM program should have account access to every computer involved in the pool of processors that will be executing parts of the program. This access will use either the `rsh` or `rlogin` commands or `ssh`. The program to be executed must be available on each host and the PVM environment must be aware of what the hosts are and where the binaries will be installed.

Figure 6–3   An example of a PVM host file.

```
# Comment lines start with # (empty lines are ignored)
# lines starting with & allow the machine to be loaded into
# the PVM at a later time.  If the machine's host name is
# not preceded by & it will be loaded automatically by the
# PVM environment

flavius
marcus
&cambius lo=romulus
&karsius
# The * marks default options for following hosts

* dx=/export/home/fred/pvm3/lib/pvmd
&octavius

# if the computers involved are part of a typical linux
# cluster then  the host names as defined in the hosts
# file can be used to include the nodes of the cluster
# with the other nodes in a PVM
```

6.2.4   Combining the C++ Runtime Library and the PVM Library

Since access to the PVM is provided through a collection of library routines, a C++ program treats the PVM as any other library. Keep in mind that each PVM program is a standalone C++ program with its own `main()` function. This means that each PVM program has its own address space. When a PVM task is spawned, a new process is created. Each PVM program will have its own process and process id. The PVM processes are visible to the `ps` utility. Although two or more PVM tasks may be working together to solve some problem, they will have their own copies of the C++ runtime library. Each program has its own `iostream`, template library, algorithms, and so on. The scope of global C++ variables do not cross address space. This means global variables in one PVM task will be invisible to the other PVM tasks involved in the processing. Message passing is used to communicate between these separate tasks. Notice that this is in contrast to multithreaded programs where threads share the same address space and may communicate through parameter passing and global variables. If the PVM programs are executing on a single computer that has multiple processors, then the programs may share a file system and can use pipes, fifos, shared memory, and files as additional means to communicate. While message passing is the premier method of communicating between PVM tasks, nothing prevents the use of shared file systems, clipboards, or even command-line arguments as supplemental methods of communication between tasks. The PVM library adds to rather than restricts the capabilities of the C++ runtime library.

6.2.5   Approaches to Using PVM Tasks

The work a C++ program performs can be distributed between functions, objects, or combinations of functions and objects. The units of work in a program usually fall into logical categories: input/output, user interface, database processing, signal processing, error handling, numerical computation, and so on. Also, we try to keep user interface code separated from file processing code and printing routine code separated from the numerical computation code. Therefore, not only do we divide up the work our program does between functions or objects, we try to keep categories of functionality together. These logical groupings are organized into libraries, modules, object patterns, components, and frameworks. We maintain this type of organization when introducing PVM tasks into a C++ program. We can arrive at the WBS (Work Breakdown Structures) using either a bottom-up or top-down approach. In either case, the parallelism should naturally fit within the work that a function, module, or object has to do.

It is not a good idea to attempt to force parallelism in a program. Forced parallelism produces awkward program architectures that are hard to understand by making them hard to maintain and often hard to determine program correctness. So when a program uses PVM tasks, they should be a result of the natural division within the program. Each PVM task should be traceable to one of the categories of work within the program. For instance, if we have an application that has NLP (Natural Language Processing) and TTS (Text to Speech) processing as part of its user interface and inferencing as part of its data retrieval, then the parallelism that is natural within the NLP component should be represented as tasks within the NLP module or object that is responsible for NLP. Likewise, the parallelism within the inferencing component should be represented as tasks within the data retrieval module or the object or framework that is responsible for data retrieval. That is, we identify PVM tasks where they logically fit within the work that the program is doing as opposed to dividing the work the program does into a set of generic PVM tasks.

The notion of logic first, parallelism second, has several implications for C++ programs. It means that we might spawn PVM tasks from the `main()` function. We might spawn PVM tasks from subroutines called from `main()` or from other subroutines. We might spawn PVM tasks from within methods belonging to objects. Where we spawn the tasks depends on the concurrency requirements of the function, module, or object that is performing the work. The PVM tasks generally fall into two categories: SPMD (a derivative of SIMD) and MPMD (a derivative of MIMD). In the SPMD model, the tasks will execute the same set of instructions but on different pieces of data. In the MPMD model, each task executes different instructions on different data. Whether we are using the SPMD model or the MPMD model, the spawning of the task should be from the relevant areas of the program. Figure 6–4 shows some possible configurations for spawning PVM tasks.

6.2.5.1   Using the SPMD (*SIMD*) Model with PVM and C++

In Figure 6–4, Case 1 represents the situation where the function `main()` spawns from 1 to N tasks where each task performs the same set of instruc-

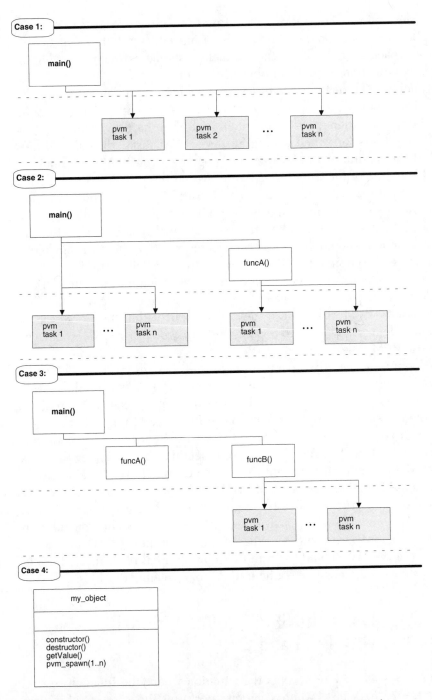

Figure 6–4 Some possible configurations for spawning PVM tasks.

tions but on different data sets. There are several options for implementing this scenario. Example 6.1 shows `main()` using the `pvm_spawn` routine.

```
// Example 6.1 Calling the pvm_spawn routine from main().

int main(int argc, char *argv[])
{
   int TaskId[10];
   int TaskId2[5];
   pvm_spawn("set_combination",NULL,0,"",10,TaskId); // 1rst Spawn
   pvm_spawn("set_combination",argv,0,"",5,TaskId2); // 2nd Spawn
   //...
}
```

In Example 6.1, the first spawn creates 10 tasks. Each task will execute the same set of instructions contained in the `set_combination` program. The `TaskId` array will contain the task identifiers for the PVM tasks if the spawn was successful. Once the program in Example 6.1 has the `TaskIds`, then it can use the `pvm_send()` routines to send specific data for each program to work on. This is possible because the `pvm_send()` routine contains the task identifier of the receiving task. The second spawn in Example 6.1 creates five tasks but in this case it passes each task information through the `argv` parameter. This is an additional method to pass information to tasks during startup. This is another way for a child task to uniquely identify itself by using values it receives in the `argv` parameter. In Example 6.2, the `main()` function uses multiple calls to `pvm_spawn()` to create *N* tasks as opposed to a single call.

```
// Example 6.2 Using multiple calls to pvm_spawn from main().

int main(int argc, char *argv[])
{
   int Task1;
   int Task2;
   int Task3;
   //...
   pvm_spawn("set_combination", NULL,1,"host1",1,&Task1);
   pvm_spawn("set_combination",argv,1,"host2",1,&,Task2);
   pvm_spawn("set_combination",argv++,1,"host 3",1,&,Task3);
   //...
}
```

The approach used in Example 6.2 can be used when you want the tasks to execute on specific computers. This is one of the advantages of the PVM environment. A program can take advantage of some particular resource on a particular computer, for example, special math processor, graphics processor, or MPP capabilities. Notice in Example 6.2 each host is executing the same set of instructions but each host received a different command-line argument. Case 2 in Figure 6–4 represents the scenario where the `main()` function does not spawn the PVM tasks. In this scenario the PVM tasks are logically related to `funcB()` and therefore `funcB()` spawns the tasks. The `main()` function and `funcA()` don't need to know anything about the PVM tasks so there is no reason to put any of the PVM housekeeping code in those functions. Case 3 in Figure 6–4 represents the scenario where the `main()` function and other functions in the program have natural parallelism. In this case the other function is `funcA()`. Also the PVM tasks executed by `main()` and the PVM tasks executed by `funcA()` execute different code. Although the tasks that `main()` spawns execute identical code and the tasks that `funcA()` spawns executes identical code, the two sets of tasks are different. This illustrates that a C++ program may use collections of tasks to solve different problems simultaneously. There is no reason that the program has to be restricted to one problem at a time. In Case 4 from Figure 6–4, the parallelism is contained within an object, therefore one of the object's methods spawns the PVM tasks. Here, the logical place to initiate the parallelism was within a class as opposed to some free-floating function.

As in the other cases, the PVM tasks spawned in Case 4 all execute the same instructions but with different data. This SPMD (Single Program Multiple Data) method is a commonly used technique for parallelization of certain kinds of problem solving. The fact that C++ has support for objects and generic programming using templates makes C++ a particularly powerful choice for this kind of programming. The objects and templates allow the C++ programmer to represent very general and flexible solutions to entire classes of problems with a single piece of code. This single piece of code fits in nicely with the SPMD model of parallelism. The notion of a class extends the SPMD model so that an entire class of problems can be solved. The templates allow the class of problems to be solved for virtually any data type. So although each task in the SPMD model is executing the same piece of code, it might be for an object or any of its descendants and it might be for different data types (different objects!). For example, Example 6.1 uses four PVM tasks to generate four sets in which each has C(n,r) elements: C(24,9), C(24,12), C(7,4), and C(7,3). Specifically, Example 6.3 enumerates the combinations of a set of 24 colors taken 9 and 12 at a time. It also enumerates the combinations of a set of 7 floating point numbers taken 4 at a time and 3 at a time. For an explanation of the notation C(n,r), see Sidebar 6.1.

```
// Example 6.3 Creating combinations of sets.

int main(int argc,char *argv[])
{
    int RetCode,TaskId[4];
    RetCode = pvm_spawn("pvm_generic_combination",NULL,0,"",4,TaskId);
    if(RetCode == 4){
        colorCombinations(TaskId[0],9);
        colorCombinations(TaskId[1],12);
        numericCombinations(TaskId[2],4);
        numericCombinations(TaskId[3],3);
        saveResult(TaskId[0]);
        saveResult(TaskId[1]);
        saveResult(TaskId[2]);
        saveResult(TaskId[3]);
        pvm_exit();
    }
    else{
        cerr << "Error Spawning ChildProcess" << endl;
            pvm_exit();
    }
    return(0);
}
```

Notice in Example 6.3 we spawn four PVM tasks:

```
pvm_spawn("pvm_generic_combination",NULL,0,"",4,TaskId);
```

Each task will execute the program named `pvm_generic_combination`. The NULL argument in our `pvm_spawn` call means that we are not passing any options via the `argv[]` parameter. The 0 in our `pvm_spawn` call means we don't care which computer the tasks execute on. `TaskId` is an array of four integers and will contain the task identifiers for each of the PVM tasks spawned if the call is successful. Notice in Example 6.3 we call `colorCombinations()` and `numericCombinations()`. These two functions assign the PVM tasks work. Example 6.4 contains the function definition for `colorCombinations()`.

```
// Example 6.4 Definition of the colorCombinations() function.

void colorCombinations(int TaskId,int Choices)
{
   int MessageId =1;
   char *Buffer;
   int Size;
   int N;
   string Source("blue purple green red yellow orange
                 silver gray ");
   Source.append("pink black white brown light_green
                 aqua beige cyan ");
   Source.append("olive azure magenta plum orchid violet
   maroon lavender");
   Source.append("\n");
   Buffer = new char[(Source.size() + 100)];
   strcpy(Buffer,Source.c_str());
   N = pvm_initsend(PvmDataDefault);
   pvm_pkint(&Choices,1,1);
   pvm_send(TaskId,MessageId);
   N = pvm_initsend(PvmDataDefault);
   pvm_pkbyte(Buffer,strlen(Buffer),1);
   pvm_send(TaskId,MessageId);
   delete Buffer;
}
```

Notice in Example 6.3 there are two calls to `colorCombinations()`. Each call assigns a PVM task a different number of color combinations to enumerate: C(24,9) and C(24,12). The first PVM task will produce 1,307,504 color combinations and the second task will produce 2,704,156 color combinations. The program named in the `pvm_spawn()` call does all the work. Each color is represented by a string. Therefore, when the `pvm_generic_combination` program is producing combinations it does so using a set of strings as the input. This is in contrast to the `numericCombinations()` function shown in Example 6.5. The code in Example 6.3 makes two calls to the `numericCombinations()` function. The first generates C(7,4) combinations and the second generates C(7,3) combinations.

```
// Example 6.5 Using PVM tasks to produce numeric combinations.

void numericCombinations(int TaskId,int Choices)
{
   int MessageId = 2;
   int N;
```

```
    double ImportantNumbers[7] = {3.00e+8,6.67e-11,1.99e+30,
                                  1.67e-27,6.023e+23,6.63e-34,
                                  3.14159265359};
    N = pvm_initsend(PvmDataDefault);
    pvm_pkint(&Choices,1,1);
    pvm_send(TaskId,MessageId);
    N = pvm_initsend(PvmDataDefault);
    pvm_pkdouble(ImportantNumbers,5,1);
    pvm_send(TaskId,MessageId);
}
```

In the `numericCombinations()` function in Example 6.4, the PVM task is sent an array of floating point numbers as opposed to an array of bytes representing strings. So the `colorCombinations()` function sends its data to the PVM tasks using:

```
pvm_pkbyte(Buffer,strlen(Buffer),1);
pvm_send(TaskId,MessageId);
```

The `numericCombination()` function sends its data to the PVM tasks using:

```
pvm_pkdouble(ImportantNumbers,5,1);
pvm_send(TaskId,MessageId);
```

The `colorCombinations()` function in Example 6.4 builds a string of colors and then copies that string of colors into an array of `char` called `Buffer`. The array of `char` is then packed and sent to the PVM task using the `pvm_pkbyte()` and `pvm_send()` functions. The `numericCombinations()` function in Example 6.5 creates an array of `doubles` and sends it to the PVM task using the `pvm_pkdouble()` and `pvm_send()` functions. One function sends a character array; the other function sends an array of `doubles`. In both cases the PVM tasks are executing the same program `pvm_generic_combination`. This is where the advantage of using C++ templates and genericity comes in. The same tasks are able to do work not only with different data but on different data types without a code change. The template facility in C++ helps to make the SPMD model more flexible and efficient. The `pvm_generic_combination` program is *almost* unaware of what data types it will be working with. The use of C++ container classes allows it to generate combinations of any `vector<T>` of objects. The `pvm_generic_combination` program does know that it will be working with two data types. Example 6.6 shows a section of code from the `pvm_generic_combination` program.

```
// Example 6.6 Using the MessageId tag to distinguish
//              data types.

pvm_bufinfo(N,&NumBytes,&MessageId,&Ptid);
if(MessageId == 1){
   vector<string> Source;
   Buf = new char[NumBytes];
   pvm_upkbyte(Buf,NumBytes,1);
   strstream Buffer;
   Buffer << Buf << ends;
   while(Buffer.good())
   {
      Buffer >> Color;
      if(!Buffer.eof()){
         Source.push_back(Color);
      }
   }
   generateCombinations<string>(Source,Ptid,Value);
   delete Buf;
}
if(MessageId == 2){
   vector<double> Source;
   double *ImportantNumber;
   NumBytes = NumBytes / sizeof(double);
   ImportantNumber = new double[NumBytes];
   pvm_upkdouble(ImportantNumber,NumBytes,1);
   copy(ImportantNumber,ImportantNumber +(NumBytes + 1),
   inserter(Source,Source.begin()));
   generateCombinations<double>(Source,Ptid,Value);
   delete ImportantNumber;

}
```

Here we use the `MessageId` tag to distinguish which data type we are working with. But in C++ we can do better. If the `MessageId` tag contains a 1, then we are working with strings. Therefore, we make the declaration:

```
vector<string> Source;
```

If the `MessageId` tag contains a 2, then we know we are working with floating point numbers, and we make the declaration:

```
vector<double> Source;
```

Once we declare what type of data the vector source will contain, the rest of the function in the `pvm_generic_combination` is generalized. Notice in Example 6.6 that each `if()` statement calls the `generateCombinations()` function. This `generateCombinations()` function is a template function. This template architecture helps us to achieve the genericity that will extend the SPMD and the MPMD scenarios for our PVM programs. We will come back to the discussion of our `pvm_generic_combination` program after we present the basic mechanics of the PVM environment. It is important to note that C++ container classes, stream classes, and template algorithms add flexibility to PVM programming that cannot be easily implemented in other PVM environments. This flexibility creates opportunities for sophisticated yet elegant parallel architectures.

6.2.5.2   Using the MPMD (MIMD) Model with PVM and C++

Whereas the SPMD model uses the `pvm_spawn()` function to create some number of tasks executing the same program but on potentially different data or resources, the MPMD model will use the `pvm_spawn()` function to create tasks that are executing different programs each with their own data sets. Example 6.7 shows how a single C++ program could implement a MPMD model of computation using PVM calls.

```
// Example 6.7 Using PVM to implement the MPMD model of
//             computation.

int main(int argc, char *argv[])
{
   int Task1[20];
   int Task2[50];
   int Task3[30];
   //...
   pvm_spawn("pvm_generic_combination", NULL,1,"host1",20,Task1);
   pvm_spawn("generate_plans",argv,0,"",50,Task2);
   pvm_spawn("agent_filters",argv++,1,"host 3",30,&Task3);
   //...
}
```

The code in Example 6.7 creates 100 tasks. The first 20 tasks are generating combinations. The next 50 tasks are generating plans from the combinations as the combinations are being created. The last 30 tasks are filtering the best plans from the set of plans being generated by the set of 50 tasks. This is in contrast to the SPMD model, where all of the programs spawned by the `pvm_spawn()` function were the same. Here, we have `pvm_generic_combination`, `generate_plans`, and `agent_filters` performing the work of the PVM tasks. They are all executing concurrently. They each have their own set of data; although they are working with transformations of the data. The `pvm_generic_combination` transforms its input into something that `generate_plans` can use. The `generate_plans` program transforms its input into something that `agent_filters` can use. Obviously these tasks will send messages to each other. The messages will represent input and control information between the processes. Also notice in Example 6.7 that we used the `pvm_spawn()` routine to allocate 20 `pvm_generic_combination` on a computer named `host1`. The `generate_plans` task was allocated to 50 anonymous proces-

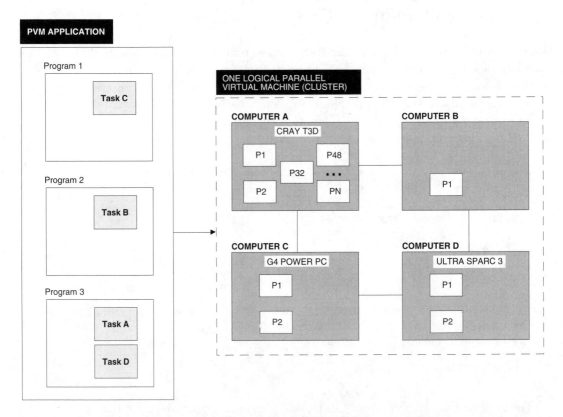

Figure 6–5 Some options available for MPMD configurations using the PVM environment.

sors, but each of the 50 tasks received the same command-line argument through the argv parameter. The `agent_filters` tasks were also directed to a particular computer. In this case, the computer was `host 3`, and each task received the same command-line argument through the `argv` parameter. This emphasizes the flexibility and power of the PVM library. Figure 6–5 shows some options available for MPMD configurations using the PVM environment.

We can take advantage of particular resources of particular computers if so desired. We can use arbitrary anonymous computers in other cases. In addition, we can assign different work to different tasks simultaneously. In Figure 6–5 Computer A is a MPP (Massively Parallel Processor) computer, and Computer B has a number of specialized numeric processors. Also notice that the PVM in Figure 6–5 consists of PowerPCs, Sparcs, Crays, and so on. In some cases we don't care what specific capabilities of the computers in a PVM are, but in other cases we do. The `pvm_spawn()` routine allows the C++ programmer to use the anonymous approach by simply not

---

S 6.1. | **Combination Notation**

Suppose we wish to choose a team of eight programmers from a pool of 24 candidates. How many different teams of eight programmers could we come up with? One of the results that follow from the Fundamental Principle of Counting tells us there are 735,471 different teams consisting of eight programmers that can be selected from a pool of 24. The notation C(n,r) is read the number of combination of n choose r. That is, the number of choices taken r at a time from n items. C(n,r) is calculated by the formula:

$$\frac{n!}{r!(n-r)!}$$

When we have a set that represents a combination, for example, {a,b,c} would be considered the same as the set {b,a,c}, or {c,b,a}. That is, we don't care about the order of the members in the set; we are only concerned about the members in the set. Many parallel programs, search algorithms, heuristics, and artificial intelligence–based programs have to deal with large sets of combinations and their close relative, permutations.

specifying which computer to create the tasks on. On the other hand, if there is something special about some member of the PVM, then that feature can be exploited by specifying the particular member using `pvm_spawn()`.

6.3   The Basic Mechanics of the PVM

The PVM environment consists of two components: the PVM daemon (pvmd) and the pvmd library. One `pvmd` daemon runs on each host computer in the virtual machine. The `pvmd` serves as a message router and controller. A `pvmd` is used to start additional `pvmds`. Each `pvmd` manages the lists of PVM tasks on its host machine. The `pvmd` performs process control, some minimal authentication, and fault tolerance. Usually the first `pvmd` is started manually. This `pvmd` then starts the other `pvmds`. Only the original `pvmd` may start additional `pvmds`. Only the original `pvmd` may unconditionally stop another `pvmd`.

The pvmd library contains the routines that allow one PVM task to interact with other PVM tasks.The library also contains routines that allow the PVM task to communicate with its `pvmd`. Figure 6–6 shows the basic architecture of the PVM environment.

The PVM environment will consist of two or more PVM tasks. Each task will contain one or more send buffers. However, only one send buffer may be active at a time. This is called the active send buffer. Each task has an active receive buffer. Notice in Figure 6–6 that communication between PVM tasks is actually accomplished using TCP sockets. The `pvm_send()` routines make socket access transparent. The programmer does not access the TCP socket calls directly. Figure 6–6 also shows PVM tasks communicating to their `pvmds` using TCP sockets and `pvmds` communicating between themselves using UDP sockets. Again, the socket calls are performed by the PVM routines. The programmer does not have to do low-level socket programming. The PVM routines we use in this book fit into four categories:

- Process Management and Control
- Messaging Packing and Sending
- Message Unpacking and Receiving
- Message Buffer Management

Simplified Architecture of a PVM Program

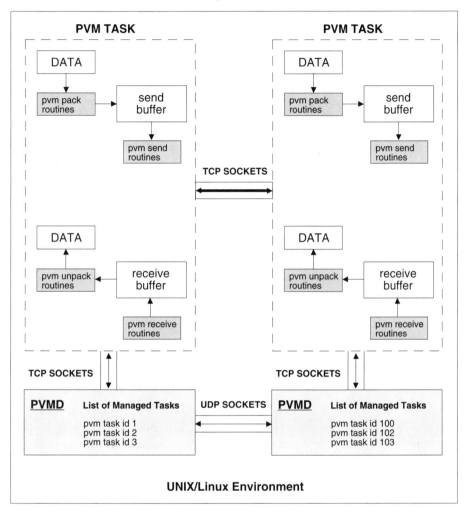

Figure 6-6 Basic architecture of the PVM environment.

While there are other categories of PVM routines, such as the Information and Utility Functions and the Group Operations, we focus on the message processing and process management routines. We will discuss any other routines in the context of the programs in which they are used.

6.3.1   Process Management and Control Routines

There are six commonly used process management and control routines.

Synopsis

```
#include "pvm3.h"

int pvm_spawn(char *task, char **argv, int flag, char *location,
            int ntask,int *taskids);
int pvm_kill(int taskid);
int pvm_exit(void);
int pvm_addhosts(char **hosts,int nhosts,int *status);
int pvm_delhosts(char **hosts,int nhosts,int *status);
int pvm_halt(void);
```

The `pvm_spawn()` routine is used to create new PVM tasks. The routine can specify how many tasks to create, where to create the tasks, and arguments to be passed to each task. For example:

```
pvm_spawn("agent_filters",argv++,1,"host 3",30,&Task3);
```

The `task` parameter should contain the name of the program that the `pvm_spawn()` is to execute. Since the program that is executed by the `pvm_spawn()` routine is a standalone program, command-line arguments may be required. The `argv` parameter is used to pass any command-line arguments to the program. The `location` parameter specifies which host the task is to be executed on. The `taskids` parameter will contain either the task identifiers for the spawned tasks or status codes representing any error conditions that might have been created during the spawn process. The `ntasks` parameter specifies how many instances of the task to create. The `pvm_kill()` routine is used to kill tasks other than the calling task. The `taskid` passed to `pvm_kill()` can reference any other user-defined task in the PVM. This routine works by sending the SIGTERM signal to the PVM task to be killed. The `pvm_exit()` routine is used to cause the calling task to be removed from the PVM. While the task can be removed from the PVM, the process that the task belonged to may continue to execute. Keep in mind that a task executing PVM calls may have other work to perform that is not related to the PVM. The `pvm_exit()` routine should be called by any task that no longer has work relevant to the PVM processing. The `pvm_addhosts()` allows the caller to dynamically add more computers to an existing PVM. Typically, the `pvm_addhosts()` is called with a list of one or more host-names:

```
int Status[3];
char *Hosts[] = {"porthos", "dartagnan","athos"};
pvm_addhosts("porthose",1,&Status);

//... or ...

pvm_addhosts(Hosts,3,Status);
```

The `Hosts` parameter will usually contain the names of one or more hosts listed in the `.rhosts` file or the `.xpvm_hosts` file. The `nhost` parameter will contain the number of hosts to be added to the PVM, and the `status` parameter will contain a value = to `nhosts` if the call was successful. If the call was not able to add any hosts, the return value will be less than `1`. If the call was only partially successful, the return value will represent the number of hosts added. Likewise, the `pvm_delhosts()` allows the caller to dynamically remove one or more computers from an existing PVM. The hosts parameter will contain a list of one or more hosts. The `nhosts` parameter will contain the number of hosts to be removed. For instance:

```
pvm_delhosts("dartagnan",1);
```

causes the computer with hostname `dartagnan` to be removed from the PVM environment. The `pvm_addhosts()` and `pvm_delhosts()` may be called during runtime. This allows the programmer to have a dynamically sizeable PVM. Any PVM task running on a host computer that is deleted from the PVM will be killed. If there are any `pvmds` running on the computers that are deleted from the PVM, the `pvmds` will be stopped also. If a host fails for some reason, the PVM environment will automatically delete the host. The return values for `pvm_delhosts` are the same as they are `pvm_addhosts()`. The `pvm_halt()` routine shuts down the entire PVM system. All tasks and `pvmds` are stopped.

6.3.2   Message Packing and Sending

Geist, Beguelin, and colleagues state the message model of the PVM environment accordingly:

PVM daemons and tasks can compose and send messages of arbitrary lengths containing typed data. The data can be converted using XDR[1] when passing between hosts with incompatible data formats. Messages are tagged at send time with a user-defined integer code and can be selected for receipt by source address or tag. The sender of a message does not wait for an acknowledgement from the receiver, but continues as soon as the message has been handed to the network and the message buffer can be safely deleted or reused. Messages are buffered at the receiving end until received. PVM reliably delivers messages, provided the destination exists. Message order from each sender to each receiver in the system is preserved; if one entity sends several messages to another, they will be received in the same order.

The PVM library consists of a family of routines used to pack the various data types into a send buffer. There are pack routines for character arrays, `doubles`, `floats`, `ints`, `longs`, `bytes`, and so on. Table 6–3 shows the list of `pvmpk` routines by type.

Table 6–3   **pvmpk** Routines

Message Packing Functions

bytes
```
int pvm_pkbyte(char *cp, int count, int std);
```
complex/double complex
```
int pvm_pkcplx(float *xp, int count, int std);
int pvm_pkdcplx(double *zp, int count, int std);
```
double
```
int pvm_pkdouble(double *dp, int count, int std);
```
float
```
int pvm_pkfloat(float *fp, int count, int std);
```
int
```
int pvm_pkint(int *np, int count, int std);
```
long
```
int pvm_pklong(long *np, int count, int std);
```
short
```
int pvm_pkshort(short *np, int count, int std);
```
string
```
int pvm_pkstr(char *cp);
```

Each of the pack routines in Table 6–3 are used to store an array of data in the send buffer. Notice in Figure 6–6 that each PVM task will have at least one send and receive buffer. Each of the pack routines takes a pointer to an array of the appropriate data type. Every pack routine except for pvm_pkstr() takes the total number of items to be stored in the array (not the number of bytes!). The pvm_pkstr() routine assumes the character array it is working with will be NULL terminated. Each pack routine except the pvm_pkstr() has as the last parameter a value that represents how to traverse the source array as items are selected to be packed into the send buffer. The parameter is often referred to as the *stride*. For instance, if the stride is four, then every fourth element will be selected from the source to be stored in the send buffer. It is important to note that the pvm_initsend() routine should be used prior to sending each message. The pvm_initsend() routine clears the buffer and prepares it to send the next message. The pvm_init-send() routine prepares the buffer to send the message in one of three formats: XDR, Raw, or In Place.

XDR (External Data Representation) is a standard used to describe and encode data. Keep in mind that the hosts involved in a PVM can be different machine types. For instance, a PVM might consist of Sun, Macintosh, Crays, and AMD machines. These machines might have different word sizes and may store data types differently. In some instance the bit ordering might be different from one machine to another. The XDR standard is used to allow the machines to exchange data in an architecture-independent way. The Raw format is used to send the data in the native format of the sending machine. No special encoding is used. The in place format really does not pack the data in the send buffer. Instead, only pointers to the data and size of the data is sent. The receiving task copies the data directly. These three types of encoding are represented by three constants in the PVM library:

PvmDataDefault	XDR
PvmDataRaw	No special encoding
PvmDataInPlace	Only pointers and sizes copied to send buffer

For example:

```
int BufferId;
BufferId = pvm_initsend(PvmDataRaw);
//...
```

specifies that data be packed into the send buffer as is, that is, with no special encoding. If the `pvm_initsend()` call is successful, it will return the number of the send buffer in `BufferId`. It is important to remember that although only one send buffer can be active at a time, a PVM task can have multiple send buffers. Each buffer will have a number associated with it. The PVM library defines several `send` routines.

Synopsis

```
#include "pvm3.h"

int pvm_send(int taskid, int messageid);
int pvm_psend(int taskid, int messageid,char *buffer,int len,
              int datatype);
int pvm_mcast(int *taskid,int ntask,int messageid);
```

In each of these routines, `taskid` is the task identifier of the PVM task that receives the message. In the case of `pvm_mcast()`, the `taskid` refers to a collection of tasks represented by the task identifiers passed in the array `*taskid`. The `messageid` parameter specifies which message to send. The message identifiers are integers and are user-defined. They are used by the sender and receiver to identify which message will be waited on by the receiver and which message will be sent by the sender. For example:

```
pvm_bufinfo(N,&NumBytes,&MessageId,&Ptid);

//...

switch(MessageId)
{
    case 1 : // do something
            break;

    case 2 : // do something else
            break
            //...
}
```

In this case, the `pvm_bufinfo()` routine is used to get information about the last message received by receive buffer `N`. We can get the number of bytes, the `messageid`, and who sent the message. Once we get the messageid we can execute the appropriate logic. The pvm_send() routine performs a pseudo-blocking send to the specified task, that is, the task only blocks as long as it takes to make sure that the message has been properly sent. The task does not wait for the receiver to actually receive the task. The pvm_psend() routine sends the message directly to the specified task. Notice that the pvm_psend() routine has a buffer parameter used to contain the message to be sent. The pvm_mcast() is used to send a message to multiple tasks simultaneously. The arguments for the pvm_mcast() will include an array of taskids that receives the message, the number of tasks involved in the multicast, and the messageid to identify the message sent. Figure 6–6 shows that each PVM task has its own send buffer. The buffer exists just long enough for the message to be guaranteed to be on its way.

With the exception of control messages, the meaning of the messages between any two PVM tasks is application defined, that is, the sending and the receiving task must have a predefined use for each message. The messages are asynchronous, of arbitrary data types, and of arbitrary length. This pro-

---

Synopsis

```
#include "pvm3.h"

int pvm_recv(int taskid, int messageid);
int pvm_nrecv(int taskid, int messageid);
int pvm_precv(int taskid, int messageid, char *buffer,
              int size, int type, int sender, int messagetag,
              int messagelength);
int pvm_trecv(int taskid, int messageid,
              struct timeval *timeout);
int pvm_probe(int taskid , int messageid);
```

---

vides for maximum flexibility within the application. The counterparts to the pvm_send messages are the PVM receive messages. There are five important functions in the receive family of routines.

The pvm_recv() routine is used to receive messages from other PVM tasks. This routine creates a new active buffer that will contain the message received. The taskid parameter specifies the task identifier of the sending task. The messageid parameter identifies the message that is being sent from the sender. Keep in mind that a task may send multiple messages, each with different or the same `messageid`. If the `taskid = -1`, then the `pvm_recv()` routine will accept a message from any task. If the `messageid` parameter `= -1`, then the routine will accept any message. The `pvm_recv()` routine return value will be the buffer id of the new active buffer if the call is successful and will be a `value < 0` if an error has occurred. When a task calls the `pvm_recv()` routine will block and wait until the message has been received. After the message is received, it is retrieved from the active message buffer using one of the unpack routines. For instance:

```
//...
float Value[10];
pvm_recv(400002,2);
pvm_unpkfloat(400002, Value,1);
cout << Value..
```

The `pvm_recv()` routine causes this code to wait on a message from a task identified as `400002`. The `messageid` received from `400002` must be 2 before the routine unblocks. The `unpack` routine is then used to retrieve the array of `floats`. Whereas the `pvm_recv()` routine causes the task to wait until it receives a message, the `pvm_nrecv()` routine is a nonblocking receive. If the appropriate message has not arrived, the `pvm_nrecv()` routine will immediately return. If the message has arrived, the `pvm_nrecv()` will return immediately and the active buffer will contain the message. If an error condition occurs, then `pvm_nrecv()` will return a value < 0. If the message has not arrived, the routine returns 0. If the message has arrived, the number for the new active buffer will be returned. The `taskid` parameter will contain the task identifier for the sending task. The `messageid` parameter will contain a user-defined message id. If the `taskid = -1`, then the `pvm_nrecv()` routine will accept a message from any task. If the `messageid = -1`, or then the routine will receive any message. When messages are received in the active buffer by either `pvm_recv()` or `pvm_nrecv()`, a new active buffer is created and the current receive buffer is cleared.

Whereas the `pvm_recv()`, `pvm_nrecv()`, and the `pvm_trecv()` receive their messages into a new active buffer, the `pvm_precv()` routine receives its message directly into a user-defined buffer. The `taskid` parameter contains the task identifier for the sending task. The `messageid` parameter identifies which message is being received. The `buffer` parameter will contain the actual message. So instead of getting the message from the active buffer using one of the unpack routines, the message is retrieved directly from the buffer parameter. The size parameter contains the length in bytes of the message.

The type parameter specifies the data type of the message. The values for data type are:

PVM_STR	PVM_BYTE
PVM_SHORT	PVM_INT
PVM_FLOAT	PVM_DOUBLE
PVM_LONG	PVM_USHORT
PVM_CPLX	PVM_DCPLX
PVM_UINT	PVM_ULONG

The pvm_trecv() is an important routine that allows the programmer to use a timed receive. The pvm_trecv() routine causes the calling task to block and wait for the message, but only for the amount of time specified for the timeout parameter. The specified parameter is a structure of type timeval defined time.h. For example:

```
#include "pvm3.h"

//...

struct timeval TimeOut;
TimeOut.tv_sec = 1000;
int TaskId;
int MessageId;
TaskId = pvm_parent();
MessageId = 2;
pvm_trecv(TaskId,MessageId,&TimeOut);
//...
```

the TimeOut variable has the tv_sec member set to 1000 seconds. The timeval struct can be used to set the timeout values in seconds and microseconds. The timeval is a struct has the structure:

```
struct timeval{
   long tv_sec;  // seconds
   long tv_usec; // microseconds
};
```

This means the pvm_trecv() routine will block the calling task for at the most 1000 seconds. If this message gets there before the 1000 seconds have expired, the routine will return. This routine can be used to help prevent indefinite postponement and deadlock. If pvm_trecv() is successful, it will return the number of the new active buffer. If an error occurs, then a value < 0 will be returned. If taskid = -1, the routine will accept a message from any sender. If the messageid parameter = -1, it will accept any message.

The pvm_probe() routine determines whether a particular message has arrived from the specified sender. The taskid parameter identifies the sender. The messageid parameter identifies the particular message. If the pvm_probe() routine sees the specified message, then the routine returns the buffer number for the new active buffer. If the specified message has not

---

Synopsis

```
#include "pvm3.h"

int pvm_getsbuf(void);
int pvm_getrbuf(void);
int pvm_setsbuf(int bufferid);
int pvm_setrbuf(int bufferid);
int pvm_mkbuf(int Code);
int pvm_freebuf(int bufferid);
```

---

arrived, the routine returns a 0. If an error condition has occurred, the routine will return a value < 0.

There are six useful buffer management routines that can be used for setting, identifying, and dynamically creating the send and receive buffers. The pvm_getsbuf() routine is used to get the number for the active send buffer. If there is no current buffer, this routine will return 0. The pvm_getrbuf() routine is used to get the id number for the active receive buffer. Keep in mind that every time a message is received, a new active receive buffer is created and the current receive buffer is cleared. If there is no current receive buffer, pvm_getrbuf() will return 0. The pvm_setsbuf() routine sets the active send buffer to bufferid. Typically, a PVM task has only one send buffer. However, sometimes multiple send buffers are required. Although only one send buffer can be active at a time, a PVM task may create additional send buffers using the pvm_mkbuf() routine. The pvm_setsbuf() can be used to set the active buffer to send buffers that have been created at runtime. This routine returns the buffer identifier for the previous active send buffer. The pvm_setrbuf() sets the active receive buffer to bufferid. Remember that the PVM unpack routines work with the active receive buffer. If there is more than one buffer, then the pvm_setrbuf() can be used to set the current buffer to be used by the unpack routines. If the call to `pvm_setrbuf()` is successful, it will return the buffer id of the previous buffer. If the buffer identifier passed to `pmv_setrbuf()` is not valid or does not exist, then the routine can return one of the following error messages: `PvmBadParam` or `PvmNoSuchbuf`. The `pvm_mkbuf()` routine is used to create a new message buffer. The `Code` parameter specifies whether the buffer will be set up to contain data encoded as XDR format, native machine format, or pointers and sizes. The `Code` parameter can be one of three values:

`PvmDataDefault`	XDR
`PvmDataRaw`	Machine dependent (no encoding)
`PvmDataInPlace`	Pointers to the data and sizes of data only used

If the `pvm_mkbuf()` routine is successful, it will return the buffer id of the new active buffer. If an error occurs, the function will return a value < 0. For every call to `pvm_mkbuf()` there should be a call made to `pvm_freebuf()` when the send buffer is no longer needed. The memory allocated by the `pvm_mkbuf()` routine is released by `pvm_freebuf()`. `pvm_freebuf()` should only be used on a buffer that is no longer needed, for example, after the message has been sent.

6.4   Accessing Standard Input (`stdin`) and Standard Output (`stdout`) within PVM Tasks

A PVM environment ties a collection of machines together and presents them to the program as one logical machine with multiple processors. Which machine in the PVM should act as the console? When a PVM task inserts data into the `cout ostream` object, where will the data be displayed? If a PVM task attempts to get data from a keyboard, which keyboard will it read the data from? The `stdout` for each child process is intercepted and sent to a designated PVM task as a PVM message. Each child process inherits information that determines which task will receive information written to `stdout` and how that information should be identified. Each child process's `stdin` is tied to `/dev/null`. Anything written to `/dev/null` disappears. If `/dev/null` is opened for reading, the equivalent of end-of-file is returned.

This means child processes should not be designed to rely on input from stdin (cin) or on sending output to stdout (cout). When designing input and output processing, this behavior of stdin and stdout in a PVM environment must be considered. However, stdin and stdout for the main or parent task behaves as expected. PVM tasks use messages to communicate. Input may be retrieved from messages, pipes, shared memory, environment variables, command-line arguments, or files. Output may be written to messages, pipes, shared memory, and files.

6.4.1   Retrieving Standard Output (cout) from a Child Task

Output written to stdout or inserted into cout behaves differently for PVM-spawned children. The parent decides what ultimately happens to the output. When output from a spawned child is inserted into cout or cerr, it is intercepted by the pvmd for that task and is packaged into standard PVM messages and sent to a TaskId specified by the parent. The parent associates a pair (TaskId, Code) to the cout and cerr of its children. This is done using the pvm_setopt() routine. This routine is called before the children are spawned. If the TaskId is 0, the messages will go to the master pvmd, where they will be written to its error log. A spawned child may only set the TaskId to 0, the value inherited from its parent, or its own TaskId. This means the parent ultimately controls where cout or cerr would write to. A child PVM designate other PVM tasks to receive data inserted into cout or cerr. The typical approach is to let the spawning task manage any important data written to stdout or stdin and let the master pvmd take everything else.

Summary

The PVM library is a flexible library that supports the major models of parallel programming. The advantage of a PVM environment is its ability to work with heterogeneous collections of computers that may consist of different processor speeds, sizes, and architectures. Besides hardware compatibility, it works nicely with the C++ standard library and with the UNIX/Linux system library. When combined with the C++ template capabilities, object-oriented programming capabilities, and collection of algorithms, the power of the

PVM environment is increased considerably. The template facility has a nice application to SPMD programming. The containers and algorithms can be used to enhance the MIMD (MPMD) capabilities of the PVM. In Chapter 13, we dig a little deeper into the PVM and show how it can be used to help implement blackboards using C++. The blackboard is one of our primary choices for implementing parallel problem solving.

7 Error Handling, Exceptions, and Software Reliability

> "It is always possible to invent over-elaborate models to explain a set of observable facts, but the scientist, if not the philosopher, will always accept the simplest theory that is consistent with all the data."
>
> —*Alastair Rae, Quantum Physics Illusion or Reality*

In this Chapter

What is Software Reliability? • Failures in Software Layers and Hardware Components • Definitions of Defects Depend on Software Specifications • Recognizing Where to Handle Defects versus Where to Handle Exceptions • Software Reliability: A Simple Plan • Using Map Objects in Error Handling • Exception Handling Mechanisms in C++ • Event Diagrams, Logic Expressions, and Logic Diagrams • Summary

One of the primary goals of software design and engineering is to produce software that meets the user's requirements correctly and reliably. Users demand reliable and correct software regardless of the software's function. Gamers have high expectations for their software in the same way as users in a business environment. Unreliable software, whether in financial, industrial, medical, scientific, or military applications, can have devastating ramifications. The dependency on software by people and machines at all levels in our society requires that every effort be made to produce reliable, robust, and fault-tolerant software. This necessity presents additional challenges to the software designer and developer who has to develop systems that contain concurrency. Programs that contain concurrency or components that execute in distributed environments contain more layers of software. The more layers involved, the more complexity that must be managed. The more complexity that needs to be managed, the greater possibility that software defects will go undiscovered. The more defects a piece of software contains, the stronger the guarantee that the software will fail, doing so at the worst possible time.

Programs divided into concurrently executing or distributed tasks have the additional challenges that are found in the process of correctly identifying the WBS (Work Breakdown Structure) of a solution. Also, the problems that are inherently part of network communications have to be handled. In addition to WBS and communication problems, synchronization woes such as deadlock and data race must be tackled. Concurrent programming is almost by definition more complex than sequential programming and therefore the error handling and exception handling for concurrent programs require more thought, more effort, and more coding. The interesting thing to note here is that the trend for software development is toward applications that require parallel and distributed programming. The Internet and the intranet model are pervasive in today's software design. General-purpose computers with multiple processors are becoming the norm rather than the exception. Embedded and industrial computing devices are becoming more sophisticated with more onboard computing power and multiple processors. The notion of the cluster is quickly becoming the de facto standard for server deployment. It is our contention that today's software designer and developer have little choice but to understand how to design and develop reliable software for parallel processor or networked environments. The requirements for software are growing in complexity and sophistication.

In many of the code examples in this book we do not show the necessary error handling or exception handling code because it would detract from some idea or concept that we are presenting. It is important to keep in mind that the examples presented in this book are introductory in nature. In practice, the amount of error handling and exception handling code for programs that require concurrency or distribution is significant. Error handling and exception handling must be part of the design of the software at every phase of its development. We advocate a modeling approach toward discovering the parallelism within a problem domain or solution domain. It is during this modeling phase that the exception handling and error handling models need to be developed. In Chapter 10, we discuss how the UML (Unified Modeling Language) can be used to visualize the design of systems requiring concurrency or distributed programming. The design of error handling and exception handling techniques can also take advantage of the UML and visualization process. There is no real substitute for this visualization process. Therefore, as an initial goal you want to see your software's reliability using tools like the UML, event diagrams, event expressions, synchronization diagrams, and so on. In this chapter we take advantage of several design techniques that aid with the visualization of error and exception handling design. We also take advantage of C++'s exception handling facilities, including the exception class hierarchy, to act as a foundation for developing reliable and robust software.

7.1   What is Software Reliability?

Software reliability is the probability of failure-free operation of a computer program for a specified time in a specified environment. Ideally, that probability should be as close to 100% as necessary. When failure is not an option, the software must be designed using the techniques of fault-tolerant programming. A *fault-tolerant system* is one that corrects or survives software faults. A fault is a program defect that can cause a piece of software to fail. We define "software failure" as the execution of some component of software that deviates from system specifications. We rely on Musa, Iannino, and Okumoto in their work *Software Reliability* for a complete characterization of faults and failures:

> A fault is the defect in the program that when executed under particular conditions, causes a failure. There can be different sets of conditions that cause failures, or the conditions can be repeated. Hence a fault can be the source of more than one failure. A fault is a property of the program rather than a property of its execution or behavior. It is what we are really referring to in general when we use the term "bug." A fault is created when a programmer makes an *error*.

The errors that a programmer or software developer makes may be from a misinterpretation of the software requirements, or from a poor, incorrect, or incomplete translation of the software requirements into code. When the programmer makes these kinds of errors, he or she introduces defects or faults into the software. When those defects or faults are executed, they can cause software failure. Software failure can only occur during the execution. The process of testing and debugging software removes faults from software, thereby preventing the possibility of software failure. Note that we use the terms "defect" and "fault" interchangeably. We use the term "error" to refer to the mistakes that the programmer makes that introduce faults (defects) into the software. *Fault tolerance* is a property that allows a piece of software to survive and recover from the software failures caused by faults introduced into the software as a result of human error. The most robust fault tolerance can even correct these failures.

Some failures are the result of software faults. Other failures are the result of exceptional conditions (not necessarily due to human error) that can occur in either hardware or software. For instance, a network card damaged as a result of a power surge can cause the software that depends on it to fail. A virus may corrupt a data transmission that will cause the software that depends on the data transmission to fail. A user may inadvertently remove critical components of a system, thereby causing the software to fail. These kinds of failures are not due to defects in the software, but are created by conditions that we call *exceptions*. An *exception* is an abnormal condition, exceptional circumstance, or an extraordinary occurrence that the software encounters that causes all or part of the software to fail. Although both defects and exceptions cause software failure, it is important to distinguish between them. The techniques for dealing with defects and exceptions can be and usually are different. While the end result of applying those techniques is reliable software, exception handling and error (defect) handling use different design approaches and coding constructs.

7.2   Failures in Software Layers and Hardware Components

Designing reliable fault-tolerant software requires that we design software that continues to operate even after some of its components fail. These components can be either hardware or software components. If our software is fault tolerant, it will have features that counter the effects of hardware or software faults. At the very minimum, our fault-tolerant designs should provide for graceful degradation of service as opposed to immediate interruption of service. If our software is fault tolerant and it encounters failed component(s), it should continue to function but at reduced levels. The failures that our software must handle can be divided into two categories: software and hardware. Figure 7–1 contains a breakdown of some of the hardware components as well as the layers of software that may be involved in failure.

In Figure 7–1, we make a distinction between the hardware components and the software layers because the techniques for handling hardware failures are often different from the techniques used to handle software failures. Also in Figure 7–1, there are several software layers involved. Some of the software layers are beyond the direct control of the developer and require

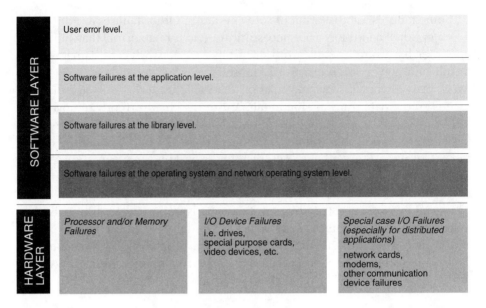

Figure 7-1   A breakdown of some of the hardware components and layers of software involved in failure.

special consideration during exception and error handling. The software design, development, and testing phases have to take into account the kinds of problems caused by hardware failures and the software layers where failure can occur. Programs that require parallelism or that consist of distributed components have additional hardware failures to consider. For instance, distributed programs rely on communications hardware and software. Failure in a communication component can cause the entire system to fail. Programs designed for parallel processors may fail if the anticipated number of processors is not available. Also, if communications or processors are available during startup, failure may occur at some time after the program has begun to execute. Exceptions may occur with any of the hardware components and in any of the software layers. In addition, each software layer may contain defects that must be handled. During the software design phase it is useful to approach exception and error handling layer by layer. The options for recovery or repair for an application that faces failure at layer 2 are different from the options that are available at layer 3. In addition to the failures that may occur in the various software layers and hardware components, the failures may also be characterized by location. Figure 7–2 depicts how as the dis-

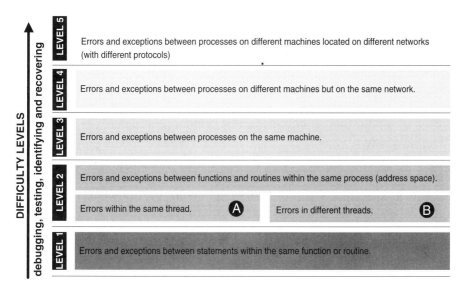

DIFFICULTY LEVELS
debugging, testing, identifying and recovering

LEVEL 5 Errors and exceptions between processes on different machines located on different networks (with different protocols)

LEVEL 4 Errors and exceptions between processes on different machines but on the same network.

LEVEL 3 Errors and exceptions between processes on the same machine.

LEVEL 2 Errors and exceptions between functions and routines within the same process (address space).
Errors within the same thread. **A**   Errors in different threads. **B**

LEVEL 1 Errors and exceptions between statements within the same function or routine.

Figure 7–2   Contrasting the increase of distance between location of tasks and the increase of the level of difficulty of error and exception handling.

tance between the tasks increases, so does the level of difficulty of error and exception handling.

The more distance in software or hardware components between the concurrently executing tasks, the more sophistication required when designing exception and error handling components. So from Figures 7–1 and 7–2, we can see that in order to design and develop reliable software, we will have to make provisions for the *what* and *where* of defects and exceptions.

7.3   Definitions of Defects Depend on Software Specifications

A software specification is the measuring stick that we use to decide whether a piece of software has defects. We cannot determine a software component's correctness without access to the software's specification. The specification contains the description and requirements for what a software component is supposed to do and what it is not supposed to do. It is important to note that complete, thorough, and accurate specifications are notoriously difficult to produce. Specifications typically fall between two extremes: The specification may come as a set of formal documents and requirements compiled by end users, analysts, user interface engineers, domain specialists, and others, or it may only have been a set of goals and loosely defined objectives verbally communicated to the software designers and developers. The deviation of a software component from the software specification is a defect or fault. The higher the quality of the specification, the easier it is to define what a defect is or to identify where the programmer made mistakes. When a project's specification is vague, and the elements are poorly defined and the requirements are not definitive, then the definition of a software defect for that project is a moving target. If the specifications are ambiguous, we cannot say what is defective and what is not. We cannot state with certainty whether the developer is correct. Vaguely defined specifications lead to vaguely defined defects. Fault-tolerant and reliable software is not possible under these situations.

7.4   Recognizing Where to Handle Defects versus Where to Handle Exceptions

In general, software defects (which are the result of programmer error) should be detected and corrected during the testing phases defined in Table 7–1.

Through the process of testing and debugging, defects should be identified and removed. On the other hand, exceptions are handled during execution of the program at runtime. We also distinguish between exceptional conditions and unwanted conditions. For instance, if we have designed a program that will add a list of numbers typed in by the user and the user types in some numbers and some characters that are not numbers, then this is an unwanted condition, not an exceptional condition. We should design programs to be robust through input validation so that the user is forced to enter the data that our program requires for proper execution. If part of a program that we design saves information to external storage and the program encounters an out-of-space condition, then the out-of-space condition is an unwanted situation, not an exceptional or extraordinary condition. We reserve exception handling for the unusual, not the unwanted. We reserve exception handling techniques for the unanticipated. Situations that are unwanted but

Table 7–1 Types of Testing Used During the Software Development Process	
Types of Testing	*Description*
Unit testing	The software is tested one component or unit at a time. A unit is described as a software module, a collection of modules, a function, a procedure, an algorithm, an object, or a program.
Integration testing	An assembly of components of the software is tested. The components are collected into logical groups and each group is tested as a unit. The groups can be subjected to the same tests. As groups pass the test, they are added to an assembly, which in turn must be tested. The number of elements that must be tested will grow combinatorially.
Regression testing	Modules are retested once they are changed. Regression testing guarantees the changes to the component do not cause it to lose any functionality.
Stress testing	Testing that pushes a component or system to and beyond its limits. This will include testing boundary conditions, which help in determining what happens at the boundaries.
Operational testing	Test the system in full operation. The software is placed in a live environment to be tested under a complete system load. This testing is also used to determine performance in a totally foreign environment.
Specification testing	The component is audited against the original specifications. The specification dictates what components are involved in the system and the relationships between those components. This is part of the software verification process.
Acceptance testing	Testing performed by the end user of the module, component, or system to determine performance. This is part of the software validation process.

have a reasonable probability should be handled by ordinary program logic such as the following:

```
If Input data not acceptable then
  request input data again
else
  perform required operation
end if
```

Checking conditions in this way is part of the fundamental art of programming. This kind of programming prevents problems from happening. It certainly doesn't rise to the definition of exception. There is a difference between defects and exceptions and between exceptions and unwanted conditions. Defects are dealt with using testing and debugging. Unwanted conditions are handled within the confines of the regular program logic and exceptions are handled using exception handling programming techniques. Table 7–2 contrasts the difference between the characteristics of error handling, exception handling, and the handling of unwanted conditions.

Table 7–2　Differences between the Characteristics of Error and Exception Handling and the Handling of Unwanted Conditions

Error Handling	*Exception Handling*	*Handling Unwanted Conditions*
• Logical errors discovered during design and testing • Correct programs do not contain errors • Use program logic to anticipate and correct errors • Normal flow of control is maintained	• Describes unanticipated conditions during execution time • Correct programs can encounter exceptions • Use exception handling to recover from exceptions • Normal flow of control is disrupted	• Describes unwanted conditions that have a reasonable probability of occurring during execution time • Correct programs may encounter unwanted conditions • Use program logic to correct unwanted conditions • Attempt to maintain normal flow of control

The goal is to build error handling and exception handling components that can then be integrated with the other components that make up our parallel or distributed programs. The error handling and exception handling components must have the capability of identifying and reporting what the problem is as well as recovering from or correcting the problem. The recovery and correction can involve everything from prompting the user to reenter the data to restarting a subsystem within the software. Recovery and correction efforts can involve extensive file processing, database backouts, network rerouting, processor masking, device reinitialization, and for some systems, even hardware part replacements. Error and exception handling components can take on a range of forms, from simple assertion statements to smart agents whose sole purpose it is to anticipate failures and prevent them before they happen. A significant portion of any serious piece of software will be de-

SIMPLIFIED ERROR HANDLING COMPONENT

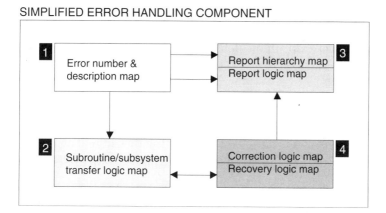

Figure 7-3   Architecture of a simplified error handling component.

voted to the error and exception handling components. Figure 7–3 shows the architecture for a simple error handling component.

Component 1 in Figure 7–3 is a simple map component that contains a list of error numbers and their descriptions. Component 2 contains a map object that maps the error numbers to jump locations, functions, or subsystems. Depending on what the error number is, component 2 is used to determine where to transfer. Component 3 is a map that maps the error numbers to the report hierarchy and report logic. The report hierarchy contains who or what should be notified of the error. The report logic determines what the notification should be. Component 4 contains two map objects. The first object maps the error numbers to objects whose purpose it is to correct some failure condition. The second object maps error numbers to objects who will return the system to a stable or at least a partially stable state. The simple error handling component in Figure 7–3 can be applied to software of all sizes and shapes. How the error handling and exception handling components are used will be determined by the amount of software reliability desired.

7.5 Software Reliability: A Simple Plan

Keep in mind that we distinguish between error conditions and inconvenient/unwanted conditions. Inconvenient or unwanted conditions should be handled by the normal program logic. Errors (defects) require special processing. *C++ Programming Language* (Stroustrup, 1997) lists four basic alternative actions that a program can take when it encounters an error. According to Stroustrup, upon detecting a problem that cannot be handled locally, the program could:

Option 1. Terminate the program.

Option 2. Return a value representing an "error."

Option 3. Return a legal value and leave the program in an illegal state.

Option 4. Call a function supplied to be called in case of error.

These four alternatives are generally seen in producer-consumer relationships of all sizes. The producer is typically a piece of code that implements a library function, class, class library, or application framework. The consumer is typically a piece of code that calls a library function, class, class library, or application framework. The consumer makes a request. The producer encounters an error in attempting to fulfill the request, and the four alternatives immediately become applicable. The problem with these four alternatives is that none of them is applicable in every situation.

Obviously terminating the program every time an error occurs is simply not acceptable. We agree with Stroustrup. We can and must do better than program termination upon encountering an error. With option 2, simply returning an error value may help in some situations but not in others. Not every return value can be interpreted as success or failure. For example, if a function has a return value of floats and the range of the function includes both negative and positive values, then which value of the function can be used to represent error? This is not always possible. As far as we are concerned, option 3 is also unacceptable. The assumption will be if the value is legal, then the operation worked. This will cause problems. Option 4 is where most of the effort should be spent whether we are discussing error or exception handling.

7.5.1   Plan A: The Resumption Model, Plan B: The Termination Model

Once an error or exception is encountered, there are two basic plans of attack for implementing option 4. The first plan of attack is to attempt to correct the condition or adjust for the condition that caused the failure, then resume execution at the point where the error or exception was encountered. This approach is called *resumption*. The second approach is to acknowledge the error or exception and perform a graceful exit of the subsystem or subroutine that caused the problem. The graceful exit is accomplished by closing the appropriate files, destroying the appropriate objects, logging the error (if possible), deallocating the appropriate memory, and handling any devices that need to be dealt with. This approach is called *termination*, not to be confused with the notion of just abruptly exiting the program. Both plans are valid and are useful in different situations. Before we discuss how to implement resumption or termination, lets look at the support C++ has for error handling and exception handling.

7.6 Using Map Objects in Error Handling

A map is a simple component that can be used as a part of any error handling or exception handling strategy. A map associates one item with another. For example, a map can be used to associate error numbers with descriptions:

```
//...
map<int,string> ErrorTable;
ErrorTable[123] = "division by zero";
ErrorTable[4556] = "no dial tone";
//...
```

Here, the number 123 is associated with "division by zero." If we write:

```
cout << ErrorTable[123] << endl;
```

Then "division by zero" will be written to cout.

In addition to mapping built-in data types, we may also map user-defined objects with built-in types. Instead of simply returning a message description for each error number, we may return an object with each error number. The object can have methods designed for error correction, error reporting, and error logging. For example, if we have a user-defined object called

defect_response:

```
class defect_response{
protected:
    //...
    int DefectNo;
    string Explanation;
```

```
public:
   bool operator<(defect_response &X);
   virtual int doSomething(void);
   string explanation(void);
   //...
};
```

We can add `defect_response` objects to the map using something like:

```
//...
map<int,defect_reponse *> ErrorTable;
defect_response * Response;
Response = new defect_response;
ErrorTable[123] = Response;
//...
```

This associates a response object with error number 123. Using polymorphism, the map object can contain pointers to any `defect_response` object or any object that is descended from defect response. For instance, if we have a class:

```
class exception_response : public defect_response{
   //...
public:
   int doSomething(void)
   //...
};
```

called `exception_response` that is descended from `defect_response`, then we may also add pointers to type `exception_response` to the `ErrorTable` object.

```
//...
map<int,defect_reponse *> ErrorTable;
defect_response * Response;
exception_response *Response2;
Response = new defect_response;
Respone2 = new exception_response;
ErrorTable[123] = Response;   // Stores an object of type
                                     defect_response
ErrorTable[456] = Response2;  // Stores an object of type
                                     exception_response
//...
```

This shows that the `ErrorTable` object can map different objects with different explanations and capabilities with the appropriate error number. Therefore, the references to the `doSomething()` method:

```
//...
defect_response *ProblemSolver;
ProblemSovler = ErrorTable[123];
ProblemSolver->doSomething();
ProblemSovler = ErrorTable[456];
ProblemSovler->doSomething();
//...
```

will each cause the `ProblemSolver` object to execute a different set of instructions. Although `ProblemSolver` is a pointer to a `defect_response` object, polymorphisms allow `ProblemSolver` to also point to an `exception_response` object or any other object descended from `defect_response`. Because the `doSomething()` method is declared virtual in the `defect_response` class, the compiler can do dynamic binding. This will ensure that the correct `doSomething()` method will be called at runtime. This dynamic binding is important because each descendant of `defect_response` will define its own `doSomething()` method. We want the `doSomething()` method to be called based on which descendant of `defect_response` is referenced. This technique allows us to associate error numbers with objects that are specialized in handling certain error conditions. Using this technique, we can make the error handling code simpler. Example 7.1 shows how the return value from some function can be used to summon the appropriate error handling object:

```
//Example 7.1 Using a function's return values to determine
//             the correct ErrorHandler object to access.

void importantOperation(void)
{
   //...
   Result = reliableOperation();
   if(Result != Success){
      defect_response *Solver;
      Solver = ErrorTable[Result];
      Solver->doSomething();
   }
   else{
      // continue processing
   }
   //...
}
```

Notice in Example 7.1 that we do not have a series of `if()` statements or `case` statements. The map object allows us to directly access the error handling object we want by index. The `doSomething()` method called in Example 7.1 will depend on the value of `Result`. Obviously this is an oversimplification of the processing. For example, Example 7.1 doesn't show who's responsible for memory management of the dynamically allocated objects stored in the `ErrorTable` map. Also, both the `reliableOperation()` routine and the `doSomething()` function might fail. So things can be a little more complicated than what is shown in Example 7.1. However, the example does illustrate how a single piece of code can handle many error situations. We can do better: Example 7.1 assumes that all the errors will be addressed by objects in `ErrorTable`. The objects in `ErrorTable` are either `defect_response` objects or objects descended from `defect_response`. What if we have multiple families of error handling classes? Example 7.2 shows how we can make the `importantOperation()` more general using templates.

```
// Example 7.2 Using a template in the
//             importantOperation() function.

template<class T,class U> int importantOperation(void)
{
   T ErrorTable;
   //...
   U *Solver;
   //...
   Solver = ErrorTable[Result];
   Solver->doSomething();
   //...
};
```

In Example 7.2, `ErrorTable` is not restricted to `defect_response` objects. This technique allows us to further simplify and expand the flexibility of our error handling code. This example uses both vertical and horizontal polymorphism. This kind of polymorphism is extremely useful in SPMD and MPMD programs. See Chapter 9 for a discussion on simplifying programs that require concurrency using templates and polymorphism. Using map objects and error handling objects are important steps in the direction of increasing software reliability. We can also take advantage of the exception handling mechanism and the exception handling classes in C++. These facilities add exception handling to error handling techniques.

7.7 Exception Handling Mechanisms in C++

Ideally, the testing and debugging process will remove all defects from the software or at least as many defects as possible from the software. Unwanted and inconvenient conditions should be handled by regular program logic. After defects are removed and unwanted or inconvenient conditions are handled, everything left is an exception. Exception handling is supported in C++ by three keywords: `try`, `throw`, and `catch`. Any code that encounters an exceptional condition that it cannot cope with throws an exception hoping that some exception handler (somewhere) can handle the problem (Stroustrup, 1997). The `throw` keyword is used to throw an object of some type. Throwing the object transfers control to an exception handler coded to deal with the type of object thrown. The `catch` keyword is used to identify handlers designed to catch exception objects. For example:

```
void importantOperation
{
    // executeImportCode()
    // the Impossible Happens Somehow
    impossible_condition ImpossibleCondition;
    throw ImpossibleCondition;
    //...
}

catch (impossible_condition &E)
{
    // Do something about E
    //...
}
```

The `importantOperation()` routine attempts to do its work and encounters an unusual condition that it cannot cope with. In our example, it creates an object of type `impossible_condition` and uses the keyword `throw` to throw the object. The block of code that uses the `catch` keyword is designed to catch objects of type `impossible_condition`. This block of code is called an *exception handler*. Exception handlers are associated with blocks of code contained within a `try` expression. A `try` block is used to surround code that possibly contains a routine that will encounter some exceptional situation. A `catch` block may only follow a `try` block or another `catch` block. So we might have:

```
try{
   //...
   importantOperation()
   //...
}

catch(impossible_condition &E)
{
   // do something about E
   //...
}
```

Here, either the routine `importantOperation()` or one of the routine `importantOperation()` calls have the potential to encounter some condition that it simply cannot cope with. The routine will throw an exception. Control will be transferred to the first exception handler that accepts an error of type `impossible_condition`. Either that routine will handle the exception or throw the exception to be handled by another exception handler. The objects thrown can be user-defined objects that can form simple to sophisticated error codes and messages. They may contain code that will help the exception handler perform its work. If we used objects like `exception_response` objects from Examples 7.1 and 7.2, they may be used by the exception handler to either correct the problem or allow the program to somehow recover its state. We may also use the built-in exception classes to create exception objects.

7.7.1   The Exception Classes

The standard C++ class library has nine exception classes divided into two basic groups. Table 7–3 shows the runtime error group and the logic error group. The runtime error group represents errors that are somewhat difficult

Table 7–3 Runtime and Logic Error Classes	
runtime error Classes	*logic error Classes*
range_error	domain_error
underflow_error	invalid_argument
overflow_error	length_error
	out_of_range

to prevent. The logic error group represents errors that are "theoretically preventable."

7.7.1.1   The **runtime_error** Classes

Figure 7–4 shows the class relationship diagram for the runtime_error family of classes. The runtime_error family of classes is derived from the exception class. Three classes are derived from runtime_error: range_error, overflow_error, and underflow_error. The runtime_error classes report internal computation or arithmetic errors. The runtime_error classes get their primary functionality from the exception class ancestor. The what() method, assignment operator=(), and the constructors for the exception handling class provide the capability of the runtime_error classes. The runtime_error classes provide an exception framework and architectural blueprint to build upon.

They offer little inherent functionality—the programmer must specialize them through inheritance. For example, the defect_response and exception_response classes created in Examples 7.1 and 7.2 might be derived from either runtime_error or logic_error classes. Let's look at how the basic exception classes work with no specialization. Example 7.3 shows how an exception object and a logic_error object can be thrown.

```
// Example 7.3. Throwing an exception object and a
//              logic_error object.

try{
    exception X;
    throw(X);
}
```

Figure 7–4   The class relationship diagram for the runtime_error family of classes.

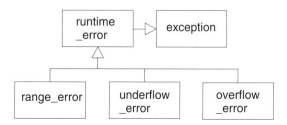

```
catch(const exception &X)
{
    cout << X.what() << endl;
}

try{
    logic_error Logic("Logic Mistake");
    throw(Logic);
}

catch(const exception &X)
{
    cout << X.what() << endl;
}
```

The basic exception classes have only construction, destruction, assignment, copy, and simple reporting capabilities. They do not contain the capability to correct a fault that has occurred. The error message returned by the what() method of the exception classes will be determined by the string passed to the constructor for the logic_error object. In Example 7.3, the string "Logic Mistake" passed to the constructor will be returned by the what() message in the catch block.

7.7.1.2   The **logic_error** Classes

The logic_error family of classes is derived from the exception class. In fact, most of the functionality of the logic_error family of classes is also inherited from the exception class. The exception class contains the what() method, used to report to the user a description for the error being thrown. Each class in the logic_error family contains a constructor used to tailor a message specific to that class. Figure 7–5 shows the class relationship diagram for the logic_error classes.

Figure 7–5   The class relationship diagram for the logic_error family of classes.

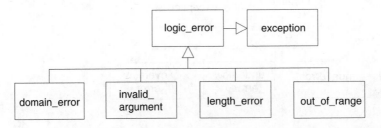

Like the `runtime_error` classes, these classes are really designed to be specialized. Unless the user adds some functionality to these classes, they cannot do anything other than report the error and the type. The nine generic exception classes provide no corrective action or error handling.

7.7.1.3   Deriving New Exception Classes

The exception classes can be used as-is, that is, they can be used simply to report an error message describing the error that has occurred. However, this is virtually useless as an exception handling technique. Simply knowing what the exception was doesn't do much to increase software reliability. The real value of the exception class hierarchy is the architectural road map that they provide for the designer and the developer. The exception classes provided basic error types that the developer can specialize. Many of the exceptions that occur in a runtime environment can be placed into either the `logic_error` or `runtime_error` family of classes. To demonstrate how to specialize an `exception` class, lets use the `runtime_error` class as an example. The `runtime_error` class is a descendant of the `exception` class. We can specialize the `runtime_error` class through inheritance. For instance:

```
class file_access_exception : public runtime_error{
protected:
    //...
    int ErrorNumber;
    string DetailedExplanation;
    string FileName;
    //...
public:
    virtual int takeCorrectiveAction(void)
    string detailedExplanation(void);
    //...
};
```

Here, the `file_access_exception` inherits `runtime_error` and specializes it by adding a number of data members and member functions. Specifically, the `takeCorrectiveAction()` method is added. This method can be used to help the exception handler perform its recovery and correction work. This `file_access_exception` object knows how to identify deadlock and how to break deadlock. It also has specialized logic for dealing with viruses that can damage files as well as specialized knowledge for dealing with file transfers that get unexpectedly interrupted. Each of these situations can introduce runtime exceptions. We can use our `file_access_exception` objects with the throw, catch, and try facilities of C++. For instance:

```
try{
   //...
   fileProcessingOperation();
   //...
}

catch(file_access_exception &E)
{
   cerr << E.what() << endl;
   cerr << E.detailedExplanation() << endl;
   E.takeCorrectiveAction();
   // Handler Take Additional Corrective Action
   //...
}
```

This technique allows you to create `ExceptionTable` map objects similar to the `ErrorTable` map objects used in Examples 7.1 and 7.2. Using vertical and horizontal polymorphism will also simplify exception handler processing.

7.7.1.4   Protecting the Exception Classes from Exceptions

The exception objects are thrown when some software component encounters a software or hardware anomaly. But note, the exception objects themselves do not throw exception. This has many implications. If the processing of the exception is complex enough to potentially cause another exception to be generated, then the exception processing should be redesigned and simplified where possible. The exception handling mechanism is unnecessarily complicated when exception handling code can generate exceptions. Therefore, most of the methods in the exception classes contain the empty `throw()` specification.

```
// Class declaration for exception class

class exception {
public:
   exception() throw() {}
   exception(const exception&) throw() {}
   exception& operator=(const exception&) throw()
      {return *this;}
   virtual ~exception() throw() {}
   virtual const char* what() const throw();
};
```

Note the `throw()` declarations with empty arguments. The empty argument shows that the method cannot throw an exception. If the method attempts to throw an exception, a compile-time error message is generated. If the base class cannot throw an exception, then the corresponding method in any derived class cannot throw an exception.

7.8 Event Diagrams, Logic Expressions, and Logic Diagrams

Exception handling should be used as the last line of defense because the mechanism totally alters the natural flow of control within the program. There are schemes that try to mask this fact, but those schemes are typically not flexible enough to scale to our programs that require concurrency or distribution. In the vast majority of situations where the temptation is to use catchall exception handlers, the logic can be made more robust by solid error handling or through improving the logic of a program. It is often useful to use an event diagram to help identify those components of an application that are critical to an acceptable completion of the application's work. Event diagrams can show which components can be potentially bypassed and which components lead to system failure. In some applications a single component's failure does not necessarily lead to system failure. Where a single component's failure would lead to system failure, then exception handling techniques can be used in conjunction with error handling techniques to provide the *failure-is-not-an-option* feature. Figure 7–6 shows a simple event diagram.

We use the event diagram to come up with a scheme to use in exception handling. Figure 7–6 depicts a system that consists of seven tasks labeled A, B, C, D, E, F, and H. Notice that each label is located at a switch. If switches are closed, then the component is functioning; otherwise, the component is not functioning. The terminal point at the left represents the beginning execution

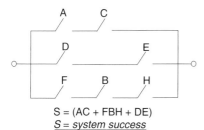

S = (AC + FBH + DE)
S = system success

Figure 7-6   A simple event diagram.

and the terminal at the right represents the end of execution. In order for the program to successfully end, a path through functioning components must be found. We can illustrate how this can be applied to our exception handling situation. Lets say that we start the program executing at A. In order for the program to successfully complete, A and C must both function properly. That is, the A switch and the C switch must be closed. In this event diagram both A and C are on the same branch. This means that A and C are executing concurrently. If either A or C fails, then an exception is thrown. The exception handler could possibly start A and C again. However, our event diagram tells us that this operation will be successful if either AC or DE or FBH is successful. Therefore, we design our exception handler to execute one of an alternative set of components (e.g., DE or FBH). There is an OR relationship between AC, DE, and FBH. This means that either set of these components concurrently executing represents success. The simple event diagram in Figure 7–6 indicates how we can approach our exception handler. The expression:

```
S = (AC + FBH + DE)
```

in Figure 7–6 is often referred to as a logic expression or boolean expression. This expression means that (A and C) or (F and B and H) or (D and E) must successfully execute in order for the system to be in a reliable state. The event diagram can also be used to tell us which combinations of component failure can lead to system failure. For instance, if only the components E and B fail, then the system may still successfully execute if components A and C are functioning. However, if components A, H, and D were to fail, then the entire system fails. The event diagram and the logic expression are useful tools for describing concurrently dependent and independent components. They are also good for determining how to approach processing in the exception handler. For example, from Figure 7–6, we can use:

```
try{
    start(task A and B)
}

catch(mysterious_condition &E){
    try{
        if(!(A && B)){
            start(F and B and H)
        }
    }
    catch(mysterious_condition &E){
        start(D and E)
    }
};
```

This kind of strategy aims at improving software reliability. Also note that the concurrency and opportunities for fault tolerant planning can be seen in the traditional logic diagram shown in Figure 7–7.

Figure 7–7 shows three AND gates and how they are OR'ed together to get to the S that represents the success of the system. The event diagram in Figure 7–6 and the logic diagram in Figure 7–7 are examples of simple techniques that can be used to visualize the critical paths and critical components in a piece of software. Once the critical paths and components are correctly identified, the developer must design software responses in case any of the critical components fail. If the termination model is used, then the exception handling does not attempt to resume execution at the point where the exception occurred; rather, the function or procedure where the exception occurred is exited, and steps are taken to put the system in as stable a state as possible. However, if the resumption model is used, the condition(s) that created the exception are either corrected or adjusted and the program resumes from the point where the exception occurred. It is important to note that the resumption model carries with it several challenges. For example, if we have a succession of nested procedure calls such as:

```
try{
    A calls B
        B calls C
            C calls D
                D calls E
                    E encounters an anomaly that it cannot cope with
}
catch(exception Q)
{

}
```

Figure 7–7   A logic diagram showing three AND gates OR'ed with OR gates to obtain the success of the system.

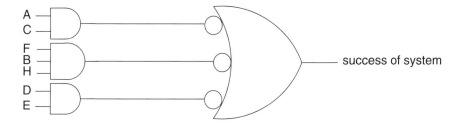

and an anomaly occurs in E and an exception is thrown, then there is the issue of what to do about the call stack. There are also object destruction issues and suspended return values that need to be resolved. What happens if C and D are recursive? Even if we fix the condition that caused the exception in procedure E, how can we return the program to the state it was in just prior to the exception? We will have to keep stack information, object construction and destruction tables, interrupt tables, and so on. This requires a lot of overhead and cooperation between the callee and the caller. These issues represent only the surface. It is because of the complexity of implementing the resumption model and the fact that large-scale systems can be developed without it that the termination model was chosen for C++. In *The Design and Evolution of C++*, Stroustrup (1994) presents a complete rationale about why the ANSI committee eventually selected the termination model of exception handling. While the resumption model does present challenges, if the reliability and the continuity of the software are critical enough, then the effort to implement a resumption model will have to be expended and the exception handling facilities in C++ can be used to implement a resumption model.

Summary

Producing reliable software is serious business. Exception handling and defect removal should be approached with extreme rigor. Thorough testing then debugging of a software component should be the primary defense against software defects. Exception handling should be added to the software system or subsystem after the software has undergone rigorous testing. Throwing exceptions should not be used as a generic error handling technique because it destroys the flow of control of the program. Exceptions should only be thrown after all of the measures have been exhausted. The standard exception handling classes should be used as architectural road maps for the programmer who wishes to design more complete and useful exception classes. If not specialized through inheritance, the standard classes can only report errors. More useful exception classes can be built that have corrective functionality as well as more information. In general, both the termination and resumption models allow the program to continue to execute. Both models resist simply aborting the program when an error occurs. For a more complete discussion of exception handling, see *The Design and Evolution of C++* (Stroustrup, 1994).

8

Distributed Object-Oriented Programming in C++

"So a basic naively determined difference between the human situation and the android situation is that the human being comes equipped with an ego, whereas the robot does not."

—*Cary G deBessonet*, Towards A Sentential 'Reality' for the Android

In this Chapter

Decomposition and Encapsulation of the Work • Accessing Objects in Other Address Spaces • The Anatomy of a Basic CORBA Consumer • The Anatomy of a CORBA Producer • The Basic Blueprint of a CORBA Application • A Closer Look at Object Adapters • Implementation and Interface Repositories • Simple Distributed Web Services Using CORBA • The Trading Service • The Client/Server Paradigm • Summary

Distributed objects are objects that are part of the same application but reside in different *address spaces*. The address spaces may be on the same computer or on different computers connected by a network or another form of communication. The objects involved in the application could have been designed originally to work together or they may have been designed by different departments, divisions, companies, or organizations at different times and for different purposes. A distributed object-oriented application can be anything from a one-time collaborative effort by a collection of unrelated objects to a multigenerational application whose objects are spread over the entire Internet. The location of the objects can be intermixed between intranets, extranets, and the Internet. In the most general description of distributed objects, the object may be implemented in different languages such as C++, Java, Eiffel, and Smalltalk. Distributed objects play a number of roles. In some situations an object or collection of objects is used as a server that can provide database, application, or communication services. In other situations objects play the part of clients. Distributed objects can be used in collaborative problem-solving models such as blackboards and multiagent systems. Besides collaborative problem-solving models, distributed objects can be used to implement parallel programming paradigms such as SPMD and MPMD. Objects within the same application don't need any special protocol to communicate. The communication is achieved through normal method invocation, parameter passing, and global variables. Since distributed objects reside in different address spaces, interprocess communication techniques are required and in many cases network programming is necessary.

Applications that require distribution can be necessary for several reasons:

- Resources needed (e.g., databases, special processors, modems, printers, etc.) are located on different computers. Client objects interact with server objects in order to access these resources.
- Objects developed at different times, by different parties, which reside in different locations need to interoperate in order to perform some necessary work or solve some problem.
- Agents implemented as objects are highly specialized and each agent requires its own address space because it is started as a separate process.
- Objects are used as the basic unit of modularity and the modules have been implemented as separate programs, each with its own address space.
- Objects have been implemented in a SPMD or MPMD architecture in order to facilitate parallel programming, and the objects are located in different processes and on different computers.

In an object-oriented application, the work that a program does is divided between a number of objects. These objects are models of some real-world person, place, thing, or idea. The execution of an object-oriented program causes its objects to interact with each other according to the models they represent. In a distributed object-oriented application, some interacting objects will have been created by different programs possibly running on different computers. Recall from Chapter 3 that each executing program has one or more processes associated with it. Each process has its own resources. For instance, each process has its own memory, file handles, stack space, process id, and so on. Tasks executing in one process do not have direct access to the resources owned by another process. If the tasks executing in one process need information stored in the memory of another process, then the two processes must explicitly exchange the information either through files, pipes, shared memory, environment variables, or sockets. Objects that reside in different processes that need to interact must also explicitly exchange information in one of these ways. The challenges for the C++ developer that wants to do distributed object-oriented programming include:

- Decomposition and encapsulation of the problem and solution into a set of objects, with the realization that some of the objects will belong to different processes and may be located on different computers.
- Communication between objects residing in different processes (address spaces).
- Synchronization of the interaction between the local and the remote objects.
- Error and exception handling in the distributed environment.

8.1 Decomposition and Encapsulation of the Work

Object-oriented software design is the process of translating the software requirements into a blueprint where objects model each aspect of the system to be developed and work to be done. The blueprint is centered around the structure and hierarchy of collections of objects and their relationships and interactions. The C++ `class` keyword is used to support the notion of a software model. There are two basic types of models. The first type of model is a scaled representation of some process, concept, or idea. This type of model is used for the sake of analysis or experimentation. For example, a class can be used to develop a molecular model. The hypothesis and structure of some chemical process within molecules can be modeled using C++'s class concept. A molecule's behavior when new groups of atoms are introduced can then be studied in software. The second type of software model is a reproduction in software of some real-world task, process, or idea. The purpose of this model is to function as its real-world counterpart as a part of some system or application. The software takes the place of some component in a manual system, or some physical thing. For example, we may use the class concept to model an adding machine. Once we have correctly modeled all of the characteristics and behavior of the adding machine, then an object can be instantiated from that class and used in place of a real adding machine. The software adding machine takes the place of the real-world adding machine. The modeled class serves as a virtual stand-in for some real-world person, place, thing, or idea. The software model captures the essence of the real thing.

For our purposes, *decomposition* is the process of dividing a problem and its solution into units of work, collections of objects, and the relationships between those objects. Likewise, *encapsulation* is the capturing or modeling of the characteristics, attributes, and behavior of some person, place, thing, or idea using the C++ `class` construct. This modeling (encapsulation) and decomposition is part of the object-oriented software design phase. Object-oriented applications that contain distributed objects add an additional layer to the design considerations. In one view of the design, the locations of objects within an application should not affect the design of the attributes and characteristics of those objects. The class is a model and unless location is part of that model, the ultimate location of the objects that will instantiate that class should not matter. On the other hand, objects don't exist in a vacuum. They interact and communicate with other objects. If some of the objects that communicate are located on different computers, possibly different networks, then this consideration has to be part of the original software design process. Although there is a lot of disagreement as to where in the design process distribution needs to be considered, it must be considered. The error handling and exception handling between objects located in different processes or computers are different from the error handling and exception handling between objects that are part of the same process. Also, the communication and interaction between objects located within the same process is performed differently if those objects are located in different processes where the processes may be on different computers. This must be taken into account during the design phase. In a distributed object-oriented application, the work that must be done is divided between the objects in the application and is implemented as member functions of the various objects. The objects will be logically divided into some WBM (Work Breakdown Model). They may be divided into a client-server, producer–consumer, peer-to-peer, blackboard, or multiagent model. Figure 8–1 shows the logical structure of each of these models and how the objects are distributed in each model.

In each model shown in Figure 8–1, the objects involved may or may not be on the same computer. However, they will be in different processes. The fact that they are in different processes is what makes them *distributed*.[1]

---

[1]We do not include multithreaded programs in the category of distributed programs.

PRODUCER CONSUMER MODEL:

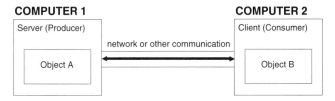

PEER-TO-PEER MODEL:

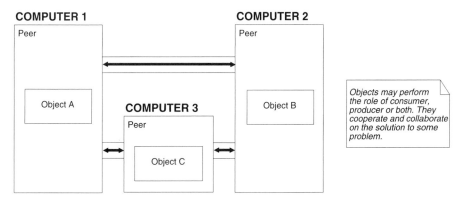

BLACKBOARD/MULTIAGENT MODEL:

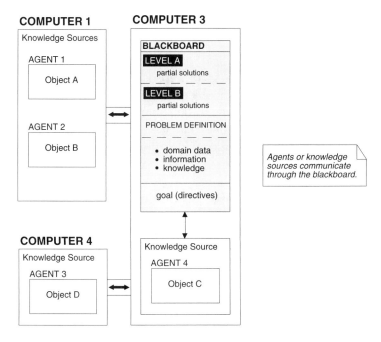

Figure 8–1 The logical structure and distribution of objects in the producer–consumer, peer-to-peer, blackboard, and multiagent models.

Each model represents a different approach to the division of work between the objects.

8.1.1   Communication between Distributed Objects

If the objects are located within the same process, then parameter passing, regular method invocation, and global variables can be used as a means of communication. If the objects are located in different processes on the same computer, then files, pipes, fifos, shared memory, clipboards, or environment variables are needed to facilitate communication between the objects. If the objects are located on different computers, then sockets, remote procedure calls, and other types of network programming will be required to facilitate communication. Not only must we be concerned with *how* the objects in a distributed application communicate, we must also be concerned with *what* they communicate. Object-oriented applications can include anything from simple to complex user-defined classes. These classes are often communicated between objects. So not only do distributed objects need to communicate simple built-in data types such as `ints`, `floats`, and `doubles`, they also need to communicate any type of user-defined class that might be necessary to allow some object to complete its work. Also, one object needs a way to be able to invoke methods of another object located in another address space. To complicate matters, there needs to be some way for one object to know the methods of a remote object. While C++ does support pure object-oriented programming, it does not have distributed communication facilities built in. It does not have built-in methods for locating and querying remote objects.

There are several important protocols for distributed object communication. Two of the most important protocols are IIOP (Internet Inter-ORB Protocol; pronounced "eye-op"), and the RMI (Remote Method Invocation). Using these protocols, objects located virtually anywhere on any network can communicate. In this chapter, we will discuss techniques for implementing distributed object-oriented programs using these protocols and the CORBA (Common Object Request Broker Architecture) specification. The CORBA specification is the industry standard for specifying the relationships, the interaction, and the communication between distributed objects. IIOP and GIOP are the two primary protocols that the CORBA specification works with. These protocols operate well with TCP/IP. CORBA is the easiest and most flexible way to add distributed programming to the C++ environment. The facilities provided by a CORBA implementation support the two major models of object-oriented parallelism that we use in this book: blackboards and multiagent systems. Because the CORBA specification reflects object-oriented programming, applications ranging from the small to the very large can be reasonably implemented. In this book we use MICO[2] which is an open-source implementation of the CORBA specification. The MICO implementation supports the major CORBA components and services. C++ interacts with MICO through a collection of classes and class libraries. CORBA supports distributed object-oriented modeling at every level.

8.1.2 Synchronization of the Interaction between the Local and the Remote Objects

Mutexes and semaphores can be used to help synchronize data and resource access between two or more objects located in different processes but on the same computer. This is because each process, although segregated, still has access to the computer's system memory. This system memory acts as a kind of shared memory between processes. However, multiple computers don't have any memory in common and therefore synchronization schemes must be implemented differently when the processes are distributed across different computers. Synchronizing access depending on the WBM used can require considerable communication between the distributed objects. For synchronization we will enhance the traditional methods of synchronization with CORBA's communication abilities.

8.1.3 Error and Exception Handling in the Distributed Environment

Perhaps one of the most challenging areas of exception or error handling in a distributed environment is the area of partial failure. In a distributed system, one or more components may fail while the other components operate under

---

[2]Any CORBA examples in this book are implemented using MICO 2.3.3 on SuSE Linux and MICO 2.3.7 on Solaris 8.

the assumption that everything is fine. In a local application where all of the components are within the same process, if one function or routine fails, it is not difficult for the entire application to know about it. This is not so for distributed applications. A network card might fail on one computer and the other objects executing on other computers will have no knowledge that a failure has happened. What happens if one of the objects needs to communicate or interact with an object whose network communications have been mysteriously interrupted? In a peer-to-peer model of problem solving where we have groups of objects working on various facets of some problem and one of the groups fails, how will the other groups know? Furthermore, what do we do about it? Should a single component's failure lead to system failure? If one client fails, should we shut the server down? If the server fails, should we shut the client down? What if the server or the clients only partially fail? So, in addition to data race and deadlock, we must also find ways to cope with partial failure of a distributed system where one or more of the components in the system have totally or partially failed. Again, what is necessary is a distributed approach to C++'s exception handling mechanism. The CORBA facilities provide a sufficient start.

8.2   Accessing Objects in Other Address Spaces

Objects that share the same scope can interact. They can access each other through their names, aliases for their names, or through pointers. An object can only be accessed where its name or a pointer to it is visible. Scope determines the visibility of object names. C++ has four basic levels of scope:

- block scope
- function scope
- file scope
- class scope

Recall that a block is defined in C++ by {} so that assigning Y to X in Example 8.1 would be illegal because Y is only visible within the block that it is declared in. The function main() does not know the name Y after the closing brace of the block where Y was declared.

```
// Example 8.1  Simple example of block scope.

int main(int argc, char argv[])
{
   int X;
   int Z;
   {
      int Y;
      Z = Y;    // Legal
      //...
   }
   X = Y ;      //  Illegal, Y is no longer defined
}
```

However, the name Y is visible to any other code that occurs in the same block where Y is declared. A name has function scope when it is declared within the function or the function's declaration. In Example 8.1, X and Z are visible only to the function `main()` and cannot be accessed by other functions. File scope refers to source files. Since a C++ program can consist of multiple files, we can have objects that are visible within one file but not in another. Names that have file scope visibility are visible from the point they are declared until the end of the source file. Names with file scope visibility will not be declared in any particular function. They are usually referred to as global variables. Names that have object scope are visible to any member function declared as part of the object. We use scope as the first level of access to an object's capabilities. The object's private, protected, and public interfaces determine the second level. Although an object's name may be visible, private and protected members still have restricted access. Scope simply tells us if the object's name is visible. In a nondistributed program, scope is associated with a single address space. Two objects in the same address space can refer to each other by name or pointer and can interact simply by invoking each other's methods.

```
// Example 8.2 Using objects which invoke methods of other
//             objects of the same address space.

//...
some_object    A;
another_object B;
dynamic_object *C;
C = new dynamic_object;

//...
B.doSomething(A.doSomething());
A.doSomething(B.doSomething());
C->doMore(A.doSomething());
//...
```

In Example 8.2, objects A and B are within the same scope, B is visible to A and A is visible to B. A may call B's member functions and vice versa. How is scope affected when two objects are on different machines? What happens when B is created by another program and is in a totally different address space? How will A know of B's existence? More importantly, how will A know B's name and interface? How can A call member functions that belong to B if B is part of another program? In Example 8.2, objects A and B are created at compile time and object C is created at runtime. They are part of the same program, they have the same scope, and their addresses are part of the same process. In order for a process to execute an instruction, it needs to know the address of the instruction. When the program in Example 8.2 is compiled, the addresses of objects A and B are stored in the executable. Therefore, the process that executes the program in Example 8.2 will know where objects A and B can be found. The address for object C is assigned during runtime. The exact location of the object C is unknown until the new() function has been called. However, the pointer C does have an address within the same space as objects A and B and therefore the process will use the pointer to get to the object. We have access to each object because we have access to their addresses either directly or indirectly. The object's variable name is simply an alias for the object's address. If the object's name is within our scope then we may access it. The trick is how we associate a remote object with our local scope. If we want to access object D that is in another address space we need some way to introduce the address of the remote object to our executing process. We need some way to associate the remote object with our local scope. We need a visible name that is an alias for an address in another process that might even be on another machine. In some cases the other machine might be on another network! It would be convenient if we could simply ask for the remote object by some agreed-upon description and receive a reference for the address of the remote object. Once we had the reference, we could then interact with the remote object in our local scope. Here is where a CORBA implementation can be used to do distributed programming.

8.2.1   IOR Access to Remote Objects

The IOR (Interoperable Object Reference) is the standard object reference format for distributed objects. Each CORBA Object has an IOR. The IOR is a handle that uniquely identifies the object. Whereas a pointer contains a simple machine address for an object, an IOR can contain a port number, a host name, an object key, and more. In C++ we use a pointer to access dynamically created objects. The pointer tells where the object is located in memory. When an object's pointer is dereferenced, the address is used to access the services of that object. The dereferencing process requires more effort when the object to be accessed is located in a different address space and possibly on a different computer. The pointer must contain enough information to resolve the object's exact location. If the object is located on another network, then the pointer must contain either directly or indirectly a network address, a network protocol, hostname, port address, object key, and physical address. The standard IOR acts as a kind of *distributed pointer* to a remote object. Figure 8–2 shows a high-level breakdown of some component contained in an IOR under the IIOP protocol.

The notion of a portable object reference is an important advancement in distributed computing. It allows local references to remote objects to appear virtually anywhere on the Internet or an intranet. This has important implications for multiagent systems where agents may need to travel between systems and throughout the Internet. The IOR standard creates some foundation for mobile objects and distributed agents. Once your program has access to an object's IOR, then an ORB (Object Request Broker) can be used to interact with the remote object through method invocation, parameter passing, return values, and so on.

8.2.2   ORBS (Object Request Brokers)

The ORB acts on behalf of your program. It sends messages to the remote object and returns messages from the remote object. The ORB acts as a middleman between your objects and the remote objects. The ORB takes care of all the details involved in routing a request from your program to the remote

Figure 8–2   A high-level breakdown of some component contained in an IOR under the IIOP protocol.

Logical Components of an IOR

HOST	PORT	OBJECT KEY	OTHER COMPONENTS
Identifies the Internet host.	Contains the TCP/IP port number where the target object is listening for requests.	A value that maps unambiguously to a particular object.	Additional information that may be used in making invocations, e.g., security.

object, and routing the response from the remote object back to your program. It makes the communications between systems virtually transparent. The ORB removes the need to do socket programming between processes on different computers. Similarly, it removes the need to do pipe or fifo programming between processes on the same computer. It takes care of much of the network programming that is required for distributed programs. Furthermore, it hides the differences between operating systems, computer languages, and hardware. The local objects are not aware of what language the remote objects have been implemented in, what platform they are running on, or whether they are located on the Internet or some local intranet. The ORB uses the IOR to help facilitate communications between machines, networks, and objects. Notice in Figure 8–2 that an IOR does contain information that can be used to make TCP/IP connections. We present only a high-level partial description of the IOR because the IOR is meant to be a black box for the developer. The ORB uses the IOR to locate the target object. Once the target object is located, the ORB activates it and transmits any arguments that are necessary to call the object. The ORB waits for the request to complete and returns the necessary information to the calling object or an exception if the method invocation or call fails. Figure 8–3 contains a simplified overview of the steps that an ORB uses on behalf of a local object.

The steps in Figure 8–3 present a simplified overview of what the ORB does during an interaction with a remote object. These steps are almost transparent to the local object. The local object invokes one of the methods of the remote object and the ORB performs these steps on behalf of the local object. The ORB does a lot of processing with a few simple lines of code. Typically, a distributed object-oriented application requires at least two programs. Each program has one or more objects that will interact with each

Figure 8–3   The simplified overview of the steps that an ORB uses on behalf of a local object.

SIMPLIFIED ORB METHOD INVOCATION STEPS
1) Locate the remote object.
2) Activate the module containing the target object if it is not already activated.
3) Transmit arguments to the remote object.
4) Wait for response from the invocation of the remote object's method.
5) Return information to the local object or exception if the remote method invocation failed.

other across address spaces. The object interaction may be client-server, producer-consumer, or peer-to-peer in nature. Therefore, if we have two programs, one will act as the client and the other as the server, or one as the producer and the other as the consumer, or they will both be peers. Program 8.1 implements a consumer that invokes a simple remote adding machine object. The program shows how a remote object may be accessed and how an ORB is initialized and used.

```
//Program 8.1

 1   using namespace std;
 2   #include "adding_machine_impl.h"
 3   #include <iostream>
 4   #include <fstream>
 5   #include <string>
 6
 7
 8   int main(int argc, char *argv[])
 9   {
10       CORBA::ORB_var Orb = CORBA::ORB_init(argc,argv,"mico-local-orb");
11       CORBA::BOA_var Boa = Orb->BOA_init(argc,argv,"mico-local-boa");
12       ifstream In("adding_machine.objid");
13       string Ref;
14       if(!In.eof()){
15       In >> Ref;
16       }
17       In.close();
18       CORBA::Object_var Obj = Orb->string_to_object(Ref.data());
19       adding_machine_var Machine = adding_machine::_narrow(Obj);
20       Machine->add(700);
21       Machine->subtract(250);
22       cout << "Result is " << Machine->result() << endl;
23       return(0);
24   }
25
26
```

On line 10 the ORB is initialized. On line 15 the IOR for the adding_machine object is read from a file. One of the nice features of the IOR is that it can be stored as a simple string and communicated to other programs. Transmitting the IOR through command line arguments, stdin, environment variables, or files are the simplest methods. An IOR can be sent using e-mail or ftp. IORs can be shared through common file systems and can be downloaded from Web pages. Once a program has an IOR for a remote object, then an ORB can be used to access the remote object. We shall cover other techniques for communicating IORs later in this chapter. But the file system technique is enough to get us started. The IOR was originally converted from an object reference to its stringified form by the remote adding machine's ORB and written to a file. On line 18 the local Orb object converts the stringified IOR back to an object reference. On line 19 the object reference is used to instantiate an adding_machine object. The interesting thing about this adding_machine object is that when its methods are invoked they will cause code on the remote machine to execute. The calls on line 20, 21, and 22

```
Machine->add(700);
Machine->subtract(250);
cout << "Result is " << Machine->result() << endl;
```

although made in our local scope, refer to executable code in another address space and in this case on another machine. To the developer the Machine object's location is transparent. After the object has been created on line 19 it is used like any other C++ object. Although there are very specific differences between local object invocations and remote object invocations,[3] the object-oriented metaphor is maintained, and from the object-oriented programming perspective remote objects look and feel like local objects. The code in Program 8.1 is client code or consumer code because it uses the services of the adding_machine object. In order for this simple adding machine application to be complete, we need the code that implements the adding_machine object. The code in Program 8.2 shows the second component to our simple adding machine application.

```
// Program 8.2

1   #include <iostream>
2   #include <fstream>
3   #include "adding_machine_impl.h"
4
5
6
7
8   int main(int argc, char *argv[])
9   {
```

---

[3]Remote objects invocation introduces latency, security requirements, and the possibility of partial failure.

```
10    CORBA::ORB_var Orb = CORBA::ORB_init
                          (argc,argv,"mico-local-orb");
11    CORBA::BOA_var Boa = Orb->BOA_init(argc,argv,"mico-local-boa");
12    adding_machine_impl *AddingMachine = new adding_machine_impl;
13    CORBA::String_var Ref = Orb->object_to_string(AddingMachine);
14    ofstream Out("adding_machine.objid");
15    Out << Ref << endl;
16    Out.close();
17    Boa->impl_is_ready(CORBA::ImplementationDef::_nil());
18    Orb->run();
19    CORBA::release(AddingMachine);
20    return(0);
21    }
22
23
```

Notice on line 10 that the producer program also has to initialize an `Orb` object. This is an important requirement for CORBA-based programs. Each program communicates with the aid of an ORB. Initializing the ORB is one of the first things that a CORBA program must do. On line 12, the actual `adding_machine` object is declared. This is the object that Program 8.1 will actually communicate with. On line 13, the object reference for the actual `adding_machine` object is converted to its stringified form. It's then written to a simple text file that can be easily read. Once the IOR is written to the file, the `Orb` object waits for a request. Each time one of its methods is called, it performs the necessary addition or subtraction to a persistent value. This value is accessed by calling the `adding_machine`'s `result()` method. Programs 8.1 and 8.2 represent barebones CORBA programs that show the basic structure that CORBA programs will have. The code that makes the `adding_machine` object distributed begins with its CORBA class declaration. Each CORBA object starts out as an IDL (Interface Definition Language) design.

8.2.3 Interface Definition Language (IDL): A Closer Look at CORBA Objects

The IDL is the standard object-oriented design language used to design classes that will be used for distributed programming. It is used to express class interfaces and class relationships. It is used to specify member function prototypes, parameter types, and return types. One primary function of the IDL is to separate the class interface from the implementation. Therefore, the actual definitions of methods are not specified with the IDL. Neither the

Table 8–1 IDL Keywords			

IDL Keywords

abstract	enum	native	struct
any	factory	Object	supports
attribute	FALSE	octet	typedef
boolean	fixed	oneway	unsigned
case	float	out	union
char	in	raises	ValueBase
const	inout	readonly	valuetype
cell	interface	sequence	void
double	long	short	wchar
exception	module	string	

implementation of member functions nor data members are specified using IDL. The IDL only specifies the function interface. Table 8–1 contains the commonly used keywords in the IDL.

The keywords in Table 8–1 are reserved words in a CORBA program. In addition to specifying the function interface for a class, the IDL is used to specify relationships between classes. The IDL supports:

- user-defined types
- user-defined sequences
- array types
- recursive types
- exception semantics
- modules (similar to namespaces)
- single and multiple interitance
- bitwise and arithmetic operators

Here is the IDL definition for `adding_machine` class from Example 8.2:

```
interface adding_machine{
   void add(in unsigned long X);
   void subtract(in unsigned long X);
   long result();
};
```

It begins with the CORBA keyword `interface`. Notice that this `adding_machine` declaration does not include any variables to hold the result of the additions and subtractions. Its `add()` and `subtract()` methods accept a single `unsigned long` as a parameter. The parameter is accompanied by the CORBA keyword `in` to denote that the parameter is an input parameter. This class declaration is stored in a separate source file and named `adding_ma-chine.idl`. Source files containing IDL definitions must end in the `.idl` suffix. The source file containing the IDL declaration must be converted to C++ before it can be used. This conversion can be done using a preprocessor step or by a standalone program. All CORBA implementations include an IDL compiler. There are IDL compilers for C, Smalltalk, C++, Java, and so on. The IDL compiler converts IDL definitions into the appropriate language. In our case the IDL compiler converts the interface declaration into legitimate C++ code. Depending on the implementation of CORBA that you use, the IDL compiler is called with syntax that will be similar to:

```
idl  adding_machine.idl
```

This command will produce a file that contains C++ code. Since our IDL definition is saved in a file named `adding_machine.idl`, the MICO IDL compiler produces a file named `adding_machine.h` that contains several C++ skeleton classes and some CORBA data types. Table 8–2 contains the basic IDL data types.

Table 8–2   Basic IDL Data Types

IDL Datatypes	Range	Size
long	-2^{31} to $2^{31} - 1$	> = 32 bits
short	-2^{15} to $2^{15} - 1$	> = 16 bits
unsigned long	0 to $2^{32} - 1$	> = 32 bits
unsigned short	0 to $2^{16} - 1$	> = 16 bits
float	IEEE single-precision	> = 32 bits
double	IEEE double-precision	> = 64 bits
char	ISO Latin-1	> = 8 bits
string	ISO Latin-1, except ASCII NULL	Variable length
boolean	TRUE or FALSE	Unspecified
octet	0-255	> = 8 bits
any	Runtime identifiable arbitrary type	Variable length

Even after the IDL compiler creates C++ code from the interface class, the implementation for the interface class methods are still undefined. The IDL compiler produces several C++ skeletons that are to be used as base classes. Example 8.3 shows two of several classes generated by our MICO IDL compiler from the file `adding_machine.idl`.

```
// Example 8.3 Two classes generated by MICO IDL compiler
//             from the adding_machine.idl.

class adding_machine : virtual public CORBA::Object{
public:
   virtual ~adding_machine();

   #ifdef HAVE_TYPEDEF_OVERLOAD
   typedef adding_machine_ptr _ptr_type;
   typedef adding_machine_var _var_type;
   #endif
   static adding_machine_ptr _narrow( CORBA::Object_ptr obj );
   static adding_machine_ptr _narrow( CORBA::AbstractBase_ptr
                                      obj );
   static adding_machine_ptr _duplicate( adding_machine_ptr
                                         _obj );
   {
      CORBA::Object::_duplicate (_obj);
      return _obj;
   }

   static adding_machine_ptr _nil()
   {
      return 0;
   }

   virtual void *_narrow_helper( const char *repoid );
   static vector<CORBA::Narrow_proto> *_narrow_helpers;
   static bool _narrow_helper2( CORBA::Object_ptr obj );
   virtual void add( CORBA::ULong X ) = 0;
   virtual void subtract( CORBA::ULong X ) = 0;
   virtual CORBA::Long result() = 0;

protected:
   adding_machine() {};
private:
   adding_machine( const adding_machine& );
   void operator=( const adding_machine& );
};

class adding_machine_stub : virtual public adding_machine{
public:
   virtual ~adding_machine_stub();
```

```
  void add( CORBA::ULong X );
  void subtract( CORBA::ULong X );
  CORBA::Long result();

private:
  void operator=( const adding_machine_stub& );
};
```

adding_machine.idl is input to the compiler and adding_machine.h along with its skeleton classes is output from the compiler. The developer uses inheritance to actually provide implementations for the function interfaces declared in the IDL source file. For instance, Example 8.4 shows the user-defined class that provides the implementation for one of the skeleton classes produced by the IDL compiler.

```
// Example 8.4 User-defined class implementation of skeleton
                classes.

class adding_machine_impl : virtual public adding_machine_skel{
private:
  CORBA::Long  Result;
public:
  adding_machine_impl(void)
  {
    Result = 0;
  };
  void add(CORBA::ULong X)
  {
    Result = Result + X;
  };
  void subtract(CORBA::ULong X)
  {
    Result = Result - X;
  };
  CORBA::Long result(void)
  {
    return(Result);
  };
};
```

One of the skeletons that IDL compiler creates from the adding_machine interface class is named adding_machine_skel. Notice that the IDL uses the name used in the interface definition to derive new classes. Our adding_machine_impl class provides the implementation for the function interfaces declared using the IDL. First, the adding_machine_impl class declares a data member named Result. Second, it declares the actual implementations for the add(), subtract(), and the result() methods. So while the adding_ `machine` interface class specifies the declaration of these methods, the `adding_` `machine_impl` class provides implementation of the methods. The user-defined `adding_machine_impl` class will inherit a lot of functionality useful for distributed programming from the base class. This is the basic scheme when doing CORBA programming. An interface class is designed that represents the interfaces to be used. The IDL compiler is called to generate real C++ class skeletons from the interface definition. The developer derives a class from one of the skeletons and provides implementations for the methods defined in the interface class and data members that will be used to hold attributes of the object. Generating real C++ classes from IDL is a three-step process:

1. Design the class interfaces, relationships, and hierarchies using the IDL.

2. Use the IDL Compiler to generate real C++ skeletons from the IDL classes.

3. Use inheritance to create descendants from one or more of the skeleton classes and implement the interface methods inherited from the skeleton classes.

We'll discuss this process in more detail later in this chapter. First, let's take a closer look at the basic structure of a consumer program.

8.3   The Anatomy of a Basic CORBA Consumer

One of the most common models for distributed programming is the *consumer-producer* model. In this model, one program plays the role of producer and another plays the role of consumer. The producer creates some service or data used by a consumer. For example, we could have a program that generates unique license plate numbers upon demand. The consumer is the program that makes requests for new license plate numbers and the producer is the program that generates the license plate numbers. Typically, the consumer and producer are located in different address spaces. Figure 8–4 shows several components and steps that most CORBA consumer programs contain.

To communicate with objects on other computers or in different address spaces, each program involved in the communication must declare an ORB object. Once the `Orb` object is declared, then the consumer program has access to its member functions. In Figure 8–4, the ORB is initialized using the call:

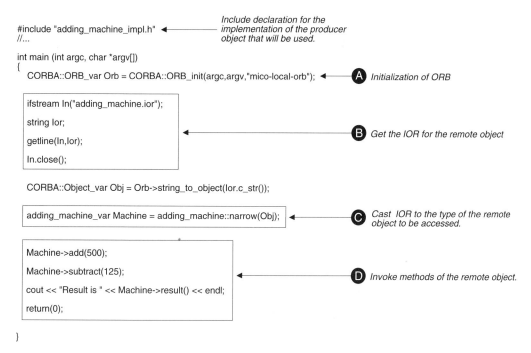

Figure 8–4 Components and steps used by a CORBA consumer program.

```
CORBA::ORB_var Orb = CORBA::ORB_init(argc,argv,"mico-local-orb");
```

This initializes an ORB object. The `CORBA::ORB_var` type is a handle to an object of type ORB. In CORBA implementations, objects that have the `_var` designation take care of deallocating its underlying reference. This is in contrast to the objects that have the `_ptr` designation. The command-line arguments are passed to the ORB's constructor along with an `orb_id`. In our case, the `orb_id` is "`mico-local-orb`". The string passed to the `ORB_init()` function that names the ORB to be initialized is implementation specific and can differ between implementations. The derived object is referred to as the *servant* object.

Once the ORB and the object adapter are initialized, the next basic component that any CORBA application will need is the IOR for the remote object(s). In Figure 8–4, the IOR is retrieved from a file named `adding_machine.ior`. The IOR has been written in its stringified form to the file. The ORB object is used to convert the IOR from a string back to its object form using its `string_to_object()` method. In Figure 8–4, this is accomplished by the call:

```
CORBA::Object_var Obj = Orb->string_to_object(Ior.c_str());
```

Here, `Ior.c_str()` returns the stringified IOR and `Obj` will be a reference to the object form of the IOR. The object form of the IOR is then *narrowed*. This narrowing process is analogous to C++ type casting. The narrowing process *sizes* an object reference to the appropriate object type. In this case, the appropriate type is `adding_machine`. The consumer program in Figure 8–4 narrows the IOR object using the call:

```
adding_machine_var Machine = adding_machine::_narrow(Obj);
```

This process creates a reference to an `adding_machine` object. The consumer program can now call the methods defined in the IDL interface for the `adding_machine` class. For instance:

```
Machine->add(500);
Machine->subtract(125);
```

call the `add()` and `subtract()` methods of the remote object. Although the consumer program in Figure 8–4 is an oversimplified consumer, it does show the basic components of a typical CORBA consumer or client program. The consumer program requires a producer program in order for the application to be complete. We will look at a simplified CORBA program that acts as the producer for the program in Figure 8–4.

8.4   The Anatomy of a CORBA Producer

The producer is responsible for providing either data, routines, or services to its consumer programs. The producer, together with the consumer, make a complete distributed application. Each CORBA producer program is designed with the assumption that there will be consumer programs to invoke its services. Therefore, each producer program will create servant objects and provide IORs so that the objects may be accessed. Figure 8–5 contains a simple producer program used in conjunction with the consumer program from Figure 8–4. Figure 8–5 contains the basic components that any CORBA producer program will contain.

Notice that part A for the consumer program and the producer program are essentially the same. Both the consumer and the producer program re-

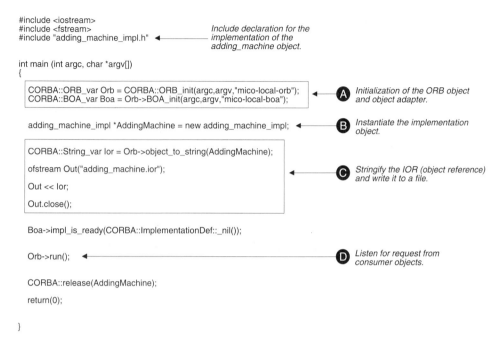

```
#include <iostream>
#include <fstream>
#include "adding_machine_impl.h"     ◀─────── Include declaration for the
                                              implementation of the
                                              adding_machine object.

int main (int argc, char *argv[])
{
    CORBA::ORB_var Orb = CORBA::ORB_init(argc,argv,"mico-local-orb");   ◀──── Ⓐ  Initialization of the ORB object
    CORBA::BOA_var Boa = Orb->BOA_init(argc,argv,"mico-local-boa");                and object adapter.

    adding_machine_impl *AddingMachine = new adding_machine_impl;   ◀──── Ⓑ  Instantiate the implementation
                                                                             object.

    CORBA::String_var Ior = Orb->object_to_string(AddingMachine);

    ofstream Out("adding_machine.ior");                            ◀──── Ⓒ  Stringify the IOR (object reference)
                                                                             and write it to a file.
    Out << Ior;

    Out.close();

    Boa->impl_is_ready(CORBA::ImplementationDef::_nil());

    Orb->run();    ◀─────────────────────────────────────────────────── Ⓓ  Listen for request from
                                                                             consumer objects.
    CORBA::release(AddingMachine);

    return(0);

}
```

Figure 8–5   Basic components of a CORBA producer program.

quire an ORB to communicate. The ORB is used to get a reference to an *object adapter*. Figure 8–5 contains the call:

```
CORBA::BOA_var Boa = Orb->BOA_init(argc,argv,"mico-local-boa");
```

This call is used to get a reference to an object adapter. The object adapter is a middleman between the ORB and the object that implements the services to be called. Keep in mind that CORBA objects start as interface declarations only. At some point in the development process, a derived class provides the implementation for the CORBA interface. The object adapter acts as the middleman between the interface that the ORB interacts with and the real methods implemented by the derived class. The object adapters are used to access servant and implementation objects. The producer in Figure 8–5 creates an implementation object in part B using:

```
adding_machine_impl *AddingMachine = new adding_machine_impl;
```

This is the object that will provide the implementation for the services that the client or consumer objects will request. Also notice that in part C in Figure 8–5, the producer program uses the Orb object to convert the IOR to a string and writes the string to a file named `adding_machine.ior`. This file can be transmitted to the producer through `ftp`, e-mail, over `http` using Web pages, via NFS mounts and so on. There are other ways to communicate the IOR, but the file method provides a simple introduction. After the IOR is written the producer program simply waits for requests from client or consumer programs. The producer program in Figure 8–5 is also an oversimplification of the CORBA producer or server program, but it does contain the basic components that a typical producer program will have.

8.5   The Basic Blueprint of a CORBA Application

We can see from the programs in Figures 8–4 and 8–5 that a barebones CORBA application will require two ORBs, an object adapter, a method for communicating an IOR, and at least one servant object. Figure 8–6 shows the logical structure of a barebones CORBA application.

After the IOR is obtained and narrowed, the remote method invocation in the consumer or client program looks just like regular method calls in a C++ program. In the CORBA examples in this book, the IIOP (Internet Inter ORB Protocol) is assumed. Therefore, the ORBs in Figure 8–6 are communicating using a TCP/IP protocol. The IOR will contain enough information about the remote object's location to facilitate the TCP/IP communication. The object adapter in Figure 8–6 will typically be a portable object adapter. However, some older or simpler programs may use the basic object adapter. We will describe the difference between these two adapters later in this chapter. Each CORBA application has one or more servant objects that implements the interface designed in the IDL class. The simple consumer and producer programs shown in Figures 8–4 and 8–5 can execute on the same computer in different processes or on different computers. If the programs are executed on the same computer then the file `adding_machine.ior` should be accessible from both programs. If the programs are executed on different computers, then the file will have to be sent to the client computer via `ftp`, e-mail, `http`, and so on. The compilation and execution details for the programs shown in Figure 8–4 and 8–5 are shown in Profile 8.1 and 8.2.

Blueprint for Simple CORBA Application

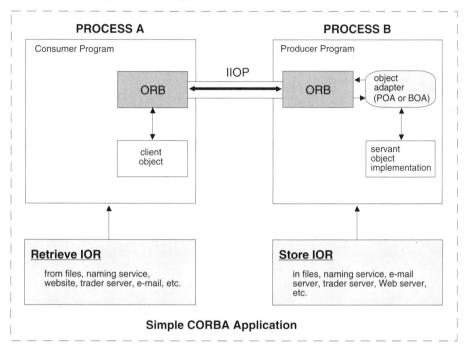

Figure 8-6   The logical structure of a barebones CORBA application.

Program Profile 8.1

Program Name
adding_machine_client_impl.cc

Description
This program is a simple consumer program. It connects to the CORBA producer program shown in Figure 8–5. It adds 500 to the adding machine and then subtracts 125. It sends the result of the operations to cout using the results() method.

Libraries Required
mico2.3.3 or mico2.3.7

Headers Required
None

Compile & Link Instructions

```
idl -poa  adding_machine.idl
mico-c++  -g -c adding_machine.cc -o adding_machine.o
mico-c++  -g -c adding_machine_impl.cc -o adding_machine_impl.o
mico-c++ -g -c adding_machine_client_impl.cc -o
adding_machine_client_impl.o
mico-ld -g -o adding_machine_client adding_machine_client_impl.o
adding_machine_impl.o adding_machine.o -lmico2.3.3
```

Test Environment

SuSE Linux 7.1 gnu C++ 2.95.2, Solaris 8 Workshop 7, MICO 2.3.3, MICO 2.3.7

Execution Instructions

Execute the binary named `adding_machine_client` (e.g., `./adding_machine_client`). The CORBA producer program needs to be started first. The producer program is shown in Figure 8–5 and is named `adding_machine_server`.

Notes

The CORBA producer program should be running at the time `adding_machine_client` is invoked.

Program Profile 8.2

Program Name

`adding_machine_server_impl.cc`

Description

This program is a simple server program shown in Figure 8–5. It accepts requests for additions and subtractions and produces the results of those requests.

Libraries Required

mico2.3.3 or mico2.3.7

Headers Required

None

Compile and Link Instructions

```
idl -poa  adding_machine.idl
mico-c++  -g -c adding_machine.cc -o adding_machine.o
mico-c++  -g -c adding_machine_impl.cc -o adding_machine_impl.o
mico-c++ -g -c adding_machine_server_impl.cc -o
adding_machine_server_impl.o
```

```
mico-ld  -g -o adding_machine_server adding_machine_server_impl.o
adding_machine_impl.o adding_machine.o -lmico2.3.3
```

Test Environment

SuSE Linux 7.1 gnu C++ 2.95.2, Solaris 8 Workshop 7, MICO 2.3.3, MICO 2.3.7

Execution Instructions

Execute the binary named `adding_machine_server` (e.g., `./adding_machine_server`)

Notes

None

8.5.1   The IDL Compiler

The IDL compiler is a tool used to translate IDL Class definitions into C++ code. This code consists of a collection of class skeletons, enumerated types, and template classes. The IDL compiler used for the CORBA programs in this book is the MICO IDL compiler. Table 8–3 contains some commonly used command-line options to the IDL compiler.

Table 8–3   Some Commonly Used Command-Line Options to the IDL Compiler

IDL Complier Command-Line Options	Description
`--boa`	Generates skeletons that use the basic object adapter (BOA). This is the default.
`--no-boa`	Turns off code generation of skeletons for the BOA.
`--poa`	Generates skeletons that use the portable object adapter (POA).
`--no-poa`	Turns off code generation of skeletons for the POA. This is currently the default.
`--gen-included-defs`	Generate code that was included using the `#include`.
`--version`	Prints the version of MICO.
`-D<define>`	Defines a preprocessor macro. This option is equivalent to the `-D` switch of most UNIX C-compilers.
`-I<path>`	Defines a search path for `#include` directives. This option is equivalent to the `-I` switch of most UNIX C-compilers.

The −boa and −poa switches in Table 8–3 can be used to determine what kind of adapter skeletons will be produced. For example, typing the command:

```
idl   −poa  −no-boa   adding_machine.idl
```

will produce a file named adding_machine.h that contains skeletons for the poa (portable object adapter) and it will turn off the production of skeletons for the boa (basic object adapter). Typing the command:

```
idl -h
```

generates a complete list of the IDL compiler switches. If the man pages for the MICO distribution have been properly installed, then typing the command:

```
man   idl
```

will provide a complete explanation of the IDL switches available. Designing the IDL classes is the first step in CORBA programming. The next major step in a CORBA program is determining how the IORs for remote objects will be stored and retrieved.

8.5.2   Obtaining IOR for Remote Objects

The ORB class has two member functions that can be used for converting IOR objects between strings and Object_ptrs. The methods are string_to_object() and object_to_string(). The string_to_object() member function takes a const char * and converts it to an Object_ptr. The object_to_string() member function takes an Object_ptr and converts it to a char *. These methods are part of the ORB class interface. The object_to_string() method is used to stringify object IORs. Once the IOR has been stringified it can be transmitted to client and consumer programs through a variety of techniques, including:

E-mail	Shared file systems (NFS mounts)
ftp	Embedded within html documents
Java applets/servlets	Command-line arguments
Shared memory	Traditional IPC (i.e., pipes, fifos)
Environment variables	CGI get and post commands

The receiving program then takes the stringified IOR and uses its ORB's string_to_object() member function to convert the IOR to a CORBA object ptr. The CORBA object ptr is then *narrowed* and used to initialize the local object. Programs 8.1 and 8.2 use stringified objects and a file to communicate the IOR between the consumer program and the producer program. The stringified IOR can be used to facilitate very flexible connections to remote objects that can reside virtually anywhere on the Internet or on any intranet or extranet. In fact, the MIWCO (Wireless Mico) is an open-source implementation of wCORBA,[4] the wireless CORBA standard, and can be used to enhance the mobility of objects. The wireless specification enables mobility through a MIOR (Mobile IOR). The wireless specification has support for TCP, UDP, and WAP WDP (Wireless Application Protocol Wireless Datagram Protocol) transports. Multiagent and distributed agent systems can also benefit by taking advantage of the IOR standards. The IOR and MIOR are part of the building blocks for the next generation of object-oriented Web services. It is important to note that although the stringified IOR provides a flexible and portable object reference, it may not be ideal for all situations and configurations. Moving a file containing the IOR may not be practical for many installations. Forcing client and server applications to share the same file system or network may not be practical. Security concerns might exclude the stringified IOR as an option. If a client-server application is large and diverse enough, then the stringified IOR sharing may be too restricting. The CORBA specification includes two other standards for obtaining or communicating object references: naming services, and trading services.

8.6   The Naming Service

The naming service standard provides a mechanism for mapping names to object references. The requester of an IOR provides a name to the naming service and the naming service returns the object reference associated with that name.

The naming service acts as a kind of telephone directory, in which the name is used to look up the number. It allows client and consumer programs to look up object references by name. The naming service can be used to map other application resources in addition to providing simple IOR maps. A mapping from a name to an object reference is called *name binding*. A collection of name bindings is associated with a *naming context* object. To illustrate the notion of a naming context, lets say we have an application that does travel planning that consists of a large and diverse collection of objects. We can organize these groups of objects according to function. Some objects are associated with file I/O, some object with secu-

---

[4]wCorba is the CORBA standard for wireless remote object interaction. White papers and case studies for the wireless CORBA standard are available at *www.omg.org*.

rity. Other objects are specifically related to transportation: train, bus, car, and bicycle objects. Each grouping forms a context. For instance, to logically group the transportation related objects together we can create a *transportation context,* and associate each of our forms of transportation with that context. This grouping forms a *naming context.* We bind the name of each form of transportation with its IOR. This is *name binding.* We then associate that binding with the transportation context. We use contexts to logically organize groups of related objects. Furthermore, a collection of connected *naming contexts* forms a *naming graph.* Naming contexts are represented by objects. Since a naming context is implemented as an object, it can participate in name binding just like any other object. This means that a naming context can potentially contain other naming contexts. For instance, Figure 8–7 contains several contexts including a logical representation for our transportation context.

Notice that the last entry in the `transportation` context is the name `airborne`. The `airborne` name maps to another context named `flying_machines`. The `flying_machines` context contains bindings of several objects related by function. The `transportation` context, together with the `flying_machines` context, form a naming graph. Notice in Figure 8–7 that the last object in the `flying_machines` context is named `sonic`. The `sonic` name maps to the `fast_flying_machines` context. That is, the `sonic` name has an object reference of `8888`. This adds another context to the naming graph. This is an example of one naming context containing another naming context. The naming graph can be used to represent the "big picture" of the structure of the relationships within a distributed object-oriented application. The naming graph captures the *landscape* of a distributed application. For multiagent systems the naming graph can be used as a kind of semantic network (see sidebar 8.1). Although the objects involved may be scattered among diverse hardware platforms, operating systems, programming languages, and geographical locations, the naming graph can present a single logical structure of the relationships and connections between the objects. Figure 8–8 shows an alternative representation of the naming graph from Figure 8–7. Figure 8–8 has the same naming contexts as Figure 8–7 and it clearly shows the relationships between the naming contexts. Figure 8–8 also demonstrates that there is a path from the `transportation` context to the `fast_flying_machines` context and then back to the `transportation` context.

Graph traversal algorithms can even be employed to traverse through the naming graph in the process of distributed problem solving. Using traversal in this way, various paths through a naming graph can represent solutions to problems. The naming service provides the requester access to naming con-

TRANSPORTATION CONTEXT

Object Name	Object Reference
boat	1234
car	5678
train	9876
bicycle	2345
airborne	9999 ──────▶ 9999

FLYING MACHINES CONTEXT

Object Name	Object Reference
helicopter	9331
kite	9221
balloon	0911
sonic	8888 ──────▶ 8888

FAST FLYING MACHINES CONTEXT

Object Name	Object Reference
jet	9898
shuttle	8899
starship	8889

Figure 8-7   Several different naming contexts.

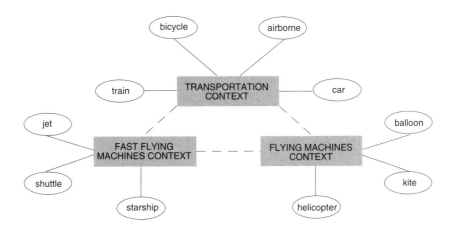

Figure 8-8   An alternative representation of the naming graph.

texts and naming graphs. Naming contexts can be accessed through naming graphs. Bindings can be accessed through naming contexts. The binding provides a direct association between a name and an object reference. Program 8.3 shows a simple producer that creates a name binding and associates that name binding with a naming context.

```
// Program 8.3

 1   #include <iostream>
 2   #include <fstream>
 3   #include "permutation_impl.h"
 4   #define MICO_CONF_IMR
 5   #include <CORBA-SMALL.h>
 6   #include <iostream.h>
 7   #include <fstream.h>
 8   #include <unistd.h>
 9   #include <mico/CosNaming.h>
10
11
12   int main(int argc, char *argv[])
13   {
14       CORBA::ORB_var Orb = CORBA::ORB_init
                             (argc,argv,"mico-local-orb");
15       CORBA::Object_var PoaObj =
             Orb->resolve_initial_references("RootPOA");
16       PortableServer::POA_var Poa =
                       PortableServer::POA::_narrow(PoaObj);
17       PortableServer::POAManager_var Mgr = Poa->the_POAManager();
18       inversion Server;
19       PortableServer::ObjectId_var Oid =
                       Poa->activate_object(&Server);
20       Mgr->activate();
21       permutation_ptr ObjectReference = Server._this();
22       CORBA::Object_var NameService =
             Orb->resolve_initial_references ("NameService");
23       CosNaming::NamingContext_var NamingContext =
          CosNaming::NamingContext::_narrow (NameService);
24       CosNaming::Name name;
25       name.length (1);
26       name[0].id = CORBA::string_dup ("Inflection");
27       name[0].kind = CORBA::string_dup ("");
28       NamingContext->bind (name, ObjectReference);
29       Orb->run();
30       Poa->destroy(TRUE,TRUE);
31       return(0);
32   }
```

33

34

S 8.1.

Semantic Networks

A semantic network or semantic net is one of the oldest and easiest to understand knowledge representation schemes. A semantic network is basically a graphic depiction of knowledge that shows the hierarchical relationships between objects. Sidebar Figure 8–1 shows a simple semantic network that conveys knowledge about vehicles in general and knowledge about certain vehicles in particular.

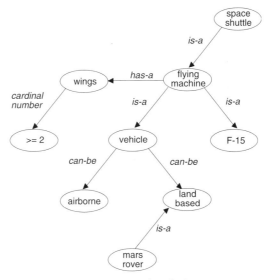

Sidebar Figure 8–1   A simple vehicle semantic network.

The circles in the semantic net are called nodes. *The lines are called* links. *The links represent some kind of relationship between the nodes. The nodes are used to represent objects and facts or descriptors. Links are used to represent relationships and connections. Some links are definitional while other links can be computational. The links can be used to show inheritance or subordination. Together the nodes and the links convey chunks of knowledge. For example, from the semantic network in Sidebar Figure 8–1, we know that a F-15 is a vehicle and a flying machine that has at least two wings. Semantic networks are used to understand and design the knowledge needed by problem-solving software.*

8.6.1 Using the Naming Service and Creating Naming Contexts

On line 22, the server program gets a reference to the naming service:

```
CORBA::Object_var NameService = Orb->resolve_initial_
references ("NameService");
```

In addition to returning object references for the Implementation Repository and the Interface Repository, the `resolve_initial_references()` method of the ORB is used to return a reference to the naming service. After obtaining a reference to the naming service, the server program creates a naming context from the object reference of the naming service on line 23:

```
CosNaming::NamingContext_var NamingContext =
CosNaming::NamingContext::_narrow(NameService);
```

This technique provides a naming context referred to as the *initial naming context*. The initial naming context plays the part of a default context. Once the naming service is located and the initial naming context is created, then the server program can add name/object reference pairs (name bindings) to the context. The names may be domain objects or other contexts. To add a name/object pair to a context, a name must first be created. Names are implemented in the CORBA standard by the `NameComponent` structure:

```
struct NameComponent {
   //...
   Istring_var id;
   Istring_var kind;
}
```

The MICO implementation of CORBA declaring the `NameComponent` structure is the `CosNaming.h` file. The `NameComponent` structure has two attributes: `id` and `kind`. The first attribute is used to hold the text of the name and the second attribute is an identifier that can be used to classify the object. For example:

```
//...
CosNaming::Name ObjectName;
ObjectName.length(1);
ObjectName.id = Corba::string_dup("train");
ObjectName.kind = Corba::string_dup("land_transportation");
NamingContext->bind(ObjectName,ObjectReference);
//...
```

Declares a NameComponent object. The id attribute is set to "train" and the kind attribute is set to land_transportation. Obviously the id attribute should be descriptive of the object. The kind attribute can be used to describe the context or the logical group that the object belongs to. In this case, it classifies train as a land_transportation object. The bind() method maps the ObjectName to the ObjectReference and associates it with the initial naming context. A name can consist of multiple NameComponent objects. If the name only consists of a single NameComponent, it is called a simple name. If it consists of multiple NameComponent objects, it is called a component name. If the name is a compound name, then the kind attribute can be used to describe a relationship. This technique is discussed further in Chapter 12. Program 8.3 binds its object with an object reference and associates it with a naming context. Once it is associated with the naming context, then the client object may access it through the name service. In Programs 8.1 and 8.2, we used a file to communicate a stringified IOR between the consumer program and the producer program. The naming service is used for communication with the client for Program 8.3.

The details for installing and executing the naming service is implementation specific. The MICO environment contains a program named nsd that implements a COS-compliant naming service. The nsd program requires the micod daemon to be running and appropriate entries to be made to the Implementation Repository before the naming service will be available to the consumer program. See the man pages for nsd, micod, and imr for a description of these programs and the MICO manual for a description of how they are used. Furthermore, the MICO distribution is accompanied by a wealth of examples of how to use the imr, nsd, micod, and ird programs. Example 8–5 is an excerpt from the shell script used to set up the server in Program 8.3 so that the name service would be available to the consumer program.

```
// Example 8.5    Shell script that adds an entry to the
//               Implementation Repository and starts the
//               naming service.

micod -ORBIIOPAddr inet:hostname:portnumber —forward &
imr create NameService poa `which nsd` IDL:omg.org/CosNaming/
NamingContext:1.0#NameService \
    -ORBImplRepoAddr inet:hostname:portnumber \
    -ORBNamingAddr inet:hostname:hostname:portnumberportnumber

imr create permutation persistent "`pwd`/permutation_server \
    -ORBImplRepoAddr inet:hostname:portnumber \
```

```
-ORBNamingAddr inet:hostname:portnumber" IDL:permutation:1.0  \
   -ORBImplRepoAddr inet:hostname:portnumber \
-ORBNamingAddr inet:hostname:portnumber
imr activate permutation -ORBImplRepoAddr inet:hostname:portnumber  \
   -ORBNamingAddr inet:hostname:portnumber
```

This shell script can be used in conjunction with the server in Program 8.3. In fact, this script actually helps to automatically start the server program named `permutation_server`. Note that `hostname` and `portnumber` in Example 8.5 need to be replaced by the `hostname` of the computer where the server is running and an appropriate port number.

8.6.2   A Name Service Consumer/Client

Program 8.3 associates the name of an object with a naming context. Program 8.4 contains a consumer program that uses the naming service to access the object/reference bindings that were created in Program 8.3. Program 8.3 produces a permutation of any string of characters that it receives. Permutations are creating by inflections of the characters within a string. For instance:

      Objcte   JbOetc   tbOjec

      Ojbect   JObetc

      Ojbcet   JtObec

are permutations of the string *Object*. The client gives the server a string to permute and the server generates N permutations. The server associates the name "`Inflection`" with the naming context. This name is the name that the client program will have to specify in order to get the object reference from the naming context.

```
// Program 8.4

1   int main(int argc, char *argv[])
2   {
3
4     try{
5            CORBA::ORB_var Orb = CORBA::ORB_init
                (argc,argv,"mico-local-orb");
6            object_reference Remote("NameService",Orb);
7            Remote.objectName("Inflection");
8            permutation_var Client =
                permutation::_narrow(Remote.objectReference());
```

```
9              char Value[1000];
10             strcpy(Value,"Common Object Request Broker");
11             Client->original(Value);
12             int N;
13             for(N = 0;N < 15;N++)
14             {
15                cout << "Value of nextPermutation() "
                      << Client->nextPermutation() << endl;
16             }
17         }
18     catch (CosNaming::NamingContext::NotFound_catch &exc) {
19             cerr << " Object NotFound exception" << endl;
20         }
21     catch (CosNaming::NamingContext::InvalidName_catch &exc) {
22             cerr << "InvalidName exception" << endl;
23         }
24
25     return(0);
26 }
```

Three steps the consumer program must take to access the appropriate object in the naming context are:

1. Get a reference to the name service.
2. Obtain a reference to the appropriate naming context through the name service.
3. Obtain a reference to the appropriate object through the naming context.

Step 1 is accomplished by calling the `resolve_initial_references()` method:

```
//...
CORBA::Object_var NameService;
NameService = Orb->resolve_initial_references ("NameService");
//...
```

This will return an object reference to the name service. In Step 2 this reference is used to get an object reference for the naming context:

```
CosNaming::NamingContext_var NameContext;
NameContext = CosNaming::NamingContext::_narrow (NameService);
```

The value of `NameService` is narrowed in Step 3, resulting in an object reference for `NameContext`. The consumer program needs the `NameContext` object so that it may call the `NameContext`'s `resolve()` method. The technique from Program 8.3 lines 24–27 is used to construct the name that will passed to the NameContext's resolve() method:

```
Name.length (1);
Name[0].id = CORBA::string_dup ("Inflection");
Name[0].kind = CORBA::string_dup ("");
try {
        ObjectReference = NameContext->resolve (Name);
}
```

The resolve() method will return the object reference associated with the name. In this case, the object's name is "Inflection." Note that this is the same name associated with the naming context on line 28 from Program 8.3. Once the consumer program has this object reference, it can be narrowed and then the remote object can be accessed by the consumer program. The process of obtaining an object reference for a remote object is such a common event that it makes sense to simplify the process by encapsulating the components within a class.

```
class object_reference{
//...
protected:
    CORBA::Object_var NameService;
    CosNaming::NamingContext_var NameContext;
    CosNaming::Name  Name;
    CORBA::Object_var ObjectReference;
public:
    object_reference(char *Service,CORBA::ORB_var Orb);
    CORBA::Object_var objectReference(void);
    void objectName(char *FileName,CORBA::ORB_var Orb);
    void objectName(char *OName);
//...
}
```

Program 8.4 takes advantage of the simple skeleton object_reference class that we have created for this purpose.

Notice on line 6 from Program 8.4 that an object named Remote of type object_reference is created. On line 8, this object is used to obtain a reference to the remote object using the method call:

```
Remote.objectReference();
```

After making this call the consumer program has access to the remote object. The object_reference class hides some of the work that needs to be done and therefore makes writing the consumer program easier. The constructor for the `object_reference` class is called on line 6 of Program 8.4. The constructor is implemented as:

```
object_reference::object_reference(char *Service,CORBA::ORB_var Orb)
{
    NameService = Orb->resolve_initial_references (Service);
    NameContext = CosNaming::NamingContext::_narrow (NameService);
}
```

The constructor gets a reference to the name service and instantiates the `NameContext` object. On line 7, the object's name is passed to the method `objectName()`. This process will using the naming context to retrieve the object reference associated with the object's name. The `objectName()` method is implemented as:

```
void object_reference::objectName(char *OName)
{
    Name.length (1);
    Name[0].id = CORBA::string_dup (OName);
    Name[0].kind = CORBA::string_dup ("");
    try {
            ObjectReference = NameContext->resolve (Name);
    }
    catch(...){
        cerr << "  Problem resolving Name  " << endl;
    throw;
    }
}
```

After the `objectName()` method is called the consumer program has access to the remote object's reference. All that is left to do is to call the `objectReference()` method. This occurs on line 8 of Program 8.4. The `resolve()` function does most of the work in the `objectName()` method. Programs 8.3 and 8.4 form a simple distributed client/server application that uses the naming service instead of stringified IORs to communicate object references. Both the naming service approach and the stringified IOR can be used in an intranet or on the Internet. Both can be used as support structure components within the context of the new Web services model.

8.7   A Closer Look
at Object Adapters

In addition to the name service and naming context object, the server in Program 8.3 also uses a portable object adapter. Recall from Figure 8–6 that the adapter acts as a kind of middleman between the ORB and the servant object that actually does the work of the CORBA object. We can compare a servant object to a ghost writer that writes a book on behalf of a celebrity. The publicists, marketers, and lawyers interact with the celebrity. The celebrity gets all the credit, but the ghost writer does the actual work and writing involved. The CORBA object publishes an interface to the outside world and is the celebrity in a CORBA program. The client or producer program interacts with the interface that the CORBA object provides, however, it's the servant object playing the part of the ghost writer that actually does the real work. The servant object has its own protocol. This protocol might be different from the one presented by the CORBA object. The CORBA object might present a C++ interface to the client. The servant object might be implemented in Java, Smalltalk, Fortran and so on. The object adapter provides an interface to the servant object. It adapts the interface so that the implementation of the servant object is transparent to the ORB and the client program. A CORBA implementation will normally have support for two types of object adapters: the Basic Object Adapter (BOA) and the Portable Object Adapter (POA). The BOA was the original adapter specified by the CORBA standard. The POA was designed to replace the BOA and is considerably more flexible and most commonly used. The BOA is a barebones adapter that has minimal capabilities. However, the BOA can be used to activate object implementations based on information stored in the Implementation Repository. Table 8–4 contains some of the commonly found elements in an Implementation Repository.

The BOA uses the activation mode and the path from the Implementation Repository to start the execution of a producer or server object. Although some of the simpler examples in this chapter used the BOA, we recommend that you use the POA for any serious CORBA development. The POA:

- Supports transparent object activation
- Supports transient objects
- Supports implicit activation of servant objects
- Supports persistent objects across server boundaries

Table 8–4 Some Commonly Found Elements in an Implementation Repository	
Implementation Repository Elements	*Description*
object name	Unique identifier for each object.
activation mode	Shared, unshared, persistent, `permethod` library.
path	Name and path of the binary.
list of repository IDs	

Perhaps the most important function of the POA is to interact with *servant objects*. The CORBA specification defines a servant accordingly:

> A servant is a programming language object or entity that implements requests on one or more objects. Servants generally exist within the context of a server process. Requests made on an object's references are mediated by the ORB and transformed into invocations on a particular servant. In the course of an object's lifetime it may be associated with multiple servants.

Every servant object will have at least one POA. However, other configurations are possible. Figure 8–9 shows the configuration possibilities between POAs and servants.

POAs are managed in part by POA manager objects. The CORBA specification defines a POA manager accordingly.

> A POA manager is an object that encapsulates the processing state of one or more POAs. Using operation on a POA manager, the developer can cause requests for the associated POAs to be queued or discarded. The developer can also use the POA manager to deactivate the POAs.

The server in Program 8.3 provides a simple example of how to use POAs and POA manager objects. A complete discussion of the POA is beyond the scope of this book. For a thorough discussion of POAs, see *Advanced CORBA Programming with C++* by Michi Henning and Steve Vinoski. The MICO distribution also contains several examples of how to use some of the more advanced features of the POA.

POA/SERVANT CONFIGURATION 1:   POA/SERVANT CONFIGURATION 2:

POA/SERVANT CONFIGURATION 3:

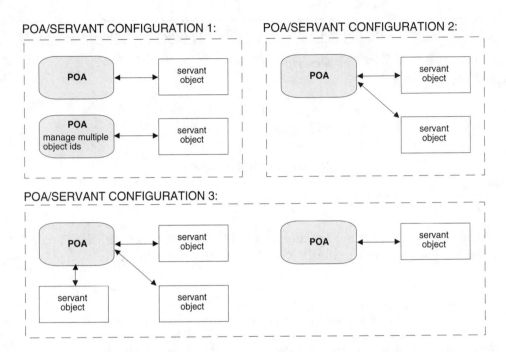

Figure 8–9   Configuration possibilities between POAs and servants.

8.8   Implementation and Interface Repositories

The ORB uses the Implementation Repository to locate objects when stringified IORs are not available. Implementation Repositories are normally ORB specific and are used as a convenient place to store environment-specific information (e.g., security information, debugging information, etc.). The Implementation Repository will contain enough information to allow the ORB to locate the object's path and binary executable. The `imr` tool is used with MICO distributions to manage the Implementation Repository. The `imr` tool is used to display, list, add, and delete entries from the Implementation Repository. For example:

```
imr create permutation persistent "`pwd`/permutation_server \
    -ORBImplRepoAddr inet:hostname:portnumber \
    -ORBNamingAddr inet:hostname:portnumber" IDL:permutation:1.0  \
```

Adds an entry to the repository with the name permutation. The executable file is located at `'pwd'/permutation_server`. The entry also includes the `hostname` and the `portnumber` that the program should be executed on. The Implementation Repository is a good place to store this type of information about an object. This entry is also given the mode of persistent. The ORB uses the information in this entry to properly initiate the execution of the program named `permutation_server`. See the man pages for a complete list of options available for the `imr` tool. The Interface Repository is used in addition to the Implementation Repository to store runtime information about each object. The Interface Repository can be used to discover the interface to CORBA objects dynamically because the IDL information about CORBA objects can be stored in the Interface Repository. The `ird` tool implements the Interface Repository for MICO distributions of CORBA. Although the CORBA specification describes the logical features of the Implementation Repository and the Interface Repository, the specifics are environment, distribution, and vendor specific. Also, the manner in which information is placed into and managed within an Implementation and Interface Repository will be vendor specific.

8.9   Simple Distributed Web Services Using CORBA

The addresses for Implementation Repositories and naming services can be imbedded within HTML and used as part of a CGI call to a Web server. This technique can be used to implement simple distributed Web services using CORBA. Example 8.6 shows a simple HTML entry. When the link is clicked, a CORBA client executes. The CORBA client can then get to the server using the address of the Implementation Repository and the naming service that was passed from the HTML CGI command.

```
// Example 8.6   A HTML document with an embedded call to a
//               CORBA client program.

<HTML>
<HEAD>
<TITLE> CORBA</TITLE>
</HEAD>
<BODY>
```

```
<a href="http://www.somewhere.org/cgi-bin/client?-
ORBImplRepoAddr+inet:hostname:port+-
ORBNamingAddr+inet:hostname:port">Click</a>
<P>
</HTML>
```

Here the client refers to a program that will access a CORBA producer or server program. The client has the name of the object that needs to be accessed and uses the naming service to resolve the reference. This technique does not require code to be downloaded to the user's computer. Instead, the client code is executed on the Web server and will access the CORBA-based server program whether it is on an intranet connected to a Web server or somewhere else on the Internet. The client program will respond to the HTML browser using the appropriate CGI protocol. Figure 8–10 shows a simple Web services configuration using CORBA components.

Figure 8–10   A simple Web services configuration using CORBA components.

Simple Web Services Architecture

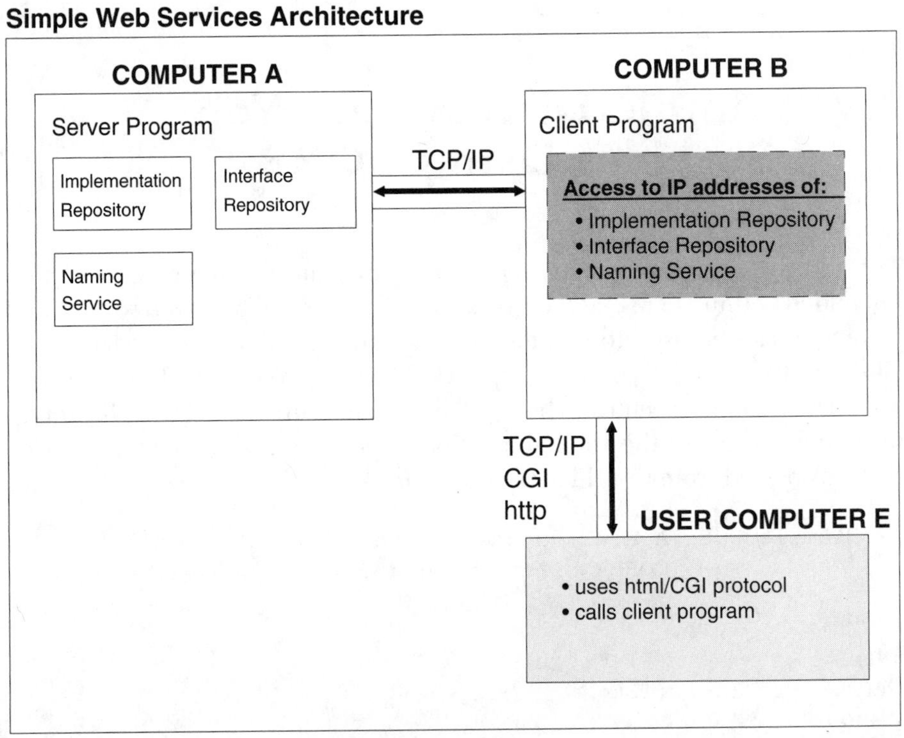

In addition to `http`, `telnet` can be used to launch CORBA-based clients and servers. The `http` protocol and the `telnet` protocol can be used to support global distribution of CORBA components. It is important to remember software, data, and system security when considering the design of distributed components that will be used across the Internet or intranet. Although security implementations and requirements are beyond the scope of this book, we mention it as a fundamental consideration in any distributed design. The Implementation Repository can be used to store security-type information. A CORBA implementation can be used in conjunction with `SSL` (Secure Socket Layer) and `SSH` (Secure Shell).

8.10   The Trading Service

In addition to stringified IORs and the naming service, the CORBA specification includes a more advanced and dynamic method of obtaining object references called the *trading service*. The trading service offers a more *discovery-based* approach to interacting with remote objects. Instead of interacting with a naming service, the client interacts with a trader. A trader has access to object references in the same manner as a naming service. However, the trader associates descriptions, and interfaces with the object references instead of a simple name. Whereas the naming service contains name/reference pairs, the trader contains descriptions-interfaces/reference pairs. Clients can describe the object they are looking for to the trader and the trader responds with an object reference if a match is found. This a very powerful search method. Not only can the client be unaware of the object's location, it can also be unaware of the object's name. This allows the client to query a trader based on a list of services that it needs instead of looking for a particular object. This allows the client to have a *I-don't-care-who-or-where* approach. The CORBA specification defines a trader accordingly:

> A trader is an object that supports the trading object service in a distributed environment. It can be viewed as an object through which other objects can advertise their capabilities and match their needs against advertised capabilities. Advertising a capability or offering a service is called "export." Matching against the needs or discovering services is called "import." Export and import facilitate dynamic discovery of, and late binding to, services.

Client-Server Application Using Trader Objects

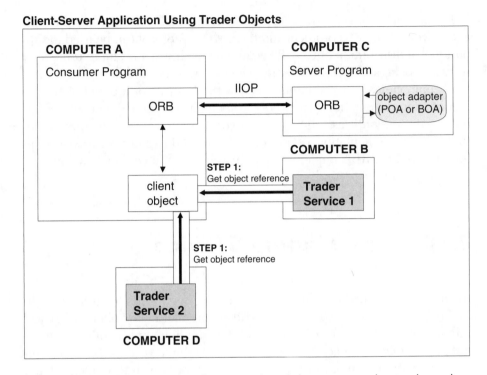

Figure 8-11 Basic architecture of a CORBA-based client-server application that makes requests of traders.

In the same way that connecting two or more naming contexts produce naming graphs, connecting two or more traders produce trading graphs. Naming and trading graphs are powerful methods of knowledge and capability representation. Naming graphs and trading graphs provide the foundations for global Web services and telnet services. Traversing naming and trading graphs might include hops that have the potential to visit anywhere on the local network, intranet, extranet, or the Internet. Like naming contexts, traders typically represent certain kinds of objects. For instance, we might have some traders that have access to credit card objects while other traders have access to compression and encryption objects. We can have traders that deal in weather and geography objects. We can have traders that deal in financial and insurance services. If each of these traders were linked, we would have a trading graph. If one trader trades on behalf of other traders, we would have what is known as a *trade federation*. When a client describes the services that it needs to one trader and that trader then contacts other traders to locate the required services, the client and the trader are involved with a trade federation. This is the most powerful and flexible form of *I-don't-care-who-or-where* request that the client can perform. When a trade federation returns an object reference it can literally be from anywhere and may be implemented by a servant object(s) whose operating system and language are totally foreign to the client program. Federations of traders provide access to very large and diverse collections of services. Keep in mind that the CORBA standard includes a wireless specification wCORBA. This has tremendous implications for the design of mobile agent and multiagent systems. Figure 8–11 shows the basic architecture of a CORBA-based client/server application that makes requests of traders.

A client program may interact directly with a trader or traders or indirectly with a trader through the federation. Notice in Figure 8–11 that the object reference is obtained and then the interaction with the ORB occurs. Table 8–5 shows common terms used with trader programming.

Table 8–5 Common Trader Programming Terms	
Trader Programming Terms	*Description*
Exporter	Advertises a service with a trader. An exporter can be the service provider or it can advertise a service on behalf of another.
Importer	Uses a trader to search for services matching some criteria. An importer can be the potential service client or it can import a service on behalf of another.
Service offer	Contains a description of the service being advertised. It contains a service type name, object reference, and object properties.

8.11   The Client/Server Paradigm

The terms "client" and "server" are applied in many ways to many different kinds of software applications. The client/server paradigm divides a patten of work between two parties represented by either processes or threads. One party, the client, makes requests for data or for action. The other party, the server, fulfills the requests. The roles of requester and request satisfier are common themes found in many different software applications. The terms client/server are used at the operating-system level to describe many producer–consumer relationships that can occur between processes. For instance, when a fifo is used to connect two processes, one of the processes takes on the role of server and the other of client. Sometimes a client can take on the role of server when it receives requests. Similarly, a server may take on the role of client when it needs to make requests of another program. The client/server configuration is the most fundamental architecture for distributed programming. The type of server involved usually characterizes the entire application. Table 8–6 shows the most commonly found types of software servers.

Blackboards and multiagent systems are the two primary architectures that we use in this book to support parallel and distributed programming. We place special emphasis on the logic server defined in Table 8–6. The logic server is a special type of an application server, and is used to perform problem solving that requires intense symbolic and possibly parallel computation. The process of inference and deduction is often processor intensive and can benefit from parallel processors. Usually the more processors available to logic servers, the better. The Agent and Blackboard architectures that we discuss in Chapter 12 and 13 rely on the notion of distributed logic servers that can cooperatively solve problems over a network, an intranet, or the Internet. Although the Blackboard and Agents form more of a peer-to-peer architecture, they are clients to the logic servers that they access. Distributed objects are used to implement all of the components involved. CORBA is used to facilitate the network programming.

Summary

Distributed programming involves programs that execute in different processes. Each process can potentially reside on a different computer and possibly on a different network with different network protocols. Distributed programming techniques allow the developer to divide an application into separately executing modules that will either have some kind of producer–consumer relationship or peer-to-peer relationship. The modules each have their own address space and computer resources. Distributed programming can be used to take advantage of special processors, peripherals, and other computer resources (i.e., database servers, applications servers,

Table 8–6 Common Types of Software Servers	
Types of Software Servers	**Description**
Application servers	Used to provide multiple clients with access to an application. It divides work in an application between the client and the server. The majority of the work is done on the server and the client (with its own processor) performs part of the work.
File servers	Acts as a central repository for shared documents, multimedia files, databases, and so on. The clients are usually terminals or workstations on a network. The client makes requests for files or records within the files, then the file server transmits the request to the client. The file server maintains data integrity and enforces file access security.
Database servers	Splits the processing of an application between different machines in a network environment. A client makes requests for an item of data, then the database server locates the data and transmits the request to the client. The database server can process complex information queries that may require joins and intersections of multiple databases.
Transaction servers	Used to perform transactions that take place on the machine or machines that contain the transaction server. Every action or update completes in its entirety without interruption. If any problems are encountered, all actions or updates are undone and the transaction is tried again.
Logic servers	Used to perform problem solving that requires intense symbolic computation. It is able to find both implicit and explicit information within a database. The logic server is able to deduce or infer information that has not been explicitly entered into the database. It consists of a database with one or more built-in inference engines. The inference engine is used to obtain conclusions and inferences from the server. The database consists of rules, theorems, axioms, and procedures. Queries submitted to the logic server causes it to perform deduction, induction, abduction, or some combination.

e-mail servers, etc.). CORBA is the standard for distributed object-oriented programming. We provide an introduction to some of the simple basics of CORBA programming. However, this chapter barely scratches the surface of the CORBA specification and CORBA services. It provides only enough to see what the basic components look like and how a simple distributed program can be constructed. The CORBA specifications for Web services, MAF, naming services, and so on, can be obtained from *www.omg.org*. Michi Henning and Steve Vionosk provide a detailed resource in their *Advanced CORBA Programming with C++*. The naming and trader graphs provide the basis for powerful distributed knowledge representation that can be used in conjunction with multiagent programming. They provide the basis for the next level of smart Web services.

9 SPMD and MPMD Using Templates and the MPI

"There must be an essentially non-algorithmic ingredient in the action of consciousness."

—*Roger Penrose,* The Emperor's New Mind

In this Chapter

Work Breakdown Structure for the MPI • Using Template Functions to Represent MPI Tasks • Simplifying MPI Communications • Summary

Templates support the notion of parameterized programming. The basic idea of parameterized programming is to maximize software reuse by implementing software designs in as general a form as possible. Function templates support generic procedural abstractions and class templates support generic data abstractions. Typically, computer programs are already general solutions to specific problems. A program that adds two numbers is usually designed to add any two numbers. However, if the program only performed the operation of addition, we could generalize this program by allowing it to perform different operations on any two numbers. If we want the most general program, can we stop with simply allowing it to perform different operations on any two numbers? What if the numbers are of different types, that is, complex numbers and `float`s? We may wish to design the program so that not only can it perform different operations on any two numbers but on different types or classes of numbers (i.e., `int`s, `float`s, `double`s, complex numbers, etc.). In addition, we would like the program to perform any kind of binary operation on any pair of numbers so long as that operation is legal for those two numbers. Once we have implemented such a program, the opportunities for reuse are significant. Function and class templates give this capability to the C++ programmer. This kind of generalization can be accomplished using parameterized programming.

The parameterized programming paradigm supported by C++, combined with the object-oriented paradigm that is also supported by C++, provide some unique approaches to MPI programming. As we discussed in Chapter

1, the MPI (Message Passing Interface) is a standard of communication used in implementing programs that require parallelism. The MPI is implemented as a collection of more than 300 routines. The MPI functions include everything from spawning tasks to barrier synchronization to set operations. There is also a C++ representation for the MPI functions that encapsulate the functionality of the MPI into a set of classes. However, many of the advantages found in the object-oriented paradigm are not used in the MPI library. The advantages of parameterized programming are also absent. So while the MPI has important value as a standard, it does not go a long way to simplify parallel programming. It does insulate the programmer from socket programming and many of the pitfalls of network programming. That insulation is not enough. Cluster, SMP, and MPP application programming can be made easier. The template facilities in C++, and the support for true object-oriented programming, can be used to help us accomplish this goal. In this chapter, we use templates and techniques from object-oriented programming, to simplify the basic SPMD and MPMD approaches used with MPI programming.

9.1   Work Breakdown Structure for the MPI

One of the advantages of using the MPI over traditional UNIX/Linux processes and sockets is the ability of an MPI environment to launch multiple executables simultaneously. An MPI implementation can launch multiple executables, establish a basic relationship between the executables, and identify each executable. In this book we use the MPICH[1] implementation of MPI. The command:

```
$ mpirun -np 16 /tmp/mpi_example1
```

tells the MPI runtime to launch 16 processes. Each process will execute the program named mpi_example1. Each process may use a different processor if the processor is available. Also, each process may be on a different ma-

---

[1]All the MPI examples in this book were implemented using MPICH 1.1.2 and MPICH 1.2.4 in the Linux environment.

chine if the MPI is run in a cluster-type environment. The processes will execute concurrently. The `mpirun` command is a shell script that is responsible for starting MPI jobs on the necessary processors. This script insulates the user from details of starting concurrent processes on different machines. Here it will launch 16 copies of the program `mpi_example1`. Although the MPI-2 standard does specify spawn routines that can be used to dynamically add programs to an executing MPI application, this technique is not encouraged. In general, the number of processes needed are created at the start of an MPI application. This means that the code is replicated N number of times during startup. This scheme easily supports the SPMD (SIMD) model for concurrency because the same program is launched simultaneously on multiple processors. The data that each program needs to work on can be determined after the programs are running. This technique of starting the same program on multiple processors also has implications if the MPMD model is desired. The work that a MPI program will do is divided between the number of processes launched on startup. Which process does what and which process works on which data is coded in the executable. The computers that can be involved in the process are listed in the `machines.arch` (`machines.Linux` in our case) file by host name. The location of this file is implementation dependent. Depending on your installation, the computers listed in the file will either be able to communicate using `ssh` or the UNIX/Linux 'r' commands.

9.1.1 Differentiating Tasks by Rank

During the startup of the processes involved in an MPI application, the MPI environment assigns each process a rank and a communication group. The rank is stored as an `int`. The rank serves as a kind of process id for each MPI task. The communication group determines which processes can engage in point-to-point communications. Initially, all MPI processes are assigned to a default communication group. The members of a communication group can be changed after the application has started. After each process is started, one of the first things that it should do is determine its rank. This is done with the `MPI_Comm_rank()` routine. The `MPI_Comm_rank()` routine returns the rank of the calling process. The calling process specifies what communicator it is associated with in the first argument to the routine and the rank is returned in the second argument. Example 9.1 shows how the `MPI_Comm_rank()` routine is used.

```
// Example 9.1 Using the MPI_Comm_rank() routine.

//...
int Tag = 33;
int WorldSize;
int TaskRank;
MPI_Status Status;
MPI_Init(&argc,&argv);
MPI_Comm_rank(MPI_COMM_WORLD,&TaskRank);
MPI_Comm_size(MPI_COMM_WORLD,&WorldSize);
//...
```

The MPI_COMM_WORLD communicator is the default communicator that all MPI tasks are assigned upon startup. MPI tasks are grouped by communicators. The communicator is what identifies a *communication group*. In Example 9.1 the rank is returned in the variable TaskRank. Each process will have a unique rank. Once the rank is determined, then the appropriate data may be given to that task or the appropriate code for that task to execute may be determined. For instance, in Case 1:

Case 1: Simple MPMD	*Case 2: Simple SIMD*

```
if(TaskRank == 1){            if(TaskRank == 1){
  // do something                // use this data
}                             }


if (TaskRank == 2){           if(TaskRank == 2){
  // do something else           // use that data
}                             }
```

the rank is used to differentiate which process will do which work and in Case 2 the rank is used to differentiate which data each process will work on. Although each MPI executable starts out with the same code, MPMD (MIMD) may be achieved by using the rank and performing a branch. Likewise, once the rank is determined, data types may be assigned to the data of a process or specific data that a given process needs to work with may be identified. The rank is also used in message passing. MPI tasks identify each other in a communication exchange by ranks and communicators. The MPI_Send() and MPI_Recv() routines use rank for destination and source, respectively. The call:

```
MPI_Send(Buffer,Count,MPI_LONG,TaskRank,Tag,Comm);
```

will send Count number of longs to a MPI process with rank = TaskRank. The Buffer is a pointer to the data to be sent to the process

`TaskRank`. `Count` represents the number of items in the `Buffer`, not the size of `Buffer`. Each message has a tag. The tag can be used to differentiate one message from another, to group messages into classes, to associate certain messages with certain communicators, and so on. The tag is an `int` and its value is user-defined. The `Comm` parameter represents the communicator that the process is assigned to or associated with. If the rank and communicator of a task are known, then messages may be sent to that task. The call:

```
MPI_Recv(Buffer,Count,MPI_INT,TaskRank,Tag,Comm,&Status);
```

will receive `Count` `ints` from a process with `rank` = `TaskRank`. This routine will cause the caller to block until it receives a message from a process with `TaskRank` and the appropriate value for `Tag`. The MPI does support wildcards for the rank and tag parameters. These wildcards are `MPI_ANY_TAG` and `MPI_ANY_SOURCE`. If these values are used, the calling process will accept the next message that it receives regardless of the source and tag of that message. The `Status` parameter is of type `MPI_Status`. Information about the receive operation can be retrieved from the `Status` object. Three fields contained in status are `MPI_SOURCE`, `MPI_TAG`, and `MPI_ERROR`. Therefore, the `Status` object can be used to determine what the tag and source of the sending process were. Once the processes know how many processes are involved, they can determine who to send messages to and who to receive messages from. Naturally, which task receives messages and which task sends messages will depend on the application. How the work is divided up between the processes will also be application dependent. Another piece of information that is determined immediately by each process before the work starts is how many other processes are involved in the application. This is done by a call to:

```
MPI_Comm_size(MPI_COMM_WORLD,&WorldSize);
```

This routine determines the size of the group of processes associated with a particular communicator. In this case, the communicator is the default communication `MPI_COMM_WORLD`. The number of processes involved are returned in the `WorldSize` parameter. This parameter is an `int`. Once each process has the `WorldSize`, it knows how many processes are associated with its communicator and what its rank is relative to the other processes.

9.1.2   Grouping Tasks by Communicators

In addition to ranks, processes are also associated with communicators. The communicator specifies a communication domain for a set of processes. All processes with the same communicator are in the same *communication group*. The work that a MPI program does can be divided between communicator groups. MPI_COMM_WORLD is the default communicator group that all processes are in initially. MPI_Comm_create() can be used to create new communicators. Table 9–1 shows a list of short descriptions for the routines used to work with communicators.

Through the use of the rank and the communicator, MPI tasks are identified and differentiated. The rank and the communicator allow us to structure a program as SPMD or MPMD or some combination. We use the rank and the communicator in conjunction with paramaterized programming and object-oriented techniques to simplify the code written for a MPI program. The templates can accommodate not only the *different data* aspect of SIMD but different *data types* may also be specified using templates. This greatly simplifies the many computational-intensive applications that do the same work but with different data types. We recommend runtime polymorphism (supported by objects), parametric polymorphism (supported by templates), function objects, and predicates to achieve MPMD (MIMD). These techniques are used in conjunction with the rank and the communicator of a MPI process to accomplish the division and assignment of work in an MPI application. When using an object-oriented approach, the work of a program is divided between families of objects. The families of objects are each associated with different communicators. Associating families of objects with different communicators helps with modularity in the design of an MPI application. This kind of division also helps with understanding how the parallelism can be applied. We have found that the object-oriented approach makes MPI programs more extensible, maintainable, and easier to debug and test.

9.1.3   The Anatomy of an MPI Task

Figure 9–1 contains a skeleton MPI program. The tasks involved in this MPI program simply report their ranks to the MPI task whose rank == 0.

Every MPI program should at least have MPI_Init() and MPI_Finalize(). The MPI_Init routine initializes the MPI environment for the calling task. The MPI_Finalize() routine deallocates resources from the MPI task.

Table 9–1 Routines Used to Work with Communicators	
MPI Communicator Routines `#include "mpi.h"`	*Description*

`int MPI_Intercomm_create`
`(MPI_Comm LocalComm,`
` int LocalLeader,`
` MPI_Comm PeerComm,`
` int remote_leader,`
` int MessageTag,`
` MPI_Comm *CommOut);`
	Creates an intercommunicator from two intracommunicators.

`int MPI_Intercomm_merge`
`(MPI_Comm Comm,int High,`
` MPI_Comm *CommOut);`
	Creates an intracommunicator from an intercommunicator.

`int MPI_Cartdim_get` `(MPI_Comm Comm,int *NDims);`	Returns Cartesian topology information associated with a communicator.

`int MPI_Cart_create`
`(MPI_Comm CommOld,int NDims,`
` int *Dims,int *Periods,`
` int Reorder,`
` MPI_Comm *CommCart);`
	Creates a new communicator to which topology information has been attached.

`int MPI_Cart_sub`
`(MPI_Comm Comm,`
` int *RemainDims,`
` MPI_Comm *CommNew);`
	Divides a communicator up into subgroups, which form lower dimensional Cartesian subgrids.

`int MPI_Cart_shift`
`(MPI_Comm Comm, int Direction,`
` int Display,int *Source,`
` int *Destination);`
	Retrieves the shifted source and destination ranks, given a shift direction and amount.

`int MPI_Cart_map`
`(MPI_Comm CommOld,`
` int NDims,int *Dims,`
` int *Periods,int *Newrank);`
	Maps process to Cartesian topology information.

`int MPI_Cart_get`
`(MPI_Comm Comm,int MaxDims,`
` int *Dims,int *Periods,`
` int *Coords);`
	Returns Cartesian topology information associated with a communicator.

`int MPI_Cart_coords`
`(MPI_Comm Comm, int Rank,`
` int MaxDims, int *Coords);`
	Calculates process coords in Cartesian topology given rank in group.

(continued)

Table 9–1   (cont.)

MPI Communicator Routines `#include "mpi.h"`	Description

`int MPI_Comm_create`
`(MPI_Comm Comm,`
` MPI_Group Group,`
` MPI_Comm *CommOut);`
	Creates a new communicator.

`int MPI_Comm_rank` `(MPI_Comm Comm,int *Rank );`	Calculates and returns the rank of the calling process in the communicator.

`int MPI_Cart_rank`
`(MPI_Comm Comm,int *Coords,`
` int *Rank );`
	Calculates and returns the process rank in a communicator given Cartesian location.

`int MPI_Comm_compare`
`(MPI_Comm Comm1,`
` MPI_Comm Comm2,`
` int *Result);`
	Compares two communicators, `Comm1` and `Comm2`.

`int MPI_Comm_dup`
`(MPI_Comm CommIn,`
` MPI_Comm *CommOut);`
	Duplicates an already existing communicator along with all its cached information.

`int MPI_Comm_free` `(MPI_Comm *Comm);`	Marks the communicator object to be deallocated.

`int MPI_Comm_group`
`(MPI_Comm Comm,`
` MPI_Group *Group);`
	Accesses the group associated with the given communicator.

`int MPI_Comm_size` `(MPI_Comm Comm,int *Size);`	Calculates and returns the size of the group associated with a communicator.

`int MPI_Comm_split`
`(MPI_Comm Comm,int Color,`
` int Key,MPI_Comm *CommOut);`
	Creates new communicators based on colors and keys.

`int MPI_Comm_test_inter` `(MPI_Comm Comm,int *Flag);`	Determines if a communicator is an intercommunicator.

`int MPI_Comm_remote_group`
`(MPI_Comm Comm,`
` MPI_Group *Group);`
	Accesses the remote group associated with the given intercommunicator.

`int MPI_Comm_remote_size` `(MPI_Comm Comm,int *Size);`	Calculates and returns the size of the remote group associated with an intercommunicator.

```
#include <mpi.h>  ◄————————————— MPI header file
int Dest;
int Tag = 50;
int WorldSize;
int TaskRank;
string M;
char MessageIn[1000];
int N;
strstream Buffer;
MPI_Status Status;
MPI_Init(&argc,&argc);  ◄————————————— Initialization routine
MPI_Comm_rank(MPI_COMM_WORLD,TaskRank);  ◄————————————— Get task rank
MPI_Comm_size(MPI_COMM_WORLD,&WorldSize);  ◄————————————— Get # of MPI tasks
Dest = 0;  ◄————————————— Tells who receives the message
N = 1;
if(TaskRank != 0){
   Buffer << "Ready To Work From Rank#" << TaskRank << ends;
   getline(Buffer,M);
   MPI_Send(const_char<char*>(M.data()),M.size()+1,MPI_CHAR,Dest,Tag,MPI_COMM_WORLD);  ◄————————————— Send message
}
else{
     do{
          cout << "From Supervisor" << endl;
          MPI_Recv(MessageIn,100,MPI_CHAR,N,Tag,MPI_COMM_WORLD,&Status);  ◄————————————— Receive message
          cout << MessageIn << endl;
          cout << "Received From " << MessageIn << endl;
          N++;
     } while(N < WorldSize);
   }
   MPI_Finalize();  ◄————————————— Finish up MPI
}
```

Figure 9-1   A MPI program.

Every MPI task should call the `MPI_Finalize()` routine prior to exiting. Notice the calls to `MPI_COMM_rank()` and `MPI_COMM_Size()` in Figure 9–1. They are used to get the rank and the number of processes that belong to an MPI application. Most MPI applications should call this function. The remaining MPI functions will depend on the application. The MPI environment supports over 300 functions. Consult your man pages for a complete listing and discussion of the MPI functions.

9.2   Using Template Functions to Represent MPI Tasks

Function templates allow us to generalize a procedure for any type. Let's look at a multiplication procedure that works for any data type for which multiplication is defined:

```
template<class T>  T multiplies(T X, T Y)
{
   return( X * Y);
}
```

To use a template function such as this one we provide the necessary parameters for the type `T`. `T` is a stand-in for some data type that will be supplied when the template is instantiated. So we can instantiate `multiplies()` accordingly:

```
//...
multiplies<double>(3.2,4.5);
multiplies<int>(7,2);
multiplies<rational>("7/2","3/4");
//...
```

with `T` instantiated to `double`, `int`, and `rational`, thereby determining the exact implementation of the multiplication operation. Multiplication is defined differently for each data type. So the specification of the data type causes slightly different code to be executed. The template function allows us to write the `multiplies()` operation once and apply it to many different data types.

9.2.1 Instantiating Templates and SPMD (Datatypes)

Parameterized functions can be used with the MPI to handle situations where each process is executing the same code but is working with a different type of data. So once we have determined the TaskRank of the process, we can differentiate what data and type of data the process should work with. Example 9.2 shows how to instantiate different tasks for different ranks.

```
//Example 9.2 Using template functions to designate what the
//            MPI task will do.

int main(int argc, char *argv[])
{
   //...
   int Tag = 2;
   int WorldSize;
   int TaskRank;
   MPI_Status Status;
   MPI_Init(&argc,&argv);
   MPI_Comm_rank(MPI_COMM_WORLD,&TaskRank);
   MPI_Comm_size(MPI_COMM_WORLD,&WorldSize);
   //...
   switch(TaskRank)
   {
      case 1:  multiplies<double>(3.2,4.6);
               break;
      case 2:  multiplies<complex>(X,Y)
               break;

      //case n:

      //...
   }

}
```

Since no two tasks have the same rank, each branch in the case statement in Example 9.2 will be executed by a different MPI task. Also, you may extend this type of parameterization to container arguments for template functions. This allows you to pass different containers of objects containing different types of objects to the same generic template function. For instance Example 9.3 contains a generic search() template.

```
//Example 9.3   Using container templates as arguments to
//              template functions.

template<T> bool search(T Key,graph<T>)
{
   //...
   locate(Key)
   //...
}

//...
MPI_Comm_rank(MPI_COMM_WORLD,&TaskRank);
//...
switch(TaskRank)
{

   case 1:
        {
            graph<string> bullion;
            search<string> search("gold", bullion)
        }
        break;
   case 2:
        {
            graph<complex>  Coordinates;
            search<complex>((X,Y),Coordinates);
        }
        break;

//...
```

In Example 9.3, the process with TaskRank == 1 searches a graph named bullion that contains string objects and the process with TaskRank == 2 searches a graph named Coordinates containing complex numbers. We did not have to change the search() routine to accommodate the different data or data types and the MPI program is made simpler because we can reuse the search function template to search a graph container containing any type. Using templates simplifies SPMD programming. The more generic we make the MPI task, the more flexible it is. Also, once the template is debugged and tested, the reliability of all of the MPI tasks are increased since they all execute the same code.

9.2.2 Using Polymorphism to Implement MPMD

Polymorphism is a primary characteristic of object-oriented programming. In order for a language to support true object-oriented programming, the language must support encapsulation, inheritance, and polymorphism. *Polymorphism* is the ability of an object to take on many forms. Polymorphism supports the notion of "one interface, multiple implementations." A user uses one name or interface implemented in different ways by different objects. To illustrate the concept of polymorphism, lets look at a `vehicle` class, its descendants, and a simple function called `travel()` that uses the `vehicle` class. Figure 9–2 shows the simple hierarchy for our `vehicle` class family.

Airplanes, helicopters, cars, and submarines are all descendants of type `vehicle`. A `vehicle` object can start its engine, move forward, turn right, turn left, stop, and so on. Example 9.4 demonstrates how the travel function uses a `vehicle` object to make a computerized trip.

Figure 9–2 The `vehicle` class family hierarchy.

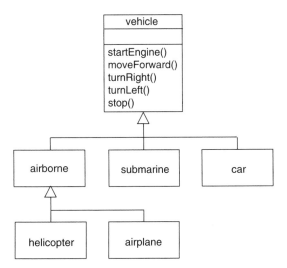

```
// Example 9.4 The travel() function using a vehicle object.

void travel(vehicle *Transport)
{

    Transport->startEngine();
    Transport->moveForward();
    Transport->turnLeft();
    //...
    Transport-> stop();
}

int main(int argc, char *argv[])
{
    //...
    car *Car;
    Transportation = new Vechicle();
    travel(Car);
    //...
}
```

The travel() function accepts a pointer to a vehicle object. The travel() function invokes the appropriate methods of the vehicle object. Notice that the main() function in Example 9.4 declares an object of type car and not type vehicle. A car object is passed to the function travel() instead of a vehicle object. This is possible because in C++ a pointer to a class can point to an object of that type or any objects that are descendants of that type. Since car inherits vehicle, a vehicle pointer can point to an object of type car. The function travel() is written without the knowledge of what types of vehicle object it will manipulate. The travel() function simply requires that its vehicle objects have the capability of starting an engine, moving forward, turning left and right, and so on. As long as its vehicle object can perform those actions, then the travel() function can do its work. Notice in Figure 9–2 that the methods of the vehicle class have been declared as virtual. Declaring the methods as virtual in a base class is necessary for runtime polymorphism to work. The car, helicopter, submarine, and airplane class will each define:

```
startEngine();
moveForward();
turnLeft();
turnRight();
stop();
//...
```

relative to their type of machine. Although each type of vehicle moves forward, the method in which a car moves forward is different from the way a submarine moves forward. The way an airplane turns right is different from the way a car turns right. Therefore, each `vehicle` type has to implement the necessary operations to complete its class. Since these operations are declared as `virtual` in the base class, they are candidates for polymorphism. When the `travel()` function's `vehicle` pointer actually points to a `car` object, then the `startEngine()`, `moveForward()`, and so on called will be those methods defined in the `car` class. If the `travel ()` function's `vehicle` pointer was assigned a pointer to an `airplane` class, then the `startEngine()`, `moveForward()`, and so on methods that belonged to the `airplane` class would be called. This is where the *many forms*, or *single interface multiple implementations,* come in. Although the `travel()` function only calls a single set of methods, the behavior of those methods can be radically different depending on what type of `vehicle` has been assigned to the `vehicle` pointer. In this way `travel()` is polymorphic because it may do something very different each time it is called. In fact, as long as the `travel()` function uses a pointer to a `vehicle` type, it may be used in the future for vehicle types that were unknown or that did not exist at the time the `travel()` function was designed. As long as the future `vehicle` classes inherit `vehicle` and define the necessary methods then they can be manipulated by the `travel()` function. This type of polymorphism is called *runtime polymorphism.* It's called runtime polymorphism because the `travel()` function does not know exactly which `startEngine()`, `moveForward()`, or `turnLeft()` functions it will call until the program is executing.

This type of polymorphism is useful when implementing MPI programs that use a MPMD model. If the work that the MPI tasks perform manipulate pointers to base classes, then polymorphism allows the MPI class to also manipulate any derived classes of the base class. If instead of pointers, the `travel()` function in Example 9.4 had a declaration:

```
void travel(vehicle Transport);
```

then the `startEngine()`, `moveForward()`, and so on calls would belong to the `vehicle` class and there wouldn't be an easy way to manipulate derived classes. The pointer to the `vehicle` class and the fact that the methods in the `vehicle` class are declared `virtual` are what makes the polymorphism work. MPI tasks that manipulate pointers to base classes can take advantage of polymorphism in the same way that the `travel()` function is able to work with any kind of `vehicle` object present or future. This technique holds a lot of promise for the future of cluster, smp, and mpp applications that will need to implement MPMD models. To see how this MPMD works in a MPI context, let's use our `travel()` function as a MPI task that is part of a search and rescue simulation. Each MPI task is responsible for performing a search and rescue mission with a different type of `vehicle` object. Each vehicle will obviously have different means of mobility. Although the problem to be solved requires that each MPI task perform a search, the code is different because each task uses a different kind of `vehicle` object that works different and requires different data. Example 9.5 would be launched in our MPICH environment using:

$ mpirun -np 16   /tmp/search_n_rescue

```
//Example 9.5   MPI tasks implementing simple search and
//              rescue simulation.

template<T>  bool travel(vehicle *Transport,set<T> Location,
                         T Object)
{

   //...
   Transport->startEngine();
   Transport->moveForward(XDegrees);
   Transport->turnLeft(YDegrees);
   //...
   if (Location.find(Transport->location() == Object){
      //... rescue()
   }
   //...
}

int main(int argc, char *argv[])
{
   //...
   int Tag = 2;
   int WorldSize;
   int TaskRank;
   MPI_Status Status;
   MPI_Init(&argc,&argv);
   MPI_Comm_rank(MPI_COMM_WORLD,&TaskRank);
   MPI_Comm_size(MPI_COMM_WORLD,&WorldSize);
   //...
   switch(TaskRank)
   {
       case 1:
          {
```

```
            //...
            car * Car;
            set<streets> SearchSpace
            travel<streets>(Car, SearchSpace,Street);
            //...
        }
        break;
    case 2:
        {
            //...
            helicopter *BlueThunder;
            set<air_space>  NationalAirSpace;
            travel<air_space>(BlueThunder,NationalAirSpace,
                              AirSpace);
            //...
        }

    //case n:

    //...
    }


}
```

This will cause search_n_rescue to be launched in 16 processes, with each process potentially running on a different processor and each processor potentially on a different computer. Although each process is executing the same executable, the work (code) and data that each process works with is radically different. Templates and polymorphism are used to differentiate what each MPI task will do and what data it will use. Notice in Example 9.5 that the MPI process that has a TaskRank == 1 will use a Car object to perform a search and rescue with a container that contains street objects. The MPI process that has a TaskRank == 2 will perform its simulation using helicopters and air_space objects. Both tasks call the travel() template function. Since the travel() template function manipulates pointers to the vehicle class, it can take advantage of polymorphism and perform its operations with any descendant of type vehicle. This means that although each MPI task is calling the same travel() function, the operation that the travel() function performs will not be the same. Notice there are no case statements or if statements in the travel() function that attempt to identify what type of vehicle it is working with. The particular vehicle object it is working with is determined by the type that vehicle is pointing to. This MPI application would work with potentially 16 different vehicles, each with its own type of mobility and search space. There are other techniques that can be used to implement MPMD within a MPI environment but the polymorphic approaches generally require less code.

The two primary types of polymophism we demonstrate are *dynamic binding polymorphism* supported by inheritance and `virtual` methods and *parametric polymorphism* supported by templates. The `travel()` function in Example 9.5 uses both types of polymorphism. The inheritance-based polymorphism is demonstrated by the use of the `vehicle *Transport`. The parameterized polymorphism is demonstrated by the use of `set<T>`, and `T Object`. Parametric polymorphism is the mechanism by which the same code is used on different types passed as parameters. Table 9–2 lists the different types of polymorphism that may be used to simplify MPI tasks and shorten the code required to implement an MPI program.

Table 9–2   Different Types of Polymorphism That May Be Used to Simplify MPI Tasks

Types of Polymorphism	Mechanisms	Description
Runtime (dynamic)	inheritance virtual methods	All information needed to determine which function is to be executed is not known until runtime.
Parametric	templates	A mechanism in which the same code is used on different types that are passed as parameters.

9.2.3   Adding MPMD with Function Objects

Function objects are also used by the standard algorithms to implement a kind of horizontal polymorphism. The polymorphism implemented using `vehicle *Transport` in Example 9.5 is vertical because in order for it to work the classes must all be related through inheritance. When horizontal polymorphism is used, the classes are not related by inheritance but by interface. Function objects each has the `operator()` defined. Function objects would allow MPI tasks to be designed with the general form:

```
// function object
class some_class{
   //...
   operator();
   //
};

template<class T>   T  mpiTask(T  X)
{
   //...
   T Result;
   Result =  X()
   //...

}
```

The `mpiTask()` template function will then work with any type `T` that has the `operator()` function appropriately defined:

```
//...
MPI_Init(&argc,&argv);
MPI_Comm_rank(MPI_COMM_WORLD,&TaskRank);
MPI_Comm_size(MPI_COMM_WORLD,&WorldSize);
//...

if(TaskRank == 0){
   //...
   user_defined_type  M;
   mpiTask(M);
   //...
}

if(TaskRank == N){
   //...
   some_other_userdefined_type N;
   mpiTask(N);
}
//....
```

This horizontal polymorphism does not rely on inheritance or virtual functions. So if our MPI task gets its rank and then declares any type of object that has the `operator()` defined, then when `mpiTask()` is called its behavior will be dictated by whatever functionality is found in the `operator()` method. So although each process launched with the `mpirun` script is identical, the polymorphism of templates and the function objects allow each MPI task to perform different work on different data.

9.3   Simplifying MPI Communications

In addition to simplifying and shortening the code of the MPI task with polymorphism and templates, we can also simplify the communication between MPI tasks by taking advantage of operator overloading. The `MPI_Send()` and `MPI_Recv()` class of functions have the form:

```
MPI_Send(Buffer,Count,MPI_LONG,TaskRank,Tag,Comm);
MPI_Recv(Buffer,Count,MPI_INT,TaskRank,Tag,Comm,&Status);
```

where the calls require that the user specify the data type involved in the call and a buffer that will hold the data to be sent or received. The specification of the data type for each call of the send and receive routines can be tedious and can introduce subtle errors if the wrong types are passed. Table 9–3 contains short descriptions for each of the MPI send and receive functions and their prototypes.

The goal is to make the data types and buffers as transparent as possible during send and receive operations. We would like to send and receive MPI data using the stream metaphor of the `iostream` classes. We would like to send data using syntax such as:

```
//...
int  X;
float Y;
user_defined_type Z;

cout << X << Y << Z;

//...
```

Here, the developer does not have to specify the types when inserting data into `cout`. The three data types to be displayed each have the operator `<<` defined. These definitions specify how to translate the type during the insertion into the `cout` stream. Likewise, extraction from the `cin` stream:

```
//...

int  X;
float Y;
user_defined_type Z;

cin  >>  X  >>  Y  >>  Z;
//...
```

occurs without specifying the types involved. Operator overloading allows the developer to use this technique for MPI tasks. The `cout` stream is instan-

Table 9–3   MPI Send and Receive Functions and Their Prototypes

MPI Send and Receive Routines `#include "mpi.h"`	*Description*

`int MPI_Send`
`(void *Buffer,int Count,`
` MPI_Datatype Type,`
` int Destination,`
` int MessageTag,`
` MPI_Comm Comm);`
	Performs a basic send.

`int MPI_Send_init`
`(void *Buffer,int Count,`
` MPI_Datatype Type,`
` int Destination,`
` int MessageTag,`
` MPI_Comm Comm,`
` MPI_Request *Request);`
	Initializes a handle for a standard send.

`int MPI_Ssend`
`(void *Buffer,int Count,`
` MPI_Datatype Type,`
` int Destination,`
` int MessageTag,`
` MPI_Comm Comm);`
	Performs a basic synchronous send.

`int MPI_Ssend_init`
`(void *Buffer,int Count,`
` MPI_Datatype Type,`
` int Destination,`
` int MessageTag,`
` MPI_Comm Comm,`
` MPI_Request *Request);`
	Initializes a handle for a synchronous send.

`int MPI_Rsend`
`(void *Buffer, int Count,`
` MPI_Datatype Type,`
` int Destination,`
` int MessageTag,`
` MPI_Comm Comm);`
	Performs basic ready send.

(continued)

Table 9–3 *(cont.)*

MPI Send and Receive Routines `#include "mpi.h"`	Description

`int MPI_Rsend_init`
`(void *Buffer,int Count,`
` MPI_Datatype Type,`
` int Destination,`
` int MessageTag,`
` MPI_Comm Comm,`
` MPI_Request *Request);`
	Initializes a handle for a ready send.

`int MPI_Isend`
`(void *Buffer,int Count,`
` MPI_Datatype Type,`
` int Destination,`
` int MessageTag,`
` MPI_Comm Comm,`
` MPI_Request *Request );`
	Starts a nonblocking send.

`int MPI_Issend`
`(void *Buffer,int Count,`
` MPI_Datatype Type,`
` int Destination,`
` int MessageTag,`
` MPI_Comm Comm,`
` MPI_Request *Request);`
	Starts a nonblocking synchronous send.

`int MPI_Irsend`
`(void *Buffer, int Count,`
` MPI_Datatype Type,`
` int Destination,`
` int MessageTag,`
` MPI_Comm Comm,`
` MPI_Request *Request);`
	Starts a nonblocking ready send.

`int MPI_Recv`
`(void *Buffer,int Count,`
` MPI_Datatype Type,`
` int source,int MessageTag,`
` MPI_Comm Comm,`
` MPI_Status *Status);`
	Performs a basic receive.

Table 9–3 (cont.)	

MPI Send and Receive Routines `#include "mpi.h"`	*Description*

`int MPI_Recv_init`
`(void *Buffer,int Count,`
` MPI_Datatype Type,`
` int source,int MessageTag,`
` MPI_Comm Comm,`
` MPI_Request *Request);`
	Initializes a handle for a receive.

`int MPI_Irecv`
`(void *Buffer,int Count,`
` MPI_Datatype Type,`
` int source,int MessageTag,`
` MPI_Comm Comm,`
` MPI_Request *Request);`
	Begins a nonblocking receive.

`int MPI_Sendrecv`
`(void *sendBuffer,`
` int SendCount,`
` MPI_Datatype SendType,`
` int Destination,int SendTag,`
` void *recvBuffer,`
` int RecvCount,`
` MPI_Datatype RecvYype,`
` int Source, int RecvTag,`
` MPI_Comm Comm,`
` MPI_Status *Status);`
	Sends and receives a message.

`int MPI_Sendrecv_replace`
`(void *Buffer,int Count,`
` MPI_Datatype Type,`
` int Destination,int SendTag,`
` int Source,int RecvTag,`
` MPI_Comm Comm,`
` MPI_Status *Status);`
	Sends and receives using a single buffer.

tiated from an `ostream` class and `cin` is instantiated from an `istream` class. These classes define the operator `<<` and `>>` for the built-in C++ data types. For instance, the `ostream` class contains a number of overloaded operator `<<` functions:

```
//...
ostream& operator<<(char c);
ostream& operator<<(unsigned char c);
ostream& operator<<(signed char c);
ostream& operator<<(const char *s);
ostream& operator<<(const unsigned char *s);
ostream& operator<<(const signed char *s);
ostream& operator<<(const void *p);
ostream& operator<<(int n);
ostream& operator<<(unsigned int n);
ostream& operator<<(long n);
ostream& operator<<(unsigned long n);
//...
```

These definitions allow the user of the `ostream` and the `istream` classes to use `cout` and `cin` objects without having to specify the data types involved in the operations. This overloading technique can be used to simplify MPI communications. We explored the idea of a PVM stream in Chapter 6. Here we employ the same approach to create an MPI stream. We can use the structure of an `istream` and `ostream` as a guide for creating an `mpi_stream` class. The stream classes consist of a state component, buffer component, and translation component. The state component is captured by the `ios` class. The buffer component is represented by the `streambuf`, `stringbuf`, or `filebuf` classes. The translator classes are `istream`, `ostream`, `istringstream`, `ostringstream`, `ifstream`, and `ofstream`. The state component is responsible for encapsulating the state of the stream. The format of the stream, whether the stream is in a good state or failed state, or whether the stream is at `eof`, and so on are captured by the `ios` component. The buffer components are used to hold the data that is being read or written. The translation classes translate types into streams of bytes and streams of bytes back into built-in types. Figure 9–3 shows the UML class diagram for the `iostream` family classes.

9.3.1   Overloading the << and >> Operators for MPI Communication

The relationships and functionality of the classes in Figure 9–3 are used as a guideline for designing `mpi_streams`. Although going through the trouble of designing MPI stream classes is more work up front than using the `MPI_Recv()` and `MPI_Send()` routines directly, it will make MPI develop-

iostream HIERARCHY

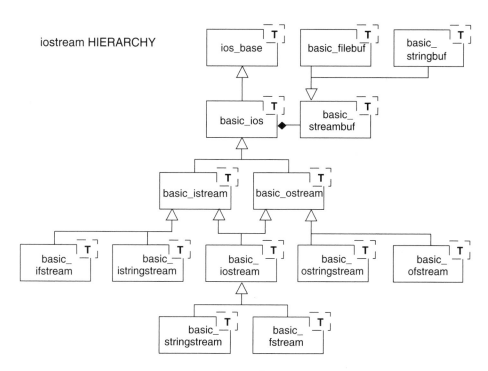

Figure 9–3 UML class diagram for iostream family classes.

ment considerably simpler in the long run. Where parallel programs can be made simpler, they should. Reducing the complexity of programs is usually a noteworthy goal. We only present a skeleton on an mpi_stream class here. We present enough to demonstrate how the construction of an MPI stream class can be approached. Once an mpi_stream class is designed it can be used to simplify communications in most any MPI program. Example 9.6 contains an excerpt from the declaration of a mpi_stream class.

```
// Example 9.6  Contains an excerpt from the declaration of a
//             mpi_stream class.

class mpios{
protected:
    int Rank;
    int Tag;
    MPI_Comm Comm;
    MPI_Status Status;
    int BufferCount;
    //...
public:
```

```
        int tag(void);
        //...

    }

    class mpi_stream public mpios{
    protected:
        mpi_buffer Buffer;
        //...

    public:
        //...
        mpi_stream(void);
        mpi_stream(int R,int T,MPI_Comm C);
        void rank(int R);
        void tag(int T);
        void comm(MPI_Comm C);
        mpi_stream &operator<<(int X);
        mpi_stream &operator<<(float X);
        mpi_stream &operator<<(string X);
        mpi_stream &operator<<(vector<long> &X);
        mpi_stream &operator<<(vector<int> &X);
        mpi_stream &operator<<(vector<float> &X);
        mpi_stream &operator<<(vector<string> &X);
        mpi_stream &operator>>(int &X);
        mpi_stream &operator>>(float &X);
        mpi_stream &operator>>(string &X);
        mpi_stream &operator>>(vector<long> &X);
        mpi_stream &operator>>(vector<int> &X);
        mpi_stream &operator>>(vector<float> &X);
        mpi_stream &operator>>(vector<string> &X);
        //...
    };
```

For exposition purposes we have combined the `impi_stream` and `ompi_stream` class into a single `mpi_stream` class. In the same manner that the `istream` and `ostream` classes overload the << and >> operators, we overload those operators as well. Example 9.7 shows these overloaded operators can be defined:

```
// Example 9.7 Definition of << and >> operators.

//...
mpi_stream &operator<<(string X)
{
    MPI_Send(const_cast<char*>(X.data()),X.size(),MPI_CHAR,Rank,Tag,Comm);
    return(*this);
```

```
}
// Over simplification of  buffer
mpi_stream &operator<<(vector<long> &X)
{
    long *Buffer;
    Buffer = new long[X.size()];
    copy(X.begin(),X.end(),Buffer);
    MPI_Send(Buffer,X.size(),MPI_LONG,Rank,Tag,Comm);
    delete Buffer;
    return(*this);
}

// Over simplification of  buffer

mpi_stream &operator>>(string &X)
{

    char Buffer[10000];
    MPI_Recv(Buffer,10000,MPI_CHAR,Rank,Tag,Comm,&Status);
    MPI_Get_count(&Status,MPI_CHAR,&BufferCount);
    X.append(Buffer);
    return(*this);

}
```

The mpios class in Example 9.7 serves a similar purpose to that of the ios class for the iostream. The purpose of the mpios class is to maintain the state of the mpi_stream classes. Each data type that will be used within your MPI applications should have the operators << and >> overloaded for them. Here, we show a few simple overloaded operators. In each case we present an over-simplification of the buffer management. In practice, exception handling and memory allocation issues are handled by template classes and allocator classes. Notice in Example 9.7 that the mpios class holds the communicator, status of the mpi_stream, the buffer count, and the value for rank and tag. This is only one possible configuration for a mpi_stream class—there are many others. Once an mpi_stream class is defined it can be reused in any MPI program. Communication between MPI tasks can be written as:

```
//...
int X;
float Y;
vector<float> Z;
mpi_stream  Stream(Rank,Tag,MPI_WORLD_COMM);
Stream << X << Z;
Stream << Y;
//...
Stream >> Z;
```

This notation allows the programmer to maintain the stream metaphor and simplifies the MPI code. Of course the appropriate error checking and exception handling must be included within the definitions of the << and >> operators.

Summary

Implementations of the SPMD and MPMD models of concurrency have much to be gained by using templates and taking advantage of polymorphism. While the MPI does include bindings for C++ it does not take advantage of object-oriented programming techniques. This presents an opportunity and challenge to developers using the MPI standard. Inheritance and polymorphism can be used to simplify MPMD programming. Parameterized or genericity programming that is supported using the template facilities of C++ can be used to simplify SPMD programming with the MPI. Dividing a program's work between objects is a natural way to discover and exploit the parallelism within an application. Families of objects can be associated with communicators to facilitate communication in the MPI between multiple groups that have different work responsibilities. Operator overloading can be used to maintain a stream metaphor with the MPI. Using object-oriented programming techniques and parameterized programming techniques within the same MPI application is a multiparadigm approach that simplifies and in most cases shortens the code. It leads to programs that are easier to debug, test, and maintain. MPI tasks implemented by template functions tend to be more reliable across different data types than separately defined functions that have to perform type casting.

10 Visualizing Concurrent and Distributed System Design

"Unnamed thinking which I would like to suggest may be common with us. Our brainwaves are very often wordless. We often quite suddenly perceive correct solutions to problems with which we have been striving for a long time before we have decided we will name them in one language or another. . . . Very many ideas come to us in wordless form . . ."

—*O. Koehler*, The Ability of Birds to Count

In this Chapter

Visualizing Structures • Visualizing Concurrent Behavior • Visualizing the Whole System • Summary

A model of a system is the body of information gathered for the purpose of studying the system so it can be better understood by the developers and maintainers of the system. When a system is modeled, the boundaries and identification of the entities, attributes, and the activities performed by the system can be determined. Modeling is an important tool in the design process of any system. It is essential that developers fully understand the system they are developing. Modeling can reveal the concurrency embedded in the system and where distribution can be appropriately applied.

The UML (United Modeling Language) is a graphical notation used to design, visualize, model, and document the artifacts of a software system. It is the de facto standard for communicating and modeling object-oriented systems. The modeling language uses symbols and notations to represent the artifacts of a software system from different views and different focuses. The UML brings together the approaches of Grady Booch, James Rumbaugh, and Ivar Jacobson's object-oriented analysis and design methods developed in the 1980s and 1990s. It was adopted by the OMG (Object Management Group), an international organization consisting of software developers and information system vendors with over 800 members. The adoption and conformance to the UML give software developers a consistent language and tool for object analysis, specification, visualization, and documentation.

In this chapter, we show you how to visualize and model your concurrent and distributed system using the UML. Besides helping you in the design of your system, modeling will help you identify where concurrency emerges, when synchronization and communication are needed, and how and where objects can be distributed. We discuss diagramming techniques used to visualize and model concurrent systems from the structural and behavioral perspectives. Please note the classes, objects, and systems used as examples in this chapter are used for exposition purposes and may or may not necessarily reflect actual classes, objects, or structures used in an actual system.

10.1   Visualizing Structures

The structural view of a system focuses on the static parts of that system. This view examines how the elements in the system are constructed. It examines its attributes, properties, and operations along with its organization, composition, and relationship with other elements in the system. The diagraming techniques discussed in this section are the ones used to model:

- class, objects, templates, processes, and threads
- organization of objects that work together

The elements documented can be conceptual or physical.

10.1.1   Classes and Objects

A class is a model of a construct with its attributes and behaviors. It is a description of a set of things or objects that share the same attributes. A class is the basic component of any object-oriented system. Classes can be used to represent real-world, conceptual, hardware, and software constructs. A *class diagram* is used to represent the classes, the objects, and the relationships that exist between them within your concurrent and/or distributed system. The class diagram is used to show the attributes and the services a class provides and the restrictions that apply to the manner in which these classes/objects are connected.

The UML provides a graphical representation of a class. The simplest representation of a class is a rectangular box that contains the name of the class. The name alone is the *simple name*. The class diagram can also show the attributes and services provided to the user of the class. To include attributes and services, a rectangle is drawn displaying three horizontal compartments. The top compartment displays the simple name of the class, the middle compartment displays the attributes, and the bottom compartment displays the services. The attributes and services compartments can be labeled *"attributes"* and *"services,"* respectively, in order to identify each compartment. Besides the name of the class, if the attributes or services are to be shown, then the other compartment is displayed as empty. Figure 10–1 shows the various ways a class can be represented.

In Figure 10–1, the class `student_schedule` is represented. Figure 10–1(a) shows the class in its simplest representation, (b) shows the class name and its attributes and services, and (c) shows the class name and its services. The compartment that contains the attributes is empty in order to communicate that the class has attributes but they are not shown.

An additional compartment can be used to describe the *responsibility of the class*. This compartment appears under the services compartment and can be omitted. The responsibility of the class is what the class will perform. It is displayed as contractual statements. These responsibilities are transformed into services and attributes. Attributes are transformed into datatypes and data structures and services are transformed into methods. This compartment can be labeled *"responsibilities."* The responsibilities of the `student_schedule` class can be stated as: "returns the schedule for a student for any day of the week, the student number, the year, and term of the stored schedule." The responsibilities of the class are displayed as text in its compartment where each responsibility is listed as a short statement or paragraph.

The class diagram can show an object, an instance of a class. Like a class, the simplest representation of an object is a rectangle that contains the name of the object underlined. This is called a *named instance* of a class. A named instance of a class can be shown with or without its class name:

`mySchedule`   named instance

`mySchedule:student_schedule`   named instance with class name

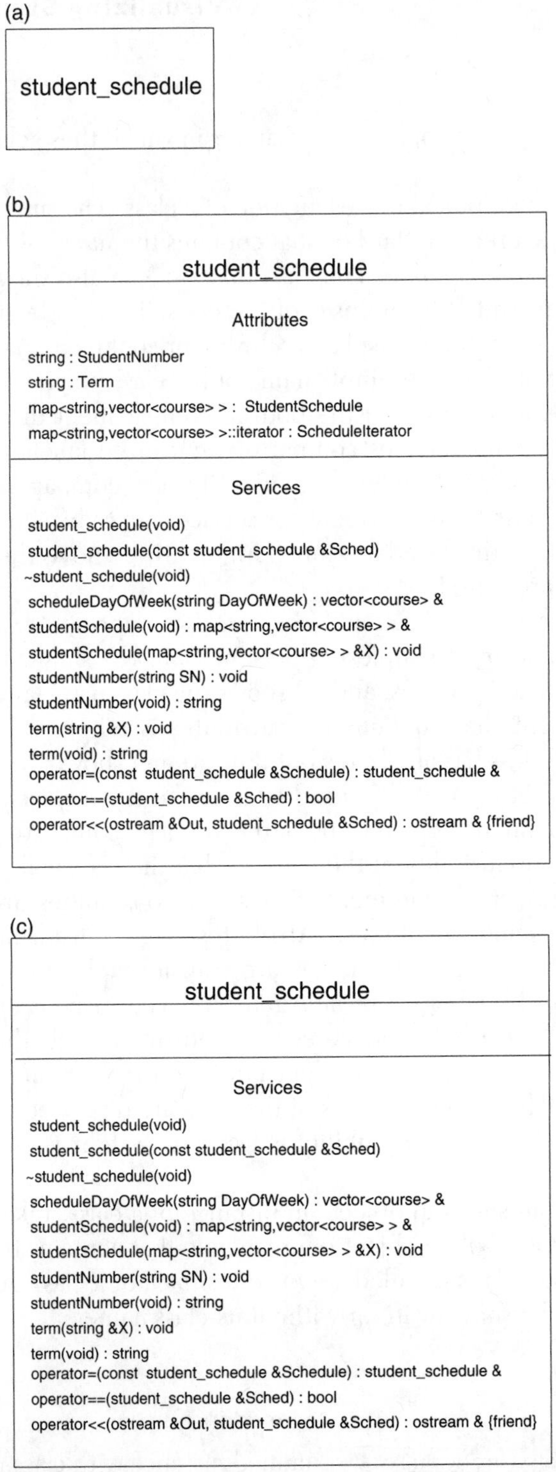

student_schedule

student_schedule

Attributes

string : StudentNumber
string : Term
map<string,vector<course> > : StudentSchedule
map<string,vector<course> >::iterator : ScheduleIterator

Services

student_schedule(void)
student_schedule(const student_schedule &Sched)
~student_schedule(void)
scheduleDayOfWeek(string DayOfWeek) : vector<course> &
studentSchedule(void) : map<string,vector<course> > &
studentSchedule(map<string,vector<course> > &X) : void
studentNumber(string SN) : void
studentNumber(void) : string
term(string &X) : void
term(void) : string
operator=(const student_schedule &Schedule) : student_schedule &
operator==(student_schedule &Sched) : bool
operator<<(ostream &Out, student_schedule &Sched) : ostream & {friend}

student_schedule

Services

student_schedule(void)
student_schedule(const student_schedule &Sched)
~student_schedule(void)
scheduleDayOfWeek(string DayOfWeek) : vector<course> &
studentSchedule(void) : map<string,vector<course> > &
studentSchedule(map<string,vector<course> > &X) : void
studentNumber(string SN) : void
studentNumber(void) : string
term(string &X) : void
term(void) : string
operator=(const student_schedule &Schedule) : student_schedule &
operator==(student_schedule &Sched) : bool
operator<<(ostream &Out, student_schedule &Sched) : ostream & {friend}

Figure 10-1 The various ways to represent a class.

Since the actual name of the object may be known only to the program that declares it, you may want to represent *anonymous instances* of classes in your system documentation. You can label an object as anonymous in this way:

`:student schedule`

This type of labeling may be convenient where there are several instances of a class in your system. Several instances of a class can be represented in two ways: as objects and as classes.

The number of instances a class may have is called *multiplicity*. The number of instances of a class can be noted in a class diagram. A class may have zero to an infinite number of instances. A class with zero instances is a *pure abstract class*. It cannot have any objects explicitly declared of its type. The number of instances may have an upper or lower bound, which may also be expressed in the diagram of a class. Figure 10–2 shows how several instances of a class can be represented in a class diagram as objects or with multiplicity notation.

In Figure 10–2, the multiplicity of the `student_schedule` class is `1..7`, meaning the least number of student schedules in our system is 1 and the

Figure 10–2 Mutiple instances of a class represented graphically and using multiplicity notation.

student_schedule

student_schedule	1..7

Services
student_schedule(void)
student_schedule(const student_schedule &Sched)
~student_schedule(void)
scheduleDayOfWeek(string DayOfWeek) : vector<course> &
studentSchedule(void) : map<string,vector<course> > &
studentSchedule(map<string,vector<course> > &X) : void
studentNumber(string SN) : void
studentNumber(void) : string
term(string &X) : void
term(void) : string
operator=(const student_schedule &Schedule) : student_schedule &
operator==(student_schedule &Sched) : bool
operator<<(ostream &Out, student_schedule &Sched) : ostream & {friend}

most that can exist is 7. Here are more examples of multiplicity notation and their meaning:

1	One instance
1..n	One to a specified number n
1..*	One to an infinite number
0..1	0 to 1
0..*	0 to an infinite number
*	An infinite number

Of course, an infinite number of instances will be limited by internal memory or external storage.

10.1.1.1   Displaying Specifics about Attributes and Services

The class diagram can specify more details about the attributes and services of the class. The attributes compartment can specify the datatype and/or default value (if there is one) for classes and values of attributes for objects. For example, the datatypes for the attributes of the `student_schedule` class can be displayed:

```
StudentNumber : string
Term : string
StudentSchedule : map <string,vector<course> >
ScheduleIterator :  map <string,vector<course> >::iterator
```

For the `myschedule` object, these attributes can take on values:

```
StudentNumber : string = "102933"
Term : string = "Spring"
```

Methods can be shown with parameters and return type:

```
studentSchedule(&X : map <string,vector<course> >) : void
studentNumber() : string
```

The `studentSchedule()` function accepts the courses of the student. `course` is a class that models a single course. The courses for each day of the week are stored in a `vector`. The `map` container maps a `string` (day of the week) with the `vector` of courses for that particular day. The `studentSchedule()` function returns `void` where the `studentNumber()` function returns a `string`.

The properties of attributes and methods can be displayed in the class diagram. Properties help describe how an attribute or operation can be used. Property labels can be used to describe attributes that are constant or modifiable. There are three properties used to describe attributes: `changeable`, `addOnly`, and `frozen`. Table 10–1 lists these properties with a brief description. There are four properties used to define methods: `isQuery`, `sequential`, `guarded`, and `concurrent`. They are also listed in Table 10–1. `sequential`, `guarded`, and `concurrent` properties are concerned with the concurrency of a method. The `sequential` property describes a concurrent operation where synchronization is the responsibility of the callers of the operation. These operations do not guarantee the integrity of the object. The `guarded` property describes a concurrent operation where synchronization is

Table 10–1   Properties for Attributes and Operations

Properties for Attributes	*Description*
`{changeable}`	No restrictions on modifying the values of this type of attribute.
`{addOnly}`	For attributes with multiplicity > 1, additional values can be added. Once created a value cannot be removed or changed.
`{frozen}`	Attribute's value cannot be changed once the object has been initialized.
Properties for Methods	
`{isQuery}`	Execution of this type of method leaves the state of the object unchanged. This method returns values.
`{sequential}`	Users of the object must use synchronization to ensure sequential access to this method. Multiple concurrent access to this method jeopardizes the integrity of the object.
`{guarded}`	Synchronized sequential access to this method is built in the object; integrity of the object is guaranteed.
`{concurrent}`	Multiple concurrent access is permitted; integrity of the object is guaranteed.

already built in. guarded operations mean callers invoke the operation one at a time. The concurrent property describes an operation that permits simultaneous use. The guarded and concurrent operations guarantee the integrity of the object. Guaranteeing the integrity of an object is applicable to operations that change the state of the object.

guarded and concurrent properties for methods can be used to reflect the PRAM (Parallel Random-Access Machine) model. If a method is reading and/or writing memory that is accessible to another method that is also reading and/or writing that same memory, then that method can be described as a PRAM algorithm. The properties can be appropriately used. For example:

PRAM Algorithms	*Properties*
CR (Concurrent Read)	concurrent
CW (Concurrent Write)	concurrent
CRCW (Concurrent Read Concurrent Write)	concurrent
EW (Exclusive Write)	guarded
ER (Exclusive Read)	guarded
EREW (Exclusive Read Exclusive Write)	guarded

The student_schedule class can further describe how its attributes and services can be used by using property labels:

attributes

```
StudentNumber : string {frozen}
Term : string {changeable}
StudentSchedule : map <string,vector<course> > {changeable}
```

operations

```
scheduleDayOfWeek(&X : vector<course>, Day : string) :
                void {guarded}
studentNumber() : string {isQuery, concurrent}
```

StudentNumber is a string constant. Once an object assigns a value, it cannot be changed. If the student_schedule object is used for the same student but for different terms, then Term and StudentSchedule would be modifiable attributes. The scheduleDayOfWeek() operation accepts a vector of courses for a particular day of the week stored in the string

Day. This operation is `guarded`. It inserts a student schedule for a particular day of the week into the `map` object `StudentSchedule`, changing the state of the object. Synchronization is built into the object by using mutexes. The `studentNumber()` operation has two properties: `isQuery` and `concurrent`. It returns the constant `StudentNumber` and is safe for simultaneous access. Calling this method does not change the state of the object thus using the `isQuery` property.

Another important property that can be shown is the *visibility* of attributes and operations. A visibility property describes who can access the attribute or invoke the operation. This property uses a character or symbol to represent the level of visibility. Visibility maps to the access specifiers of C++:

Access Specifiers	*Visibility Symbols*
`public`	(+) Anyone has access.
`protected`	(#) The class itself and its descendants have access.
`private`	(-) Only the class itself has access.

The symbol is prepended to the service, method, or attribute name.

10.1.1.2   Ordering the Attributes and Services

It may be best when representing a class with many attributes and operations to organize them within their compartments. Order helps to identify and navigate through the attributes and operations. The organization can be alphabetical, by access, or by category. Alphabetical order is not helpful in identifying what attributes or operations can be called (if the documentation is targeted to users of the system) or which of them are not defined (if documentation is used in the development process). Ordering by access is very useful. It communicates to the user which attributes and operations are publicly accessible. Knowing which members are protected will assist users who need to extend or specialize the class through inheritance. This can be done by using the visibility symbols, +, -, and #, or by using the C++ access specifiers, `protected`, `public`, and `private`.

There are several ways to categorize the attributes and operations. The *minimal standard interface* defines categories for operations that in turn define attributes that support these operations. The minimal standard interface is based on the concept that all classes should define certain operations and services in order for a class to be useful. These operations are:

- default constructor
- destructor
- copy constructor
- assignment operations
- equality operations
- input and output operations
- hash operations
- query operations

These can be used as categories to classify the operations of a class. Other categories can be used to help organize attributes and operations:

attributes

```
static
const
```

operations

```
virtual
pure virtual
friend
```

These categories should be used based upon what best describes the services offered by the class. The category name is embraced in left and right double angle brackets, (<< . . .>>). Figure 10–3 shows the two ways attributes and operations can be organized for the student_schedule class: (a) using the visibility symbols, access specifiers, and (b) using categorization based on the minimal standard interface.

10.1.1.3   Template Classes

A *template* class is a mechanism that allows a type to be a parameter in the definition of the class. The template defines services that manipulate what-

(a) visibility symbols and access specifiers

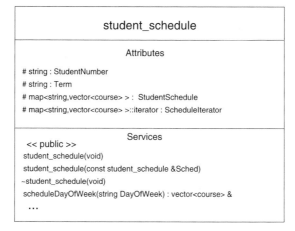

(b) categorization based on minimal standard interface

Figure 10–3 Two ways attributes and services can be organized in a class diagram.

ever datatype that is passed to it. The parameterized class is created in C++ by using the `template` keyword:

```
template <class Type > classname {...};
```

`Type` parameter represents any type passed to the template. `Type` can be a built-in datatype or a user-defined class. When `Type` is declared, the template is bound by the element passed to it as the parameterized type. For example, the `student_schedule` class has a `map` container that contains `vectors` of `course` objects for each day of the week. Both the `map` and the `vector` are template classes:

```
map <string,vector<course> > StudentSchedule;
```

The `map` container has `string` as a key and `vector` as the value. The `vector` container contains a user-defined `course` object. The `map` container can map any datatype to any other datatype and `vector` containers can contain any datatype:

`map <int, vector <string> >`	Maps a number to a vector of strings
`map <int, string> >`	Maps a number to a string
`vector <student_schedule>`	A vector of `student_schedule` objects
`vector <map <int,string> >`	A vector of maps that maps a number to a string

Template classes are also represented as rectangular boxes. The parameterized type is represented as a dashed box displayed in the upper right-hand corner. The template class can be unbound or bound. When representing an unbound template class, the dashed box displays a capital `T` to represent the unbound parameterized type. There are two ways to represent a bound template class. One approach is to use the class symbol containing the C++ syntax for declaring and binding a template class:

```
vector <string>
```

This is called *implicit binding*. Another approach uses a dependency stereotype, `bind`. The stereotype specifies the source instantiating the template class by using the actual parameterized type. This is called *explicit binding*. The template object is the instantiation of the template class. It has a dependency relationship with the template class. The stereotype specifies the name of the parameter types. Inside the dashed box, datatypes are displayed. The template object can also be considered as a *refinement* of the template class. Refinement is a general term to indicate a greater level of de-

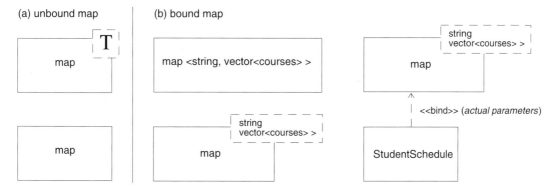

Figure 10–4   The ways to represent a bound and unbound template class.

tail of something that already exists. The stereotype indicator <<bind>> re-fines the template class by instantiating the parameterized type. Figure 10–4 depicts the ways a template class can be represented, unbound and bound, for a map container.

10.1.2   The Relationship between Classes and Objects

The UML defines three types of relationships between classes:

- dependencies
- generalizations
- associations

Dependency defines a relationship between two classes. When one class depends on another class, this means a change to the independent class may affect the dependent class. *Generalization* is a relationship between a general construct and a more specific type of that construct. The general construct is the *parent* or *superclass* and the more specific construct is the *child* or *subclass*. The child inherits the properties, attributes, and operations of the parent and may define other attributes and operations of its own. The child is derived from the parent and can be used as a substitute for the parent class. A class that has no parent is called the *root* or *base* class. *Association* is a structural relationship that specifies that objects of one type are connected to objects of another type. Associations between objects are bidirectional. For example, if object 1 is associated with object 2, then object 2 is associated with object 1. An association between two elements (classes, etc.) is called a *binary association*. An association between *n* elements is called *n-ary association*.

Table 10–2 Stereotypes That Can Be Applied to Dependencies	
Dependency SOURCE ----> TARGET	*Description*
stereotype `<< bind >>`	Stipulates that the source instantiates the template target using the actual parameters.
stereotype `<< friend >>`	Stipulates that the source is given visibility into the target.
stereotype `<< instanceOf >>`	Stipulates that the source is an instance of the target; used to define relationships between classes and objects.
stereotype `<< instantiate >>`	Stipulates that the source creates instances of the target; used to define relationships beween classes and objects.
stereotype `<< refine >>`	Stipulates that the source is a greater level of detail than the target; used to define relationships between derived and base classes.
stereotype `<< use >>`	Stipulates that the source depends on the public interface of the target.
stereotype `<< become >>`	Stipulates that the target object is the same object as the source, but at a later time in the object's lifetime; target may have different values, states, etc.
stereotype `<< call >>`	Stipulates that the source object invokes the target's method.
stereotype `<< copy >>`	Stipulates that the target object is an exact independent copy of the source object.
stereotype `<< access >>`	Stipulates that the source package is the given the right to reference the elements of the target package.
stereotype `<< extend >>`	Stipulates that the target use case extends the behavior of the source use case.
stereotype `<< include >>`	Stipulates that the source use case can include the behavior of the target use case at a location named by the source use case.

Dependency, generalization, and association are actually classifications of relationships. There are many types of dependencies, generalizations, and associations that exist and can be defined. Each relationship classification has its own symbol of representation. That symbol is a solid or dashed line segment between the elements and may be accompanied with some type of arrowhead. To further define that relationship to a specific type, stereotypes or adornments are used in conjunction with the line segment. *Stereotypes* are labels used to further describe a UML element. It is rendered as a name enclosed by guillemets and placed above or next to the element. For example:

```
<<bind>>
```

was placed next to the arrow, which depicts dependency when describing the template object in Figure 10–4. Adornments are textual or graphical items added to an element's basic representation and are used to document details about that element's specifications. For example, an association is depicted as a solid line between elements. Aggregation is a type of association that expresses a "whole–part" relationship. To depict aggregation, a hollow diamond *adorns* the solid line at the whole end.

Dependency is rendered as a dashed directed line (has a arrow) pointing to the construct being depended on. Use a dependency relationship when one construct uses another. Generalization is rendered as a solid directed line with a large open arrowhead pointing to the parent or superclass. Use a

Table 10–3 Stereotypes and Constraints That Can Be Applied to Generalizations	
Generalization CHILD ⟶ PARENT	*Description*
stereotype `<< implementation >>`	Stipulates that the child inherits the implementation of the parent but does not make public nor support the parent's interfaces.
constraint `{complete}`	Stipulates that all children in the generalization have been named and no more additional children can be derived.
constraint `{incomplete}`	Stipulates that not all children in the generalization have been named and additional children can be derived.
constraint `{disjoint}`	Stipulates that the parent's objects may have no more than one of its children as a type.
constraint `{overlapping}`	Stipulates that the parent's objects may have more than one of its children as a type.

generalization relationship when one construct is derived from another construct. Association is rendered as a solid line connecting the same or different constructs. Use an association relationship when one construct is structurally related to another. Table 10–2 lists some of the stereotypes and constraints that can be applied to dependencies. These stereotypes are used to show dependencies between classes, interactive objects, states, and packages. Tables 10–3 and 10–4 list the stereotypes and constraints that can be applied to generalizations and associations. If any of the stereotypes use graphical adornments, they are shown.

Table 10–4   Stereotypes, Constraints, and Adornments That Can Be Applied to Associations

Association	Description
OBJECT 1 ——— OBJECT 2	
type navigation OBJECT 1 ----> OBJECT 2	Describes a one-direction association where object 1 is associated with object 2 but object 2 is not associated with object 1.
type aggregation PART ——◇ WHOLE	Describes a containment (whole–part relationship) where the part is not associated with just one whole for its lifetime.
type composition PART ◀—◆ WHOLE	Describes a containment (whole–part relationship) where the part can only be associated with one whole for its lifetime.
constraints {implicit}	Stipulates that the relationship is conceptual.
constraints {ordered}	Stipulates that the objects at one end of the association has an order.
property {changeable}	Describes what can be added, deleted, and changed between two objects.
property {addOnly}	Decribes new links that can be added to an object on the opposite end of the association.
property {frozen}	Describes a link that once added to an object on the opposite end of the association, cannot be changed or deleted.

Associations have another level of detail that can be applied to a general association or stereotype listed in Table 10–4:

name   An association can have a name that is used to describe the nature of the relationship. A direction triangle can be added to the name to ensure its meaning. The triangle points in the direction the name is intended to be read.

role   A role is the face the class at the near end of the association presents to the class at the other end of the association.

multiplicity   Multiplicity notation can be used to state how many objects may be connected across an association. Multiplicity can be shown at both ends of an association.

navigation   Navigation across an association can be directed where object 1 is associated with object 2 but object 2 is not associated with object 1.

10.1.2.1   Interface Classes

An *interface class* is used to modify the interface of another class or set of classes. The modification makes the class easier to use, more functional, safer, or semantically correct. An example of an interface class are the container *adaptors* that are part of the Standard Template Library. The adaptors provide a new public interface for the deque, vector, and list containers. Example 10.1 shows the stack class. It is used as an interface class to modify a vector class.

```
//Example 10.1  Using the stack class as an interface class.

template < class Container >
class stack{
//...
public:
   typedef Container::value_type value_type;
   typedef Container::size_type size_type;
protected:
   Container c;
public:
   bool empty(void) const {return c.empty();}
   size_type size(void) const {return c.size(); }
   value_type& top(void) {return c.back(); }
   const value_type& top const {return c.back(); }
   void push(const value_type& x) {c.push.back(x); }
   void pop(void) {c.pop.back(); }
};
```

The `stack` is declared by specifying the `Container` type:

```
stack < vector< T> > Stack;
```

In this case, the `Container` is a `vector` but any container that defines these operations:

```
empty()
size()
back()
push.back()
pop.back()
```

can be used as the implementation class for the `stack` interface class. The `stack` class supplies the semantically correct interface traditionally accepted for stacks.

There are multiple ways to depict an interface. A circle with the name of the interface class outside the circle is one way to represent an interface class. This is depicted in Figure 10–5(a), showing the `stack` as an interface class. The class symbol can also be used to show the operations of the stack class, Figure 10–5(b). Here the stereotype indicator `<<interface>>` is displayed above the name of the class to denote that this is an interface class. The letter `I` can be prepended to the name of the interface class and all of its operations to further distinguish it from other classes.

Realization can be used to show the relationship between the `stack` and the `vector` class. Realization is a semantic relationship between classes in which one specifies a contract (interface class) and the other class carries it out (implementation class). In our example, the `stack` class specifies the contract and the `vector` class carries it out. A realization relationship is depicted as a dashed line between the two classes with a large open arrowhead pointing to the interface class or the class that specifies the contract, which is depicted in Figure 10–5(c). It is read "The stack class is realized by the vector class." The relationship between the interface class and its implementer can also be depicted with the interface lollipop notation, as shown in Figure 10–5(d). The `stack` class can be the interface to or realized by a `vector`, `list`, or `deque`.

10.1.3   The Organization of Interactive Objects

As you can see, classes and interfaces can be used as building blocks to create more complex classes and interfaces. In a distributed or parallel system, there may be many large and complex structures collaborating with other

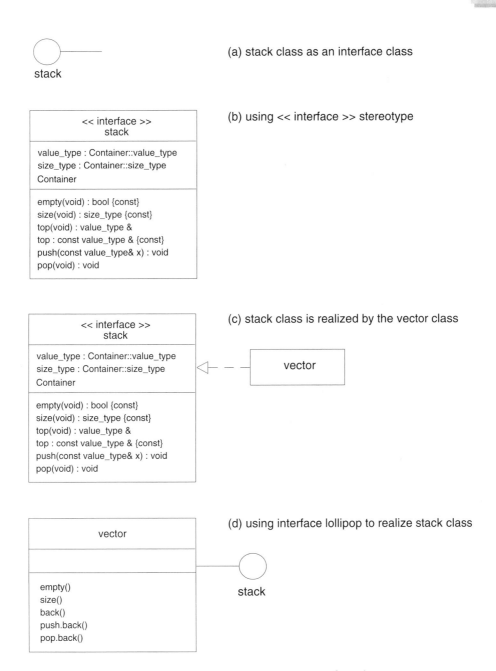

(a) stack class as an interface class

(b) using << interface >> stereotype

(c) stack class is realized by the vector class

(d) using interface lollipop to realize stack class

Figure 10–5   Ways to represent an interface class.

structures, thus creating a society of classes and interfaces working together to accomplish the goals of the system. In the UML, this is called a *collaboration*. These building blocks can include both the structural and behavioral elements of the system. A particular task requested by a user may involve many objects working together to accomplish that task. Those same objects working with other elements are used to accomplish other tasks. This collection of elements, together with their interactions, form a *collaboration*. The collaboration has two parts: a *structural part*, which focuses on the way the collaborating elements are organized and constructed, and a *behavioral part*, which focuses on the interaction between the elements. This will be discussed in the next section.

A collaboration is depicted as an ellipse with dashed lines containing the name of the collaboration. A collaboration name is unique. It is a noun or short noun phrase based on the vocabulary of the system being modeled. Zooming inside the collaboration ellipse is the structural and behavioral parts of the collaboration. Figure 10–6 shows an example of the structural part of the *course adviser system*. The structural part of the collaboration consists of any combination of classes and interfaces, components and nodes. In Figure

Figure 10–6   A collaboration diagram for a course adviser system.

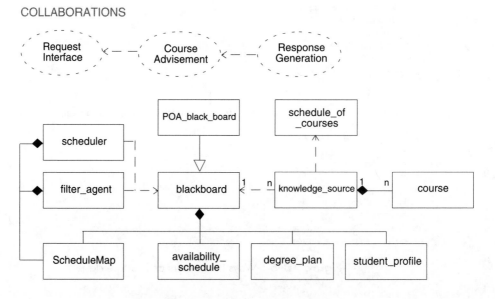

10–6, a system may contain many collaborations. A single collaboration is unique in the system but the elements of a collaboration are not. The elements of one collaboration may be used in another collaboration using a different organization.

10.2   Visualizing Concurrent Behavior

The behavioral view of a system focuses on the dynamic aspects of that system. This view examines how the elements in the system behave as it interacts with other elements of the system. Here is where concurrency will emerge as elements interact with other elements. The diagramming techniques discussed in this section are the ones used to model:

- the lifetime of the behavior of an object
- the behavior of objects that work together for a particular purpose
- flows of control focusing on action or sequence of actions
- synchronization and communication between elements

This section also covers diagraming techniques used to model distributed objects.

10.2.1   Collaborating Objects

Collaborating objects are objects involved with each other to perform some specific task. They do not form a permanent relationship. The same objects can be involved with other objects working together to perform other tasks. Collaborating objects can be represented in a *collaboration diagram*. Collaboration diagrams have a structural part and an interactive part. The structural part has already been discussed. The interaction part is a graph where all of the participating objects are vertices. The connections between the objects are the arcs. The arcs can be adorned with messages passed between the objects, method invocations, and stereotype indicators that express more details about the nature of the connection.

The connection between two objects is a *link*. A link is a type of association. When two objects are linked, actions can be performed between them. The action may result in a change of the state of one or both objects. These are examples of the types of actions that can take place:

create	An object can be created.
destroy	An object can be destroyed.
call	An operation of an object can be invoked by another object or itself.
return	A value is returned to an object.
send	A signal may be sent to an object.

When any method is invoked, the parameters and the return value can be expressed. Other actions can take place if specified.

These actions can take place if the receiving object is visible to the calling object. Stereotypes can be used to specify why the object is visible:

association	The object is visible because an association exists (very general).
parameter	The object is visible because it is a parameter to the calling object.
local	The object is visible because it has local scope to the calling object.
global	The object is visible because it has global scope to the calling object.
self	The object calls its own method.

Other stereotypes and adornments appropriate for associations can be expressed.

When a method is invoked, this may cause a number of other methods to be invoked by other objects. The sequence in which the operations are performed can be shown by using a sequence number combination and a colon separator prepended to the method. The sequence number combination expresses what sequence the method is associated with and the time order number in which the operation takes place. For example, Figure 10–7 shows a collaboration diagram that uses the sequence numbers.

In Figure 10–7, MainObject performs two operations in sequence:

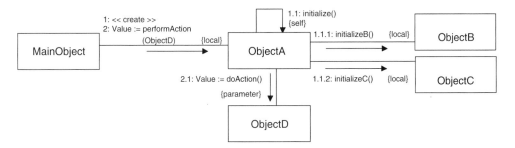

Figure 10–7   A collaboration diagram using sequence numbers.

```
1: <<create>>
2: Value := performAction(ObjectF)
```

In operation 1, `MainObject` creates `ObjectA`. `ObjectA` is local to the `MainObject` by containment. This initiates the first sequence of operations in a nested flow of control. All operations apart from this sequence use the number 1 followed by the time order number in which the operation takes place. The first operation of sequence 1 is:

```
1.1: initialize()
```

`ObjectA` invokes its own operation. This is expressed by linking the object to itself and by using the `{self}` stereotype indicator. The `ObjectA::ini-tialize()` operation also causes the beginning of another sequence of actions:

```
1.1.1: initializeB()
1.1.2: initializeC()
```

in which two other objects local to `ObjectA` initialize methods are called. The operation:

```
2: performAction(ObjectD)
```

is the beginning of another nested sequence. `ObjectD` is passed to `ObjectA`. `ObjectA` invokes `ObjectD`'s operation:

```
2.1: doAction()
```

`ObjectA` can invoke this operation because `ObjectD` is a parameter (passed by `MainObject`), as the stereotype `{parameter}` indicates. A value is returned to `ObjectA` and a value is returned to `MainObject`. Besides sequence number combinations, these nested flows of control are further enhanced by using a line with a solid arrowhead pointing in the direction of the flow of the sequence.

10.2.1.1   Processes and Threads

A process is a unit of work created by the operating system. It has one or more flows of control executing within its address space. Each process has at least one thread, the main thread, but can have many threads executing within its address space. Each thread represents a process's flow of control. Multiple processes can execute concurrently. Threads within the address space of a process can execute concurrently with threads of other processes.

When using the UML, each independent flow of control is considered an *active object*. An active object is an object that owns a process or thread. Each active object can initiate control activity. An *active class* is a class whose objects are active. Active classes can be used to model a group of processes or threads that share the same data members and methods. The objects of your system may not have a one-to-one correlation with active objects. As discussed in Chapters 3 and 4, when dividing your program up into processes and threads along object lines, an object's methods may execute in a separate process or execute on separate threads. Therefore, when modeling such an object, it may be represented by several active objects. This relationship between static and active objects can be represented by using an interaction diagram. Your system may have several PVM or MPI tasks or processes. Each of them can be represented directly as an active object.

The UML represents an active object or class the same way a static object is represented, except it has a heavier line tracing the perimeter of the rectangle. Two stereotypes can also be used:

```
process
thread
```

These stereotype indicators can be displayed to show the distinction between the two types of active objects. Figure 10–8 shows a PVM task as an active class and an active object. A collaboration diagram can consist of active objects.

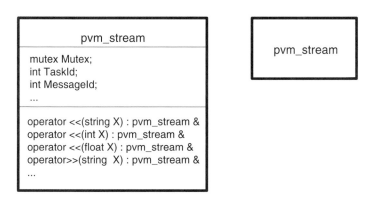

Figure 10–8 An active object and class.

10.2.1.2 Showing the Multiple Flows of Control and Communication

In a concurrent and distributed system, there will be multiple flows of control. Each flow of control is based on a process or a thread controlling the activity. These processes and threads may be executing on a single computer system with multiple processors or the processes may be distributed among several different computers. An active object or class is used to represent each flow of control. When the active object is created, an independent flow of control is initiated. When the active object is destroyed, the flow of control is terminated. Modeling the multiple flows of control in your system will help in the management, synchronization, and communication between them.

In a collaboration diagram, sequence numbers and solid arrows are used to identify flows of control. In a collaboration diagram that consists of active objects in a concurrent system, the name of the active object is preprended to the sequence numbers of the operations peformed by the active object. Active objects can invoke methods in other objects and suspend execution until the function returns or can continue to execute. Arrows are used not to just show the direction of the flow of control but the nature of it. A solid arrowhead is used to represent a synchronous call and a half-stick arrowhead is used to represent an asynchronous call. Since more than one active object can invoke the operation of a single object, the method properties:

```
sequential
guarded
concurrent
```

can be used to describe the synchronization property of that method.

Figure 10–9 shows a collaboration of several active objects. In this diagram, these objects are working together to produce a student schedule. The `blackboard` object is used to record and coordinate the preliminary work and resultant schedule produced by the active object problem solvers, in this case called *agents*:

MajorAgent   Produces a list of major courses available.

MinorAgent   Produces a list of minor courses available.

Figure 10–9 A collaboration diagram of static and active objects in the course adviser system.

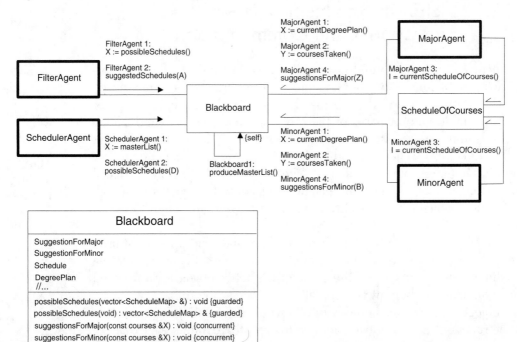

FilterAgent   Filters the list of courses and produces a list of possible courses.

ScheduleAgent   Produces several schedules based on the list of possible courses.

The `schedule_of_courses` object contains all the courses available.

The `blackboard` and `schedule_of_courses` objects are accessed concurrently by several agents. Both objects are visible to all the agents in this collaboration. The `MajorAgent`, `MinorAgent`, `FilterAgent`, and `ScheduleAgent` invoke methods of the `blackboard` object. `MajorAgent` and `MinorAgent` invoke methods of the `schedule_of_courses` object. `MajorAgent` and `MinorAgent` have a similar sequence of calls to the `blackboard` and `schedule_of_courses` objects:

```
MajorAgent1:currentDegreePlan()      MinorAgent1:currentDegreePlan()
MajorAgent2:coursesTaken()           MinorAgent2:coursesTaken()
MajorAgent3:scheduleOfCourses()      MinorAgent3:scheduleOfCourses()
MajorAgent4:suggestionsForMajor()    MinorAgent4:suggestionsForMinor()
```

As you can see, the name of the active object that invokes these operations are prepended to the sequence number. Both objects are concurrently invoking `blackboard` and `schedule_of_courses` operations. All these operations have concurrent synchronization and are safe to call simultaneously. `masterList()` and `possibleCourses()` have a `guarded` property. The objects supplying these courses may be writing them as these objects are attempting to read them. They are guarded by only allowing sequential access (EREW).

10.2.2   Message Sequences between Objects

Where a collaboration diagram focuses on the structural organization and interaction of objects working together to perform a task, operation, or realize a use case, a *sequence diagram* focuses on the time ordering of method invocation or procedures involved in a particular task, operation, or use case. In a sequence diagram, the name of each object or construct involved is displayed in its own rectangular box. The boxes are placed at the top along the x-axis of the diagram. You should only include the major players involved and the most important function calls because the diagram can quickly become too complicated. The objects are ordered from left to right starting from the object or procedure that initiates the action to the most subordinate objects or procedures. The calls are placed along the y-axis from top to bottom in time order. Vertical lines are placed under each box representing the lifeline of the object. Solid arrowhead lines are drawn from the lifeline of one object to the lifeline of another representing a function call or method invocation from the caller to the receiver. Stick arrowhead lines are drawn from the receiver back to the caller representing a return from a function or method. Each function call is labeled at the minimum with the function or method name. The arguments and control information, like the condition in which the method is invoked, can also be displayed. For example:

```
[list != empty]
getResults()
```

The function or method will not be performed unless the condition is true. Methods that are to be invoked several times on an object, like reading values from a structure, are preceded by an *iteration marker* ($*$).

Figure 10–10 shows a sequence diagram of some of the objects involved in the course adviser system. Only some of the objects are shown to avoid a complicated diagram. When using the sequence diagram for concurrent objects or procedures, activation symbols are used. An activation symbol is a rectangle that appears on the object's lifeline. This indicates the object or procedure is active. These are used when an object makes a call to another object or procedure and does not block. This shows that the object or procedure is continuing to execute or be active. In Figure 10–10, the blackboard object is always active. It spawns a schedule_agent object and does not block. The schedule_agent calls blackboard.masterList() and waits for the method to return the list of courses. A return arrow is used to indicate the method has returned. The schedule_agent then calls one of its own methods createSchedules(). To indicate an object has called one of its own methods, a *self-delegation* symbol is used. This is a combination of an activation symbol and a call arrow. An activation symbol is overlapped on the existing activation symbol. A line proceeds from the original activation symbol with an arrow pointing to the added activation symbol. Once schedule_agent posts its results by calling blackboard.possible-Schedule(), the blackboard object kills it. This is indicated with the large X at the end of its lifeline. A call arrow from the blackboard object points to this X, indicating it has killed the object. The blackboard object spawns a filter_agent object and does not block. The filter_agent calls blackboard.possibleSchedules() and waits for the method to return the schedules. The filter_agent then calls one of its own methods

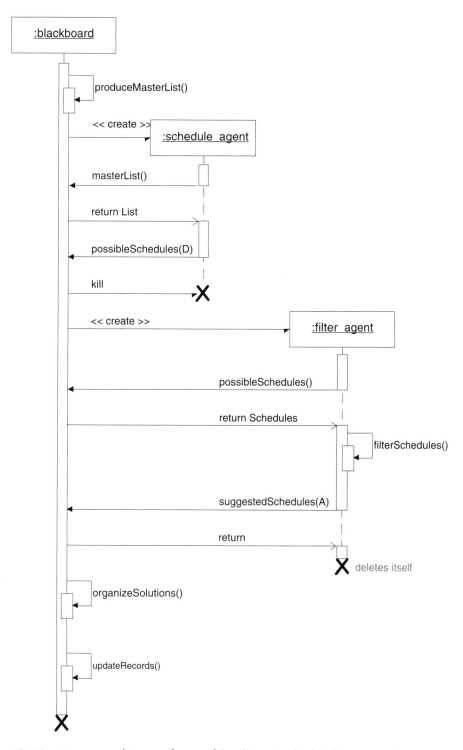

Figure 10–10 A sequence diagram of some of the objects involved in the course adviser system.

filterCourses(). Once filter_agent posts its results, it deletes itself. The blackboard object calls its own organizeSolution() and updateRecords() then deletes itself.

10.2.3   The Activities of Objects

The UML can be used to model the activities performed by objects involved in a specific operation or use case. This is called an *activity diagram*. It is a flowchart showing the sequential and concurrent actions or activities involved in a specific task, step-by-step. The arrows trace the flow of control for the activities represented in the diagram. Collaboration diagrams emphasize the flow of control from object to object, sequence diagrams emphasize the flow of control in time order, and the activity diagram emphasizes the flow of control from one action or activity to another. The actions or activities change the state of the object or returns a value. The containment of the action or activity is called an *action* or *activity state*. They represent the state of the object at a particular instant in the flow of control.

Actions and activities differ. Actions cannot logically be decomposed or interrupted by other actions or events. Examples of actions are creating or destroying an object, invoking an object's method, or calling a function in a procedure. An activity can be decomposed into other activities or even another activity diagram. An example of an activity is a program, a use case, or a procedure. Activities can be interrupted by an event or other activities or actions.

An activity diagram is a graph in which the nodes are actions or activities and the arcs are triggerless transitions. Triggerless transitions require no event to cause the transition to occur. The transition occurs when the previous action or activity has completed. The diagram comprises decision branches, starts, stops, and synchronization bars that join or fork several actions or activities. Both action and activity states are represented the same way. To represent an action or activity state, the UML uses the standard flowchart symbol used to show the enter and exit point of the flowchart. This symbol is used regardless of the type of action or activity occurring. We prefer to use the standard flowchart symbols that distinguish input/output actions (parallelogram) from processing or transformation actions (rectangle). The description of the action or activity as a function call, expression, phrase, use case, or program name is displayed in the action symbol used. An activity state may in addition show the entry and/or exit action. The entry action is the action that takes place when the activity state is entered. The exit action

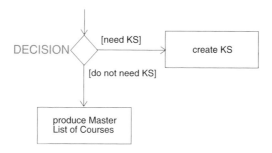

Figure 10–11 The decision symbol used in determining whether a knowledge source should be constructed.

is the action that takes place just before exiting the activity state. They are the first and last actions to be executed in the activity state, respectively.

Once an action has completed, a transition occurs in which the next action takes place immediately. The transition is represented as a directed line from one state with a stick arrow pointing to the next state. A transition pointing to a state is inbound and a transition leading from a state is outbound. Before the outbound transition occurs, the exit action, if it exists, executes. After an inbound transition, the entry action for the state, if it exists, executes. The start of the flow of control is represented as a large solid dot. The first transition leads from the solid dot to the first state in the diagram. The stopping point or stop state of the activity diagram is represented as a large solid dot inside a circle.

Activity diagrams, like flowcharts, have a decision symbol. The decision symbol is a diamond with one inbound transition and two or more outbound transitions. The outbound transitions are guarded conditions that determine the path of the flow of control. The guarded condition is a simple boolean expression. All of the outbound transitions should cover all of the possible paths from the branch. Figure 10–11 shows the decision symbol used in determining whether a knowledge source should be constructed.

You may find that there exists more than one flow of a sequence of actions or activities occurring concurrently after an action or activity has completed. Unlike a flowchart, the UML defines a symbol that can be used to represent the instant where multiple flows of control occur concurrently. A *synchronization bar* is used to show where a single path branches off or forks into parallel paths and where parallel paths join. It is a thick horizontal line in which there can be multiple outbound transitions (forking) or multiple

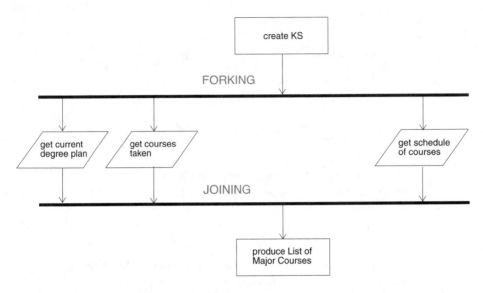

Figure 10–12   An example of forking and joining from or to the synchronization bar.

inbound transitions (joining). Each transition represents a different path. Outbound transitions from a synchronization bar signify an action or activity state has caused multiple flows of control to occur. Inbound transitions into a synchronization bar signify the multiple flows of control need to be synchronized. A synchronization bar is used to show the paths are waiting for all paths to meet and join into a single flow or path. Figure 10–12 shows an example of forking and joining.

In Figure 10–12, creating `MajorAgent` invokes its constructor, which forks three flows of control. After these three actions have completed, they are joined again into a single flow of control in which the action "produce list of major courses" is executed.

The diagram can be divided into separate sections called *swimlanes*. In each swimlane, the actions or activities of a particular object, component, or use case occurs. Swimlanes are vertical lines that partition the diagram into sections. A swimlane for a particular object, component, or use case specifies the focus of activities. An action or activity can only occur in a single swimlane. Transitions and synchronization bars can cross one or more swimlanes. Actions or activities in the same lane or different lanes but at the same level are concurrent. Figure 10–13 shows the activity diagram with swimlanes.

The purpose of this activity diagram is to model the sequence of actions involved in a `blackboard` object producing the master list for our course

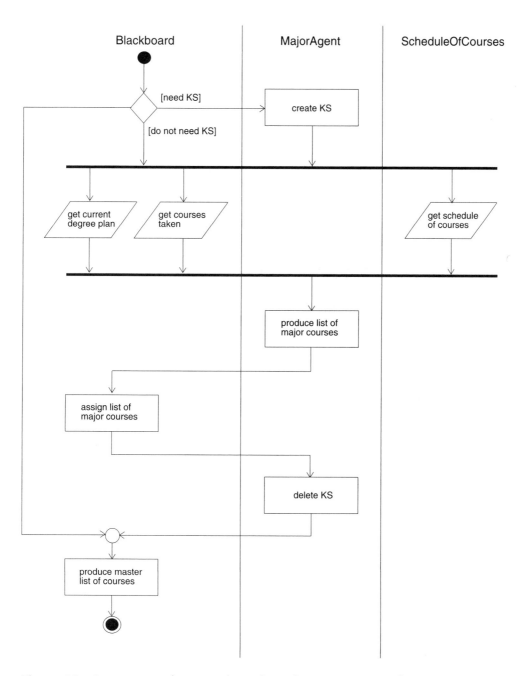

Figure 10–13 An activity diagram with swimlanes showing a sequence of actions in the course advisor system.

adviser system. In Figure 10–13, the `blackboard` object first makes the decision whether the `MajorAgent` object should be constructed. If so, the constructor for `MajorAgent` is invoked. This causes a fork of three flows of control. Two of the actions are executed by the `blackboard` object, "get current degree plan" and "get courses taken," and one action is executed by the `ScheduleofCourses` object, "get schedule of courses." These are all input actions, as the symbol represents. The multiple paths are joined again and `MajorAgent` performs an action "produce list of major courses." The `blackboard` performs an action "receive list of major courses" followed by the deletion of the `MajorAgent` object. The `blackboard` object "produces master list of courses," then the activities stop.

10.2.4   State Machines

State machines depict the behavior of a single construct specifying the sequence of transformations during its lifetime as it responds to internal and external events. The single construct can be a system, a use case, or an object. State machines are used to model the behavior of a single entity. An entity can respond to events such as procedures, functions, operations, and signals. An entity can also respond to elapses in time. Whenever an event takes place, the entity responds by performing some activity or taking some action resulting in a change of the state of the entity or the production of some artifact. The action or activity performed will depend upon the current state of the entity. A state is a condition the entity is in during its lifetime as a result of performing some action or responding to some event.

A state machine can be represented in a table or directed graph called a *state diagram*. Figure 10–14 shows a UML state diagram for the state machine of a process. Figure 10–14 shows the states some process progresses go through while it is active in the system. The process can have four states: ready, running, sleeping, and stopped. There are eight events that cause the four states of the process. Three of the events only occur if a condition is met. The *block* event occurs only if the process requests I/O or it is waiting for an event to occur. If the *block* event occurs, it triggers the process to transform from a running state to a sleeping state. The *wakeup* event occurs only if the event takes place or the I/O has been completed. If the *wakeup* event occurs, it triggers the process to transform from a *sleeping* state (source state) to a ready state (target state). The *exit* event occurs only if the process has executed all its instructions. If the *exit* event occurs, it triggers

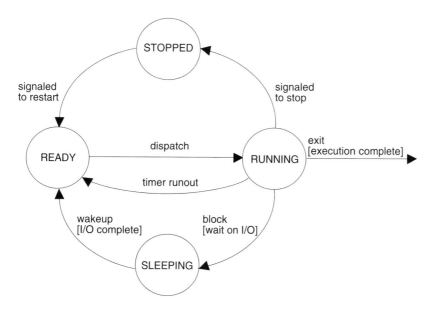

Figure 10–14   State diagram for processes.

the process to transform from a *running* state to a *sleeping state*. The remaining events are external events and not under the control of the process. They occur for some external reason triggering the process to transform from a source to a target state.

The state diagrams are used to model the dynamic aspects of an object, use case, or system. The sequence, activity, and interactive collaboration diagrams and now the state diagram are used to model the behavior of the system or object when it is active. Structural collaboration and class diagrams are used to model the structural organization of an object or system. State diagrams are good to use to describe the behavior of an object regardless of the use case. They should not be used to describe the behavior of several interacting or collaborating objects. They should be used to describe the behavior of an object, system, or use case that goes through a number of transformations and more than one event may cause a single transformation to occur. These are constructs that are very reactive to internal and external events.

In the state diagram, the nodes are states and the arcs are transitions. The states are represented as rounded-corner rectangles in which the name of the state is displayed. The transitions are lines connecting the source and target states with a stick arrow pointing to the target state. There are *initial* and *final states.* The initial state is the default starting point for the state machine. It is represented as a solid black dot with a transition to the first state of the state machine. The final state is the ending state of the state machine, indicating it has completed or the system, use case, or object has reached the end of its lifeline. It is represented as a solid dot embedded in a circle.

Table 10–5 Parts of a State	
Parts of a State	*Description*
Name	The unique name of the state that distinguishes it from other states; a state may have no name.
Entry / exit actions	Actions executed when entering the state (entry state) or executed when exiting the state (exit action).
Substates	A nested state; the substates are the disjointed states that can be activated sequentially or concurrently. The composite or superstate is the state that contains the substates.
Internal transitions	Transitions that occur within the state that are handled without causing a change in the state.
Self-transitions	Transitions that occur within the state that are handled without causing a change in the state but causes the exit then the entry actions to execute.
Deferred events	A list of events that occurs while the object is in that state but is queued and handled when the object is in another state.

A state has several parts. Table 10–5 lists the parts of a state. A state can be represented simply by displaying the name of the state at the center of the state symbol. If other actions are to be shown inside the state symbol, the name of the state should appear at the top in a separate compartment. The actions and activities are listed below this compartment and are displayed in this format:

```
label [Guard] / action or activity
```

For example:

```
do / validate(data)
```

The `do` is the label used for an activity to be performed while the object is in this state. The `validate(data)` function is called with `data` as the argument. If an action or activity is a call to a function or method, the arguments can be displayed.

The Guard is an expression that evaluates to true or false. If a condition evaluates to true, the action or activity takes place. For example:

```
exit [data valid] / send(data)
```

The exit action send(data) is guarded. The expression data valid is evaluated to be true or false. Upon exiting the state, if the expression is true, then the send(data) function is called. The Guard is always optional.

Transitions occur when an event takes place. This causes the object, system, or use case to transform from one state to another. There are two transitions that can occur that does not cause a change in the state of the object, system, or use case: self-transition and internal transition.

With a *self-transition*, when a particular event occurs, this triggers the object to leave the current state. When exiting, it performs the exit action (if any), then performs whatever action is associated with the self-transition (if any). The object reenters the state and the entry action (if any) is performed. With an *internal transition*, the object does not leave the state and therefore no entry or exit actions are performed. Figure 10–15 shows the general structure of a state with exit and entry actions, do activity along with internal and self-transitions. A self-transition is represented as a directed line that points back to the same state.

A transition between different states indicates that there is a relationship or path that exists between them. From one state an event can occur or a condition can be met that causes the object to be transformed from one state (source state) to another state (target state). The event triggers the transition of the object. A transition may have several concurrently existing source states. If so, they are joined before the transition occurs. A transition may have several concurrently existing target states in which a fork has occurred. Table 10–6 lists the parts of a transition. A transition is rendered as a directed

Figure 10–15 The general structure of a state with an exit action, entry action, do activity, and internal–self-transitions.

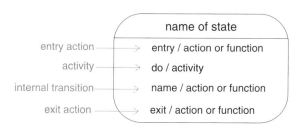

line from the source state pointing to the target state. The name of the event trigger is displayed next to the transition. Like actions and activities, events for transitions can also be guarded. A transition can be *triggerless,* meaning no special event occurs that causes the transition to take place. Exiting the source state, the object immediately makes the transition and enters the target state.

Table 10–6   Parts of a Transition

Parts of a Transition	*Description*
Source state	The original state of the object; when a transition occurs the object leaves the source state.
Target state	The state the objects enter after a transition occurs.
Event trigger	The event that causes the transition to occur. A transition may be triggerless, in which the transition occurs as soon as the object has completed all activities in the source state.
Guard condition	A boolean expression associated with an event trigger that when evaluated to True, the transition occurs.
Action	An action executed by the object that takes place during a transition; it may be associated with an event trigger and/or guard condition.

10.2.4.1   Concurrent Substates

A substate can be used to further simplify the depiction of modeling the behavior of a concurrent system. A *substate* is a state contained inside another state called a *superstate* or *composite state*. This representation means a state can be further broken down into one or more substates. These substates can be sequential or concurrent. With concurrent substates, each state machine represented exists in parallel as different but concurrently existing flows of control. This means the object is engaged in two independent sets of behavior. This is true for our blackboard object. As it is processing each possible schedule, it has to also update its appropriate structures and perform other maintenance. Each substate is contained in a separate compartment. The substates are synchronized and joined before exiting the composite state. When one substate has reached its final state, it waits for the other state to

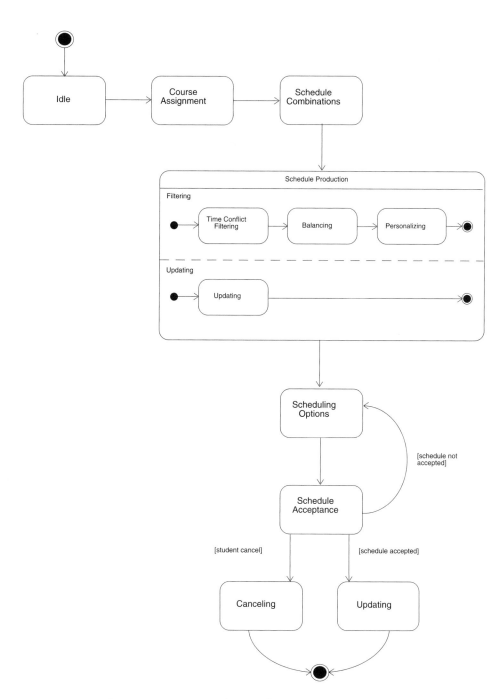

Figure 10–16   State diagram for the `blackboard` object.

reach its final state, then the substates are joined back into one flow. Figure 10–16 shows a state diagram for the `blackboard` object that produces a student schedule.

In Figure 10–16, the *schedule production* is a composite state. It has concurrent substates called *filtering* and *maintenance*. Each substate is separated by a dashed line and is represented by its own state machine, each having an initial and final state. In the filtering substate, the object goes through the time conflict filtering, balancing, and then personalizing states. In the maintenance substate, the object goes through one state: updating. When both substates have reached their final states, filtering and maintenance are joined before exiting the composite state schedule production.

10.2.5   Distributed Objects

Distributed objects are objects executing on different processors on different machines. A *deployment diagram* is used to model the view of the system that shows the physical relationships between the software and hardware components in the delivered system. They are used to show how the components and objects are routed in the distributed system. Components can be executable programs, libraries, or databases. You may want to specify where a particular component or object resides in the system. Determining how to distribute the concurrent components of your system will be difficult. Modeling how the components are distributed will help in managing the configuration, functionality, and throughput of the system.

A deployment diagram consists of nodes and the objects or components that reside on the nodes. A *node* is a computational unit or a piece of hardware that has some memory and processing capability, whether it be a device, a computer, a mainframe, or a cluster of computers. The nodes are related by dependency. These dependencies represent how the components communicate with each other. The direction of the dependency indicates which component is aware of the other component. Even if there is communication in both directions, one component may not be aware of whom they are communicating with.

There are two ways to model the location of components or objects in a UML deployment diagram: nesting or tagged value.

They reflect the approach of listing the components that reside on a node in the node symbol or displaying the location of the components in the com-

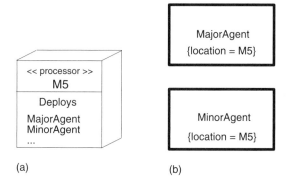

Figure 10–17 Approaches to show the location of a component in a distributed system.

ponent symbol. Nodes are a part of a deployment diagram. The node symbol is a cube. The cube can have two separate compartments: one contains the stereotype indicator describing the type of node and the other contains the list of components that reside on that node. The approach uses the component symbol and displays a *location* tag assigning the name of the node where the component resides. A location tag has this format:

```
{location = name of node}
```

The location tag can be a part of any diagram in which the location of the component is appropriate (e.g., collaboration, object, or activity diagram). Figure 10–17 shows the two approaches of showing the location components in a distributed system. In Figure 10–17, (a) shows the node symbol listing the components that reside on it and (b) shows the active object symbol using the location tag.

10.3 Visualizing the Whole System

A system is composed of many elements, including subsystems organized into a collaboration to accomplish some purpose. It is an aggregation of constructs joined in some regular interaction. The diagraming techniques discussed in this chapter allow the developer to model a single system from different viewpoints, from different levels, and from different flows of control to assist in the design and development of the system. In this section, we discuss modeling and documenting the system as a whole. This means at the highest level the major components or functional elements can be depicted. The diagraming techniques discussed in this section are the ones used to model the delivered system and the architecture of the system. Although this is the last section in this chapter, modeling and documenting the whole system would be the first level of designing and developing a system.

10.3.1   *Visualizing Deployment of Systems*

The deployment of a system is the last step in system development. Deployment is the delivery of the system. When a system is to be deployed, you may want to model the actual physical components of the runtime version of your system. A deployment diagram depicts the configuration of runtime processing elements and the software components that execute on them. The software components are actual executable modules such as active objects (processes), libraries, databases, and so on. A deployment diagram consists of nodes and components. The components used in a deployment diagram are runtime entities. Runtime entities are the physical implementations of logical elements. A class is a logical element that may be implemented as one or several components. A class may be divided into processes or threads. Each process or thread can be a component in a deployment diagram. The components of a class may be executed on different nodes on a single machine (threads/processes) or different machines (processes).

A node is represented by a cube. Nodes are connected by dependencies or associations. Components and nodes can be connected by dependencies as well. As discussed earlier, a node can list its components or a component can be depicted separate from a node showing the relationship between them. A component can be represented as a rectangle with tags on the left side. The name of the component is contained inside the symbol.

Components can be grouped together to create larger chunks such as packages or subsystems. Figure 10–18 shows a deployment diagram. In Figure 10–18, the users connect to the system via intranet. The nodes are the part of a cluster of PCs. They are grouped into a package. The user connects to the cluster as a whole. Each node lists the components that reside on them. The communication between nodes is by means of a network node.

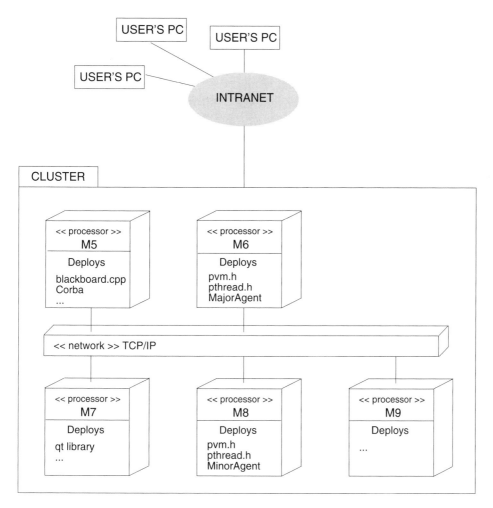

Figure 10–18   A deployment diagram using packages.

10.3.2   *The Architecture of a System*

When modeling and documenting the architecture of a system, the view of the system is at the highest level. Booch, Rumbaugh, and Jacobson define *architecture* as:

> The set of significant decisions about the organization of a software system, the selection of the structural elements and their interfaces by which the system is composed, together with their behavior as specified in the collaboration among

those elements, the composition of these structural and behavioral elements into progressively larger subsystems, and the architectural style that guides this organization—these elements and their interfaces, their collaborations, and their composition.

Modeling and documenting the architecture will capture the system's logical and physical elements along with the structure and behavior of the system at the highest level.

The architecture of the system is a description of the system from a distinct view that focuses on the structure and organization of the system from that aspect. The views are as follows:

use case	Describes the behavior of the system presented to end users.
process	Describes the processes and threads used in the system's mechanisms of concurrency and synchronization.
design	Describes the services and functions provided to the end user.
implementation	Describes the components used to create the physical system.
deployment	Describes the software components and the nodes on which they are executing in the delivered system.

As you can see, these views overlap and interact with each other. Use cases can be used in the design view. Processes can show up as components in the implementation view. Software components are used in both implementation and deployment views. When designing the architecture of the system, diagrams that reflect each of these views should be constructed.

A system can be decomposed into subsystems and modules. The subsystems or modules will be further broken down into components, nodes, classes, objects, and interfaces. In the UML, subsystems or modules used at the architectural level of documentation are called *packages*. A package can be used to organize elements into a group that describes the general purpose of those elements. A package is represented as a rectangle with a tab on the upper left corner. The package symbol contains the name of the package. The packages in the system can be connected by means of composition, aggregation, dependency, and associations relationships. Stereotype indicators can be used to distinguish one type of package from another. Figure 10–19 shows the packages involved in the course adviser system. The system pack-

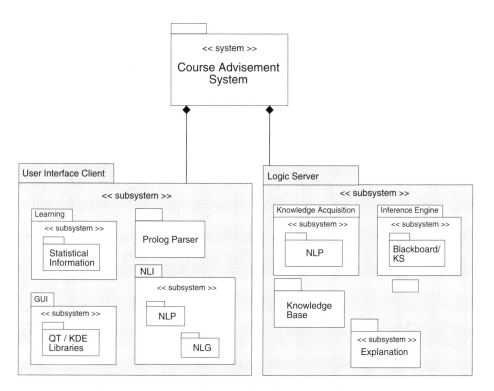

Figure 10–19 Packages used in the course adviser system.

age uses a `<<system>>` indicator to distinguish it from the *User Interface Client* and *Logic Server* subsystems, which use the `<<subsystem>>` indicator. Because they are subsystems, they are related to the system by aggregation relationship.

Packages can contain other packages. If a package contains other packages, then the name of the package is placed in the tab. Figure 10–19 also shows the content of each subsystem.

Summary

A model of a system is the body of information gathered for the purpose of studying the system. Documentation is a tool used in modeling a system. The UML, Unified Modeling Language, is a graphical notation used to design, visualize, model, and document the artifacts of a software system created by

Grady Booch, James Rumbaugh, and Ivar Jacobson. It is the de facto standard for communicating and modeling object-oriented systems. The UML can be used to model concurrent and distributed systems from the structural and behavioral perspectives.

UML diagrams can be used to model to most basic units, the object, to the whole system. An object is the basic unit used in many UML diagrams. Dependency, inheritance, aggregation, and composition are some of the relationships that can exist between objects. Interaction diagrams are used to show the behavior of an object and identify concurrency in the system. Objects can interact with other objects by communicating and invoking methods. Collaboration diagrams depict the interactions between objects working together to perform some particular task. Sequence diagrams are used to represent the interactions between objects in time sequence. Statecharts are used to depict the actions of a single object over its lifetime. Objects that are distributed can be tagged with the location of the node on which it resides.

Deployment diagrams are used to model the delivered system. The basic units of a deployment diagram are nodes and components. A node represents hardware and components are software. Nodes can be depicted to show what objects or components reside on them. When modeling the whole system, the basic unit is a package. A package can be used to represent systems and subsystems. Packages can have relationships with other packages such as composition or some type of association.

Designing Components That Support Concurrency

"As we cross the divide to instantiate ourselfs into our computational technology, our indentity will be based on our evolving mind file. We will be software, not hardware."

—*Ray Kurzweil,* The Age of Spiritual Machines

In this Chapter

Taking Advantage of Interface Classes • A Closer Look at Object-Oriented Mutual Exclusion and Interface Classes • Maintaining the Stream Metaphor • User-Defined Classes Designed to Work with PVM Streams • Object-Oriented Pipes and fifos as Low-Level Building Blocks • Framework Classes Components for Concurrency • Summary

As a rule of thumb the requirement for parallelism and concurrency within a piece of software should be discovered and not introduced. Sometimes the goal of speeding up a program is not enough justification to force parallelism into logic that is naturally sequential. The parallelism within a design should be a natural consequence of the requirements of a system. Once concurrency is identified in the system requirements, then architectures and algorithms that support parallelism should be considered. In other cases the need for parallelism will emerge within an existing system that was originally designed with only sequential processing in mind. This is often the case for systems that started as single-user systems and grew into multiuser systems or systems that have evolved functionally far beyond the original specifications. In these systems the requirement for parallelism is after the fact and the system architecture must be augmented to support concurrency. In this book we are concerned with describing techniques for implementing natural parallelism. That is, once we know we need parallelism, how do we do it using C++?

We present an architectural approach to managing parallelism within a program. We take advantage of the C++ support for object-oriented programming and genericity. Particularly C++'s support for inheritance, polymorphism, and templates is used to cleanly implement architectures and components that support concurrency. Object-oriented programming techniques supply support for 10 class types shown in Table 11–1.

Table 11–1 Types of Object-Oriented Classes	
Types of Classes	*Description*
Template classes	A parameterized type containing generic code that can use or manipulate any type; an actual type is the parameter for the code body.
Container class	A class used to hold objects in memory or external storage.
Virtual base class	A base class where during multiple inheritance, the class is the indirect and/or direct base of a derived class; only one copy of the class is shared by all the derived classes.
Abstract class	A class that supplies the interface for derived classes that can only be used as a base class; used as the layout for the construction of other classes.
Interface class	A class used to adjust the interface of other classes.
Node class	A class that has added new services or functionality beyond the services inherited from its base class.
Domain class	A class created to simulate some entity within a specific domain; the meaning of the class is relative to the domain.
Aggregate class	A class that contains other classes; has a "whole–part" relationship with other classes.
Concrete class	A complete class whose implementation is defined and instances of the class can be declared; not intended to be a base class and no attempt to create operations of commonality.
Framework class	A class or collection of classes that has a predefined structure and represents a generalized pattern of work.

These class types prove to be especially useful for designs that require concurrency. This is because these class types aid with the building-block approach. We start with primitive components, using them to build synchronization classes. We use the synchronization classes to build concurrency-safe container classes and framework classes. The framework classes are the building blocks for higher level parallel architectures such as multiagent systems and blackboards. At each level the complexity of the parallel and distributed programming is reduced with the help of the various class types in Table 11–1.

We start our discussion with the interface class. An interface or adapter class is used to modify or enhance the interface of another class or set of classes. The interface class may also act as a wrapper around one or more functions that are not members of any particular class. This use of the interface class allows us to provide an object-oriented interface to software that is not necessarily object-oriented. Furthermore, interface classes allow us to simplify the interfaces of function libraries such as POSIX threads, PVM and MPI. We can either wrap a non-object-oriented function in an object-oriented interface; or we might want to wrap a piece of data, encapsulate it, and give it an object-oriented interface. In addition to simplifying the complexity of some function libraries, the interface classes are used to present a consistent API (Application Programmer Interface) to the developers. For example, C++ programmers that have grown accustomed to the advantages of the iostreams classes tend to think of input and output in terms of object-oriented streams. The learning curve is minimized when new input and output techniques can be presented within the iostream metaphor. For instance, we might present the MPI message passing library as a collection of streams:

```
mpi_stream  Stream1;
mpi_stream  Stream2;

Stream1 << Message1 << Message2 << Message3;
Stream2 >> Message4;
//...
```

In this way, the programmer can focus on the logic of the program without getting bogged down in the syntax requirements of the MPI library.

11.1 Taking Advantage of Interface Classes

It is often advantageous to use encapsulation to hide the details of function libraries and to provide self-contained components that can be reused. Let's take for example the mutex that we discussed in Chapter 7. Recall that a mutex is a special kind of variable used for synchronization. Mutexes are used to provide safe access to a critical section of data or code within a program. There are six basic functions that can be performed on a `pthread_mutex_t` (POSIX Threads Mutex) variable.

Synopsis

#include <pthread.h>

pthread_mutex_destroy(pthread_mutex_t *mutex);
pthread_mutex_init(pthread_mutex_t *mutex, pthread_mutexattr_t *attr);
pthread_mutex_lock(pthread_mutex_t *mutex);
pthread_mutex_timedlock(pthread_mutex_t *mutex);
pthread_mutex_trylock(pthread_mutex_t *mutex);
pthread_mutex_unlock(pthread_mutex_t *mutex);

Each of these functions take at least a pointer to a pthread_mutex_t variable. An interface class can be used to encapsulate access to the pthread_mutex_t variable and to simplify the function calls that access the pthread_mutex_t variable. In Example 11.1, we can declare a class called mutex.

```
//Example 11.1 Declaration of the mutex class.

class mutex{
protected:
    pthread_mutex_t *Mutex;
    pthread_mutexattr_t *Attr;
public:
    mutex(void)
    int lock(void);
    int unlock(void);
    int trylock(void);
    int timedlock(void);
};
```

Once this mutex class is declared, we can use it to define mutex variables. We can declare arrays of these mutexes. We use these variables as members of user-defined classes. By encapsulating the pthread_mutex_t variable and its functions, we can take advantage of the object-oriented programming techniques. These mutex variables can now be used as parameter arguments and function return values. And since the functions are now bound to the pthread_mutex_t variable, wherever we pass the mutex variable the functions are also available.

The member functions for the class mutex are defined by wrapping the calls to the corresponding Pthread routines, for instance:

```
//Example 11.2 Member functions for the mutex class.

mutex::mutex(void)
    {
```

```
try{
      int Value;
      Value = pthread_mutexattr_int(Attr);
      //...
      Value = pthread_mutex_init(Mutex,Attr);
      //...
   }
}

int mutex::lock(void)
{
   int RetValue;
   RetValue = pthread_mutex_lock(Mutex);
   //...
   return(ReturnValue);
}
```

We also protect the `pthread_mutex_t *` and the `pthread_mutexattr_t *` through encapsulation. In other words, when we invoke the `lock()`, `unlock()`, `trylock()`, and so on methods, we don't have to worry about which mutex variable or which attribute variables these functions will be applied to. The availability of information hiding through encapsulation allows the programmer to write safer code. With the free floating versions of Pthread mutex functions, any `pthread_mutex_t` variable may be passed to these functions. Simply passing the wrong mutex to one of these functions can lead to deadlock or indefinite postponement. Encapsulating the `pthread_mutex_t` variable and the `pthread_mutexattr_t` variable within the `mutex` class gives the programmer complete control over which functions have access to those particular variables.

Now we can use an embedded interface class like `mutex` within other user-defined classes to provide thread-safe classes. Let's say that we wanted to make a thread-safe queue and a thread-safe `pvm_stream` class. The queue is used to store incoming events for multiple threads within a program. Some of the threads have the responsibility of sending messages to various PVM tasks. The PVM tasks and the threads are executing concurrently. The multiple threads share a single PVM stream and a single event queue. Figure 11–1 shows the relationship between threads, PVM tasks, event queue, and `pvm_stream`.

The queue in Figure 11–1 is a critical section because it is shared between multiple executing threads. The `pvm_stream` in Figure 11–1 is also a critical section because it is shared between multiple executing threads. If these critical sections are not synchronized and protected, then we can end up with corrupted data in the queue and `pvm_stream`. The fact that multiple threads can update either the queue or the `pvm_stream` introduces an environment for

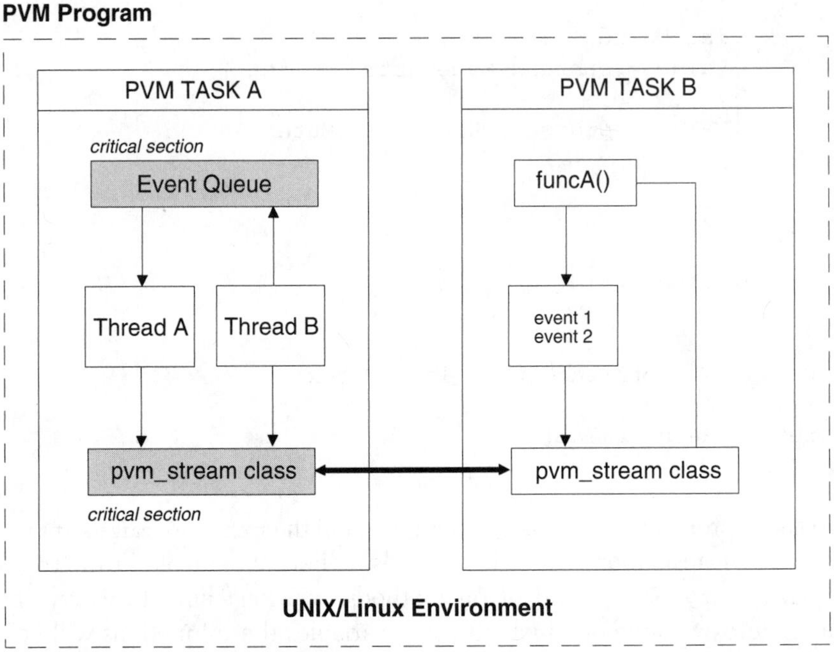

PVM Program

Figure 11-1   The relationship between threads, PVM tasks, event queue, and the `pvm_stream` class within a PVM program.

race conditions. To help manage the race conditions we design our queue and `pvm_stream` class with built-in lock and unlock functionality. The lock and unlock functionality is supplied by our `mutex` class. Figure 11–2 shows the class diagram for our user-defined `x_queue` and `pvm_stream` classes.

Notice that the `x_queue` class contains a `mutex` class. This is a *has-a* or aggregation relationship between `x_queue` and `mutex`, that is, `x_queue` has a `mutex` class. Any operation that changes the state of our `x_queue` class can cause a race condition if that operation is not synchronized. Therefore, the operations that add an object to the queue or that remove an object from the queue are candidates for synchronization. Example 11.3 contains the declaration of our `x_queue` class as a template class.

```
//Example  11.3  Declaration of the x_queue class.

template <class T> x_queue  class{
protected:
   queue<T>  EventQ;
   mutex  Mutex;
   //...
public:
```

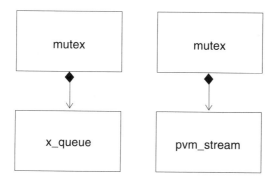

Figure 11-2 The class diagram for our user-
defined x_queue class and
pvm_stream class.

```
bool  enqueue(T Object);
T dequeue(void);
//...
};
```

The `enqueue()` method is used to add items to the queue and the `de-queue()` method is used to remove items from the queue. Each of these methods will use the `Mutex` object. The `enqueue()` and `dequeue()` methods are defined in Example 11.4.

```
//Example 11.4 Defintion of enqueue() method.

template<class T> bool x_queue<T>::enqueue(T Object)
{
   Mutex.lock();
   EventQ.push(Object);
   Mutex.unlock();
}

template<class T> T x_queue<T>::dequeue(void)
{

   T Object;
   //...
   Mutex.lock();
   Object = EventQ.front()
   EventQ.pop();
   Mutex.unlock();
   //...
   return(Object);
}
```

Now items can be added to and removed from our queue in a multithreaded environment. Thread B in Figure 11–1 adds items to the queue and Thread A in Figure 11–1 removes items. The `mutex` class is an interface class. It wraps the `pthread_mutex_lock()`, `pthread_mutex_unlock()`, `pthread_mutex_init()`, and `pthread_mutex_trylock()` functions. The `x_queue` class is also an interface class because it adapts the interface for the built-in `queue<T>` class. First, it changes the `push()` and `pop()` method interfaces to `enqueue()` and `dequeue()`. Furthermore, it wraps the insertion and removal of items with the `Mutex.lock()` and `Mutex.unlock()` methods. So in the first case we use the interface class to encapsulate `pthread_mutex_t *` and `pthread_mutexattr_t *` variables. We also wrap several functions from the Pthread library. In the second case, we use the interface class to adapt the interface of the `queue<T>` class. Another advantage of the mutex class is that it can be easily reused in other classes that contain critical sections or critical regions.

In Figure 11–1 the PVM stream is also a critical section because both Thread A and Thread B have access to the stream. A possible race condition exists because Thread A and Thread B may both try to access the stream at the same time. Therefore, we use the `mutex` class in our user-defined `pvm_stream` class to provide synchronization.

```
//Example 11.5 Declaration of pvm_stream class.

class pvm_stream{
protected:
   mutex Mutex;
   int TaskId;
   int MessageId;
   //...
public:
   pvm_stream & operator <<(string X);
   pvm_stream & operator <<(int X);
   pvm_stream &operator <<(float X);
   pvm_stream &operator>>(string  X);
   //...
};
```

As with the `x_queue` class, the `Mutex` object is used with the functions that can change the state of a `pvm_stream` object. For example, we might define one of the << operators as:

```
//Example 11.6 Definition of the << operator for the
             pvm_stream class.

pvm_stream &pvm_stream::operator<<(string X)
{
```

```
//...
pvm_pkbyte(const_cast<char *>(X.data()),X.size(),1);
Mutex.lock();
pvm_send(TaskId,MessageId);
Mutex.unlock();
//...
return(*this);
}
```

The `pvm_stream` class uses `Mutex` objects to synchronize access to its critical section in the same manner as was done with the `x_queue` class. It's important to note that in both cases the `pthread_mutex` functions are hidden. The programmer does not have to be concerned about their syntax. A simpler `lock()` and `unlock()` interface is used. Furthermore, there is no confusion about which `pthread_mutex_t *` is being used with the `pthread_mutex` functions. In addition to these advantages, the programmer may declare multiple instances of the `mutex` class without having to call Pthread mutex functions over again. We made reference to the Pthread functions once within the method definitions of the `mutex` class. Now only the methods of the `mutex` class need be called.

11.2   A Closer Look at Object-Oriented Mutual Exclusion and Interface Classes

To confront some of the complexity with writing and maintaining programs that require concurrency, we try to streamline and simplify the API to the parallel libraries. Some systems may require the use of the Pthreads library, the MPI library, the standard semaphore, and shared memory functions as part of a single solution. Each of these libraries and functions have their own protocols and syntax. However, often they have similar functionality. We can use interface classes, inheritance, and polymorphism to present a simplified and consistent interface to the programmer. We can also hide the details of library-specific implementation from our applications. If the application only relies on the methods used in our interface classes, then our application is shielded from implementation changes, library updates, and other under-the-hood restructuring. Ultimately the work that you do in providing interface classes to concurrency components and function libraries and function data will allow you to reduce the complexity of parallel programming. Let's take a closer look at how we can approach the design of interface classes that support concurrency.

11.2.1   *Semi-Fat Interfaces that Support Concurrency*

The basic POSIX semaphore is used to synchronize access to a critical section between two or more processes. The basic POSIX thread is used to synchronize access to a critical section between two or more threads. In both cases, there are synchronization variables involved and a number of functions available on the synchronization variables. The MPI library and the PVM library both contain message-passing primitives. Both have the capabilities of spawning tasks. However, the interfaces of these two libraries are different. The application programmer wants to focus on the logic and structure of the program. This is difficult when the semantics of a program are obscured by multiple libraries that happen to perform similar functions but whose syntax and protocols are very different. What is needed is a generalized interface that can be used across libraries.

There are at least a couple of approaches to designing an interface for a family of classes or a collection of classes. The object-oriented approach starts with the general and moves to the specific by means of inheritance. That is, we take the minimal core set of characteristics and attributes that every member of the family of classes should have and, through lineage of inheritance, we specialize those characteristics for each class. In this approach, the interface grows more narrow as you move down the class hierarchy. The second approach is often used in template collections. Template-based approaches start with the specific and move to the general through fat interfaces. The fat interface includes a generalization of all of the characteristics and attributes under discussion (see Stroustrup, 1997). If we were to apply narrow and fat interfaces to our concurrency libraries, the narrow interface approach would take intersection between each library, generalize it, and put it in a base class. The fat interface approach would take the union of the functionality within each library, generalize it, and put in a base class. The set intersection would produce a smaller, less useful class. The set union would produce a large, possibly unwieldy class. For our discussion we are interested in a position somewhere in the middle. We want semi-fat interfaces. We start with a narrow approach and generalize as much as we can within a single class hierarchy. We then use the narrow interface as a basis for a collection of classes that are not related by inheritance but that are related by function. The narrow interface acts as a sort of policy to constrain how fat a semi-fat interface can become. In other words, we don't want a union of every characteristic and attribute under discussion; we only want a union of the things that are logically related to our narrow interface. Let's illustrate this point with a simple design of interface classes for the Pthread mutex, Pthread read-write lock variable, and the POSIX semaphore.

Regardless of the implementation details, the operations of lock, unlock, and trylock are characteristic of synchronization variables. So we make a base class that will act as a pattern for a family of classes. The `synchronization_variable` class is declared in Example 11.7.

```
//Example 11.7 Declaration of the synchronization_variable class.

class synchronization_variable{
protected:
   runtime_error Exception;
   //...
public:
   int virtual lock(void) = 0;
   int virtual unlock(void) = 0;
   int virtual trylock(void) = 0;
   //...
};
```

Notice that the methods of the `synchronization_variable` class are declared virtual and are initialized to `0`. This means these methods are pure virtual methods, making the `synchronization_variable` class an abstract class. An object cannot be directly created from any class that has one or more pure virtual functions. In order to use this class a new class must be derived from it and the new class must provide definitions for each of the pure virtual functions. The abstract class acts as a kind of policy that says what functions a derived class must define. It provides an interface blueprint for derived classes. It doesn't dictate how the methods should be implemented, only that the methods must be present and cannot be pure virtuals. We can get hints of the proposed behavior from the names of the methods. The blueprint interface class provides an interface without any implementation. This type of class is used to provide a foundation for future classes. The blueprint class guarantees that the interface will have a certain look (Caroll & Ellis, 1995). The `synchronization_variable` class provides a blueprint interface policy for our family of synchronization variables. We use inheritance to provide implementations for the interface. The Pthread mutex is a good candidate for an interface class, so we define a `mutex` class derived from `synchronization_variable`:

```
// Example 11.8 Declaration of a mutex class that inherits the
//              synchronization_variable class.

class mutex : public synchronization_variable{
protected:
    pthread_mutex_t *Mutex;
    pthread_mutexattr_t *MutexAttr;
    //...
public:
    int lock(void);
    int unlock(void);
    int trylock(void);
    //...
};
```

The `mutex` class will provide implementations for each of the pure virtual functions. Once the functions are defined, the policy suggested by the abstract base class has been met. The `mutex` class is not considered an abstract class, therefore `mutex` and any of its descendants can be instantiated as objects. Each of the methods of `mutex` wraps the corresponding Pthread function. For instance:

```
int mutex::trylock(void)
{
    //...
    return(pthread_mutex_trylock(Mutex);
    //...
}
```

provides an interface to the `pthread_mutex_trylock()` function. The `lock()`, `unlock()`, and `trylock()` interface simplifies the Pthread function calls. Our goal is to use encapsulation and inheritance to eventually define a complete family of mutex classes. The inheritance process is a specialization process. The derived class provides additional attributes or characteristics that distinguish it from its ancestors. Each attribute or characteristic added to the derived class specializes it. Now we can design a specialization of the `mutex` class through inheritance by adding the notion of a read/write `mutex` class. Our generic `mutex` class is designed to protect a critical section from access. Once a thread has locked the mutex, it has access to the critical section the mutex protects. Sometimes this is too extreme. There are times when it is okay to allow multiple threads to access the same data at the same time, so long as none of the threads modify or change the data in any way. That is, there are times that we may want to relax the lock on the critical section and only lock out access to actions that want to modify or change the data and allow access to actions that only read or copy the data. This is called a *read lock*. The read lock allows concurrent read access to a critical section. The critical section may already be locked by one thread and another thread may also obtain a lock so long as it does not want to modify the data. The critical section may be locked for writing by some thread, and another thread may request a lock for reading the critical section.

The blackboard architecture is a good example of a structure that can take advantage of read mutexes and the stronger, more generic mutex. The blackboard is a common region shared by concurrently executing routines. The blackboard is used to hold solutions to some problem that the group of routines is collaboratively solving. As each routine makes progress toward the solution to the problem, it writes its progress to the blackboard. Each routine also reads the blackboard to see if there are any results generated by the other routines that might be useful. The blackboard structure is a critical section. We really only want one routine at a time to update the blackboard. On the other hand, we can allow any number of routines to simultaneously read the blackboard. Also, if we have multiple routines reading the blackboard, we don't want the blackboard updated until all the routines that are reading are done. The read mutex is an appropriate mutex for this situation because it can lock access to the blackboard and only allow blackboard readers while denying access to blackboard writers. However, the blackboard will need to be updated if a solution to the problem is ever to be achieved. When the blackboard is being updated, we do not want any readers to have access to the blackboard. We want to block the readers until the routine that is updating the blackboard is done. Therefore, we need a write mutex. Only one routine may hold a write mutex at a time. So we distinguish between a mutex that is locked for reading and no writing and a mutex that is locked for writing and no reading. With a read mutex we can have multiple concurrent reads, and with a write mutex we may only have one writer. This is part of the CREW (Concurrent Read Exclusive Write) approach to parallel programming.

Synopsis

```
#include <ptrhead.h>

int pthread_rwlock_init(pthread_rwlock_t *,
                        const pthread_rwlockattr_t *);
int pthread_rwlock_destroy(pthread_rwlock_t *);
int pthread_rwlock_rdlock(pthread_rwlock_t *);
int pthread_rwlock_tryrdlock(pthread_rwlock_t *);
int pthread_rwlock_wrlock(pthread_rwlock_t *);
int pthread_rwlock_trywrlock(pthread_rwlock_t *);
int pthread_rwlock_unlock(pthread_rwlock_t *);
int pthread_rwlockattr_init(pthread_rwlockattr_t *);
int pthread_rwlockattr_destroy(pthread_rwlockattr_t *);
int pthread_rwlockattr_getpshared(const pthread_rwlockattr_t *,
                                  int *);
int pthread_rwlockattr_setpshared(pthread_rwlockattr_t *, int);
```

To design our specialization of the mutex class, we need to add the ability to perform read locks and write locks. The pthreads library has a read/write mutex variable and attribute variable:

`pthread_rwlock_t and  pthread_rwlockattr_t`

These variables are used in conjunction with the 11 `pthread_rwlock()` functions. We use our interface `class rw_mutex` to encapsulate the `pthread_rwlock_t` and `pthread_rwlockattr_t` variables and to wrap the Pthread read/write mutex functions.

```
// Example 11.9 Declaration of rw_mutex class that contains
//              pthread_rwlock_ t and pthread_rwlockattr_t
//              objects.

class rw_mutex : public mutex{
protected:
   struct pthread_rwlock_t *RwLock;
   struct pthread_rwlockattr_t *RwLockAttr;
public:
   //...
   int read_lock(void);
   int write_lock(void);
   int try_readlock(void);
   int try_writelock(void);
   //...
};
```

The rw_mutex class inherits the mutex class. Figure 11–3 shows the class relationships between our rw_mutex class, mutex class, synchronization_variable class and our runtime_error class.

So far we have a somewhat narrow interface. We are only interested in providing the core minimum set of attributes and characteristics needed to generalize our mutex class using the mutex types and functions from the Pthread library. However, once we are done with this narrow interface for this mutex class we use that interface as a basis for our semi-fat interface. The narrow interface typically is used with classes that are all related through inheritance in some way. The fat interfaces tend to be used with classes that are related by functionality and not by inheritance. We can use the interface class to simplify the interface on classes or functions that belong to different libraries but have similar functionality. The interface class will provide the programmer with a consistent look and feel. We take each of the libraries or classes that have sim-

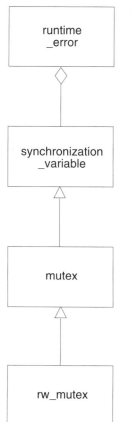

Figure 11–3 The class relationships between rw_mutex, mutex, synchronization_variable, and runtime_error classes.

ilar functionality, collect all of the common functions and variables, then generalize that functionality into a large class that contains all of the required functions and attributes. This will define a class with a fat interface. However, if we just include the functions and data we are interested in, we (e.g., rw_mutex class) then have a semi-fat interface. It has some of the advantages of the fat interface by allowing us to access objects that are only related by functionality and it restricts the set of methods the programmer has to deal with to the methods contained in the narrow interface class. This can be very important when integrating large function libraries like MPI and PVM with the POSIX facilities for concurrency. The combination of the MPI, PVM, and POSIX facilities represents hundreds of functions that all have very similar goals. Taking the time to streamline this functionality into interface classes will allow the programmer to reduce some of the complexity involved with parallel and distributed programming. Also, these interface classes become reusable components that support concurrency.

To see how we approach our semi-fat interface, lets provide an interface class for the POSIX semaphore. Although the semaphore is not part of the Pthread library, it certainly has similar uses within a multithreaded environment. However, it can be used in an environment that includes concurrently executing processes as well as threads. So in some cases it is a more general synchronization variable than our mutex class.

We might define our semaphore class in Example 11.10 as:

```
//Example 11.10 Declaration of semaphore class.

class semaphore : public synchronization_variable{
protected:
    sem_t   *Semaphore;
public:
    //...
    int lock(void);
    int unlock(void);
    int trylock(void);
    //...
};
```

Synopsis

```
<semaphore.h>

int   sem_init(sem_t *, int, unsigned int);
int   sem_destroy(sem_t *);
```

```
sem_t *sem_open(const char *, int, ...);
int    sem_close(sem_t *);
int    sem_unlink(const char *);
int    sem_wait(sem_t *);
int    sem_trywait(sem_t *);
int    sem_post(sem_t *);
int    sem_getvalue(sem_t *, int *);
```

Notice that it has the same interface as our mutex class. What's the difference? First there are several important POSIX semaphore functions. Although the interfaces of mutex and semaphore are the same, the implementation of the lock(), unlock(), trylock(), and so on functions will be calls to the POSIX semaphore functions. For instance:

```
// Example 11.11 Definitions of lock(), unlock(), and trylock()
//                methods for the semaphore class.

int semaphore::lock(void)
{
    //...
    return(sem_wait(Semaphore));
}
int semaphore::unlock(void)
{
    //...
    return(sem_post(Semaphore));
}
```

So the lock(), unlock(), trylock(), and so on, functions will wrap POSIX semaphore functions instead of Pthread functions. It is very important to note that a semaphore and a mutex are not the same thing. However, they can be used in similar situations. Often from the point of view of instructions that are implementing parallelism, the lock() and the unlock() mechanisms serve the same purpose. Table 11–2 shows some of the fundamental differences between a mutex and a semaphore.

While the differences in semantics in Table 11–2 are important, they are often not enough to justify a completely different interface to semaphore and mutexes. Therefore, we keep our lock(), unlock(), and trylock() semi-fat interface with the caveat that the programmer must know the differences between a mutex and a semaphore. This is similar to the situation that arises with the fat interfaces of the container classes such as deque, queue, set, multiset, and so on. The container classes are related by interface but their semantics are different in certain areas. Using the notion of an interface

Table 11–2   Fundamental Differences between Mutexes and Semaphores

Characteristics of Mutexes	*Characteristics of Semaphores*
Mutexes and condition variables are shared between threads.	Semaphores are typically shared between processes, but may also be shared between threads.
A mutex is unlocked by the same threads that locked it.	A semaphore post can be performed by other than the original thread or process that held it.
A mutex is either locked or unlocked.	A semaphore is managed by its reference count state.
	The POSIX standard includes named semaphores.

class, synchronization components can be designed for mutexes, condition variables, read/write mutexes, and semaphores. Once we have these components, we can design concurrency-safe container classes, domain classes, and framework classes. We can also use the interface classes to provide a single interface to different versions of the same function library, where both versions need to be used within the same application for some reason. Sometimes the interface class can be used to bridge the gap between deprecated, obsolete functions and new functionality. We often want to insulate the application programmer from the difference between operating systems. When the System V semaphores or POSIX semaphores are used, the programmer can be provided with a consistent API using an interface class.

11.3   Maintaining the Stream Metaphor

Besides using interface classes to simplify and to create new fat interfaces for the parallel and message-passing libraries, we may also want to extend existing interfaces. For instance, the object-oriented stream metaphor can be extended to pipes, fifos, and the message passing libraries like PVM and MPI. These components are used to accomplish IPC (Inter-Process Communication), ITC (Inter-Thread Communication), and in some cases OTOC (Object-to-Object Communicaton). When communication occurs between concurrently executing threads or processes, then the communication channel may be a critical section. That is, if two or more routines are attempting to update the same pipe, fifo, or message buffer at the same time, then a race condition is present. If we are going to extend the object-oriented stream in-

terface to include components from the PVM or MPI library, then we need
to make sure that the streams we design are concurrency safe. Here is where
our synchronization components that were designed as interface classes
come in handy. Let's look at a simple `pvm_stream` class.

```
// Example 11.12 Declaration of pvm_stream class that inherits
//               mios class.

class pvm_stream : public mios{
protected:
   int TaskId;
   int MessageId;
   mutex  Mutex;
   //...
public:
   void taskId(int Tid);
   void messageId(int Mid);
   pvm_stream(int Coding = PvmDataDefault);
   void reset(int Coding = PvmDataDefault);
   pvm_stream &operator<<(string &Data);
   pvm_stream &operator>>(string &Data);
   pvm_stream &operator>>(int &Data);
   pvm_stream &operator<<(int &Data);
   //...
 };
```

This stream class will be used to encapsulate the state of the active buffer
in a PVM task. The inserter operator << and the extractor operator >> will be
used to send and retrieve messages between PVM processes. Here we only
show operators for string and `int` types. The interface for this class is far from
complete. Since this class could possibly be used with any datatype, we have
to expand the inserter and extractor definitions. Since we plan to use the
`pvm_stream` class within a multithreaded program, we want to make sure that
the `pvm_stream` object is thread safe. Therefore, we include a `mutex` class as
a member of our `pvm_stream` class. The `pvm_stream` class also encapsulates
the active buffer for the PVM task. The stream can direct the message to a
particular PVM task. The goal is to use the `ostream` and `istream` classes as a
guide for the type of functionality that the `pvm_stream` class should have. Recall that `istream` and `ostream` classes are translator classes. They translate
datatypes into generic streams of bytes for output and from generic streams of
bytes to specific datatypes on input. Using the `istream` and `ostream` classes,
the programmer does not have to get bogged down in details of what datatype
is being inserted or extracted from a stream. We want the `pvm_stream` to be-

have in the same manner. The PVM has a different function for every type that needs to be packed into or unpacked from a send or receive buffer. For instance:

```
pvm_pkdouble()
pvm_pkint()
pvm_pkfloat()
```

Figure 11–4 The class diagram showing the relationship between the major classes in the iostream class library and the class diagram for the `pvm_stream` class.

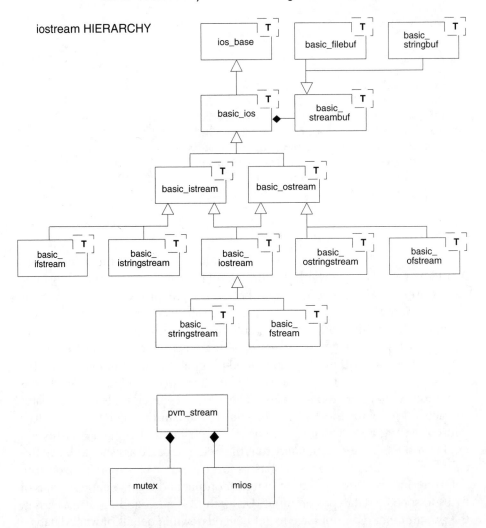

are used to pack `doubles`, `ints`, and `floats`. There are similar functions for the other datatypes that C++ uses. We would like to retain our stream metaphor where input and output is seen as a generic stream of bytes moving into or out of the program. Therefore, we define the `<<` inserter operator and the `>>` extractor operator for every type we wish to exchange between PVM tasks. Furthermore, we also model the stream state after `istream` and `ostream` classes. The `istream` and `ostream` classes have an `ios` component that is used to hold the state of the stream. The stream may be in an error state, or the stream may be in one of several different numeric states such as octal, decimal, and hexadecimal. The stream may be in a good state, a locked state, an end-of-file state, and so on. The `pvm_stream` class should have a component that maintains the state of the stream and should have methods that set, reset, and report the PVM stream state. Our `pvm_stream` class contains a `mios` component for this purpose. The `mios` component maintains the state of the stream and the active send and receive buffer. Figure 11–4 contains a class diagram showing the relationships between the major classes in the iostream class library and how the `pvm_stream` class compares.

Notice that the `istream` and `ostream` classes inherit an `ios` class. The `ios` class maintains the stream state and buffer state of the `istream` and `ostream` class. Our `mios` class plays the same role for the `pvm_stream` class. The `istream` and `ostream` classes contain the definitions for the inserter `<<` and extractor `>>` operators. The operators are defined by our `pvm_stream` class. So although our `pvm_stream` class is not related to the iostream classes by inheritance, it is related by interface. We use the interface of the iostream classes to dictate a semi-fat interface for the `pvm_stream` and `mios` classes. Notice in Figure 11–4 that the `mios` class is inherited by the `pvm_stream` class. We want to maintain the stream metaphor with the `pvm_stream` class. The notion of an interface class is used to accomplish this.

11.3.1   Overloading the <<, >> Operators for PVM Streams

Let's take a look at how the `<<` inserter operators and `>>` extractor operators are defined for the `pvm_stream` class. The `<<` inserter operator is used to wrap the `pvm_send` and `pvm_pk` routines. A method definition that looks something like:

```
// Example 11.13 Definition of <<operator for the pvm_stream
//                  class.

pvm_stream &pvm_stream::operator<<(int Data)
{
    //...
    reset();
    pvm_pkint(&Data,1,1);
    pvm_send(TaskId,MessageId);
    //...
    return(*this);
}
```

is provided for each type that will be used with the pvm_stream class. The reset() method is inherited from the mios class. This method is used to clear or initialize the send buffer. TaskId and MessageId are data members of the pvm_stream class and are set with the taskId() and messageId() methods. The inserter method allows us to send data to a PVM task with the standard stream notation:

```
int  Value = 2004;
pvm_stream   MyStream;
//...
MyStream    << Value;
//...
```

The >> extractor operators are used in a similar manner to receive messages from PVM tasks. The >> operator is used to wrap the pvm_recv() and pvmupk routines. Extractor operators can be defined as:

```
// Example 11.14 Definition of operator
//                  >> for the pvm_stream class.

pvm_stream &pvm_stream::operator>>(int &Data)
{
    int BufId;
    //...
    BufId = pvm_recv(TaskId,MessageId);
    StreamState = pvm_upkint(&Data,1,1);
    //...
    return(*this);
}
```

This type of definition will allow us to receive messages from PVM tasks using the extractor operator.

```
int Value;
pvm_stream MyStream;

MyStream >> Value;
```

Because the operator returns a reference to the `pvm_stream`, the insertion and extraction operators may be strung together:

```
Mystream << Value1 << Value2;
Mystream >>  Value3 >> Value4;
```

Using this syntax, the programmer is isolated from the more cumbersome syntax of the `pvm_send`, `pvm_pk`, `pvm_upk`, and `pvm_recv` routines and the more familiar object-oriented stream metaphor can be used. In this case, the stream represents a message buffer and the items that are inserted and extracted from the streams represent messages that are being exchanged between PVM processes. Recall that each PVM process has a separate address space. So not only do the << insertion and >> extraction operators disguise the `pvm_send` and `pvm_recv` calls, they also mask the underlying socket activity. Since the `pvm_stream` class might be used in a multithreaded environment, the insertion and extraction operators need to be thread safe.

The class diagram in Figure 11–4 shows that the `pvm_stream` class contains a `mutex` class. The `mutex` class can be used to protect the critical sections that are present in the `pvm_stream` class. The `pvm_stream` class

Figure 11–5 The interaction between the threads, the `pvm_stream` class, and the `pvm_send` and `pvm_receive` buffers.

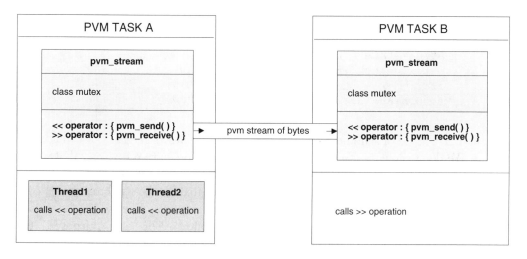

encapsulates access to the send buffer and the receive buffer. Figure 11–5 shows how threads and the `pvm_stream` class interact with the `pvm_send` and `pvm_receive` buffers.

Not only are the send and receive buffers critical sections, the `mios` class used to store the state of the `pvm_stream` class is also a critical section. The `mutex` class can be used to protect this component as well.

The `Mutex` object can be used in the call to the insertion and extraction operators.

```
// Example 11.15 Definition of operator << and operator >> for
//               the pvm_stream class.

pvm_stream &pvm_stream::operator<<(int Data)

{
   //...
   Mutex.lock();
   reset();
   pvm_pkint(&Data,1,1);
   pvm_send(TaskId,MessageId);
   Mutex.unlock();
   //...
   return(*this);

}

pvm_stream &pvm_stream::operator>>(int &Data)
{
    int BufId;
    //...
    Mutex.lock();
    BufId = pvm_recv(TaskId,MessageId);
    StreamState = pvm_upkint(&Data,1,1);
    Mutex.unlock();
    //...
    return(*this);
}
```

This kind of scheme can be used to make the `pvm_stream` class thread safe. We don't show the exception handling code or the extra processing that would be included to prevent indefinite postponement or deadlock. The idea here is to focus on the components and architectures that can be used to support concurrency. The `mutex` interface class and the `pvm_stream` class can be reused and both support concurrency programming. For our purposes, the `pvm_stream` objects are assumed to be used by the receiving and the sending PVM task. However, this is not a strict requirement. In order for the user to use the `pvm_stream` class concept with user-defined classes, the insertion operator (<<) and the extraction operator (>>) must be defined for the user-defined class.

11.4   User-Defined Classes Designed to Work with PVM Streams

To see how the user-defined class can be used with the `pvm_stream` class, we will improve on the PVM palette producing routines introduced in Chapter 6. The palette class represents a simple collection of colors. For convenience, we store the colors in a `vector<string>` named `Colors`.

We begin by declaring a `spectral_palette` class that contains friend declarations for the << inserter and >> extractor operators.

```
//Example 11.16 Declaration of spectral_palette class.

class spectral_palette : public pvm_object{
protected:
   //...
   vector<string> Colors;
public:
   spectral_palette(void);
   //...
   friend pvm_stream &operator>>(pvm_stream &In,
                                 spectral_palette &Obj);
   friend pvm_stream &operator<<(pvm_stream &Out,
                                 spectral_palette &Obj);
   //...
};
```

Notice this `spectral_palette` class in Example 11.16 inherits a `pvm_object` class. The `pvm_object` class provides the `spectral_palette` class with member access to a task id and message id. Recall that the task id and message id are used in many PVM routines. With the definition of the << operator and >> operator, `spectral_palette` objects can be sent between concurrently executing PVM tasks. The technique used with the `spectral_palette` class is a simplified approach that can be used with any user-defined class. Since the `pvm_stream` class will have operators for the built-in datatypes and for containers that hold built-in datatypes, a user-defined class need only define the << operator and >> operator to translate its representation to either a built-in datatype or a standard container that holds built-in datatypes. For instance, the << operator for the `spectral_palette` class is defined in Example 11.17.

```
//Example 11.17 Definition of operator<< for the
//               spectral_palette class.

pvm_stream &operator<<(pvm_stream &Out, spectral_palette &Obj)
{
   int N;
   string Source;
   for(N = 0;N < Obj.Colors.size();N++)
   {
      Source.append(Obj.Colors[N]);
      if( N <Obj.Colors.size() - 1){
         Source.append(" ");
      }
   }
   Out.reset();
   Out.taskId(Obj.TaskId);
   Out.messageId(Obj.MessageId);
   Out << Source;
   return(Out);
}
```

Let's closely examine the definition of this insertion operation in Example 11.17. Since the `pvm_stream` class only works with built-in types, the goal of the user-defined << operator is to *translate* the user-defined object into a sequence of user-defined datatypes. This translation process is one of the primary responsibilities of the stream classes. Here, the `spectral_palette` class will be translated into a string of colors separated by a blank. The list of colors is stored in a string named `Source`. This translation process allows the class to be used with the `pvm_stream` << operator that has been defined for the string datatype. Once these operators are defined, the programmer's API is considerably more consistent than it would be if the native versions of the Pthread library, POSIX semaphore library, and MPI library routines were called. A `spectral_palette` object can be sent to another PVM task using an << insertion operator as:

```
//Example 11.18 Using the pvm_stream and spectral_palette
//               objects.

pvm_stream  TaskStream;
spectral_palette  MyColors;

//...
TaskStream.taskId(20001);
TaskStream.messageId(1);
//...
TaskStream << MyColors;
//...
```

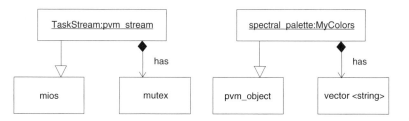

Figure 11–6 The components used to support the `TaskStream` and `MyColors` objects.

The `MyColors` object is sent to the appropriate PVM task. Figure 11–6 contains the components used to support the `TaskStream` and `MyColors` objects. Each component in Figure 11–6 can be refined and optimized individually. Each layer provides an additional level of insulation from the complexity of these components. At the highest level the programmer is only concerned about the application domain. This high level of abstraction allows the programmer to naturally represent the parallelism that the application domain requires without getting bogged down in syntax and complicated function call sequences. The components in Figure 11–6 represent the beginnings of a class library that can be used for PVM programs and multithreaded PVM programs. These same techniques can be used to communicate between concurrently executing tasks that are not part of a PVM. There are many applications that require concurrency but that do not need the complete machinery of the PVM environment. For these applications the `exec()`, `fork()`, or `pvm_spawn()` functions are sufficient. Applications that only require a few concurrently executing processes and client-server applications are good examples. Interprocess communication is also required for these non-PVM or non-MPI applications. We would also like to maintain the stream metaphor for concurrently executing processes created with the `fork-exec` sequence or `pvm_spawn`. The notion of the object-oriented stream can be extended to cover pipes and fifos.

11.5 Object-Oriented Pipes and fifos as Low-Level Building Blocks

To arrive at a design for object-oriented pipes, we start with basic characteristics and behavior that all pipes have in common. A pipe is a channel of communication between two or more processes. In order for the processes to communicate, they will transmit some sort of information between them. The information may represent data or commands to be performed. Typically, the information is translated into a sequence of data and inserted into the pipe and retrieved by a process on the other side of the pipe. The data is reassembled into meaningful data by the retrieving process. Whatever the data represents, there must be somewhere to store the data while it is in transit from one process to another. We call the storage area for the information a data buffer. Insertion and extraction operations are needed to place data into and extract data from the buffer. Before any insertion into the data buffer or extraction from a data buffer can begin, the data buffer must first exist. Object-oriented piping facilities must support an operation that creates and initializes a data buffer. Once the communications between processes have been completed, the data buffer used to hold the information will no longer be necessary. This means that our object-oriented pipe must be able to remove the data buffer after it is no longer needed. This suggests there are at least five basic components that any object-oriented piping facility should have:

- Buffer
- Insertion operation
- Extraction operation
- Creation/initialization operation
- Destruction operation

In addition to these five basic components, a pipe will have two ends. One end of the pipe will be for inserting data. The other end of the pipe will be for extracting data. These two ends can be accessed from different processes. To complete our notion of a pipe we must include an input port and an output port, which could be connected to separate processes. This gives seven basic components needed to describe our object-oriented pipe:

- Input port
- Output port
- Buffer
- Insertion operation
- Extraction operation
- Creation/initialization operation
- Buffer destruction operation

These components represent minimal core requirements for our description of a pipe. Once we have the basic components, we can identify how existing system APIs or data structures can be used to help us design an object-oriented pipe. In the same way that we use encapsulation and operator overloading to design a pvm_stream, we use the same techniques to wrap the pipe and fifo functions.

Notice that five of the seven basic components are common to many basic I/O data structures and container types. Most UNIX/Linux file services support:

- Buffers
- Buffer insertion operations
- Buffer extraction operations
- Buffer creation operations
- Buffer destruction operations

We use the notion of C++ interface classes to encapsulate the functionality provided by UNIX/Linux system services. We build object-oriented versions of the input/output services. Whereas we had to start from scratch with the pvm_stream class for the PVM library, here we can take advantage of the existing C++ standard library and the iostreams. Recall that the iostreams class library supports an object-oriented model of input and output streams. Furthermore, this object-oriented library has support for the data buffer no-

Figure 11-7 Class diagram for the major components of the iostream class.

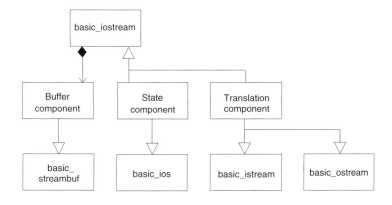

tion and all the operations upon the data buffer. Figure 11–7 shows a simple class diagram of the iostream class.

The major components of the iostream class can be described by three kinds of classes: a buffer component, a translation component, and a state component (see Hughes & Hughes, 1999). The buffer component is used as a holding area for bytes that are in transit. The translation component is responsible for translating anonymous sequences of bytes into the appropriate datatypes and data structures, and for translating data structures and datatypes in anonymous sequences of bytes. The translation component is responsible for providing the programmer with a stream of bytes metaphor where all I/O regardless of source or destination is treated as a stream of bytes. The state component encapsulates the state of the object-oriented stream. The state component maintains what type of formatting is applicable to the data bytes that are in the buffer component. The state component also maintains whether a stream has been opened in the append mode, create mode, exclusive read, exclusive write, or whether numbers will be interpreted as hexadecimal, octal, or binary. The state component also can be used to determine the error state of I/O operations on the buffer component. By querying the state component the programmer can determine if the buffer component is in a good or bad state. These three components are objects and can be used together to form a complete object-oriented stream, or separately as support objects in other tasks.

Five of the basic requirements for our pipe are already implemented in the iostreams class library. All we need to add is the notion of the input port and output port. To do this, we can examine the system services that support the use of pipes. The UNIX/Linux system calls create a pipe.

```
// Example 11.19 Using system call to create a pipe.

int main(int argc, char *argv[])
{
   //...
   int Fd[2];
   pipe(Fd);
   //...
}
```

The pipe function call is used to create a pipe data structure, which can be used between parent and child processes to communicate. If the call to pipe is successful, it will return two file descriptors. File descriptors are integers used to identify successfully opened files. In this case, the descriptors are stored in the array Fd. Fd[0] will be open for reading, and Fd[1] will be open for writing. Once these two file descriptors are created, they can be used with regular `read( )` and `write( )` functions. The `write( )` function will cause data to be inserted into the pipe via `Fd[1]`, and the `read( )` function will cause data to be extracted from the pipe via `Fd[0]`. Because the `pipe()` function returns file descriptors, access to a pipe can be accomplished using system file services. The `sysconf(_SC_OPEN_MAX)` system call can be used to determine the maximum allowable file descriptors open by a process. The `pathconf(_PC_PIPE_BUF)` call can be used to find the size of the pipe.

These two file descriptors represent our logical input port and output port, respectively. We also use these two file descriptors to provide links to the iostream class library. Specifically, they provide a link to the buffer class. The buffer component of the iostream classes has three families of classes. Table 11–3 lists the three types of buffer classes and their descriptions.

Table 11–3 Three Types of Buffer Classes	
Types of Buffer Classes	*Description*
`basic_streambuf`	Describes the behavior of various stream buffers in order to control input and output sequences of characters.
`basic_stringbuf`	Associates input and output sequences with a sequence of arbitrary characters that can be initialized from or made available as a string object.
`basic_filebuf`	Associates input and output sequences of characters with a file.

We are interested in the `filebuf` class. Whereas the `basic_streambuf` class is used as an object-oriented buffer in I/O from standard in and standard out, and the `basic_stringbuf` class is used for object-oriented memory buffers, the `filebuf` class is used as object-oriented buffers for files. By examining the interface for the `filebuf` class and the interface for its translator classes, `ifstream`, `ofstream`, and `fstream`, we can find a way to connect the file descriptors returned from the `pipe()` system call to the `iostream` objects. Figure 11–8 shows the class diagrams for the fstream family of classes.

Notice that the `ifstream`, `ofstream`, and `fstream` classes all contain the `filebuf` class. Therefore, we can use any class from the fstream family of classes to help us in creating object-oriented pipe facilities. We can connect the file descriptors returned by the `pipe()` system call either through constructors, or through the `attach()` member function.

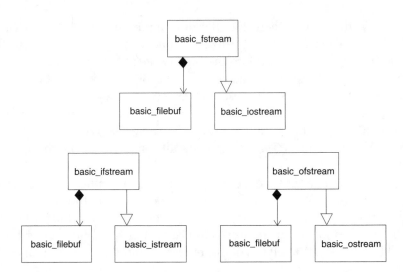

Figure 11-8 The class diagrams for the fstream family of classes.

```
Synopsis

#include <fstream>

//  UNIX systems
ifstream(int fd)
fstream(int fd)
ofstream(int fd)

//  gnu C++
void attach(int fd);
```

11.5.1 Connecting Pipes to *iostream* Objects Using File Descriptors

There are three iostream classes that we can use to connect to a pipe. They are ifstream, ofstream, and fstream. An ifstream object is used for input and an ofstream object is used for output. An fstream object can be used for both input and output. Although direct support for file descriptors and the iostreams is not yet part of the ISO standard, most UNIX and Linux C++ environments support iostream access to file descriptors. The GNU C++ iostreams library supports a file descriptor in one of the ifstream, of-stream, and fstream constructors and with the attach() method of the ifstream and ofstream classes. UNIX compilers such as Sun's C++ compiler supports file descriptors through one of the ifstream, ofstream, and fstream constructors. So the sequence of code:

```
//...
int Fd[2];
Pipe(Fd);
ifstream IPipe(Fd[0]);
ofstream OPipe(Fd[1]);
```

will create to object-oriented pipes. IPipe will be an input stream and OPipe will be an output stream. Once these streams are created they can be used to communicate between concurrently executing processes using the stream metaphor and the inserter << and >> extractor operators. For the C++ environments that support the attach() method, the file descriptor can be attached to an ifstream, ofstream, or fstream object using the syntax:

```
// Example 11.20 Creating a pipe and using the attach() function.

int Fd[2];
ofstream OPipe;
//...
pipe(Fd);
//...
OPipe.attach(Fd[1]);
//...
OPipe << Value << endl;
```

This usage of object-oriented pipes assumes the existence of some child process that can read the pipe. Program 11.1 uses the fork command to create two processes. The parent process sends a value to the child process using an iostreams-based pipe.

```
// Program 11.1

1 #include <unistd.h>
2 #include <iostream.h>
3 #include <fstream.h>
4 #include <math.h>
5 #include <sys/wait.h>
6
7
8
9
10 int main(int argc, char *argv[])
11 {
12
```

```
13    int Fd[2];
14    int Pid;
15    float Value;
16    int Status;
17    if(pipe(Fd) != 0){
18       cerr << "Error Creating Pipe " << endl;
19       exit(1);
20    }
21    Pid = fork();
22    if(Pid == 0){
23       ifstream IPipe(Fd[0]);
24       IPipe >> Value;
25       cout << "Value Received From Parent " << Value << endl;
26       IPipe.close();
27    }
28    else{
29          ofstream OPipe(Fd[1]);
30          OPipe << M_PI << endl;
31          wait(&Status);
32          OPipe.close();
33
34    }
35
36     }
```

Recall that when a fork() call is made, the return value of 0 belongs to the child process. In Program 11.1 the pipe is created on line 17. On line 29 the parent process opens the pipe for writing. The file descriptor Fd[1] is the write end of the pipe. This end of the pipe is attached to an ofstream object through the constructor on line 29. The read end of the pipe is attached to an ifstream object on line 23. The child process opens the pipe for reading. The child process has access to the file descriptor because along with the parent's environment, file descriptors are also inherited. Therefore, any files that are open in the parent will be opened in the child unless explicit instructions are given to the operating system using the fcntl system call. Besides open files being inherited, the position markers within the files remain where they are during the spawning of the child process so that the child process also has access to the position marker. When the position is moved in the parent, the marker in the child process is also moved. In this case, we were able to accomplish the stream metaphor without creating an interface class. Simply by attaching the pipe's file descriptors to the ofstream and ifstream objects we are able to use the << inserter and >> extractor operators. Likewise, any class that has the >> extraction or << insertion operators defined can be extracted from or inserted into the pipe without requiring any further work from the programmer. The parent inserts the value M_PI into the pipe on line 30. The child extracts the value from the pipe using the >> operator on line 24. The details for executing and compiling this program are contained in Program Profile 11.1.

Program Profile 11.1

Program Name
program11-1.cc

Description
Program 11.1 demonstrates the use of an object-oriented stream metaphor with anonymous system pipes. The program uses the fork() program to create two processes that will communicate using the << inserter and >> extractor operators.

Headers Required
<wait.h>, <unistd.h>, <iostream.h>, <fstream.h>, <math.h>

Compile and Link Instructions
c++ -o program11-1 program11-1.cc

Test Environment
Solaris 8, SuSE Linux 7.1

Execution Instructions
./program11-1

The gnu C++ compiler also supports the attach() method. We could use this method to connect the file descriptors to the ifstream and ofstream objects. For instance:

```
//Example 11.21 Connecting file descriptors to an ofstream
//               object.

int  main (int argc, char *argv[])
{
   int Fd[2];
   ofstream Out;
   pipe(Fd);
   Out.attach(Fd[1]);
   //...
   // Interprocess Communication
   //...
   Out.close( );
}
```

The `Out.attach(Fd[1])` call attaches an `ofstream` object to a pipe file descriptor. Now any information that is inserted into the `Out` object is actually being written to a pipe. Using extractors and insertors to perform automatic format translation is a major advantage of using the fstream family of classes in conjunction with the pipe communication. The ability to use user-defined extractors and insertors removes some of the difficulty encountered with pipe programming. So instead of requiring the explicit enumeration of data sizes of everything written and read from the pipe we use the number of elements to control read/write access, which makes the entire process simpler. In addition, this cost savings makes the parallel programming efforts easier. The technique we recommend is to use architecture to support a divide-and-conquer approach to parallelization. Once the correct components are in place, the programming becomes easier. For instance, since the pipe is tied to `ofstream` and `ifstream` objects, we are able to use the information retained by the `ios` component to determine the state of the pipe. The translation components of the iostreams can be used to perform automatic conversions as the data is inserted into one end of the pipe and extracted out of the other end. Using the pipes with the iostreams also allows the programmer to integrate the standard containers and algorithms with pipe interprocess communication. Figure 11–9 shows the relationship between the `ifstream`, `ofstream`, extractor, insertor, pipe, and the inserter and extractor when iostreams are used for interprocess communication.

Figure 11–9   The relationships between `ifstream` and `ofstream` objects, pipe, and the inserter and extractor when the iostreams are used for interprocess communication.

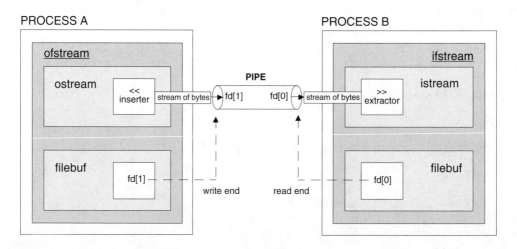

The fstream family of classes can also use the `read( )` and `write( )` member functions to read data to a pipe, and write data from a pipe.

11.5.2   Accessing Anonymous Pipes Using the `ostream_iterator`

We can also use the pipe with the `ostream_iterator` and `istream_iterator`. These iterators are generic object-oriented pointers. The `ostream_iterator` will allow you to transfer entire containers (i.e., lists, vectors, sets, queues, etc.) across the pipe. Without the use of iostreams and `ostream_iterator`, transferring containers of objects would be a very tedious and error-prone process. Table 11–4 lists the set of operations that are available on the `ostream_iterator` and `istream_iterator` class.

Table 11–4 Set of Operations Available on the `ostream_iterator` and `istream_iterator`		
Iterators	*Operations*	*Description*
`istream_iterator`	a == b	Equivalence relation
	a != b	Nonequivalence relation
	*a	Dereference
	++ r	Preincrementation
	r ++	Postincrementation
`ostream_iterator`	++ r	Preincrementation
	r ++	Postincrementation

Typically, these iterators are used with the iostreams classes and the standard algorithms. The `ostream_iterator` is a sequential write-only iterator. Once an item has been accessed, the programmer cannot go back to it without starting the iteration over. The pipe is treated like a sequence container when used with these iterators. This means that when the pipe is connected to the iostreams through `ostream_iterator` and the file descriptors, we can apply standard algorithm type processing to the input from a pipe or the input to a pipe. The reason these iterators can be used in conjunction with pipes is the connection between the iterators and the iostream classes. The diagram in Figure 11–10 shows the relationship between the I/O iterators and the iostream classes.

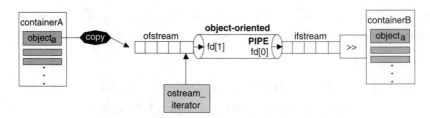

Figure 11–10   The relationship between the I/O iterators and the iostream classes.

Figure 11–10 also shows how these classes interact with the notion of our object-oriented pipe. Let's take a close look at how the `ostream_iterator` is used with an `ostream` object. If a pointer is incremented, we expect it to point at the next location in memory. When the `ostream_iterator` is incremented, it moves or points to the next position in the output stream. When we assign a value to a dereferenced pointer, we are placing that value at the location that the pointer points to. When we assign a value to an `ostream_iterator`, we are placing that value in the output stream. If that output stream is connected to `cout`, then the value will be displayed on the standard out. If we declare an `ostream_iterator` object such as:

```
ostream_iterator<int>  X(cout,"\n");
```

Then X is an object of type `ostream_iterator`. The increment operation:

```
X++;
```

causes X to move to the next position in the output stream. The statement:

```
*X = Y;
```

causes Y to be displayed on standard out. This is because the assignment operator = has been overloaded to use an `ostream` object. The declaration:

```
ostream_iterator<int>  X(cout, "\n");
```

caused X to be constructed with a `cout` as the stream. The other argument in the constructor is the delimiter that will automatically be placed after every int that is inserted into the stream. The declaration for the `ostream_iterator` looks like this:

```
//Example 11.22 Declaration of the ostream_iterator class.

template <class _Tp>
class ostream_iterator {
protected:
    ostream* _M_stream;
    const char* _M_string;
```

```
public:
   typedef output_iterator_tag iterator_category;
   typedef void                value_type;
   typedef void                difference_type;
   typedef void                pointer;
   typedef void                reference;

   ostream_iterator(ostream& __s) : _M_stream(&__s), _M_string(0) {}
   ostream_iterator(ostream& __s, const char* __c)
    : _M_stream(&__s), _M_string(__c)   {}
    ostream_iterator<_Tp>& operator=(const _Tp& __value) {
    *_M_stream << __value;
   if (_M_string) *_M_stream << _M_string;
      return *this;
   }
   ostream_iterator<_Tp>& operator*() { return *this; }
   ostream_iterator<_Tp>& operator++() { return *this; }
   ostream_iterator<_Tp>& operator++(int) { return *this; }
};
```

The constructor for the `ostream_iterator` accepts a reference to an `os-tream` object. The `ostream_iterator` class has an aggregate relationship with the `ostream` class. The `istream_iterator` has just the opposite use of the `ostream_iterator`. It is used with `istream` objects instead of `ostream` objects. If `istream_iterator` and `ostream_iterator` objects are connected to `iostream` objects that in turn are connected to pipe file descriptors, then every time the `istream_iterator` is incremented, the pipe is being read, and every time the `ostream_iterator` is incremented, the pipe is being written. To demonstrate how these components work together, we have two programs: Programs 11.2 and 11.2b that use anonymous pipes to communicate. Program 11.2 is the parent and Program 11.2b is the child. The parent uses the `fork()` and `execl()` system calls to create the child process. Although file descriptors are inherited by the child, their values are immediately available to Program 11.2b because an `execl()` call has been made.

```
// Program 11.2

10 int main(int argc, char *argv[])
11 {
12
13    int Size,Pid,Status,Fd1[2],Fd2[2];
14    pipe(Fd1); pipe(Fd2);
15    strstream Buffer;
16    char Value[50];
17    float Data;
```

```
18    vector<float> X(5,2.1221), Y;
19    Buffer << Fd1[0] << ends;
20    Buffer >> Value;
21    setenv("Fdin",Value,1);
22    Buffer.clear();
23    Buffer << Fd2[1] << ends;
24    Buffer >> Value;
25    setenv("Fdout",Value,1);
26    Pid = fork();
27    if(Pid != 0){
28       ofstream OPipe;
29       OPipe.attach(Fd1[1]);
30       ostream_iterator<float> OPtr(OPipe,"\n");
31       OPipe << X.size() << endl;
32       copy(X.begin(),X.end(),OPtr);
33       OPipe << flush;
34       ifstream IPipe;
35       IPipe.attach(Fd2[0]);
36       IPipe >> Size;
37       for(int N = 0; N < Size;N++)
38       {
39          IPipe >> Data;
40          Y.push_back(Data);
41       }
42       wait(&Status);
43       ostream_iterator<float> OPtr2(cout,"\n");
44       copy(Y.begin(),Y.end(),OPtr2);
45       OPipe.close();
46       IPipe.close();
47    }
48    else{
49          execl("./program11-2b","program11-2b",NULL);
50    }
51
52    return(0);
53 }
```

In lines 21 and 25, the setenv() system call is used to pass the values of file descriptors to the child. This is possible because the child process inherits the environment of the parent process. We can set environment variables within a program using the setenv() system calls. So, in this case, we set:

```
Fdin=filedesc;
Fdout=filedesc;
```

The child process then uses the `getenv()` system call to retrieve the values of `Fdin` and `Fdout`. The value in `Fdin` will be the read end of the pipe for the child and the value of `Fdout` will be the write end. Using the `setenv()` and `getenv()` system calls provide a simple form of IPC between parent and child processes. The pipes are created on line 14. On line 29 the parent attaches to one end of the pipe for writing using the `attach()` method. Once the attach is performed, any data inserted into the `OPipe` `ofstream` object will be written to the pipe. An `ostream_iterator` is connected to the `OPipe` object on line 30 using:

```
ostream_iterator<float> OPtr(OPipe,"\n");
```

This causes the iterator `OPtr` to refer to `OPipe`. The `"\n"` will be inserted as a delimiter after every insertion. Using `OPtr` we may insert any number of `float` values to the pipe. We can attach more than one iterator with different types to pipe. However, this does require that on the receiving end data is extracted using the appropriate types. In Program 11.2 the number of elements is first inserted into the pipe using:

```
OPipe <<  X.size() << endl;
```

The actual elements are sent using one of the C++ standard algorithms.

```
copy(X.begin(),X.end(),OPtr);
```

The `copy()` algorithm copies the contents of its container into the container associated with the target iterator. Here the target iterator is `OPtr`. `OPtr` is connected to the `OPipe` so `copy()` causes the entire contents of the container to be written to the pipe in one line of code. This demonstrates how the standard algorithms can be used to help with the communication in parallel programming or distributed programming environments. Here the copy is sending information from one process to another process in a different address space. These processes are executing concurrently and the `copy()` algorithm makes the communication between the processes considerably easier. We emphasize this approach because everything that can be done to make the logic for a parallel or distributed program simpler should be done. Interprocess communication is one of the issues that complicates parallel and distributed programming. The C++ algorithms, the iostreams, and the `ostream_iterator` help to reduce that complexity. The `flush` manipulator on line 33 ensures that the data is moved along the pipe.

Program Profile 11.2

Program Name
program11-2.cc

Description
Program uses the iostreams and the ostream_iterator to send the contents of a vector container over an anonymous pipe.

Headers Required
<algorithm>, <fstream>, <vector>, <iterator>, <stdlib.h>, <string.h>,<unistd.h>

Compile and Link Instructions
c++ -o program11-2   program11-2.cc

Test Environment
SuSE Linux 7.1, 6.2

Execution Instructions
./program11-2

In Program 11-2b on line 36 the child will get the number of elements to be retrieved from the pipe first and then it uses the istream object IPipe to retrieve the objects from the pipe.

```
// Program 11.2b

11 class multiplier{
12   float X;
13 public:
14   multiplier(float Value) { X = Value;}
15   float &operator()(float Y) {   X = (X * Y);return(X);}
16 };
17
18
19 int main(int argc,char *argv[])
20 {
21   char Value[50];
22   int Fd[2];
23   float Data;
24   vector<float> X;
25   int NumElements;
26   multiplier N(12.2);
27   strcpy(Value,getenv("Fdin"));
```

```
28    Fd[0] = atoi(Value);
29    strcpy(Value,getenv("Fdout"));
30    Fd[1] = atoi(Value);
31    ifstream IPipe;
32    ofstream OPipe;
33    IPipe.attach(Fd[0]);
34    OPipe.attach(Fd[1]);
35    ostream_iterator<float> OPtr(OPipe,"\n");
36    IPipe >> NumElements;
37    for(int N = 0;N < NumElements;N++)
38    {
39      IPipe >> Data;
40      X.push_back(Data);
41    }
42    OPipe << X.size() << endl;
43    transform(X.begin(),X.end(),OPtr,N);
44    OPipe << flush;
45    return(0);
46
47 }
```

The child process retrieves the items from the pipe, inserts them into a vector class, and then performs a mathematical transformation on each element of the vector as it is sending it back to the parent. The mathematical transformation occurs on line 43 using the standard C++ transform algorithm and a user-defined multiplier class. The transform algorithm applies an operation to each element in a container and then inserts the results into the target container. Here, the target container is Optr, which is connected to an OPipe object. The required headers for Program 11.2b are shown in Program Profile 11.2b.

Program Profile 11.2b

Program Name
program11-2b.cc

Description
Child process that is launched by Program 11.2. This program uses an ifstream object to receive the contents of a container that are sent from Program 11.2. The program uses a ostream_iterator object and the standard transform algorithm to send information back through the pipe to the parent.

Headers Required

```
<iostream>, <algorithm>, <fstream>, <vector>, <iterator>,
<stdlib.h>, <string.h>, <unistd.h>
```

Compile and Link Instructions

```
c++ -o program11-2b program11-2b.cc
```

Execution Instructions

This program is spawned by Program 11.2.

Although the iostreams classes, istream_iterator, and ostream_iterator make pipe programming easy, they do not change the behavior of the system pipe construct. The blocking issues and the issues concerning the correct order to open and close the pipes discussed in Chapter 5 still apply. The underlying mechanisms of the same object-oriented programming techniques reduce the complexity of parallel and distributed programming.

11.5.3   fifos (Named Pipes), iostreams, and the ostream_iterator Classes

The techniques we used to implement object-oriented anonymous pipes had two setbacks. First, any processes involved in interprocess communication need access to the file descriptors returned from the pipe() system call. So there is the issue of getting these file descriptors to all of the processes involved. This was straightforward because the processes that were created in Programs 11.1, 11.2a, and 11.2b had parent–child relationships, which leads us to the second problem. The processes using unnamed pipes need to be related, although this requirement could be subverted with a descriptor-passing scheme. The fifo (First In-First Out) structure is the solution to the problem. Its most important advantage is it can be accessed by unrelated processes. The processes do need to be on the same machine but otherwise don't require any relationship. The processes may be running programs implemented in different languages using different programming paradigms (e.g., generic and object-oriented). Crowd computations and other peer-to-peer configurations can take advantage of fifo (sometimes called the named pipe) because in the UNIX and Linux environment the fifo has a user-defined filename in the system and is somewhat of a permanent structure (in contrast to anonymous pipes). The fifo is a one-way structure, that is, the user of a named pipe in the UNIX environment should open it for either reading or writing, but not both. Named pipes created in the UNIX environment remain in the file system until they are explicitly removed using `unlink( )` from within a program, or some form of deletion at the command prompt such as the rm command. Named pipes are given the equivalent of a file-name when they are created. Any process that knows the name of a pipe and has the necessary access permissions can open, read, and write the pipe.

To connect the anonymous pipes to the `ifstream` and `ofstream` objects, we used the nonstandard file descriptor connection. File descriptors and the iostreams are not yet tightly coupled by the ISO C++ standard. We are a lot safer using the fifo. The special file type fifo is accessed through a filename in the file system. The connection with the C++ `ifstream` and `ofstream` classes is supported. So in the same way that we simplified IPC using iostream classes with the anonymous pipe, we make fifo access easy. So the fifo that has the same basic functionality as the anonymous pipe allows us to extend the communication between unrelated classes. However, each program involved will still have to know the names of the fifos. It seems like the same restriction as we encountered with the file descriptors. However, the fifo is a definite improvement. First, only the system determines what the available file descriptors are when the anonymous pipe is opened. This is out of the programmer's control. Second, there is a limit to the number of file descriptors the system has. Third, since fifos are user-defined names, there is no limit to the names that may be used. The file descriptors must belong to previously and successfully opened files. fifo names are just names. The fifo name is user-specified; file descriptors are system-specified. Filenames are associated with `ifstream`, `fstream`, and `ofstream` objects using either the constructor or the `open()` method. Program 11.3a uses the constructor to associate the `ofstream` and `ifstream` objects with the fifo.

```
// Program 11.3

14 using namespace std;
15
16 const int FMode = S_IRUSR | S_IWUSR | S_IRGRP | S_IROTH;
17
18 int main(int argc, char *argv[])
19 {
20
21    int Pid,Status,Size;
22    double  Value;
25    mkfifo("/tmp/channel.1",FMode);
26    mkfifo("/tmp/channel.2",FMode);
```

```
28    vector<double> X(100,13.0);
29    vector<double> Y;
30    ofstream OPipe("/tmp/channel.1",ios::app);
31    ifstream IPipe("/tmp/channel.2");
32    OPipe << X.size() << endl;
33    ostream_iterator<double> Optr(OPipe,"\n");
34    copy(X.begin(),X.end(),Optr);
35    OPipe << flush;
36    IPipe >> Size;
37    for (int N = 0;N < Size; N++)
38    {
39       IPipe >> Value;
40       Y.push_back(Value);
41    }
42
43    IPipe.close();
44    OPipe.close();
45    unlink("/tmp/channel.1");
46    unlink("/tmp/channel.2");
47    cout <<  accumulate(Y.begin(),Y.end(),-13.0) << endl;
48
49    return(0);
50 }
```

There are two fifos in Program 11.3a. Recall that fifos are one-way communication components. So if processes are to exchange data, at least two fifos are necessary. In Program 11.3a the fifos are called `channel.1` and `channel2`. Notice on line 16 the permissions flags that will be set for the fifos. These are the most generic settings for UNIX/Linux setting. These permissions indicate that the owner of the fifo has read and write access and all others have read-only access to the fifo. On line 30 `channel.1` is open for *output only*. We could have also accomplished this by:

```
OPipe.open("/tmp/channel.1", ios::app);
```

This says that the fifo will be opened in append mode. Program 11-3a uses the `copy()` algorithm to insert the objects into the `OPipe fstream` object and indirectly into the fifo. We could also use a `fstream` object here if we declare it as:

```
fstream  OPipe("/tmp/channel.1", ios::out | ios::app);
```

This restricts the communication to output only in append mode. If we don't use the `ios::app` flag, the `ofstream` object on line 30 will make a failed attempt at creating the fifo. Unfortunately, this will not work. Creation of fifos is the province of the `mkfifo()` routine. Lines 40 and 41 Program 11.3a deletes the fifos from the file system. At this point in the processing any processes that happen to still have the fifo open will continue to be able to access it. However, the name will be removed. So those processes will not be able to call `open()` or construct any new `ofstream` or `ifstream` objects based on the filename that has been unlinked. On lines 32–34, `ostream_iterator` and `ofstream` objects are used to insert items into the fifo. Notice that Program 11.3a does not do any forking and does not have any child processes to communicate with. Program 11.3 depends on some other program to read from `channel.1` or at least to write to `channel.2`. If there is no program executing at the time to access the fifo, then Program 11.3a will block. The implementation specifics are contained in Program Profile 11.3a.

Program Profile 11.3a

Program Name
`program11-3.cc`

Description
Uses an `ostream_iterator` object and an `ofstream` object to send a container object through a fifo. Extracts information from a fifo using an `ifstream` object.

Headers Required
`<unistd.h>`, `<iomanip>`, `<algorithm>`, `<fstream.h>`, `<vector>`, `<iterator>`
`<strstream.h>`, `<stdlib.h>`, `<sys/wait.h>`, `<sys/types.h>`, `<sys/stat.h>`
`<fcntl.h>`, `<numeric>`

Compile and Link Instructions
`c++ -o program11-3 program11-3.cc`

Test Environment
SuSE Linux 7.1, gcc 2.95.2, Solaris 8, Sun Workshop 6

Execution Instructions
`./program11-3 & program11-3b`

Notes
Start Program 11.3a first. Program 11.3b has a sleep statement to account for the lack of real synchronization.

Program 11.3b reads from `channel.1` and writes to `channel.2`.

```
//Program 11.3b Reads from channel1 and write to channel2.

10 using namespace std;
11
12 class multiplier{
13   double X;
14 public:
15   multiplier(double Value) { X = Value;}
16   double &operator()(double Y) {   X = (X * Y);return(X);}
17 };
18
19
20 int main(int argc,char *argv[])
21 {
22
23   double Size;
24   double Data;
25   vector<double> X;
26   multiplier R(1.5);
27   sleep(15);
28   fstream IPipe("/tmp/channel.1");
29   ofstream OPipe("/tmp/channel.2",ios::app);
30   if(IPipe.is_open()){
31   IPipe >> Size;
32   }
33   else{
34        exit(1);
35   }
36   cout << "Number of Elements " << Size << endl;
37   for(int N = 0;N < Size;N++)
38   {
39     IPipe >> Data;
40     X.push_back(Data);
41   }
42   OPipe << X.size()   << endl;
43   ostream_iterator<double> Optr(OPipe,"\n");
44   transform(X.begin(),X.end(),Optr,R);
45   OPipe << flush;
46   OPipe.close();
47   IPipe.close();
48   return(0);
49
50 }
```

Notice that Program 11.3a opens `channel.1` for output and Program 11.3b opens `channel.1` for input. Keep in mind that fifos are one-way communication mechanisms. Don't try to send data both ways! Another advantage of using iostreams in conjunction with fifos is that you have access to the iostream methods as they would be applied to the fifo. For instance, on line 30 we use the `basic_filebuf()` method `is_open()` to determine whether the fifo is open. If it isn't Program 11.3b doesn't continue any further. The implementation specifics for Programs 11.3a and 11.3b are provided in Program Profiles 11.3a and 11.3b.

Program Profile 11.3b

Program Name
program11-3b.cc

Description
This program reads objects from the fifo using a `ifstream` object. It uses the `ostream_iterator` and the standard `transform` algorithm to send information through the fifo.

Headers Required
`<unistd.h>`, `<iomanip>`, `<algorithm>`, `<fstream.h>`, `<vector>`
`<iterator>`, `<strstream.h>`,`<stdlib.h>`, `<sys/wait.h>`,
`<sys/types.h>`, `<sys/stat.h>`, `<fcntl.h>`, `<numeric>`

Compile and Link Instructions
c++ -o program11-3b program11-3b.cc

Test Environment
SuSE Linux 7.1 , gcc 2.95.2, Solaris 8, Sun Workshop 6.0

Execution Instructions
program11.3 & program11-3b

Notes
Start Program 11.3a first. Program 11.3b has a sleep statement to account for the lack of real synchronization.

11.5.3.1   fifo Interface Classes

In addition to simplifying the IPC using `iostreams`, `istream_iterator`, and `ostream_iterator`, we can also simplify matters by encapsulating the fifo into a fifo class.

```
// Example 11.23 Declaration of the fifo class.

class fifo{
   mutex Mutex;
   //...
protected:
   string  Name;
public:
   fifo &operator<<(fifo &In, int X);
   fifo &operator<<(fifo &In, char X);
   fifo &operator>>(fifo &Out, float X);
   //...
};
```

Using this technique, we can easily create fifos in the constructor. We can pass them easily as parameters and return values. We can use them in conjunction with the standard container classes. The construction of such a component greatly reduces the amount of code needed to use fifos. It provides opportunities for type safety and generally allows the programmer to work at a higher level.

11.6   Framework Classes Components for Concurrency

A framework is a class or collection of classes that has a predefined structure and represents a generalized pattern of work. In the same manner that programs provide general solutions to specific problems, frameworks provide specific solutions to classes of problems. That is, an application framework captures the *general flow of control* for an entire range of programs that all solve or represent problems in a similar fashion. Put another way, an application framework represents a single solution to a family of problems. Frameworks are generic *mini self-contained* applications. The framework serves as a blueprint for the mini-application. It embodies the fundamental structure or skeleton that the application will have without providing the application details. The framework class specifies the relationships, responsibilities, patterns of work, and protocols between software parts in an object-oriented architecture without providing the implementation details. For instance, we can design a language processor class that captures the general pattern of work for an entire range of applications. The specific *pattern of work* that the language processor captures is the work involved in taking some input language and translating that language to some output form. This framework consists of a few common software parts:

- Validation components
- Tokenizer components
- Parser components
- Syntax analysis components
- Lexical analysis components

These software parts can be combined to form a very familiar pattern of work:

```
// Example 11.24 Declarations for the language_processor
//               class and definition for the process_input
//               method.

class  language_processor {
   //...
protected:
   virtual bool getString(void) = 0;
   virtual bool validateString(void) = 0;
   virtual bool parseString(void) = 0;
   //...
public:
   bool process_input(void);
};

bool language_processor::process_input(void)
{
   getString();
   validateString();
   parseString();
   //...
   compareTokens();
   //...
}
```

First, the `language_processor` class is an abstract base class because it contains pure virtual functions:

```
virtual bool getString(void) = 0;
virtual bool validateString(void) = 0;
virtual bool parseString(void) = 0;
```

This means it is not meant to be used directly. It serves as a blueprint for derived classes. The other important thing to note is the `process_input()` method. This method captures the general pattern of work that the `language_processor` class is meant to generalize. In many ways this is what distinguishes framework classes from other types of classes. The framework not only contains generalized structure and relationships between components, it also captures predefined patterns of work and sequences of action. It provides the skeleton for the pattern of work without providing the implementation details. In this case, the pattern of work is specified by a set of pure virtual functions. So the framework class does not specify how these things are to be done—it only specifies that they should be done and they should be done in a certain order. The derived class has to provide the implementations for the pure virtual functions. The framework class emphasizes the responsibilities of the derived class. Framework classes by definition are contract classes. They require two parties in order to work properly. The framework class does its part but the derived class must provide the implementation details for the pure virtual functions. The commonly found sequence of actions performed by the `process_input()` method are found in:

Compilers	Command interpreters
Natural language processors	Encryption/decryption routines
Compression/decompression	File transfer protocols
Graphical user interfaces	Device control, etc.

So by properly designing the `language_processssor` class, the pattern of work for an entire range of applications is captured. If the sequence can be properly recorded and tested and debugged, then a wide range of applications can be developed faster by reusing the `language_processor` framework class.

The notion of a framework class is also useful in developing applications that have concurrency requirements. Specifically, the use of agent frameworks and blackboard frameworks captures the basic structure of concurrency and patterns of work within those structures. Michael Wooldridge, in *Reasoning About Rational Agents*, gives us a generalized agent control loop:

```
Algorithm: Agent control Loop

B = B0
while true do
  get next percept p
  B = brf(B,p)
  I = deliberate(B)
```

```
   Π  = plan(B,I)
   execute(Π)
end while
```

This pattern of work is performed by a wide range of rational agents. If you are developing a program that uses rational agents, then the chances are good that this sequence of actions will be found in your program. This is exactly the type of sequence of action that frameworks are good at capturing. For the agent control loop, the `brf()`, `deliberate()`, `plan()` functions will be pure abstract virtual. The agent control loop specifies what order these functions should be called and how they should be called, and the fact that they should be called. However, what the functions actually do will be determined by a derived class. Once this agent control loop is properly defined, then an entire class of problems has been solved. It turns out that systems consisting of multiple agents executing concurrently are becoming a standard for implementing parallel programming applications. These systems are often called *multiagent systems.* We discuss agent-oriented architectures in Chapter 12. It is important to note that agent framework classes help to reduce the complexity of developing multiagent systems and multiagent systems are becoming the preferred architecture for implementing medium- to large-scale applications that require concurrency or massive parallelism.

In addition to providing the pattern of work that will be useful for parallel or distributed systems, the framework class can capture the structure with respect to synchronization components such as object-oriented mutexes, semaphores, and message streams. The blackboard stucture is a useful medium for multiple agents to communicate through. The blackboard will be a critical region because multiple agents will be able to read and write to it simultaneously. Therefore, the framework class should provide the basic structure for the relationships between the agents, the synchronization components, and the blackboard. For instance, Example 11.25 contains two methods that the framework could use to access the blackboard.

```
// Example 11.25 Definition of recordMessge() and getMessage()
//               methods for the agent_framework class.

 int agent_framework::recordMessage(void)
{

   Mutex.lock();
   BlackBoardStream <<  Agent[N].message();
   Mutex.unlock();
}
```

```
int agent_framework::getMessage(void)
{
   Mutex.lock();
   BlackBoardStream >> Values;
   Agent[N].perceive(Values);
   Mutex.unlock();
}
```

Figure 11-11   The basic structure of the `agent_framework` class and how it relates to the blackboard.

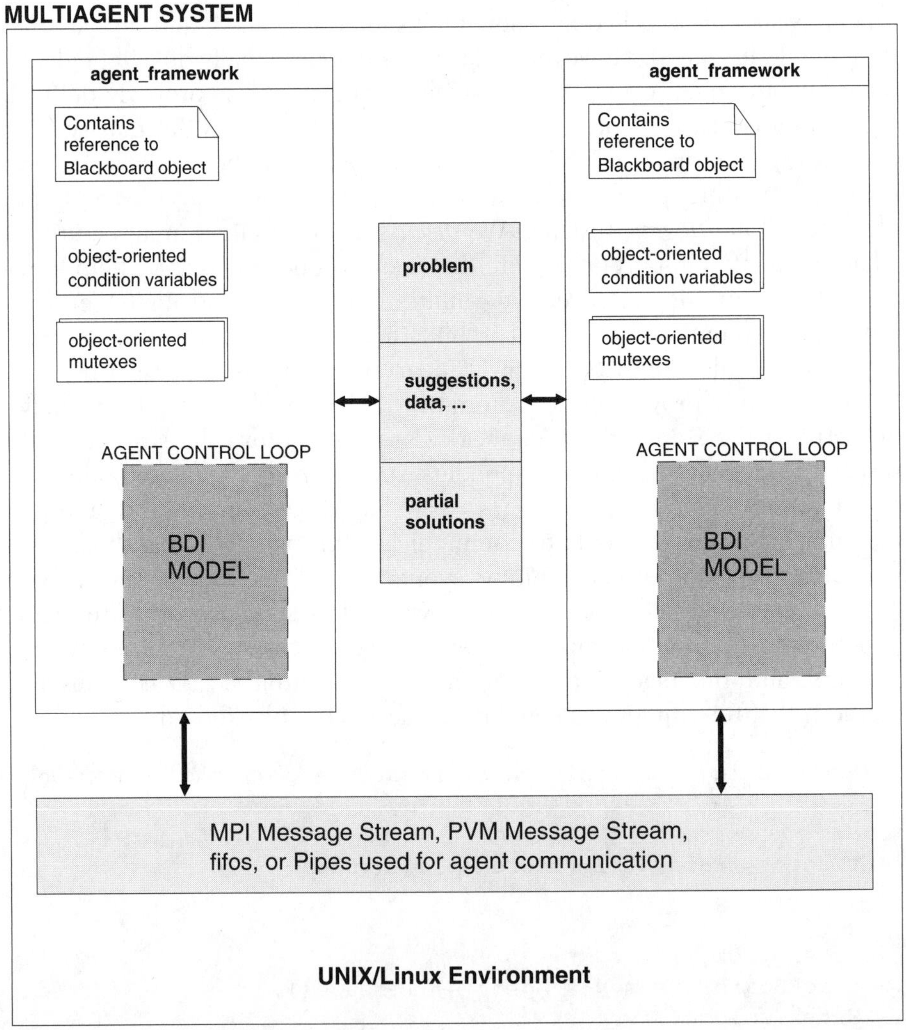

MULTIAGENT SYSTEM

Here the framework class will protect the access to the blackboard by using synchronization objects. So when agents read messages from or write messages to the blackboard, the synchronization is already provided by the framework. The programmer does not have to worry about synchronizing blackboard access. Figure 11–11 contains the basic structure of our agent framework and how the framework relates to a blackboard.

Notice that the framework encapsulates the object-oriented mutexes and condition variables. The agent framework in Figure 11–11 will use either MPI or PVM message streams to communicate in a MPI- or PVM-based system. Recall these message streams were designed as interface classes and allow the programmer to use the iostream metaphor to access the PVM or MPI class. If MPI or PVM are not used, the agents can communicate using sockets, pipes, or even shared memory. In either case, we recommend that the synchronization primitives be implemented using interface classes since that will make them simpler to use. The blackboard in Figure 11–11 is object-oriented and takes advantage of the genericity provided by template classes. This also simplifies the concurrency requirements. The agents executing concurrently provide an effective model for parallel and distributed programming.

Summary

The challenges to parallel programming introduced in Chapter 2 can be reasonably approached using the building blocks that we introduced in this chapter. The importance of the interface class in simplifying the use of function libraries cannot be overstated. The interface class introduces consistency of API by wrapping the function calls of libraries such as MPI or PVM. Type safety and reuse is introduced through interface classes. The interface class allows the programmer to work with a familiar metaphor, as in the case of PVM streams or MPI streams. IPC is simplified by connecting pipe or message streams to iostreams and overriding the << inserter and >> extractor operators for user-defined classes. The `ostream_iterator` class proves to be very useful in sending entire container objects and their contents between processes. The `ostream_iterator` and `istream_iterator` also provide the glue between the standard algorithms and IPC components and techniques. Since a large number of parallel or distributed applications use the message-passing model, any technique that simplifies passing various datatypes between processes will simplify the programming required for the application. Using iostreams, the `ostream_iterator` and `istream_iterator` does this simplification. The framework class is introduced here as the basic building block of concurrency applications. We consider classes like the mutex classes, condition variable classes, and the stream classes to low-level components that should be hidden from the programmer within the framework class (where possible!). When building medium- to large-scale applications that require concurrency, the programmer should not have to focus on these low-level components. Ideally, the framework will be the base-level building block for concurrency approaches, which we introduce in the remainder of this book. The framework will provide us with patterns for peer-to-peer and client-server interaction. We can have numeric frameworks, database frameworks, agent frameworks, blackboard frameworks, GUI frameworks, and so on. The approach that we advocate for implementing concurrency requirements builds applications from a collection of frameworks that already have the proper synchronization components wired into the proper relationships. In Chapters 12 and 13, we take a closer look at frameworks that support concurrency. We also introduce the use of standard C++ algorithms, containers, and function objects to manage the creation and spawning of multiple tasks or threads in applications that require concurrency.

12 Implementing Agent-Oriented Architectures

Much remains to be done before we understand how people construct their problem representations and the role those representations play in problem solving. But we know enough already to suggest that the representations people use—both propositional and pictorial—can be simulated by computers.

—*Herbert A. Simon*, Machine as Mind (Android Epistemology)

In this Chapter

What are Agents? • What is Agent-Oriented Programming? • Basic Agent Components • Implementing Agents in C++ • Multiagent Systems • Summary

If sequential (procedure-based) programming solutions were practical in every situation, then there would be no need for parallel or distributed programming techniques. In many situations, sequential programming techniques are simply inadequate for the demands and the sophistication of today's computer users. As developers scramble for new approaches to meet the growing challenges that user requirements present, alternative software models are created. Better ways to organize and think about how software should be constructed are discovered. Structured programming was presented as an improvement over procedureless goto/jump-filled programming. Object-oriented programming was presented as an improvement over structured programming. In many ways agents and agent-oriented programming is an improvement over object-oriented programming. Agents present yet another (more sophisticated) method for organizing and thinking about distributed/parallel programs.

12.1   What are Agents?

There was a lot of controversy over what constituted an object when object programming was initially introduced. There is a similar controversy over exactly what constitutes an agent. Many proponents define agents as autonomous, continuously executing programs that act on behalf of a user. However, this definition can be applied to some UNIX daemons, or even some device drivers. Others add the requirements that the agent must have special knowledge of the user, must execute in an environment inhabited by other agents, and must function only within the specified environment. These requirements would exclude other programs considered to be agents by some. For instance, many e-mail agents act alone and may function in multiple environments. In addition to agent requirements, various groups in the agent community have introduced terms like *softbot, knowbot, software broker,* and *smart object* to describe agents. We define the term *agent* iteratively in this chapter. We start with some simple, agreed-upon partial definitions and construct a definition that is practical for C++ programmers.

One commonly found definition defines an agent *as an entity that functions continuously and autonomously in an environment in which other processes take place and other agents exist.* Although it is tempting to accept this definition and move on, we cannot because it too easily describes other kinds of software constructions. Many object-oriented components function continuously and autonomously in an environment in which other processes take place and other objects exist. In fact, many CORBA-based client-server systems fit this description! So if we exchange the word *object* for *agent* in this definition it accurately describes many object-oriented systems. A look at a more formal source, the Foundation for Intelligent Physical Agents (FIPA) specification defines the term *agent* accordingly:

> An Agent is the fundamental actor in a domain. It combines one or more service capabilities into a unified and integrated execution model which can include access to external software, human users and communication facilities.

While this definition has a more structured feel, it also needs further clarification because many servers (some object-oriented and some not) fit this definition. This definition as is would include too many types of programs and software constructs to be useful. Although we rely on the FIPA specification where we discuss agents, this basic definition requires further work.

12.1.1   Agents: A First-Cut Definition

One of the reasons that the word *object* can in so many instances replace the word *agent* in so many definitions and descriptions of agent is because agents are inherently based on objects. In fact, our initial requirement on the definition for an agent is that it first fit the definition of an object[1], that is, we designate an agent as a certain kind of object. This chapter is largely about what makes an agent different from other classes of objects. In the same sense that C++ has support for interface classes, container classes, and framework classes, we can also designate *agent* classes. This brings us to our second requirement on the definition of agents within a C++ environment. In C++ an agent is implemented using the notion of a class. The different types of classes are distinguished by how they function or how they are structured. For instance, a container class describes an object used to hold or contain other objects. An interface class is used to describe an object that transforms or adapts the interface of another object. A framework class describes an object that contains a pattern of work that is common to a family of other objects. An agent class will be used to define objects that have what Yohav Shoham (1997) describes as a mental state: "The mental state will contain such components as beliefs, capabilities, choices, and commitments." This mental state is often partially summarized by the Belief Desires and Intentions (BDI) model. We extend the BDI model to include *actions*. So in our first-cut definition of agents, we define an agent as a piece of software meeting the following three requirements:

1. A certain type of object (not all objects are agents)
2. Implemented using the notion of a class (encapsulation, inheritance, and polymorphism are important for agents!)
3. Contains a set of behaviors and attributes that *must* include *beliefs, desires, intentions,* and *actions*

For our purposes, agents are by definition *rational software components.* Before we define agents further, lets look at the types of agents that are commonly implemented.

---

[1]When we use the term object in the definition of agent we include its AI cousins: actor and frame.

12.1.2   Types of Agents

Several categories of agents have emerged. Although not every agent fits into one of these categories, the categories are generally descriptive of the majority of agents in practical use. Table 12–1 contains five major categories of agents. Obviously there are hybrid agents that fit into more than one category at the same time. There are no hard and fast rules that determine which agents fit into any particular category. These categories are presented for convenience and as a starting point when trying to classify agents that you may have to develop or work with.

Table 12–1   Five Major Categories of Agents

Agent Categories	Description
Interface agents	Represent the next generation of human–computer interaction. These agents provide new user interfaces to the computer.
Search agents	Perform various types of information retrieval.
Monitor/control agents	Patrol, observe, audit, manage, and monitor devices and conditions, data, and processes.
Acquisition agents	Authorized to acquire some good or service on behalf of the user.
Decision support agents	Provide analysis, information synthesis, condition and data interpretation, planning, and evaluation.

Table 12–1 represents a functional breakdown of the agent categories. It does not specify any particular components that the agents must have. It only specifies the types of activities that the agents engage in. In fact, these categories are not the exclusive domain of agents. Other classes of software such as expert systems and object-oriented systems have categorizations very similar to these. In some cases, the only difference is that we are talking about agents as opposed to objects or expert systems.

12.1.3   What is the Difference between Objects and Agents?

One of the fundamental requirements for an agent is that it first meets the conditions of object orientation. So agents and objects have more things in common than many of the agent proponents would like to admit. It is the function and construction of the object that places it into the agent column. Objects are by definition self-contained and exhibit a certain amount of autonomy. Once the degree of autonomy crosses a certain threshold and the object is given cognitive data structures such as those found in the BDI model, then the object is an agent. An autonomous rational object is an agent.[2] An object is considered rational when it has:

- Methods that implement some form of deduction, induction, or abduction
- Data members that are implementations of cognitive data structures

Keep in mind that in object-oriented programming, the routines defined for a class are called *methods* and in C++ they are called *member functions*. The variables or data components defined for a class are called *attributes* and in C++ they are called *data members*. If some of the member functions are used to perform deduction, induction, or abduction on the data members that are implementations of cognitive data structures, then the object is rational. If the rational object also crosses a certain threshold of autonomy, then it is an agent.

Cognitive data structures are structures used to represent mental constructs like beliefs, intentions, commitments, decisions, moods, and knowledge. For instance, we could designate a believe structure using a C++ set:

```
set<statements>  Beliefs;

struct   statement{
//...
   float ArrivalTime;
   float DepartureTime;
   string Destination;
   //...
};
```

where the statements are about schedule some form of public transportation. A collection of these statements is stored within `set<statements>` and represents the agent's beliefs. This is what we mean by data members that are implementations of cognitive data structures. The agent would declare the data member accordingly:

---

[2]We intentionally avoid the term *intelligent*. It is not currently known whether we will ever produce intelligent software. However, we can undoubtedly produce rational software based on well understood, logical formalisms.

S 12.1. Deduction, Induction, and Abduction

Deduction, induction, and abduction are processes used to draw conclusions from a set of statements or a collection of data. The process of deduction allows the reasoner to deduce a conclusion from a set of statements. If the statements are true and the reasoner follows the proper rules of inference, then the conclusion is said to be necessarily true or that it follows by necessity. For instance:

All three-sided figures are triangles.

This is a three-sided figure.

This is a triangle. ← *Conclusion arrived at by deduction*

The rules of inference are guidelines and restrictions that determine how the reasoner may move from one statement to another. The rules of inference determine when statements are logically equivalent and the conditions under which one statement may be transformed into another. Sidebar Figure 12–1 contains the eight most basic rules of inference.

The process of induction allows the reasoner to induce the conclusion from a set of statements taken to be facts. For instance:

It rained yesterday.

It rained the day before.

It rained all last week.

It will rain tomorrow. ← *Conclusion arrived at by induction*

Whereas the conclusions in the deductive process are said to be necessarily true (if the rules of inference were applied correctly), the conclusions in an inductive process have only a probability of being true. How close that probability is to 100% will depend on the nature and context of the statements and data they are drawn from. The process of abduction allows the reasoner to draw the most plausible conclusion based on a set of statements or data. For instance:

Articles of the defendant's clothing were found at the scene of the crime.

The defendant and the deceased recently had a violent argument.

The defendant's DNA was found at the scene of the crime.

The defendant is the perpetrator of the crime ← Conclusion arrived at by abduction

Deduction, induction, and abduction are the three fundamental processes found in logic. They provide for logic what calculation and arithmetic provide for mathematics. The ability to correctly move from premises (statements, data, and facts) to conclusions is the process that we call reasoning.

1. Modus Ponens

$p > q$
p
_____
$\therefore q$

2. Modus Tollens

$p > q$
$\sim q$
_____
$\therefore \sim p$

3. Hypothetical Syllogisms

$p > q$
$q < r$
_____
$\therefore p > r$

4. Disjunctive Syllogism

$p > q$
$\sim p$
_____
$\therefore q$

5. Constructive Dilemma

$(p > q) \bullet (r > s)$

_____
$\therefore q \vee s$

6. Absorption

$p > q$
_____
$\therefore p > (p \bullet q)$

7. Simplication

$p \bullet q$
_____
$\therefore p$

8. Conjunction

p
q
_____
$\therefore p \bullet q$

9. Addition

p
_____
$\therefore p \vee q$

Sidebar Figure 12.1   Rules of inference taken from the back inside cover of COPI symbolic reasoning.

```
class agent{
    //...
    set<statements>  Beliefs;
    //...
};
```

The agent class uses deduction, induction, or abduction to process its `Beliefs` in order to form intentions, commitments, or plans. A closer look at our definition of agents states that if it is a rational autonomous object, it is an agent. If it is not rational, then its not an agent, it's just an object. The degree of autonomy is another area of debate and we will examine it closely later in this chapter.

12.2   What is Agent-Oriented Programming?

Agent-oriented programming is the process of assigning the work a program has to one or more agents. The WBS (Work Breakdown Structure) consists only of agents. If all the work that a program does can be assigned to one or more agents, then it is a pure agent-oriented program and all of the design and development involved only requires agent-oriented programming. In many situations, agents will be involved with other kinds of objects and systems that are not agent-oriented and therefore the entire programming effort is not called agent-oriented programming, which is often the case when agents are involved with database servers, application servers, and other types of object-oriented systems. Whether producing software systems that are completely agent-oriented or only partially agent-oriented, agent-oriented programming produces rational object-oriented software components.

12.2.1   Why Agents Work for Distributed Programming

Practical distributed programs rise out of necessity. Typically, there is some resource located on another computer or network separated from the program that needs it. These resources often take the form of databases, Web servers, e-mail servers, application servers, printers, and large storage devices. The resources are usually managed by a piece of software called a *server*. The software that needs access to the resources is referred to a client. The fact that the resources are located on different computers than the client leads to distributed architectures. In most cases, it does not make sense to attempt to combine these programs into one large program that runs on a single computer and in a single address space. Furthermore, there are many programs developed at different times, by different developers, and for different purposes that end up taking advantage of each other's services. The application that uses these programs evolved over time and the result was a distrusted application. Since these programs are separate, they will each have their own address space and resources. When these programs are used together to form a single application or collectively solve a program they form a distributed program. It turns out that the distributed program architecture provides very flexible architectures that can be used for large-scale applications. In so many practical applications, the requirements for distribution are discovered after the fact. However, good software engineering and design techniques can be used to identify when applications should be distributed. Once you know that you need to develop a distributed application, the next question is how it should be distributed. What model should be used? Although there are very many different client-server and peer-to-peer models available in this book, we focus on only two: blackboard architectures and multiagent architectures.

Both of these architectures can take advantage of agents because agents are inherently self-contained, autonomous, and rational software structures. Because agents are rational it means they know their purpose. Regular objects have a purpose and agents know what that purpose is. Identifying the purpose of each aspect of a piece of software is a natural process. It is straightforward to recognize the purpose of a piece of software during the design phase. Assigning that purpose to an agent is an easy form of software decomposition. The WBS becomes a matter of which class of agent to delegate the work to. Since the agent is the unit of modularity in an AOP (agent-oriented program), the work of distribution is reduced to finding means for multiple agents to communicate. The process of designing the original agent class hides the effort required for identifying the WBS of a distributed program. Once we get over the hurdles that agents are really rational objects, we can then take advantage of the CORBA specification to design truly distributed multiagent systems. CORBA hides the complexity of distributed programming and communication over networks, intranets, and the Internet. Chapter 8 contains a simple overview of distributed programming using CORBA. Since agents are objects, the entire discussion of CORBA is applicable. Chapter 6 introduces the PVM (Parallel Virtual Machine). PVM can also be used to greatly simplify the communication between agents executing on different processes or on different computers. Agents can be implemented as CORBA objects, or they can be assigned to separate PVM processes. In both cases, the communication is simple and straightforward. When two or more agents are involved within a single application they are *multiagent systems*. The agents may still use CORBA, PVM, or the MPI (Message Passing Interface) to communicate if they are on the same computer. Agents within different processes may also use traditional methods of IPC such as fifos, shared memory, and pipes to communicate. There are three fundamental challenges in distributed programming:

1. Identifying the WBS of the distributed solution
2. Implementing effective and efficient communication between the distributed components
3. Dealing with exceptions, errors, and partial failures

While there is nothing inherent within the notion of an agent class to deal with item 2, items 1 and 3 are almost implicit in the agent design itself. Each agent's rationality defines its purpose and thereby the part that it is to play in the software solution. Since agents are self-contained and autonomous, a good agent class design will include the necessary fault tolerance.

12.2.2   Agents and Parallel Programming

Agents deployed in an environment where multiple processors or concurrently executing threads offer the same advantages as they do in distributed programming, with the addition that cooperation between agents is much easier to program. The PVM and MPI environments can also be used for message passing between agents that are collectively solving some kind of problem. Again, the rationality of the agents makes it easier to understand to design the WBS for parallelism. The common obstacles encountered in parallel programming are:

1. Dividing the work effectively and efficiently between two or more software components
2. Coordinating the concurrently executing software components
3. Designing appropriate communication (where needed) between the components
4. Dealing with exceptions, errors, and partial failures (if the agents are on separate computers)

Multiagent parallel architectures tend to be loosely coupled, that is, the communication and the interdependency is minimal. Each agent knows its purpose and has methods to accomplish its purpose. Whereas obstacle 3 is not inherently dealt with by the agent class, obstacles 1, 2, and 4 are easily managed by the implicit capabilities of the agent classes. For example, the impact of obstacle 2 is reduced because each agent is rational, has a purpose, and has the ways and means to accomplish its purpose. So the responsibility is shifted away from some coordination and control algorithm to the actions of each agent. The impact of obstacle 4 is reduced because agents are self-contained, rational, and autonomous and a good class design will include the necessary fault tolerance. Since the agent's state is encapsulated, the responsibility to protect critical sections within the agent object is the responsibility of the agent class. The agent will enforce its own data access policies. Table 12–2 shows the state access polices from which agents can choose.

Table 12–2 State Access Policies	
Read-Write Algorithm Types	*Meaning*
EREW	Exclusive Read Exclusive Write
CREW	Concurrent Read Exclusive Write
ERCW	Exclusive Read Concurrent Write
CRCW	Concurrent Read Concurrent Write

Each agent's class will determine which access policy is acceptable in a multiagent environment. In some cases, combinations of the access policies in Table 12–2 are implemented. This makes the parallel programming easier. The developer can work at a higher level without having to worry about mutexes, semaphores, and so on. Multiagent solutions allow the developer to work at a higher level without getting bogged down with the minutia of coordinating every function call and data access. Each agent has a purpose. Each agent is rational and therefore has a logic for achieving its purpose. The programming process looks alot more like task delegation as opposed to the typical task coordination paradigms for traditional parallel programming. Since agent-oriented programming is a specific kind of object-oriented programming, agents use a more declarative mode of parallel programming than the traditional procedural-based programming that is often implemented in languages such as Fortran or C. The developer specifies what needs to be done and which agents should do it and the parallelism almost takes care of itself. There is always some amount of coordination and communication programming required, but agent-oriented programming keeps it to a minimum. However, all these advantages depend on the existence of agent classes. Someone has to design and code the agent classes. Let's now look at what an agent class will contain.

12.3   Basic Agent Components

An agent is declared using the `class` keyword. The components of an agent will consist of C++ data members and member functions. Figure 12–1 shows the logical layout of an agent class.

The class attributes and methods in Figure 12–1 refer to the typical initialization, read, and write methods that any object would have. The attributes would include state variables that define the object. The methods would include constructors, destructors, assignment operators, exception handlers, and so on. If we stopped with these attributes and methods we would have only a traditional object. The cognitive data structures and the inference methods make up the rational component. It is the rational component that transforms an object into an agent.

12.3.1   Cognitive Data Structures

A *data structure* is a set of rules for logically organizing data and the rules for accessing that logical organization. It is a method of organization that specifies both how the data should be conceptually structured and how access op-

Figure 12–1   Logical layout of an agent class.

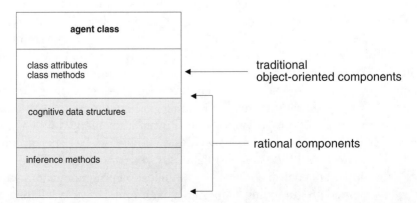

erations are allowed to be applied to that structure. Whereas datatypes and ADTs (abstract datatypes) focus on *what*, data structures focus on *how*. For example, the integer datatype specifies an entity that has a data component and a number of arithmetic operations (i.e., addition, subtraction, multiplication, division, modulo, etc.). That data component does not have a fractional part. The data component consists of negative and positive numbers, and so on. The datatype specification does not mention how the integers should be used or accessed. On the other hand, a data structure specification such as a stack specifies a list of elements stored in a LIFO (last-in-first-out) order. The stack data structure also specifies that elements may only be taken out one at a time from the top of the stack, that is, the last element inserted must be removed before any other elements can be accessed. So not only does the stack data structure specify how the elements are organized, it also specifies how the elements are accessed (i.e., visited, read, changed, deleted, etc.). Cognitive data structures restrict the rules for organizing and accessing data to those found in the fields of logic and epistemology. The rules of inference, the methods of inference (i.e., deduction, induction, and abduction), the notions of epistemic data, knowledge, justification, belief, premises, propositions, fallacies, and conclusions are the defining features of cognitive data structures.[3] Whereas algorithms for sorting, searching, and iterating are commonplace for traditional data structures, inference methods are more commonplace for cognitive data structures. The ADTs used with cognitive data structures often include:

Questions	Events
Facts	Time
Propositions	Fallacies
Beliefs	Purpose
Statements	Justification
Conclusions	

Of course, other datatypes can be used with a cognitive data structure but these are characteristic of programs that use rational software components such as agents. These ADTs are normally implemented as datatypes using the `struct` or `class` keywords. For instance:

---

[3]Mentalistic concepts such as imagination, paranoia, anxiety, happiness, sadness, and so on are intentionally excluded from our definition of cognitive data structures. Our focus is on rational epistemic software, not intelligent software.

```
struct question{                        class justification{
   //...                                   //...
   string RequiredInformation;            time   EventTime;
   target_object  QuestionDomain;         bool   Observed;
   string Tense;                          bool   Present;
   string Mood;                           //...
   //...                                };
};
```

The C++ template and container classes can be used to organize cognitive data structures such as knowledge. For instance:

```
class  preliminary_knowledge{
   //...
   map<question,belief>  Opinion;
   map<conclusion,justification>  SimpleKnowledge;
   set<propositions>  Argument;
   //...
};
```

12.3.1.2 Inference Methods

The inference methods in Figure 12–1 refer to deduction, induction, and abduction. (See Sidebar 12.1 for an explanation of these methods.) While inference methods are called for in an agent architecture, there is no specific mention on how the inference methods are implmented. Deduction, induction, and abduction are high-level processes. The details of how to implement these processes are up to the software developer. Inference is the process of deriving logical conclusions from premises known or assumed to be true. There is no one right way to implement an inferencing process, sometimes called an inference engine. However, there are several commonly used methods for implementing inference. Forward-chaining or backward-chaining techniques can be used. Means–end analysis techniques can be used. Graph traversal algorithms such as DFS (Depth First Search) and BFS (Breadth First Search) can also be used. There is a host of theorem-proving techniques that can be used to implement inference methods and inference engines. The important point to note here is that an agent class will have one or more inference methods. Table 12–3 contains descriptions for the most basic techniques used to implement the inference methods.

These techniques are well understood and widely available in many libraries, frameworks, and some programming languages. These techniques are the building blocks for the basic inference methods. To see how this in-

Table 12–3	Tables for Descriptions of the Most Basic Inference Implementation Techniques

Inference Implementation Techniques	*Description*
Backward Chaining	Purpose- or goal-driven approach in which a process starts from a proposition, statement, or hypothesis and searches for supporting evidence.
Forward Chaining	Data-driven approach that starts from available data or facts and moves toward conclusions.
Means-end Analysis	Uses a set of operators to solve one subproblem at a time until the entire problem is solved (opportunistic).

ferencing works lets use one of the rules of inference Modus Ponens and build a simple inference method to support it. Take the following statement: If there is a bus trip from Detroit to New York then John will go on vacation. If we establish that there is a bus trip from Detroit to New York, then we know that John will go on vacation. The Modus Ponens form of this is:

$$P \rightarrow Q$$
$$P$$
$$\overline{\qquad\qquad}$$
$$Q$$

where:

P = If there is a bus trip from Detroit to New York

Q = John will go on vacation

We could design a simple decision support agent to tell us whether John will go on vacation or not. That agent would need to know something about possible bus trips. Let's say we have a list of bus trips:

Toledo to Cleveland	Detroit to Chicago	Youngstown to New York
Cleveland to Columbus	Cincinnati to Detroit	Detroit to Toledo
Columbus to New York	Cincinnati to Youngstown	

Each of these trips represents commitments by the ABC Bus Company. If our agent has access to the ABC Bus Company's schedule, then this list of trips can be used to represent part of our agent's beliefs. The question is, how do we get from a list of trips to beliefs? First, lets design a simple statement structure.

```
struct existing_trip{
   //...
   string From;
   time  Departure;
   string To;
   time  Arrival;
   //...
};
```

Next let's use a container class that will represent our agent's beliefs about bus trips.

```
set<existing_trips>  BusTripKnowledge;
```

If the bus trip is contained in the set `BusTripKnowledge`, then our agent believes that the bus trip will take place from a certain origin to a certain destination at a certain time. So we might construct a trip accordingly:

```
//...
existing_trip  Trip;
Trip.From.append("Toledo");
Trip.To.append("Cleveland");
Trip.Departure("4:30");
Trip.Arrival("5:45");
BusTripKnowledge.insert(Trip);
//...
```

If we place each trip into the `BusTripKnowledge` set, then our agent's beliefs about the ABC Bus Company's trips are complete. Notice that there is no single trip from Detroit to New York. However, John can get to New York from Detroit if he takes the following bus trips:

Detroit to Toledo

Toledo to Cleveland

Cleveland to Columbus

Columbus to New York

So while the ABC Bus Company does not provide a one-stop trip, it does provide a multistop trip. The problem is how does our agent know this? The agent needs some way to conclude based on what it knows about bus trips that there is a trip from Detroit to New York. We use a simple chaining process. We search our `BusTripKnowledge` for the first trip leaving from Detroit. We find one: Detroit to Chicago. We check the `To` attribute of this trip. If it is equal to `"New York"`, we stop because we have found a trip. If it is not, we save this trip on a stack. We then search through the trips to see if there is another trip whose `From` attribute = `"Chicago."` We find that there are no buses leaving from Chicago. Therefore, we pop the Detroit to Chicago trip from the stack. We note that we have used this trip, and we search for the next trip leaving from Detroit to anywhere. We find a trip: Detroit to Toledo. We check to see if the `To` attribute = `"New York,"` and since it does not, we save this trip on a stack. We then search through the trips to see if there is another trip whose `From` attribute = `"Toledo."` Here we find one: Toledo to Cleveland. We then place this trip on the stack. We then search through the trips to see if there is another trip whose `From` attribute = `"Cleveland."` At each trip we check the `To` attribute. If the `To` attribute = `"New York,"` then the trips on the stack represent a bus trip from Detroit to New York, with the starting trip at the bottom of the stack and the ending trip on the top of the stack. If we go through the entire list and none of the `To` attributes = `"New York,"` or we run out of `To` attributes for the trip on top of the stack, then we pop the top element of the stack and search for the next item whose `From` attribute is equal to the `To` attribute of the element on the top of the stack. This process is repeated until either the stack is empty or we've found a trip. This process uses a simplified DFS technique to determine if there is a trip from point A to point B.

Our simple agent would use this DFS technique to establish the existence of the trip from Detroit to New York. Once this fact was established, then the agent would update its beliefs about John. The agent will now believe that John is going on vacation. Let's say we added another precondition to John's vacation:

If John adds 15 or more new clients, then his profits > 150000.

If John's profits are > 150000 and there is a bus trip from Detroit to New York, then John will go on vacation.

Here the agent must establish whether John's profits are > 150000 and whether there is a bus trip from Detroit to New York. To establish whether

John's profits are > 150000, the agent must first establish whether John has added 15 or more new clients. Suppose we convince the software agent that John has added 23 new clients. Then the agent can infer that John's profits are > 150000. From `BusTripKnowledge` the agent was able to infer that there was a trip from Detroit to New York. Using the beliefs about the bus trips, and the belief about the 23 new clients, the agent uses the process of forward chaining to deduce that John will go on vacation. We call this forward chaining from the fact that with 23 new clients added and the bus schedule facts, the agent moved to the conclusion. The inference form of this process looks like:

$$A \longrightarrow B$$
$$(B \text{ and } C) \longrightarrow D$$
$$A$$
$$C$$

$$\overline{}$$

$$D$$

where

A = If John adds 15 or more new clients
B = Profits > 150000
C = There is a bus trip from Detroit to New York
D = John will go on vacation

In this example, the agent believes A and C to be true. Using the rules of inference, B and D are established to be true. Therefore, the agent will commit to tell us that John will go on vacation. This kind of processing could be assigned to an agent in a situation where a manager has hundreds or even thousands of employees and decides to have agent software regularly schedule employee hours. The manager would then consult the agent to see who was working, who was on sick leave, who was on vacation, and so on. The agent would be given knowledge and authority to assign work schedules. Each week the agent would commit to a number of acceptable work schedules, vacations, and sick leaves. The agent in this case uses simple forward chaining and DFS to make its inferences. To implement this kind of inferencing we used `structs`, and stack and set classes. These classes are used to hold knowledge, propositions, and patterns of reasoning. They allow us to implement our CDS (Cognitive Data Structures). We used DFS techniques to move through the stack data structures and set structures to support the process of inference.

The combination of chaining and DFS produces a process whereby one proposition can be affirmed on the basis of previous propositions that have already been accepted. This is important because our agent will know that it is inherently correct when it accomplishes its objectives based on inference. This also affects parallel programming considerations. The fact that the agent is rational and moves according to rules of inference allows the developer to focus on correctly modeling the task that the agent performs instead of getting bogged down in attempts to explicitly control the parallelism in the program. The minimal requirements of parallelization DCS (decomposition, communication, and synchronization) are in large part addressed by the architecture of the agent. Each agent has a rationale for its behavior. That rationale will be based on well defined, well understood rules of inference. The decomposition happens simply as a matter of assigning the agent one or more prime directives. Thinking of the WBS in this way is natural and ultimately results in parallel or distributed programs that are easier to maintain and enhance. It is easier to think about communication between agents than communication between anonymous modules because the boundaries between agents are clear and obvious. Each agent has a purpose that is immediately apparent. The knowledge or information each agent needs to achieve its purpose is easily determined. To allow the agents to communicate, the developer can use simple MPI calls or the object communication facilities that are part of any CORBA implementation. The most challenging aspect of the communication, namely figuring out:

- what needs to be communicated
- who needs to communicate
- when the communication should occur
- what format the communication should be in

is implied in the design of the agents. All that is left is the physical implementation of the communication, which is easily handled by any of the libraries that support parallelism that we have discussed in this book. Finally, the problems of synchronization are reduced because the agent's rationale tells it when it can and should perform an action. Therefore, the complicated issues of synchronization are transformed into simpler issues of cooperation. This subtle difference is an important paradigm shift because it simplifies what the software developer has to think about. Lets look a little closer at the basic layout of an agent and how we can implement it in C++.

12.4   Implementing Agents in C++

We will explore a simplified variation of our previous example of an agent and demonstrate how it can be approached in C++. The purpose of this agent is to schedule and book vacations for the owner of the ABC Auto Repair Company. The owner has dozens of employees and therefore doesn't have time to figure out when and where to go on vacation. Furthermore, unless the owner is making a certain amount of profit, vacations are out of the question. So the owner has acquired agent software that will plan and schedule vacations at various times throughout the year if the conditions are right. As far as the owner is concerned, the primary selling feature is that the agent runs unattended. Once the agent is installed on the computer the owner doesn't have to bother with it. When the agent determines that an appropriate time for a vacation has arrived, the agent will schedule the vacation, book the hotel and transportation, and then e-mail the owner an itinerary. The only responsibility the owner has is during the setup of the agent. The owner has to specify where he would like to go and how much profit the business must make before he can go. Let's look at how this agent could be constructed. Recall from Figure 12–1 that the rational component of an agent class consists of cognitive data structures and inference methods. The cognitive data structures help to capture beliefs, propositions, notions of epistemic data, knowledge, fallacies, facts, and so on. The agent class uses inference methods to access these cognitive data structures in the process of problem solving and task performance. The standard C++ library comes with a set of container classes and algorithms that can be used to implement the CDS and the inference methods.

12.4.1   *Proposition Datatypes and Belief Structures*

This agent has beliefs about the performance of the owners auto repair business. The beliefs capture information about how many customers per hour, the bay utilization per day, and the total sales during the period. Furthermore, the agent knows that the owner only likes bus trips. Therefore, the agent keeps up on any available bus trips that the owner might enjoy. In a math-intensive program, the primary datatypes are integers and floating point numbers. In a graphics-intensive program, the primary datatypes are pixels, lines, colors, circles, and so on. In an agent-oriented program, the primary datatypes are propositions, rules, statements, literals, and strings. We will use the object-oriented support in C++ to build a few datatypes that are native to agent-oriented programming. Example 12.1 shows the declaration for a proposition class.

```
//Example 12.1  Declaration of a proposition class.

template<class C> class proposition {
//...
protected:
   list<C> UniverseOfDiscourse;
   bool TruthValue;
public:
   virtual bool operator()(void) = 0;
   bool operator&&(proposition &X);
   bool operator||(proposition &X);
   bool operator||(bool X);
   bool operator&&(bool X);
   operator void*();
   bool operator!(void);
   bool possible(proposition &X);
   bool necessary(proposition &X);
   void universe(list<C> &X);
   //...
};
```

A proposition is a statement in which the subject is affirmed or denied by the predicate. A proposition is either true or false. A proposition can be used to capture any single belief that the agent has. Also, other information that the agent does not necessarily believe but is offered to the agent will be presented as a proposition. The proposition is a cognitive datatype. It should be just as functional in an agent-oriented program as a floating point or integer datatype in a math-oriented program. Therefore, we use the operator overloading facilities of C++ to provide some of the basic operators that are applicable to propositions. Table 12–4 shows how the operators are mapped to logic operators.

The `proposition` class in Example 12.1 is a scaled-down version. The goal of this class is to allow the `proposition` datatype to be used just as eas-

Table 12–4 How the Operators are Mapped to Logical Operators	
C++ User-Defined Operators	*Commonly Used Logical Operators*
&&	∧
||	∨
!	~
possible	◆
necessary	❏

ily and naturally as any other C++ datatype. Notice that the `proposition` class has the declaration:

```
virtual bool operator()(void) = 0;
```

This is called a pure virtual method. When a class has a pure virtual method, it means the class is an abstract class and cannot be directly instantiated. This is because there is no definition for the pure virtual function in the class. The function is only declared, not defined. Abstract classes are used to define policies and blueprints for derived classes. A derived class must define any pure virtual functions that it inherits from the abstract class. Here the `proposition` class is used to define the minimum capability that any descendant will have. Another important thing to notice about the `proposition` class in Example 12.1 is it's also a template class. It contains the data member:

```
list<C> UniverseOfDiscourse;
```

This data member will be used to hold the universe of discourse that the proposition belongs to. In logic, the universe of discourse contains all of the legal things that may be considered during a discussion. Here, we use a list container. Since the topics under consideration in a universe of discourse can take on different types, we use a container class. We make the `UniverseOfDiscourse` protected instead of private so that it can be accessed by all descendants of the `proposition` class. The `proposition` class also has the capability to deal with logical necessity and possibility, the major themes in modal logic that are also useful in agent-oriented programming. Modal logic allows the agent to deal with what is *possibly* true or what is *necessarily* true. Table 12–4 lists the primary operators used for logical possibility and necessity. We provide these methods for exposition purposes only; the implementations of these methods are beyond the scope of this book. However, they are part of the proposition classes that the authors use in practice. To make the proposition class usable, we derive a new class that we name trip_announcement. The trip_announcement class is a statement about the existence of a bus trip from some point of origin to some destination. For instance: There is a bus trip from Detroit to Toledo. This makes a statement that is either true or false. If we were concerned with when this statement was true or false we might imply temporal logic. Temporal logic deals with the logic of time. Agents also employ temporal reasoning. But here all propositions refer to the current time. This statement asserts that there is currently a bus trip from Detroit to Toledo. The agent will either be able to verify this and therefore believe or reject it as a false statement. Example 12.2 shows the declaration of the trip_announcement class.

```
//Example 12.2 Declaration of the trip_announcement class.

class trip_announcement : public proposition<trip_announcement>{
//...
protected:
   string Origin;
   string Destination;
   stack<trip_announcement> Candidates;
public:
   bool operator()(void);
   bool operator==(const trip_announcement &X) const;
   void origin(string X);
   string origin(void);
   void destination(string X);
   string destination(void);
   bool directTrip(void);
   bool validTrip(list<trip_announcement>::iterator I,
                  string TempOrigin);
   stack<trip_announcement> candidates(void);
   friend bool operator||(bool X,trip_announcement &Y);
   friend bool operator&&(bool X,trip_announcement &Y);
   //...
};
```

Notice that the trip_announcement class inherits the proposition class. Recall that the proposition class is a template class and requires a parameter to determine its type. The declaration:

```
class trip_announcement : public proposition<trip_announcement>
                     {...};
```

provides the `proposition` class with a type. It is also important to note that the `trip_announcement` class defines the `operator()`. Therefore, `trip_announcement` is a concrete class as opposed to an abstract class. We may declare and use the `trip_announcement` proposition directly within our agent program. The `trip_announcement` class adds some additional data members:

```
Origin
Destination
Candidates
```

These data members are used to contain the origin and destination of a bus trip. If the bus trip requires transfers from one bus to another and multiple layovers, then the `Candidates` data member will contain the complete route involved. Therefore, the `trip_announcement` object will be a statement about a bus trip and the route involved. The `trip_announcement` class also defines some additional operators. These operators help to put the `trip_announcement` class on equal footing with built-in C++ datatypes. In addition to beliefs about trips, the agent also has beliefs about the performance of areas within the owner's business. These beliefs differ in structure but are still basically statements that will be either true or false. So, we again use the `proposition` class as a base class. Example 12.3 shows the declaration for the `peformance_statement` class.

```
//Example 12.3 Declaration for the performance_statement class.

class performance_statement : public proposition<performance_
                               statement>{
   //...
   int Bays;
   float Sales;
   float PerHour;
public:
   bool operator() (void);
   bool operator==(const performance_statement &X) const;
   void bays(int X);
   int bays(void);
   float sales(void);
   void sales(float X);
   float perHour(void);
   void perHour(float X);
   friend bool operator||(bool X,performance_statement &Y);
   friend bool operator&&(bool X,performance_statement &Y);
   //...
};
```

Notice that this class also provides the template class `proposition` with a parameter:

```
class performance_statement : public proposition<performance_
                                statement> {...}
```

With this declaration the `proposition` class is now specified for `performance_statements`. The `performance_statement` class is used to represent beliefs about how many sales, customers per hour, and bay utilization the owner's business has. Each statement corresponds to a single belief that the agent has in each area. This information is held in the data members:

```
Bays
Sales
PerHour
```

Statements such as: "Location 1 grossed $300,000 in sales, had 10 customers per hour, and had a bay utilization of 4" can be represented by the `performance_statement` class. So our agent class has two categories of beliefs implemented as datatypes derived from the `proposition` class. Figure 12–2 shows a UML class diagram for the `trip_announcement` class and the

Figure 12–2   UML class diagram for the `trip_`
`announcement` class and the
`performance_statement` class.

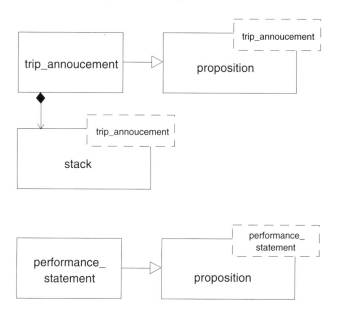

`performance_statement` class. These classes hold the structure of the agent's beliefs.

12.4.2   The Agent Class

The classes shown in Figure 12–2 provide the foundation for the CDS of the agent, the basis for what will make the agent rational. It's the fact that the agent class is rational that distinguishes it from other types of object-oriented classes. Example 12.4 shows the declaration for the agent class.

```
// Example 12.4   Declaration of the agent class.

class agent{
   //...
private:
   performance_statement Manager1;
   performance_statement Manager2;
   performance_statement Manager3;
   trip_announcement Trip1;
   trip_announcement Trip2;
   trip_announcement Trip3;
   list<trip_announcement> TripBeliefs;
   list<performance_statement>  PerformanceBeliefs;
public:
   agent(void);
   bool determineVacationAppropriate(void);
   bool scheduleVacation(void);
   void updateBeliefs(void);
   void setGoals(void);
   void displayTravelPlan(void);
   //...
};
```

As with the proposition classes, the agent class is a scaled-down version of what would be used in practice. A complete listing of the declaration of the practical versions of these classes would be three or four pages. We show enough for exposition purposes. The `agent` class contains two list containers:

```
list<trip_announcement> TripBeliefs;
list<performance_statement>  PerformanceBeliefs;
```

The list containers are standard C++ lists. Each list is used to hold a collection of what the agent currently believes about the world. Our simple agent world is restricted to knowledge about bus trips and sales performance of his owner's business. The contents of these two containers represent the complete knowledge and belief set of the agent. If there are statements in these lists that the agent no longer believes, the agent will remove them. If the agent uncovers new statements during the course of inference, they are added to these beliefs. The agent has ongoing access to information about bus trips and the performance of the owner's business. The agent is able to update its beliefs as necessary. In addition to beliefs, the agent has objectives, which are sometimes represented as desires in the BDI (Beliefs Desires Intentions) model. The objectives support the primary directives that the agent has been given by its client. In our case the objectives will be stored in statements:

```
performance_statement Manager1;
performance_statement Manager2;
performance_statement Manager3;
trip_announcement Trip1;
trip_announcement Trip2;
trip_announcement Trip3;
```

Keep in mind that this is an oversimplification of how objectives and directives are represented within an agent class. However, there is enough here to understand how these structures are built. The three Manager statements contain the performance goals that must be met before the owner can even consider going on vacation. The three Trip statements contain the bus trips that the owner would like to take if a vacation is earned. The beliefs together with the directives provide the basic cognitive datatypes that the agent has. The agent's inference methods combined with these cognitive datatypes form the agent's CDS (Cognitive Data Structure). The CDS forms the rational component and the distinguishing feature of an agent class. In addition to containers that hold beliefs and structures that in turn hold directives and objectives, most practical agent classes will have containers that hold the agent's intentions, commitments, or plans. The agent gives directives by his client. The agent uses its ability to inference and acts to fulfill its directives. The inferencing and actions that an agent does often result in a container that holds intentions, commitments, or plans. Our simple agent doesn't require a container to hold intentions or plans. However, it does keep track of the route that a bus trip vacation would take. This is stored in a container called `Candidates`. The intentions or plans would work similarly. If our agent is able to achieve its directives, it will schedule the trip and e-mail the owner the specifics. The instant our agent object is constructed, it goes to work. Example 12.5 shows an excerpt from the agent's constructor.

```
//Example 12.5  The agent class's constructor.

agent::agent(void)
{
    setGoals();
    updateBeliefs();
    if(determineVacationAppropriate()){
        displayTravelPlan();
        scheduleVacation();
        cout << "Emailed Vacation Approved and Scheduled" << endl;
    }
    else{
        cout << "Emailed Vacation Not Appropriate At this time" << endl;
    }
}
```

12.4.2.1   The Agent Loop

Many definitions for agents include requirements of continuity and autonomy. The idea is that the agent continually performs what tasks it is assigned without the need for human intervention. The agent has the capability to interact and semi-control its environment through a feedback loop. The continuity and autonomy are often implemented as an event loop where the agent continually receives messages and events. The agent uses the messages and events to update its internal model of the world, intentions, and take action. However, autonomy and continuity are relative terms. Some agents need to function from one microsecond to the next, while other agents only need to perform their services annually. In fact, with deep space mission software, an agent may have longer than an annual cycle. Multiple years may pass before the agent performs the next task. Therefore, we don't focus on physical event loops and constantly active message queues. While these work for some agents, they are not appropriate for others. We have found the notion of a logical cycle to be the most practical. The logical cycle may or may not be implemented as an event loop. The logical cycle can be anything from nanoseconds to years. Figure 12–3 shows a simple overview of a logical agent cycle.

The universe of discourse in Figure 12–3 represents everything our agent can legitimately interact with. This might include files, information from ports, or data acquisition devices. The information will be represented as some kind of proposition or statement. Notice that there is a feedback loop from the agent's outputs back to the agent's inputs. Our agent from Example 12.4 is only needed a few times a year. Therefore, it is not appropriate to put it in an event loop that constantly runs. Our agent will simply activate itself

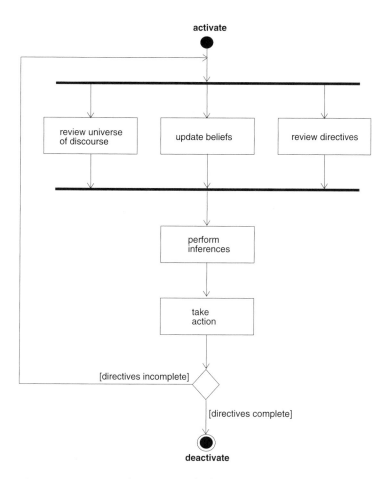

Figure 12–3   Simple overview of a logical agent cycle.

periodically during the course of the year to execute its initiatives. Example 12.5 shows the agent's constructor. When the agent activates, it sets some goals, updates its beliefs, and then determines whether a vacation is appropriate. If the vacation is appropriate, the necessary steps are taken and the owner is e-mailed. If a vacation is not appropriate at that time, then the owner is e-mailed with that fact also.

12.4.2.2   The Agent's Inference Methods

This agent has inference capabilities implemented partially by the proposition class descendants and partially by the

```
determineVacationAppropriate()
```

method. Recall that the proposition class declared the `operator()=0` as a pure virtual. They force derived classes to implement the `operator()`. We use this operator to design a proposition so the proposition itself can determine whether it is true or not, that is, the proposition classes are self-contained. This is a fundamental tenet of object-oriented programming, namely, that a class is a self-contained encapsulation of characteristics and behaviors. Therefore, one of the primary behaviors of the proposition class and its descendants is the capability to determine whether it is true or not. The operator overloading and function objects are used to accommodate this feature. Example 12.6 shows an excerpt from the proposition class and its descendant's definitions.

```
//Example 12.6   Excerpts from the definition of the
                 proposition class and its descendants.

template <class C> bool proposition<C>::operator&&(proposition &X)
{
    return((*this)() && X());
}


template <class C> bool proposition<C>::operator||(proposition &X)
{
    return((*this)() || X());
}
template<class C> proposition<C>::operator void*(void)
{
    return((void*)(TruthValue));
}


bool trip_announcement::operator()(void)
{
    list<trip_announcement>::iterator I;
    if(directTrip()){
        return(true);
    }
    I = UniverseOfDiscourse.begin();
    if(validTrip(I,Origin)){
        return(true);
    }
    return(false);
}
```

The definitions of the || and the && operators for the proposition classes determine whether the proposition is true or false. Each of these operator definitions ultimately calls the `operator()` defined for its class. Notice in Example 12.6 the definition for | |. This operator is defined as:

```
template <class C> bool proposition<C>::operator||
                                        (proposition &X)
{
   return((*this)() || X());
}
```

It allows code to be written as:

```
trip_announcement   A;
performance_statement B;
if (A || B){
   // Do Something
}
```

When A or B is evaluated, the operator definitions will cause the `operator()` to be called. Each proposition class defines behavior for the `operator()`. For example, the `trip_announcement` class defines the `operator()` as:

```
bool trip_announcement::operator()(void)
{
   list<trip_announcement>::iterator I;
   if(directTrip()){
      return(true);
   }
   I = UniverseOfDiscourse.begin();
   if(validTrip(I,Origin)){
      return(true);
   }
   return(false);
}
```

This code will determine whether there is a trip from some designated origin to some destination. For example, if the desired type is Detroit to Columbus and the universe of discourse contains:

Detroit to Toledo

Toledo to Columbus

Then a `trip_announcement` object will report that the statement that there is a trip from Detroit to Columbus is true, although the universe of discourse does not contain a statement like:

Detroit to Columbus

In fact, the `trip_announcement` class does check to see if there is a direct route from Detroit to Columbus. If there is a direct route, then it returns true. If there is no direct route, it attempts to find an indirect route. This behavior is accomplished by:

```
if(directTrip()){
    return(true);
}
I = UniverseOfDiscourse.begin();
if(validTrip(I,Origin)){
    return(true);
}
```

processing in the `operator()` for the `trip_anouncement` class. The `directTrip()` method is straightforward and simply sequentially searches through the universe to see if there is a statement that says:

Detroit to Columbus

The `validTrip()` method uses a DFS (Depth First Search) technique to determine if there is an indirect route. Example 12.7 contains definitions for `validTrip()` and `directTrip()`:

```
//Example 12.7  Definitions for validTrip and directTrip().

bool trip_announcement::validTrip(list<trip_announcement>::
                            iterator I, string TempOrigin)
{
    if(I == UniverseOfDiscourse.end()){
        if(Candidates.empty()){
            TruthValue = false;
            return(false);
        }
        else{
                trip_announcement Temp;
                Temp = Candidates.top();
                I = find(UniverseOfDiscourse.begin(),
                        UniverseOfDiscourse.end(),Temp);
                UniverseOfDiscourse.erase(I);
                Candidates.pop();
                I = UniverseOfDiscourse.begin();
                if(I != UniverseOfDiscourse.end()){
                    TempOrigin = Origin;
                }
                else{
```

```
                    TruthValue = false;
                    return(false);
               }
         }
    }
    if((*I).origin() == TempOrigin && (*I).destination() == Destination){
         Candidates.push(*I);
         TruthValue = true;
         return(true);
    }
    if((*I).origin() == TempOrigin){
              TempOrigin = (*I).destination();
              Candidates.push(*I);
    }
    I++;
    return(validTrip(I,TempOrigin));
}

bool trip_announcement::directTrip(void)
{
    list<trip_announcement>::iterator I;
    I = find(UniverseOfDiscourse.begin(),UniverseOfDiscourse.end(),*this);
    if(I == UniverseOfDiscourse.end()){
       TruthValue = false;
       return(false);
    }
    TruthValue = true;
    return(true);
}
```

Both the `validTrip()` and `directTrip()` methods make use of the `find()` algorithm from the Standard C++ library. The `UniverseOfDiscourse` is a container that contains the agent's beliefs and statements made to the agent. Recall that one of the first steps the agent took was to `updateBeliefs()`. The `updateBeliefs()` method is what ultimately populates the `UniverseOfDiscourse` container. Example 12.8 contains the definition for the `updateBeliefs()` method.

```
// Example 12.8 Update beliefs.

void agent::updateBeliefs(void)
{
    performance_statement TempP;
    TempP.sales(203.0);
    TempP.perHour(100.0);
    TempP.bays(4);
```

```
    PerformanceBeliefs.push_back(TempP);
    trip_announcement Temp;
    Temp.origin("Detroit");
    Temp.destination("LA");
    TripBeliefs.push_back(Temp);
    Temp.origin("LA");
    Temp.destination("NJ");
    TripBeliefs.push_back(Temp);
    Temp.origin("NJ");
    Temp.destination("Windsor");
    TripBeliefs.push_back(Temp);
}
```

In practice the beliefs will come from the agent's executing environment (i.e., files, sensors, ports, data acquisition devices, etc.). In Example 12.8 the information pushed into `TripBeliefs` and `PerformanceBeliefs` represent new statements that the agent is receiving about the available trips and the performance of one of the auto repair locations. These statements will be evaluated against the directives or initiatives that the agent has. The `setGoals()` method establishes what the agent's directives are. Example 12.9 shows the definition for the `setGoals()` method.

```
// Example 12.9   The set goals method.

void agent::setGoals(void)
{
    Manager1.perHour(15.0);
    Manager1.bays(8);
    Manager1.sales(123.23);
    Manager2.perHour(25.34);
    Manager2.bays(4);
    Manager2.sales(12.33);
    Manager3.perHour(34.34);
    Manager3.sales(100000.12);
    Manager3.bays(10);
    Trip1.origin("Detroit");
    Trip1.destination("Chicago");
    Trip2.origin("Detroit");
    Trip2.destination("NY");
    Trip3.origin("Detroit");
    Trip3.destination("Windsor");
}
```

These goals tell the agent that the owner would like to go from either Detroit to Chicago, Detroit to New York, or Detroit to Windsor. In addition to the trips, the financial objectives are also set. In order for a vacation to be achieved, one or more of these objectives must be met. After the goals have been set and the agent updates its beliefs, the next objective is to determine from the goals and the beliefs if a vacation can be scheduled. The second component of the agent's inference methods is invoked:

```
determineVacationAppropriate()
```

This method will pass the `UniverseOfDiscourse` to each of the proposition objects. It will then use a statement of the form:

```
(A v B v C) ^ (Q v R v S) --> W
```

which states if at least one of the statements is true from each grouping, then W is true. In the case of our agent, this means that if at least one of the sales performance goals are met and there is a bus trip that is satisfactory, then a vacation is appropriate. Example 12.10 shows the definition of the `deter-mineVacationAppropriate()` method.

```
// Example 12.10  second inference method.

bool agent::determineVacationAppropriate(void)
{
   bool TruthValue;
   Manager1.universe(PerformanceBeliefs);
   Manager2.universe(PerformanceBeliefs);
   Manager3.universe(PerformanceBeliefs);
   Trip1.universe(TripBeliefs);
   Trip2.universe(TripBeliefs);
   Trip3.universe(TripBeliefs);
   TruthValue = ((Manager1 || Manager2 || Manager3)  &&
                (Trip1 || Trip2 || Trip3));
   return(TruthValue);
}
```

Notice that the `TripBeliefs` and the `PerformanceBeliefs` are arguments to the `universe()` method of the `Trip` and `Manager` objects. This is where the propositions get the `UniverseOfDiscourse` information. Prior to the `proposition` calling their `operator()`, their `UniverseOfDiscourse` is populated. In Example 12.10 the statement:

```
((Manager1 || Manager2 || Manager3)  && (Trip1 || Trip2 ||
                                    Trip3));
```

causes six propositions to be evaluated by the `||` operator. The `||` operator for each proposition executes the `operator()` for each proposition. The `operator()` uses the `UniverseOfDiscourse` to determine whether the proposition is true or false. Examples 12.6 and 12.7 show how the `operator()` is defined for the `trip_announcement` class. Keep in mind that the `trip_announcement` class and the `performance_statement` class inherit much of their functionality from the `proposition` class. Example 12.11 shows how the `operator()` is defined for the `performance_statement` class.

```
//Example 12.11  The performance_statement class.

bool performance_statement::operator()(void)
{
   bool Satisfactory = false;
   list<performance_statement>::iterator I;
   I = UniverseOfDiscourse.begin();

   while(I != UniverseOfDiscourse.end() && !Satisfactory)
   {
       if(((*I).bays() >= Bays) || ((*I).sales() >= Sales) ||
          ((*I).perHour() >= PerHour)){
         Satisfactory = true;
       }
       I++;
   }
   return(Satisfactory);
}
```

The `operator()` for each `proposition` class plays a part in the inferencing capabilities of the agent class. Example 12.6 shows how the `operator()` is called whenever `||` or `&&` is evaluated for a `proposition` class or one of its descendants. It is the combination of the `proposition` classes' `operator()` methods and the `agent`'s methods that produce the inference methods for the `agent` class. In addition to the `||` and `&&` operator defined by the `proposition` class, the `trip_announcement` class and the `performance_statement` class define:

```
friend bool operator||(bool X,trip_announcement &Y);
friend bool operator&&(bool X,trip_announcement &Y);
```

The friend declarations allow the `propositions` to be used in longer expressions. If we have:

```
//...
trip_announcement A,B,C;
bool X;
X = A || B || C;
//...
```

then A and B will be OR'ed together and the result will be a `bool`. The next part of the evaluation tries to `||` the `bool` with the `trip_announcement` datatype:

```
bool ||   trip_announcement
```

Without the friend declararations, this would be a illegal operation. Example 12.12 shows how these friend functions are defined.

```
// Example 12.12  Operator overloading of  || and &&.

bool operator||(bool X,trip_announcement &Y)
{
   return(X || Y());
}

bool operator&&(bool X,trip_announcement &Y)
{
   return(X && Y());
}
```

Notice that the definitions of these friend functions also call the function operator() with the reference to Y(). These functions are also defined for the performance_statement class. The goal is to make the proposition classes as easy to use as the built-in datatypes. The proposition class also defines another operator that allows the proposition to be used in a natural fashion. Let's examine the code:

```
//...
trip_announcement    A;
if(A){
   //... do something
}
//...
```

How does the compiler define Test A? The if() statement is looking for an integral type or a bool. A is neither. We want the compiler to treat A as a statement that is either true or false. The function operator is not called under this circumstance. So we define the void* operator to give us the desired functionality. This function operator can be defined accordingly:

```
template<class C> proposition<C>::operator void*(void)
{
   return((void*)(TruthValue));
}
```

This definition allows any proposition type presented in standalone fashion to be tested for a truth value. For example, when our agent class is preparing to send the owner an e-mail containing the route. The agent needs to determine which trip is available. Example 12.13 shows another excerpt from the agent's trip processing methods.

```
// Example 12.13  displayTravelPlan() method.

 void agent::displayTravelPlan(void)
 {
    stack<trip_announcement> Route;
    if(Trip1){
       Route = Trip1.candidates();
    }
    if(Trip2){
       Route = Trip2.candidates();
    }
    if(Trip3){
       Route = Trip3.candidates();
    }
    while(!Route.empty())
    {
        cout << Route.top().origin() << " TO " << Route.
              top().destination() << endl;
        Route.pop();
    }
 }
```

Notice that `Trip1`, `Trip2`, and `Trip3` are tested as if they were `bools`. The `candidates()` method simply returns the route discovered for the trip. The operator overloading capabilities and the template facilities support the development of reusable inference methods and the CDS. These inference methods and the CDS make the object a rational object. A C++ programmer uses the classes construct to design agents. Container objects are often used in conjunction with the built-in algorithms to implement the CDS. A class that has a CDS is rational. A rational class is an agent.

12.4.3   Simple Autonomy

Since our simple agent class does not require the traditional *"agent loop"* to do its processing, we need other means to activate this agent without human intervention and on a period or cyclic basis. There will be many situations where an agent that you are writing only needs to run sometimes or only under limited conditions. The UNIX/Linux environments come with the `crontab` facility. The crontab facility is the user interface of the UNIX cron system. The `crontab` utility allows you to schedule one or more programs to be executed on a cyclic or periodic basis. Crontab jobs can be scheduled to the month, week, day, hour, and minute. To use `crontab` a file must be created that contains the schedule for when the agent is to be activated. The file is a simple text file set up in the following form:

minute   hour   day   month   weekday   command

Where each column can take on the following values:

minute	0–59
hour	0–23
day	1–31
month	1–12
weekday	1–7 (1 = Mon., 7 = Sun)
command	can be any UNIX/Linux command as well as the name of the file that contains your agents

Once this text file is created, it is submitted to the cron system as the command:

$crontab   *NameOfCronFile*

For example, if we have a file named `activate.agent` that is set up as follows:

```
15   8    *    *    *    agent1
0    21   *    *    6    agent2
*    *    1    12   *    agent3
```

and we execute the `crontab` command:

$crontab `activate.agent`

Then `agent1` will activate everyday at 8:15 A.M., `agent2` will activate every Saturday at 9:00 P.M. and `agent3` will activate every 1st of December. The cron files can be added or deleted as necessary. Cronfiles can contain references to other cron jobs, thus allowing an agent to reschedule itself. In fact, shell scripts can be used in conjunction with the `crontab` utility to provide extremely flexible, dynamic, and reliable activation of agents. See the man pages for a complete description of the `crontab` facility.

$man   `crontab`   or   **$man**   `at`

The `crontab` and `at` facilities are the simplest method to automate or regularly schedule agents that don't require constantly executing event loops. They are reliable and flexible. On the other extreme, the implementation repositories and object request brokers that we discussed in Chapter 8 can also be used to implement automatic agent activation. Standard CORBA implementations also provide event looping capabilities.

12.5   Multiagent Systems

Multiagent systems are systems in which two or more agents cooperate, collaborate, negotiate, or compete toward the solution to some problem. The C++ software developer has several options for implementing multiagent systems. Agents can be implemeted in separate threads using the POSIX thread API. This method divides a single program into multiple threads where each thread contains one or more agents. Therefore, each agent shares the same address space. This allows the agents to easily communicate using global variables and simple parameter passing. If the computer the program is running on contains more than one processor, then the agents can perform their activities in parallel. Obviously each agent should have the necessary synchronization objects defined, as discussed in Chapters 5 and 11, and the exception handling components, as discussed in Chapter 7. Multiagents implemented with multithreading are the easiest approach but limits the agents to a single computer. The most flexible approach to multiagents is using a CORBA implementation. The CORBA standard has a MAF (multi-agent facility) specification in addition to the core CORBA specification. The MICO implementation that we use in the CORBA examples in this book can be used to implement agents that can interact over the Internet, over intranets, and over local networks. The C++ binding of the CORBA standard has complete support for the object-oriented metaphor and therefore has inherent support for agent-oriented programming. In Chapter 13, we discuss how the PVM and MPI libraries can be used to support agents in a parallel and distributed programming context.

Summary

Agents are rational objects. Agent-oriented programming is another important approach to parallel and distributed programming. Agent-oriented programming provides a fresh approach to dealing with the age-old problems of decomposition, communication, and synchronization that are part of every parallel programming or distributed programming project. The C++ support for operator overloading, containers, and templates provide effective tools for implementing a wide range of agent classes. Future massively parallel and large complex distributed systems will rely on agent-oriented implementations because there is almost no other way to competently approach such systems. While the agent examples and techniques that we presented in this chapter were introductory, they provide the basis for understanding how practical agent systems can be built. The POSIX thread API, MICO, PVM, and MPI libraries that are freely available and widely used can be used to deploy multiagent systems. Multiagent systems can be used to implement either solutions that require parallel programming or solutions that require distributed programming. This book advocates two primary architectures for parallel programming and distributed programming: Agents provide the first architecture, and blackboards (which assume agents) provide the second. The next chapter provides a discussion of how to use blackboards to implement parallel and distributed programming solutions.

13

Blackboard Architectures Using PVM, Threads, and C++ Components

> "The human brain is far more complicated than any computer, and in any event the benchmark to be attained by some super microchip of the future is to match the performance, not of an isolated human brain, but of a brain reared in a society comprising many humans . . ."
>
> —*Timothy Ferris*, The Universe and Eye

In this Chapter

The Blackboard Model • Approaches to Structuring the Blackboard • The Anatomy of a Knowledge Source • The Control Strategies for Blackboards • Implementing the Blackboard Using CORBA Objects • Implementing the Blackboard Using Global Objects • Activating Knowledge Sources Using Pthreads • Summary

One of the primary goals in parallel programming is to divide the work a program must do into a set of tasks that may be executed with as much concurrency as necessary. This goal is an elusive one. Finding the correct WBS (Work Breakdown Structure) that will support parallelism and produce correct and efficient results can be a challenge. We use a modeling and architectural approach to achieve an acceptable WBS. In practice the process of modeling the problem and solution as naturally as possible with either objects or processes reveals any necessary parallelism. The model also identifies where the parallelism occurs within the problem or the solution. It's not necessary to introduce parallelism into a solution. If the problem and solution are appropriately modeled, then any necessary parallelism will be discovered. The blackboard architecture helps with this modeling process. In particular, the blackboard model helps to organize and conceptualize the concurrency and the communication within a system that requires parallelism or distributed programming.

13.1   The Blackboard Model

The blackboard model is an approach to collaborative problem solving. The blackboard is used to record, coordinate, and communicate the efforts of two or more software-based problem solvers. Hence there are two primary types of components in the blackboard model: the blackboard and the problem solvers.

The *blackboard* is a centralized object that each of the problem solvers has access to. The problem solvers may read the blackboard and change the contents of the blackboard. The contents of the blackboard at any given time will vary. The initial content of the blackboard will include the problem to be solved. Other information representing the initial state of the problem, problem constraints, goals, and objectives may be contained on the blackboard. As the problem solvers are working toward the solution, intermediate results, hypotheses, and conclusions are recorded on the blackboard. The intermediate results written by one problem solver on the blackboard may act as a catalyst for other problem solvers reading the blackboard. Tentative solutions are posted to the blackboard. If the solutions are determined not to be sufficient, these solutions are erased and other solutions are pursued. The problem solvers use the blackboard as opposed to direct communication to pass partial results and findings to each other. In some configurations the blackboard acts as a referee, informing the problem solvers when a solution has been reached or whether to start work or stop work. The blackboard is an active object, not simply a storage location. In some cases the blackboard determines which problem solvers to involve and what content to accept or reject. The blackboard may also organize the incremental or intermediate results of the problem solvers. The blackboard may translate or interpret the work from one set of problem solvers so that it may be used by another set of problem solvers.

The *problem solver* is a piece of software that typically has specialized knowledge or processing capabilities within some area or problem domain. The problem solver can be as simple a routine that converts from Celsius to Fahrenheit or as complex as a smart agent that handles medical diagnoses. In the blackboard model these problem solvers are called *knowledge sources*. To solve a problem using blackboards, two or more knowledge sources are needed and each knowledge source usually has a different area of focus or specialty. The blackboard is a natural fit for problems that can be divided into separate tasks that can be solved independently or semi-independently.

In the basic blackboard configuration each problem solver tackles a different part of the problem. Each problem solver only sees the part of the problem with which it is familiar. If the solutions to any parts of the problem are dependent on the solutions or partial solutions to other parts of the problem, then the blackboard is used to coordinate the problem solvers and integrate the partial solutions. A blackboard's problem solvers need not be homogeneous. Each problem solver may be implemented using different techniques. For instance, some problem solvers might be implemented using object-oriented techniques while other solvers might be implemented as functions. Furthermore, the problem solvers may employ completely different problem-solving paradigms. For example, solver A might use a backward-chaining approach to solving its problem, while solver B might use a counterpropagation approach. There is no requirement that the blackboard's problem solvers be implemented using the same programming language.

The blackboard model does not specify any particular structure or layout for the blackboard nor does it suggest how the knowledge sources should be structured. In practice, the structure of a blackboard is problem dependent.[1] The implementation of the knowledge sources is also specific to the problem being solved. The blackboard framework is a conceptual model describing relationships without describing the structures of the blackboard and knowledge sources. The blackboard model does not dictate the number or purpose of the knowledge sources. The blackboard may be a single global object or a distributed object with components on multiple computers. Blackboard systems may consist of multiple blackboards, with each blackboard dedicated to a part of the original problem. This makes the blackboard an extremely flexible model for problem solving. The blackboard model supports parallel programming and distributed programming. First, the knowledge sources may execute simultaneously, with each knowledge source working on its part of the problem. Second, the knowledge sources may be implemented in separate threads or in separate processes on the same or different computers.

The blackboard can be segmented into separate parts allowing concurrent access by multiple knowledge sources. The blackboard easily supports CREW, EREW, and MIMD. We implement the blackboard as a global object or collection of objects when the knowledge sources are implemented in

---

[1]While a blackboard may be reused for other, very similar problems, it is nontrivial to design a blackboard that can be used for completely different kinds or classes of problems. Reuse is usually limited to problems that are very similar in nature. This is because the solution space is closely mapped to the problem and the rule component is closely mapped to the solution space, which prevents the use of the blackboard for general problems.

separate threads. Since the threads share the same address space, a black-board implemented as a global object or family of objects will be accessible by each threaded knowledge source. If the knowledge sources are implemented as separate processes running on the same or different computers, the blackboard is implemented as a CORBA object or collection of CORBA objects. Recall that CORBA objects can be used to support both a parallel and distributed model of computing. Here, we use CORBA to support the blackboard as a kind of *distributed shared-memory* between tasks executing

Figure 13-1 Two memory configurations for the blackboard.

BLACKBOARD MEMORY CONFIGURATION 1:

Knowledge sources are in different address spaces.

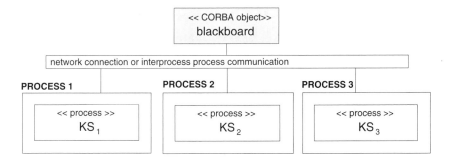

BLACKBOARD MEMORY CONFIGURATION 2:

Knowledge sources share the same address space.

PROCESS 1

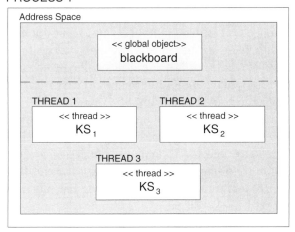

in different address spaces. The tasks can be PVM (Parallel Virtual Machine) tasks, tasks spawned by the traditional `fork-exec` functions calls, or tasks spawned by the new `posix_spawn()`. Figure 13–1 shows our two memory configurations for the blackboard.

In both the cases in Figure 13-1, all knowledge sources have access to the blackboard. Knowledge sources in different address spaces will each make a network connection to a blackboard implemented as one or more CORBA objects. Also, when the knowledge sources are implemented as PVM tasks, the knowledge sources can supplement the blackboard communication with the message-passing model. This configuration provides for an extremely flexible model of problem solving.

13.2   Approaches to Structuring the Blackboard

There is no one way to structure a blackboard. However, most blackboards will have certain characteristics and attributes in common. The original contents of the blackboard will typically contain some kind of partitioning of the solution space for the problem that is to be solved. The solution space will contain all the partial solutions and full solutions to a problem. For instance, let's say that we have a search engine that searches the Internet for pictures of cars. The search engine can process a bitmap image or vector image to determine whether it contains a picture of a car and if so, whether it is the target car. Let's say that our search engine is developed using the blackboard model. Each knowledge source has a speciality: one knowledge source is a specialist in identifying images of tires, another focuses on identifying rearview mirrors, and another is an expert in identifying car door handles, lug nuts, and so on. Each aspect of the car represents a small part of the solution space. Parts of the solution space contain full images of cars from different perspectives that is, from the top, the bottom, 45-degree angles, and so on. Other parts of the solution space only contain sections of cars, perhaps the front end, the roof, the trunk, and the back end. A bitmap or vector image is placed on the blackboard and the individual knowledge sources attempt to identify something in the image that might be part of a car. If some part of the solution space matches something in the image, that piece of the image is written to another part of the blackboard as a partial solution. One knowledge source might put an identified car door handle on the blackboard. Another may put an identified car door on the blackboard. Once these two pieces of information have been put on the blackboard, another knowledge source may use this information to aid in identifying the front end of a car in the image. Once this has been identified, the image of the front end is placed on the blackboard. Each of these various ways to identify the image of a car represents part of the solution space.

The solution space is sometimes organized in a hierarchy. In our car example, complete images of cars might be at the top of the hierarchy and the next level may consist of various views of front ends and back ends, with the next level consisting of the doors, trunks, hoods, windshields, and wheels. Each level describes a smaller, perhaps less obvious image of some part of a car. The knowledge sources may work on multiple levels within the hierarchy simultaneously. The solution space may also be organized as a graph where each node represents some part of the solution and each edge represents the relationships between two partial solutions. The solution space may be represented as one or more matrices, with each element of the matrix containing a solution or partial solution. The solution space representation is an important component of the blackboard architecture. The nature of the problem will often determine how the solution space should be partitioned. In addition to a solution space component, blackboards typically have one or more rule (heuristic) components. The rule component is used to determine which knowledge sources to deploy and what solutions to accept or reject. The rule component can also be used to translate partial solutions from one level in the solution space hierarchy to another level. The rule component may also be used to prioritize the knowledge source approaches. Some knowledge sources may go down blind alleys. The blackboard deselects one set of knowledge sources in favor of another set. The blackboard may use the rule component to suggest to the knowledge sources a more appropriate potential hypothesis based on the partial hypothesis already generated. In addition to the solution space and rule component, the blackboard will often contain initial values, constraint values, and ancillary goals. In some cases the blackboard will contain one or more event queues used to capture input from either the problem space or the knowledge sources. Figure 13–2 shows a logical layout for a basic blackboard architecture.

Figure 13–2 shows the blackboard has a number of segments, each segment having a variety of implementations. This suggests that blackboards are more than global pieces of memory or traditional databases. While Figure 13–2 shows the common core components that most blackboards have, the blackboard architecture is not limited to these components. Other useful components for blackboards include context models of the problem and

Blackboard Architecture

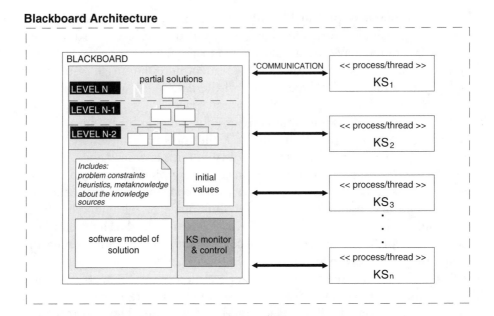

* If the KS (knowledge source) is a process, communication can be over a network or IPC
(interprocess communication). If the KS is a thread, communication may be parameter passing.

Figure 13–2   The logical layout for a basic blackboard architecture.

domain models that can be used to aid the problem solvers with navigation
through the solution space. The support C++ has for object-oriented design and programming fits nicely with the flexibility requirements of the
blackboard model. Most blackboard architectures can be modeled using
classes in C++. Recall that classes can be used to model some person,
place, thing, or idea. Blackboards are used to solve problems that involve
persons, places, things, or ideas. So using C++ classes to model the objects
that blackboards contain or the actual blackboards is a natural fit. We take
advantage of C++ container classes and the standard algorithms in our implementations of the blackboard model. In addition to the built-in classes
we construct interface classes for the mutexes and other synchronization
variables that we use with the blackboard. Because multiple knowledge
sources can access the blackboard simultaneously, this means that the
blackboard is a critical section and access needs to be synchronized. So
along with the other components that a blackboard contains, we will use
synchronization objects to the blackboard.

13.3   The Anatomy of a Knowledge Source

Knowledge sources are represented as objects, procedures, sets of rules, logic assertions, and in some cases entire programs. Knowledge sources have a condition part and an action part. When the blackboard contains some information that satisfies the condition part of some knowledge source, then the action part of the knowledge source is activated. Englemore and Morgan clearly state the responsibilities of a knowledge source in their work *Blackboard Systems:*

> Each knowledge source is responsible for knowing the conditions under which it can contribute to a solution. Each knowledge source has preconditions that indicate the condition on the blackboard that must exist before the body of the knowledge source is activated. One can view a knowledge source as a large rule. The major difference between a rule and a knowledge source is the grain size of the knowledge each holds. The condition part of this large rule is called the knowledge source precondition, and the action part is called the knowledge source body.

Here Englemore and Morgan do not specify any of the details of the condition part or the action part of a knowledge source. They are logical constructs. The condition part could be as simple as the value of some boolean flag on the blackboard or as complex as a specific sequence of events arriving in an event queue within a certain period of time. Likewise, the action part of a knowledge source can be as simple as a single statement performing an expression assignment or as involved as a forward chain in an expert system. Again, this is a statement of how flexible the blackboard model can be. The C++ class construct and the notion of an object will be sufficient for our purposes. Each knowledge source will be an object. The action part of the knowledge source will be implemented by the object's methods. The condition part of the knowledge source will be captured as data members of the object. Once the object is in a certain state then the action parts of that object will be activated. To keep things simple we will map knowledge sources to either threads or processes. Therefore, for each thread there will only be one knowledge source and for each process there will only be one knowledge source. When using the PVM with the blackboard, a knowledge source will be equivalent to a PVM task. Figure 13–3 shows the logical layout of the anatomy of a knowledge source.

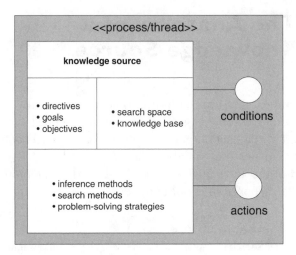

Figure 13–3   The logical layout of a knowledge source.

Each knowledge source's condition part is updated from the blackboard. Some of the knowledge source's action part updates the blackboard. Notice in Figure 13-3 there is a one-for-one correlation between process space and knowledge source or thread space and knowledge source. An important attribute of the knowledge source is its autonomy. Each knowledge source is a specialist and is largely independent from the other problem solvers. This presents one of the desired qualities for a parallel program. Ideally the tasks in a parallel program can operate concurrently without much interaction with other tasks. This is exactly the case in the blackboard model. The knowledge sources act independently and any major interaction is through the blackboard. So from the knowledge source's point of view it is acting alone and getting additional information from the blackboard and recording its findings on the blackboard. The activities of the other knowledge sources and their strategies and structures are unknown. In the blackboard model, the problem is partitioned into a number of autonomous or semi-autonomous problem solvers. This is the advantage of the blackboard model over other models. In the most flexible configuration the knowledge sources are *intelligent agents*. The agent will be completely self-sufficient and able to act on its own with minimum interaction with the blackboard. The intelligent agent presents the greatest opportunity for large-scale parallelism.

13.4 The Control Strategies for Blackboards

There are several layers of control in a blackboard implementation where the knowledge sources may be activated concurrently. At the lowest layer their synchronization schemes must protect the integrity of the blackboard. The blackboard is a critical section because it is a shared, modifiable resource. In a parallel environment the knowledge source's read and write access must be coordinated and synchronized. This coordination and synchronization can involve file locking, semaphores, mutexes, and so on. This layer of control is not directly involved in the solution the knowledge sources are working toward. This is a utility layer of control and should be independent of the problem to be solved by the blackboard. In our architectural approach, this layer of control will be implemented by interface classes like the mutex, and semaphore classes that we introduced in Chapter 11. Recall that the functionality contained in these classes is independent of the application they are used in. For concurrency implementations of blackboards, this layer selects one or more of the four types of parallel access that the knowledge source algorithms or heuristics will have to the physical implementation of the blackboard. That is, the users of the blackboard can be EREW, CREW, ERCW, or CRCW. This access determines how the synchronization primitives will be used. Table 13–1 contains the descriptions of the four types of parallel access that a model can use.

Table 13–1 Four Types of Parallel Access Used by a Model	
PRAM models	*Description*
EREW	Exclusive Read Exclusive Write
CREW	Concurrent Read Exclusive Write
ERCW	Exclusive Read Concurrent Write
CRCW	Concurrent Read Concurrent Write

The segmentation of the blackboard into parts will determine which of the types of concurrency in Table 13–1 are appropriate. The most flexible CRCW can be achieved depending on the structure of the blackboard. For instance, if 16 knowledge sources are involved in a collaborative effort and each knowledge source accesses its own segment of the blackboard, then these knowledge sources can concurrently read and write the blackboard without data race problems.

The next layer of control involves the selection of which knowledge sources to involve in the search for the solution and which aspects of the problem to focus on. This is a focus-of-attention layer. This layer of control decides to focus on a certain area of the problem and selects knowledge sources accordingly. One of the major issues to tackle in any kind of problem solving is where to start and what kind of information is needed to solve the problem. The focus/attention layer evaluates the initial conditions of the problem and then *controls* which knowledge sources to use and where they will start. The available knowledge sources will be known to the blackboard and typically the knowledge source will accept messages or parameters that dictate how it should proceed or where in the solution space it should begin the search. For parallel implementations, this layer will determine the basic model of parallelism (distribution of the problem solvers). Usually for blackboards this is the Multiple Programs Multiple Data (MPMD, a.k.a. MIMD) model because each knowledge source/problem solver has its own area of speciality. However, the nature of the problem might warrant the popular Single Program Multiple Data (SPMD) model. If this model is used, the control layer will spawn N number of the same knowledge source but pass different parameters to each.

The next layer of control involves determining what to do with the solution or partial solutions written to the blackboard. This layer of control will determine whether the knowledge sources can stop work or whether the solution generated is acceptable, unacceptable, partially acceptable, and so on. This layer of control has complete visibility of the blackboard and all the partial or tentative solutions. It *guides* the overall problem-solving strategies of the collective. As with the layout of the blackboard and the structure of the knowledge sources, the blackboard model suggests the existence of a control component but does not specify how it should be structured. Sometimes the control component is part of the blackboard. Sometimes the control component is implemented by the knowledge sources. In some cases the control component is implemented by modules external to the blackboard. The control component can also be implemented by any combination of these. The knowledge sources collectively search for *a solution* to some problem. We want to emphasize *a solution* because many problems have more than one solution. Some solutions may be deeper in the search space than others, some may cost more to find than others, and some may be deemed not good

Control component is part of the blackboard.

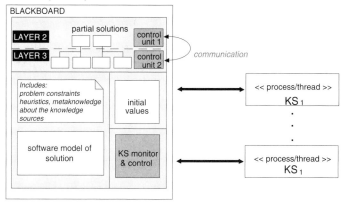

CASE 2:

Control component is part of the blackboard and the knowledge sources.

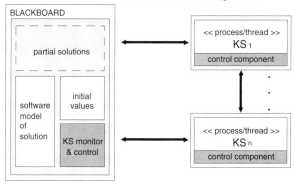

CASE 3:

Control component is external to both the blackboard and the knowledge sources.

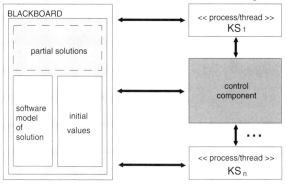

Figure 13–4 Control configurations and their layers in the blackboard architecture.

enough. The control component helps to manage the collective search strategies of the knowledge sources and monitors the tentative or partial solutions to make sure that the knowledge sources are not pursuing an impractical search strategy. The control component looks out for any infinite loops, blind alleys, or recursive regression. Furthermore, the control component is involved in selecting the best or the most appropriate knowledge sources for the problem. As the knowledge sources make progress toward a solution, the control component may relieve some knowledge sources while assigning others. The control strategy will be closely related to the search strategies used by the knowledge sources. It is important to remember that the knowledge sources may each use different search strategies and problem-solving techniques. Although they work with a common blackboard, the knowledge sources or problem solvers are essentially autonomous and self-contained. Therefore, this layer of control has a two-way communication with the knowledge sources. Figure 13–4 shows possible control configurations and their layers in a blackboard architecture.

Note the configuration in Figure 13–4 contains the control within the blackboard as opposed to a separate module or knowledge source. In this configuration, the control is designed as part of the blackboard class. Since a two-way communication is needed in Layer 2 and Layer 3, it is convenient to have the blackboard spawn the processes or threads that will contain the knowledge sources. If the blackboard spawns the processes or threads it will have easy access to the thread ids or process ids. This will allow the blackboard to easily broadcast messages to the knowledge sources, and perform process and thread management. When the blackboard needs to terminate a knowledge source for some reason, access to the thread id or process id will make this easy. Notice if Figure 13–4 that one of the options is to have the control external to the blackboard and the knowledge sources. If this configuration is used, thread ids and process ids must be communicated explicitly to the control modules.

13.5 Implementing the Blackboard Using CORBA Objects

Recall from Chapter 8 that a CORBA object is a platform-independent distributed object. CORBA objects can be accessed between processes on the same machines or processes running on different machines connected to a network. This makes CORBA objects candidates for use in PVM environments where the program is divided into a number of processes that may or may not be running on the same computer. Ordinarily the PVM environment is used for the message-passing strengths and any shared memory approaches are secondary if used at all. The notion of a network-accessible shared object adds computational power to the PVM environment. Keep in mind that CORBA objects can model anything that nondistributed objects can represent. This means PVM tasks that have shared access to CORBA objects can access container objects, framework objects, pattern objects, domain objects, and any kind of utility object. In this case, we want the PVM tasks to have access to blackboard objects. So the message-passing model is supplemented with shared access to complex objects. In addition to PVM tasks accessing distributed CORBA objects, traditional tasks spawned by the `posix_spawn()` or `fork-exec` functions can access the CORBA objects. These tasks execute in separate address spaces on the same machine but may still connect to a CORBA object that is either located on the same machine or some different machine. So while the tasks created with the `posix_spawn()` and `fork-exec` functions will all reside on the same machine, the CORBA objects can be located on any machine.

13.5.1   The CORBA Blackboard: An Example

To demonstrate our notion of a CORBA-based blackboard, we'll look at a blackboard developed at Ctest Laboratories. While providing a complete implementation of the blackboard is beyond the scope of this book and subject to other restrictions, we look closely at some of the most important aspects of the blackboard and the knowledge sources as they relate to our architectural approach to parallel programming. The blackboard implements a software-based course adviser. The blackboard solves the course scheduling problems for the typical college student. Students often encounter several obstacles to the perfect schedule. During course registration there is always a competition for seats in a class. At some point important classes are closed. So there is the infamous *first-come, first-serve* issue. So during registration where tens of thousands of students are trying to sign up for a limited number of courses, this timeliness is a factor. The student wishes to get courses that apply directly to the degree sought. Ideally these courses will be during hours that the student can attend and has open. Also, the student would like to stay within a certain course load, and keep some time open for working and other extracurricular activities. The problem is that when the student is ready to take a given course, the course may not always be offered, so substitutes or filler classes are offered to the student instead. The substitutes and filler classes add to the cost and duration of the student's education. Adding to the cost and duration are negative outcomes from the student's vantage point. However, if the substitutes or filler classes are in some way related to the student's nonacademic interests, hobbies, or goals, then the substitutes or filler classes will be reluctantly tolerated. Also, there are a number of electives and options that can be taken under the degree sought. The student wishes to have the optimum mix of courses that will allow the student to graduate either early or on time, within budget, and with the most flexibility possible. The student uses *real-time* course advisement software built with blackboard technology to solve the problem.

It is important to note that the blackboard has real-time access to the student's academic record, the current courses open or closed at any instant during the registration process. The blackboard has access to the student's degree plan, the university's requirements for the degree plan, the student availability schedule, the student's goals, and so on. Each of these items are modeled using C++ classes and CORBA classes and make up the components of the blackboard. To keep our blackboard example simple, we will look only at these four knowledge sources:

- General requirements counselor
- Major requirements counselor
- Electives counselor
- Minor requirements counselor

Example 13.1 shows an excerpt from the blackboard's CORBA interface.

```
//Example 13.1 Two CORBA declarations necessary for our
//             blackboard class.

typedef sequence<long> courses;

interface black_board{
    //...
    void suggestionsForMajor(in courses Major);
    void suggestionsForMinor(in courses Minor);
    void suggestionsForGeneral(in courses General);
    void suggestionsForElectives(in courses Electives);
    courses currentDegreePlan();
    courses suggestedSchedule();
    //...
};
```

The primary purpose of the `black_board` interface is to provide read/write access to the knowledge sources. In this case, the blackboard's partitions will include segments for each knowledge source.[2] This will allow the knowledge sources to access the blackboard with a CRCW policy with respect to each other. That is, multiple types of knowledge sources can access the blackboard at the same time, however, two or more knowledge sources of the same type will be restricted to a CREW policy. Any method or member function the knowledge sources will access should be defined in the `black_board` interface class. The class `courses` has been declared as a CORBA type and therefore it can be used as parameter and return values between the knowledge sources and the blackboard. So the `black_board` class declarations such as:

```
courses Minor;
courses Major;
```

will be used to represent information that is either being written to or read from the blackboard. The type `courses` is a CORBA `typedef` for se-quence<long>. A *sequence* in CORBA is a variable-length vector (array). This means that courses will be used to store an array of `long`s. Each `long` will be used to store a course code. Each course code represents a course offered at the university. Since C++ does not have a sequence type, the `sequence<long>` declaration is mapped to a C++ class. The class has the same name as `sequence<long>` typedef: `courses`. The mapping process from CORBA types to C++ types occurs during the idl compilation phase when building a CORBA application. The idl compiler will translate the `sequence<long>` declaration into C++ code. The C++ `courses` class will have a number of method functions automatically included:

```
allocbuf()
freebuf()
get_buffer()
length()
operator[]
release()
replace()
maximum()
```

The knowledge sources will interact with these methods. The `sequence<long>` declaration will be transparent to the knowledge sources; they only see the class `courses`. Because CORBA supports datatypes such as `struct`s, classes, arrays, and sequences, the knowledge sources can exchange

---

[2]In practice, each of the knowledge source segments will contain one or more standard C++ container classes used as data queues and event queues. Each container is made safe with synchronization components.

sophisticated objects with the blackboard. This allows the programmer to maintain the object-oriented metaphor when exchanging data with the blackboard. Maintaining the object-oriented metaphor where necessary is an important part of reducing the complexity of parallel programming. The ability to easily read and write complex objects or object hierarchies from the blackboard simplifies the programming in parallel applications. There is no need to perform the translation from primitive datatypes to complex objects. The complex objects may be exchanged directly.

13.5.2   The Implementation of the black_board Interface Class

Notice in Example 13.1 the interface class does not declare any variables. Recall the interface class in CORBA is restricted to only declaring the method interfaces. There are no storage components in the interface class. CORBA classes must be supplied with C++ implementations before any work can get done. The actual implementations of the methods and any variables are added to a derived class of the interface class. Example 13.2 shows the derived (implementation) class for the black_board interface class.

```
//Example 13.2   An excerpt from the implementation class for
//               the black_board interface class.

#include "black_board.h"
#include <set.h>

class blackboard : virtual public POA_black_board{
protected:
   //...
   set<long> SuggestionForMajor;
   set<long> SuggestionForMinor;
   set<long> SuggestionForGeneral;
   set<long> SuggestionForElective;
   courses Schedule;
   courses DegreePlan;
public:
   blackboard(void);
  ~blackboard(void);
   void suggestionsForMajor(const courses &X);
   void suggestionsForMinor(const courses &X);
   void suggestionsForGeneral(const courses &X);
   void suggestionsForElectives(const courses &X);
   courses *currentDegreePlan(void);
```

```
   courses *suggestedSchedule(void);
   //...
};
```

The implementation class is used to provide the actual implementations of the methods defined in the interface class. In addition to method implementation, the derived class may contain data components since it is not declared as an interface. Notice that the black_board implementation class in Example 13.2 does not directly inherit the black_board interface class. Instead it inherits POA_black_board, which is one of the classes that the idl compiler created on behalf of the black_board interface class. Example 13.3 contains the declaration of POA_black_board created by the idl compiler.

```
// Example 13.3  Excerpt of the POA_black_board class created
//               by the idl compiler for  the black_board
//               interface class.

class POA_black_board : virtual public PortableServer:
                        :StaticImplementation
{
public:
   virtual ~POA_black_board ();
   black_board_ptr _this ();
   bool dispatch (CORBA::StaticServerRequest_ptr);
   virtual void invoke (CORBA::StaticServerRequest_ptr);
   virtual CORBA::Boolean _is_a (const char *);
   virtual CORBA::InterfaceDef_ptr _get_interface ();
   virtual CORBA::RepositoryId _primary_interface
                 (const PortableServer::ObjectId &,
                  PortableServer::POA_ptr);

   virtual void * _narrow_helper (const char *);
   static POA_black_board * _narrow (PortableServer::Servant);
   virtual CORBA::Object_ptr _make_stub (PortableServer::
                                         POA_ptr,
                                         CORBA::Object_ptr);
   //...
   virtual void suggestionsForMajor (const courses& Major)
                               = 0;
   virtual void suggestionsForMinor (const courses& Minor)
                               = 0;
   virtual void suggestionsForGeneral (const courses& General)
                               = 0;
   virtual void suggestionsForElectives (const courses& Electives)
                               = 0;
```

```
   virtual courses* currentDegreePlan() = 0;
   virtual courses* suggestedSchedule() = 0;
   //...
protected:
   POA_black_board () {};
private:
   POA_black_board (const POA_black_board &);
   void operator= (const POA_black_board &);
};
```

Notice that the class in Example 13.3 is an abstract virtual class because it has pure virtual member functions such as:

```
virtual courses* suggestedSchedule() = 0;
```

This means that this class cannot be used directly. It must have a derived class that provides actual member functions for every pure virtual member function. The blackboard class in Example 13.2 provides the required definitions for each pure virtual member function. In the case of our blackboard class, C++ methods will be used to implement the functionality of the blackboard and invocation of the knowledge sources. However, the knowledge sources themselves are implemented partially in C++ and partially in the logic programming language Prolog.[3] But since C++ supports multilanguage and multiparadigm development, the advantages of Prolog can be intermixed with C++. In C++ we can either spawn Prolog executables using `posix_spawn()`, `fork-exec` functions, or we can access the Prolog through its foreign language interface that allows Prolog to talk directly to C++ and vice versa. Whether the actual implementation is in C++ or Prolog, the blackboard class only has to interact with C++ methods.

13.5.3   Spawning the Knowledge Sources in the Blackboard's Constructor

The blackboard is implemented as a distributed object using the CORBA protocol. One of the primary functions of the blackboard in this case is to spawn the knowledge sources. This is important because the blackboard will need access to the process ids of the tasks. The initial state of the blackboard is set in the constructor. The initial state includes information about the stu-

---

[3]This configuration is useful because Prolog has many features built in, such as unification, backtracking, and support for predicate logic that would have to be implemented from scratch in C++. For the examples in this book where we intermix C++ with Prolog, SWI-Prolog (University of Amsterdam) and its C++ interface library is used.

dent, the student's academic record, the current semester, degree require-ments and so on. The blackboard decides which knowledge sources to begin based on the initial state. As the blackboard evaluates the initial problem and state of the system it decides on a list of knowledge sources to invoke. Each knowledge source has an associated binary file. The blackboard uses a con-tainer called `Solvers` to store the names of the binaries of the knowledge sources. Later during the construction process, a function object and the `for_each()` algorithm are used to spawn the knowledge sources. Recall that any class that has the `operator()` defined can be used as a *function object*. Function objects are used with the standard algorithms in place of functions or in addition to functions. Usually where a function can be used a function object may be used instead. To define your own function object you must de-fine the `operator()` with the appropriate meaning, parameter list, and re-turn type. Our CORBA blackboard implementation can support knowledge sources implemented within PVM tasks, traditional UNIX/Linux tasks, or within separate threads using the POSIX thread libraries. The type of task spawned in the constructor determines whether the blackboard will be work-ing with POSIX threads, traditional UNIX/Linux processes, or PVM tasks.

13.5.3.1 Spawning Knowledge Sources Using PVM Tasks

Part of the constructor contains the call:

```
for_each(Solve.begin(),Solve.end(),Task);
```

The `for_each()` algorithm applies the function object operator for the task class to each element of the `Solve` container. This technique is used to spawn knowledge sources in a MIMD model, which is used when the knowl-edge sources each have a different speciality working on different data. Ex-ample 13.4 contains the declaration of the task class.

```
// Example 13.4 The declaration of the task class.

class task{
   int Tid[4];
   int N;
   //...
public:
   //...
   task(void) { N = 0; }
   void operator()(string X);
};
```

```
void task::operator()(string X)
{
    int cc;
    pvm_mytid();
    cc = pvm_spawn(const_cast<char *>(X.data()),NULL,0,"",1,
                    &Tid[N]);N++;
}

blackboard::blackboard(void)
{

    task Task;

    vector<string> Solve;
    //...
    // Determine which KS to invoke
    //...
    Solve.push_back(KS1);
    Solve.push_back(KS2);
    Solve.push_back(KS3);
    Solve.push_back(KS4);
    for_each(Solve.begin(),Solve.end(),Task);
}
```

This `Task` class encapsulates a process that has been spawned. It will contain the task ids in the case of PVM. In the case of standard UNIX/Linux processes or Pthreads, it will contain the process ids and thread ids. This class acts as an interface to the created thread or process and the blackboard. The blackboard acts as the primary control component. It can manage the PVM tasks through their task ids. Also, the blackboard can use the PVM group operations to synchronize the PVM tasks with barriers, organize the PVM tasks into logical groups that will work on certain aspects of the problem, and to signal group members with certain message tags. Table 13–2 contains the PVM group routines and their descriptions.

The `pvm_barrier()` and the `pvm_joingroup()` routines in Table 13–2 are of particular interest to our blackboard because there are situations where the blackboard does not want to launch new knowledge sources until a certain group of knowledge sources has finished their work. The `pvm_barrier()` routine can be used to block the calling process until the appropriate knowledge sources have finished their processing. For instance, the course advisor blackboard does not want to activate the scheduler knowledge source until the knowledge sources that focus on major requirements, general requirements,

Table 13–2   PVM Group Routines

PVM group operations	*Description*
`int pvm_joingroup(char *groupname);`	Enrolls the calling process in the group `groupname` and then returns an `int`, which is the instance number of this process in this group.
`int pvm_lvgroup(char *groupname);`	Unrolls the calling process from the group `groupname`.
`int pvm_gsive(char *groupname);`	Returns an `int`, which is the number of members in the group `groupname`.
`int pvm_gettid(char *groupname,` `           int inum);`	Returns an `int`, which is the task id of the process identified by the group name `groupname` and the instance number `inum`.
`int pvm_getinst(char *groupname,` `            int taskid);`	Returns an `int`, which is the instance number associated with the group name `groupname` and the process with the task id `taskid`.
`int pvm_barrier(char *groupname,` `            int count);`	Blocks the calling process until `count` members in the group `groupname` have called this function.
`int pvm_bcast(char *groupname,` `          int messageid);`	Broadcasts a message stored in the active send buffer associated with `messageid` to all the members of the group `groupname`.

`int pvm_reduce(void *operation,`
`           void *buffer,`
`           int count,`
`           int datatype,`
`           int messageid,`
`           char *groupname,`
`           int root);`
	Performs a global operation `operation` on all the processes in the group `groupname`.

minor requirements, and electives are through making their suggestions. So the blackboard will use the `pvm_barrier()` routine to wait on the PVM task group that focuses on requirements. Figure 13–5 shows a UML activity diagram that shows how the knowledge sources and the blackboard are synchronized.

In Figure 13–5, the synchronization barrier is implemented with the help of the `pvm_barrier()` and `pvm_joingroup()` routines. Example 13.5 contains the function operator of the task object.

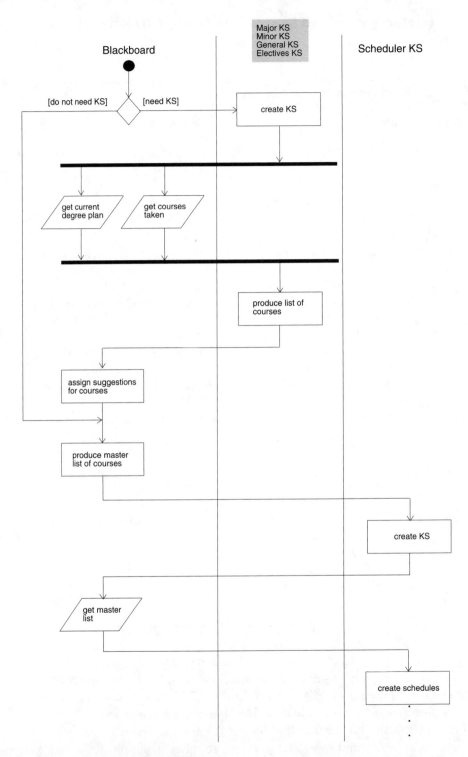

Figure 13-5 UML activity diagram showing the synchronization of the blackboard and the knowledge sources.

```
// Example 13.5 The function operator of the task object.

void task::operator()(string X)
{
   int cc;
   pvm_mytid();
   cc = pvm_spawn(const_cast<char *>(X.data()),NULL,0,"",1,
                  &Tid[N]);N++;
}
```

The function operator is used to spawn PVM tasks. The name of the task is contained in X.data(). The call to the pvm_spawn() routine in Example 13.5 creates one task and stores the task id of the task in Tid[N]. The pvm_spawn() routine and the invocation of PVM tasks are discussed in Chapter 6. The task class is used as a *function object*. The algorithm:

```
for_each(Solve.begin(),Solve.end(),Task);
```

will cause the operator() to execute for the Task object. This operation will cause a knowledge source in the Solve container to be activated. The for_each() algorithm ensures that each knowledge source will be activated. If the SIMD model is used, then the for_each() algorithm is not necessary. Instead we use a PVM spawn call directly in the constructor of the blackboard. Example 13.6 shows how a set of PVM tasks using a SIMD model can be launched from the blackboard constructor.

```
// Example 13.6 Launching PVM tasks from the task class
//              constructor.

void task::operator()(string X)
{

   int cc;
   pvm_mytid();
   cc = pvm_spawn(const_cast<char *>(X.data()),NULL,0,"",1,
                  &Tid[N]);N++;
}
```

13.5.3.2 Connecting Blackboard and the Knowledge Sources

In Example 13.6, 20 knowledge sources are spawned. Initially they will each execute the same code. After they are spawned, the blackboard will send messages to them representing what part they are to play in the problem-solving process. With this configuration the knowledge sources and the blackboard are part of the PVM. After the knowledge sources are created, they will be able to interact with the blackboard by connecting to the port that the blackboard is located on, or to the address the blackboard is at on an intranet or the Internet. The knowledge sources will need the object reference for the blackboard. These references may be coded within the knowledge sources, or the knowledge sources might read them from a configuration file, or get them from a naming service. Once the knowledge source has the reference the knowledge source interacts with the ORB (Object Request Broker) to locate the actual knowledge and activate it. For our example, we will assign the blackboard a specific port. We start the CORBA blackboard with a command:

```
blackboard -ORBIIOPAddr inet:porthos:12458
```

This command executes our blackboard program and assigns it to listen on port 12458 on host `porthos`. Starting a CORBA object will differ depending on the CORBA implementation used. Here we are using Mico,[4] an open-source implementation of CORBA. When the blackboard program executes, it instantiates the blackboard that in turn spawns the knowledge sources. When the knowledge sources are spawned by the blackboard they will have the port number hard-coded. Example 13.7 shows an excerpt from a knowledge source that connects to the CORBA-based blackboard.

```
// Example 13.7 A knowledge source that connects to the CORBA
                blackboard.

 1 #include "pvm3.h"
 2 using namespace std;
 3 #include <iostream>
 4 #include <fstream>
 5 #include <string.h>
 6 #include <strstream>
 7 #include "black_board_impl.h"
 8
 9 int main(int argc, char *argv[])
10 {
11   CORBA::ORB_var Orb = CORBA::ORB_init(argc,argv,
                                    "mico-local-orb");
12   CORBA::Object_var Obj =Orb->bind("IDL:black_board:1.0",
                                    "inet:porthos:12458");
```

---

[4]We used Mico 2.3.3 in the Linux environment and Mico 2.3.7 under Solaris 8 for all of the CORBA examples in this book.

```
13    courses Courses;
14    //...
15    //...
16    black_board_var BlackBoard = black_board::_narrow(Obj);
17
18    int Pid;
19    //...
20    //...
21
22    cout << "created the knowledge source" << endl;
23    Courses.length(2);
24    Courses[0] = 255551;
25    Courses[1] = 253212;
26    string FileName;
27    strstream Buffer;
28    Pid = pvm_mytid();
29    Buffer <<  "Result." << Pid << ends;
30    Buffer >> FileName;
31    ofstream Fout(FileName.data());
32    BlackBoard->suggestionsForMajor(Courses);
33    Fout.close();
34    pvm_exit();
35    return(0);
36 }
37
```

In line 11 in Example 13.7, the ORB runtime is initalized. Line 12 associates the `black_board` object name with the port 12458 and returns a reference to the CORBA object in the `Obj` variable. Line 16 performs a kind of cast operation so that the `Blackboard` variable is referring to the right size object. Once the knowledge source has instantiated the `Blackboard` object, any method declared in the `black_board` interface shown in Example 13.1 may be invoked. Notice on line 13 that the object `Courses` is instantiated. Recall that courses was originally defined as a CORBA sequence type. Here, the knowledge source is using the class courses created during the idl compilation. The elements are added to this class as they would be for an array. Lines 24 and 25 add two courses to the `Courses` object and line 32 contains the method invocation:

```
BlackBoard->suggestionsForMajor(Courses)
```

This call writes the courses on the blackboard. Similarly, the:

```
courses currentDegreePlan();
courses suggestedSchedule();
```

methods can be used to read information from the blackboard. So all that is needed by the knowledge source is a reference to the `Black_board` object. The `Black_board` object may be located anywhere within an intranet or the Internet. It is the ORB's responsibility to actually locate the object. (Chapter 8 discusses the process of locating and activating CORBA objects.) Because the `Black_board` object has the PVM task ids, it may perform task management and send and receive messages directly from the knowledge sources. Likewise the knowledge sources may communicate directly with each other using the more traditional PVM messaging. It is important to note that the destructor for the `Black_board` object will call `pvm_exit()` and each knowledge source should call `pvm_exit()` after there are no more PVM system calls. This will remove them from the PVM environment, although other processing may continue.

13.5.3.3   Activating Knowledge Sources Using POSIX `spawn()`

Implementing the knowledge sources or problem solvers within PVM tasks is especially useful when the tasks will run on separate computers. Each knowledge source can take advantage of any special resource that a particular computer may have. These resources can include processor speed, databases, special peripherals, processor architectures, and numbers of processors. The PVM tasks may also be used on a single computer that has multiple processors. However, since our blackboard can be implemented by connecting to ports, we can just as easily use traditional UNIX/Linux processes to contain our knowledge sources. When the knowledge sources are created in standard UNIX/Linux processes and the computer has multiple processors, then the knowledge sources may run concurrently on the processors available. Obviously if there are more knowledge sources than there are processors, then multitasking will be necessary. Figure 13–6 shows two simple architectures that can be used with the CORBA-based blackboard and UNIX/Linux processes.

In Case 1, the CORBA object is located on the same computer as the knowledge sources and each knowledge source has its own address space. That is, each knowledge source has been spawned using either the `posix_spawn()` routine or the `fork-exec` routines. In Case 2, the CORBA object is located on a different computer and the knowledge sources are each located on the same computer but in different address spaces. In both Case 1 and Case 2, the CORBA object acts as a kind of shared memory for the knowledge sources because they each have access to it and they may exchange information through

CASE 1:

Blackboard on same computer as the knowledge sources.
Each KS is in a different process.

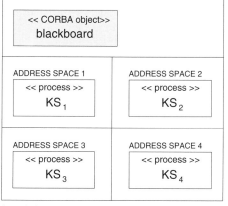

COMPUTER A

knowledge sources spawned by posix_spawn()
or fork-exec() functions

CASE 2:

Blackboard on different computer than the knowledge sources.
Each KS is in a different process.

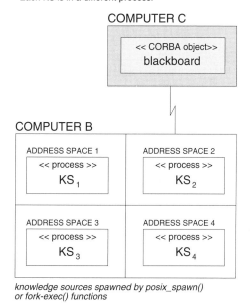

knowledge sources spawned by posix_spawn()
or fork-exec() functions

Figure 13–6   Two architectures that can be used with the CORBA-based blackboard
and UNIX/Linux processes.

the blackboard. But there is a major advantage of the CORBA object—it is far
more sophisticated than a simple block of memory locations. The blackboard is
a complete object that may consist of any type of data structure, object, or even
other blackboards. This kind of sophistication cannot be easily implemented
using the basic shared memory routines. So the CORBA gives us an ideal
method for implemented complex shared objects between processes. In section 13.5.3.1 we spawned PVM tasks that implemented the knowledge sources.
Here we change the constructor to contain calls to the `posix_spawn()` routine
or we can use our `for_each()` algorithm and the task function object to call
the `posix_spawn()` routine. In Case 1 in Figure 13-6, the blackboard can
spawn the knowledge sources from its constructor. However, in Case 2, this is
not possible because the blackboard is located on a separate computer. In Case
2, the blackboard will use some intermediary to cause the `posix_spawn()`
routine to be executed. There are several options available such as the black-

board calling another CORBA object on the computer that contains the knowledge sources, or RPC, or using a MPI or PVM task that will call a program containing a call to `posix_spawn()`. Chapter 3 contains a discussion of how to set up a call to `posix_spawn()`. Example 13.8 shows how the `posix_spawn()` routine can be used to activate one of the knowledge sources.

```
//Example 13.8 Using posix_spawn() to launch knowledge sources.

#include <spawn.h>

blackboard::blackboard(void)
{
    //...
    pid_t Pid;
    posix_spawnattr_t M;
    posix_spawn_file_actions_t N;
    posix_spawn_attr_init(&M);
    posix_spawn_file_actions_init(&N);
    char *const argv[] = {"knowledge_source1",NULL};
    posix_spawn(&Pid,"knowledge_source1",&N,&M,argv,NULL);
    //...
}
```

In Example 13.8, the spawn attributes and the spawn file actions are initialized and then the `posix_spawn()` routine is used to create a separate process that will execute `knowledge_source1`. Once this process is created the blackboard has some access to the process through the process's id stored in `Pid`. In addition to the blackboard as a means of communication, the standard IPC communication is available if the blackboard is located on the same computer as the knowledge sources. While sockets are available in the configuration where the blackboard is on a separate computer, the blackboard is the simplest means of communication between the knowledge sources. When using this configuration, the control that the blackboard has over the knowledge sources will be governed more strictly by the content of the blackboard at any given time as opposed to sending messages directly to the knowledge sources. Sending messages directly is more easily accommodated using the blackboard in conjunction with PVM tasks. Here the knowledge sources regulate themselves based on the content of the blackboard. However, the blackboard does have some level of control over the knowledge sources because the blackboard has the process ids for each process containing a knowledge source. Both the MPMD (MIMD) and SPMD (SIMD) models are also supported using the `posix_spawn()` routine. Example 13.9 shows a class that will be used as a function object with the `for_each()` algorithm.

```
// Example 13.9 The child_process will be used as a function
//                object when launching knowledge sources.
class child_process{
   string Command;
   posix_spawnattr_t M;
   posix_spawn_file_actions_t N;
   pid_t Pid;
   //...
public:
   child_process(void);
   void operator()(string X);
   void spawn(string X);
};

void child_process::operator()(string X)
{
   //...
   posix_spawnattr_init(&M);
   posix_spawn_file_actions_init(&N);
   Command.append("/tmp/");
   Command.append(X);
   char *const argv[] = {const_cast<char*>(Command.data())
                        ,NULL};
   posix_spawn(&Pid,Command.data(),&N,&M,argv,NULL);
   Command.erase(Command.begin(),Command.end());
   //...

}
```

We encapsulate the attributes for the posix_spawn() routine in a class named child_process. Encapsulating all of the information needed to use the posix_spawn() routine within a class makes it easier to use posix_spawn() and provides a natural interface to the attributes of a process that will be created using posix_spawn(). Notice in Example 13.9 that we defined the operator () for the child_process class. This means that the class can be used as a function object with the for_each() algorithm. As the blackboard decides which knowledge sources will be involved in a problem-solving effort, it stores the name of the knowledge sources in a container we call Solve. Later, during the construction of the blackboard, the knowledge sources are activated using the for_each() algorithm.

```
// Constructor
//...
```

```
child_process  Task;
for_each(Solve.begin(),Solve.end(),Task);
```

This will cause the `operator()` method shown in Example 13.9 to be executed for each element of the `Solve` container. Once these knowledge sources are activated, they access a reference to the blackboard and can begin the problem-solving process. Although these are not PVM tasks they connect to the blackboard in the same manner (see section 13.5.3.2) and they perform the work in the same manner. The difference is the interprocess communication between standard UNIX/Linux processes and the interprocess communication that is possible using the PVM environment. Also, the PVM tasks may be located on separate computers. While processes created with `posix_spawn()` exist on the same computer. If processes created by either `posix_spawn()` or the `fork-exec` routines are to be used in conjunction with the SIMD model, then the `argc` and `argv` parameters can be used in addition to the blackboard to assign the knowledge sources a specific area of the problem to solve. In the case where the blackboard is on the same computer as the knowledge sources and the blackboard activates the knowledge sources in its constructor, then technically the blackboard is the parent of the knowledge sources and the knowledge sources will inherit the environment variables of the blackboard. The environment variables of the blackboard are an additional method that can be used to pass information to the knowledge sources. These environment variables can be easily manipulated using the:

```
#include <stdlib.h>
//...
setenv();
unsetenv();
putenv();
```

routines. When the knowledge sources are implemented in processes that were created using either `posix_spawn()` or the `fork-exec` routines, the programs look like regular CORBA programs and can take advantage of all of the facilities that the CORBA protocol has to offer.

13.6   Implementing the Blackboard Using Global Objects

The choice of a CORBA-based blackboard is a natural choice when the knowledge sources will be implemented within an intranet or the Internet environment or when the knowledge sources will be implemented in separate processes for purposes of modularity, encapsulation, and so on. However, distributed blackboards are not always necessary. In the case where the knowledge sources can be implemented within the same process and on the same computer, multiple threads provide a superior solution because they will be faster, have less overhead, and are easier to use and set up. The communication between multiple threads is also easier because the threads share the same address space and can use global variables. In fact, with threads the blackboard will be instantiated as a global object available to all of the threads within the process. There is no need for interprocess communication, socket communication, or any other kind of network communication when the knowledge sources are implemented as threads within a single program. Also, the added layer of the CORBA protocol is not necessary and the objects may be designed as regular C++ classes. If the program is running on a machine that has multiple processors, then the threads may run concurrently on as many processors as are available. The thread's configuration of the blackboard is very attractive in SMP and MPP systems. In general, threads will have the best performance. Threads are often referred to as *lightweight processes* because they don't require the same overhead as traditional UNIX/Linux processes. The POSIX threads (Pthreads) library offers virtually everything needed for knowledge source creation and management. Figure 13–7 contrasts the three basic configurations for process distributions for blackboards and knowledge sources.

Because the blackboard is implemented within a multithread environment, then Pthread mutexes and condition variables may be used to synchronize access to the blackboard. Of course the mutexes and condition variables should be encapsulated within interface classes, as discussed in Chapter 11. Also, `pthread_cond_signal()` and `pthread_cond_broadcast()` can be used to coordinate and synchronize the work that the knowledge sources are performing. Since the blackboard creates the threads it will have easy access to the thread id of each knowledge source. This means the blackboard can cancel a thread if necessary with `pthread_cancel()`. Also, the blackboard will be able to synchronize on the various knowledge sources using the `pthread_join()` routine. In addition to the performance and ease-of-use advantages of threads and global blackboards, there is also the issue of error and exception management. In general, it is easier to deal with errors and exceptions within the same process than between different processes, and with errors on the same machine than between different machines. Figure 13–8 shows the exception and error level difficulty when handling errors and difficulties within a program.

PROCESS DISTRIBUTION 1:

Knowledge sources are implemented as threads within the same process
sharing the blackboard as a global object.

SINGLE PROCESS

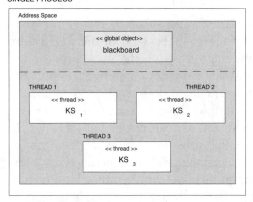

PROCESS DISTRIBUTION 2:

Knowledge sources are implemented as processes running on the same computer using IPC to communicate
with the blackboard as a CORBA object running on the same computer.

SINGLE COMPUTER WITH MULTIPLE PROCESSES

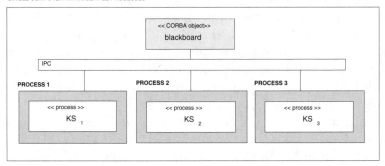

PROCESS DISTRIBUTION 3:

Knowledge sources are implemented as processes running on different computers using IIOP to communicate
with the blackboard as a CORBA object.

MULTIPLE PROCESSES ON MULTIPLE COMPUTERS

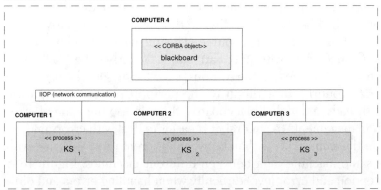

Figure 13–7 Contrasts of the three basic configurations for process
distribution for blackboards and knowledge sources.

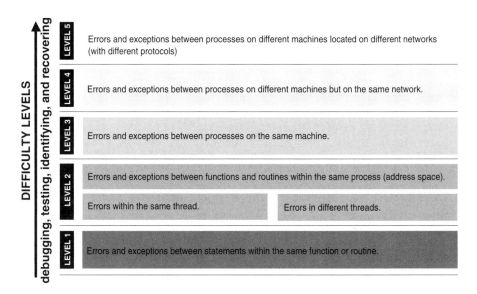

Figure 13-8 The exception and error level difficulty.

Since the knowledge sources are implemented within separate threads within the same process, any errors or exceptions that occur will be at Level 2. Whenever programs that require concurrency are designed and developed, the complexity of handling and recovering from errors and exceptions must be considered. The blackboard implemented as a global object and the knowledge sources implemented as threads are the simplest architecture when using the blackboard model for concurrency. Example 13.10 contains an excerpt declaration from our course advisor blackboard.

```
//Example 13.10 An excerpt from the course advisor blackboard
//              designed for a threaded environment.

class blackboard{
protected:
   //...
   set<long> SuggestionForMajor;
   set<long> SuggestionForMinor;
   set<long> SuggestionForGeneral;
   set<long> SuggestionForElective;
   set<long> Schedule;
   set<long>  DegreePlan;
   mutex Mutex[10];
   //...
```

```
public:
   blackboard(void);
  ~blackboard(void);
   void suggestionsForMajor(set<long> &X);
   void suggestionsForMinor(set<long> &X);
   void suggestionsForGeneral(set<long> &X);
   void suggestionsForElectives(set<long> &X);
   set<long> currentDegreePlan(void);
   set<long> suggestedSchedule(void);
   //...
};
```

This `blackboard` class is designed to be instantiated as a global object accessible to all the threads within a program. Notice that the `blackboard` class in Example 13.10 has an array of mutexes. These mutexes will be used to protect the critical sections within the blackboard. The knowledge sources are virtually unaware of the synchronized access to the critical sections because the synchronization is encapsulated within the blackboard.

13.7   Activating Knowledge Sources Using Pthreads

The knowledge sources are implemented within separate threads. The blackboard's constructor creates the threads and assigns each thread a specific knowledge source. This gives the blackboard its MIMD model. Example 13.11 contains part of the constructor for the blackboard.

```
//Example 13.11 The blackboard's constructor used to create
//              the threads that will contain the
//              knowledge sources.

blackboard::blackboard(void)
{
    pthread_t Tid[4];
    //...
    try{
        pthread_create(&Tid[0],NULL,suggestionForMajor,
                       NULL);
        pthread_create(&Tid[1],NULL,suggestionForMinor,
                       NULL);
```

```
          pthread_create(&Tid[2],NULL,suggestionForGeneral,
                    NULL);
          pthread_create(&Tid[3],NULL,suggestionForElective,
                    NULL);
          pthread_join(Tid[0],NULL);
          pthread_join(Tid[1],NULL);
          pthread_join(Tid[2],NULL);
          pthread_join(Tid[3],NULL);
      }

   //...
}
```

Notice that the constructor calls the `pthread_join()` routine. This causes the constructor to wait for these four threads to terminate before it continues. These threads can be activated from other member functions of the blackboard. However, the particular processing these knowledge sources are performing for the constructor is a preliminary kind of initialization for the blackboard, so it is totally appropriate for the blackboard to wait on these threads before it continues to construct the object. This technique of creating threads within the constructor also raises error handling and exception handling issues. What happens if the threads fail for some reason? Since constructors don't have return values, exception handling must be used.

Each thread is associated with a function. In this case:

```
void *suggestionForMajor(void *X);
void *suggestionForMinor(void *X);
void *suggestionForGeneral(void *X);
void *suggestionForElective(void *X);
```

These four functions are used by the threads to implement the functionality of these particular knowledge sources. Since the blackboard is a global object, each of these functions has immediate access to the blackboard's member functions. So the knowledge sources may call the blackboard's member functions directly, such as:

```
//...
Combination.generateCombinations(1,9,Courses);
Result = Combination.element(9);
//...
Blackboard.suggestionsForMinor(Value);
//...
```

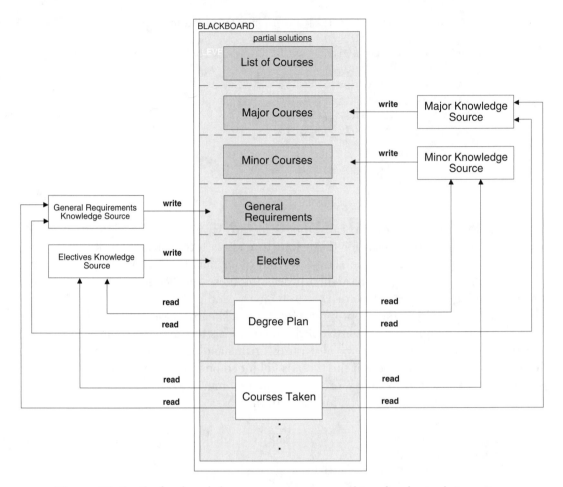

Figure 13–9   The four knowledge sources may concurrently read and write their section of the blackboard.

Since some divisions of the blackboard are restricted to a particular knowledge source, these divisions of the blackboard may be accessed using CRCW policies, as shown in Figure 13–9.

The type of parallelism shown in Figure 13–9 is a natural scheme in blackboard systems because the blackboard is often divided into sections, with each section referring to a certain part of the problem or subproblem. There is typically one knowledge source per problem area, so these sections may be accessed concurrently.

Summary

The blackboard model supports concurrency. The concurrency is inherent in the structure of the blackboard and the relationship between the blackboard and the knowledge sources and between the knowledge sources and each other. The blackboard is a problem-solving model. The problem is divided up into knowledge-specific areas. Each area is assigned a knowledge source or problem solver. The knowledge sources and problem solvers are typically self-contained and require little interaction with the other knowledge sources. The communication that is necessary occurs through the blackboard. Therefore, the knowledge sources and problem solvers serve to modularize the processing within the program. These modules can be treated separately and they can execute concurrently without complex synchronization needs. The blackboard may be implemented using CORBA objects. When the blackboard is implemented as CORBA objects, the knowledge sources can be distributed across intranets or the Internet. The blackboard acts as a kind of shared distributed memory for tasks within a PVM-type environment. The blackboard model easily supports MPMD (MIMD) and the SPMD (SIMD) model. The concept of the blackboard motivates the designer to break down the work that a program needs to do along *knowledge lines*. This results in the program having a WBS of knowledge specialists. The blackboard will contain software models of the problem domain and the solution space. These software models help the designer and developer to discover any parallelism that is necessary within a program that will be implemented. Alongside of the classic client-server model of distributed programming the blackboard model is one of the most powerful models available for both distributed and parallel programming. The knowledge sources or problem solvers in the blackboard model are often implemented as agents. In the next chapter we will take a closer look at how to implement agents and how to deploy multiagent systems to achieve concurrency.

Appendix A

T his appendix provides a quick reference to the UML diagrams used throughout this book. The UML (United Modeling Language) is a graphical notation used to design, visualize, model, and document the artifacts of a software system. It is the de facto standard for communicating and modeling object-oriented systems. The modeling language uses symbols and notations to represent the artifacts of a software system from different views and different focuses. Although there are other graphical notations and artifacts used in this book, this appendix provides a quick way the reader can become familiar with the basic UML notations and symbols they may require in documenting their software systems.

A.1   Class and Object Diagrams

Class and object diagrams are the most common diagrams used in modeling an object-oriented system. Class diagrams can be use to represent each type of class in your system, including template classes and interface classes. Class diagrams can include the details of the class (e.g., attributes, services). Class and object diagrams can show the datatype, value of variables, and return types of functions. Object diagrams can show the object name. Both types of diagrams can depict the number of classes or objects used in the system along with their relationships between classes and objects.

REPRESENTING A CLASS

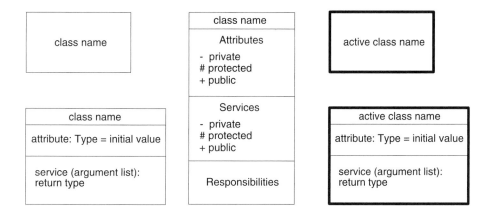

class name
class name
attribute: Type = initial value
service (argument list): return type

class name
Attributes
- private
protected
+ public
Services
- private
protected
+ public
Responsibilities

active class name

active class name
attribute: Type = initial value
service (argument list): return type

REPRESENTING AN OBJECT

object name: class name

active object name: class name

Figure A-1   The multiple ways a class or object can be represented. Classes can show services, attributes, and visibility. Active classes or objects use a heavier line.

REPRESENTING MULTIPLE INSTANCES

class name

multiple classes

object name: class name

multiple objects

class name 1..7	multiplicity notation
Attributes
- private
protected
+ public
Services
- private
protected
+ public
Responsibilities

Figure A-2   Multiple instances of classes and objects. Multiple instances can be shown graphically or by using multiplicity notation.

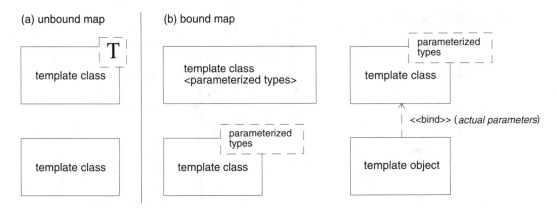

Figure A-3   The ways to represent bound or unbound template or parameterized classes.

A.2   Interaction Diagrams

Interaction diagrams show the interaction between objects. It consists of a set of objects, their relationship, and the messages exchanged between them. Interaction diagrams include collaboration, sequence, and activity diagrams.

A.2.1   Collaboration Diagrams

Collaboration diagrams are used to show a set of objects working together to perform some work. The collaboration in the system is a temporary cooperation between a set of objects. Collaboration diagrams can depict the organization of the collaboration or can depict the structure of the collaboration. This involves showing all the objects in the set, their links, and the messages sent and received between them.

A.2.2   Sequence Diagrams

Sequence diagrams are used to emphasize the time ordering of messages received and sent by objects in a system.

REPRESENTING AN INTERFACE CLASS

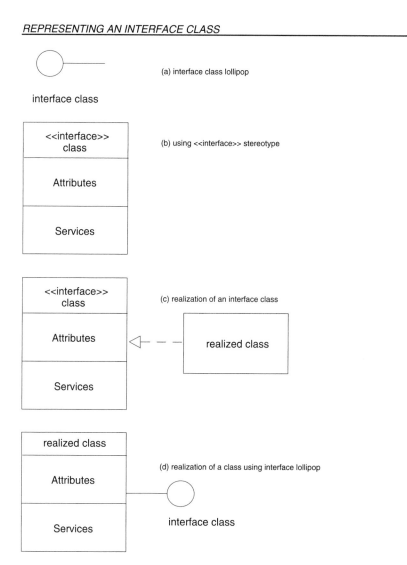

(a) interface class lollipop

interface class

(b) using <<interface>> stereotype

(c) realization of an interface class

(d) realization of a class using interface lollipop

interface class

Figure A–4   The ways to represent an interface class. An interface class can be represented using a lollipop symbol or as a regular class displaying the <<interface>> stereotype. The relationship between the interface class and the realization of the class can also be depicted.

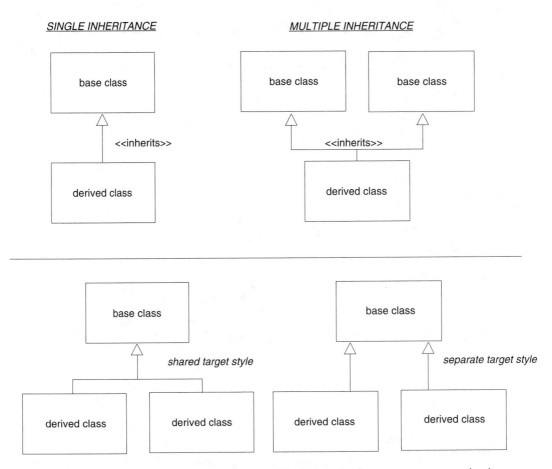

SINGLE INHERITANCE

MULTIPLE INHERITANCE

Figure A–5   The ways to represent single and multiple inheritance. There are two target styles that can be used when multiple classes are involved in a relationship: shared and separate. With the shared target style, multiple classes are tied to a single inheritance symbol that points to the target class. With the separate target style, each class has its own inheritance symbol.

A.2.3 Activity Diagrams

Activity diagrams show the flow of control from one activity to another. Activities are actions performed by objects. Actions include processing input/output, creating or destroying objects, or performing computations. Activity diagrams are similar to flowcharts.

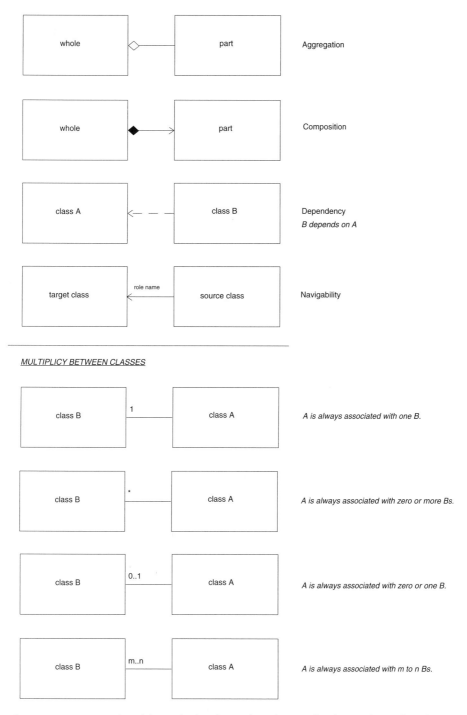

Figure A–6 Examples of the multiple relationships that can be depicted in a class diagram. Multiplicity notation can be used to show the number of instances between classes and objects.

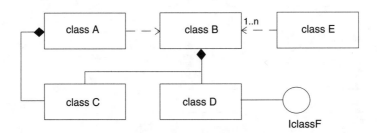

Figure A–7 A collaboration diagram showing the organization of collaborations within a system and the structural relationship of objects within a collaboration.

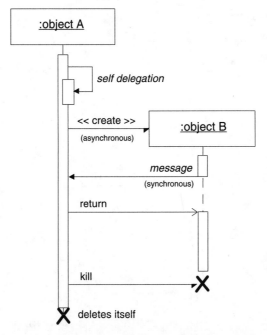

Figure A–8 A sequence diagram is used to emphasize the time ordering of messages passed between objects. The active objects are placed at the top on the *x*-axis of the diagram. The messages passed between the objects are placed on the *y*-axis of the diagram. The diagram can depict synchronous and asynchronous messaging. The time ordering of messages is demonstrated by reading the messages from top to bottom along the *y*-axis.

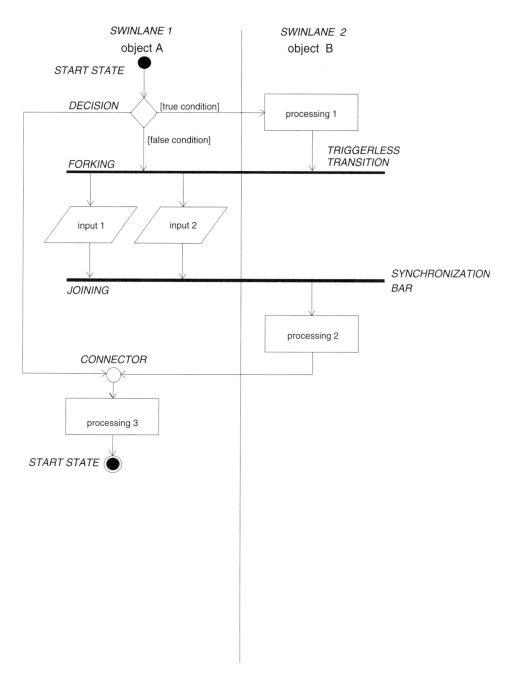

Figure A-9 Activity diagrams show the action of objects as it flows from the focus of control of one object to another. It depicts the forking of multiple flows of control (concurrency) and joining of flows of control with a synchronization bar. Swimlanes are used to show which object is performing the action. Transitions may cut across swimlanes. A synchronization bar may also cut across swimlanes, indicating multiple flows of control reside in different objects performing actions concurrently.

A.3   State Diagrams

A state diagram is used to emphasize the state of objects and their transitions to those states. A state is a condition that an object occupies at some point in its lifetime. An object can be transformed into many different states in its lifetime. The objects transform into a state if some condition is met, some action is performed, or some event has taken place.

Figure A-10 State diagrams show the states and transitions of an object during its lifetime. A state diagram has an initial state and a final state. A state has several parts. States can also be a composite of other states or even another state diagram. Substates that execute in parallel within a single entity are called concurrent substates.

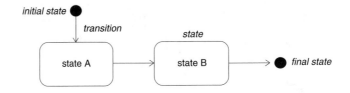

ADVANCED STATES AND TRANSITIONS

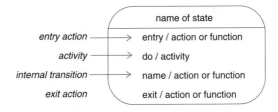

COMPOSITE STATE

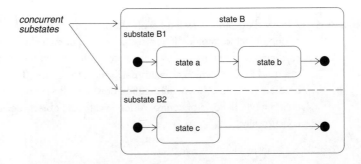

A.4   Package Diagrams

Package diagrams are used to organize entities into groups.

Figure A-11   Package diagrams can be used to organize elements of a system. The stereotypes <<system>> or <<subsystem>> can be used. The tab on the left can hold the name of the package if the package contains other entities.

RELATIONSHIPS BETWEEN SYSTEMS

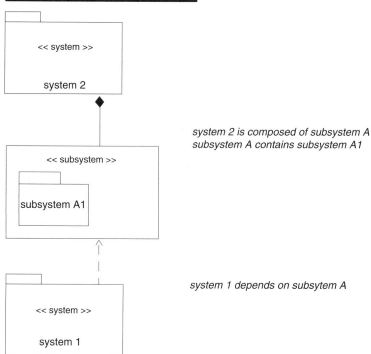

*system 2 is composed of subsystem A
subsystem A contains subsystem A1*

system 1 depends on subsytem A

Appendix B

28273 **NAME**

28274   posix_spawn, posix_spawnp—spawn a process (**ADVANCED REALTIME**)

28275 **SYNOPSIS**

28276 SPN
```
#include <spawn.h>
```

```
int posix_spawn (pid_t *restrict pid, const char *restrict path,
      const posix_spawn_file_actions_t *file_actions,
      const posix_spawnattr_t *restrict attrp,
      char *const argv[restrict], char *const envp[restrict]);
int posix_spawnp (pid_t *restrict pid, const char *restrict file,
      const posix_spawn_file_actions_t *file_actions,
      const posix_spawnattr_t *restrict attrp,
      char *const argv[restrict], char * const envp[restrict]);
```

DESCRIPTION

The *posix_spawn*() and *posix_spawnp*() functions shall create a new process (child process) from the specified process image. The new process image shall be constructed from a regular executable file called the new process image file.

When a C program is executed as the result of this call, it shall be entered as a C-language function call as follows:

```
int main (int argc, char *argv[]);
```

where *argc* is the argument count and *argv* is an array of character pointers to the arguments themselves. In addition, the following variable:

```
extern char **environ;
```

shall be initialized as a pointer to an array of character pointers to the environment strings.

The argument *argv* is an array of character pointers to null-terminated strings. The last member of this array shall be a null pointer and is not counted in *argc*. These strings constitute the argument list available to the new process image. The value in *argv*[0] should point to a filename that is associated with the process image being started by the *posix_spawn*() or *posix_spawnp*() function.

The argument *envp* is an array of character pointers to null-terminated strings. These strings constitute the environment for the new process image. The environment array is terminated by a null pointer.

The number of bytes available for the child process' combined argument and environment lists is {ARG_MAX}. The implementation shall specify in the system documentation (see the Base Definitions volume of IEEE Std 1003.1-2001, Chapter 2, Conformance) whether any list overhead, such as length words, null terminators, pointers, or alignment bytes, is included in this total.

28310
28311

The *path* argument to *posix_spawn()* is a pathname that identifies the new process image file to execute.

28312
28313
28314
28315
28316
28317

The *file* parameter to *posix_spawnp()* shall be used to construct a pathname that identifies the new process image file. If the *file* parameter contains a slash character, the *file* parameter shall be used as the pathname for the new process image file. Otherwise, the path prefix for this file shall be obtained by a search of the directories passed as the environment variable *PATH* (see the Base Definitions volume of IEEE Std 1003.1-2001, Chapter 8, Environment Variables). If this environment variable is not defined, the results of the search are implementation-defined.

28318
28319
28320
28321

If *file_actions* is a null pointer, then file descriptors open in the calling process shall remain open in the child process, except for those whose close-on-*exec* flag FD_CLOEXEC is set (see *fcntl()*). For those file descriptors that remain open, all attributes of the corresponding open file descriptions, including file locks (see *fcntl()*), shall remain unchanged.

28322
28323
28324
28325

If *file_actions* is not NULL, then the file descriptors open in the child process shall be those open in the calling process as modified by the spawn file actions object pointed to by *file_actions* and the FD_CLOEXEC flag of each remaining open file descriptor after the spawn file actions have been processed. The effective order of processing the spawn file actions shall be:

28326
28327
28328

1. The set of open file descriptors for the child process shall initially be the same set as is open for the calling process. All attributes of the corresponding open file descriptions, including file locks (see *fcntl()*), shall remain unchanged.

28329
28330

2. The signal mask, signal default actions, and the effective user and group IDs for the child process shall be changed as specified in the attributes object referenced by *attrp*.

28331
28332

3. The file actions specified by the spawn file actions object shall be performed in the order in which they were added to the spawn file actions object.

28333

4. Any file descriptor that has its FD_CLOEXEC flag set (see *fcntl()*) shall be closed.

28334
28335

The **posix_spawnattr_t** spawn attributes object type is defined in <**spawn.h**>. It shall contain at least the attributes defined below.

28336
28337
28338
28339

If the POSIX_SPAWN_SETPGROUP flag is set in the *spawn-flags* attribute of the object referenced by *attrp*, and the *spawn-pgroup* attribute of the same object is non-zero, then the child's process group shall be as specified in the *spawn-pgroup* attribute of the object referenced by *attrp*.

28340
28341
28342

As a special case, if the POSIX_SPAWN_SETPGROUP flag is set in the *spawn-flags* attribute of the object referenced by *attrp*, and the *spawn-pgroup* attribute of the same object is set to zero, then the child shall be in a new process group with a process group ID equal to its process ID.

28343
28344

If the POSIX_SPAWN_SETPGROUP flag is not set in the *spawn-flags* attribute of the object referenced by *attrp*, the new child process shall inherit the parent's process group.

28345 PS
28346
28347
28348

If the POSIX_SPAWN_SETSCHEDPARAM flag is set in the *spawn-flags* attribute of the object referenced by *attrp*, but POSIX_SPAWN_SETSCHEDULER is not set, the new process image shall initially have the scheduling policy of the calling process with the scheduling parameters specified in the *spawn-schedparam* attribute of the object referenced by *attrp*.

28349
28350
28351
28352
28353

If the POSIX_SPAWN_SETSCHEDULER flag is set in the *spawn-flags* attribute of the object referenced by *attrp* (regardless of the setting of the POSIX_SPAWN_SETSCHEDPARAM flag), the new process image shall initially have the scheduling policy specified in the *spawn-schedpolicy* attribute of the object referenced by *attrp* and the scheduling parameters specified in the *spawn-schedparam* attribute of the same object.

28354 The POSIX_SPAWN_RESETIDS flag in the *spawn-flags* attribute of the object referenced by *attrp*
28355 governs the effective user ID of the child process. If this flag is not set, the child process shall
28356 inherit the parent process' effective user ID. If this flag is set, the child process' effective user ID
28357 shall be reset to the parent's real user ID. In either case, if the set-user-ID mode bit of the new
28358 process image file is set, the effective user ID of the child process shall become that file's owner
28359 ID before the new process image begins execution.

28360 The POSIX_SPAWN_RESETIDS flag in the *spawn-flags* attribute of the object referenced by *attrp*
28361 also governs the effective group ID of the child process. If this flag is not set, the child process
28362 shall inherit the parent process' effective group ID. If this flag is set, the child process' effective
28363 group ID shall be reset to the parent's real group ID. In either case, if the set-group-ID mode bit
28364 of the new process image file is set, the effective group ID of the child process shall become that
28365 file's group ID before the new process image begins execution.

28366 If the POSIX_SPAWN_SETSIGMASK flag is set in the *spawn-flags* attribute of the object
28367 referenced by *attrp*, the child process shall initially have the signal mask specified in the *spawn-*
28368 *sigmask* attribute of the object referenced by *attrp*.

28369 If the POSIX_SPAWN_SETSIGDEF flag is set in the *spawn-flags* attribute of the object referenced
28370 by *attrp*, the signals specified in the *spawn-sigdefault* attribute of the same object shall be set to
28371 their default actions in the child process. Signals set to the default action in the parent process
28372 shall be set to the default action in the child process.

28373 Signals set to be caught by the calling process shall be set to the default action in the child
28374 process.

28375 Except for SIGCHLD, signals set to be ignored by the calling process image shall be set to be
28376 ignored by the child process, unless otherwise specified by the POSIX_SPAWN_SETSIGDEF flag
28377 being set in the *spawn-flags* attribute of the object referenced by *attrp* and the signals being
28378 indicated in the *spawn-sigdefault* attribute of the object referenced by *attrp*.

28379 If the SIGCHLD signal is set to be ignored by the calling process, it is unspecified whether the
28380 SIGCHLD signal is set to be ignored or to the default action in the child process, unless
28381 otherwise specified by the POSIX_SPAWN_SETSIGDEF flag being set in the *spawn_flags*
28382 attribute of the object referenced by *attrp* and the SIGCHLD signal being indicated in the
28383 *spawn_sigdefault* attribute of the object referenced by *attrp*.

28384 If the value of the *attrp* pointer is NULL, then the default values are used.

28385 All process attributes, other than those influenced by the attributes set in the object referenced
28386 by *attrp* as specified above or by the file descriptor manipulations specified in *file_actions*, shall
28387 appear in the new process image as though *fork*() had been called to create a child process and
28388 then a member of the *exec* family of functions had been called by the child process to execute the
28389 new process image.

28390 THR It is implementation-defined whether the fork handlers are run when *posix_spawn*() or
28391 *posix_spawnp*() is called.

28392 **RETURN VALUE**
28393 Upon successful completion, *posix_spawn*() and *posix_spawnp*() shall return the process ID of the
28394 child process to the parent process, in the variable pointed to by a non-NULL *pid* argument, and
28395 shall return zero as the function return value. Otherwise, no child process shall be created, the
28396 value stored into the variable pointed to by a non-NULL *pid* is unspecified, and an error number

28397 shall be returned as the function return value to indicate the error. If the *pid* argument is a null
28398 pointer, the process ID of the child is not returned to the caller.

28399 **ERRORS**

28400 The *posix_spawn*() and *posix_spawnp*() functions may fail if:

28401 [EINVAL]   The value specified by *file_actions* or *attrp* is invalid.

28402 If this error occurs after the calling process successfully returns from the *posix_spawn*() or
28403 *posix_spawnp*() function, the child process may exit with exit status 127.

28404 If *posix_spawn*() or *posix_spawnp*() fail for any of the reasons that would cause *fork*() or one of
28405 the *exec* family of functions to fail, an error value shall be returned as described by *fork*() and
28406 *exec*, respectively (or, if the error occurs after the calling process successfully returns, the child
28407 process shall exit with exit status 127).

28408 If POSIX_SPAWN_SETPGROUP is set in the *spawn-flags* attribute of the object referenced by
28409 *attrp*, and *posix_spawn*() or *posix_spawnp*() fails while changing the child's process group, an
28410 error value shall be returned as described by *setpgid*() (or, if the error occurs after the calling
28411 process successfully returns, the child process shall exit with exit status 127).

28412 PS If POSIX_SPAWN_SETSCHEDPARAM is set and POSIX_SPAWN_SETSCHEDULER is not set
28413 in the *spawn-flags* attribute of the object referenced by *attrp*, then if *posix_spawn*() or
28414 *posix_spawnp*() fails for any of the reasons that would cause *sched_setparam*() to fail, an error
28415 value shall be returned as described by *sched_setparam*() (or, if the error occurs after the calling
28416 process successfully returns, the child process shall exit with exit status 127).

28417 If POSIX_SPAWN_SETSCHEDULER is set in the *spawn-flags* attribute of the object referenced by
28418 *attrp*, and if *posix_spawn*() or *posix_spawnp*() fails for any of the reasons that would cause
28419 *sched_setscheduler*() to fail, an error value shall be returned as described by *sched_setscheduler*()
28420 (or, if the error occurs after the calling process successfully returns, the child process shall exit
28421 with exit status 127).

28422 If the *file_actions* argument is not NULL, and specifies any *close*, *dup2*, or *open* actions to be
28423 performed, and if *posix_spawn*() or *posix_spawnp*() fails for any of the reasons that would cause
28424 *close*(), *dup2*(), or *open*() to fail, an error value shall be returned as described by *close*(), *dup2*(),
28425 and *open*(), respectively (or, if the error occurs after the calling process successfully returns, the
28426 child process shall exit with exit status 127). An open file action may, by itself, result in any of
28427 the errors described by *close*() or *dup2*(), in addition to those described by *open*().

28428 **EXAMPLES**

28429 None.

28430 **APPLICATION USAGE**

28431 These functions are part of the Spawn option and need not be provided on all implementations.

28432 **RATIONALE**

28433 The *posix_spawn*() function and its close relation *posix_spawnp*() have been introduced to
28434 overcome the following perceived difficulties with *fork*(): the *fork*() function is difficult or
28435 impossible to implement without swapping or dynamic address translation.

28436 • Swapping is generally too slow for a realtime environment.

28437 • Dynamic address translation is not available everywhere that POSIX might be useful.

28438 • Processes are too useful to simply option out of POSIX whenever it must run without
28439   address translation or other MMU services.

28440
28441

Thus, POSIX needs process creation and file execution primitives that can be efficiently implemented without address translation or other MMU services.

28442
28443
28444
28445
28446

The *posix_spawn*() function is implementable as a library routine, but both *posix_spawn*() and *posix_spawnp*() are designed as kernel operations. Also, although they may be an efficient replacement for many *fork*()/*exec* pairs, their goal is to provide useful process creation primitives for systems that have difficulty with *fork*(), not to provide drop-in replacements for *fork*()/*exec*.

28447
28448
28449
28450
28451
28452
28453
28454

This view of the role of *posix_spawn*() and *posix_spawnp*() influenced the design of their API. It does not attempt to provide the full functionality of *fork*()/*exec* in which arbitrary user-specified operations of any sort are permitted between the creation of the child process and the execution of the new process image; any attempt to reach that level would need to provide a programming language as parameters. Instead, *posix_spawn*() and *posix_spawnp*() are process creation primitives like the *Start_Process* and *Start_Process_Search* Ada language bindings package *POSIX_Process_Primitives* and also like those in many operating systems that are not UNIX systems, but with some POSIX-specific additions.

28455
28456
28457
28458

To achieve its coverage goals, *posix_spawn*() and *posix_spawnp*() have control of six types of inheritance: file descriptors, process group ID, user and group ID, signal mask, scheduling, and whether each signal ignored in the parent will remain ignored in the child, or be reset to its default action in the child.

28459
28460
28461
28462
28463

Control of file descriptors is required to allow an independently written child process image to access data streams opened by and even generated or read by the parent process without being specifically coded to know which parent files and file descriptors are to be used. Control of the process group ID is required to control how the child process' job control relates to that of the parent.

28464
28465
28466

Control of the signal mask and signal defaulting is sufficient to support the implementation of *system*(). Although support for *system*() is not explicitly one of the goals for *posix_spawn*() and *posix_spawnp*(), it is covered under the "at least 50%" coverage goal.

28467
28468
28469
28470
28471
28472
28473
28474
28475

The intention is that the normal file descriptor inheritance across *fork*(), the subsequent effect of the specified spawn file actions, and the normal file descriptor inheritance across one of the *exec* family of functions should fully specify open file inheritance. The implementation need make no decisions regarding the set of open file descriptors when the child process image begins execution, those decisions having already been made by the caller and expressed as the set of open file descriptors and their FD_CLOEXEC flags at the time of the call and the spawn file actions object specified in the call. We have been assured that in cases where the POSIX *Start_Process* Ada primitives have been implemented in a library, this method of controlling file descriptor inheritance may be implemented very easily.

28476
28477
28478
28479
28480
28481
28482
28483

We can identify several problems with *posix_spawn*() and *posix_spawnp*(), but there does not appear to be a solution that introduces fewer problems. Environment modification for child process attributes not specifiable via the *attrp* or *file_actions* arguments must be done in the parent process, and since the parent generally wants to save its context, it is more costly than similar functionality with *fork*()/*exec*. It is also complicated to modify the environment of a multi-threaded process temporarily, since all threads must agree when it is safe for the environment to be changed. However, this cost is only borne by those invocations of *posix_spawn*() and *posix_spawnp*() that use the additional functionality. Since extensive

28484 modifications are not the usual case, and are particularly unlikely in time-critical code, keeping
28485 much of the environment control out of *posix_spawn*() and *posix_spawnp*() is appropriate design.

28486 The *posix_spawn*() and *posix_spawnp*() functions do not have all the power of *fork*()/*exec*. This is
28487 to be expected. The *fork*() function is a wonderfully powerful operation. We do not expect to
28488 duplicate its functionality in a simple, fast function with no special hardware requirements. It is
28489 worth noting that *posix_spawn*() and *posix_spawnp*() are very similar to the process creation
28490 operations on many operating systems that are not UNIX systems.

28491 **Requirements**

28492 The requirements for *posix_spawn*() and *posix_spawnp*() are:

28493 • They must be implementable without an MMU or unusual hardware.

28494 • They must be compatible with existing POSIX standards.

28495 Additional goals are:

28496 • They should be efficiently implementable.

28497 • They should be able to replace at least 50% of typical executions of *fork*().

28498 • A system with *posix_spawn*() and *posix_spawnp*() and without *fork*() should be useful, at least
28499 for realtime applications.

28500 • A system with *fork*() and the *exec* family should be able to implement *posix_spawn*() and
28501 *posix_spawnp*() as library routines.

28502 **Two-Syntax**

28503 POSIX *exec* has several calling sequences with approximately the same functionality. These
28504 appear to be required for compatibility with existing practice. Since the existing practice for the
28505 *posix_spawn*°() functions is otherwise substantially unlike POSIX, we feel that simplicity
28506 outweighs compatibility. There are, therefore, only two names for the *posix_spawn*°() functions.

28507 The parameter list does not differ between *posix_spawn*() and *posix_spawnp*(); *posix_spawnp*()
28508 interprets the second parameter more elaborately than *posix_spawn*().

28509 **Compatibility with POSIX.5 (Ada)**

28510 The *Start_Process* and *Start_Process_Search* procedures from the *POSIX_Process_Primitives*
28511 package from the Ada language binding to POSIX.1 encapsulate *fork*() and *exec* functionality in a
28512 manner similar to that of *posix_spawn*() and *posix_spawnp*(). Originally, in keeping with our
28513 simplicity goal, the standard developers had limited the capabilities of *posix_spawn*() and
28514 *posix_spawnp*() to a subset of the capabilities of *Start_Process* and *Start_Process_Search*; certain
28515 non-default capabilities were not supported. However, based on suggestions by the ballot group
28516 to improve file descriptor mapping or drop it, and on the advice of an Ada Language Bindings
28517 working group member, the standard developers decided that *posix_spawn*() and *posix_spawnp*()
28518 should be sufficiently powerful to implement *Start_Process* and *Start_Process_Search*. The
28519 rationale is that if the Ada language binding to such a primitive had already been approved as
28520 an IEEE standard, there can be little justification for not approving the functionally-equivalent
28521 parts of a C binding. The only three capabilities provided by *posix_spawn*() and *posix_spawnp*()
28522 that are not provided by *Start_Process* and *Start_Process_Search* are optionally specifying the
28523 child's process group ID, the set of signals to be reset to default signal handling in the child
28524 process, and the child's scheduling policy and parameters.

28525 For the Ada language binding for *Start_Process* to be implemented with *posix_spawn*(), that
28526 binding would need to explicitly pass an empty signal mask and the parent's environment to

28527 *posix_spawn*() whenever the caller of *Start_Process* allowed these arguments to default, since
28528 *posix_spawn*() does not provide such defaults. The ability of *Start_Process* to mask user-specified
28529 signals during its execution is functionally unique to the Ada language binding and must be
28530 dealt with in the binding separately from the call to *posix_spawn*().

Process Group

28532 The process group inheritance field can be used to join the child process with an existing process
28533 group. By assigning a value of zero to the *spawn-pgroup* attribute of the object referenced by
28534 *attrp*, the *setpgid*() mechanism will place the child process in a new process group.

Threads

28536 Without the *posix_spawn*() and *posix_spawnp*() functions, systems without address translation
28537 can still use threads to give an abstraction of concurrency. In many cases, thread creation
28538 suffices, but it is not always a good substitute. The *posix_spawn*() and *posix_spawnp*() functions
28539 are considerably "heavier" than thread creation. Processes have several important attributes that
28540 threads do not. Even without address translation, a process may have base-and-bound memory
28541 protection. Each process has a process environment including security attributes and file
28542 capabilities, and powerful scheduling attributes. Processes abstract the behavior of non-
28543 uniform-memory-architecture multi-processors better than threads, and they are more
28544 convenient to use for activities that are not closely linked.

28545 The *posix_spawn*() and *posix_spawnp*() functions may not bring support for multiple processes to
28546 every configuration. Process creation is not the only piece of operating system support required
28547 to support multiple processes. The total cost of support for multiple processes may be quite high
28548 in some circumstances. Existing practice shows that support for multiple processes is
28549 uncommon and threads are common among "tiny kernels". There should, therefore, probably
28550 continue to be AEPs for operating systems with only one process.

Asynchronous Error Notification

28552 A library implementation of *posix_spawn*() or *posix_spawnp*() may not be able to detect all
28553 possible errors before it forks the child process. IEEE Std 1003.1-2001 provides for an error
28554 indication returned from a child process which could not successfully complete the spawn
28555 operation via a special exit status which may be detected using the status value returned by
28556 *wait*() and *waitpid*().

28557 The *stat_val* interface and the macros used to interpret it are not well suited to the purpose of
28558 returning API errors, but they are the only path available to a library implementation. Thus, an
28559 implementation may cause the child process to exit with exit status 127 for any error detected
28560 during the spawn process after the *posix_spawn*() or *posix_spawnp*() function has successfully
28561 returned.

28562 The standard developers had proposed using two additional macros to interpret *stat_val*. The
28563 first, WIFSPAWNFAIL, would have detected a status that indicated that the child exited because
28564 of an error detected during the *posix_spawn*() or *posix_spawnp*() operations rather than during
28565 actual execution of the child process image; the second, WSPAWNERRNO, would have
28566 extracted the error value if WIFSPAWNFAIL indicated a failure. Unfortunately, the ballot group
28567 strongly opposed this because it would make a library implementation of *posix_spawn*() or
28568 *posix_spawnp*() dependent on kernel modifications to *waitpid*() to be able to embed special
28569 information in *stat_val* to indicate a spawn failure.

28570 The 8 bits of child process exit status that are guaranteed by IEEE Std 1003.1-2001 to be
28571 accessible to the waiting parent process are insufficient to disambiguate a spawn error from any
28572 other kind of error that may be returned by an arbitrary process image. No other bits of the exit
28573 status are required to be visible in *stat_val*, so these macros could not be strictly implemented at
28574 the library level. Reserving an exit status of 127 for such spawn errors is consistent with the use
28575 of this value by *system*() and *popen*() to signal failures in these operations that occur after the
28576 function has returned but before a shell is able to execute. The exit status of 127 does not
28577 uniquely identify this class of error, nor does it provide any detailed information on the nature
28578 of the failure. Note that a kernel implementation of *posix_spawn*() or *posix_spawnp*() is permitted
28579 (and encouraged) to return any possible error as the function value, thus providing more
28580 detailed failure information to the parent process.

28581 Thus, no special macros are available to isolate asynchronous *posix_spawn*() or *posix_spawnp*()
28582 errors. Instead, errors detected by the *posix_spawn*() or *posix_spawnp*() operations in the context
28583 of the child process before the new process image executes are reported by setting the child's
28584 exit status to 127. The calling process may use the WIFEXITED and WEXITSTATUS macros on
28585 the *stat_val* stored by the *wait*() or *waitpid*() functions to detect spawn failures to the extent that
28586 other status values with which the child process image may exit (before the parent can
28587 conclusively determine that the child process image has begun execution) are distinct from exit
28588 status 127.

28589 **FUTURE DIRECTIONS**
28590 None.

28591 **SEE ALSO**
28592 *alarm*(), *chmod*(), *close*(), *dup*(), *exec*, *exit*(), *fcntl*(), *fork*(), *kill*(), *open*(),
28593 *posix_spawn_file_actions_addclose*(), *posix_spawn_file_actions_adddup2*(),
28594 *posix_spawn_file_actions_addopen*(), *posix_spawn_file_actions_destroy*(), <REFERENCE
28595 UNDEFINED>(posix_spawn_file_actions_init), *posix_spawnattr_destroy*(), *posix_spawnattr_init*(),
28596 *posix_spawnattr_getsigdefault*(), *posix_spawnattr_getflags*(), *posix_spawnattr_getpgroup*(),
28597 *posix_spawnattr_getschedparam*(), *posix_spawnattr_getschedpolicy*(), *posix_spawnattr_getsigmask*(),
28598 *posix_spawnattr_setsigdefault*(), *posix_spawnattr_setflags*(), *posix_spawnattr_setpgroup*(),
28599 *posix_spawnattr_setschedparam*(), *posix_spawnattr_setschedpolicy*(), *posix_spawnattr_setsigmask*(),
28600 *sched_setparam*(), *sched_setscheduler*(), *setpgid*(), *setuid*(), *stat*(), *times*(), *wait*(), the Base
28601 Definitions volume of IEEE Std 1003.1-2001, **<spawn.h>**

28602 **CHANGE HISTORY**
28603 First released in Issue 6. Derived from IEEE Std 1003.1d-1999.

28604 IEEE PASC Interpretation 1003.1 #103 is applied, noting that the signal default actions are
28605 changed as well as the signal mask in step 2.

28606 IEEE PASC Interpretation 1003.1 #132 is applied.

28607 **NAME**

28608   posix_spawn_file_actions_addclose, posix_spawn_file_actions_addopen — add close or open
28609   action to spawn file actions object (**ADVANCED REALTIME**)

28610 **SYNOPSIS**

28611 SPN
```
#include <spawn.h>
```

28612
28613
```
int posix_spawn_file_actions_addclose (posix_spawn_file_actions_t *
    file_actions, int fildes);
```
28614
28615
28616
```
int posix_spawn_file_actions_addopen (posix_spawn_file_actions_t *
    restrict file_actions, int fildes,
    const char *restrict path, int oflag, mode_t mode);
```
28617

28618 **DESCRIPTION**

28619   These functions shall add or delete a close or open action to a spawn file actions object.

28620   A spawn file actions object is of type **posix_spawn_file_actions_t** (defined in <**spawn.h**>) and is
28621   used to specify a series of actions to be performed by a *posix_spawn*() or *posix_spawnp*()
28622   operation in order to arrive at the set of open file descriptors for the child process given the set of
28623   open file descriptors of the parent. IEEE Std 1003.1-2001 does not define comparison or
28624   assignment operators for the type **posix_spawn_file_actions_t**.

28625   A spawn file actions object, when passed to *posix_spawn*() or *posix_spawnp*(), shall specify how
28626   the set of open file descriptors in the calling process is transformed into a set of potentially open
28627   file descriptors for the spawned process. This transformation shall be as if the specified sequence
28628   of actions was performed exactly once, in the context of the spawned process (prior to execution
28629   of the new process image), in the order in which the actions were added to the object;
28630   additionally, when the new process image is executed, any file descriptor (from this new set)
28631   which has its FD_CLOEXEC flag set shall be closed (see *posix_spawn*()).

28632   The *posix_spawn_file_actions_addclose*() function shall add a *close* action to the object referenced
28633   by *file_actions* that shall cause the file descriptor *fildes* to be closed (as if *close*(*fildes*) had been
28634   called) when a new process is spawned using this file actions object.

28635   The *posix_spawn_file_actions_addopen*() function shall add an *open* action to the object referenced
28636   by *file_actions* that shall cause the file named by *path* to be opened (as if *open*(*path, oflag, mode*)
28637   had been called, and the returned file descriptor, if not *fildes*, had been changed to *fildes*) when a
28638   new process is spawned using this file actions object. If *fildes* was already an open file descriptor,
28639   it shall be closed before the new file is opened.

28640   The string described by *path* shall be copied by the *posix_spawn_file_actions_addopen*() function.

28641 **RETURN VALUE**

28642   Upon successful completion, these functions shall return zero; otherwise, an error number shall
28643   be returned to indicate the error.

28644 **ERRORS**

28645   These functions shall fail if:

28646   [EBADF]   The value specified by *fildes* is negative or greater than or equal to
28647   {OPEN_MAX}.

28648   These functions may fail if:

28649   [EINVAL]   The value specified by *file_actions* is invalid.

28650   [ENOMEM]   Insufficient memory exists to add to the spawn file actions object.

28651   It shall not be considered an error for the *fildes* argument passed to these functions to specify a
28652   file descriptor for which the specified operation could not be performed at the time of the call.
28653   Any such error will be detected when the associated file actions object is later used during a
28654   *posix_spawn*() or *posix_spawnp*() operation.

28655 **EXAMPLES**
28656   None.

28657 **APPLICATION USAGE**
28658   These functions are part of the Spawn option and need not be provided on all implementations.

28659 **RATIONALE**
28660   A spawn file actions object may be initialized to contain an ordered sequence of *close*(), *dup2*(),
28661   and *open*() operations to be used by *posix_spawn*() or *posix_spawnp*() to arrive at the set of open
28662   file descriptors inherited by the spawned process from the set of open file descriptors in the
28663   parent at the time of the *posix_spawn*() or *posix_spawnp*() call. It had been suggested that the
28664   *close*() and *dup2*() operations alone are sufficient to rearrange file descriptors, and that files
28665   which need to be opened for use by the spawned process can be handled either by having the
28666   calling process open them before the *posix_spawn*() or *posix_spawnp*() call (and close them after),
28667   or by passing filenames to the spawned process (in *argv*) so that it may open them itself. The
28668   standard developers recommend that applications use one of these two methods when practical,
28669   since detailed error status on a failed open operation is always available to the application this
28670   way. However, the standard developers feel that allowing a spawn file actions object to specify
28671   open operations is still appropriate because:

28672   1. It is consistent with equivalent POSIX.5 (Ada) functionality.
28673   2. It supports the I/O redirection paradigm commonly employed by POSIX programs
28674   designed to be invoked from a shell. When such a program is the child process, it may not
28675   be designed to open files on its own.
28676   3. It allows file opens that might otherwise fail or violate file ownership/access rights if
28677   executed by the parent process.

28678   Regarding 2. above, note that the spawn open file action provides to *posix_spawn*() and
28679   *posix_spawnp*() the same capability that the shell redirection operators provide to *system*(), only
28680   without the intervening execution of a shell; for example:

28681   `system ("myprog <file1 3<file2");`

28682   Regarding 3. above, note that if the calling process needs to open one or more files for access by
28683   the spawned process, but has insufficient spare file descriptors, then the open action is necessary
28684   to allow the *open*() to occur in the context of the child process after other file descriptors have
28685   been closed (that must remain open in the parent).

28686   Additionally, if a parent is executed from a file having a "set-user-id" mode bit set and the
28687   POSIX_SPAWN_RESETIDS flag is set in the spawn attributes, a file created within the parent
28688   process will (possibly incorrectly) have the parent's effective user ID as its owner, whereas a file
28689   created via an *open*() action during *posix_spawn*() or *posix_spawnp*() will have the parent's real
28690   ID as its owner; and an open by the parent process may successfully open a file to which the real
28691   user should not have access or fail to open a file to which the real user should have access.

28692   **File Descriptor Mapping**

28693   The standard developers had originally proposed using an array which specified the mapping of
28694   child file descriptors back to those of the parent. It was pointed out by the ballot group that it is
28695   not possible to reshuffle file descriptors arbitrarily in a library implementation of *posix_spawn*()
28696   or *posix_spawnp*() without provision for one or more spare file descriptor entries (which simply
28697   may not be available). Such an array requires that an implementation develop a complex
28698   strategy to achieve the desired mapping without inadvertently closing the wrong file descriptor
28699   at the wrong time.

28700   It was noted by a member of the Ada Language Bindings working group that the approved Ada
28701   Language *Start_Process* family of POSIX process primitives use a caller-specified set of file
28702   actions to alter the normal *fork*()/*exec* semantics for inheritance of file descriptors in a very
28703   flexible way, yet no such problems exist because the burden of determining how to achieve the
28704   final file descriptor mapping is completely on the application. Furthermore, although the file
28705   actions interface appears frightening at first glance, it is actually quite simple to implement in
28706   either a library or the kernel.

28707   **FUTURE DIRECTIONS**
28708   None.

28709   **SEE ALSO**
28710   *close*(),   *dup*(),   *open*(),   *posix_spawn*(),   *posix_spawn_file_actions_adddup2*(),
28711   *posix_spawn_file_actions_destroy*(),   *posix_spawnp*(),   the   Base   Definitions   volume   of
28712   IEEE Std 1003.1-2001, <**spawn.h**>

28713   **CHANGE HISTORY**
28714   First released in Issue 6. Derived from IEEE Std 1003.1d-1999.

28715   IEEE PASC Interpretation 1003.1 #105 is applied, adding a note to the DESCRIPTION that the
28716   string pointed to by *path* is copied by the *posix_spawn_file_actions_addopen*() function.

28717 **NAME**

28718   posix_spawn_file_actions_adddup2 — add dup2 action to spawn file actions object

28719   **(ADVANCED REALTIME)**

28720 **SYNOPSIS**

28721 SPN   `#include <spawn.h>`

```
28722    int posix_spawn_file_actions_adddup2 (posix_spawn_file_actions_t *
28723        file_actions, int fildes, int newfildes);
28724
```

28725 **DESCRIPTION**

28726   The *posix_spawn_file_actions_adddup2()* function shall add a *dup2()* action to the object
28727   referenced by *file_actions* that shall cause the file descriptor *fildes* to be duplicated as *newfildes* (as
28728   if *dup2(fildes, newfildes)* had been called) when a new process is spawned using this file actions
28729   object.

28730   A spawn file actions object is as defined in *posix_spawn_file_actions_addclose()*.

28731 **RETURN VALUE**

28732   Upon successful completion, the *posix_spawn_file_actions_adddup2()* function shall return zero;
28733   otherwise, an error number shall be returned to indicate the error.

28734 **ERRORS**

28735   The *posix_spawn_file_actions_adddup2()* function shall fail if:

28736   [EBADF]   The value specified by *fildes* or *newfildes* is negative or greater than or equal to
28737   {OPEN_MAX}.

28738   [ENOMEM]   Insufficient memory exists to add to the spawn file actions object.

28739   The *posix_spawn_file_actions_adddup2()* function may fail if:

28740   [EINVAL]   The value specified by *file_actions* is invalid.

28741   It shall not be considered an error for the *fildes* argument passed to the
28742   *posix_spawn_file_actions_adddup2()* function to specify a file descriptor for which the specified
28743   operation could not be performed at the time of the call. Any such error will be detected when
28744   the associated file actions object is later used during a *posix_spawn()* or *posix_spawnp()*
28745   operation.

28746 **EXAMPLES**

28747   None.

28748 **APPLICATION USAGE**

28749   The *posix_spawn_file_actions_adddup2()* function is part of the Spawn option and need not be
28750   provided on all implementations.

28751 **RATIONALE**

28752   Refer to the RATIONALE in *posix_spawn_file_actions_addclose()*.

28753 **FUTURE DIRECTIONS**

28754   None.

28755 **SEE ALSO**

28756   *dup()*, *posix_spawn()*, *posix_spawn_file_actions_addclose()*, *posix_spawn_file_actions_destroy()*,
28757   *posix_spawnp()*, the Base Definitions volume of IEEE Std 1003.1-2001, <**spawn.h**>

28758 **CHANGE HISTORY**

28759   First released in Issue 6. Derived from IEEE Std 1003.1d-1999.

28760   IEEE PASC Interpretation 1003.1 #104 is applied, noting that the [EBADF] error can apply to the
28761   *newfildes* argument in addition to *fildes*.

28773 **NAME**

28774   posix_spawn_file_actions_destroy, posix_spawn_file_actions_init — destroy and initialize
28775   spawn file actions object (**ADVANCED REALTIME**)

28776 **SYNOPSIS**

28777 SPN `#include <spawn.h>`

28778   `int posix_spawn_file_actions_destroy (posix_spawn_file_actions_t *`
28779   `file_actions);`
28780   `int posix_spawn_file_actions_init (posix_spawn_file_actions_t *`
28781   `file_actions);`

28782

28783 **DESCRIPTION**

28784   The *posix_spawn_file_actions_destroy*() function shall destroy the object referenced by *file_actions*;
28785   the object becomes, in effect, uninitialized. An implementation may cause
28786   *posix_spawn_file_actions_destroy*() to set the object referenced by *file_actions* to an invalid value. A
28787   destroyed spawn file actions object can be reinitialized using *posix_spawn_file_actions_init*(); the
28788   results of otherwise referencing the object after it has been destroyed are undefined.

28789   The *posix_spawn_file_actions_init*() function shall initialize the object referenced by *file_actions* to
28790   contain no file actions for *posix_spawn*() or *posix_spawnp*() to perform.

28791   A spawn file actions object is as defined in *posix_spawn_file_actions_addclose*().
28792   The effect of initializing an already initialized spawn file actions object is undefined.

28793 **RETURN VALUE**

28794   Upon successful completion, these functions shall return zero; otherwise, an error number shall
28795   be returned to indicate the error.

28796 **ERRORS**

28797   The *posix_spawn_file_actions_init*() function shall fail if:

28798   [ENOMEM]   Insufficient memory exists to initialize the spawn file actions object.

28799   The *posix_spawn_file_actions_destroy*() function may fail if:

28800   [EINVAL]   The value specified by *file_actions* is invalid.

28801 **EXAMPLES**

28802   None.

28803 **APPLICATION USAGE**

28804   These functions are part of the Spawn option and need not be provided on all implementations.

28805 **RATIONALE**

28806   Refer to the RATIONALE in *posix_spawn_file_actions_addclose*().

28807 **FUTURE DIRECTIONS**

28808   None.

28809 **SEE ALSO**

28810   *posix_spawn*(), *posix_spawnp*(), the Base Definitions volume of IEEE Std 1003.1-2001, <**spawn.h**>

28811 **CHANGE HISTORY**

28812   First released in Issue 6. Derived from IEEE Std 1003.1d-1999.

28813   In the SYNOPSIS, the inclusion of <**sys/types.h**> is no longer required.

28814 **NAME**

28815   posix_spawnattr_destroy, posix_spawnattr_init—destroy and initialize spawn attributes object

28816   (**ADVANCED REALTIME**)

28817 **SYNOPSIS**

28818 SPN   ```#include <spawn.h>```

28819   ```int posix_spawnattr_destroy (posix_spawnattr_t *attr);```
28820   ```int posix_spawnattr_init (posix_spawnattr_t *attr);```

28821

28822 **DESCRIPTION**

28823   The *posix_spawnattr_destroy*() function shall destroy a spawn attributes object. A destroyed *attr*
28824   attributes object can be reinitialized using *posix_spawnattr_init*(); the results of otherwise
28825   referencing the object after it has been destroyed are undefined. An implementation may cause
28826   *posix_spawnattr_destroy*() to set the object referenced by *attr* to an invalid value.

28827   The *posix_spawnattr_init*() function shall initialize a spawn attributes object *attr* with the default
28828   value for all of the individual attributes used by the implementation. Results are undefined if
28829   *posix_spawnattr_init*() is called specifying an already initialized *attr* attributes object.

28830   A spawn attributes object is of type **posix_spawnattr_t** (defined in <**spawn.h**>) and is used to
28831   specify the inheritance of process attributes across a spawn operation. IEEE Std 1003.1-2001 does
28832   not define comparison or assignment operators for the type **posix_spawnattr_t**.

28833   Each implementation shall document the individual attributes it uses and their default values
28834   unless these values are defined by IEEE Std 1003.1-2001. Attributes not defined by
28835   IEEE Std 1003.1-2001, their default values, and the names of the associated functions to get and
28836   set those attribute values are implementation-defined.

28837   The resulting spawn attributes object (possibly modified by setting individual attribute values),
28838   is used to modify the behavior of *posix_spawn*() or *posix_spawnp*(). After a spawn attributes
28839   object has been used to spawn a process by a call to a *posix_spawn*() or *posix_spawnp*(), any
28840   function affecting the attributes object (including destruction) shall not affect any process that
28841   has been spawned in this way.

28842 **RETURN VALUE**

28843   Upon successful completion, *posix_spawnattr_destroy*() and *posix_spawnattr_init*() shall return
28844   zero; otherwise, an error number shall be returned to indicate the error.

28845 **ERRORS**

28846   The *posix_spawnattr_init*() function shall fail if:

28847   [ENOMEM]   Insufficient memory exists to initialize the spawn attributes object.

28848   The *posix_spawnattr_destroy*() function may fail if:

28849   [EINVAL]   The value specified by attr is invalid.

28850 **EXAMPLES**

28851   None.

28852 **APPLICATION USAGE**

28853   These functions are part of the Spawn option and need not be provided on all implementations.

28854 **RATIONALE**

28855 The original spawn interface proposed in IEEE Std 1003.1-2001 defined the attributes that specify
28856 the inheritance of process attributes across a spawn operation as a structure. In order to be able
28857 to separate optional individual attributes under their appropriate options (that is, the *spawn-*
28858 *schedparam* and *spawn-schedpolicy* attributes depending upon the Process Scheduling option), and
28859 also for extensibility and consistency with the newer POSIX interfaces, the attributes interface
28860 has been changed to an opaque data type. This interface now consists of the type
28861 **posix_spawnattr_t**, representing a spawn attributes object, together with associated functions to
28862 initialize or destroy the attributes object, and to set or get each individual attribute. Although the
28863 new object-oriented interface is more verbose than the original structure, it is simple to use,
28864 more extensible, and easy to implement.

28865 **FUTURE DIRECTIONS**

28866 None.

28867 **SEE ALSO**

28868 *posix_spawn*(), *posix_spawnattr_getsigdefault*(), *posix_spawnattr_getflags*(),
28869 *posix_spawnattr_getpgroup*(), *posix_spawnattr_getschedparam*(), *posix_spawnattr_getschedpolicy*(),
28870 *posix_spawnattr_getsigmask*(), *posix_spawnattr_setsigdefault*(), *posix_spawnattr_setflags*(),
28871 *posix_spawnattr_setpgroup*(), *posix_spawnattr_setsigmask*(), *posix_spawnattr_setschedpolicy*(),
28872 *posix_spawnattr_setschedparam*(), *posix_spawnp*(), the Base Definitions volume of
28873 IEEE Std 1003.1-2001, **<spawn.h>**

28874 **CHANGE HISTORY**

28875 First released in Issue 6. Derived from IEEE Std 1003.1d-1999.

28876 IEEE PASC Interpretation 1003.1 #106 is applied, noting that the effect of initializing an already
28877 initialized spawn attributes option is undefined.

28878 **NAME**

28879   posix_spawnattr_getflags, posix_spawnattr_setflags — get and set the spawn-flags attribute of a
28880   spawn attributes object (**ADVANCED REALTIME**)

28881 **SYNOPSIS**

28882 SPN
```
#include <spawn.h>
```

28883
28884
```
int posix_spawnattr_getflags (const posix_spawnattr_t *restrict attr,
    short *restrict flags);
```
28885
```
int posix_spawnattr_setflags (posix_spawnattr_t *attr, short flags);
```
28886

28887 **DESCRIPTION**

28888   The *posix_spawnattr_getflags*() function shall obtain the value of the *spawn-flags* attribute from
28889   the attributes object referenced by *attr*.

28890   The *posix_spawnattr_setflags*() function shall set the *spawn-flags* attribute in an initialized
28891   attributes object referenced by *attr*.

28892   The *spawn-flags* attribute is used to indicate which process attributes are to be changed in the
28893   new process image when invoking *posix_spawn*() or *posix_spawnp*(). It is the bitwise-inclusive
28894   OR of zero or more of the following flags:

28895   POSIX_SPAWN_RESETIDS
28896   POSIX_SPAWN_SETPGROUP
28897   POSIX_SPAWN_SETSIGDEF
28898   POSIX_SPAWN_SETSIGMASK
28899 PS   POSIX_SPAWN_SETSCHEDPARAM
28900   POSIX_SPAWN_SETSCHEDULER
28901

28902   These flags are defined in <**spawn.h**>. The default value of this attribute shall be as if no flags
28903   were set.

28904 **RETURN VALUE**

28905   Upon successful completion, *posix_spawnattr_getflags*() shall return zero and store the value of
28906   the *spawn-flags* attribute of *attr* into the object referenced by the *flags* parameter; otherwise, an
28907   error number shall be returned to indicate the error.

28908   Upon successful completion, *posix_spawnattr_setflags*() shall return zero; otherwise, an error
28909   number shall be returned to indicate the error.

28910 **ERRORS**

28911   These functions may fail if:

28912   [EINVAL]   The value specified by *attr* is invalid.

28913   The *posix_spawnattr_setflags*() function may fail if:

28914   [EINVAL]   The value of the attribute being set is not valid.

28915 **EXAMPLES**

28916   None.

28917 **APPLICATION USAGE**

28918   These functions are part of the Spawn option and need not be provided on all implementations.

28919 **RATIONALE**

28920 None.

28921 **FUTURE DIRECTIONS**

28922 None.

28923 **SEE ALSO**

28924 *posix_spawn*(), *posix_spawnattr_destroy*(), *posix_spawnattr_init*(), *posix_spawnattr_getsigdefault*(),

28925 *posix_spawnattr_getpgroup*(), *posix_spawnattr_getschedparam*(), *posix_spawnattr_getschedpolicy*(),

28926 *posix_spawnattr_getsigmask*(), *posix_spawnattr_setsigdefault*(), *posix_spawnattr_setpgroup*(),

28927 *posix_spawnattr_setschedparam*(), *posix_spawnattr_setschedpolicy*(), *posix_spawnattr_setsigmask*(),

28928 *posix_spawnp*(), the Base Definitions volume of IEEE Std 1003.1-2001, <**spawn.h**>

28929 **CHANGE HISTORY**

28930 First released in Issue 6. Derived from IEEE Std 1003.1d-1999.

28931 **NAME**

28932   posix_spawnattr_getpgroup, posix_spawnattr_setpgroup — get and set the spawn-pgroup

28933   attribute of a spawn attributes object (**ADVANCED REALTIME**)

28934 **SYNOPSIS**

28935 SPN   `#include <spawn.h>`

28936   `int posix_spawnattr_getpgroup (const posix_spawnattr_t *restrict attr,`

28937   `pid_t *restrict pgroup);`

28938   `int posix_spawnattr_setpgroup (posix_spawnattr_t *attr, pid_t pgroup);`

28939

28940 **DESCRIPTION**

28941   The *posix_spawnattr_getpgroup*() function shall obtain the value of the *spawn-pgroup* attribute

28942   from the attributes object referenced by *attr*.

28943   The *posix_spawnattr_setpgroup*() function shall set the *spawn-pgroup* attribute in an initialized

28944   attributes object referenced by *attr*.

28945   The *spawn-pgroup* attribute represents the process group to be joined by the new process image

28946   in a spawn operation (if POSIX_SPAWN_SETPGROUP is set in the *spawn-flags* attribute). The

28947   default value of this attribute shall be zero.

28948 **RETURN VALUE**

28949   Upon successful completion, *posix_spawnattr_getpgroup*() shall return zero and store the value of

28950   the *spawn-pgroup* attribute of *attr* into the object referenced by the *pgroup* parameter; otherwise,

28951   an error number shall be returned to indicate the error.

28952   Upon successful completion, *posix_spawnattr_setpgroup*() shall return zero; otherwise, an error

28953   number shall be returned to indicate the error.

28954 **ERRORS**

28955   These functions may fail if:

28956   [EINVAL]   The value specified by *attr* is invalid.

28957   The *posix_spawnattr_setpgroup*() function may fail if:

28958   [EINVAL]   The value of the attribute being set is not valid.

28959 **EXAMPLES**

28960   None.

28961 **APPLICATION USAGE**

28962   These functions are part of the Spawn option and need not be provided on all implementations.

28963 **RATIONALE**

28964   None.

28965 **FUTURE DIRECTIONS**

28966   None.

28967 **SEE ALSO**

28968   *posix_spawn*(), *posix_spawnattr_destroy*(), *posix_spawnattr_init*(), *posix_spawnattr_getsigdefault*(),

28969   *posix_spawnattr_getflags*(), *posix_spawnattr_getschedparam*(), *posix_spawnattr_getschedpolicy*(),

28970   *posix_spawnattr_getsigmask*(), *posix_spawnattr_setsigdefault*(), *posix_spawnattr_setflags*(),

28971   *posix_spawnattr_setschedparam*(), *posix_spawnattr_setschedpolicy*(), *posix_spawnattr_setsigmask*(),
28972   *posix_spawnp*(), the Base Definitions volume of IEEE Std 1003.1-2001, **<spawn.h>**

28973 **CHANGE HISTORY**
28974   First released in Issue 6. Derived from IEEE Std 1003.1d-1999.

28975 **NAME**

28976   posix_spawnattr_getschedparam, posix_spawnattr_setschedparam — get and set the spawn-
28977   schedparam attribute of a spawn attributes object (**ADVANCED REALTIME**)

28978 **SYNOPSIS**

28979 SPN PS `#include <spawn.h>`
28980   `#include <sched.h>`

28981   `int posix_spawnattr_getschedparam (const posix_spawnattr_t *`
28982   `    restrict attr, struct sched_param *restrict schedparam);`
28983   `int posix_spawnattr_setschedparam (posix_spawnattr_t *restrict attr,`
28984   `    const struct sched_param *restrict schedparam);`
28985

28986 **DESCRIPTION**

28987   The *posix_spawnattr_getschedparam*() function shall obtain the value of the *spawn-schedparam*
28988   attribute from the attributes object referenced by *attr*.

28989   The *posix_spawnattr_setschedparam*() function shall set the *spawn-schedparam* attribute in an
28990   initialized attributes object referenced by *attr*.

28991   The *spawn-schedparam* attribute represents the scheduling parameters to be assigned to the new
28992   process image in a spawn operation (if POSIX_SPAWN_SETSCHEDULER or
28993   POSIX_SPAWN_SETSCHEDPARAM is set in the *spawn-flags* attribute). The default value of this
28994   attribute is unspecified.

28995 **RETURN VALUE**

28996   Upon successful completion, *posix_spawnattr_getschedparam*() shall return zero and store the
28997   value of the *spawn-schedparam* attribute of *attr* into the object referenced by the *schedparam*
28998   parameter; otherwise, an error number shall be returned to indicate the error.

28999   Upon successful completion, *posix_spawnattr_setschedparam*() shall return zero; otherwise, an
29000   error number shall be returned to indicate the error.

29001 **ERRORS**

29002   These functions may fail if:

29003   [EINVAL]   The value specified by *attr* is invalid.

29004   The *posix_spawnattr_setschedparam*() function may fail if:

29005   [EINVAL]   The value of the attribute being set is not valid.

29006 **EXAMPLES**

29007   None.

29008 **APPLICATION USAGE**

29009   These functions are part of the Spawn and Process Scheduling options and need not be provided
29010   on all implementations.

29011 **RATIONALE**

29012   None.

29013 **FUTURE DIRECTIONS**

29014   None.

29015 **SEE ALSO**

29016   *posix_spawn()*, *posix_spawnattr_destroy()*, *posix_spawnattr_init()*, *posix_spawnattr_getsigdefault()*,

29017   *posix_spawnattr_getflags()*, *posix_spawnattr_getpgroup()*, *posix_spawnattr_getschedpolicy()*,

29018   *posix_spawnattr_getsigmask()*, *posix_spawnattr_setsigdefault()*, *posix_spawnattr_setflags()*,

29019   *posix_spawnattr_setpgroup()*, *posix_spawnattr_setschedpolicy()*, *posix_spawnattr_setsigmask()*,

29020   *posix_spawnp()*, the Base Definitions volume of IEEE Std 1003.1-2001, **<sched.h>, <spawn.h>**

29021 **CHANGE HISTORY**

29022   First released in Issue 6. Derived from IEEE Std 1003.1d-1999.

29023 **NAME**

29024   posix_spawnattr_getschedpolicy, posix_spawnattr_setschedpolicy — get and set the spawn-schedpolicy

29025   attribute of a spawn attributes object (**ADVANCED REALTIME**)

29026 **SYNOPSIS**

29027 SPN   ```
#include <spawn.h>
```
29028    ```
#include <sched.h>
```

29029   ```
int posix_spawnattr_getschedpolicy (const posix_spawnattr_t *
```
29030    ```
    restrict attr, int *restrict schedpolicy);
```
29031   ```
int posix_spawnattr_setschedpolicy (posix_spawnattr_t *attr,
```
29032    ```
    int schedpolicy).;
```

29033

29034 **DESCRIPTION**

29035   The *posix_spawnattr_getschedpolicy*() function shall obtain the value of the *spawn-schedpolicy*

29036   attribute from the attributes object referenced by *attr*.

29037   The *posix_spawnattr_setschedpolicy*() function shall set the *spawn-schedpolicy* attribute in an

29038   initialized attributes object referenced by *attr*.

29039   The *spawn-schedpolicy* attribute represents the scheduling policy to be assigned to the new

29040   process image in a spawn operation (if POSIX_SPAWN_SETSCHEDULER is set in the *spawn-flags*

29041   attribute). The default value of this attribute is unspecified.

29042 **RETURN VALUE**

29043   Upon successful completion, *posix_spawnattr_getschedpolicy*() shall return zero and store the

29044   value of the *spawn-schedpolicy* attribute of *attr* into the object referenced by the *schedpolicy*

29045   parameter; otherwise, an error number shall be returned to indicate the error.

29046   Upon successful completion, *posix_spawnattr_setschedpolicy*() shall return zero; otherwise, an

29047   error number shall be returned to indicate the error.

29048 **ERRORS**

29049   These functions may fail if:

29050   [EINVAL]   The value specified by *attr* is invalid.

29051   The *posix_spawnattr_setschedpolicy*() function may fail if:

29052   [EINVAL]   The value of the attribute being set is not valid.

29053 **EXAMPLES**

29054   None.

29055 **APPLICATION USAGE**

29056   These functions are part of the Spawn and Process Scheduling options and need not be provided

29057   on all implementations.

29058 **RATIONALE**

29059   None.

29060 **FUTURE DIRECTIONS**

29061   None.

29062 **SEE ALSO**

29063　*posix_spawn()*, *posix_spawnattr_destroy()*, *posix_spawnattr_init()*, *posix_spawnattr_getsigdefault()*,

29064　*posix_spawnattr_getflags()*, *posix_spawnattr_getpgroup()*, *posix_spawnattr_getschedparam()*,

29065　*posix_spawnattr_getsigmask()*, *posix_spawnattr_setsigdefault()*, *posix_spawnattr_setflags()*,

29066　*posix_spawnattr_setpgroup()*, *posix_spawnattr_setschedparam()*, *posix_spawnattr_setsigmask()*,

29067　*posix_spawnp()*, the Base Definitions volume of IEEE Std 1003.1-2001, **<sched.h>**, **<spawn.h>**

29068 **CHANGE HISTORY**

29069　First released in Issue 6. Derived from IEEE Std 1003.1d-1999.

29070 **NAME**

29071   posix_spawnattr_getsigdefault, posix_spawnattr_setsigdefault — get and set the spawn-sigdefault
29072   attribute of a spawn attributes object (**ADVANCED REALTIME**)

29073 **SYNOPSIS**

29074 SPN   `#include <signal.h>`
29075   `#include <spawn.h>`

29076   `int posix_spawnattr_getsigdefault (const posix_spawnattr_t *`
29077   `    restrict attr, sigset_t *restrict sigdefault);`
29078   `int posix_spawnattr_setsigdefault (posix_spawnattr_t *restrict attr,`
29079   `    const sigset_t *restrict sigdefault);`
29080

29081 **DESCRIPTION**

29082   The *posix_spawnattr_getsigdefault*() function shall obtain the value of the *spawn-sigdefault*
29083   attribute from the attributes object referenced by *attr*.

29084   The *posix_spawnattr_setsigdefault*() function shall set the *spawn-sigdefault* attribute in an
29085   initialized attributes object referenced by *attr*.

29086   The *spawn-sigdefault* attribute represents the set of signals to be forced to default signal handling
29087   in the new process image (if POSIX_SPAWN_SETSIGDEF is set in the *spawn-flags* attribute) by a
29088   spawn operation. The default value of this attribute shall be an empty signal set.

29089 **RETURN VALUE**

29090   Upon successful completion, *posix_spawnattr_getsigdefault*() shall return zero and store the value
29091   of the *spawn-sigdefault* attribute of *attr* into the object referenced by the *sigdefault* parameter;
29092   otherwise, an error number shall be returned to indicate the error.

29093   Upon successful completion, *posix_spawnattr_setsigdefault*() shall return zero; otherwise, an error
29094   number shall be returned to indicate the error.

29095 **ERRORS**

29096   These functions may fail if:

29097   [EINVAL]   The value specified by *attr* is invalid.

29098   The *posix_spawnattr_setsigdefault*() function may fail if:

29099   [EINVAL]   The value of the attribute being set is not valid.

29100 **EXAMPLES**

29101   None.

29102 **APPLICATION USAGE**

29103   These functions are part of the Spawn option and need not be provided on all implementations.

29104 **RATIONALE**

29105   None.

29106 **FUTURE DIRECTIONS**

29107   None.

29108 **SEE ALSO**

29109   *posix_spawn*(), *posix_spawnattr_destroy*(), *posix_spawnattr_init*(), *posix_spawnattr_getflags*(),
29110   *posix_spawnattr_getpgroup*(), *posix_spawnattr_getschedparam*(), *posix_spawnattr_getschedpolicy*(),

29111 *posix_spawnattr_getsigmask*(), *posix_spawnattr_setflags*(), *posix_spawnattr_setpgroup*(),
29112 *posix_spawnattr_setschedparam*(), *posix_spawnattr_setschedpolicy*(), *posix_spawnattr_setsigmask*(),
29113 *posix_spawnp*(), the Base Definitions volume of IEEE Std 1003.1-2001, **<signal.h>**, **<spawn.h>**

29114 **CHANGE HISTORY**
29115 First released in Issue 6. Derived from IEEE Std 1003.1d-1999.

29116 **NAME**

29117 posix_spawnattr_getsigmask, posix_spawnattr_setsigmask—get and set the spawn-sigmask
29118 attribute of a spawn attributes object (**ADVANCED REALTIME**)

29119 **SYNOPSIS**

29120 SPN
```
#include <signal.h>
```
29121
```
#include <spawn.h>
```

29122
```
int posix_spawnattr_getsigmask (const posix_spawnattr_t *restrict attr,
```
29123
```
    sigset_t *restrict sigmask);
```
29124
```
int posix_spawnattr_setsigmask (posix_spawnattr_t *restrict attr,
```
29125
```
    const sigset_t *restrict sigmask);
```
29126

29127 **DESCRIPTION**

29128 The *posix_spawnattr_getsigmask*() function shall obtain the value of the *spawn-sigmask* attribute
29129 from the attributes object referenced by *attr*.

29130 The *posix_spawnattr_setsigmask*() function shall set the *spawn-sigmask* attribute in an initialized
29131 attributes object referenced by *attr*.

29132 The *spawn-sigmask* attribute represents the signal mask in effect in the new process image of a
29133 spawn operation (if POSIX_SPAWN_SETSIGMASK is set in the *spawn-flags* attribute). The
29134 default value of this attribute is unspecified.

29135 **RETURN VALUE**

29136 Upon successful completion, *posix_spawnattr_getsigmask*() shall return zero and store the value
29137 of the *spawn-sigmask* attribute of *attr* into the object referenced by the *sigmask* parameter;
29138 otherwise, an error number shall be returned to indicate the error.

29139 Upon successful completion, *posix_spawnattr_setsigmask*() shall return zero; otherwise, an error
29140 number shall be returned to indicate the error.

29141 **ERRORS**

29142 These functions may fail if:

29143 [EINVAL] The value specified by *attr* is invalid.

29144 The *posix_spawnattr_setsigmask*() function may fail if:

29145 [EINVAL] The value of the attribute being set is not valid.

29146 **EXAMPLES**

29147 None.

29148 **APPLICATION USAGE**

29149 These functions are part of the Spawn option and need not be provided on all implementations.

29150 **RATIONALE**

29151 None.

29152 **FUTURE DIRECTIONS**

29153 None.

29154 **SEE ALSO**

29155 *posix_spawn*(), *posix_spawnattr_destroy*(), *posix_spawnattr_init*(), *posix_spawnattr_getsigdefault*(),
29156 *posix_spawnattr_getflags*(), *posix_spawnattr_getpgroup*(), *posix_spawnattr_getschedparam*(),

29157   *posix_spawnattr_getschedpolicy*(), *posix_spawnattr_setsigdefault*(), *posix_spawnattr_setflags*(),
29158   *posix_spawnattr_setpgroup*(), *posix_spawnattr_setschedparam*(), *posix_spawnattr_setschedpolicy*(),
29159   *posix_spawnp*(), the Base Definitions volume of IEEE Std 1003.1-2001, <**signal.h**>, <**spawn.h**>

29160 **CHANGE HISTORY**

29161   First released in Issue 6. Derived from IEEE Std 1003.1d-1999.

31104 **NAME**
31105   pthread_attr_destroy, pthread_attr_init — destroy and initialize the thread attributes object

31106 **SYNOPSIS**
31107 THR   `#include <pthread.h>`

31108   `int pthread_attr_destroy (pthread_attr_t *attr);`
31109   `int pthread_attr_init (pthread_attr_t *attr);`
31110

31111 **DESCRIPTION**
31112   The *pthread_attr_destroy*() function shall destroy a thread attributes object. An implementation
31113   may cause *pthread_attr_destroy*() to set *attr* to an implementation-defined invalid value. A
31114   destroyed *attr* attributes object can be reinitialized using *pthread_attr_init*(); the results of
31115   otherwise referencing the object after it has been destroyed are undefined.

31116   The *pthread_attr_init*() function shall initialize a thread attributes object *attr* with the default
31117   value for all of the individual attributes used by a given implementation.

31118   The resulting attributes object (possibly modified by setting individual attribute values) when
31119   used by *pthread_create*() defines the attributes of the thread created. A single attributes object can
31120   be used in multiple simultaneous calls to *pthread_create*(). Results are undefined if
31121   *pthread_attr_init*() is called specifying an already initialized *attr* attributes object.

31122 **RETURN VALUE**
31123   Upon successful completion, *pthread_attr_destroy*() and *pthread_attr_init*() shall return a value of
31124   0; otherwise, an error number shall be returned to indicate the error.

31125 **ERRORS**
31126   The *pthread_attr_init*() function shall fail if:

31127   [ENOMEM]   Insufficient memory exists to initialize the thread attributes object.

31128   These functions shall not return an error code of [EINTR].

31129 **EXAMPLES**
31130   None.

31131 **APPLICATION USAGE**
31132   None.

31133 **RATIONALE**
31134   Attributes objects are provided for threads, mutexes, and condition variables as a mechanism to
31135   support probable future standardization in these areas without requiring that the function itself
31136   be changed.

31137   Attributes objects provide clean isolation of the configurable aspects of threads. For example,
31138   "stack size" is an important attribute of a thread, but it cannot be expressed portably. When
31139   porting a threaded program, stack sizes often need to be adjusted. The use of attributes objects
31140   can help by allowing the changes to be isolated in a single place, rather than being spread across
31141   every instance of thread creation.

31142   Attributes objects can be used to set up "classes" of threads with similar attributes; for example,
31143   "threads with large stacks and high priority" or "threads with minimal stacks". These classes
31144   can be defined in a single place and then referenced wherever threads need to be created.
31145   Changes to "class" decisions become straightforward, and detailed analysis of each
31146   *pthread_create*() call is not required.

The attributes objects are defined as opaque types as an aid to extensibility. If these objects had been specified as structures, adding new attributes would force recompilation of all multi-threaded programs when the attributes objects are extended; this might not be possible if different program components were supplied by different vendors.

Additionally, opaque attributes objects present opportunities for improving performance. Argument validity can be checked once when attributes are set, rather than each time a thread is created. Implementations often need to cache kernel objects that are expensive to create. Opaque attributes objects provide an efficient mechanism to detect when cached objects become invalid due to attribute changes.

Since assignment is not necessarily defined on a given opaque type, implementation-defined default values cannot be defined in a portable way. The solution to this problem is to allow attributes objects to be initialized dynamically by attributes object initialization functions, so that default values can be supplied automatically by the implementation.

The following proposal was provided as a suggested alternative to the supplied attributes:

1. Maintain the style of passing a parameter formed by the bitwise-inclusive OR of flags to the initialization routines (*pthread_create*(), *pthread_mutex_init*(), *pthread_cond_init*()). The parameter containing the flags should be an opaque type for extensibility. If no flags are set in the parameter, then the objects are created with default characteristics. An implementation may specify implementation-defined flag values and associated behavior.

2. If further specialization of mutexes and condition variables is necessary, implementations may specify additional procedures that operate on the **pthread_mutex_t** and **pthread_cond_t** objects (instead of on attributes objects).

The difficulties with this solution are:

1. A bitmask is not opaque if bits have to be set into bitvector attributes objects using explicitly-coded bitwise-inclusive OR operations. If the set of options exceeds an **int**, application programmers need to know the location of each bit. If bits are set or read by encapsulation (that is, get and set functions), then the bitmask is merely an implementation of attributes objects as currently defined and should not be exposed to the programmer.

2. Many attributes are not Boolean or very small integral values. For example, scheduling policy may be placed in 3-bit or 4-bit, but priority requires 5-bit or more, thereby taking up at least 8 bits out of a possible 16 bits on machines with 16-bit integers. Because of this, the bitmask can only reasonably control whether particular attributes are set or not, and it cannot serve as the repository of the value itself. The value needs to be specified as a function parameter (which is non-extensible), or by setting a structure field (which is non-opaque), or by get and set functions (making the bitmask a redundant addition to the attributes objects).

Stack size is defined as an optional attribute because the very notion of a stack is inherently machine-dependent. Some implementations may not be able to change the size of the stack, for example, and others may not need to because stack pages may be discontiguous and can be allocated and released on demand.

The attribute mechanism has been designed in large measure for extensibility. Future extensions to the attribute mechanism or to any attributes object defined in this volume of IEEE Std 1003.1-2001 has to be done with care so as not to affect binary-compatibility.

31191   Attributes objects, even if allocated by means of dynamic allocation functions such as *malloc()*,
31192   may have their size fixed at compile time. This means, for example, a *pthread_create()* in an
31193   implementation with extensions to **pthread_attr_t** cannot look beyond the area that the binary
31194   application assumes is valid. This suggests that implementations should maintain a size field in
31195   the attributes object, as well as possibly version information, if extensions in different directions
31196   (possibly by different vendors) are to be accommodated.

31197   **FUTURE DIRECTIONS**
31198   None.

31199   **SEE ALSO**
31200   *pthread_attr_getstackaddr()*, *pthread_attr_getstacksize()*, *pthread_attr_getdetachstate()*,
31201   *pthread_create()*, the Base Definitions volume of IEEE Std 1003.1-2001, **<pthread.h>**

31202   **CHANGE HISTORY**
31203   First released in Issue 5. Included for alignment with the POSIX Threads Extension.

31204   **Issue 6**
31205   The *pthread_attr_destroy()* and *pthread_attr_init()* functions are marked as part of the Threads
31206   option.

31207   IEEE PASC Interpretation 1003.1 #107 is applied, noting that the effect of initializing an already
31208   initialized thread attributes object is undefined.

31209 **NAME**

31210   pthread_attr_getdetachstate, pthread_attr_setdetachstate — get and set the detachstate attribute

31211 **SYNOPSIS**

31212 THR   `#include <pthread.h>`

```
31213     int pthread_attr_getdetachstate (const pthread_attr_t *attr,
31214         int *detachstate);
31215     int pthread_attr_setdetachstate (pthread_attr_t *attr, int detachstate);
31216
```

31217 **DESCRIPTION**

31218   The *detachstate* attribute controls whether the thread is created in a detached state. If the thread
31219   is created detached, then use of the ID of the newly created thread by the *pthread_detach*() or
31220   *pthread_join*() function is an error.

31221   The *pthread_attr_getdetachstate*() and *pthread_attr_setdetachstate*() functions, respectively, shall
31222   get and set the *detachstate* attribute in the *attr* object.

31223   For *pthread_attr_getdetachstate*(), *detachstate* shall be set to either
31224   PTHREAD_CREATE_DETACHED or PTHREAD_CREATE_JOINABLE.

31225   For *pthread_attr_setdetachstate*(), the application shall set *detachstate* to either
31226   PTHREAD_CREATE_DETACHED or PTHREAD_CREATE_JOINABLE.

31227   A value of PTHREAD_CREATE_DETACHED shall cause all threads created with *attr* to be in
31228   the detached state, whereas using a value of PTHREAD_CREATE_JOINABLE shall cause all
31229   threads created with *attr* to be in the joinable state. The default value of the *detachstate* attribute
31230   shall be PTHREAD_CREATE_JOINABLE.

31231 **RETURN VALUE**

31232   Upon successful completion, *pthread_attr_getdetachstate*() and *pthread_attr_setdetachstate*() shall
31233   return a value of 0; otherwise, an error number shall be returned to indicate the error.

31234   The *pthread_attr_getdetachstate*() function stores the value of the *detachstate* attribute in *detachstate*
31235   if successful.

31236 **ERRORS**

31237   The *pthread_attr_setdetachstate*() function shall fail if:

31238   [EINVAL]   The value of *detachstate* was not valid

31239   These functions shall not return an error code of [EINTR].

31240 **EXAMPLES**

31241   None.

31242 **APPLICATION USAGE**

31243   None.

31244 **RATIONALE**

31245   None.

31246 **FUTURE DIRECTIONS**

31247   None.

31248 **SEE ALSO**

31249   *pthread_attr_destroy*(), *pthread_attr_getstackaddr*(), *pthread_attr_getstacksize*(), *pthread_create*(), the
31250   Base Definitions volume of IEEE Std 1003.1-2001, **<pthread.h>**

31251 **CHANGE HISTORY**

31252   First released in Issue 5. Included for alignment with the POSIX Threads Extension.

31253 **Issue 6**

31254   The *pthread_attr_setdetachstate*() and *pthread_attr_getdetachstate*() functions are marked as part of
31255   the Threads option.
31256   The DESCRIPTION is updated to avoid use of the term "must" for application requirements.

31257 **NAME**

31258 pthread_attr_getguardsize, pthread_attr_setguardsize — get and set the thread guardsize
31259 attribute

31260 **SYNOPSIS**

31261 XSI   #include <pthread.h>

```
31262    int pthread_attr_getguardsize (const pthread_attr_t *restrict attr,
31263        size_t *restrict guardsize);
31264    int pthread_attr_setguardsize (pthread_attr_t *attr,
31265        size_t guardsize);
31266
```

31267 **DESCRIPTION**

31268 The *pthread_attr_getguardsize*() function shall get the *guardsize* attribute in the *attr* object. This
31269 attribute shall be returned in the *guardsize* parameter.

31270 The *pthread_attr_setguardsize*() function shall set the *guardsize* attribute in the *attr* object. The new
31271 value of this attribute shall be obtained from the *guardsize* parameter. If *guardsize* is zero, a guard
31272 area shall not be provided for threads created with *attr*. If *guardsize* is greater than zero, a guard
31273 area of at least size *guardsize* bytes shall be provided for each thread created with *attr*.

31274 The *guardsize* attribute controls the size of the guard area for the created thread's stack. The
31275 *guardsize* attribute provides protection against overflow of the stack pointer. If a thread's stack is
31276 created with guard protection, the implementation allocates extra memory at the overflow end
31277 of the stack as a buffer against stack overflow of the stack pointer. If an application overflows
31278 into this buffer an error shall result (possibly in a SIGSEGV signal being delivered to the thread).

31279 A conforming implementation may round up the value contained in *guardsize* to a multiple of
31280 the configurable system variable {PAGESIZE} (see **<sys/mman.h>**). If an implementation
31281 rounds up the value of *guardsize* to a multiple of {PAGESIZE}, a call to *pthread_attr_getguardsize*()
31282 specifying *attr* shall store in the *guardsize* parameter the guard size specified by the previous
31283 *pthread_attr_setguardsize*() function call.

31284 The default value of the *guardsize* attribute is {PAGESIZE} bytes. The actual value of {PAGESIZE}
31285 is implementation-defined.

31286 If the *stackaddr* or *stack* attribute has been set (that is, the caller is allocating and managing its
31287 own thread stacks), the *guardsize* attribute shall be ignored and no protection shall be provided
31288 by the implementation. It is the responsibility of the application to manage stack overflow along
31289 with stack allocation and management in this case.

31290 **RETURN VALUE**

31291 If successful, the *pthread_attr_getguardsize*() and *pthread_attr_setguardsize*() functions shall return
31292 zero; otherwise, an error number shall be returned to indicate the error.

31293 **ERRORS**

31294 The *pthread_attr_getguardsize*() and *pthread_attr_setguardsize*() functions shall fail if:

31295 [EINVAL]   The attribute *attr* is invalid.

31296 [EINVAL]   The parameter *guardsize* is invalid.

31297 These functions shall not return an error code of [EINTR].

31298 **EXAMPLES**
31299   None.

31300 **APPLICATION USAGE**
31301   None.

31302 **RATIONALE**
31303   The *guardsize* attribute is provided to the application for two reasons:

31304   1. Overflow protection can potentially result in wasted system resources. An application
31305   that creates a large number of threads, and which knows its threads never overflow their
31306   stack, can save system resources by turning off guard areas.

31307   2. When threads allocate large data structures on the stack, large guard areas may be needed
31308   to detect stack overflow.

31309 **FUTURE DIRECTIONS**
31310   None.

31311 **SEE ALSO**
31312   The Base Definitions volume of IEEE Std 1003.1-2001, **<pthread.h>** , **<sys/mman.h>**

31313 **CHANGE HISTORY**
31314   First released in Issue 5.

31315 **Issue 6**
31316   In the ERRORS section, a third [EINVAL] error condition is removed as it is covered by the
31317   second error condition.

31318   The **restrict** keyword is added to the *pthread_attr_getguardsize*() prototype for alignment with the
31319   ISO/IEC 9899: 1999 standard.

31320 **NAME**

31321   pthread_attr_getinheritsched, pthread_attr_setinheritsched — get and set the inheritsched
31322   attribute (**REALTIME THREADS**)

31323 **SYNOPSIS**

31324 THR TPS   `#include <pthread.h>`

```
31325      int pthread_attr_getinheritsched (const pthread_attr_t *restrict attr,
31326          int *restrict inheritsched);
31327      int pthread_attr_setinheritsched (pthread_attr_t *attr,
31328          int inheritsched);
31329
```

31330 **DESCRIPTION**

31331   The *pthread_attr_getinheritsched*(), and *pthread_attr_setinheritsched*() functions, respectively, shall
31332   get and set the *inheritsched* attribute in the *attr* argument.

31333   When the attributes objects are used by *pthread_create*(), the *inheritsched* attribute determines
31334   how the other scheduling attributes of the created thread shall be set.

31335   PTHREAD_INHERIT_SCHED
31336   Specifies that the thread scheduling attributes shall be inherited from the creating thread,
31337   and the scheduling attributes in this *attr* argument shall be ignored.

31338   PTHREAD_EXPLICIT_SCHED
31339   Specifies that the thread scheduling attributes shall be set to the corresponding values from
31340   this attributes object.

31341   The symbols PTHREAD_INHERIT_SCHED and PTHREAD_EXPLICIT_SCHED are defined in
31342   the <**pthread.h**> header.

31343   The following thread scheduling attributes defined by IEEE Std 1003.1-2001 are affected by the
31344   *inheritsched* attribute: scheduling policy (*schedpolicy*), scheduling parameters (*schedparam*), and
31345   scheduling contention scope (*contentionscope*).

31346 **RETURN VALUE**

31347   If successful, the *pthread_attr_getinheritsched*() and *pthread_attr_setinheritsched*() functions shall
31348   return zero; otherwise, an error number shall be returned to indicate the error.

31349 **ERRORS**

31350   The *pthread_attr_setinheritsched*() function may fail if:

31351   [EINVAL]   The value of *inheritsched* is not valid.

31352   [ENOTSUP]   An attempt was made to set the attribute to an unsupported value.

31353   These functions shall not return an error code of [EINTR].

31354 **EXAMPLES**

31355   None.

31356 **APPLICATION USAGE**

31357   After these attributes have been set, a thread can be created with the specified attributes using
31358   *pthread_create*(). Using these routines does not affect the current running thread.

31359 **RATIONALE**

31360   None.

31361 **FUTURE DIRECTIONS**

31362   None.

31363 **SEE ALSO**

31364   *pthread_attr_destroy*(), *pthread_attr_getscope*(), *pthread_attr_getschedpolicy*(),

31365   *pthread_attr_getschedparam*(), *pthread_create*(), the Base Definitions volume of

31366   IEEE Std 1003.1-2001, **<pthread.h>**, **<sched.h>**

31367 **CHANGE HISTORY**

31368   First released in Issue 5. Included for alignment with the POSIX Threads Extension.

31369   Marked as part of the Realtime Threads Feature Group.

31370 **Issue 6**

31371   The *pthread_attr_getinheritsched*() and *pthread_attr_setinheritsched*() functions are marked as part
31372   of the Threads and Thread Execution Scheduling options.

31373   The [ENOSYS] error condition has been removed as stubs need not be provided if an
31374   implementation does not support the Thread Execution Scheduling option.

31375   The **restrict** keyword is added to the *pthread_attr_getinheritsched*() prototype for alignment with
31376   the ISO/IEC 9899: 1999 standard.

31377 **NAME**

31378 pthread_attr_getschedparam, pthread_attr_setschedparam — get and set the schedparam
31379 attribute

31380 **SYNOPSIS**

31381 THR `#include <pthread.h>`

31382 `int pthread_attr_getschedparam (const pthread_attr_t *restrict attr,`
31383 `    struct sched_param *restrict param);`
31384 `int pthread_attr_setschedparam (pthread_attr_t *restrict attr,`
31385 `    const struct sched_param *restrict param);`
31386

31387 **DESCRIPTION**

31388 The *pthread_attr_getschedparam*(), and *pthread_attr_setschedparam*() functions, respectively, shall
31389 get and set the scheduling parameter attributes in the *attr* argument. The contents of the *param*
31390 structure are defined in the **<sched.h>** header. For the SCHED_FIFO and SCHED_RR policies,
31391 the only required member of *param* is *sched_priority*.

31392 TSP For the SCHED_SPORADIC policy, the required members of the *param* structure are
31393 *sched_priority*,   *sched_ss_low_priority*,   *sched_ss_repl_period*,   *sched_ss_init_budget*,   and
31394 *sched_ss_max_repl*. The specified *sched_ss_repl_period* must be greater than or equal to the
31395 specified *sched_ss_init_budget* for the function to succeed; if it is not, then the function shall fail.
31396 The value of *sched_ss_max_repl* shall be within the inclusive range [1.{SS_REPL_MAX}] for the
31397 function to succeed; if not, the function shall fail.

31398 **RETURN VALUE**

31399 If successful, the *pthread_attr_getschedparam*() and *pthread_attr_setschedparam*() functions shall
31400 return zero; otherwise, an error number shall be returned to indicate the error.

31401 **ERRORS**

31402 The *pthread_attr_setschedparam*() function may fail if:

31403 [EINVAL]   The value of *param* is not valid.

31404 [ENOTSUP]   An attempt was made to set the attribute to an unsupported value.

31405 These functions shall not return an error code of [EINTR].

31406 **EXAMPLES**

31407 None.

31408 **APPLICATION USAGE**

31409 After these attributes have been set, a thread can be created with the specified attributes using
31410 *pthread_create*(). Using these routines does not affect the current running thread.

31411 **RATIONALE**

31412 None.

31413 **FUTURE DIRECTIONS**

31414 None.

31415 **SEE ALSO**

31416 *pthread_attr_destroy*(), *pthread_attr_getscope*(), *pthread_attr_getinheritsched*(),
31417 *pthread_attr_getschedpolicy*(), *pthread_create*(), the Base Definitions volume of
31418 IEEE Std 1003.1-2001, **<pthread.h>**, **<sched.h>**

31419 **CHANGE HISTORY**

31420   First released in Issue 5. Included for alignment with the POSIX Threads Extension.

31421 **Issue 6**

31422   The *pthread_attr_getschedparam*() and *pthread_attr_setschedparam*() functions are marked as part
31423   of the Threads option.

31424   The SCHED_SPORADIC scheduling policy is added for alignment with IEEE Std 1003.1d-1999.

31425   The **restrict** keyword is added to the *pthread_attr_getschedparam*() and
31426   *pthread_attr_setschedparam*() prototypes for alignment with the ISO/IEC 9899: 1999 standard.

31427 **NAME**

31428   pthread_attr_getschedpolicy, pthread_attr_setschedpolicy — get and set the schedpolicy
31429   attribute (**REALTIME THREADS**)

31430 **SYNOPSIS**

31431 THR TPS `#include <pthread.h>`

31432   `int pthread_attr_getschedpolicy (const pthread_attr_t *restrict attr,`
31433   `int *restrict policy);`
31434   `int pthread_attr_setschedpolicy (pthread_attr_t *attr, int policy);`
31435

31436 **DESCRIPTION**

31437   The *pthread_attr_getschedpolicy*() and *pthread_attr_setschedpolicy*() functions, respectively, shall
31438   get and set the *schedpolicy* attribute in the *attr* argument.

31439   The supported values of *policy* shall include SCHED_FIFO, SCHED_RR, and SCHED_OTHER,
31440   which are defined in the **<sched.h>** header. When threads executing with the scheduling policy
31441 TSP SCHED_FIFO, SCHED_RR, or SCHED_SPORADIC are waiting on a mutex, they shall acquire
31442   the mutex in priority order when the mutex is unlocked.

31443 **RETURN VALUE**

31444   If successful, the *pthread_attr_getschedpolicy*() and *pthread_attr_setschedpolicy*() functions shall
31445   return zero; otherwise, an error number shall be returned to indicate the error.

31446 **ERRORS**

31447   The *pthread_attr_setschedpolicy*() function may fail if:

31448   [EINVAL]   The value of *policy* is not valid.

31449   [ENOTSUP]   An attempt was made to set the attribute to an unsupported value.

31450   These functions shall not return an error code of [EINTR].

31451 **EXAMPLES**

31452   None.

31453 **APPLICATION USAGE**

31454   After these attributes have been set, a thread can be created with the specified attributes using
31455   *pthread_create*(). Using these routines does not affect the current running thread.

31456 **RATIONALE**

31457   None.

31458 **FUTURE DIRECTIONS**

31459   None.

31460 **SEE ALSO**

31461   *pthread_attr_destroy*(), *pthread_attr_getscope*(), *pthread_attr_getinheritsched*(),
31462   *pthread_attr_getschedparam*(), *pthread_create*(), the Base Definitions volume of
31463   IEEE Std 1003.1-2001, **<pthread.h>**, **<sched.h>**

31464 **CHANGE HISTORY**

31465   First released in Issue 5. Included for alignment with the POSIX Threads Extension.

31466   Marked as part of the Realtime Threads Feature Group.

31467 **Issue 6**

31468 The *pthread_attr_getschedpolicy*() and *pthread_attr_setschedpolicy*() functions are marked as part of
31469 the Threads and Thread Execution Scheduling options.

31470 The [ENOSYS] error condition has been removed as stubs need not be provided if an
31471 implementation does not support the Thread Execution Scheduling option.

31472 The SCHED_SPORADIC scheduling policy is added for alignment with IEEE Std 1003.1d-1999.

31473 The **restrict** keyword is added to the *pthread_attr_getschedpolicy*() prototype for alignment with
31474 the ISO/IEC 9899: 1999 standard.

31983 **NAME**

31984   pthread_cancel — cancel execution of a thread

31985 **SYNOPSIS**

31986 THR   `#include <pthread.h>`

31987   `int pthread_cancel (pthread_t thread);`

31988

31989 **DESCRIPTION**

31990   The *pthread_cancel*() function shall request that *thread* be canceled. The target thread's
31991   cancelability state and type determines when the cancelation takes effect. When the cancelation
31992   is acted on, the cancelation cleanup handlers for *thread* shall be called. When the last cancelation
31993   cleanup handler returns, the thread-specific data destructor functions shall be called for *thread*.
31994   When the last destructor function returns, *thread* shall be terminated.

31995   The cancelation processing in the target thread shall run asynchronously with respect to the
31996   calling thread returning from *pthread_cancel*().

31997 **RETURN VALUE**

31998   If successful, the *pthread_cancel*() function shall return zero; otherwise, an error number shall be
31999   returned to indicate the error.

32000 **ERRORS**

32001   The *pthread_cancel*() function may fail if:

32002   [ESRCH]   No thread could be found corresponding to that specified by the given thread
32003   ID.

32004   The *pthread_cancel*() function shall not return an error code of [EINTR].

32005 **EXAMPLES**

32006   None.

32007 **APPLICATION USAGE**

32008   None.

32009 **RATIONALE**

32010   Two alternative functions were considered for sending the cancelation notification to a thread.
32011   One would be to define a new SIGCANCEL signal that had the cancelation semantics when
32012   delivered; the other was to define the new *pthread_cancel*() function, which would trigger the
32013   cancelation semantics.

32014   The advantage of a new signal was that so much of the delivery criteria were identical to that
32015   used when trying to deliver a signal that making cancelation notification a signal was seen as
32016   consistent. Indeed, many implementations implement cancelation using a special signal. On the
32017   other hand, there would be no signal functions that could be used with this signal except
32018   *pthread_kill*(), and the behavior of the delivered cancelation signal would be unlike any
32019   previously existing defined signal.

32020   The benefits of a special function include the recognition that this signal would be defined
32021   because of the similar delivery criteria and that this is the only common behavior between a
32022   cancelation request and a signal. In addition, the cancelation delivery mechanism does not have
32023   to be implemented as a signal. There are also strong, if not stronger, parallels with language
32024   exception mechanisms than with signals that are potentially obscured if the delivery mechanism
32025   is visibly closer to signals.

32026   In the end, it was considered that as there were so many exceptions to the use of the new signal
32027   with existing signals functions it would be misleading. A special function has resolved this
32028   problem. This function was carefully defined so that an implementation wishing to provide the
32029   cancelation functions on top of signals could do so. The special function also means that
32030   implementations are not obliged to implement cancelation with signals.

32031   **FUTURE DIRECTIONS**
32032   None.

32033   **SEE ALSO**
32034   *pthread_exit*(), *pthread_cond_timedwait*(), *pthread_join*(), *pthread_setcancelstate*(), the Base
32035   Definitions volume of IEEE Std 1003.1-2001, **<pthread.h>**

32036   **CHANGE HISTORY**
32037   First released in Issue 5. Included for alignment with the POSIX Threads Extension.

32038   **Issue 6**
32039   The *pthread_cancel*() function is marked as part of the Threads option.

32040 **NAME**

32041   pthread_cleanup_pop, pthread_cleanup_push — establish cancelation handlers

32042 **SYNOPSIS**

32043 THR   `#include <pthread.h>`

32044   `void pthread_cleanup_pop (int execute);`

32045   `void pthread_cleanup_push (void (* routine) (void*), void *arg);`

32046

32047 **DESCRIPTION**

32048   The *pthread_cleanup_pop*() function shall remove the routine at the top of the calling thread's
32049   cancelation cleanup stack and optionally invoke it (if *execute* is non-zero).

32050   The *pthread_cleanup_push*() function shall push the specified cancelation cleanup handler *routine*
32051   onto the calling thread's cancelation cleanup stack. The cancelation cleanup handler shall be
32052   popped from the cancelation cleanup stack and invoked with the argument *arg* when:

32053   • The thread exits (that is, calls *pthread_exit*()).

32054   • The thread acts upon a cancelation request.

32055   • The thread calls *pthread_cleanup_pop*() with a non-zero *execute* argument.

32056   These functions may be implemented as macros. The application shall ensure that they appear
32057   as statements, and in pairs within the same lexical scope (that is, the *pthread_cleanup_push*()
32058   macro may be thought to expand to a token list whose first token is '{' with
32059   *pthread_cleanup_pop*() expanding to a token list whose last token is the corresponding '}').

32060   The effect of calling *longjmp*() or *siglongjmp*() is undefined if there have been any calls to
32061   *pthread_cleanup_push*() or *pthread_cleanup_pop*() made without the matching call since the jump
32062   buffer was filled. The effect of calling *longjmp*() or *siglongjmp*() from inside a cancelation
32063   cleanup handler is also undefined unless the jump buffer was also filled in the cancelation
32064   cleanup handler.

32065 **RETURN VALUE**

32066   The *pthread_cleanup_push*() and *pthread_cleanup_pop*() functions shall not return a value.

32067 **ERRORS**

32068   No errors are defined.

32069   These functions shall not return an error code of [EINTR].

32070 **EXAMPLES**

32071   The following is an example using thread primitives to implement a cancelable, writers-priority
32072   read-write lock:

```
32073    typedef struct {
32074        pthread_mutex_t lock;
32075        pthread_cond_t rcond,
32076            wcond;
32077        int lock_count; /* < 0 .. Held by writer. */
32078                        /* > 0 .. Held by lock_count readers. */
32079                        /* = 0 .. Held by nobody. */
32080        int waiting_writers; /* Count of waiting writers. */
32081    } rwlock;
```

```
32082    void
32083    waiting_reader_cleanup (void. *arg).
32084    {
32085        rwlock *1;

32086        1 = (rwlock *) arg;
32087        pthread_mutex_unlock (&1->lock);
32088    }

32089    void
32090    lock_for_read (rwlock *1)
32091    {
32092        pthread_mutex_lock (&1->lock);
32093        pthread_cleanup_push (waiting_reader_cleanup, 1);
32094        while ((1->lock_count < 0) && (1->waiting_writers ! = 0))
32095            pthread_cond_wait (&1->rcond, &1->lock);
32096        1->lock_count++;
32097       /*
32098        * Note the pthread_cleanup_pop executes
32099        * waiting_reader_cleanup.
32100        */
32101        pthread_cleanup_pop(1);
32102    }

32103    void
32104    release_read_lock (rwlock *1)
32105    {
32106        pthread_mutex_lock (&1->lock);
32107        if (--1->lock_count == 0)
32108            pthread_cond_signal (&1->wcond);
32109        pthread_mutex_unlock (1);
32110    }

32111    void
32112    waiting_writer_cleanup (void *arg)
32113    {
32114        rwlock *1;

32115        1 = (rwlock *) arg;
32116        if ((--1->waiting_writers == 0) && (1->lock_count >= 0)) {
32117           /*
32118            * This only happens if we have been canceled.
32119            */
32120            pthread_cond_broadcast (&1->wcond);
32121        }
32122        pthread_mutex_unlock (&1->lock);
32123    }

32124    void
32125    lock_for_write (rwlock *1)
```

```
32126      {
32127          pthread_mutex_lock (&1->lock);
32128          1->waiting_writers++;
32129          pthread_cleanup_push (waiting_writer_cleanup, 1);
32130          while (1->lock_count ! = 0)
32131              pthread_cond_wait (&1->wcond, &1->lock);
32132          1->lock_count = -1;
32133          /*
32134           * Note the pthread_cleanup_pop executes
32135           * waiting_writer_cleanup.
32136           */
32137          pthread_cleanup_pop (1);
32138      }
32139  void
32140  release_write_lock (rwlock *1)
32141  {
32142          pthread_mutex_lock (&1->lock);
32143          1->lock_count = 0;
32144          if (1->waiting_writers == 0)
32145              pthread_cond_broadcast (&1->rcond)
32146          else
32147              pthread_cond_signal (&1->wcond);
32148          pthread_mutex_unlock (&1->lock);
32149  }
32150  /*
32151   * This function is called to initialize the read/write lock.
32152   */
32153  void
32154  initialize_rwlock (rwlock *1)
32155  {
32156          pthread_mutex_init (&1->lock, pthread_mutexattr_default);
32157          pthread_cond_init (&1->wcond, pthread_condattr_default);
32158          pthread_cond_init (&1->rcond, pthread_condattr_default);
32159          1->lock_count = 0;
32160          1->waiting_writers = 0;
32161  }
32162  reader_thread()
32163  {
32164          lock_for_read (&lock);
32165          pthread_cleanup_push (release_read_lock, &lock);
32166          /*
32167           * Thread has read lock.
32168           */
32169          pthread_cleanup_pop (1);
32170      }
```

```
32171    writer_thread()
32172    {
32173        lock_for_write (&lock);
32174        pthread_cleanup_push (release_write_lock, &lock);
32175        /*
32176         * Thread has write lock.
32177         */
32178    pthread_cleanup_pop (1);
32179    }
```

APPLICATION USAGE

The two routines that push and pop cancelation cleanup handlers, *pthread_cleanup_push*() and *pthread_cleanup_pop*(), can be thought of as left and right parentheses. They always need to be matched.

RATIONALE

The restriction that the two routines that push and pop cancelation cleanup handlers, *pthread_cleanup_push*() and *pthread_cleanup_pop*(), have to appear in the same lexical scope allows for efficient macro or compiler implementations and efficient storage management. A sample implementation of these routines as macros might look like this:

```
#define pthread_cleanup_push (rtn, arg) { \
    struct _pthread_handler_rec __cleanup_handler, **__head; \
    __cleanup_handler.rtn = rtn; \
    __cleanup_handler.arg = arg; \
    (void) pthread_getspecific (_pthread_handler_key, &__head); \
    __cleanup_handler.next = *__head; \
    *__head = &__cleanup_handler;

#define pthread_cleanup_pop (ex) \
    *__head = __cleanup_handler.next; \
    if (ex) (*__cleanup_handler.rtn) (_cleanup_handler.arg); \
}
```

A more ambitious implementation of these routines might do even better by allowing the compiler to note that the cancelation cleanup handler is a constant and can be expanded inline.

This volume of IEEE Std 1003.1-2001 currently leaves unspecified the effect of calling *longjmp*() from a signal handler executing in a POSIX System Interfaces function. If an implementation wants to allow this and give the programmer reasonable behavior, the *longjmp*() function has to call all cancelation cleanup handlers that have been pushed but not popped since the time *setjmp*() was called.

Consider a multi-threaded function called by a thread that uses signals. If a signal were delivered to a signal handler during the operation of *qsort*() and that handler were to call *longjmp*() (which, in turn, did *not* call the cancelation cleanup handlers) the helper threads created by the *qsort*() function would not be canceled. Instead, they would continue to execute and write into the argument array even though the array might have been popped off the stack.

Note that the specified cleanup handling mechanism is especially tied to the C language and, while the requirement for a uniform mechanism for expressing cleanup is language-independent, the mechanism used in other languages may be quite different. In addition, this

32215   mechanism is really only necessary due to the lack of a real exception mechanism in the C
32216   language, which would be the ideal solution.

32217   There is no notion of a cancelation cleanup-safe function. If an application has no cancelation
32218   points in its signal handlers, blocks any signal whose handler may have cancelation points while
32219   calling async-unsafe functions, or disables cancelation while calling async-unsafe functions, all
32220   functions may be safely called from cancelation cleanup routines.

32221 **FUTURE DIRECTIONS**
32222   None.

32223 **SEE ALSO**
32224   *pthread_cancel*(), *pthread_setcancelstate*(), the Base Definitions volume of IEEE Std 1003.1-2001,
32225   **<pthread.h>**

32226 **CHANGE HISTORY**
32227   First released in Issue 5. Included for alignment with the POSIX Threads Extension.

32228 **Issue 6**
32229   The *pthread_cleanup_pop*() and *pthread_cleanup_push*() functions are marked as part of the
32230   Threads option.

32231   The APPLICATION USAGE section is added.

32232   The DESCRIPTION is updated to avoid use of the term "must" for application requirements.

32233 **NAME**

32234   pthread_cond_broadcast, pthread_cond_signal—broadcast or signal a condition

32235 **SYNOPSIS**

32236 THR   `#include <pthread.h>`

32237   `int pthread_cond_broadcast (pthread_cond_t *cond);`
32238   `int pthread_cond_signal (pthread_cond_t *cond);`

32239

32240 **DESCRIPTION**

32241   These functions shall unblock threads blocked on a condition variable.

32242   The *pthread_cond_broadcast*() function shall unblock all threads currently blocked on the
32243   specified condition variable *cond*.

32244   The *pthread_cond_signal*() function shall unblock at least one of the threads that are blocked on
32245   the specified condition variable *cond* (if any threads are blocked on *cond*).

32246   If more than one thread is blocked on a condition variable, the scheduling policy shall determine
32247   the order in which threads are unblocked. When each thread unblocked as a result of a
32248   *pthread_cond_broadcast*() or *pthread_cond_signal*() returns from its call to *pthread_cond_wait*() or
32249   *pthread_cond_timedwait*(), the thread shall own the mutex with which it called
32250   *pthread_cond_wait*() or *pthread_cond_timedwait*(). The thread(s) that are unblocked shall contend
32251   for the mutex according to the scheduling policy (if applicable), and as if each had called
32252   *pthread_mutex_lock*().

32253   The *pthread_cond_broadcast*() or *pthread_cond_signal*() functions may be called by a thread
32254   whether or not it currently owns the mutex that threads calling *pthread_cond_wait*() or
32255   *pthread_cond_timedwait*() have associated with the condition variable during their waits;
32256   however, if predictable scheduling behavior is required, then that mutex shall be locked by the
32257   thread calling *pthread_cond_broadcast*() or *pthread_cond_signal*().

32258   The *pthread_cond_broadcast*() and *pthread_cond_signal*() functions shall have no effect if there are
32259   no threads currently blocked on *cond*.

32260 **RETURN VALUE**

32261   If successful, the *pthread_cond_broadcast*() and *pthread_cond_signal*() functions shall return zero;
32262   otherwise, an error number shall be returned to indicate the error.

32263 **ERRORS**

32264   The *pthread_cond_broadcast*() and *pthread_cond_signal*() function may fail if:

32265   [EINVAL]   The value *cond* does not refer to an initialized condition variable.

32266   These functions shall not return an error code of [EINTR].

32267 **EXAMPLES**

32268   None.

32269 **APPLICATION USAGE**

32270   The *pthread_cond_broadcast*() function is used whenever the shared-variable state has been
32271   changed in a way that more than one thread can proceed with its task. Consider a single
32272   producer/multiple consumer problem, where the producer can insert multiple items on a list
32273   that is accessed one item at a time by the consumers. By calling the *pthread_cond_broadcast*()
32274   function, the producer would notify all consumers that might be waiting, and thereby the

application would receive more throughput on a multi-processor. In addition, *pthread_cond_broadcast*() makes it easier to implement a read-write lock. The *pthread_cond_broadcast*() function is needed in order to wake up all waiting readers when a writer releases its lock. Finally, the two-phase commit algorithm can use this broadcast function to notify all clients of an impending transaction commit.

It is not safe to use the *pthread_cond_signal*() function in a signal handler that is invoked asynchronously. Even if it were safe, there would still be a race between the test of the Boolean *pthread_cond_wait*() that could not be efficiently eliminated.

Mutexes and condition variables are thus not suitable for releasing a waiting thread by signaling from code running in a signal handler.

RATIONALE

Multiple Awakenings by Condition Signal

On a multi-processor, it may be impossible for an implementation of *pthread_cond_signal*() to avoid the unblocking of more than one thread blocked on a condition variable. For example, consider the following partial implementation of *pthread_cond_wait*() and *pthread_cond_signal*(), executed by two threads in the order given. One thread is trying to wait on the condition variable, another is concurrently executing *pthread_cond_signal*(), while a third thread is already waiting.

```
pthread_cond_wait (mutex, cond):
    value = cond->value; /* 1 */
    pthread_mutex_unlock (mutex); /* 2 */
    pthread_mutex_lock (cond->mutex); /* 10 */
    if (value == cond->value) { /* 11 */
        me->next_cond = cond->waiter;
        cond->waiter = me;
        pthread_mutex_unlock (cond->mutex);
        unable_to_run (me);
    } else
        pthread_mutex_unlock (cond->mutex); /* 12 */
    pthread_mutex_lock (mutex); /* 13 * /
pthread_cond_signal (cond):
    pthread_mutex_lock (cond->mutex); /* 3 */
    cond->value++; /* 4 */
    if (cond->waiter) { /* 5 */
        sleeper = cond->waiter; /* 6 */
        cond->waiter = sleeper->next_cond; /* 7 */
        able_to_run (sleeper); /* 8 */
    }
    pthread_mutex_unlock (cond->mutex); /* 9 */
```

The effect is that more than one thread can return from its call to *pthread_cond_wait*() or *pthread_cond_timedwait*() as a result of one call to *pthread_cond_signal*(). This effect is called "spurious wakeup". Note that the situation is self-correcting in that the number of threads that are so awakened is finite; for example, the next thread to call *pthread_cond_wait*() after the sequence of events above blocks.

32319 While this problem could be resolved, the loss of efficiency for a fringe condition that occurs
32320 only rarely is unacceptable, especially given that one has to check the predicate associated with a
32321 condition variable anyway. Correcting this problem would unnecessarily reduce the degree of
32322 concurrency in this basic building block for all higher-level synchronization operations.

32323 An added benefit of allowing spurious wakeups is that applications are forced to code a
32324 predicate-testing-loop around the condition wait. This also makes the application tolerate
32325 superfluous condition broadcasts or signals on the same condition variable that may be coded in
32326 some other part of the application. The resulting applications are thus more robust. Therefore,
32327 IEEE Std 1003.1-2001 explicitly documents that spurious wakeups may occur.

32328 **FUTURE DIRECTIONS**
32329 None.

32330 **SEE ALSO**
32331 *pthread_cond_destroy*(),   *pthread_cond_timedwait*(),   the   Base   Definitions   volume   of
32332 IEEE Std 1003.1-2001, **<pthread.h>**

32333 **CHANGE HISTORY**
32334 First released in Issue 5. Included for alignment with the POSIX Threads Extension.

32335 **Issue 6**
32336 The *pthread_cond_broadcast*() and *pthread_cond_signal*() functions are marked as part of the
32337 Threads option.

32338 The APPLICATION USAGE section is added.

32339 **NAME**

32340   pthread_cond_destroy, pthread_cond_init — destroy and initialize condition variables

32341 **SYNOPSIS**

32342 THR   `#include <pthread.h>`

32343   `int pthread_cond_destroy (pthread_cond_t *cond);`
32344   `int pthread_cond_init (pthread_cond_t *restrict cond,`
32345   `const pthread_condattr_t *restrict attr);`
32346   `pthread_cond_t cond = PTHREAD_COND_INITIALIZER;`
32347

32348 **DESCRIPTION**

32349   The *pthread_cond_destroy()* function shall destroy the given condition variable specified by *cond*;
32350   the object becomes, in effect, uninitialized. An implementation may cause *pthread_cond_destroy()*
32351   to set the object referenced by *cond* to an invalid value. A destroyed condition variable object can
32352   be reinitialized using *pthread_cond_init()*; the results of otherwise referencing the object after it
32353   has been destroyed are undefined.

32354   It shall be safe to destroy an initialized condition variable upon which no threads are currently
32355   blocked. Attempting to destroy a condition variable upon which other threads are currently
32356   blocked results in undefined behavior.

32357   The *pthread_cond_init()* function shall initialize the condition variable referenced by *cond* with
32358   attributes referenced by *attr*. If *attr* is NULL, the default condition variable attributes shall be
32359   used; the effect is the same as passing the address of a default condition variable attributes
32360   object. Upon successful initialization, the state of the condition variable shall become initialized.

32361   Only *cond* itself may be used for performing synchronization. The result of referring to copies of
32362   *cond* in calls to *pthread_cond_wait()*, *pthread_cond_timedwait()*, *pthread_cond_signal()*,
32363   *pthread_cond_broadcast()*, and *pthread_cond_destroy()* is undefined.

32364   Attempting to initialize an already initialized condition variable results in undefined behavior.

32365   In cases where default condition variable attributes are appropriate, the macro
32366   PTHREAD_COND_INITIALIZER can be used to initialize condition variables that are statically
32367   allocated. The effect shall be equivalent to dynamic initialization by a call to *pthread_cond_init()*
32368   with parameter *attr* specified as NULL, except that no error checks are performed.

32369 **RETURN VALUE**

32370   If successful, the *pthread_cond_destroy()* and *pthread_cond_init()* functions shall return zero;
32371   otherwise, an error number shall be returned to indicate the error.

32372   The [EBUSY] and [EINVAL] error checks, if implemented, shall act as if they were performed
32373   immediately at the beginning of processing for the function and caused an error return prior to
32374   modifying the state of the condition variable specified by *cond*.

32375 **ERRORS**

32376   The *pthread_cond_destroy()* function may fail if:

32377   [EBUSY]   The implementation has detected an attempt to destroy the object referenced
32378   by *cond* while it is referenced (for example, while being used in a
32379   *pthread_cond_wait()* or *pthread_cond_timedwait()* by another thread.
32380   [EINVAL]   The value specified by *cond* is invalid.

32381   The *pthread_cond_init*() function shall fail if:

32382   [EAGAIN]   The system lacked the necessary resources (other than memory) to initialize
32383   another condition variable.

32384   [ENOMEM]   Insufficient memory exists to initialize the condition variable.

32385   The *pthread_cond_init*() function may fail if:

32386   [EBUSY]   The implementation has detected an attempt to reinitialize the object
32387   referenced by *cond*, a previously initialized, but not yet destroyed, condition
32388   variable.

32389   [EINVAL]   The value specified by *attr* is invalid.

32390   These functions shall not return an error code of [EINTR].

32391   **EXAMPLES**

32392   A condition variable can be destroyed immediately after all the threads that are blocked on it are
32393   awakened. For example, consider the following code:

```
32394     struct list {
32395          pthread_mutex_t lm;
32396          ...
32397     }

32398     struct elt {
32399          key k;
32400          int busy;
32401          pthread_cond_t notbusy;
32402          ...
32403     }

32404     /* Find a list element and reserve it. */
32405     struct elt *
32406     list_find (struct list *lp, key k)
32407     {
32408          struct elt *ep;

32409          pthread_mutex_lock (&lp->lm);
32410          while ((ep = find_elt (1, k) ! = NULL) && ep->busy)
32411               pthread_cond_wait (&ep->notbusy, &lp->lm);
32412          if (ep != NULL)
32413               ep->busy = 1;
32414          pthread_mutex_unlock (&lp->lm);
32415          return (ep);
32416     }

32417     delete_elt (struct list *lp, struct elt *ep)
32418     {
32419          pthread_mutex_lock (&lp->lm);
32420          assert (ep->busy);
32421          ... remove ep from list ...
32422          ep->busy = 0; /* Paranoid. */
32423  (A) pthread_cond_broadcast (&ep->notbusy);
32424          pthread_mutex_unlock (&lp->lm);
```

```
32425    (B) pthread_cond_destroy (&rp->notbusy);
32426        free (ep);
32427    }
```

32428 In this example, the condition variable and its list element may be freed (line B) immediately
32429 after all threads waiting for it are awakened (line A), since the mutex and the code ensure that no
32430 other thread can touch the element to be deleted.

32431 **APPLICATION USAGE**

32432 None.

32433 **RATIONALE**

32434 See *pthread_mutex_init*(); a similar rationale applies to condition variables.

32435 **FUTURE DIRECTIONS**

32436 None.

32437 **SEE ALSO**

32438 *pthread_cond_broadcast*(), *pthread_cond_signal*(), *pthread_cond_timedwait*(), the Base Definitions
32439 volume of IEEE Std 1003.1-2001, **<pthread.h>**

32440 **CHANGE HISTORY**

32441 First released in Issue 5. Included for alignment with the POSIX Threads Extension.

32442 **Issue 6**

32443 The *pthread_cond_destroy*() and *pthread_cond_init*() functions are marked as part of the Threads
32444 option.

32445 IEEE PASC Interpretation 1003.1c #34 is applied, updating the DESCRIPTION.

32446 The **restrict** keyword is added to the *pthread_cond_init*() prototype for alignment with the
32447 ISO/IEC 9899: 1999 standard.

32456 **NAME**

32457   pthread_cond_timedwait, pthread_cond_wait—wait on a condition

32458 **SYNOPSIS**

32459 THR   `#include <pthread.h>`

32460   `int pthread_cond_timedwait (pthread_cond_t *restrict cond,`
32461   `pthread_mutex_t *restrict mutex,`
32462   `const struct timespec *restrict abstime);`
32463   `int pthread_cond_wait (pthread_cond_t *restrict cond,`
32464   `pthread_mutex_t *restrict mutex);`
32465

32466 **DESCRIPTION**

32467   The *pthread_cond_timedwait*() and *pthread_cond_wait*() functions shall block on a condition
32468   variable. They shall be called with *mutex* locked by the calling thread or undefined behavior
32469   results.

32470   These functions atomically release *mutex* and cause the calling thread to block on the condition
32471   variable *cond*; atomically here means "atomically with respect to access by another thread to the
32472   mutex and then the condition variable". That is, if another thread is able to acquire the mutex
32473   after the about-to-block thread has released it, then a subsequent call to *pthread_cond_broadcast*()
32474   or *pthread_cond_signal*() in that thread shall behave as if it were issued after the about-to-block
32475   thread has blocked.

32476   Upon successful return, the mutex shall have been locked and shall be owned by the calling
32477   thread.

32478   When using condition variables there is always a Boolean predicate involving shared variables
32479   associated with each condition wait that is true if the thread should proceed. Spurious wakeups
32480   from the *pthread_cond_timedwait*() or *pthread_cond_wait*() functions may occur. Since the return
32481   from *pthread_cond_timedwait*() or *pthread_cond_wait*() does not imply anything about the value
32482   of this predicate, the predicate should be re-evaluated upon such return.

32483   The effect of using more than one mutex for concurrent *pthread_cond_timedwait*() or
32484   *pthread_cond_wait*() operations on the same condition variable is undefined; that is, a condition
32485   variable becomes bound to a unique mutex when a thread waits on the condition variable, and
32486   this (dynamic) binding shall end when the wait returns.

32487   A condition wait (whether timed or not) is a cancelation point. When the cancelability enable
32488   state of a thread is set to PTHREAD_CANCEL_DEFERRED, a side effect of acting upon a
32489   cancelation request while in a condition wait is that the mutex is (in effect) re-acquired before
32490   calling the first cancelation cleanup handler. The effect is as if the thread were unblocked,
32491   allowed to execute up to the point of returning from the call to *pthread_cond_timedwait*() or
32492   *pthread_cond_wait*(), but at that point notices the cancelation request and instead of returning to
32493   the caller of *pthread_cond_timedwait*() or *pthread_cond_wait*(), starts the thread cancelation
32494   activities, which includes calling cancelation cleanup handlers.

32495   A thread that has been unblocked because it has been canceled while blocked in a call to
32496   *pthread_cond_timedwait*() or *pthread_cond_wait*() shall not consume any condition signal that
32497   may be directed concurrently at the condition variable if there are other threads blocked on the
32498   condition variable.

32499   The *pthread_cond_timedwait*() function shall be equivalent to *pthread_cond_wait*(), except that an
32500   error is returned if the absolute time specified by *abstime* passes (that is, system time equals or
32501   exceeds *abstime*) before the condition *cond* is signaled or broadcasted, or if the absolute time
32502   specified by *abstime* has already been passed at the time of the call.

32503 CS   If the Clock Selection option is supported, the condition variable shall have a clock attribute
32504   which specifies the clock that shall be used to measure the time specified by the *abstime*
32505   argument. When such timeouts occur, *pthread_cond_timedwait*() shall nonetheless release and
32506   re-acquire the mutex referenced by *mutex*. The *pthread_cond_timedwait*() function is also a
32507   cancelation point.

32508   If a signal is delivered to a thread waiting for a condition variable, upon return from the signal
32509   handler the thread resumes waiting for the condition variable as if it was not interrupted, or it
32510   shall return zero due to spurious wakeup.

32511 **RETURN VALUE**
32512   Except in the case of [ETIMEDOUT], all these error checks shall act as if they were performed
32513   immediately at the beginning of processing for the function and shall cause an error return, in
32514   effect, prior to modifying the state of the mutex specified by *mutex* or the condition variable
32515   specified by *cond*.

32516   Upon successful completion, a value of zero shall be returned; otherwise, an error number shall
32517   be returned to indicate the error.

32518 **ERRORS**
32519   The *pthread_cond_timedwait*() function shall fail if:

32520   [ETIMEDOUT]   The time specified by *abstime* to *pthread_cond_timedwait*() has passed.

32521   The *pthread_cond_timedwait*() and *pthread_cond_wait*() functions may fail if:

32522   [EINVAL]   The value specified by *cond, mutex*, or *abstime* is invalid.
32523   [EINVAL]   Different mutexes were supplied for concurrent *pthread_cond_timedwait*() or
32524   *pthread_cond_wait*() operations on the same condition variable.
32525   [EPERM]   The mutex was not owned by the current thread at the time of the call.

32526   These functions shall not return an error code of [EINTR].

32527 **EXAMPLES**
32528   None.

32529 **APPLICATION USAGE**
32530   None.

32531 **RATIONALE**
32532   **Condition Wait Semantics**

32533   It is important to note that when *pthread_cond_wait*() and *pthread_cond_timedwait*() return
32534   without error, the associated predicate may still be false. Similarly, when
32535   *pthread_cond_timedwait*() returns with the timeout error, the associated predicate may be true
32536   due to an unavoidable race between the expiration of the timeout and the predicate state change.

32537   Some implementations, particularly on a multi-processor, may sometimes cause multiple
32538   threads to wake up when the condition variable is signaled simultaneously on different
32539   processors.

32540   In general, whenever a condition wait returns, the thread has to re-evaluate the predicate
32541   associated with the condition wait to determine whether it can safely proceed, should wait
32542   again, or should declare a timeout. A return from the wait does not imply that the associated
32543   predicate is either true or false.

32544   It is thus recommended that a condition wait be enclosed in the equivalent of a "while loop"
32545   that checks the predicate.

32546   **Timed Wait Semantics**

32547   An absolute time measure was chosen for specifying the timeout parameter for two reasons.
32548   First, a relative time measure can be easily implemented on top of a function that specifies
32549   absolute time, but there is a race condition associated with specifying an absolute timeout on top
32550   of a function that specifies relative timeouts. For example, assume that *clock_gettime*() returns
32551   the current time and *cond_relative_timed_wait*() uses relative timeouts:

```
32552   clock_gettime (CLOCK_REALTIME, &now)
32553   reltime = sleep_til_this_absolute_time -now;
32554   cond_relative_timed_wait (c, m, &reltime);
```

32555   If the thread is preempted between the first statement and the last statement, the thread blocks
32556   for too long. Blocking, however, is irrelevant if an absolute timeout is used. An absolute timeout
32557   also need not be recomputed if it is used multiple times in a loop, such as that enclosing a
32558   condition wait.

32559   For cases when the system clock is advanced discontinuously by an operator, it is expected that
32560   implementations process any timed wait expiring at an intervening time as if that time had
32561   actually occurred.

32562   **Cancelation and Condition Wait**

32563   A condition wait, whether timed or not, is a cancelation point. That is, the functions
32564   *pthread_cond_wait*() or *pthread_cond_timedwait*() are points where a pending (or concurrent)
32565   cancelation request is noticed. The reason for this is that an indefinite wait is possible at these
32566   points—whatever event is being waited for, even if the program is totally correct, might never
32567   occur; for example, some input data being awaited might never be sent. By making condition
32568   wait a cancelation point, the thread can be canceled and perform its cancelation cleanup handler
32569   even though it may be stuck in some indefinite wait.

32570   A side effect of acting on a cancelation request while a thread is blocked on a condition variable
32571   is to re-acquire the mutex before calling any of the cancelation cleanup handlers. This is done in
32572   order to ensure that the cancelation cleanup handler is executed in the same state as the critical
32573   code that lies both before and after the call to the condition wait function. This rule is also
32574   required when interfacing to POSIX threads from languages, such as Ada or C++, which may
32575   choose to map cancelation onto a language exception; this rule ensures that each exception
32576   handler guarding a critical section can always safely depend upon the fact that the associated
32577   mutex has already been locked regardless of exactly where within the critical section the
32578   exception was raised. Without this rule, there would not be a uniform rule that exception
32579   handlers could follow regarding the lock, and so coding would become very cumbersome.

32580   Therefore, since *some* statement has to be made regarding the state of the lock when a
32581   cancelation is delivered during a wait, a definition has been chosen that makes application
32582   coding most convenient and error free.

32583 When acting on a cancelation request while a thread is blocked on a condition variable, the
32584 implementation is required to ensure that the thread does not consume any condition signals
32585 directed at that condition variable if there are any other threads waiting on that condition
32586 variable. This rule is specified in order to avoid deadlock conditions that could occur if these two
32587 independent requests (one acting on a thread and the other acting on the condition variable)
32588 were not processed independently.

32589 **Performance of Mutexes and Condition Variables**

32590 Mutexes are expected to be locked only for a few instructions. This practice is almost
32591 automatically enforced by the desire of programmers to avoid long serial regions of execution
32592 (which would reduce total effective parallelism).

32593 When using mutexes and condition variables, one tries to ensure that the usual case is to lock the
32594 mutex, access shared data, and unlock the mutex. Waiting on a condition variable should be a
32595 relatively rare situation. For example, when implementing a read-write lock, code that acquires a
32596 read-lock typically needs only to increment the count of readers (under mutual-exclusion) and
32597 return. The calling thread would actually wait on the condition variable only when there is
32598 already an active writer. So the efficiency of a synchronization operation is bounded by the cost
32599 of mutex lock/unlock and not by condition wait. Note that in the usual case there is no context
32600 switch.

32601 This is not to say that the efficiency of condition waiting is unimportant. Since there needs to be
32602 at least one context switch per Ada rendezvous, the efficiency of waiting on a condition variable
32603 is important. The cost of waiting on a condition variable should be little more than the minimal
32604 cost for a context switch plus the time to unlock and lock the mutex.

32605 **Features of Mutexes and Condition Variables**

32606 It had been suggested that the mutex acquisition and release be decoupled from condition wait.
32607 This was rejected because it is the combined nature of the operation that, in fact, facilitates
32608 realtime implementations. Those implementations can atomically move a high-priority thread
32609 between the condition variable and the mutex in a manner that is transparent to the caller. This
32610 can prevent extra context switches and provide more deterministic acquisition of a mutex when
32611 the waiting thread is signaled. Thus, fairness and priority issues can be dealt with directly by the
32612 scheduling discipline. Furthermore, the current condition wait operation matches existing
32613 practice.

32614 **Scheduling Behavior of Mutexes and Condition Variables**

32615 Synchronization primitives that attempt to interfere with scheduling policy by specifying an
32616 ordering rule are considered undesirable. Threads waiting on mutexes and condition variables
32617 are selected to proceed in an order dependent upon the scheduling policy rather than in some
32618 fixed order (for example, FIFO or priority). Thus, the scheduling policy determines which
32619 thread(s) are awakened and allowed to proceed.

32620 **Timed Condition Wait**

32621 The *pthread_cond_timedwait*() function allows an application to give up waiting for a particular
32622 condition after a given amount of time. An example of its use follows:

```
32623  (void) pthread_mutex_lock (&t. mn);
32624        t.waiters++;
32625     clock_gettime (CLOCK_REALTIME, &ts);
```

```
32626          ts.tv_sec += 5;
32627          rc = 0;
32628          while (! mypredicate (&t) && rc == 0)
32629              rc = pthread_cond_timedwait (&t.cond, &t.mn, &ts);
32630          t.waiters- -;
32631          if (rc == 0) setmystate (&t);
32632     (void) pthread_mutex_unlock (&t.mn);
```

32633   By making the timeout parameter absolute, it does not need to be recomputed each time the
32634   program checks its blocking predicate. If the timeout was relative, it would have to be
32635   recomputed before each call. This would be especially difficult since such code would need to
32636   take into account the possibility of extra wakeups that result from extra broadcasts or signals on
32637   the condition variable that occur before either the predicate is true or the timeout is due.

32638 **FUTURE DIRECTIONS**
32639   None.

32640 **SEE ALSO**
32641   *pthread_cond_signal*(), *pthread_cond_broadcast*(), the Base Definitions volume of
32642   IEEE Std 1003.1-2001, **<pthread.h>**

32643 **CHANGE HISTORY**
32644   First released in Issue 5. Included for alignment with the POSIX Threads Extension.

32645 **Issue 6**
32646   The *pthread_cond_timedwait*() and *pthread_cond_wait*() functions are marked as part of the
32647   Threads option.

32648   The Open Group Corrigendum U021/9 is applied, correcting the prototype for the
32649   *pthread_cond_wait*() function.

32650   The DESCRIPTION is updated for alignment with IEEE Std 1003.1j-2000 by adding semantics for
32651   the Clock Selection option.

32652   The ERRORS section has an additional case for [EPERM] in response to IEEE PASC
32653   Interpretation 1003.1c #28.

32654   The **restrict** keyword is added to the *pthread_cond_timedwait*() and *pthread_cond_wait*()
32655   prototypes for alignment with the ISO/IEC 9899: 1999 standard.

32656 **NAME**

32657 pthread_condattr_destroy, pthread_condattr_init—destroy and initialize the condition variable
32658 attributes object

32659 **SYNOPSIS**

32660 THR
```
#include <pthread.h>
```
32661
32662
```
int pthread_condattr_destroy (pthread_condattr_t *attr);
int pthread_condattr_init (pthread_condattr_t *attr);
```
32663

32664 **DESCRIPTION**

32665 The *pthread_condattr_destroy*() function shall destroy a condition variable attributes object; the
32666 object becomes, in effect, uninitialized. An implementation may cause *pthread_condattr_destroy*()
32667 to set the object referenced by *attr* to an invalid value. A destroyed *attr* attributes object can be
32668 reinitialized using *pthread_condattr_init*(); the results of otherwise referencing the object after it
32669 has been destroyed are undefined.

32670 The *pthread_condattr_init*() function shall initialize a condition variable attributes object *attr* with
32671 the default value for all of the attributes defined by the implementation.

32672 Results are undefined if *pthread_condattr_init*() is called specifying an already initialized *attr*
32673 attributes object.

32674 After a condition variable attributes object has been used to initialize one or more condition
32675 variables, any function affecting the attributes object (including destruction) shall not affect any
32676 previously initialized condition variables.

32677 This volume of IEEE Std 1003.1-2001 requires two attributes, the *clock* attribute and the *process-*
32678 *shared* attribute.

32679 Additional attributes, their default values, and the names of the associated functions to get and
32680 set those attribute values are implementation-defined.

32681 **RETURN VALUE**

32682 If successful, the *pthread_condattr_destroy*() and *pthread_condattr_init*() functions shall return
32683 zero; otherwise, an error number shall be returned to indicate the error.

32684 **ERRORS**

32685 The *pthread_condattr_destroy*() function may fail if:

32686 [EINVAL]   The value specified by *attr* is invalid.

32687 The *pthread_condattr_init*() function shall fail if:

32688 [ENOMEM]   Insufficient memory exists to initialize the condition variable attributes object.

32689 These functions shall not return an error code of [EINTR].

32690 **EXAMPLES**

32691 None.

32692 **APPLICATION USAGE**

32693 None.

32694 **RATIONALE**

32695 See *pthread_attr_init*() and *pthread_mutex_init*().

32696   A *process-shared* attribute has been defined for condition variables for the same reason it has been
32697   defined for mutexes.

32698 **FUTURE DIRECTIONS**
32699   None.

32700 **SEE ALSO**
32701   *pthread_attr_destroy*(), *pthread_cond_destroy*(), *pthread_condattr_getpshared*(), *pthread_create*(),
32702   *pthread_mutex_destroy*(), the Base Definitions volume of IEEE Std 1003.1-2001, **<pthread.h>**

32703 **CHANGE HISTORY**
32704   First released in Issue 5. Included for alignment with the POSIX Threads Extension.

32705 **Issue 6**
32706   The *pthread_condattr_destroy*() and *pthread_condattr_init*() functions are marked as part of the
32707   Threads option.

32753 **NAME**
32754   pthread_condattr_getpshared, pthread_condattr_setpshared — get and set the process-shared
32755   condition variable attributes

32756 **SYNOPSIS**
32757 THR TSH `#include <pthread.h>`

```
32758       int pthread_condattr_getpshared (const pthread_condattr_t *restrict attr,
32759           int *restrict pshared);
32760       int pthread_condattr_setpshared (pthread_condattr_t *attr,
32761           int pshared);
32762
```

32763 **DESCRIPTION**
32764   The *pthread_condattr_getpshared*() function shall obtain the value of the *process-shared* attribute
32765   from the attributes object referenced by *attr*. The *pthread_condattr_setpshared*() function shall set
32766   the *process-shared* attribute in an initialized attributes object referenced by *attr*.

32767   The *process-shared* attribute is set to PTHREAD_PROCESS_SHARED to permit a condition
32768   variable to be operated upon by any thread that has access to the memory where the condition
32769   variable is allocated, even if the condition variable is allocated in memory that is shared by
32770   multiple processes. If the *process-shared* attribute is PTHREAD_PROCESS_PRIVATE, the
32771   condition variable shall only be operated upon by threads created within the same process as the
32772   thread that initialized the condition variable; if threads of differing processes attempt to operate
32773   on such a condition variable, the behavior is undefined. The default value of the attribute is
32774   PTHREAD_PROCESS_PRIVATE.

32775 **RETURN VALUE**
32776   If successful, the *pthread_condattr_setpshared*() function shall return zero; otherwise, an error
32777   number shall be returned to indicate the error.

32778   If successful, the *pthread_condattr_getpshared*() function shall return zero and store the value of
32779   the *process-shared* attribute of *attr* into the object referenced by the *pshared* parameter. Otherwise,
32780   an error number shall be returned to indicate the error.

32781 **ERRORS**
32782   The *pthread_condattr_getpshared*() and *pthread_condattr_setpshared*() functions may fail if:

32783   [EINVAL]   The value specified by *attr* is invalid.

32784   The *pthread_condattr_setpshared*() function may fail if:

32785   [EINVAL]   The new value specified for the attribute is outside the range of legal values
32786   for that attribute.

32787   These functions shall not return an error code of [EINTR].

32788 **EXAMPLES**
32789   None.

32790 **APPLICATION USAGE**
32791   None.

32792 **RATIONALE**
32793   None.

32794 **FUTURE DIRECTIONS**

32795 None.

32796 **SEE ALSO**

32797 *pthread_create*(), *pthread_cond_destroy*(), *pthread_condattr_destroy*(), *pthread_mutex_destroy*(), the

32798 Base Definitions volume of IEEE Std 1003.1-2001, **<pthread.h>**

32799 **CHANGE HISTORY**

32800 First released in Issue 5. Included for alignment with the POSIX Threads Extension.

32801 **Issue 6**

32802 The *pthread_condattr_getpshared*() and *pthread_condattr_setpshared*() functions are marked as part

32803 of the Threads and Thread Process-Shared Synchronization options.

32804 The **restrict** keyword is added to the *pthread_condattr_getpshared*() prototype for alignment with

32805 the ISO/IEC 9899: 1999 standard.

32832 **NAME**

32833   pthread_create — thread creation

32834 **SYNOPSIS**

32835 THR   `#include <pthread.h>`

```
32836    int pthread_create (pthread_t *restrict thread,
32837        const pthread_attr_t *restrict attr,
32838        void * (*start_routine) (void*), void *restrict arg);
```

32839

32840 **DESCRIPTION**

32841   The *pthread_create*() function shall create a new thread, with attributes specified by *attr*, within a
32842   process. If *attr* is NULL, the default attributes shall be used. If the attributes specified by *attr* are
32843   modified later, the thread's attributes shall not be affected. Upon successful completion,
32844   *pthread_create*() shall store the ID of the created thread in the location referenced by *thread*.

32845   The thread is created executing *start_routine* with *arg* as its sole argument. If the *start_routine*
32846   returns, the effect shall be as if there was an implicit call to *pthread_exit*() using the return value
32847   of *start_routine* as the exit status. Note that the thread in which *main*() was originally invoked
32848   differs from this. When it returns from *main*(), the effect shall be as if there was an implicit call
32849   to *exit*() using the return value of *main*() as the exit status.

32850   The signal state of the new thread shall be initialized as follows:

32851   • The signal mask shall be inherited from the creating thread.

32852   • The set of signals pending for the new thread shall be empty.

32853   The floating-point environment shall be inherited from the creating thread.

32854   If *pthread_create*() fails, no new thread is created and the contents of the location referenced by
32855   *thread* are undefined.

32856 TCT   If _POSIX_THREAD_CPUTIME is defined, the new thread shall have a CPU-time clock
32857   accessible, and the initial value of this clock shall be set to zero.

32858 **RETURN VALUE**

32859   If successful, the *pthread_create*() function shall return zero; otherwise, an error number shall be
32860   returned to indicate the error.

32861 **ERRORS**

32862   The *pthread_create*() function shall fail if:

32863   [EAGAIN]   The system lacked the necessary resources to create another thread, or the
32864   system-imposed limit on the total number of threads in a process
32865   {PTHREAD_THREADS_MAX} would be exceeded.
32866   [EINVAL]   The value specified by *attr* is invalid.
32867   [EPERM]   The caller does not have appropriate permission to set the required
32868   scheduling parameters or scheduling policy.

32869   The *pthread_create*() function shall not return an error code of [EINTR].

32870 **EXAMPLES**

32871   None.

APPLICATION USAGE

None.

RATIONALE

A suggested alternative to *pthread_create*() would be to define two separate operations: create and start. Some applications would find such behavior more natural. Ada, in particular, separates the "creation" of a task from its "activation".

Splitting the operation was rejected by the standard developers for many reasons:

- The number of calls required to start a thread would increase from one to two and thus place an additional burden on applications that do not require the additional synchronization. The second call, however, could be avoided by the additional complication of a start-up state attribute.

- An extra state would be introduced: "created but not started". This would require the standard to specify the behavior of the thread operations when the target has not yet started executing.

- For those applications that require such behavior, it is possible to simulate the two separate steps with the facilities that are currently provided. The *start_routine*() can synchronize by waiting on a condition variable that is signaled by the start operation.

An Ada implementor can choose to create the thread at either of two points in the Ada program: when the task object is created, or when the task is activated (generally at a "begin"). If the first approach is adopted, the *start_routine*() needs to wait on a condition variable to receive the order to begin "activation". The second approach requires no such condition variable or extra synchronization. In either approach, a separate Ada task control block would need to be created when the task object is created to hold rendezvous queues, and so on.

An extension of the preceding model would be to allow the state of the thread to be modified between the create and start. This would allow the thread attributes object to be eliminated. This has been rejected because:

- All state in the thread attributes object has to be able to be set for the thread. This would require the definition of functions to modify thread attributes. There would be no reduction in the number of function calls required to set up the thread. In fact, for an application that creates all threads using identical attributes, the number of function calls required to set up the threads would be dramatically increased. Use of a thread attributes object permits the application to make one set of attribute setting function calls. Otherwise, the set of attribute setting function calls needs to be made for each thread creation.

- Depending on the implementation architecture, functions to set thread state would require kernel calls, or for other implementation reasons would not be able to be implemented as macros, thereby increasing the cost of thread creation.

- The ability for applications to segregate threads by class would be lost.

Another suggested alternative uses a model similar to that for process creation, such as "thread fork". The fork semantics would provide more flexibility and the "create" function can be implemented simply by doing a thread fork followed immediately by a call to the desired "start routine" for the thread. This alternative has these problems:

32913   • For many implementations, the entire stack of the calling thread would need to be
32914   duplicated, since in many architectures there is no way to determine the size of the calling
32915   frame.

32916   • Efficiency is reduced since at least some part of the stack has to be copied, even though in
32917   most cases the thread never needs the copied context, since it merely calls the desired start
32918   routine.

32919 **FUTURE DIRECTIONS**
32920   None.

32921 **SEE ALSO**
32922   *fork*(), *pthread_exit*(), *pthread_join*(), the Base Definitions volume of IEEE Std 1003.1-2001,
32923   **<pthread.h>**

32924 **CHANGE HISTORY**
32925   First released in Issue 5. Included for alignment with the POSIX Threads Extension.

32926 **Issue 6**
32927   The *pthread_create*() function is marked as part of the Threads option.

32928   The following new requirements on POSIX implementations derive from alignment with the
32929   Single UNIX Specification:

32930   • The [EPERM] mandatory error condition is added.

32931   The thread CPU-time clock semantics are added for alignment with IEEE Std 1003.1d-1999.

32932   The **restrict** keyword is added to the *pthread_create*() prototype for alignment with the
32933   ISO/IEC 9899: 1999 standard.

32934   The DESCRIPTION is updated to make it explicit that the floating-point environment is
32935   inherited from the creating thread.

32936 **NAME**
32937   pthread_detach — detach a thread

32938 **SYNOPSIS**
32939 THR   `#include <pthread.h>`

32940   `int pthread_detach (pthread_t thread);`
32941

32942 **DESCRIPTION**
32943   The *pthread_detach*() function shall indicate to the implementation that storage for the thread
32944   *thread* can be reclaimed when that thread terminates. If *thread* has not terminated,
32945   *pthread_detach*() shall not cause it to terminate. The effect of multiple *pthread_detach*() calls on
32946   the same target thread is unspecified.

32947 **RETURN VALUE**
32948   If the call succeeds, *pthread_detach*() shall return 0; otherwise, an error number shall be returned
32949   to indicate the error.

32950 **ERRORS**
32951   The *pthread_detach*() function shall fail if:

32952   [EINVAL]   The implementation has detected that the value specified by *thread* does not
32953   refer to a joinable thread.
32954   [ESRCH]   No thread could be found corresponding to that specified by the given thread
32955   ID.

32956   The *pthread_detach*() function shall not return an error code of [EINTR].

32957 **EXAMPLES**
32958   None.

32959 **APPLICATION USAGE**
32960   None.

32961 **RATIONALE**
32962   The *pthread_join*() or *pthread_detach*() functions should eventually be called for every thread that
32963   is created so that storage associated with the thread may be reclaimed.

32964   It has been suggested that a "detach" function is not necessary; the *detachstate* thread creation
32965   attribute is sufficient, since a thread need never be dynamically detached. However, need arises
32966   in at least two cases:

32967   1. In a cancelation handler for a *pthread_join*() it is nearly essential to have a *pthread_detach*()
32968   function in order to detach the thread on which *pthread_join*() was waiting. Without it, it
32969   would be necessary to have the handler do another *pthread_join*() to attempt to detach the
32970   thread, which would both delay the cancelation processing for an unbounded period and
32971   introduce a new call to *pthread_join*(), which might itself need a cancelation handler. A
32972   dynamic detach is nearly essential in this case.
32973   2. In order to detach the "initial thread" (as may be desirable in processes that set up server
32974   threads).

32975 **FUTURE DIRECTIONS**
32976   None.

32977 **SEE ALSO**

32978   *pthread_join*(), the Base Definitions volume of IEEE Std 1003.1-2001, **<pthread.h>**

32979 **CHANGE HISTORY**

32980   First released in Issue 5. Included for alignment with the POSIX Threads Extension.

32981 **Issue 6**

32982   The *pthread_detach*() function is marked as part of the Threads option.

33016 **NAME**

33017 pthread_exit—thread termination

33018 **SYNOPSIS**

33019 THR `#include <pthread.h>`

33020 `void pthread_exit (void *value_ptr);`

33021

33022 **DESCRIPTION**

33023 The *pthread_exit*() function shall terminate the calling thread and make the value *value_ptr*
33024 available to any successful join with the terminating thread. Any cancelation cleanup handlers
33025 that have been pushed and not yet popped shall be popped in the reverse order that they were
33026 pushed and then executed. After all cancelation cleanup handlers have been executed, if the
33027 thread has any thread-specific data, appropriate destructor functions shall be called in an
33028 unspecified order. Thread termination does not release any application visible process resources,
33029 including, but not limited to, mutexes and file descriptors, nor does it perform any process-level
33030 cleanup actions, including, but not limited to, calling any *atexit*() routines that may exist.

33031 An implicit call to *pthread_exit*() is made when a thread other than the thread in which *main*()
33032 was first invoked returns from the start routine that was used to create it. The function's return
33033 value shall serve as the thread's exit status.

33034 The behavior of *pthread_exit*() is undefined if called from a cancelation cleanup handler or
33035 destructor function that was invoked as a result of either an implicit or explicit call to
33036 *pthread_exit*().

33037 After a thread has terminated, the result of access to local (auto) variables of the thread is
33038 undefined. Thus, references to local variables of the exiting thread should not be used for the
33039 *pthread_exit*() *value_ptr* parameter value.

33040 The process shall exit with an exit status of 0 after the last thread has been terminated. The
33041 behavior shall be as if the implementation called *exit*() with a zero argument at thread
33042 termination time.

33043 **RETURN VALUE**

33044 The *pthread_exit*() function cannot return to its caller.

33045 **ERRORS**

33046 No errors are defined.

33047 **EXAMPLES**

33048 None.

33049 **APPLICATION USAGE**

33050 None.

33051 **RATIONALE**

33052 The normal mechanism by which a thread terminates is to return from the routine that was
33053 specified in the *pthread_create*() call that started it. The *pthread_exit*() function provides the
33054 capability for a thread to terminate without requiring a return from the start routine of that
33055 thread, thereby providing a function analogous to *exit*().

33056 Regardless of the method of thread termination, any cancelation cleanup handlers that have
33057 been pushed and not yet popped are executed, and the destructors for any existing thread-specific

33058 data are executed. This volume of IEEE Std 1003.1-2001 requires that cancelation
33059 cleanup handlers be popped and called in order. After all cancelation cleanup handlers have
33060 been executed, thread-specific data destructors are called, in an unspecified order, for each item
33061 of thread-specific data that exists in the thread. This ordering is necessary because cancelation
33062 cleanup handlers may rely on thread-specific data.

33063 As the meaning of the status is determined by the application (except when the thread has been
33064 canceled, in which case it is PTHREAD_CANCELED), the implementation has no idea what an
33065 illegal status value is, which is why no address error checking is done.

33066 **FUTURE DIRECTIONS**
33067 None.

33068 **SEE ALSO**
33069 *exit*(), *pthread_create*(), *pthread_join*(), the Base Definitions volume of IEEE Std 1003.1-2001,
33070 **<pthread.h>**

33071 **CHANGE HISTORY**
33072 First released in Issue 5. Included for alignment with the POSIX Threads Extension.

33073 **Issue 6**
33074 The *pthread_exit*() function is marked as part of the Threads option.

33075 **NAME**

33076   pthread_getconcurrency, pthread_setconcurrency — get and set the level of concurrency

33077 **SYNOPSIS**

33078 XSI   ```
#include <pthread.h>
```

33079     ```
int pthread_getconcurrency (void);
```
33080   ```
int pthread_setconcurrency (int new_level);
```
33081

33082 **DESCRIPTION**

33083        Unbound threads in a process may or may not be required to be simultaneously active. By
33084        default, the threads implementation ensures that a sufficient number of threads are active so that
33085        the process can continue to make progress. While this conserves system resources, it may not
33086        produce the most effective level of concurrency.

33087        The *pthread_setconcurrency*() function allows an application to inform the threads
33088        implementation of its desired concurrency level, *new_level*. The actual level of concurrency
33089        provided by the implementation as a result of this function call is unspecified.

33090        If *new_level* is zero, it causes the implementation to maintain the concurrency level at its
33091        discretion as if *pthread_setconcurrency*() had never been called.

33092        The *pthread_getconcurrency*() function shall return the value set by a previous call to the
33093        *pthread_setconcurrency*() function. If the *pthread_setconcurrency*() function was not previously
33094        called, this function shall return zero to indicate that the implementation is maintaining the
33095        concurrency level.

33096        A call to *pthread_setconcurrency*() shall inform the implementation of its desired concurrency
33097        level. The implementation shall use this as a hint, not a requirement.

33098        If an implementation does not support multiplexing of user threads on top of several kernel-
33099        scheduled entities, the *pthread_setconcurrency*() and *pthread_getconcurrency*() functions are
33100        provided for source code compatibility but they shall have no effect when called. To maintain
33101        the function semantics, the *new_level* parameter is saved when *pthread_setconcurrency*() is called
33102        so that a subsequent call to *pthread_getconcurrency*() shall return the same value.

33103 **RETURN VALUE**

33104        If successful, the *pthread_setconcurrency*() function shall return zero; otherwise, an error number
33105        shall be returned to indicate the error.

33106        The *pthread_getconcurrency*() function shall always return the concurrency level set by a previous
33107        call to *pthread_setconcurrency*(). If the *pthread_setconcurrency*() function has never been called,
33108        *pthread_getconcurrency*() shall return zero.

33109 **ERRORS**

33110        The *pthread_setconcurrency*() function shall fail if:

33111        [EINVAL]        The value specified by *new_level* is negative.
33112        [EAGAIN]        The value specific by *new_level* would cause a system resource to be exceeded.

33113        These functions shall not return an error code of [EINTR].

33114 **EXAMPLES**

33115        None.
```

33116 **APPLICATION USAGE**
33117   Use of these functions changes the state of the underlying concurrency upon which the
33118   application depends. Library developers are advised to not use the *pthread_getconcurrency*() and
33119   *pthread_setconcurrency*() functions since their use may conflict with an applications use of these
33120   functions.

33121 **RATIONALE**
33122   None.

33123 **FUTURE DIRECTIONS**
33124   None.

33125 **SEE ALSO**
33126   The Base Definitions volume of IEEE Std 1003.1-2001, **<pthread.h>**

33127 **CHANGE HISTORY**
33128   First released in Issue 5.

33161 **NAME**

33162   pthread_getschedparam, pthread_setschedparam — dynamic thread scheduling parameters
33163   access **(REALTIME THREADS)**

33164 **SYNOPSIS**

33165 THR TPS `#include <pthread.h>`

```
33166    int pthread_getschedparam (pthread_t thread, int *restrict policy,
33167        struct sched_param *restrict param);
33168    int pthread_setschedparam (pthread_t thread, int policy,
33169        const struct sched_param *param);
```
33170

33171 **DESCRIPTION**

33172   The *pthread_getschedparam*() and *pthread_setschedparam*() functions shall, respectively, get and set
33173   the scheduling policy and parameters of individual threads within a multi-threaded process to
33174   be retrieved and set. For SCHED_FIFO and SCHED_RR, the only required member of the
33175   **sched_param** structure is the priority *sched_priority*. For SCHED_OTHER, the affected
33176   scheduling parameters are implementation-defined.

33177   The *pthread_getschedparam*() function shall retrieve the scheduling policy and scheduling
33178   parameters for the thread whose thread ID is given by *thread* and shall store those values in
33179   *policy* and *param*, respectively. The priority value returned from *pthread_getschedparam*() shall be
33180   the value specified by the most recent *pthread_setschedparam*(), *pthread_setschedprio*(), or
33181   *pthread_create*() call affecting the target thread. It shall not reflect any temporary adjustments to
33182   its priority as a result of any priority inheritance or ceiling functions. The *pthread_setschedparam*()
33183   function shall set the scheduling policy and associated scheduling parameters for the thread
33184   whose thread ID is given by *thread* to the policy and associated parameters provided in *policy*
33185   and *param*, respectively.

33186   The *policy* parameter may have the value SCHED_OTHER, SCHED_FIFO, or SCHED_RR. The
33187   scheduling parameters for the SCHED_OTHER policy are implementation-defined. The
33188   SCHED_FIFO and SCHED_RR policies shall have a single scheduling parameter, *priority*.

33189 TSP   If _POSIX_THREAD_SPORADIC_SERVER is defined, then the *policy* argument may have the
33190   value SCHED_SPORADIC, with the exception for the *pthread_setschedparam*() function that if the
33191   scheduling policy was not SCHED_SPORADIC at the time of the call, it is implementation-
33192   defined whether the function is supported; in other words, the implementation need not allow
33193   the application to dynamically change the scheduling policy to SCHED_SPORADIC. The
33194   sporadic server scheduling policy has the associated parameters *sched_ss_low_priority*,
33195   *sched_ss_repl_period*, *sched_ss_init_budget*, *sched_priority*, and *sched_ss_max_repl*. The specified
33196   *sched_ss_repl_period* shall be greater than or equal to the specified *sched_ss_init_budget* for the
33197   function to succeed; if it is not, then the function shall fail. The value of *sched_ss_max_repl* shall
33198   be within the inclusive range [1,SS_REPL_MAX] for the function to succeed; if not, the function
33199   shall fail.

33200   If the *pthread_setschedparam*() function fails, the scheduling parameters shall not be changed for
33201   the target thread.

33202 **RETURN VALUE**

33203   If successful, the *pthread_getschedparam*() and *pthread_setschedparam*() functions shall return zero;
33204   otherwise, an error number shall be returned to indicate the error.

33205 **ERRORS**

33206   The *pthread_getschedparam*() function may fail if:

33207   [ESRCH]   The value specified by *thread* does not refer to an existing thread.

33208   The *pthread_setschedparam*() function may fail if:

33209   [EINVAL]   The value specified by *policy* or one of the scheduling parameters associated
33210   with the scheduling policy *policy* is invalid.

33211   [ENOTSUP]   An attempt was made to set the policy or scheduling parameters to an
33212   unsupported value.

33213 TSP   [ENOTSUP]   An attempt was made to dynamically change the scheduling policy to
33214   SCHED_SPORADIC, and the implementation does not support this change.

33215   [EPERM]   The caller does not have the appropriate permission to set either the
33216   scheduling parameters or the scheduling policy of the specified thread.

33217   [EPERM]   The implementation does not allow the application to modify one of the
33218   parameters to the value specified.

33219   [ESRCH]   The value specified by *thread* does not refer to a existing thread.

33220   These functions shall not return an error code of [EINTR].

33221 **EXAMPLES**
33222   None.

33223 **APPLICATION USAGE**
33224   None.

33225 **RATIONALE**
33226   None.

33227 **FUTURE DIRECTIONS**
33228   None.

33229 **SEE ALSO**
33230   *pthread_setschedprio*(), *sched_getparam*(), *sched_getscheduler*(), the Base Definitions volume of
33231   IEEE Std 1003.1-2001, **<pthread.h>**, **<sched.h>**

33232 **CHANGE HISTORY**
33233   First released in Issue 5. Included for alignment with the POSIX Threads Extension.

33234 **Issue 6**

33235   The *pthread_getschedparam*() and *pthread_setschedparam*() functions are marked as part of the
33236   Threads and Thread Execution Scheduling options.

33237   The [ENOSYS] error condition has been removed as stubs need not be provided if an
33238   implementation does not support the Thread Execution Scheduling option.

33239   The Open Group Corrigendum U026/2 is applied, correcting the prototype for the
33240   *pthread_setschedparam*() function so that its second argument is of type **int.**

33241   The SCHED_SPORADIC scheduling policy is added for alignment with IEEE Std 1003.1d-1999.

33242   The **restrict** keyword is added to the *pthread_getschedparam*() prototype for alignment with the
33243   ISO/IEC 9899: 1999 standard.

33244   The Open Group Corrigendum U047/1 is applied.

33245   IEEE PASC Interpretation 1003.1 #96 is applied, noting that priority values can also be set by a
33246   call to the *pthread_setschedprio*() function.

33302 **NAME**
33303   pthread_join — wait for thread termination

33304 **SYNOPSIS**

33305 THR `#include <pthread.h>`

33306   `int pthread_join (pthread_t thread, void **value_ptr);`
33307

33308 **DESCRIPTION**
33309   The *pthread_join*() function shall suspend execution of the calling thread until the target *thread*
33310   terminates, unless the target *thread* has already terminated. On return from a successful
33311   *pthread_join*() call with a non-NULL *value_ptr* argument, the value passed to *pthread_exit*() by
33312   the terminating thread shall be made available in the location referenced by *value_ptr*. When a
33313   *pthread_join*() returns successfully, the target thread has been terminated. The results of multiple
33314   simultaneous calls to *pthread_join*() specifying the same target thread are undefined. If the
33315   thread calling *pthread_join*() is canceled, then the target thread shall not be detached.

33316   It is unspecified whether a thread that has exited but remains unjoined counts against
33317   {PTHREAD_THREADS_MAX}.

33318 **RETURN VALUE**
33319   If successful, the *pthread_join*() function shall return zero; otherwise, an error number shall be
33320   returned to indicate the error.

33321 **ERRORS**
33322   The *pthread_join*() function shall fail if:

33323   [EINVAL]   The implementation has detected that the value specified by *thread* does not
33324   refer to a joinable thread.

33325   [ESRCH]   No thread could be found corresponding to that specified by the given thread
33326   ID.

33327   The *pthread_join*() function may fail if:

33328   [EDEADLK]   A deadlock was detected or the value of *thread* specifies the calling thread.

33329   The *pthread_join*() function shall not return an error code of [EINTR].

33330 **EXAMPLES**
33331   An example of thread creation and deletion follows:

```
33332      typedef struct {
33333          int *ar;
33334          long n;
33335      } subarray;

33336      void *
33337      incer (void *arg)
33338      {
33339          long i;

33340          for (i = 0; i < ((subarray *)arg) ->n; i++)
33341              ((subarray *) arg) ->ar[i]++;
33342      }
```

```
33343    int main (void)
33344    {
33345        int         ar[1000000];
33346        pthread_t th1, th2;
33347        subarray sb1, sb2;
33348        sb1.ar = &ar[0];
33349        sb1.n = 500000;
33350        (void) pthread_create(&th1, NULL, incer, &sb1);
33351        sb2.ar = &ar[500000];
33352        sb2.n = 500000;
33353        (void) pthread_create(&th2, NULL, incer, &sb2);
33354        (void) pthread_join(th1, NULL);
33355        (void) pthread_join(th2, NULL);
33356        return 0;
33357    }
```

APPLICATION USAGE

None.

RATIONALE

The *pthread_join*() function is a convenience that has proven useful in multi-threaded applications. It is true that a programmer could simulate this function if it were not provided by passing extra state as part of the argument to the *start_routine*(). The terminating thread would set a flag to indicate termination and broadcast a condition that is part of that state; a joining thread would wait on that condition variable. While such a technique would allow a thread to wait on more complex conditions (for example, waiting for multiple threads to terminate), waiting on individual thread termination is considered widely useful. Also, including the *pthread_join*() function in no way precludes a programmer from coding such complex waits. Thus, while not a primitive, including *pthread_join*() in this volume of IEEE Std 1003.1-2001 was considered valuable.

The *pthread_join*() function provides a simple mechanism allowing an application to wait for a thread to terminate. After the thread terminates, the application may then choose to clean up resources that were used by the thread. For instance, after *pthread_join*() returns, any application-provided stack storage could be reclaimed.

The *pthread_join*() or *pthread_detach*() function should eventually be called for every thread that is created with the *detachstate* attribute set to PTHREAD_CREATE_JOINABLE so that storage associated with the thread may be reclaimed.

The interaction between *pthread_join*() and cancelation is well-defined for the following reasons:

• The *pthread_join*() function, like all other non-async-cancel-safe functions, can only be called with deferred cancelability type.

• Cancelation cannot occur in the disabled cancelability state.

Thus, only the default cancelability state need be considered. As specified, either the *pthread_join*() call is canceled, or it succeeds, but not both. The difference is obvious to the application, since either a cancelation handler is run or *pthread_join*() returns. There are no race conditions since *pthread_join*() was called in the deferred cancelability state.

33386 **FUTURE DIRECTIONS**

33387   None.

33388 **SEE ALSO**

33389   *pthread_create*(), *wait*(), the Base Definitions volume of IEEE Std 1003.1-2001, **<pthread.h>**

33390 **CHANGE HISTORY**

33391   First released in Issue 5. Included for alignment with the POSIX Threads Extension.

33392 **Issue 6**

33393   The *pthread_join*() function is marked as part of the Threads option.

33621 **NAME**
33622   pthread_mutex_destroy, pthread_mutex_init — destroy and initialize a mutex

33623 **SYNOPSIS**
33624 THR `#include <pthread.h>`

33625   `int pthread_mutex_destroy (pthread_mutex_t *mutex);`
33626   `int pthread_mutex_init (pthread_mutex_t *restrict mutex,`
33627   `const pthread_mutexattr_t *restrict attr);`
33628   `pthread_mutex_t mutex = PTHREAD_MUTEX_INITIALIZER;`
33629

33630 **DESCRIPTION**
33631   The *pthread_mutex_destroy*() function shall destroy the mutex object referenced by *mutex*; the
33632   mutex object becomes, in effect, uninitialized. An implementation may cause
33633   *pthread_mutex_destroy*() to set the object referenced by *mutex* to an invalid value. A destroyed
33634   mutex object can be reinitialized using *pthread_mutex_init*(); the results of otherwise referencing
33635   the object after it has been destroyed are undefined.

33636   It shall be safe to destroy an initialized mutex that is unlocked. Attempting to destroy a locked
33637   mutex results in undefined behavior.

33638   The *pthread_mutex_init*() function shall initialize the mutex referenced by *mutex* with attributes
33639   specified by *attr*. If *attr* is NULL, the default mutex attributes are used; the effect shall be the
33640   same as passing the address of a default mutex attributes object. Upon successful initialization,
33641   the state of the mutex becomes initialized and unlocked.

33642   Only *mutex* itself may be used for performing synchronization. The result of referring to copies
33643   of *mutex* in calls to *pthread_mutex_lock*(), *pthread_mutex_trylock*(), *pthread_mutex_unlock*(), and
33644   *pthread_mutex_destroy*() is undefined.

33645   Attempting to initialize an already initialized mutex results in undefined behavior.

33646   In cases where default mutex attributes are appropriate, the macro
33647   PTHREAD_MUTEX_INITIALIZER can be used to initialize mutexes that are statically allocated.
33648   The effect shall be equivalent to dynamic initialization by a call to *pthread_mutex_init*() with
33649   parameter *attr* specified as NULL, except that no error checks are performed.

33650 **RETURN VALUE**
33651   If successful, the *pthread_mutex_destroy*() and *pthread_mutex_init*() functions shall return zero;
33652   otherwise, an error number shall be returned to indicate the error.

33653   The [EBUSY] and [EINVAL] error checks, if implemented, act as if they were performed
33654   immediately at the beginning of processing for the function and shall cause an error return prior
33655   to modifying the state of the mutex specified by *mutex*.

33656 **ERRORS**
33657   The *pthread_mutex_destroy*() function may fail if:

33658   [EBUSY]   The implementation has detected an attempt to destroy the object referenced
33659   by *mutex* while it is locked or referenced (for example, while being used in a
33660   *pthread_cond_timedwait*() or *pthread_cond_wait*()) by another thread.
33661   [EINVAL]   The value specified by *mutex* is invalid.

33662   The *pthread_mutex_init*() function shall fail if:

33663 [EAGAIN]   The system lacked the necessary resources (other than memory) to initialize
33664   another mutex.

33665 [ENOMEM]   Insufficient memory exists to initialize the mutex.

33666 [EPERM]   The caller does not have the privilege to perform the operation.

33667 The *pthread_mutex_init*() function may fail if:

33668 [EBUSY]   The implementation has detected an attempt to reinitialize the object
33669   referenced by *mutex*, a previously initialized, but not yet destroyed, mutex.

33670 [EINVAL]   The value specified by *attr* is invalid.

33671 These functions shall not return an error code of [EINTR].

33672 **EXAMPLES**

33673 None.

33674 **APPLICATION USAGE**

33675 None.

33676 **RATIONALE**

33677 **Alternate Implementations Possible**

33678 This volume of IEEE Std 1003.1-2001 supports several alternative implementations of mutexes.
33679 An implementation may store the lock directly in the object of type **pthread_mutex_t**.
33680 Alternatively, an implementation may store the lock in the heap and merely store a pointer,
33681 handle, or unique ID in the mutex object. Either implementation has advantages or may be
33682 required on certain hardware configurations. So that portable code can be written that is
33683 invariant to this choice, this volume of IEEE Std 1003.1-2001 does not define assignment or
33684 equality for this type, and it uses the term "initialize" to reinforce the (more restrictive) notion
33685 that the lock may actually reside in the mutex object itself.

33686 Note that this precludes an over-specification of the type of the mutex or condition variable and
33687 motivates the opaqueness of the type.

33688 An implementation is permitted, but not required, to have *pthread_mutex_destroy*() store an
33689 illegal value into the mutex. This may help detect erroneous programs that try to lock (or
33690 otherwise reference) a mutex that has already been destroyed.

33691 **Tradeoff Between Error Checks and Performance Supported**

33692 Many of the error checks were made optional in order to let implementations trade off
33693 performance *versus* degree of error checking according to the needs of their specific applications
33694 and execution environment. As a general rule, errors or conditions caused by the system (such as
33695 insufficient memory) always need to be reported, but errors due to an erroneously coded
33696 application (such as failing to provide adequate synchronization to prevent a mutex from being
33697 deleted while in use) are made optional.

33698 A wide range of implementations is thus made possible. For example, an implementation
33699 intended for application debugging may implement all of the error checks, but an
33700 implementation running a single, provably correct application under very tight performance
33701 constraints in an embedded computer might implement minimal checks. An implementation
33702 might even be provided in two versions, similar to the options that compilers provide: a full-checking,
33703 but slower version; and a limited-checking, but faster version. To forbid this
33704 optionality would be a disservice to users.

By carefully limiting the use of "undefined behavior" only to things that an erroneous (badly coded) application might do, and by defining that resource-not-available errors are mandatory, this volume of IEEE Std 1003.1-2001 ensures that a fully-conforming application is portable across the full range of implementations, while not forcing all implementations to add overhead to check for numerous things that a correct program never does.

Why No Limits are Defined

Defining symbols for the maximum number of mutexes and condition variables was considered but rejected because the number of these objects may change dynamically. Furthermore, many implementations place these objects into application memory; thus, there is no explicit maximum.

Static Initializers for Mutexes and Condition Variables

Providing for static initialization of statically allocated synchronization objects allows modules with private static synchronization variables to avoid runtime initialization tests and overhead. Furthermore, it simplifies the coding of self-initializing modules. Such modules are common in C libraries, where for various reasons the design calls for self-initialization instead of requiring an explicit module initialization function to be called. An example use of static initialization follows.

Without static initialization, a self-initializing routine *foo*() might look as follows:

```
static pthread_once_t foo_once = PTHREAD_ONCE_INIT;
static pthread_mutex_t foo_mutex;
void foo_init ()
{
pthread_mutex_init (&foo_mutex, NULL);
}

void foo()
{
  pthread_once (&foo_once, foo_init);
  pthread_mutex_lock (&foo_mutex);
  /* Do work. */
  pthread_mutex_unlock (&foo_mutex);
}
```

With static initialization, the same routine could be coded as follows:

```
static pthread_mutex_t foo_mutex = PTHREAD_MUTEX_INITIALIZER;
void foo()
{
  pthread_mutex_lock(&foo_mutex);
  /* Do work. */
  pthread_mutex_unlock(&foo_mutex);
}
```

Note that the static initialization both eliminates the need for the initialization test inside *pthread_once*() and the fetch of &*foo_mutex* to learn the address to be passed to *pthread_mutex_lock*() or *pthread_mutex_unlock*().

33747 Thus, the C code written to initialize static objects is simpler on all systems and is also faster on a
33748 large class of systems; those where the (entire) synchronization object can be stored in
33749 application memory.

33750 Yet the locking performance question is likely to be raised for machines that require mutexes to
33751 be allocated out of special memory. Such machines actually have to have mutexes and possibly
33752 condition variables contain pointers to the actual hardware locks. For static initialization to work
33753 on such machines, *pthread_mutex_lock*() also has to test whether or not the pointer to the actual
33754 lock has been allocated. If it has not, *pthread_mutex_lock*() has to initialize it before use. The
33755 reservation of such resources can be made when the program is loaded, and hence return codes
33756 have not been added to mutex locking and condition variable waiting to indicate failure to
33757 complete initialization.

33758 This runtime test in *pthread_mutex_lock*() would at first seem to be extra work; an extra test is
33759 required to see whether the pointer has been initialized. On most machines this would actually
33760 be implemented as a fetch of the pointer, testing the pointer against zero, and then using the
33761 pointer if it has already been initialized. While the test might seem to add extra work, the extra
33762 effort of testing a register is usually negligible since no extra memory references are actually
33763 done. As more and more machines provide caches, the real expenses are memory references, not
33764 instructions executed.

33765 Alternatively, depending on the machine architecture, there are often ways to eliminate *all*
33766 overhead in the most important case: on the lock operations that occur *after* the lock has been
33767 initialized. This can be done by shifting more overhead to the less frequent operation:
33768 initialization. Since out-of-line mutex allocation also means that an address has to be
33769 dereferenced to find the actual lock, one technique that is widely applicable is to have static
33770 initialization store a bogus value for that address; in particular, an address that causes a machine
33771 fault to occur. When such a fault occurs upon the first attempt to lock such a mutex, validity
33772 checks can be done, and then the correct address for the actual lock can be filled in. Subsequent
33773 lock operations incur no extra overhead since they do not "fault". This is merely one technique
33774 that can be used to support static initialization, while not adversely affecting the performance of
33775 lock acquisition. No doubt there are other techniques that are highly machine-dependent.

33776 The locking overhead for machines doing out-of-line mutex allocation is thus similar for
33777 modules being implicitly initialized, where it is improved for those doing mutex allocation
33778 entirely inline. The inline case is thus made much faster, and the out-of-line case is not
33779 significantly worse.

33780 Besides the issue of locking performance for such machines, a concern is raised that it is possible
33781 that threads would serialize contending for initialization locks when attempting to finish
33782 initializing statically allocated mutexes. (Such finishing would typically involve taking an
33783 internal lock, allocating a structure, storing a pointer to the structure in the mutex, and releasing
33784 the internal lock.) First, many implementations would reduce such serialization by hashing on
33785 the mutex address. Second, such serialization can only occur a bounded number of times. In
33786 particular, it can happen at most as many times as there are statically allocated synchronization
33787 objects. Dynamically allocated objects would still be initialized via *pthread_mutex_init*() or
33788 *pthread_cond_init*().

33789 Finally, if none of the above optimization techniques for out-of-line allocation yields sufficient
33790 performance for an application on some implementation, the application can avoid static
33791 initialization altogether by explicitly initializing all synchronization objects with the

corresponding *pthread_°_init*() functions, which are supported by all implementations. An implementation can also document the tradeoffs and advise which initialization technique is more efficient for that particular implementation.

Destroying Mutexes

A mutex can be destroyed immediately after it is unlocked. For example, consider the following code:

```
struct obj {
pthread_mutex_t om;
    int refcnt;
    ...
};
obj_done (struct obj *op)
{
    pthread_mutex_lock (&op- >om);
    if (- -op- >refcnt == 0) {
        pthread_mutex_unlock (&op- >om);
(A)     pthread_mutex_destroy (&op- >om);
(B)     free(op);
    } else
(C)     pthread_mutex_unlock (&op->om);
}
```

In this case *obj* is reference counted and *obj_done*() is called whenever a reference to the object is dropped. Implementations are required to allow an object to be destroyed and freed and potentially unmapped (for example, lines A and B) immediately after the object is unlocked (line C).

FUTURE DIRECTIONS

None.

SEE ALSO

pthread_mutex_getprioceiling(), *pthread_mutex_lock*(), *pthread_mutex_timedlock*(), *pthread_mutexattr_getpshared*(), the Base Definitions volume of IEEE Std 1003.1-2001, **<pthread.h>**

CHANGE HISTORY

First released in Issue 5. Included for alignment with the POSIX Threads Extension.

Issue 6

The *pthread_mutex_destroy*() and *pthread_mutex_init*() functions are marked as part of the Threads option.

The *pthread_mutex_timedlock*() function is added to the SEE ALSO section for alignment with IEEE Std 1003.1d-1999.

IEEE PASC Interpretation 1003.1c #34 is applied, updating the DESCRIPTION.

The **restrict** keyword is added to the *pthread_mutex_init*() prototype for alignment with the ISO/IEC 9899: 1999 standard.

33833 **NAME**

33834   pthread_mutex_getprioceiling, pthread_mutex_setprioceiling — get and set the priority ceiling

33835   of a mutex (**REALTIME THREADS**)

33836 **SYNOPSIS**

33837 THR TPP `#include <pthread.h>`

33838   ```
int pthread_mutex_getprioceiling (const pthread_mutex_t *restrict mutex,
```

33839     ```
    int *restrict prioceiling) ;
```

33840   ```
int pthread_mutex_setprioceiling (pthread_mutex_t *restrict mutex,
```

33841     ```
    int prioceiling, int *restrict old_ceiling);
```

33842

33843 **DESCRIPTION**

33844   The *pthread_mutex_getprioceiling*() function shall return the current priority ceiling of the mutex.

33845   The *pthread_mutex_setprioceiling*() function shall either lock the mutex if it is unlocked, or block

33846   until it can successfully lock the mutex, then it shall change the mutex's priority ceiling and

33847   release the mutex. When the change is successful, the previous value of the priority ceiling shall

33848   be returned in *old_ceiling*. The process of locking the mutex need not adhere to the priority

33849   protect protocol.

33850   If the *pthread_mutex_setprioceiling*() function fails, the mutex priority ceiling shall not be

33851   changed.

33852 **RETURN VALUE**

33853   If successful, the *pthread_mutex_getprioceiling*() and *pthread_mutex_setprioceiling*() functions shall

33854   return zero; otherwise, an error number shall be returned to indicate the error.

33855 **ERRORS**

33856   The *pthread_mutex_getprioceiling*() and *pthread_mutex_setprioceiling*() functions may fail if:

33857   [EINVAL]   The priority requested by *prioceiling* is out of range.

33858   [EINVAL]   The value specified by *mutex* does not refer to a currently existing mutex.

33859   [EPERM]   The caller does not have the privilege to perform the operation.

33860   These functions shall not return an error code of [EINTR].

33861 **EXAMPLES**

33862   None.

33863 **APPLICATION USAGE**

33864   None.

33865 **RATIONALE**

33866   None.

33867 **FUTURE DIRECTIONS**

33868   None.

33869 **SEE ALSO**

33870   *pthread_mutex_destroy*(), *pthread_mutex_lock*(), *pthread_mutex_timedlock*(), the Base Definitions

33871   volume of IEEE Std 1003.1-2001, <**pthread.h**>

33872 **CHANGE HISTORY**

33873   First released in Issue 5. Included for alignment with the POSIX Threads Extension.

33874   Marked as part of the Realtime Threads Feature Group.

33875 **Issue 6**

33876   The *pthread_mutex_getprioceiling*() and *pthread_mutex_setprioceiling*() functions are marked as
33877 part of the Threads and Thread Priority Protection options.

33878   The [ENOSYS] error condition has been removed as stubs need not be provided if an
33879 implementation does not support the Thread Priority Protection option.

33880   The [ENOSYS] error denoting non-support of the priority ceiling protocol for mutexes has been
33881 removed. This is because if the implementation provides the functions (regardless of whether
33882 _POSIX_PTHREAD_PRIO_PROTECT is defined), they must function as in the DESCRIPTION
33883 and therefore the priority ceiling protocol for mutexes is supported.

33884   The *pthread_mutex_timedlock*() function is added to the SEE ALSO section for alignment with
33885 IEEE Std 1003.1d-1999.

33886   The **restrict** keyword is added to the *pthread_mutex_getprioceiling*() and
33887 *pthread_mutex_setprioceiling*() prototypes for alignment with the ISO/IEC 9899: 1999 standard.

33898 **NAME**

33899   pthread_mutex_lock, pthread_mutex_trylock, pthread_mutex_unlock — lock and unlock a

33900   mutex

33901 **SYNOPSIS**

33902 THR   `#include <pthread.h>`

33903   `int pthread_mutex_lock (pthread_mutex_t *mutex);`
33904   `int pthread_mutex_trylock (pthread_mutex_t *mutex);`
33905   `int pthread_mutex_unlock (pthread_mutex_t *mutex);`
33906

33907 **DESCRIPTION**

33908   The mutex object referenced by *mutex* shall be locked by calling *pthread_mutex_lock()*. If the
33909   mutex is already locked, the calling thread shall block until the mutex becomes available. This
33910   operation shall return with the mutex object referenced by *mutex* in the locked state with the
33911   calling thread as its owner.

33912 XSI   If the mutex type is PTHREAD_MUTEX_NORMAL, deadlock detection shall not be provided.
33913   Attempting to relock the mutex causes deadlock. If a thread attempts to unlock a mutex that it
33914   has not locked or a mutex which is unlocked, undefined behavior results.

33915   If the mutex type is PTHREAD_MUTEX_ERRORCHECK, then error checking shall be provided.
33916   If a thread attempts to relock a mutex that it has already locked, an error shall be returned. If a
33917   thread attempts to unlock a mutex that it has not locked or a mutex which is unlocked, an error
33918   shall be returned.

33919   If the mutex type is PTHREAD_MUTEX_RECURSIVE, then the mutex shall maintain the
33920   concept of a lock count. When a thread successfully acquires a mutex for the first time, the lock
33921   count shall be set to one. Every time a thread relocks this mutex, the lock count shall be
33922   incremented by one. Each time the thread unlocks the mutex, the lock count shall be
33923   decremented by one. When the lock count reaches zero, the mutex shall become available for
33924   other threads to acquire. If a thread attempts to unlock a mutex that it has not locked or a mutex
33925   which is unlocked, an error shall be returned.

33926   If the mutex type is PTHREAD_MUTEX_DEFAULT, attempting to recursively lock the mutex
33927   results in undefined behavior. Attempting to unlock the mutex if it was not locked by the calling
33928   thread results in undefined behavior. Attempting to unlock the mutex if it is not locked results in
33929   undefined behavior.

33930   The *pthread_mutex_trylock()* function shall be equivalent to *pthread_mutex_lock()*, except that if
33931   the mutex object referenced by *mutex* is currently locked (by any thread, including the current
33932   thread), the call shall return immediately. If the mutex type is PTHREAD_MUTEX_RECURSIVE
33933   and the mutex is currently owned by the calling thread, the mutex lock count shall be
33934   incremented by one and the *pthread_mutex_trylock()* function shall immediately return success.

33935 XSI   The *pthread_mutex_unlock()* function shall release the mutex object referenced by *mutex*. The
33936   manner in which a mutex is released is dependent upon the mutex's type attribute. If there are
33937   threads blocked on the mutex object referenced by *mutex* when *pthread_mutex_unlock()* is called,
33938   resulting in the mutex becoming available, the scheduling policy shall determine which thread
33939   shall acquire the mutex.

33940 XSI (In the case of PTHREAD_MUTEX_RECURSIVE mutexes, the mutex shall become available
33941 when the count reaches zero and the calling thread no longer has any locks on this mutex.)

33942 If a signal is delivered to a thread waiting for a mutex, upon return from the signal handler the
33943 thread shall resume waiting for the mutex as if it was not interrupted.

33944 **RETURN VALUE**

33945 If successful, the *pthread_mutex_lock*() and *pthread_mutex_unlock*() functions shall return zero;
33946 otherwise, an error number shall be returned to indicate the error.

33947 The *pthread_mutex_trylock*() function shall return zero if a lock on the mutex object referenced by
33948 *mutex* is acquired. Otherwise, an error number is returned to indicate the error.

33949 **ERRORS**

33950 The *pthread_mutex_lock*() and *pthread_mutex_trylock*() functions shall fail if:
33951 [EINVAL]　　　　The *mutex* was created with the protocol attribute having the value
33952 　　　　　　　　PTHREAD_PRIO_PROTECT and the calling thread's priority is higher than
33953 　　　　　　　　the mutex's current priority ceiling.

33954 The *pthread_mutex_trylock*() function shall fail if:

33955 [EBUSY]　　　　The *mutex* could not be acquired because it was already locked.

33956 The *pthread_mutex_lock*(), *pthread_mutex_trylock*(), and *pthread_mutex_unlock*() functions may
33957 fail if:

33958 [EINVAL]　　　　The value specified by *mutex* does not refer to an initialized mutex object.
33959 XSI [EAGAIN]　　　　The mutex could not be acquired because the maximum number of recursive
33960 　　　　　　　　locks for *mutex* has been exceeded.

33961 The *pthread_mutex_lock*() function may fail if:

33962 [EDEADLK]　　　　The current thread already owns the mutex.

33963 The *pthread_mutex_unlock*() function may fail if:

33964 [EPERM]　　　　The current thread does not own the mutex.

33965 These functions shall not return an error code of [EINTR].

33966 **EXAMPLES**
33967 None.

33968 **APPLICATION USAGE**
33969 None.

33970 **RATIONALE**

33971 Mutex objects are intended to serve as a low-level primitive from which other thread
33972 synchronization functions can be built. As such, the implementation of mutexes should be as
33973 efficient as possible, and this has ramifications on the features available at the interface.

33974 The mutex functions and the particular default settings of the mutex attributes have been
33975 motivated by the desire to not preclude fast, inlined implementations of mutex locking and
33976 unlocking.

33977 For example, deadlocking on a double-lock is explicitly allowed behavior in order to avoid
33978 requiring more overhead in the basic mechanism than is absolutely necessary. (More "friendly"
33979 mutexes that detect deadlock or that allow multiple locking by the same thread are easily

33980 constructed by the user via the other mechanisms provided. For example, *pthread_self*() can be
33981 used to record mutex ownership.) Implementations might also choose to provide such extended
33982 features as options via special mutex attributes.

33983 Since most attributes only need to be checked when a thread is going to be blocked, the use of
33984 attributes does not slow the (common) mutex-locking case.

33985 Likewise, while being able to extract the thread ID of the owner of a mutex might be desirable, it
33986 would require storing the current thread ID when each mutex is locked, and this could incur
33987 unacceptable levels of overhead. Similar arguments apply to a *mutex_tryunlock* operation.

33988 **FUTURE DIRECTIONS**
33989 None.

33990 **SEE ALSO**
33991 *pthread_mutex_destroy*(),   *pthread_mutex_timedlock*(),   the   Base   Definitions   volume   of
33992 IEEE Std 1003.1-2001, **<pthread.h>**

33993 **CHANGE HISTORY**
33994 First released in Issue 5. Included for alignment with the POSIX Threads Extension.

33995 **Issue 6**
33996 The *pthread_mutex_lock*(), *pthread_mutex_trylock*(), and *pthread_mutex_unlock*() functions are
33997 marked as part of the Threads option.

33998 The following new requirements on POSIX implementations derive from alignment with the
33999 Single UNIX Specification:

34000 • The behavior when attempting to relock a mutex is defined.

34001 The *pthread_mutex_timedlock*() function is added to the SEE ALSO section for alignment with
34002 IEEE Std 1003.1d-1999.

34013 **NAME**

34014   pthread_mutex_timedlock — lock a mutex (**ADVANCED REALTIME**)

34015 **SYNOPSIS**

34016 THR TMO
```
#include <pthread.h>
```
34017
```
#include <time.h>
```

34018
```
int pthread_mutex_timedlock (pthread_mutex_t *restrict mutex,
```
34019
```
    const struct timespec *restrict abs_timeout);
```
34020

34021 **DESCRIPTION**

34022   The *pthread_mutex_timedlock*() function shall lock the mutex object referenced by *mutex*. If the
34023   mutex is already locked, the calling thread shall block until the mutex becomes available as in
34024   the *pthread_mutex_lock*() function. If the mutex cannot be locked without waiting for another
34025   thread to unlock the mutex, this wait shall be terminated when the specified timeout expires.

34026   The timeout shall expire when the absolute time specified by *abs_timeout* passes, as measured by
34027   the clock on which timeouts are based (that is, when the value of that clock equals or exceeds
34028   *abs_timeout*), or if the absolute time specified by *abs_timeout* has already been passed at the time
34029   of the call.

34030 TMR   If the Timers option is supported, the timeout shall be based on the CLOCK_REALTIME clock; if
34031   the Timers option is not supported, the timeout shall be based on the system clock as returned
34032   by the *time*() function.

34033   The resolution of the timeout shall be the resolution of the clock on which it is based. The
34034   **timespec** data type is defined in the <**time.h**> header.

34035   Under no circumstance shall the function fail with a timeout if the mutex can be locked
34036   immediately. The validity of the *abs_timeout* parameter need not be checked if the mutex can be
34037   locked immediately.

34038   As a consequence of the priority inheritance rules (for mutexes initialized with the
34039   PRIO_INHERIT protocol), if a timed mutex wait is terminated because its timeout expires, the
34040   priority of the owner of the mutex shall be adjusted as necessary to reflect the fact that this
34041   thread is no longer among the threads waiting for the mutex.

34042 **RETURN VALUE**

34043   If successful, the *pthread_mutex_timedlock*() function shall return zero; otherwise, an error
34044   number shall be returned to indicate the error.

34045 **ERRORS**

34046   The *pthread_mutex_timedlock*() function shall fail if:

34047   [EINVAL]   The mutex was created with the protocol attribute having the value
34048   PTHREAD_PRIO_PROTECT and the calling thread's priority is higher than
34049   the mutex' current priority ceiling.
34050   [EINVAL]   The process or thread would have blocked, and the *abs_timeout* parameter
34051   specified a nanoseconds field value less than zero or greater than or equal to
34052   1000 million.
34053   [ETIMEDOUT]   The mutex could not be locked before the specified timeout expired.

34054   The *pthread_mutex_timedlock*() function may fail if:

34055   [EINVAL]   The value specified by *mutex* does not refer to an initialized mutex object.

34056 XSI [EAGAIN]   The mutex could not be acquired because the maximum number of recursive
34057   locks for *mutex* has been exceeded.

34058   [EDEADLK]   The current thread already owns the mutex.

34059   This function shall not return an error code of [EINTR].

34060 **EXAMPLES**
34061   None.

34062 **APPLICATION USAGE**
34063   The *pthread_mutex_timedlock*() function is part of the Threads and Timeouts options and need
34064   not be provided on all implementations.

34065 **RATIONALE**
34066   None.

34067 **FUTURE DIRECTIONS**
34068   None.

34069 **SEE ALSO**
34070   *pthread_mutex_destroy*(), *pthread_mutex_lock*(), *pthread_mutex_trylock*(), *time*(), the Base
34071   Definitions volume of IEEE Std 1003.1-2001, **<pthread.h>**, **<time.h>**

34072 **CHANGE HISTORY**
34073   First released in Issue 6. Derived from IEEE Std 1003.1d-1999.

34083 **NAME**

34084   pthread_mutexattr_destroy, pthread_mutexattr_init — destroy and initialize the mutex
34085   attributes object

34086 **SYNOPSIS**

34087 THR   #include <pthread.h>

34088   int pthread_mutexattr_destroy (pthread_mutexattr_t *attr);
34089   int pthread_mutexattr_init (pthread_mutexattr_t *attr);
34090

34091 **DESCRIPTION**

34092   The *pthread_mutexattr_destroy*() function shall destroy a mutex attributes object; the object
34093   becomes, in effect, uninitialized. An implementation may cause *pthread_mutexattr_destroy*() to
34094   set the object referenced by *attr* to an invalid value. A destroyed *attr* attributes object can be
34095   reinitialized using *pthread_mutexattr_init*(); the results of otherwise referencing the object after it
34096   has been destroyed are undefined.

34097   The *pthread_mutexattr_init*() function shall initialize a mutex attributes object *attr* with the
34098   default value for all of the attributes defined by the implementation.

34099   Results are undefined if *pthread_mutexattr_init*() is called specifying an already initialized *attr*
34100   attributes object.

34101   After a mutex attributes object has been used to initialize one or more mutexes, any function
34102   affecting the attributes object (including destruction) shall not affect any previously initialized
34103   mutexes.

34104 **RETURN VALUE**

34105   Upon successful completion, *pthread_mutexattr_destroy*() and *pthread_mutexattr_init*() shall
34106   return zero; otherwise, an error number shall be returned to indicate the error.

34107 **ERRORS**

34108   The *pthread_mutexattr_destroy*() function may fail if:

34109   [EINVAL]   The value specified by *attr* is invalid.

34110   The *pthread_mutexattr_init*() function shall fail if:

34111   [ENOMEM]   Insufficient memory exists to initialize the mutex attributes object.

34112   These functions shall not return an error code of [EINTR].

34113 **EXAMPLES**

34114   None.

34115 **APPLICATION USAGE**

34116   None.

34117 **RATIONALE**

34118   See *pthread_attr_init*() for a general explanation of attributes. Attributes objects allow
34119   implementations to experiment with useful extensions and permit extension of this volume of
34120   IEEE Std 1003.1-2001 without changing the existing functions. Thus, they provide for future
34121   extensibility of this volume of IEEE Std 1003.1-2001 and reduce the temptation to standardize
34122   prematurely on semantics that are not yet widely implemented or understood.

34123   Examples of possible additional mutex attributes that have been discussed are *spin_only*,
34124   *limited spin, no_spin, recursive*, and *metered*. (To explain what the latter attributes might mean:

34125 recursive mutexes would allow for multiple re-locking by the current owner; metered mutexes
34126 would transparently keep records of queue length, wait time, and so on.) Since there is not yet
34127 wide agreement on the usefulness of these resulting from shared implementation and usage
34128 experience, they are not yet specified in this volume of IEEE Std 1003.1-2001. Mutex attributes
34129 objects, however, make it possible to test out these concepts for possible standardization at a
34130 later time.

Mutex Attributes and Performance

34131

34132 Care has been taken to ensure that the default values of the mutex attributes have been defined
34133 such that mutexes initialized with the defaults have simple enough semantics so that the locking
34134 and unlocking can be done with the equivalent of a test-and-set instruction (plus possibly a few
34135 other basic instructions).

34136 There is at least one implementation method that can be used to reduce the cost of testing at
34137 lock-time if a mutex has non-default attributes. One such method that an implementation can
34138 employ (and this can be made fully transparent to fully conforming POSIX applications) is to
34139 secretly pre-lock any mutexes that are initialized to non-default attributes. Any later attempt to
34140 lock such a mutex causes the implementation to branch to the "slow path" as if the mutex were
34141 unavailable; then, on the slow path, the implementation can do the "real work" to lock a non-default
34142 mutex. The underlying unlock operation is more complicated since the implementation
34143 never really wants to release the pre-lock on this kind of mutex. This illustrates that, depending
34144 on the hardware, there may be certain optimizations that can be used so that whatever mutex
34145 attributes are considered "most frequently used" can be processed most efficiently.

Process Shared Memory and Synchronization

34146

34147 The existence of memory mapping functions in this volume of IEEE Std 1003.1-2001 leads to the
34148 possibility that an application may allocate the synchronization objects from this section in
34149 memory that is accessed by multiple processes (and therefore, by threads of multiple processes).

34150 In order to permit such usage, while at the same time keeping the usual case (that is, usage
34151 within a single process) efficient, a *process-shared* option has been defined.

34152 If an implementation supports the _POSIX_THREAD_PROCESS_SHARED option, then the
34153 *process-shared* attribute can be used to indicate that mutexes or condition variables may be
34154 accessed by threads of multiple processes.

34155 The default setting of PTHREAD_PROCESS_PRIVATE has been chosen for the *process-shared*
34156 attribute so that the most efficient forms of these synchronization objects are created by default.

34157 Synchronization variables that are initialized with the PTHREAD_PROCESS_PRIVATE *process-*
34158 *shared* attribute may only be operated on by threads in the process that initialized them.
34159 Synchronization variables that are initialized with the PTHREAD_PROCESS_SHARED *process-*
34160 *shared* attribute may be operated on by any thread in any process that has access to it. In
34161 particular, these processes may exist beyond the lifetime of the initializing process. For example,
34162 the following code implements a simple counting semaphore in a mapped file that may be used
34163 by many processes.

```
34164 /* sem.h */
34165 struct semaphore {
34166     pthread_mutex_t lock;
34167     pthread_cond_t nonzero;
34168     unsigned count;
```

```
34169        };
34170        typedef struct semaphore semaphore_t;

34171        semaphore_t *semaphore_create (char *semaphore_name);
34172        semaphore_t *semaphore_open (char *semaphore_name);
34173        void semaphore_post (semaphore_t *semap);
34174        void semaphore_wait (semaphore_t *semap);
34175        void semaphore_close (semaphore_t *semap);

34176        /* sem.c */
34177        #include <sys/types.h>
34178        #include <sys/stat.h>
34179        #include <sys/mman.h>
34180        #include <fcntl.h>
34181        #include <pthread.h>
34182        #include "sem.h"

34183        semaphore_t *
34184        semaphore_create (char *semaphore_name)
34185        {
34186        int fd;
34187            semaphore_t *semap;
34188            pthread_mutexattr_t psharedm;
34189            pthread_condattr_t psharedc;

34190            fd = open(semaphore_name, O_RDWR | O_CREAT | O_EXCL, 0666);
34191            if (fd <0)
34192                return (NULL);
34193            (void) ftruncate (fd, sizeof (semaphore_t));
34194            (void) pthread_mutexattr_init (&psharedm);
34195            (void) pthread_mutexattr_setpshared (&psharedm,
34196                PTHREAD_PROCESS_SHARED);
34197            (void) pthread_condattr_init (&psharedc);
34198            (void) pthread_condattr_setpshared (&psharedc,
34199                PTHREAD_PROCESS_SHARED);
34200            semap = (semaphore_t *) mmap (NULL, sizeof (semaphore_t),
34201                    PROT_READ | PROT_WRITE, MAP_SHARED,
34202                    fd, 0);
34203            close (fd);
34204            (void) pthread_mutex_init (&semap->lock, &psharedm);
34205            (void) pthread_cond_init (&semap->nonzero, &psharedc);
34206            semap->count = 0;
34207            return (semap);
34208        }

34209        semaphore_t *
34210        semaphore_open (char *semaphore_name)
34211        {
34212            int fd;
34213            semaphore_t *semap;
```

```
34214          fd = open (semaphore_name, O_RDWR, 0666);
34215          if (fd <0)
34216              return (NULL);
34217          semap = (semaphore_t *) mmap (NULL, sizeof (semaphore_t),
34218                  PROT_READ | PROT_WRITE, MAP_SHARED,
34219                  fd, 0);
34220          close (fd);
34221          return (semap);
34222      }

34223      void
34224      semaphore_post (semaphore_t *semap)
34225      {
34226          pthread_mutex_lock (&semap->lock);
34227          if (semap->count == 0)
34228              pthread_cond_signal (&semapx->nonzero);
34229          semap->count++;
34230          pthread_mutex_unlock (&semap->lock);
34231      }

34232      void
34233      semaphore_wait (semaphore_t *semap)
34234      {
34235          pthread_mutex_lock (&semap->lock);
34236          while (semap->count == 0)
34237              pthread_cond_wait (&semap->nonzero, &semap->lock);
34238          semap->count--;
34239          pthread_mutex_unlock (&semap->lock);
34240      }

34241      void
34242      semaphore_close (semaphore_t *semap)
34243      {
34244          munmap ((void *) semap, sizeof (semaphore_t));
34245      }
```

34246   The following code is for three separate processes that create, post, and wait on a semaphore in
34247   the file **/tmp/semaphore**. Once the file is created, the post and wait programs increment and
34248   decrement the counting semaphore (waiting and waking as required) even though they did not
34249   initialize the semaphore.

```
34250      /* create.c */
34251      #include "pthread.h"
34252      #include "sem.h"

34253      int
34254      main()
34255      {
34256          semaphore_t *semap;

34257          semap = semaphore_create("/tmp/semaphore");
34258          if (semap == NULL)
```

```
34259          exit(1);
34260      semaphore_close (semap);
34261      return (0);
34262    }
34263    /* post */
34264    #include "pthread.h"
34265    #include "sem.h"
34266    int
34267    main()
34268    {
34269        semaphore_t *semap;
34270        semap = semaphore_open ("/tmp/semaphore");
34271        if (semap == NULL)
34272            exit (1);
34273        semaphore_post (semap);
34274        semaphore_close (semap);
34275        return (0);
34276    }
34277    /* wait */
34278    #include "pthread.h"
34279    #include "sem.h"
34280    int
34281    main ()
34282    {
34283        semaphore_t *semap;
34284        semap = semaphore_open ("/tmp/semaphore");
34285        if (semap == NULL)
34286            exit (1);
34287        semaphore_wait (semap);
34288        semaphore_close (semap);
34289        return (0);
34290    }
```

34291 **FUTURE DIRECTIONS**

34292   None.

34293 **SEE ALSO**

34294   *pthread_cond_destroy*(), *pthread_create*(), *pthread_mutex_destroy*(), *pthread_mutexattr_destroy*(), the
34295   Base Definitions volume of IEEE Std 1003.1-2001, **<pthread.h>**

34296 **CHANGE HISTORY**

34297   First released in Issue 5. Included for alignment with the POSIX Threads Extension.

34298 **Issue 6**

34299   The *pthread_mutexattr_destroy*() and *pthread_mutexattr_init*() functions are marked as part of the
34300   Threads option.

34301   IEEE PASC Interpretation 1003.1c #27 is applied, updating the ERRORS section.

34302 **NAME**
34303   pthread_mutexattr_getprioceiling, pthread_mutexattr_setprioceiling — get and set the
34304   prioceiling attribute of the mutex attributes object (**REALTIME THREADS**)

34305 **SYNOPSIS**
34306 THR TPP `# include <pthread.h>`

```
34307    int pthread_mutexattr_getprioceiling (const pthread_mutexattr_t *
34308        restrict attr, int *restrict prioceiling);
34309    int pthread_mutexattr_setprioceiling (pthread_mutexattr_t *attr,
34310        int prioceiling);
34311
```

34312 **DESCRIPTION**
34313   The *pthread_mutexattr_getprioceiling*() and *pthread_mutexattr_setprioceiling*() functions,
34314   respectively, shall get and set the priority ceiling attribute of a mutex attributes object pointed to
34315   by *attr* which was previously created by the function *pthread_mutexattr_init*().

34316   The *prioceiling* attribute contains the priority ceiling of initialized mutexes. The values of
34317   *prioceiling* are within the maximum range of priorities defined by SCHED_FIFO.

34318   The *prioceiling* attribute defines the priority ceiling of initialized mutexes, which is the minimum
34319   priority level at which the critical section guarded by the mutex is executed. In order to avoid
34320   priority inversion, the priority ceiling of the mutex shall be set to a priority higher than or equal
34321   to the highest priority of all the threads that may lock that mutex. The values of *prioceiling* are
34322   within the maximum range of priorities defined under the SCHED_FIFO scheduling policy.

34323 **RETURN VALUE**
34324   Upon   successful   completion,   the   *pthread_mutexattr_getprioceiling*()   and
34325   *pthread_mutexattr_setprioceiling*() functions shall return zero; otherwise, an error number shall be
34326   returned to indicate the error.

34327 **ERRORS**
34328   The *pthread_mutexattr_getprioceiling*() and *pthread_mutexattr_setprioceiling*() functions may fail if:
34329   [EINVAL]   The value specified by *attr* or *prioceiling* is invalid.
34330   [EPERM]   The caller does not have the privilege to perform the operation.

34331   These functions shall not return an error code of [EINTR].

34332 **EXAMPLES**
34333   None.

34334 **APPLICATION USAGE**
34335   None.

34336 **RATIONALE**
34337   None.

34338 **FUTURE DIRECTIONS**
34339   None.

34340 **SEE ALSO**
34341   *pthread_cond_destroy*(), *pthread_create*(), *pthread_mutex_destroy*(), the Base Definitions volume of
34342   IEEE Std 1003.1-2001, **<pthread.h>**

34343 **CHANGE HISTORY**

34344 First released in Issue 5. Included for alignment with the POSIX Threads Extension.

34345 Marked as part of the Realtime Threads Feature Group.

34346 **Issue 6**

34347 The *pthread_mutexattr_getprioceiling*() and *pthread_mutexattr_setprioceiling*() functions are
34348 marked as part of the Threads and Thread Priority Protection options.

34349 The [ENOSYS] error condition has been removed as stubs need not be provided if an
34350 implementation does not support the Thread Priority Protection option.

34351 The [ENOTSUP] error condition has been removed since these functions do not have a *protocol*
34352 argument.

34353 The **restrict** keyword is added to the *pthread_mutexattr_getprioceiling*() prototype for alignment
34354 with the ISO/IEC 9899: 1999 standard.

34355 **NAME**

34356   pthread_mutexattr_getprotocol, pthread_mutexattr_setprotocol — get and set the protocol
34357   attribute of the mutex attributes object (**REALTIME THREADS**)

34358 **SYNOPSIS**

34359 THR   `# include <pthread.h>`

34360 TPP|TPI   `int pthread_mutexattr_getprotocol (const pthread_mutexattr_t *`
34361   `restrict attr, int *restrict protocol);`
34362   `int pthread_mutexattr_setprotocol (pthread_mutexattr_t * attr,`
34363   `int protocol);`
34364

34365 **DESCRIPTION**

34366   The *pthread_mutexattr_getprotocol*() and *pthread_mutexattr_setprotocol*() functions, respectively,
34367   shall get and set the protocol attribute of a mutex attributes object pointed to by *attr* which was
34368   previously created by the function *pthread_mutexattr_init*().

34369   The *protocol* attribute defines the protocol to be followed in utilizing mutexes. The value of
34370   *protocol* may be one of:

34371   PTHREAD_PRIO_NONE
34372 TPI   PTHREAD_PRIO_INHERIT
34373 TPP   PTHREAD_PRIO_PROTECT
34374

34375   which are defined in the **<pthread.h>** header.

34376   When a thread owns a mutex with the PTHREAD_PRIO_NONE *protocol* attribute, its priority
34377   and scheduling shall not be affected by its mutex ownership.

34378 TPI   When a thread is blocking higher priority threads because of owning one or more mutexes with
34379   the PTHREAD_PRIO_INHERIT *protocol* attribute, it shall execute at the higher of its priority or
34380   the priority of the highest priority thread waiting on any of the mutexes owned by this thread
34381   and initialized with this protocol.

34382 TPP   When a thread owns one or more mutexes initialized with the PTHREAD_PRIO_PROTECT
34383   protocol, it shall execute at the higher of its priority or the highest of the priority ceilings of all
34384   the mutexes owned by this thread and initialized with this attribute, regardless of whether other
34385   threads are blocked on any of these mutexes or not.

34386   While   a   thread   is   holding   a   mutex   which   has   been   initialized   with   the
34387   PTHREAD_PRIO_INHERIT or PTHREAD_PRIO_PROTECT protocol attributes, it shall not be
34388   subject to being moved to the tail of the scheduling queue at its priority in the event that its
34389   original priority is changed, such as by a call to *sched_setparam*(). Likewise, when a thread
34390   unlocks a mutex that has been initialized with the PTHREAD_PRIO_INHERIT or
34391   PTHREAD_PRIO_PROTECT protocol attributes, it shall not be subject to being moved to the tail
34392   of the scheduling queue at its priority in the event that its original priority is changed.

34393   If a thread simultaneously owns several mutexes initialized with different protocols, it shall
34394   execute at the highest of the priorities that it would have obtained by each of these protocols.

34395 TPI   When a thread makes a call to *pthread_mutex_lock*(), the mutex was initialized with the protocol
34396   attribute having the value PTHREAD_PRIO_INHERIT, when the calling thread is blocked

34397 because the mutex is owned by another thread, that owner thread shall inherit the priority level
34398 of the calling thread as long as it continues to own the mutex. The implementation shall update
34399 its execution priority to the maximum of its assigned priority and all its inherited priorities.
34400 Furthermore, if this owner thread itself becomes blocked on another mutex, the same priority
34401 inheritance effect shall be propagated to this other owner thread, in a recursive manner.

34402 **RETURN VALUE**

34403 Upon successful completion, the *pthread_mutexattr_getprotocol*() and
34404 *pthread_mutexattr_setprotocol*() functions shall return zero; otherwise, an error number shall be
34405 returned to indicate the error.

34406 **ERRORS**

34407 The *pthread_mutexattr_setprotocol*() function shall fall if:

34408 [ENOTSUP]   The value specified by *protocol* is an unsupported value.

34409 The *pthread_mutexattr_getprotocol*() and *pthread_mutexattr_setprotocol*() functions may fail if:

34410 [EINVAL]   The value specified by *attr* or *protocol* is invalid.
34411 [EPERM]   The caller does not have the privilege to perform the operation.

34412 These functions shall not return an error code of [EINTR].

34413 **EXAMPLES**

34414 None.

34415 **APPLICATION USAGE**

34416 None.

34417 **RATIONALE**

34418 None.

34419 **FUTURE DIRECTIONS**

34420 None.

34421 **SEE ALSO**

34422 *pthread_cond_destroy*(), *pthread_create*(), *pthread_mutex_destroy*(), the Base Definitions volume of
34423 IEEE Std 1003.1-2001, **<pthread.h>**

34424 **CHANGE HISTORY**

34425 First released in Issue 5. Included for alignment with the POSIX Threads Extension.

34426 Marked as part of the Realtime Threads Feature Group.

34427 **Issue 6**

34428 The *pthread_mutexattr_getprotocol*() and *pthread_mutexattr_setprotocol*() functions are marked as
34429 part of the Threads option and either the Thread Priority Protection or Thread Priority
34430 Inheritance options.

34431 The [ENOSYS] error condition has been removed as stubs need not be provided if an
34432 implementation does not support the Thread Priority Protection or Thread Priority Inheritance
34433 options.

34434 The **restrict** keyword is added to the *pthread_mutexattr_getprotocol*() prototype for alignment
34435 with the ISO/IEC 9899:1999 standard.

34436 **NAME**

34437   pthread_mutexattr_getpshared, pthread_mutexattr_setpshared — get and set the process-shared
34438   attribute

34439 **SYNOPSIS**

34440 THR TSH   `#include <pthread.h>`

34441   `int pthread_mutexattr_getpshared (const pthread_mutexattr_t *`
34442   `    restrict attr, int *restrict pshared);`
34443   `int pthread_mutexattr_setpshared(pthread_mutexattr_t *attr,`
34444   `    int pshared);`
34445

34446 **DESCRIPTION**

34447   The *pthread_mutexattr_getpshared*() function shall obtain the value of the *process-shared* attribute
34448   from the attributes object referenced by *attr*. The *pthread_mutexattr_setpshared*() function shall
34449   set the *process-shared* attribute in an initialized attributes object referenced by *attr*.

34450   The *process-shared* attribute is set to PTHREAD_PROCESS_SHARED to permit a mutex to be
34451   operated upon by any thread that has access to the memory where the mutex is allocated, even if
34452   the mutex is allocated in memory that is shared by multiple processes. If the *process-shared*
34453   attribute is PTHREAD_PROCESS_PRIVATE, the mutex shall only be operated upon by threads
34454   created within the same process as the thread that initialized the mutex; if threads of differing
34455   processes attempt to operate on such a mutex, the behavior is undefined. The default value of
34456   the attribute shall be PTHREAD_PROCESS_PRIVATE.

34457 **RETURN VALUE**

34458   Upon successful completion, *pthread_mutexattr_setpshared*() shall return zero; otherwise, an error
34459   number shall be returned to indicate the error.

34460   Upon successful completion, *pthread_mutexattr_getpshared*() shall return zero and store the value
34461   of the *process-shared* attribute of *attr* into the object referenced by the *pshared* parameter.
34462   Otherwise, an error number shall be returned to indicate the error.

34463 **ERRORS**

34464   The *pthread_mutexattr_getpshared*() and *pthread_mutexattr_setpshared*() functions may fail if:

34465   [EINVAL]   The value specified by *attr* is invalid.

34466   The *pthread_mutexattr_setpshared*() function may fail if:

34467   [EINVAL]   The new value specified for the attribute is outside the range of legal values
34468   for that attribute.

34469   These functions shall not return an error code of [EINTR].

34470 **EXAMPLES**
34471   None.

34472 **APPLICATION USAGE**
34473   None.

34474 **RATIONALE**
34475   None.

34476 **FUTURE DIRECTIONS**

34477   None.

34478 **SEE ALSO**

34479   *pthread_cond_destroy*(), *pthread_create*(), *pthread_mutex_destroy*(), *pthread_mutexattr_destroy*(), the

34480   Base Definitions volume of IEEE Std 1003.1-2001, **<pthread.h>**

34481 **CHANGE HISTORY**

34482   First released in Issue 5. Included for alignment with the POSIX Threads Extension.

34483 **Issue 6**

34484   The *pthread_mutexattr_getpshared*() and *pthread_mutexattr_setpshared*() functions are marked as

34485   part of the Threads and Thread Process-Shared Synchronization options.

34486   The **restrict** keyword is added to the *pthread_mutexattr_getpshared*() prototype for alignment

34487   with the ISO/IEC 9899: 1999 standard.

34488 **NAME**

34489   pthread_mutexattr_gettype, pthread_mutexattr_settype — get and set the mutex type attribute

34490 **SYNOPSIS**

34491 XSI   `#include <pthread.h>`

34492   `int pthread_mutexattr_gettype (const pthread_mutexattr_t *restrict attr,`
34493   `int *restrict type);`
34494   `int pthread_mutexattr_settype (pthread_mutexattr_t *attr, int type);`
34495

34496 **DESCRIPTION**

34497   The *pthread_mutexattr_gettype*() and *pthread_mutexattr_settype*() functions, respectively, shall get
34498   and set the mutex *type* attribute. This attribute is set in the *type* parameter to these functions. The
34499   default value of the *type* attribute is PTHREAD_MUTEX_DEFAULT.

34500   The type of mutex is contained in the *type* attribute of the mutex attributes. Valid mutex types
34501   include:

34502   PTHREAD_MUTEX_NORMAL
34503   This type of mutex does not detect deadlock. A thread attempting to relock this mutex
34504   without first unlocking it shall deadlock. Attempting to unlock a mutex locked by a
34505   different thread results in undefined behavior. Attempting to unlock an unlocked mutex
34506   results in undefined behavior.

34507   PTHREAD_MUTEX_ERRORCHECK
34508   This type of mutex provides error checking. A thread attempting to relock this mutex
34509   without first unlocking it shall return with an error. A thread attempting to unlock a mutex
34510   which another thread has locked shall return with an error. A thread attempting to unlock
34511   an unlocked mutex shall return with an error.

34512   PTHREAD_MUTEX_RECURSIVE
34513   A thread attempting to relock this mutex without first unlocking it shall succeed in locking
34514   the mutex. The relocking deadlock which can occur with mutexes of type
34515   PTHREAD_MUTEX_NORMAL cannot occur with this type of mutex. Multiple locks of this
34516   mutex shall require the same number of unlocks to release the mutex before another thread
34517   can acquire the mutex. A thread attempting to unlock a mutex which another thread has
34518   locked shall return with an error. A thread attempting to unlock an unlocked mutex shall
34519   return with an error.

34520   PTHREAD_MUTEX_DEFAULT
34521   Attempting to recursively lock a mutex of this type results in undefined behavior.
34522   Attempting to unlock a mutex of this type which was not locked by the calling thread
34523   results in undefined behavior. Attempting to unlock a mutex of this type which is not
34524   locked results in undefined behavior. An implementation may map this mutex to one of the
34525   other mutex types.

34526 **RETURN VALUE**

34527   Upon successful completion, the *pthread_mutexattr_gettype*() function shall return zero and store
34528   the value of the *type* attribute of *attr* into the object referenced by the *type* parameter. Otherwise,
34529   an error shall be returned to indicate the error.

34530   If successful, the *pthread_mutexattr_settype*() function shall return zero; otherwise, an error
34531   number shall be returned to indicate the error.

34532 **ERRORS**

34533   The *pthread_mutexattr_settype*() function shall fail if:

34534   [EINVAL]   The value *type* is invalid.

34535   The *pthread_mutexattr_gettype*() and *pthread_mutexattr_settype*() functions may fail if:

34536   [EINVAL]   The value specified by *attr* is invalid.

34537   These functions shall not return an error code of [EINTR].

34538 **EXAMPLES**

34539   None.

34540 **APPLICATION USAGE**

34541   It is advised that an application should not use a PTHREAD_MUTEX_RECURSIVE mutex with
34542   condition variables because the implicit unlock performed for a *pthread_cond_timedwait*() or
34543   *pthread_cond_wait*() may not actually release the mutex (if it had been locked multiple times). If
34544   this happens, no other thread can satisfy the condition of the predicate.

34545 **RATIONALE**

34546   None.

34547 **FUTURE DIRECTIONS**

34548   None.

34549 **SEE ALSO**

34550   *pthread_cond_timedwait*(), the Base Definitions volume of IEEE Std 1003.1-2001, **<pthread.h>**

34551 **CHANGE HISTORY**

34552   First released in Issue 5.

34553 **Issue 6**

34554   The   Open   Group   Corrigendum   U033/3   is   applied.   The   SYNOPSIS   for
34555   *pthread_mutexattr_gettype*() is updated so that the first argument is of type **const**
34556   **pthread_mutexattr_t***.

34557   The **restrict** keyword is added to the *pthread_mutexattr_gettype*() prototype for alignment with
34558   the ISO/IEC 9899: 1999 standard.

34604 **NAME**
34605   pthread_once — dynamic package initialization
34606 **SYNOPSIS**
34607 THR   `#include <pthread.h>`

34608   ```
int pthread_once (pthread_once_t *once_control,
```
34609    ```
    void (*init_routine) (void));
```
34610   ```
pthread_once_t once_control = PTHREAD_ONCE_INIT;
```
34611

34612 **DESCRIPTION**
34613     The first call to *pthread_once*() by any thread in a process, with a given *once_control*, shall call the
34614     *init_routine* with no arguments. Subsequent calls of *pthread_once*() with the same *once_control*
34615     shall not call the *init_routine*. On return from *pthread_once*(), *init_routine* shall have completed.
34616     The *once_control* parameter shall determine whether the associated initialization routine has
34617     been called.

34618     The *pthread_once*() function is not a cancelation point. However, if *init_routine* is a cancelation
34619     point and is canceled, the effect on *once_control* shall be as if *pthread_once*() was never called.

34620     The constant PTHREAD_ONCE_INIT is defined in the **<pthread.h>** header.

34621     The behavior of *pthread_once*() is undefined if *once_control* has automatic storage duration or is
34622     not initialized by PTHREAD_ONCE_INIT.

34623 **RETURN VALUE**
34624     Upon successful completion, *pthread_once*() shall return zero; otherwise, an error number shall
34625     be returned to indicate the error.

34626 **ERRORS**
34627     The *pthread_once*() function may fail if:

34628     [EINVAL]          If either *once_control* or *init_routine* is invalid.

34629     The *pthread_once*() function shall not return an error code of [EINTR].

34630 **EXAMPLES**
34631     None.

34632 **APPLICATION USAGE**
34633     None.

34634 **RATIONALE**
34635     Some C libraries are designed for dynamic initialization. That is, the global initialization for the
34636     library is performed when the first procedure in the library is called. In a single-threaded
34637     program, this is normally implemented using a static variable whose value is checked on entry
34638     to a routine, as follows:

34639    ```
static int random_is_initialized = 0;
```
34640   ```
extern int initialize_random ();
```

34641    ```
int random_function ()
```
34642   ```
{
```
34643    ```
    if (random_is_initialized == 0) {
```
34644   ```
        initialize_random ();
```
34645    ```
        random_is_initialized = 1;
```

```
34646            }
34647            ... /* Operations performed after initialization. */
34648        }
```

34649   To keep the same structure in a multi-threaded program, a new primitive is needed. Otherwise,
34650   library initialization has to be accomplished by an explicit call to a library-exported initialization
34651   function prior to any use of the library.

34652   For dynamic library initialization in a multi-threaded process, a simple initialization flag is not
34653   sufficient; the flag needs to be protected against modification by multiple threads
34654   simultaneously calling into the library. Protecting the flag requires the use of a mutex; however,
34655   mutexes have to be initialized before they are used. Ensuring that the mutex is only initialized
34656   once requires a recursive solution to this problem.

34657   The use of *pthread_once*() not only supplies an implementation-guaranteed means of dynamic
34658   initialization, it provides an aid to the reliable construction of multi-threaded and realtime
34659   systems. The preceding example then becomes:

```
34660        #include <pthread.h>
34661        static pthread_once_t random_is_initialized = PTHREAD_ONCE_INIT;
34662        extern int initialize_random();
34663        int random_function()
34664        {
34665            (void) pthread_once (&random_is_initialized, initialize_random);
34666            ... /* Operations performed after initialization. */
34667        }
```

34668   Note that a **pthread_once_t** cannot be an array because some compilers do not accept the
34669   construct **&<array_name>**.

34670 **FUTURE DIRECTIONS**
34671   None.

34672 **SEE ALSO**
34673   The Base Definitions volume of IEEE Std 1003.1-2001, **<pthread.h>**

34674 **CHANGE HISTORY**
34675   First released in Issue 5. Included for alignment with the POSIX Threads Extension.

34676 **Issue 6**
34677   The *pthread_once*() function is marked as part of the Threads option.

34678   The [EINVAL] error is added as a may fail case for if either argument is invalid.

34679 **NAME**

34680   pthread_rwlock_destroy, pthread_rwlock_init — destroy and initialize a read-write lock object

34681 **SYNOPSIS**

34682 THR `#include <pthread.h>`

34683   `int pthread_rwlock_destroy(pthread_rwlock_t *rwlock);`
34684   `int pthread_rwlock_init(pthread_rwlock_t *restrict rwlock,`
34685   `const pthread_rwlockattr_t *restrict attr);`

34686

34687 **DESCRIPTION**

34688   The *pthread_rwlock_destroy*() function shall destroy the read-write lock object referenced by
34689   *rwlock* and release any resources used by the lock. The effect of subsequent use of the lock is
34690   undefined until the lock is reinitialized by another call to *pthread_rwlock_init*(). An
34691   implementation may cause *pthread_rwlock_destroy*() to set the object referenced by *rwlock* to an
34692   invalid value. Results are undefined if *pthread_rwlock_destroy*() is called when any thread holds
34693   *rwlock*. Attempting to destroy an uninitialized read-write lock results in undefined behavior.

34694   The *pthread_rwlock_init*() function shall allocate any resources required to use the read-write
34695   lock referenced by *rwlock* and initializes the lock to an unlocked state with attributes referenced
34696   by *attr*. If *attr* is NULL, the default read-write lock attributes shall be used; the effect is the same
34697   as passing the address of a default read-write lock attributes object. Once initialized, the lock can
34698   be used any number of times without being reinitialized. Results are undefined if
34699   *pthread_rwlock_init*() is called specifying an already initialized read-write lock. Results are
34700   undefined if a read-write lock is used without first being initialized.

34701   If the *pthread_rwlock_init*() function fails, *rwlock* shall not be initialized and the contents of *rwlock*
34702   are undefined.

34703   Only the object referenced by *rwlock* may be used for performing synchronization. The result of
34704   referring to copies of that object in calls to *pthread_rwlock_destroy*(), *pthread_rwlock_rdlock*(),
34705   *pthread_rwlock_timedrdlock*(),   *pthread_rwlock_timedwrlock*(),   *pthread_rwlock_tryrdlock*(),
34706   *pthread_rwlock_trywrlock*(), *pthread_rwlock_unlock*(), or *pthread_rwlock_wrlock*() is undefined.

34707 **RETURN VALUE**

34708   If successful, the *pthread_rwlock_destroy*() and *pthread_rwlock_init*() functions shall return zero;
34709   otherwise, an error number shall be returned to indicate the error.

34710   The [EBUSY] and [EINVAL] error checks, if implemented, act as if they were performed
34711   immediately at the beginning of processing for the function and caused an error return prior to
34712   modifying the state of the read-write lock specified by *rwlock*.

34713 **ERRORS**

34714   The *pthread_rwlock_destroy*() function may fail if:

34715   [EBUSY]   The implementation has detected an attempt to destroy the object referenced
34716   by *rwlock* while it is locked.
34717   [EINVAL]   The value specified by *rwlock* is invalid.

34718   The *pthread_rwlock_init*() function shall fail if:

34719   [EAGAIN]   The system lacked the necessary resources (other than memory) to initialize
34720   another read-write lock.

34721   [ENOMEM]   Insufficient memory exists to initialize the read-write lock.

34722   [EPERM]   The caller does not have the privilege to perform the operation.

34723   The *pthread_rwlock_init*() function may fail if:

34724   [EBUSY]   The implementation has detected an attempt to reinitialize the object
34725   referenced by *rwlock*, a previously initialized but not yet destroyed read-write
34726   lock.

34727   [EINVAL]   The value specified by *attr* is invalid.

34728   These functions shall not return an error code of [EINTR].

34729 **EXAMPLES**

34730   None.

34731 **APPLICATION USAGE**

34732   None.

34733 **RATIONALE**

34734   None.

34735 **FUTURE DIRECTIONS**

34736   None.

34737 **SEE ALSO**

34738   *pthread_rwlock_rdlock*(), *pthread_rwlock_timedrdlock*(), *pthread_rwlock_timedwrlock*(),
34739   *pthread_rwlock_tryrdlock*(), *pthread_rwlock_trywrlock*(), *pthread_rwlock_unlock*(),
34740   *pthread_rwlock_wrlock*(), the Base Definitions volume of IEEE Std 1003.1-2001. <**pthread.h**>

34741 **CHANGE HISTORY**

34742   First released in Issue 5.

34743 **Issue 6**

34744   The following changes are made for alignment with IEEE Std 1003.1j-2000:

34745   • The margin code in the SYNOPSIS is changed to THR to indicate that the functionality is
34746   now part of the Threads option (previously it was part of the Read-Write Locks option in
34747   IEEE Std 1003.1j-2000 and also part of the XSI extension). The initializer macro is also deleted
34748   from the SYNOPSIS.

34749   • The DESCRIPTION is updated as follows:
34750   — It explicitly notes allocation of resources upon initialization of a read-write lock object.
34751   — A paragraph is added specifying that copies of read-write lock objects may not be used.

34752   • An [EINVAL] error is added to the ERRORS section for *pthread_rwlock_init*(), indicating that
34753   the *rwlock* value is invalid.

34754   • The SEE ALSO section is updated.

34755   The **restrict** keyword is added to the *pthread_rwlock_init*() prototype for alignment with the
34756   ISO/IEC 9899: 1999 standard.

34757 **NAME**

34758   pthread_rwlock_rdlock, pthread_rwlock_tryrdlock — lock a read-write lock object for reading

34759 **SYNOPSIS**

34760 THR `#include <pthread.h>`

34761   `int pthread_rwlock_rdlock (pthread_rwlock_t *rwlock);`

34762   `int pthread_rwlock_tryrdlock (pthread_rwlock_t *rwlock);`

34763

34764 **DESCRIPTION**

34765   The *pthread_rwlock_rdlock*() function shall apply a read lock to the read-write lock referenced by
34766   *rwlock*. The calling thread acquires the read lock if a writer does not hold the lock and there are
34767   no writers blocked on the lock.

34768 TPS If the Thread Execution Scheduling option is supported, and the threads involved in the lock are
34769   executing with the scheduling policies SCHED_FIFO or SCHED_RR, the calling thread shall not
34770   acquire the lock if a writer holds the lock or if writers of higher or equal priority are blocked on
34771   the lock; otherwise, the calling thread shall acquire the lock.

34772 TSP TSP If the Threads Execution Scheduling option is supported, and the threads involved in the lock
34773   are executing with the SCHED_SPORADIC scheduling policy, the calling thread shall not
34774   acquire the lock if a writer holds the lock or if writers of higher or equal priority are blocked on
34775   the lock; otherwise, the calling thread shall acquire the lock.

34776   If the Thread Execution Scheduling option is not supported, it is implementation-defined
34777   whether the calling thread acquires the lock when a writer does not hold the lock and there are
34778   writers blocked on the lock. If a writer holds the lock, the calling thread shall not acquire the
34779   read lock. If the read lock is not acquired, the calling thread shall block until it can acquire the
34780   lock. The calling thread may deadlock if at the time the call is made it holds a write lock.

34781   A thread may hold multiple concurrent read locks on *rwlock* (that is, successfully call the
34782   *pthread_rwlock_rdlock*() function *n* times). If so, the application shall ensure that the thread
34783   performs matching unlocks (that is, it calls the *pthread_rwlock_unlock*() function *n* times).

34784   The maximum number of simultaneous read locks that an implementation guarantees can be
34785   applied to a read-write lock shall be implementation-defined. The *pthread_rwlock_rdlock*()
34786   function may fail if this maximum would be exceeded.

34787   The *pthread_rwlock_tryrdlock*() function shall apply a read lock as in the *pthread_rwlock_rdlock*()
34788   function, with the exception that the function shall fail if the equivalent *pthread_rwlock_rdlock*()
34789   call would have blocked the calling thread. In no case shall the *pthread_rwlock_tryrdlock*()
34790   function ever block; it always either acquires the lock or fails and returns immediately.

34791   Results are undefined if any of these functions are called with an uninitialized read-write lock.

34792   If a signal is delivered to a thread waiting for a read-write lock for reading, upon return from the
34793   signal handler the thread resumes waiting for the read-write lock for reading as if it was not
34794   interrupted.

34795 **RETURN VALUE**

34796   If successful, the *pthread_rwlock_rdlock*() function shall return zero; otherwise, an error number
34797   shall be returned to indicate the error.

34798   The *pthread_rwlock_tryrdlock*() function shall return zero if the lock for reading on the read-write
34799   lock object referenced by *rwlock* is acquired. Otherwise, an error number shall be returned to
34800   indicate the error.

34801 **ERRORS**

34802   The *pthread_rwlock_tryrdlock*() function shall fail if:

34803   [EBUSY]   The read-write lock could not be acquired for reading because a writer holds
34804   the lock or a writer with the appropriate priority was blocked on it.

34805   The *pthread_rwlock_rdlock*() and *pthread_rwlock_tryrdlock*() functions may fail if:

34806   [EINVAL]   The value specified by *rwlock* does not refer to an initialized read-write lock
34807   object.
34808   [EAGAIN]   The read lock could not be acquired because the maximum number of read
34809   locks for *rwlock* has been exceeded.

34810   The *pthread_rwlock_rdlock*() function may fail if:

34811   [EDEADLK]   The current thread already owns the read-write lock for writing.

34812   These functions shall not return an error code of [EINTR].

34813 **EXAMPLES**
34814   None.

34815 **APPLICATION USAGE**
34816   Applications using these functions may be subject to priority inversion, as discussed in the Base
34817   Definitions volume of IEEE Std 1003.1-2001, Section 3.285, Priority Inversion.

34818 **RATIONALE**
34819   None.

34820 **FUTURE DIRECTIONS**
34821   None.

34822 **SEE ALSO**
34823   *pthread_rwlock_destroy*(), *pthread_rwlock_timedrdlock*(), *pthread_rwlock_timedwrlock*(),
34824   *pthread_rwlock_trywrlock*(), *pthread_rwlock_unlock*(), *pthread_rwlock_wrlock*(), the Base Definitions
34825   volume of IEEE Std 1003.1-2001, **<pthread.h>**

34826 **CHANGE HISTORY**
34827   First released in Issue 5.

34828 **Issue 6**
34829   The following changes are made for alignment with IEEE Std 1003.1j-2000:

34830   • The margin code in the SYNOPSIS is changed to THR to indicate that the functionality is
34831   now part of the Threads option (previously it was part of the Read-Write Locks option in
34832   IEEE Std 1003.1j-2000 and also part of the XSI extension).

34833   • The DESCRIPTION is updated as follows:
34834   — Conditions under which writers have precedence over readers are specified.
34835   — Failure of *pthread_rwlock_tryrdlock*() is clarified.
34836   — A paragraph on the maximum number of read locks is added.

34837   • In the ERRORS sections, [EBUSY] is modified to take into account write priority, and
34838   [EDEADLK] is deleted as a *pthread_rwlock_tryrdlock*() error.

34839   • The SEE ALSO section is updated.

34840 **NAME**
34841   pthread_rwlock_timedrdlock — lock a read-write lock for reading

34842 **SYNOPSIS**
34843 THR TMO
```
#include <pthread.h>
```
34844
```
#include <time.h>
```

34845
```
int pthread_rwlock_timedrdlock (pthread_rwlock_t *restrict rwlock,
```
34846
```
        const struct timespec *restrict abs_timeout);
```
34847

34848 **DESCRIPTION**
34849   The *pthread_rwlock_timedrdlock*() function shall apply a read lock to the read-write lock
34850   referenced by *rwlock* as in the *pthread_rwlock_rdlock*() function. However, if the lock cannot be
34851   acquired without waiting for other threads to unlock the lock, this wait shall be terminated
34852   when the specified timeout expires. The timeout shall expire when the absolute time specified
34853   by *abs_timeout* passes, as measured by the clock on which timeouts are based (that is, when the
34854   value of that clock equals or exceeds *abs_timeout*), or if the absolute time specified by *abs_timeout*
34855   has already been passed at the time of the call.

34856 TMR   If the Timers option is supported, the timeout shall be based on the CLOCK_REALTIME clock. If
34857   the Timers option is not supported, the timeout shall be based on the system clock as returned
34858   by the *time*() function. The resolution of the timeout shall be the resolution of the clock on which
34859   it is based. The **timespec** data type is defined in the **<time.h>** header. Under no circumstances
34860   shall the function fail with a timeout if the lock can be acquired immediately. The validity of the
34861   *abs_timeout* parameter need not be checked if the lock can be immediately acquired.

34862   If a signal that causes a signal handler to be executed is delivered to a thread blocked on a read-write
34863   lock via a call to *pthread_rwlock_timedrdlock*(), upon return from the signal handler the
34864   thread shall resume waiting for the lock as if it was not interrupted.

34865   The calling thread may deadlock if at the time the call is made it holds a write lock on *rwlock*.
34866   The results are undefined if this function is called with an uninitialized read-write lock.

34867 **RETURN VALUE**

34868   The *pthread_rwlock_timedrdlock*() function shall return zero if the lock for reading on the read-write
34869   lock object referenced by *rwlock* is acquired. Otherwise, an error number shall be returned
34870   to indicate the error.

34871 **ERRORS**
34872   The *pthread_rwlock_timedrdlock*() function shall fail if:

34873   [ETIMEDOUT]   The lock could not be acquired before the specified timeout expired.

34874   The *pthread_rwlock_timedrdlock*() function may fail if:

34875   [EAGAIN]   The read lock could not be acquired because the maximum number of read
34876   locks for lock would be exceeded.
34877   [EDEADLK]   The calling thread already holds a write lock on *rwlock*.
34878   [EINVAL]   The value specified by *rwlock* does not refer to an initialized read-write lock
34879   object, or the *abs_timeout* nanosecond value is less than zero or greater than or
34880   equal to 1000 million.

34881   This function shall not return an error code of [EINTR].

34882 **EXAMPLES**

34883 None.

34884 **APPLICATION USAGE**

34885 Applications using this function may be subject to priority inversion, as discussed in the Base
34886 Definitions volume of IEEE Std 1003.1-2001, Section 3.285, Priority Inversion.

34887 The *pthread_rwlock_timedrdlock*() function is part of the Threads and Timeouts options and need
34888 not be provided on all implementations.

34889 **RATIONALE**

34890 None.

34891 **FUTURE DIRECTIONS**

34892 None.

34893 **SEE ALSO**

34894 *pthread_rwlock_destroy*(), *pthread_rwlock_rdlock*(), *pthread_rwlock_timedwrlock*(),
34895 *pthread_rwlock_tryrdlock*(), *pthread_rwlock_trywrlock*(), *pthread_rwlock_unlock*(),
34896 *pthread_rwlock_wrlock*(), the Base Definitions volume of IEEE Std 1003.1-2001, <**pthread.h**>,
34897 <**time.h**>

34898 **CHANGE HISTORY**

34899 First released in Issue 6. Derived from IEEE Std 1003.1j-2000.

34900 **NAME**

34901   pthread_rwlock_timedwrlock — lock a read-write lock for writing

34902 **SYNOPSIS**

34903 THR TMO   `#include <pthread.h>`

34904   `#include <time.h>`

34905   `int pthread_rwlock_timedwrlock(pthread_rwlock_t *restrict rwlock,`

34906   `const struct timespec *restrict abs_timeout);`

34907

34908 **DESCRIPTION**

34909   The *pthread_rwlock_timedwrlock*() function shall apply a write lock to the read-write lock

34910   referenced by *rwlock* as in the *pthread_rwlock_wrlock*() function. However, if the lock cannot be

34911   acquired without waiting for other threads to unlock the lock, this wait shall be terminated

34912   when the specified timeout expires. The timeout shall expire when the absolute time specified

34913   by *abs_timeout* passes, as measured by the clock on which timeouts are based (that is, when the

34914   value of that clock equals or exceeds *abs_timeout*), or if the absolute time specified by *abs_timeout*

34915   has already been passed at the time of the call.

34916 TMR   If the Timers option is supported, the timeout shall be based on the CLOCK_REALTIME clock. If

34917   the Timers option is not supported, the timeout shall be based on the system clock as returned

34918   by the *time*() function. The resolution of the timeout shall be the resolution of the clock on which

34919   it is based. The **timespec** data type is defined in the **<time.h>** header. Under no circumstances

34920   shall the function fail with a timeout if the lock can be acquired immediately. The validity of the

34921   *abs_timeout* parameter need not be checked if the lock can be immediately acquired.

34922   If a signal that causes a signal handler to be executed is delivered to a thread blocked on a read-write

34923   lock via a call to *pthread_rwlock_timedwrlock*(), upon return from the signal handler the

34924   thread shall resume waiting for the lock as if it was not interrupted.

34925   The calling thread may deadlock if at the time the call is made it holds the read-write lock. The

34926   results are undefined if this function is called with an uninitialized read-write lock.

34927 **RETURN VALUE**

34928   The *pthread_rwlock_timedwrlock*() function shall return zero if the lock for writing on the read-write

34929   lock object referenced by *rwlock* is acquired. Otherwise, an error number shall be returned

34930   to indicate the error.

34931 **ERRORS**

34932   The *pthread_rwlock_timedwrlock*() function shall fail if:

34933   [ETIMEDOUT]   The lock could not be acquired before the specified timeout expired.

34934   The *pthread_rwlock_timedwrlock*() function may fail if:

34935   [EDEADLK]   The calling thread already holds the *rwlock*.

34936   [EINVAL]   The value specified by rwlock does not refer to an initialized read-write lock

34937   object, or the *abs_timeout* nanosecond value is less than zero or greater than or

34938   equal to 1000 million.

34939   This function shall not return an error code of [EINTR].

34940 **EXAMPLES**

34941   None.

34942 **APPLICATION USAGE**

34943 Applications using this function may be subject to priority inversion, as discussed in the Base
34944 Definitions volume of IEEE Std 1003.1-2001, Section 3.285, Priority Inversion.

34945 The *pthread_rwlock_timedwrlock*() function is part of the Threads and Timeouts options and need
34946 not be provided on all implementations.

34947 **RATIONALE**

34948 None.

34949 **FUTURE DIRECTIONS**

34950 None.

34951 **SEE ALSO**

34952 *pthread_rwlock_destroy*(), *pthread_rwlock_rdlock*(), *pthread_rwlock_timedrdlock*(),
34953 *pthread_rwlock_tryrdlock*(), *pthread_rwlock_trywrlock*(), *pthread_rwlock_unlock*(),
34954 *pthread_rwlock_wrlock*(), the Base Definitions volume of IEEE Std 1003.1-2001, **<pthread.h>**,
34955 **<time.h>**

34956 **CHANGE HISTORY**

34957 First released in Issue 6. Derived from IEEE Std 1003.1j-2000.

34966 **NAME**
34967   pthread_rwlock_trywrlock, pthread_rwlock_wrlock — lock a read-write lock object for writing

34968 **SYNOPSIS**
34969 THR   `#include <pthread.h>`

34970   `int pthread_rwlock_trywrlock (pthread_rwlock_t *rwlock);`
34971   `int pthread_rwlock_wrlock (pthread_rwlock_t *rwlock);`
34972

34973 **DESCRIPTION**
34974   The *pthread_rwlock_trywrlock*() function shall apply a write lock like the *pthread_rwlock_wrlock*()
34975   function, with the exception that the function shall fail if any thread currently holds *rwlock* (for
34976   reading or writing).

34977   The *pthread_rwlock_wrlock*() function shall apply a write lock to the read-write lock referenced
34978   by *rwlock*. The calling thread acquires the write lock if no other thread (reader or writer) holds
34979   the read-write lock *rwlock*. Otherwise, the thread shall block until it can acquire the lock. The
34980   calling thread may deadlock if at the time the call is made it holds the read-write lock (whether a
34981   read or write lock).

34982   Implementations may favor writers over readers to avoid writer starvation.

34983   Results are undefined if any of these functions are called with an uninitialized read-write lock.

34984   If a signal is delivered to a thread waiting for a read-write lock for writing, upon return from the
34985   signal handler the thread resumes waiting for the read-write lock for writing as if it was not
34986   interrupted.

34987 **RETURN VALUE**
34988   The *pthread_rwlock_trywrlock*() function shall return zero if the lock for writing on the read-write
34989   lock object referenced by *rwlock* is acquired. Otherwise, an error number shall be returned to
34990   indicate the error.

34991   If successful, the *pthread_rwlock_wrlock*() function shall return zero; otherwise, an error number
34992   shall be returned to indicate the error.

34993 **ERRORS**
34994   The *pthread_rwlock_trywrlock*() function shall fail if:

34995   [EBUSY]   The read-write lock could not be acquired for writing because it was already
34996   locked for reading or writing.

34997   The *pthread_rwlock_trywrlock*() and *pthread_rwlock_wrlock*() functions may fail if:

34998   [EINVAL]   The value specified by *rwlock* does not refer to an initialized read-write lock
34999   object.

35000   The *pthread_rwlock_wrlock*() function may fail if:

35001   [EDEADLK]   The current thread already owns the read-write lock for writing or reading.

35002   These functions shall not return an error code of [EINTR].

35003 **EXAMPLES**
35004   None.

35005 **APPLICATION USAGE**

35006   Applications using these functions may be subject to priority inversion, as discussed in the Base
35007   Definitions volume of IEEE Std 1003.1-2001, Section 3.285, Priority Inversion.

35008 **RATIONALE**

35009   None.

35010 **FUTURE DIRECTIONS**

35011   None.

35012 **SEE ALSO**

35013   *pthread_rwlock_destroy*(), *pthread_rwlock_rdlock*(), *pthread_rwlock_timedrdlock*(),
35014   *pthread_rwlock_timedwrlock*(), *pthread_rwlock_tryrdlock*(), *pthread_rwlock_unlock*(), the Base
35015   Definitions volume of IEEE Std 1003.1-2001, <**pthread.h**>

35016 **CHANGE HISTORY**

35017   First released in Issue 5.

35018 **Issue 6**

35019   The following changes are made for alignment with IEEE Std 1003.1j-2000:

35020   • The margin code in the SYNOPSIS is changed to THR to indicate that the functionality is
35021   now part of the Threads option (previously it was part of the Read-Write Locks option in
35022   IEEE Std 1003.1j-2000 and also part of the XSI extension).

35023   • The [EDEADLK] error is deleted as a *pthread_rwlock_trywrlock*() error.

35024   • The SEE ALSO section is updated.

35025 **NAME**

35026   pthread_rwlock_unlock_unlock a read-write lock object

35027 **SYNOPSIS**

35028 THR   `#include <pthread.h>`

35029   `int pthread_rwlock_unlock(pthread_rwlock_t *rwlock);`

35030

35031 **DESCRIPTION**

35032   The *pthread_rwlock_unlock*() function shall release a lock held on the read-write lock object
35033   referenced by *rwlock*. Results are undefined if the read-write lock *rwlock* is not held by the
35034   calling thread.

35035   If this function is called to release a read lock from the read-write lock object and there are other
35036   read locks currently held on this read-write lock object, the read-write lock object remains in the
35037   read locked state. If this function releases the last read lock for this read-write lock object, the
35038   read-write lock object shall be put in the unlocked state with no owners.

35039   If this function is called to release a write lock for this read-write lock object, the read-write lock
35040   object shall be put in the unlocked state.

35041   If there are threads blocked on the lock when it becomes available, the scheduling policy shall
35042 TPS   determine which thread(s) shall acquire the lock. If the Thread Execution Scheduling option is
35043   supported, when threads executing with the scheduling policies SCHED_FIFO, SCHED_RR, or
35044   SCHED_SPORADIC are waiting on the lock, they shall acquire the lock in priority order when
35045   the lock becomes available. For equal priority threads, write locks shall take precedence over
35046   read locks. If the Thread Execution Scheduling option is not supported, it is implementation-
35047   defined whether write locks take precedence over read locks.

35048   Results are undefined if any of these functions are called with an uninitialized read-write lock.

35049 **RETURN VALUE**

35050   If successful, the *pthread_rwlock_unlock*() function shall return zero; otherwise, an error number
35051   shall be returned to indicate the error.

35052 **ERRORS**

35053   The *pthread_rwlock_unlock*() function may fail if:

35054   [EINVAL]   The value specified by *rwlock* does not refer to an initialized read-write lock
35055   object.

35056   [EPERM]   The current thread does not hold a lock on the read-write lock.

35057   The *pthread_rwlock_unlock*() function shall not return an error code of [EINTR].

35058 **EXAMPLES**

35059   None.

35060 **APPLICATION USAGE**

35061   None.

35062 **RATIONALE**

35063   None.

35064 **FUTURE DIRECTIONS**

35065   None.

SEE ALSO

pthread_rwlock_destroy(), *pthread_rwlock_rdlock*(), *pthread_rwlock_timedrdlock*(),
pthread_rwlock_timedwrlock(), *pthread_rwlock_tryrdlock*(), *pthread_rwlock_trywrlock*(),
pthread_rwlock_wrlock(), the Base Definitions volume of IEEE Std 1003.1-2001, <**pthread.h**>

CHANGE HISTORY

First released in Issue 5.

Issue 6

The following changes are made for alignment with IEEE Std 1003.1j-2000:

- The margin code in the SYNOPSIS is changed to THR to indicate that the functionality is now part of the Threads option (previously it was part of the Read-Write Locks option in IEEE Std 1003.1j-2000 and also part of the XSI extension).

- The DESCRIPTION is updated as follows:
  — The conditions under which writers have precedence over readers are specified.
  — The concept of read-write lock owner is deleted.

- The SEE ALSO section is updated.

35089 **NAME**

35090   pthread_rwlockattr_destroy, pthread_rwlockattr_init — destroy and initialize the read-write
35091   lock attributes object

35092 **SYNOPSIS**

35093 THR   `#include <pthread.h>`

35094   `int pthread_rwlockattr_destroy(pthread_rwlockattr_t *attr);`
35095   `int pthread_rwlockattr_init(pthread_rwlockattr_t *attr);`
35096

35097 **DESCRIPTION**

35098   The *pthread_rwlockattr_destroy*() function shall destroy a read-write lock attributes object. A
35099   destroyed *attr* attributes object can be reinitialized using *pthread_rwlockattr_init*(); the results of
35100   otherwise referencing the object after it has been destroyed are undefined. An implementation
35101   may cause *pthread_rwlockattr_destroy*() to set the object referenced by *attr* to an invalid value.

35102   The *pthread_rwlockattr_init*() function shall initialize a read-write lock attributes object *attr* with
35103   the default value for all of the attributes defined by the implementation.

35104   Results are undefined if *pthread_rwlockattr_init*() is called specifying an already initialized *attr*
35105   attributes object.

35106   After a read-write lock attributes object has been used to initialize one or more read-write locks,
35107   any function affecting the attributes object (including destruction) shall not affect any previously
35108   initialized read-write locks.

35109 **RETURN VALUE**

35110   If successful, the *pthread_rwlockattr_destroy*() and *pthread_rwlockattr_init*() functions shall return
35111   zero; otherwise, an error number shall be returned to indicate the error.

35112 **ERRORS**

35113   The *pthread_rwlockattr_destroy*() function may fail if:

35114   [EINVAL]   The value specified by *attr* is invalid.

35115   The *pthread_rwlockattr_init*() function shall fail if:

35116   [ENOMEM]   Insufficient memory exists to initialize the read-write lock attributes object.

35117   These functions shall not return an error code of [EINTR].

35118 **EXAMPLES**

35119   None.

35120 **APPLICATION USAGE**

35121   None.

35122 **RATIONALE**

35123   None.

35124 **FUTURE DIRECTIONS**

35125   None.

35126 **SEE ALSO**

35127   *pthread_rwlock_destroy*(), *pthread_rwlockattr_getpshared*(), *pthread_rwlockattr_setpshared*(), the
35128   Base Definitions volume of IEEE Std 1003.1-2001, **<pthread.h>**

35129 **CHANGE HISTORY**

35130 First released in Issue 5.

35131 **Issue 6**

35132 The following changes are made for alignment with IEEE Std 1003.1j-2000:

35133 • The margin code in the SYNOPSIS is changed to THR to indicate that the functionality is
35134 now part of the Threads option (previously it was part of the Read-Write Locks option in
35135 IEEE Std 1003.1j-2000 and also part of the XSI extension).

35136 • The SEE ALSO section is updated.

35137 **NAME**

35138   pthread_rwlockattr_getpshared, pthread_rwlockattr_setpshared — get and set the process-shared
35139   attribute of the read-write lock attributes object

35140 **SYNOPSIS**

35141 THR TSH `#include <pthread.h>`

35142   `int pthread_rwlockattr_getpshared(const pthread_rwlockattr_t *`
35143   `    restrict attr, int *restrict pshared);`
35144   `int pthread_rwlockattr_setpshared(pthread_rwlockattr_t *attr,`
35145   `    int pshared);`

35146

35147 **DESCRIPTION**

35148   The *pthread_rwlockattr_getpshared*() function shall obtain the value of the *process-shared* attribute
35149   from the initialized attributes object referenced by *attr*. The *pthread_rwlockattr_setpshared*()
35150   function shall set the *process-shared* attribute in an initialized attributes object referenced by *attr*.

35151   The *process-shared* attribute shall be set to PTHREAD_PROCESS_SHARED to permit a read-
35152   write lock to be operated upon by any thread that has access to the memory where the read-write
35153   lock is allocated, even if the read-write lock is allocated in memory that is shared by
35154   multiple processes. If the *process-shared* attribute is PTHREAD_PROCESS_PRIVATE, the read-
35155   write lock shall only be operated upon by threads created within the same process as the thread
35156   that initialized the read-write lock; if threads of differing processes attempt to operate on such a
35157   read-write lock, the behavior is undefined. The default value of the *process-shared* attribute shall
35158   be PTHREAD_PROCESS_PRIVATE.

35159   Additional attributes, their default values, and the names of the associated functions to get and
35160   set those attribute values are implementation-defined.

35161 **RETURN VALUE**

35162   Upon successful completion, the *pthread_rwlockattr_getpshared*() function shall return zero and
35163   store the value of the *process-shared* attribute of *attr* into the object referenced by the *pshared*
35164   parameter. Otherwise, an error number shall be returned to indicate the error.

35165   If successful, the *pthread_rwlockattr_setpshared*() function shall return zero; otherwise, an error
35166   number shall be returned to indicate the error.

35167 **ERRORS**

35168   The *pthread_rwlockattr_getpshared*() and *pthread_rwlockattr_setpshared*() functions may fail if:

35169   [EINVAL]   The value specified by *attr* is invalid.

35170   The *pthread_rwlockattr_setpshared*() function may fail if:

35171   [EINVAL]   The new value specified for the attribute is outside the range of legal values
35172   for that attribute.

35173   These functions shall not return an error code of [EINTR].

35174 **EXAMPLES**

35175   None.

35176 **APPLICATION USAGE**

35177   None.

35178 **RATIONALE**

35179 None.

35180 **FUTURE DIRECTIONS**

35181 None.

35182 **SEE ALSO**

35183 *pthread_rwlock_destroy*(), *pthread_rwlockattr_destroy*(), *pthread_rwlockattr_init*(), the Base
35184 Definitions volume of IEEE Std 1003.1-2001, **<pthread.h>**

35185 **CHANGE HISTORY**

35186 First released in Issue 5.

35187 **ISSUE 6**

35188 The following changes are made for alignment with IEEE Std 1003.1j-2000:

35189 • The margin code in the SYNOPSIS is changed to THR TSH to indicate that the functionality
35190   is now part of the Threads option (previously it was part of the Read-Write Locks option in
35191   IEEE Std 1003.1j-2000 and also part of the XSI extension).

35192 • The DESCRIPTION notes that additional attributes are implementation-defined.

35193 • The SEE ALSO section is updated.

35194 The **restrict** keyword is added to the *pthread_rwlockattr_getpshared*() prototype for alignment
35195 with the ISO/IEC 9899: 1999 standard.

35214 **NAME**

35215   pthread_self — get the calling thread ID

35216 **SYNOPSIS**

35217 THR   `#include <pthread.h>`

35218   `pthread_t pthread_self (void);`

35219

35220 **DESCRIPTION**

35221   The *pthread_self*() function shall return the thread ID of the calling thread.

35222 **RETURN VALUE**

35223   Refer to the DESCRIPTION.

35224 **ERRORS**

35225   No errors are defined.

35226   The *pthread_self*() function shall not return an error code of [EINTR].

35227 **EXAMPLES**

35228   None.

35229 **APPLICATION USAGE**

35230   None.

35231 **RATIONALE**

35232   The *pthread_self*() function provides a capability similar to the *getpid*() function for processes
35233   and the rationale is the same: the creation call does not provide the thread ID to the created
35234   thread.

35235 **FUTURE DIRECTIONS**

35236   None.

35237 **SEE ALSO**

35238   *pthread_create*(), *pthread_equal*(), the Base Definitions volume of IEEE Std 1003.1-2001,
35239   **<pthread.h>**

35240 **CHANGE HISTORY**

35241   First released in Issue 5. Included for alignment with the POSIX Threads Extension.

35242 **Issue 6**

35243   The *pthread_self*() function is marked as part of the Threads option.

35244
NAME

35245   pthread_setcancelstate, pthread_setcanceltype, pthread_testcancel — set cancelability state

35246 **SYNOPSIS**

35247 THR   `#include <pthread.h>`

```
35248    int pthread_setcancelstate(int state, int *oldstate);
35249    int pthread_setcanceltype(int type, int *oldtype);
35250    void pthread_testcancel(void);
35251
```

35252 **DESCRIPTION**

35253   The *pthread_setcancelstate*() function shall atomically both set the calling thread's cancelability
35254   state to the indicated *state* and return the previous cancelability state at the location referenced
35255   by *oldstate*. Legal values for *state* are PTHREAD_CANCEL_ENABLE and
35256   PTHREAD_CANCEL_DISABLE.

35257   The *pthread_setcanceltype*() function shall atomically both set the calling thread's cancelability
35258   type to the indicated *type* and return the previous cancelability type at the location referenced by
35259   *oldtype*. Legal values for *type* are PTHREAD_CANCEL_DEFERRED and
35260   PTHREAD_CANCEL_ASYNCHRONOUS.

35261   The cancelability state and type of any newly created threads, including the thread in which
35262   *main*() was first invoked, shall be PTHREAD_CANCEL_ENABLE and
35263   PTHREAD_CANCEL_DEFERRED respectively.

35264   The *pthread_testcancel*() function shall create a cancelation point in the calling thread. The
35265   *pthread_testcancel*() function shall have no effect if cancelability is disabled.

35266 **RETURN VALUE**

35267   If successful, the *pthread_setcancelstate*() and *pthread_setcanceltype*() functions shall return zero;
35268   otherwise, an error number shall be returned to indicate the error.

35269 **ERRORS**

35270   The *pthread_setcancelstate*() function may fail if:

35271   [EINVAL]   The specified state is not PTHREAD_CANCEL_ENABLE or
35272   PTHREAD_CANCEL_DISABLE.

35273   The *pthread_setcanceltype*() function may fail if:

35274   [EINVAL]   The specified type is not PTHREAD_CANCEL_DEFERRED or
35275   PTHREAD_CANCEL_ASYNCHRONOUS.

35276   These functions shall not return an error code of [EINTR].

35277 **EXAMPLES**

35278   None.

35279 **APPLICATION USAGE**

35280   None.

35281 **RATIONALE**

35282   The *pthread_setcancelstate*() and *pthread_setcanceltype*() functions control the points at which a
35283   thread may be asynchronously canceled. For cancelation control to be usable in modular fashion,
35284   some rules need to be followed.

35285 An object can be considered to be a generalization of a procedure. It is a set of procedures and
35286 global variables written as a unit and called by clients not known by the object. Objects may
35287 depend on other objects.

35288 First, cancelability should only be disabled on entry to on object, never explicitly enabled. On
35289 exit from an object, the cancelability state should always be restored to its value on entry to the
35290 object.

35291 This follows from a modularity argument: if the client of an object (or the client of an object that
35292 uses that object) has disabled cancelability, it is because the client does not want to be concerned
35293 about cleaning up if the thread is canceled while executing some sequence of actions. If an object
35294 is called in such a state and it enables cancelability and a cancelation request is pending for that
35295 thread, then the thread is canceled, contrary to the wish of the client that disabled.

35296 Second, the cancelability type may be explicitly set to either *deferred* or *asynchronous* upon entry
35297 to an object. But as with the cancelability state, on exit from an object the cancelability type
35298 should always be restored to its value on entry to the object.

35299 Finally, only functions that are cancel-safe may be called from a thread that is asynchronously
35300 cancelable.

35301 **FUTURE DIRECTIONS**
35302 None.

35303 **SEE ALSO**
35304 *pthread_cancel*(), the Base Definitions volume of IEEE Std 1003.1-2001, **<pthread.h>**

35305 **CHANGE HISTORY**
35306 First released in Issue 5. Included for alignment with the POSIX Threads Extensions.

35307 **Issue 6**
35308 The *pthread_setcancelstate*(), *pthread_setcanceltype*(), and *pthread_testcancel*() functions are marked
35309 as part of the Threads option.

35328 **NAME**

35329   pthread_setschedprio — dynamic thread scheduling parameters access (**REALTIME**

35330   **THREADS**)

35331 **SYNOPSIS**

35332 THR TPS `#include <pthread.h>`

35333   `int pthread_setschedprio(pthread_t thread, int prio);`

35334

35335 **DESCRIPTION**

35336   The *pthread_setschedprio*() function shall set the scheduling priority for the thread whose thread

35337   ID is given by *thread* to the value given by *prio*. See **Scheduling Policies** (on page 44) for a

35338   description on how this function call affects the ordering of the thread in the thread list for its

35339   new priority.

35340   If the *pthread_setschedprio*() function fails, the scheduling priority of the target thread shall not be

35341   changed.

35342 **RETURN VALUE**

35343   If successful, the *pthread_setschedprio*() function shall return zero; otherwise, an error number

35344   shall be returned to indicate the error.

35345 **ERRORS**

35346   The *pthread_setschedprio*() function may fail if:

35347   [EINVAL]   The value of *prio* is invalid for the scheduling policy of the specified thread.

35348   [ENOTSUP]   An attempt was made to set the priority to an unsupported value.

35349   [EPERM]   The caller does not have the appropriate permission to set the scheduling

35350   policy of the specified thread.

35351   [EPERM]   The implementation does not allow the application to modify the priority to

35352   the value specified.

35353   [ESRCH]   The value specified by *thread* does not refer to an existing thread.

35354   The *pthread_setschedprio*() function shall not return an error code of [EINTR].

35355 **EXAMPLES**

35356   None.

35357 **APPLICATION USAGE**

35358   None.

35359 **RATIONALE**

35360   The *pthread_setschedprio*() function provides a way for an application to temporarily raise its

35361   priority and then lower it again, without having the undesired side effect of yielding to other

35362   threads of the same priority. This is necessary if the application is to implement its own

35363   strategies for bounding priority inversion, such as priority inheritance or priority ceilings. This

35364   capability is especially important if the implementation does not support the Thread Priority

35365   Protection or Thread Priority Inheritance options, but even if those options are supported it is

35366   needed if the application is to bound priority inheritance for other resources, such as

35367   semaphores.

35368   The standard developers considered that while it might be preferable conceptually to solve this

35369   problem by modifying the specification of *pthread_setschedparam*(), it was too late to make such a

35370   change, as there may be implementations that would need to be changed. Therefore, this new
35371   function was introduced.

FUTURE DIRECTIONS
35373   None.

SEE ALSO
35375   **Scheduling Policies** (on page 44), *pthread_getschedparam*(), the Base Definitions volume of
35376   IEEE Std 1003.1-2001, **<pthread.h>**

CHANGE HISTORY
35378   First released in Issue 6. Included as a response to IEEE PASC Interpretation 1003.1 #96.

Bibliography

Audi, Robert. *Action, Intention, and Reason*. Ithaca, N.Y.: Cornell University Press, 1993.

Axford, Tom. *Concurrent Programming: Fundamental Techniques for Real-Time and Parallel Software Design*. Chichester, U.K.: John Wiley, 1989.

Baase, Sarah. *Computer Algorithms: Introduction to Design and Analysis*. 2nd ed. Reading, Mass.: Addison-Wesley, 1988.

Barfield, Woodrow, and Thomas A. Furnell III. *Virtual Environments and Advanced Interface Design*. New York: Oxford University Press, 1995.

Binkley, Robert, Bronaugh, Richard, and Ausonio Marras. *Agent, Action, and Reason*. Toronto: University of Toronto Press, 1971.

Booch, Grady, James Rumbaugh, and Ivar Jacobson. *The Unified Modeling Language User Guide*. Boston: Addison-Wesley, 1999.

Bowan, Howard, and John Derrick. *Formal Methods for Distributed Processing: A Survey of Object-Oriented Approaches*. New York: Cambridge University Press, 2001.

Brewka, Gerhard, Jurgen Diz, and Kurt Konolige. *Nonmonotonic Reasoning*. Stanford, Calif.: CSLI Publications, 1997.

Carroll, Martin D., and Margaret A. Ellis. *Designing and Coding Reusable C++*. Reading, Mass.: Addison-Wesley, 1995.

Cassell, Justine, Joseph Sullivan, Scott Prevost, and Elizabeth Churchill. *Embodied Conversational Agents*. Cambridge, Mass.: MIT Press, 2000.

Chellas, Brian F. *Modal Logic: An Introduction*. New York: Cambridge University Press, 1980.

Coplien, James O. *Multi-Paradigm Design for C++*. Reading, Mass.: Addison-Wesley, 1999.

Cormen, Thomas, Charles Leiserson, and Ronald Rivet. *Introduction to Algorithms*. Cambridge, Mass.: MIT Press, 1995.

Englemore, Robert, and Tony Morgan. *Blackboard Systems*. Wokingham, England: Addison-Wesley, 1988.

Garg, Vijay K. *Principles of Distributed Systems*. Norwell, Mass.: Kluwer Academic, 1996.

Geist, Al, Adam Beguelin, Jack Dongarra, Weicheng Jiang, Robert Manchek, and Vaidy Sinderman. *PVM: Parallel Virtual Machine*. London, England: MIT Press, 1994.

Goodheart, Berny, and James Cox. *The Magic Garden Explained: The Internals of Unix System V Release 4*. New York: Prentice Hall, 1994.

Gropp, William, Steven Huss-Lederman, Andrew Lumsdaine, Ewing Lusk, Bill Nitzberg, William Saphir, and Marc Snir. *MPI: The Complete Reference*. Vol. 2. Cambridge, Mass.: MIT Press, 1998.

Heath, Michael T. *Scientific Computing: An Introduction Survey*. New York: McGraw-Hill.

Henning, Michi, and Steve Vinoski. *Advanced COBRA Programming with C++*. Reading, Mass.: Addison-Wesley, 1999.

Hintikka, Jakko, and Merrill Hintikka. *The Logic of Epistemology and the Epistemology of Logic*. Amsterdam: Kluwer Academic, 1989.

Horty, John F. *Agency and Deontic Logic*. New York: Oxford University Press, 2001.

Hughes, Cameron, and Tracey Hughes. *Mastering the Standard C++ Classes*. New York: John Wiley, 1990.

Hughes, Cameron, and Tracey Hughes. *Object-Oriented Multithreading Using C++*. New York: John Wiley, 1997.

Hughes, Cameron, and Tracey Hughes. *Linux Rapid Application Development*. Foster City, Calif.: M & T Books, 2000.

International Standard Organization. *Information Technology: Portable Operating System Interface*. Pt. 1 System Application Program Interface. 2nd ed. Std 1003.1 ANSI/IEEE. 1996.

Josuttis, Nicolai M. *The C++ Standard*. Boston: Addison-Wesley, 1999.

Koeing, Andrew, and Barbara Moo. *Ruminations on C++*. Reading, Mass.: Addison-Wesley, 1997.

Krishnamoorthy, C.S., and S. Rajeev. *Artificial Intelligence and Expert Systems for Engineers*. Boca Raton, Fla.: CRC Press, 1996.

Lewis, Ted, Glenn Andert, Paul Calder, Erich Gamma, Wolfgang Press, Larry Rosenstein, and Kraus, Sarit. *Strategic Negotiation in Multitangent Environments*. London: MIT Press, 2001.

Luger, George F. *Artificial Intelligence*. 4th ed. England: Addison-Wesley, 2002.

Mandrioli Dino, and Carlo Ghezzi. *Theoretical Foundations of Computer Science*. New York: John Wiley, 1987.

Nielsen, Michael A., and Isaac L. Chuang. *Quantum Computation and Quantum Information*. New York: Cambridge University Press, 2000.

Patel, Mukesh J., Vasant Honavar, and Karthik Balakrishnan. *Advances in the Evolutionary Synthesis of Intelligent Agents*. Cambridge, Mass.: MIT Press, 2001.

Picard, Rosalind. *Affective Computing*. London: MIT Press, 1997.

Rescher, Nicholas, and Alasdir Urquhart. *Temporal Logic*. New York: Springer-Verlag, 1971.

Robbins, Kay A., and Steven Robbins. *Practical Unix Programming*. Upper Saddle River, N.J.: Prentice Hall, 1996.

Schmucker, Kurt, Ander Weinand, and John M. Vlissides. *Object-Oriented Application Frameworks*. Greenwich, Conn.: Manning Publications, 1995.

Singh, Harry. *Progressing to Distributed Multiprocessing*. Upper Saddle River, N.J.: Prentice Hall, 1999.

Skillicorn, David. *Foundations of Parallel Programming*. New York: Cambridge University Press, 1994.

Soukup, Jiri. *Taming C++: Pattern Classes and Persistence for Large Projects*. Reading, Mass.: Addison-Wesley, 1994.

Sterling, Thomas L., John Salmon, Donald J. Becker, and Daniel F. Savarese. *How to Build a Bewoulf: A Guide to Implementation and Application of PC Clusters*. London: MIT Press, 1999.

Stevens, Richard W. *UNIX Network Programming: Interprocess Communications*. Vol. 2, 2nd ed. Upper Saddle River: Prentice Hall, 1999.

Stroustrup, Bjarne. *The Design and Evolution of C++*. Reading, Mass.: Addison-Wesley, 1994.

Subrahmanian, V.S., Piero Bonatti, Jurgen Dix, Thomas Eiter, Sarit Kraus, Fatma Ozcan, and Robert Ross. *Heterogeneous Agent Systems*. Cambridge, Mass.: MIT Press, 2000.

Tel, Gerard. *Introduction to Distributed Algorithms*. 2nd ed. New York: Cambridge University Press, 2000.

Thompson, William J. *Computing for Scientists and Engineers*. New York: John Wiley, 1992.

Tomas, Gerald, and Christoph W. Uebeerhuber. *Visualization of Scientific Parallel Programming.* New York: Springer-Verlag, 1994.

Tracy, Kim W. and Peter Bouthoorn. *Object-Oriented: Artificial Intelligence Using C++.* New York: Computer Science Press, 1997.

Weiss, Gerhard. *Multitagent Systems.* Cambridge, Mass.: MIT Press, 1999.

Wooldridge, Michael. *Reasoning About Rational Agents.* London: MIT Press, 2000.

Index

Register
Your Book

at www.awprofessional.com/register

You may be eligible to receive:

- Advance notice of forthcoming editions of the book
- Related book recommendations
- Chapter excerpts and supplements of forthcoming titles
- Information about special contests and promotions throughout the year
- Notices and reminders about author appearances, tradeshows, and online chats with special guests

Contact us

If you are interested in writing a book or reviewing manuscripts prior to publication, please write to us at:

Editorial Department
Addison-Wesley Professional
75 Arlington Street, Suite 300
Boston, MA 02116 USA
Email: AWPro@aw.com

Visit us on the Web: http://www.awprofessional.com